Crime, Social Control and ...

Crime, Social Control and Human Rights
From moral panics to states of denial
Essays in honour of Stanley Cohen

Edited by

David Downes, Paul Rock, Christine Chinkin and Conor Gearty

WILLAN
PUBLISHING

Published by

Willan Publishing
Culmcott House
Mill Street, Uffculme
Cullompton, Devon
EX15 3AT, UK
Tel: +44(0)1884 840337
Fax: +44(0)1884 840251
e-mail: info@willanpublishing.co.uk
website: www.willanpublishing.co.uk

Published simultaneously in the USA and Canada by

Willan Publishing
c/o ISBS, 920 NE 58th Ave, Suite 300,
Portland, Oregon 97213-3786, USA
Tel: +001(0)503 287 3093
Fax: +001(0)503 280 8832
e-mail: info@isbs.com
website: www.isbs.com

First published 2007

Reprinted 2008

Hardback
ISBN 978-1-84392-228-5

Paperback
ISBN 978-1-84392-404-3

British Library Cataloguing-in-Publication Data

A catalogue record for this book is available from the British Library

Cover image
The sculpture on the front cover is by Jimmy Boyle while
imprisoned in the Special Unit at Barlinnie Prison, Glasgow.
The photograph of the sculpture is by Roger Riley.

Project managed by Deer Park Productions, Tavistock, Devon
Typeset by GCS, Leighton Buzzard, Bedfordshire
Printed and bound by T.J. International Ltd, Padstow, Cornwall

Contents

All royalties from sales of this book are being
donated to Sight Savers International
(http://www.sightsavers.org/)

Notes on editors and contributors

Editors

Christine Chinkin is Professor in International Law at the London School of Economics, and an overseas affiliated faculty member of the University of Michigan Law School. She is the author of *Third Parties in International Law* (1993) and co-author of *The Boundaries of International Law: A Feminist Analysis* (2000) with Hilary Charlesworth, which was awarded the American Society of International Law's Certificate of Merit for 'outstanding contribution to scholarship'.

David Downes is Professor Emeritus of Social Policy at the London School of Economics, where he is a former Director of the Mannheim Centre for Criminology and Criminal Justice. His main books are *The Delinquent Solution* (1966), *Contrasts in Tolerance* (1988), and (with Paul Rock) *Understanding Deviance* (1982; 5th edition, 2007). He is currently a member of the Council of Liberty and of the Centre for Crime and Justice Studies.

Conor Gearty is Rausing Director of the Centre for the Study of Human Rights and Professor of Human Rights Law at the London School of Economics. His books include *Can Human Rights Survive?* (2006), *Principles of Human Rights Adjudication* (2004), *Terror* (1991), and (with Keith Ewing) *The Struggle for Civil Liberties* (2000). He is a member of the Council of Justice and is on the board of various human rights centres and academic journals. He is a barrister in practice at Matrix Chambers.

Paul Rock was educated at the London School of Economics and the University of Oxford. He is Professor of Social Institutions at the former and occasional Visiting Professor at the University of Pennsylvania. His principal research interest has been in the development of policies for victims of crime, and he has written a number of books on the theme, beginning with *A View from the Shadows: The Ministry of the Solicitor General of Canada and the Justice for Victims of Crime Initiative*, and, most recently, *Constructing Victims' Rights: The Home Office, New Labour and Victims*. His current research focuses on the experimental introduction of victim impact statements in homicide trials in England and Wales.

Contributors

Howard S. Becker is a sociologist who lives and works in San Francisco. He is the author of *Outsiders, Art Worlds, Writing for Social Scientists, Tricks of the Trade*, and *Telling About Society*. He is collaborating with Robert R. Faulkner on a study of the jazz repertoire.

Thomas G. Blomberg is Dean and Sheldon L. Messinger Professor of Criminology at Florida State University's College of Criminology and Criminal Justice. He has published widely in the areas of penology, social control, and education and delinquency. His recent books are *American Penology* (2000) (with Karol Lucken), *Data-Driven Juvenile Justice Education* (2001) (with Gordon Waldo and Mark Yeisley), and *Punishment and Social Control* (enlarged 2nd edition, 2003) (with Stanley Cohen).

Nils Christie has for most of his life worked as Professor of Criminology at the University of Oslo, Norway. He has been the Director of the Institute of Criminology and Penal Law, and also of the Scandinavian Board of Criminology. He is the author of a great number of books and articles. His two most recent books are *Crime Control as Industry* (2000) and *A Suitable Amount of Crime* (2004), both translated into many languages. But most important here: he has been a friend of Stan for many, many good years.

Robin Cohen is Professor of Sociology at the University of Warwick and holds an ESRC Professorial Research Fellowship. Among his books are *Global Diasporas* (revised edition 2007), *Migration and Its Enemies* (2006), *Frontiers of Identity: The British and the Others* (1994), and (with Paul Kennedy) *Global Sociology* (revised edition 2007). He has held teaching positions in Nigeria and Trinidad and has recently returned from three years in South Africa, where he was Dean of Humanities at the University of Cape Town.

Ron Dudai is a research fellow at the Hotung Programme in Human Rights and Peace-Building in the Middle East, at the School of Oriental and African Studies, University of London. He was previously a researcher at B'Tselem, the Israeli Information Center for Human Rights in the Occupied Territories, and a fellow at the Institute for Justice and Reconciliation, South Africa. His recent articles have appeared in *Human Rights Quarterly* and the *Journal of Human Rights*. He has also written for the *Guardian*, *New Humanist* and the *Jewish Quarterly*.

Malcolm M. Feeley is Claire Sanders Clements Dean's Professor of Jurisprudence and Social Policy at the University of California at Berkeley, and the former director of the Center for the Study of Law and Society. Along with Jonathan Simon, he is co-editor of the journal, *Punishment and Society*, and he is the author of many articles and several books, including *The Process is the Punishment*, (with Austin Sarat) *The Policy Dilemma, Court Reform on Trial*, (with Edward Rubin) *Judicial Policy Making and the Modern State*, and *The Tragedy of Federalism*.

David Garland is the Arthur T. Vanderbilt Professor of Law and Professor of Sociology at New York University. He previously taught at Edinburgh University's School of Law. His publications include *Punishment and Modern Society: A Study in Social Theory* (1990), *Punishment and Welfare: The History of Penal Strategies* (1985), and *The Culture of Control: Crime and Social Order in Contemporary Society* (2001). He is currently writing on capital punishment and American society.

Daphna Golan-Agnon, PhD, teaches human rights at the Hebrew University Law School, where she heads the Academy–Community Partnership for Social Change. She was the founding research director of B'Tselem, the Israeli Information Center for Human Rights in the Occupied Territories, where she published with Stanley Cohen the first report on torture of Palestinian detainees in Israel. Her recent book, *Next Year in Jerusalem – Everyday Life in a Divided Land*, was published in New York and London by the New Press in 2005.

Fred Halliday is Professor of International Relations at the London School of Economics and Visiting Professor at the Institut Barcelona d'Estudis Internacionals. He is the author of works on international relations theory, revolution, and the Middle East. At the London School of Economics he has served as Convenor of the Department of

International Relations, as Academic Governor, and as the first Director of the Human Rights Centre.

Carter Hay is an Assistant Professor in the College of Criminology and Criminal Justice at Florida State University in Tallahassee. His research examines the causes of criminal involvement, as well as societal reactions to crime. His recent publications have appeared in *Criminology*, the *Journal of Research in Crime and Delinquency*, and *Sociological Perspectives*.

Ruth Jamieson is a Lecturer in Criminology at Queen's University, Belfast. Her research and writing are in the areas of gender, war, and crime and imprisonment. She is currently a member of the editorial boards of the *British Journal of Criminology*, *Critical Criminology*, and *Temida* (the journal of victimology, human rights and gender of the former Yugoslavia).

David Kretzmer is Professor Emeritus of Law at the Hebrew University of Jerusalem, where he was the founding Academic Director of the Minerva Centre for Human Rights. His most recent books are *The Occupation of Justice: The Supreme Court of Israel and the Occupied Territories* (2002), *The Legal Status of the Arabs in Israel* (2nd [Arabic] edition, 2002), and *The Concept of Human Dignity in Human Rights Discourse* (2002, edited with Eckart Klein). He is presently Professor of Law at the Academic College of Law in Ramat Gan, Israel, and at the Transitional Justice Institute, University of Ulster.

Adam Kuper is Professor of Anthropology at Brunel University. His most recent books are *Culture: The Anthropologists' Account* (Harvard University Press, 1996), and *The Reinvention of Primitive Society* (Routledge, 2005). He edited with his wife, Jessica Kuper, *The Social Science Encyclopedia* (Routledge, 3rd edition, 2005).

Nicola Lacey is Professor of Criminal Law and Legal Theory at the London School of Economics. Her principal publications are *State Punishment* (1988); with Elizabeth Frazer, *The Politics of Community* (1993); *Unspeakable Subjects* (1998); with Celia Wells and Oliver Quick, *Reconstructing Criminal Law* (3rd edition, 2003); and *A Life of H.L.A. Hart: The Nightmare and the Noble Dream* (2004). She currently holds a Leverhulme Major Research Fellowship and is working on the historical development of ideas of responsibility for crime.

Steven Lukes is Professor of Sociology at New York University. He has previously held posts at Balliol College, Oxford; the European University Institute in Florence; the University of Siena; and the London School of Economics. He is a Fellow of the British Academy and an editor of the *European Journal of Sociology*. His published works include *Emile Durkheim: His Life and Work*; *Individualism, Marxism and Morality*; *Liberals and Cannibals: The Implications of Diversity*, and *The Curious Enlightenment of Professor Caritat: A Comedy of Ideas* and *Power: A Radical View*, which recently appeared in a much expanded second edition, published by Palgrave; and he co-edited *Rationality and Relativism* and *The Category of the Person: Anthropology, Philosophy, History*.

Kieran McEvoy is Professor of Law and Transitional Justice and Director of the Institute of Criminology and Criminal Justice, School of Law, Queen's University Belfast. His books include *Paramilitary Imprisonment in Northern Ireland* (2001, Oxford University Press), *Criminology, Conflict Resolution and Restorative Justice* (2003, Palgrave, edited with T. Newburn), *Judges, Human Rights and Transition* (2007, Oxford University Press, edited with J. Morison and G. Anthony), and *Truth, Transition and Reconciliation: Dealing with the Past in Northern Ireland* (2007, Willan).

Harvey Molotch is Professor of Sociology and Metropolitan Studies at New York University. He is a former visiting professor at Essex University and a former Centennial Professor at the London School of Economics. His books include *Urban Fortunes* (new edition to appear in 2007) and *Where Stuff Comes From* (2003). He studies cities, communication, and the means of production.

Claire Moon is Lecturer in the Sociology of Human Rights in the Department of Sociology at the London School of Economics. Her research and teaching interests are in the areas of truth, justice and reconciliation; war and war trauma; genocide; and human rights. She has published on forgiveness in politics, and the narration of truth and human rights violations in political reconciliation processes, and is currently writing a book entitled *Narrating Reconciliation: South Africa's Truth and Reconciliation Commission*, due to be published in 2007.

Tim Newburn is Professor of Criminology and Social Policy and Director of the Mannheim Centre for Criminology, London School of Economics. He is the author of numerous books, the most recent of which are *Plural*

Policing (edited with Trevor Jones, 2006), *The Politics of Crime Control* (edited with Paul Rock, 2006), *Policy Transfer and Criminal Justice* (with Trevor Jones, 2007) and the *Handbook of Criminal Investigation* (with Tom Williamson and Alan Wright, 2007). He is currently President of the British Society of Criminology.

Jill Peay is a Professor of Law at the London School of Economics and Political Science. Her main interests are in mental health law and mentally disordered offenders. Her recent publications include *Decisions and Dilemmas: Working with Mental Health Law* (2003) and *Seminal Issues in Mental Health Law* (2005). She is currently involved as a member of the Mental Disability Advocacy Centre's Guardianship Advisory Board in an eight-country study of guardianship in central and eastern Europe.

Margo Picken until recently directed the Office of the UN High Commissioner for Human Rights in Cambodia. Before that she was a fellow at the Centre for International Studies, London School of Economics, where she helped to set up the School's Centre for Human Rights. She has also worked for the Ford Foundation and for Amnesty International. She is the author of several articles on human rights, including 'Ethical Foreign Policies and Human Rights: Dilemmas' (2001), in Karen E. Smith and Margot Light (eds), *Ethics and Foreign Policy*, Cambridge University Press; and 'The Betrayed People', *New York Review of Books*, 4 December 1986, vol. 33, no. 19.

Ken Plummer is Emeritus Professor of Sociology at the University of Essex and originally studied with his mentor Stan Cohen in the mid-1960s. He has published some ten books and 100 articles and founded the journal *Sexualities*. His most recent book is *Intimate Citizenship* (2003, University of Washington Press).

Robert Reiner is Professor of Criminology in the Law Department, London School of Economics. His most recent books are *The Politics of the Police* (2000, 3rd edition, Oxford University Press); *The Oxford Handbook of Criminology*, edited with Mike Maguire and Rod Morgan (2007, 4th edition, Oxford University Press); and *Law and Order: An Honest Citizen's Guide to Crime and Control* (2007, Polity Press).

Andrew Rutherford is Emeritus Professor of Law and Criminal Policy at the University of Southampton. His main publications are *Prisons and the Process of Justice* (1984), *Growing Out of Crime* (1986), *Criminal*

Justice and the Pursuit of Decency (1993), and *Transforming Criminal Policy* (1996). He was chair of the Howard League for Penal Reform (1984–99), and since 2001 he has been a member of the Parole Board of England and Wales.

Albie Sachs is a Justice of the Constitutional Court of South Africa, and the author of several books. He is also active in the fields of art and architecture.

Andrew Scull is Distinguished Professor of Sociology and Science Studies at the University of California at San Diego. He edited *Social Control and the State* (1984) with Stan Cohen, and his other books include: *Decarceration* (1977); *Museums of Madness* (1979); *Durkheim and the Law* (1984, with Steven Lukes); *Social Order/Mental Disorder* (1989); *The Asylum as Utopia* (1991); *The Most Solitary of Afflictions* (1993); *Masters of Bedlam* (1996); *Undertaker of the Mind* (2001, with Jonathan Andrews); *Customers and Patrons of the Mad Trade* (2003, with Jonathan Andrews); *Madhouse* (2005); and *The Insanity of Place/The Place of Insanity* (2006).

Richard Sennett is Academic Governor and Professor of Sociology at the London School of Economics. His most recent books are *The Culture of the New Capitalism* (2006), *Respect in a World of Inequality* (2003), and *The Corrosion of Character* (1998). In 2006 he was awarded the Hegel Prize for the social sciences.

Sharon Shalev is a human rights worker and a criminologist. She left a post with Israeli-Palestinian Physicians for Human Rights to pursue an LLM in International Human Rights Law at Essex University. Her PhD thesis, undertaken at the London School of Economics under Stan Cohen's supervision, is on Supermax prisons. Dr Shalev is currently a visiting fellow at LSE's Mannheim Centre for Criminology, and is writing a handbook on solitary confinement aimed at prison practitioners and health professionals.

Jonathan Simon is Associate Dean, Jurisprudence and Social Policy Program, and Professor of Law at Boalt Hall, School of Law, University of California at Berkeley. His most recent book is *Governing Through Crime: How the War on Crime Transformed American Democracy and Created a Culture of Fear* (New York: Oxford University Press, 2007).

Laurie Taylor is Visiting Professor in Sociology and Politics at Birkbeck College, University of London. He is also a Fellow of Birkbeck College and holds honorary degrees from the universities of Nottingham,

Leicester, Central England, and Westminster. He is an Academician of the Social Sciences and the author of 14 books on crime, deviance, and identity. His most recent book, *What Are Children For?*, was written with his son Matthew. For the last 25 years Taylor has been a regular broadcaster on BBC Radio Four and a columnist for *The Times Higher Education Supplement*.

Peter Townsend is Professor of International Social Policy at the London School of Economics. He has worked lately with UNICEF, the Department for International Development and the International Labour Organization and was consultant to the UN at the time of the World Summit for Social Development at Copenhagen in 1995. In November 2006 he spoke at the plenary session of the International Poverty Forum of the UN in New York. In the UK he helped to found the Child Poverty Action Group in 1965 and the Disability Alliance in 1973, was Chair of each of these organisations for 20 years, and continues to be President of both. He is Vice-President of the Fabian Society. His latest books are *World Poverty: New Policies to Defeat an Old Enemy* (co-editor with David Gordon, 2002); *Child Poverty in the Developing World* (with others, 2003); *Inequalities of Health: The Welsh Dimension* (2005); and *Social Security: Building Decent Societies* (edited, ILO, 2007).

Michael Welch is Professor of Criminal Justice at Rutgers University, New Jersey (USA). His recent books include *Scapegoats of September 11th: Hate Crimes and State Crimes in the War on Terror* (2006, Rutgers University Press), *Ironies of Imprisonment* (2005, Sage), and *Detained: Immigration Laws and the Expanding I.N.S. Jail Complex* (2002, Temple University Press). In 2005 and 2006–7, Welch was Visiting Fellow at the Centre for the Study of Human Rights at the London School of Economics. His website is www.professormichaelwelch.com.

Jock Young is Professor of Sociology at the University of Kent at Canterbury and Distinguished Professor of Criminal Justice at the Graduate Center, City University of New York. He was formerly Head of the Centre for Criminology at the University of Middlesex. His recent books are *The Exclusive Society* (1999) and *The Vertigo of Late Modernity* (2007). The last book in the trilogy *The Criminological Imagination* is due out late in 2007.

Foreword

Noam Chomsky

About 15 years ago, Stan Cohen wrote me about a research project he was undertaking on '"denial" – how people manage to shut out information about atrocities and human rights violation'. The project led to his remarkable work *States of Denial*, a chilling testimony to the times; one is tempted to say 'epitaph'. Throughout history, denial and historical amnesia have been a critically important instrument of domination from the smallest social groupings, like families, to international affairs. It is impressive, and deeply depressing, to see how differently history and what is happening before our eyes are refracted through the vision and sensibilities of those who hold the clubs, on the one hand, and those who are beaten by them, on the other. And no sensible person should be surprised to learn, over and over, how the balance of veracity is tilted. It would be tempting to provide examples, past and present, but any brief selection is unfair and misleading, and anything more serious would constitute another book – many parts of which have been written, rarely penetrating very deeply into the consciousness of those with the power and the privilege to shape history in their interests. One classic example, of unfortunately clear contemporary relevance, is de Tocqueville's observations about how Americans were able 'to exterminate the Indian race' while 'wholly depriving it of its rights … without violating a single great principle of morality in the eyes of the world' – at least the civilized world. But there are all too many more, wherever we turn our eyes.

   Stan's work on this topic began with his investigations of torture in Israel, surely informed by his early experiences in South Africa. He then extended them far more broadly, and with increasing depth and penetration. It is hard to overlook the fact that I am writing these words a few days after the leader of the Free World has passed legislation that empowers the executive to authorize torture at its own discretion, to deny *habeas corpus* and other rights that date back centuries, and much else, and that immunizes from accountability those responsible, to the highest level. Perhaps that is the natural response to the advice given the President several years earlier by his legal counsel, now Attorney-General, that it would be wise to rescind the Geneva Convention, which he determined to be 'quaint' and 'obsolete'. That step, he explained, 'substantially reduces the threat of domestic criminal prosecution under the War Crimes Act', passed in 1996 by a Republican Congress, which carries severe penalties for 'grave breaches' of the Conventions: the death penalty if death results to the victim. All now in the ashcan of history, already overflowing with far worse examples.

The hope for the future is that others will take up the cause that Stanley Cohen has followed with courage, dedication, and penetrating honesty. It is a privilege to be able to contribute at least a few words in honour of an exemplary life and memorable achievements.

Introduction

The Editors

Cohen the criminologist

There is no need in an introduction extensively to recapitulate Stan Cohen's work as a sociologist of crime, deviance and control. It is too well known, and too well covered in other chapters of this book, to warrant description in any detail here. What we shall do instead is chart some of those properties that have made it stimulating, original and influential. Where one is so supple and sophisticated, it is all but impossible to reduce his thought to plain statements. Stan Cohen is, as they used to say, multivocal, and we can dwell on only a few of his voices. Indeed, John Braithwaite said to one of us how difficult it is to summarise his argument: the best and perhaps the only way forward, he said, is to allow him to speak for himself in quotation.

Stan Cohen was at an important stage committed to the view that it was difficult to disentangle the personal and biographical from the professional and intellectual. He told his friend and sometime collaborator, Laurie Taylor, that he had for a long while been 'sold on the 60s idea that you could integrate every part of your life: the idea that your soul, your teaching, writing, political activity could all be harmonised into a single whole' (Taylor 2004). He later modified that view, calling it a 'kitsch theoretical synthesis' and saying that it should be replaced by no more than a linkage joining the 'private/personal with the political/public' (Cohen 2003: 2–3). But the biographical and intellectual did converge in his own life in several interesting ways. He would use himself and his circumstances reflexively as materials. It was with Laurie Taylor that he wrote *Escape Attempts*, in which they recalled how they 'took notes about our own "normal" deviance; smoking dope with our students, organising anti-Vietnam war demonstrations, watching porno movies' (1976: 2). He is a storyteller who translated his experiences into narratives embellished by literary reference (Burroughs, Kafka, Kerouac, Orwell, Rinehart and Serge loom large), powerful metaphor, and mellifluous and fluent writing (he once made the remarkable confession that he did not find writing difficult). And that is his first strength: unlike many social scientists, he is a cultivated person who can see the world through literary eyes.

Born as a Jew and trained as a social worker in the South Africa of apartheid, he came to England in 1963 to practise, but then repeatedly changed course to embark on a successful academic career in London, Durham and Essex, emigrate to Israel in 1980 and return to London in 1994. He has been a wanderer, something of a *Steppenwolf* or 'intellectual maverick' (Plummer 2003: 2), who has not always settled or been at ease. Of Britain in the 1960s and 1970s, he said that it was 'a sour, post welfare state [society] which had patently not delivered the goods' (Cohen 1987: iii). 'I was,' he recalled of his first sojourn in the country, 'acutely aware that [my] original commitments could never find a home in English politics. I couldn't read about what was happening in South Africa and Israel and then connect with the striking British trades unionists or university Trotskyists' (Taylor 2004). His fellow countryman, Adam Kuper, pronounced at a colloquium held in his honour at the London School of Economics (LSE) in June 2006 that neither he nor Stan Cohen had ever felt at home in England. Yet he was also to become an outsider in the political life of the Israel to which he and his family later removed. He came to lose his allegiance to Zionism and despair of its politics. As his former colleague, Ken Plummer, observed in an address delivered when Stan Cohen was awarded an honorary doctorate at the University of Essex in July 2003, 'in Israel he came to detest the atrocities generated through the Israeli-Arab conflicts. … This was one of the most unhappy periods of his life – although he loved the country.'

Marginal, something of an outsider looking in, he could not but experience a sense of anthropological distance, in which what others took for granted could be seen as extraordinary and problematic. Marginality may not be comfortable existentially, but it is propitious methodologically, and Stan Cohen was from the first committed to what he called a 'sceptical' approach (Cohen 1971), in which, as he later put it, there is an attempt 'to make the world look different: a strange terrain appears imperceptibly to be familiar or, just as interesting, a familiar terrain begins to look a little strange' (Cohen 1985: 1). It is at such points of transformation that questions and contrasts emerge, and they are worth cultivating. Stan Cohen has refused adamantly to accept *ab initio* the surface appearance of things, or, more important and unusually, the accounts (even the sceptical accounts) offered by others, including friends, intellectual allies and close colleagues, about how things appear. He has achieved originality and strength by the apparently simple device of remorselessly interrogating what others are content to leave unanalysed. Nothing, not even the enterprise of criminology itself (see Cohen 1988), is to be accepted outright, and certainly not because a colleague or authority says it must be so ('The golden rule is this,' he remarked, 'be suspicious whenever both sides claim to be "realists"' (Cohen 2003: 5)). Almost everything is to be dissected, patiently, honestly, unremittingly and at close quarters, to see what it might reveal, and in his teaching and writing he has coaxed the most commonplace problems into yielding intriguing answers. There is in all this not only a transparent integrity and insistence on purpose and method, but also an application of mature common sense, a practical wisdom, that refuses to bow to mere fad, cleverness or superficial show. He returns time and again with piercing observations to discomfit pretension. Of the three 'voracious gods' confronting the sociologist, he claimed, two were 'an overriding obligation to pursue honest intellectual enquiry (however sceptical, irrelevant and unrealistic) … [and] a political commitment to social justice' (Cohen 1998: 122).

That drive to integrity and justice is what made the essay introducing the second edition of *Folk Devils and Moral Panics*, the book based on his PhD dissertation, so memorable. The first edition had described the manner in which public interpretations of the confrontations between mods and rockers had been progressively elaborated to create folk monsters. The second questioned the weight of theory which other sociologists had subsequently woven around his themes of oppression, resistance and youthful culture. They had, he remarked, asked young people to bear a 'symbolic baggage … [that] is just too heavy … the interrogations are just a little forced. … [it] is an imaginative way of reading the style; but how can we be sure that it is also not imaginary?' (Cohen 1980: xv). What decisively shattered his credulity, and his credulity as a Jew above all, was the assertion that the cultural appropriation of the swastika by punks in the 1970s should not and could not be read as anything but a piece of politically innocuous mockery: 'Time and time again, we are assured that although this symbol is "on one level" intended to outrage and shock, it is *really* being employed in a meta-language: the wearers are ironically distancing themselves from the very message that the symbol is usually intended to convey. … But how are we to know this?' (Cohen 1980: xvii). Equally direct was his *riposte* to Taylor, Walton and Young's revolutionary vision of socialist diversity (1973). He had, he said, 'an aversion to the apocalyptic'

(1974: 30), and he questioned the failure of the radical criminologists closely to confront not only core problems of guilt, justice and tolerance but also the empirical evidence of how social life unfolded in countries ostensibly marked by 'socialist diversity'. Those are matters which cannot be trusted to the benign workings of a post-capitalist world. Socialist legality, he mused, tends to mean a 'model of social control in which offenders wearing sandwich boards listing their crimes before a crowd which shouts, "Down with the counter-revolutionaries!" are then led away to be publicly shot' (1979a: 44). Many of us may have entertained those sentiments in private, but it took a certain courage to voice them.

Relentless scepticism can blur into despair, and despair into *Weltschmerz*. There is at the heart of almost everything Stan Cohen writes an anguish about the human condition. He is, he said, a 'pessimist, a "miserabilist", even a depressive' (Cohen 2003: 5). 'The story of democratic society's attempts to control crime and deviance,' he came to write, 'is a depressing record of utopian visions gone sour, liberal hopes twisted into authoritarian nightmares and old promises lingering on to buttress policies long since discredited' (1979b: 250). Six years later, he wrote again that 'our private sense of what is going on around us … [centres on a] private terrain [that] is inhabited by premonitions of *Nineteen Eighty-Four*, *Clockwork Orange* and *Brave New World*, by fears about new technologies of mind control, by dark thoughts about the increasing intrusion of the state into family lives, by a general unease that more of our actions and thoughts are under surveillance and subject to control and manipulation. Social control has become Kafka-land, a paranoid landscape in which things are done to us, without our knowing when, why or by whom, or even that they are being done' (1985: 6–7). There are parallels repeatedly drawn between the prison and the pains and confinements of everyday life, men and women being trapped inside cages of their own and others' making, and the stratagems they devise to break free only evolve tragically into new forms of constraint and accommodation with power (Cohen and Taylor 1972, 1976).

Such despair is perhaps the only condition on which Stan Cohen did not fully turn his own scepticism. It is engrained and absolute, perhaps too absolute, for there are eddies and stirrings of change in criminal justice systems which might persuade one that everything is not always for the worst in the worst of all possible worlds. After all, there is in the West, for good or bad reasons, less corporal and capital punishment, less public branding and punishment, than there once was (Spierenberg 1984; Gatrell 1994). There is less formal and informal repression of many forms of deviance and crimes without victims.

There are inclusionary projects at work and a greater concern (if only for oblique reasons) with victims and victimisation.

Although it was not always apparent at the time, the late 1960s was a fertile period to emerge as a sociologist of deviance in Britain. The expansion of the universities prompted by the Robbins Report (1963), the mass hiring of new staff, and the break in generational continuities and allegiances combined with a similar efflorescence of scholarship in North America to introduce a new intellectual ferment and fluidity that were to be confirmed institutionally in the founding in 1968 of the National Deviancy Conference, an oppositional body whose members shared in common what were sometimes exaggerated views about 'official criminology ... ranging from ideological condemnation to a certain boredom' (Cohen 1979: 26). What the conference celebrated, and Stan Cohen himself did so much to foster, was a set of founding propositions about what a sociology of crime and deviance should be: 'what is necessary is to recognise,' he once said, 'the problematic nature of social control ... appreciation; the political implications of studying deviance ... [and that] the field has something to do with control, power, legitimacy, ideology' (1974: 4–5). Those were to prove contradictory themes in tension with one another, and they conduced to a debate about whether the sociology of deviance should become more politically engaged (and in a revolutionary direction); more fully theorised (and theorised in what was to be a Marxist vein); more eclectic or more inclined toward the ethnographic. Stan Cohen declared that he had no wish exclusively to adopt any of those paths (1974: 30), and he explored them all, concluding pointedly and in retrospect that 'real sociological understanding requires distance, even detachment, from your subject' (Cohen 2003: 5). But what chiefly mattered is that he had begun to make his mark *before* the new criminologies forked, and he continued to exercise influence thereafter as an ancestral father figure over all the criminological lineages: the radicals represented, say, by Stuart Henry and by Ian Taylor, Paul Walton and Jock Young; the cultural criminologists raised in Birmingham by Stuart Hall; the symbolic interactionists personified by Ken Plummer; those concerned with academically informed projects of criminal justice reform by David Downes; and others still, harder to classify, by David Garland. He now occupies an interesting place, almost above controversy, and is steadfastly admired by those who are little inclined to admire one another.

The work of Stan Cohen over four decades has thus come to acquire a classical status in the fields of criminology, sociology and human rights. His writing, research, teaching and practical engagement in these fields have been at once rigorously analytical and intellectually inspiring. It amounts to a unique contribution, immensely varied yet with several unifying themes, and it has made, and continues to make, a lasting impact around the world.

His first major work, *Folk Devils and Moral Panics* (1972), already encapsulated some key preoccupations. In it, he captured the nuances of the control of youthful deviance at one moment of British social history: the mods and rockers conflicts of the mid-1960s. But he also famously provided a template for the analysis of certain forms of reaction to crime and deviance that have universal validity. A decade later, his metaphorical creativity, post-Foucault, in the analysis of the 'dispersal of control' gave rise to concepts of 'net-widening' and the penetration of the state into civil society which have again proved lasting influences on criminological research. *Visions of Social Control* (1985) is the landmark book relating to that second phase of his thought. His third major seminal achievement was to travel intellectually, in ways that sprang from his own move to Israel for 14 years, to engage with the burgeoning field of human rights. In the process, he brought his immense knowledge about crime, deviance and control to bear on new terrain. The consummation of that transition was *States of Denial* (2003): a fusion of his own biography, his own brand of criminology, and his concern for human rights to illuminate the capacities of states as well as individuals both to inflict and to deny 'atrocities and suffering'. It won the British Academy Book Prize.

His work thus has a protean character and scope which transcend time and place. A book of essays in his honour can aim only to build on and reflect some of his many-sided contributions. Moreover, his work encompasses far more than the major themes sketched in above. There are also studies of 'psychological survival' and prison life; so-called escape attempts of resistance to everyday banality; and any number of forays into the quiddities of academic life, from the surreal essay in *Against Criminology* (1988) called 'The Last Seminar' (the subject of reflection in this Festschrift by Howard Becker) to the critique of Malcolm Bradbury's novel *The History Man* (1985) for its depiction of enfeebled liberalism. Stan Cohen has a legendary appetite for 'black humour' and is himself capable of ferocious wit. He has worked with co-authors as varied as Laurie Taylor, Andrew Scull, Paul Rock, and Steven Lukes. He has lived and worked in South Africa, Israel and the USA as well as Britain.

We aim in this volume to represent as full a range as possible of those who have worked with him or who have worked with his work in mind. That work ranges from the relatively theoretical to the empirically sophisticated and intensely practical. The book contains chapters by some of the world's leading thinkers as well as the rising generation of scholars and practitioners whose approach has been shaped in significant respects by his own.

Stan Cohen devoted a great deal of critical attention to criminology and is often regarded as an anti-criminologist, though he himself used that term ironically. Yet he has evolved his own version of criminology, which is neither 'critical' simply, nor 'radical', and it is a *corpus* which has revitalised and reanimated the field over the past four decades. What one might term 'Cohenology' draws on a Durkheimian sense of paradox, a Weberian awareness of the 'iron cage', and Foucault's somewhat doom-laden conception of the 'carceral society'. However, above all, his work is animated by a thorough grounding in the work of the inheritors of the Chicagoan tradition of symbolic interactionism, Howard Becker and David Matza in particular, for their notions of labelling and signification, the shaping of deviance by control rather than the converse. It also gave him an acute preoccupation with the crimes of the state rather than the state of crime. That also led him to search for a way ahead other than through punishment and correction, and led onto his third major creative phase: a concern for human rights agendas that transcends the formulaic and offers practical as well as ethical guides to conflict resolution.

Cohen and Human Rights

Continuing with the theme of the merging of Stan Cohen's private and public lives, this integration of human rights into his work comes as no surprise. Born and raised in apartheid South Africa and subsequently living and working in Israel, Stan Cohen directly faced some of the greatest human rights abuses of the twentieth century and familiarity with both victims and perpetrators. It was in Israel that he turned directly to human rights work – as activist as well as scholar. Stan was a founder of the Public Committee Against Torture and co-authored the important B'Tselem report in 1991 on the interrogation of Palestinian detainees, described in the chapter in this volume by David Kretzmer.

Stan's last university post before retirement was as at the LSE, first Visiting Centennial Professor and subsequently as Martin White Professor of Sociology. At the LSE, Stan was instrumental in bringing human rights into the teaching curriculum as a truly multi- and interdisciplinary subject. He was one of a small group of scholars responsible for the setting up of the Centre for the Study of Human Rights. Postgraduate study under the auspices of the Centre commenced with a single MSc course, on Key Issues in Human Rights, that has since blossomed into a MSc degree exploring human rights from the perspectives of sociology, social policy, law, international relations and anthropology. In particular, he has challenged through dialogue the contemporary colonisation of human rights by lawyers by exposing the inadequacies and dangers of legal definition: how can 'severe pain or suffering' be understood as a legal threshold for torture? How can law be used to distinguish mental and physical pain? What sense can be made of a requirement that for genocide to be committed there must be an intention to destroy 'in whole or in part a national, ethnical, racial or religious group as such'? What is added – or omitted – by those weasel words, 'as such'? Furthermore, what are the historic, social and political conditions that generate torture or genocide, when do events become so labelled, and why? Through his further writings and stimulating class debate, Stan has challenged students to identify the essence of human rights abuses, in particular the commission of torture, political massacre and genocide, to consider the politics of violations and more generally of crimes of the state and of obedience.

Focus upon commission of gross human rights abuses brings with it the need to identify how and why people come to be able to live with their past and integrate it into their present. The South African Truth and Reconciliation Commission offers one such model that is compared with those from South American states, Eastern European states and other states where such attempts have been largely bypassed. Throughout such models is the critical theme of knowing: a person's knowing what he or she has done, or has seen, or has understood to have happened, or has caused in some way to happen. But knowing is often painful and people develop complex protective, often unconscious, techniques to avoid such knowing, or the consequences of knowing. In *States of Denial*, Stan Cohen examines how individuals and states – victims, perpetrators, observers or bystanders – know about yet deny the commission of atrocities and suffering: they block out and deny the occurrence of the acts; they see only what they want to see and wear blinkers to avoid seeing unpleasant events. Members of the Security Council deny the existence of genocide in Rwanda and thus try to shrug off the obligation of responding. Understanding denial is central to the effectiveness of transitional justice, to the work of human rights NGOs (non-governmental organisations) that must overcome it in order to engage people in their work and to the concept of an international community seeking to assert international human rights values. In the same vein, Stan Cohen's very recent work on torture, and in particular his editing of a special issue of *Index on Censorship* on exactly this subject, has led him to confront those scholars drawn from the liberal tradition who would now justify, explain or otherwise redefine torture in a way that allows state brutality a free moral rein

(Cohen 2005). Steadfast under pressure and incapable of being bullied or charmed by celebrity intellectuals, Stan Cohen showed right at the end of his formal career at LSE that steeliness that, combined with his intellect and literary talent, has made him such an esteemed performer in so many different academic arenas.

Acknowledgements

The editors would like to thank Sharon Shalev and Michael Shiner of the Department of Social Policy at the London School of Economics for their valuable help at various stages in compiling this book.

References

Cohen, S. (1971) *Introduction to Images of Deviance.* Harmondsworth: Penguin Books.

Cohen, S. (1974) 'Criminology and the sociology of deviance in Britain', in P. Rock and M. McIntosh (eds) *Deviance and Social Control.* London: Tavistock.

Cohen, S. (1979a) 'Guilt, justice and tolerance', in D. Downes and P. Rock (eds) *Deviant Interpretations.* Oxford: Martin Robertson.

Cohen, S. (1979b) Review of A. Scull, *Decarceration, British Journal of Sociology,* 30: 250–1.

Cohen, S. (1980) *Folk Devils and Moral Panics* (2nd edn). Oxford: Basil Blackwell.

Cohen, S. (1985) *Visions of Social Control.* Cambridge: Polity.

Cohen, S. (1988) *Against Criminology.* New Brunswick, NJ: Transaction.

Cohen, S. (1998) 'Intellectual scepticism and political commitment: the case of radical criminology', in P. Walton and J. Young (eds) *The New Criminology Revisited.* London: Macmillan.

Cohen, S. (2003) Response to Public Orator by Professor Stanley Cohen, University of Essex, 9 July 2003.

Cohen, S. (ed.) (2005) *Torture: A User's Manual. Index on Censorship,* 34 (no. 1).

Cohen, S. and Taylor, L. (1972) *Psychological Survival: The Experience of Long-Term Imprisonment.* London: Penguin.

Cohen, S. and Taylor, L. (1976) *Escape Attempts.* London: Allen Lane.

Gatrell, V. (1994) *The Hanging Tree: Execution and the English People.* Oxford: Oxford University Press.

Plummer, K. (2003) Speech as Public Orator, University of Essex, 9 July.

Robbins (1963) *Report of the Committee on Higher Education,* Cmnd. 2154. London: HMSO.

Spierenberg, P. (1984) *The Spectacle of Suffering: Execution and the Evolution of Repression.* Cambridge: Cambridge University Press.

Taylor, I., Walton, P. and Young, J. (1973) *The New Criminology.* London: Routledge and Kegan Paul.

Taylor, L. (2004) 'The other side of the street', *New Humanist,* 119: 4. www.newhumanist.org.uk/volume119issue4.

Part 1
Seminal Influences

Chapter 1

Growing up with Stan

Adam Kuper

Stan and I have been friends almost forever. I actually attended the same kindergarten as Ruth, Stan's future wife, but (as far as I remember) Stan and I first came together at Saxonwold Primary School in Johannesburg, at the age of 5, going on 6. Together we went on to Parktown High School for Boys, on the edge of the ridge, opposite the University of the Witwatersrand. In 1959 we crossed the road to the University. And shortly after graduation we both went to Britain for postgraduate studies in the social sciences.

In the first half of 2006, Stan and I recorded four conversations about those years. We agreed that our experience of growing up in South Africa in the 1950s and early 1960s shaped us as social scientists, but we were uncertain about quite how that happened, or what had been the decisive forces that propelled us along similar paths.

Our one real disagreement, however, has to do with the question of agency. I tend to ask what made us choose one path rather than another. As we reminisced, I was haunted by Robert Frost's poem:

> I shall be telling this with a sigh
> Somewhere ages and ages hence:
> Two roads diverged in a wood, and I –
> I took the one less traveled by,
> And that has made all the difference.

'You're interested in why things happen,' Stan said to me at one point in our conversations. 'I'm interested in why people say things happen.' He is unconcerned about the road not taken. Indeed, he resists the idea that choices were made. He prefers the image of someone drifting along a stream, taken-for-granted habits and ideas propelling him more or less gently between the banks. He believes that we exercise little independent volition, however much we may go in for rationalisation.

Growing up together, we assumed that we were exactly the same sort of people, but as we talked these past few months it became apparent that our family backgrounds were different in some crucial ways – crucial, certainly, had we been British boys of the same generation.

Stan's mother was the youngest – and the only South African-born – daughter of Polish-Jewish immigrants, who lived in a rural area of the Cape. She was the only member of the family to get a high-school education. And she went on to university. Stan's father came to South Africa from Lithuania as a young man, together with four brothers and one sister. He started off as a trader in rural Zululand and learnt to read English, but not to write it. All Stan's parents' friends were small businessmen, most of them immigrants. Stan says he used to think the only difference between people was that some were in retail and others in wholesale.

My father's grandfather had come to South Africa from Lithuania in the 1880s, accompanied by six brothers and a sister. My grandfather was sufficiently integrated to have been arrested by the British as a spy during the Boer War and imprisoned in St Helena. My parents, all my uncles, several of my aunts and all my parents' friends were professionals or big businessmen. All the men and most of the women were graduates of the University of the Witwatersrand.

We were, I think, unaware of these differences – certainly unconcerned by them – and in fact they were insignificant as compared with our common experiences. We were both shaped from the start by the Judaism that enveloped us as children, by the Zionism of our adolescence, and then by our exhilarating, liberating student days at the University of the Witwatersrand during the revolutionary years in which the apartheid system was elaborated and the opposition began to crystallise.

South African society was organised above all by race, but the whites themselves were firmly divided into ethnic communities. The Jews were culturally assimilated to the Anglos, but they remained socially remarkably self-contained, even in their professional lives. Intermarriage was rare. Our own school friends were almost entirely Jewish boys. We were not much interested in the lives of other communities, let alone the wider world.

But if the Jewish world of our childhood was cohesive and absorbing, it is not easy to define the character of its Jewishness. Religion was not a matter of faith. None of us, indeed nobody in our parents' circles, was a true believer. We had to go to synagogue on Saturdays and holidays, and we studied Hebrew. But we travelled to synagogue by car. On Saturday afternoon my father drove off for his tennis game. The kitchens were kosher, but Stan's family had a special plate and knife for biltong, which could not be made from kosher beef. Stan's father's message to his sons was that he kept up the forms out of loyalty. In the wake of the Holocaust he could not allow himself to be the one to end the line of tradition. My father was also motivated mainly by a concern for solidarity, although he thought that we might be glad one day to have a religion to fall back on. My mother barely pretended to care about religion or ritual. Anyone who showed signs of religious enthusiasm was regarded by us, and by our parents, as *meshugah* (crazy).

The bedrock belief was that Jews should stick together. Zionism, which I suspect was largely a projection of the position of Jews in South Africa onto the wider world, was the one unchallenged idea, although there were terrific quarrels between Zionists of different camps. As adolescents, Stan and I belonged to Zionist youth movements – his, by chance, socialist; mine (my father's choice) not. A big attraction was that there were girls. Our parents and theirs approved. Indeed, it was taken for granted that we would eventually marry one of those girls, and most us did, as soon as we could.

University was the great break. Not because, like young Britons and Americans, we now left home for the first time. In fact, when we went to the University, at the age of 16 going on 17, we lived with our parents. But when we travelled up the hill to the University of the Witwatersrand we entered a different world. We were enchanted by our studies: history and anthropology in my case; the applied social sciences in Stan's. They helped us to understand the society that engrossed us, South Africa. And when we got there, Wits was still, just, racially integrated. Our fellow students included Africans and Indians, who took our broader education in hand. Essop Pahad, a common friend, is now Thabo Mbeki's right-hand man. Stan's best friend in his social-work class – one of the most significant friends of his student days – was Zanele Dlamini, who later married Thabo Mbeki. His friendship with Zanele was based on the fact that he was the only man in the class and she was the only black.

These were fraught times. Our years at Wits coincided with the first great crisis of the apartheid system, marked by the campaign against passbooks, Sharpeville, and the State of Emergency. We talked politics obsessively, began to find our place in the spectrum of opposition movements, marched in protest to Johannesburg Fort, in which several Witsies were among those imprisoned without trial during the Emergency, and which was conveniently just up the road from the campus.

There was never the slightest question that I was headed for one of the professions, although there was some anxiety that I might end up as an academic like my father's brother and his wife, and some of his less satisfactory cousins. Stan's parents accepted that he was a *luftmensch*, obviously not cut out for business. His decision to train as a social worker was regarded as eccentric, but his father would later be impressed when Stan and his younger brother Robin found steady jobs that required them to go to work only irregularly, and then dressed in jeans and tee-shirts.

As soon as we graduated from Wits, we left the country. Was this the one great choice we made? Stan sees it as a product of taken-for-granted assumptions. Staying in South Africa was not an option as far back as we could remember, although different reasons for emigration would be articulated, at the time and afterwards, ranging from pessimism about the political future to a desire to escape from our provincial world. In any case, most of our friends also went abroad, to study in Britain or, in a few cases, to settle in Israel.

Stan went to the LSE and he was to be marked – I think indelibly – by those radical years, although he never became a sectarian. I was committed to Africa, became an anthropologist, and spent the years from 1964 to 1970 largely in Botswana and Uganda. I missed the 1960s. Our fields of research were also very different. Yet I agree with Stan that we became social scientists of a rather peculiar type as a result of growing up as we did, when we did, in South Africa. Stan says that the issues which are so much part of him, problems of identity and marginality, deviance and conformity, resistance and injustice, all are rooted, for him, in his South African background. Perhaps one can be even more specific. 'My identity as a South African Jew is my primary identity,' Stan told me. 'If it is my primary identity, then it must, somehow, have influenced my choice of subjects and the way I did things.'

On the rest – our lives as grown-ups – I have only this to add. Neither of us became rooted in Britain, and we each spent many years in midcareer abroad, Stan in Israel, I in the Netherlands. We eventually drifted back, ending up, together again, in North London, sometimes dreaming that we might one day be able to go home, if only for an extended visit. To this day, we think of ourselves as South Africans. We both fail the cricket test.

Chapter 2

The art of exile: a study of Alexander Herzen

Richard Sennett

In the early spring of 1848, it seemed to Parisians like 'Daniel Stern' (the *nom de plume* of Marie d'Agoult, Franz Liszt's one-time companion, whose chronicles of 1848 are a vivid record of the upheaval) that the 'foreign colony will empty in a few days, as our friends return to the places which call them.'[1] Given the nationalisms being trumpeted in the press, her expectation seems logical. The political question this nationalism posed to all those who had become foreigners – émigrés, expatriates, or exiles – is, why aren't you home among your own kind? How, indeed, could you be Russian, somewhere else? Yet, by late April of 1848, Daniel Stern had noted that, oddly, few of the émigrés had left for home. 'They are still to be found arguing in the Palais Royal, receiving emissaries from abroad, hectoring; they are full of hope, but no one has packed his bags.'[2]

Perhaps the greatest of nineteenth-century exiles was a man who would make but a brief appearance on this scene yet, from observing it, would capture in indelible prose the cursed relation between nationalism and the condition of being a foreigner. Alexander Herzen was the illegitimate son of an ageing Russian nobleman and a young German woman (hence his name, which is roughly equivalent to 'of my heart' [*herzlich*]). Inspired by the uprising of 1825, he was, as a young man, active in radical Russian politics as these politics were then understood; that is, he was a proponent of constitutional monarchy and liberal reforms. For this, he suffered internal exile and eventually expulsion from the Russian Empire. Like others of his generation, he thought of himself at first as in temporary exile, expecting to return to his native land when political circumstances made it possible. But when, at last, this possibility arose, he held back. It was not social assimilation, or love for European culture, or personal ties, like those of his friend Turgenev to Pauline Viardot, that kept him from returning. He remained passionately interested in the affairs of his country but felt no longer able to live in it. He perambulated the capitals of Western Europe, passing his later years in London, where he published a famous newsletter about Russian realities called *The Bell*.

There is a certain kind of social thinking, falsely humane, which posits an inverse relation between consciousness and circumstance. In this kind of thinking, the sufferings of the poor make them intellectual victims of their necessities; poor thought is the sheer calculation of survival. The niceties of consciousness, the complexities of interpretation, are seen as luxuries of the affluent. In this way of thinking, the bastard son of an aristocrat can be no guide to the dilemmas faced by the wave upon wave of emigrants who would quit Europe in the nineteenth century, much less a guide for the conundrums faced by Mexican day workers, Korean grocers, Soviet Jews, or other foreigners today. Herzen, the friend of John Stuart Mill, diffident with the diffidence bred of attending many formal occasions, Herzen so curious about the places in which, yet, he knew he did not belong, Herzen enters the story we have to tell in April of 1848. It was at this moment of delay that Herzen joined the exile colony in Paris; he did so to move away from Rome, which was in its own first moments of nationalist awakening.

It must not be thought that Herzen or the other Parisian émigrés who did not immediately respond to the call of their own nation were cowards; the lives of many émigrés read as a long series of prior imprisonment and torture, particularly at the hands of the Austrian police. In part, the answer to their immobility was to be found in a familiar cruelty, that of events passing them by. Their web of mutual contacts abroad was outdated, just as their political plans for constitutions and government agencies had no place in the new rhetoric of the people. But more than this, as Daniel Stern noted, something had happened to the foreigners themselves in exile. 'It is as though they have looked in the mirror and seen another face than the one they thought they would see,' she wrote.[3] It puzzled the émigrés, as well as her: something in them resisted returning; something held them back.

It was exactly this connection that Herzen would, in the course of his life, take up, seeking to understand how nationalism had forced people to look in something like Manet's mirror to find a liveable, humane image of themselves. Ritual, belief, habit, and the signs of language would appear far different in this displacing mirror than at home. The foreigner might indeed have a more intelligent, more humane relation to his or her culture than the person who has never moved, who knows nothing but that which is, who has not been obliged to ponder the differences of one culture from another. But that is not the pressing business of becoming a foreigner. It is rather that one has, with one's own displaced condition, to deal creatively with the materials of identity the way an artist has to deal with the dumb facts which are things to be painted. One has to make oneself.

This was, at least, the possibility that Herzen sensed, reading newspaper accounts of a wave of violence in Slovakia directed against the Gypsies who had poured into the country, the Gypsies believing in 1848, as in 1990, that a nation which rises against its masters might promise them freedom as well; Herzen sipping wine in the Café Lamblin which even a century and a half later serves that beverage in the adulterated form which disgusted him; Herzen's companions plotting, telegraphing, arguing, and remaining; Herzen leading a foreign contingent in a march on the National Assembly, in support of the 'rights of man'. They would have to find a new way to be Russian.

On 27 June 1848, the revolution came to an end in Paris. Troops swept through the city indiscriminately shooting into crowds, deploying cannon in random barrages into working-class neighbourhoods; the forces of order had arrived. Herzen, like the other foreigners who had remained in Paris of their own free will, was now forced to leave; he went to Geneva, then back to Italy, and then back to France, arriving finally in London in August of 1852, an ailing, middle-aged man whose wife was erotically engaged elsewhere; who had set himself publicly against the Slavophiles dominating radical discourse in his homeland; and who spoke English haltingly in the manner of novels he had read by Sir Walter Scott. '[L]ittle by little I began to perceive that I had absolutely nowhere to go and no reason to go anywhere.'[4] It is not inflating his suffering to say that at this moment Herzen became something like a tragic figure, a man who felt the second scar of homelessness which will not heal.

What is instructive about Herzen's writings is the sense he comes to make about how to conduct daily life in such a condition, how to make sense of being a foreigner. 'By degrees, a revolution took place within me.' In part, he began to make a virtue of his very isolation in exile: 'I was conscious of power in myself.... I grew more independent of everyone.'[5] And so he began to reconstruct how he saw the world around him: '[N]ow the masquerade was over, the dominoes had been removed, the garlands had fallen from the heads, the masks from the faces.' To explain the consequences of this new vision of others in this personal crisis of exile, Herzen resorted to the same imagery of displaced vision that Daniel Stern had evoked. 'I saw features different from those that I had surmised.'[6]

Rather than making of his exile a reason for spiritual transcendence of the world itself, as a Christian might, Herzen stayed on the ground; he tried to understand how foreigners should cope with their own nationality. The nation, for a person who had become a foreigner, posed two dangers: one a danger of forgetting, and the other of remembering; the one a condition in which the foreigner was demeaned by the desire to assimilate, and the other a condition in which he or she was destroyed by nostalgia.

In his own experience, Herzen came, in the 1850s, to see these dangers exemplified by two men from his past in the 1830s and the early 1840s. The first, Ivan Golovin, was, like Herzen, a political refugee of those years, but he had at first seemed to Herzen simply a despicable individual, a small-time crook barred after a few years from the Paris stock exchange, an exploiter of his fellow exiles, flitting from scene to scene. Herzen now came to see his personal vices magnified by the conduct of his exile: 'What had he left Russia for? What was he doing in Europe? ... Uprooted from his native soil, he could not find a center of gravity.'[7] The importance of Golovin's character was magnified in Herzen's reflections in London. Golovin's character, Herzen wrote, 'bears the stamp of a whole class of people', those whose very desire to assimilate had led to a loss of self,

> [those] who live nomadic lives, with cards or without cards at spaces and in great cities, invariably dining well, known by everybody, and about whom everything is known, except two things: what they live on and what they live for. Golovin was a Russian officer, a French *braider* and *hobbler*, an English swindler, a German *Junker*, as well as our native Nozdrev and Khlestakov [characters from Gogol].[8]

Abroad, such people see that their new compatriots cannot understand what it was like in the place the émigrés came from, or it does not interest them – understandably so, it is all so far away, so long ago; in a word, so foreign. And so, men like Golovin, afraid to risk alienating or boring the others, act as though it never was.

Herzen was much too civilized to look at those foreigners seeking to assimilate as necessarily morally tainted. He looked at them rather as people engaged in a kind of voluntary amnesia, and he feared that from this will to forget could come other acts of denial. In the painting the foreigners were making of their lives, large patches were overpainted in white.

One might perhaps reformulate the insight Herzen had in looking at Golovin as follows: the desire for assimilation can be experienced as a force that creates a sense of shame about oneself, and so weakens one's ego strength. Of course, the capacity to assimilate requires income, and educational and occupational advantages that an aspiring 'new American', say, is likely to lack. But a person consumed by the desire to assimilate may also behave like a self-censor, screening out the full range of experiences and observations that he or she has lived; self-screening supposes there is something shameful, unacceptable, in one's past to be kept from others. For the foreigner, this cycle of censorship and shame can begin with nothing more than feeling that the gesture of touching others when one talks to them, or the smell of foreign foods on one's breath, is something that must be corrected. Shame about the fact that one's breath smells odd when one eats foods from the old country is reinforced by the very fear of breathing into the faces of people who do not eat these foods. Feeling ashamed of oneself is indeed likely to lead to the loss of judgement, if not moral probity, that Herzen observed in Golovin. It is why, for us, the famous 'melting pot' of American myth may function more like a meltdown of the ego's ethical powers.[9]

Golovin is a significant figure in Herzen's own attempt to work out what it means to be Russian somewhere else – the attempt to understand how to make a humane displacement of one's nationality. In a famous letter to the editor of the *Moscow News* from Paris on 1 February 1866, Golovin declared, 'I was a man before I was a Russian.'[10] Herzen prints this letter at the very end of his portrait of Golovin – and, indeed, of the first edition of *My Past and Thoughts*. The irony is meant to resonate. Such a declaration in the Age of Enlightenment could come from Kant; now it comes from a stock speculator and extortion artist, anxious only to fit in wherever he is. The revelations of exile surely cannot end this way. For the foreigner, the knowledge that he comes from elsewhere, rather than being a source of shame, should be a cautionary knowledge.

For Herzen, economic individualism was the great danger of the era of capitalist expansion he saw coming into being. Nationalism and capitalism could march hand in hand, as Herzen, a confirmed socialist, argued again and again in *The Bell*. By contrast, Herzen's hopes for a socialist movement were pinned on immigrants. Their very displacement gave them the experience, or at least the possibility, of looking beyond themselves, of dealing with others similarly displaced in a cooperative fashion.

As a reader of Herzen, it is here that I find him at his most compelling. Herzen would have thought it perfectly comprehensible that ethnic groups in modern America were at the centre of liberalism of the American kind, feeble version of democratic socialism in Europe that it is. He would have explained this relation between immigration and liberality, I think, by saying that the scars of displacement had liberally disposed those aware of themselves as foreigners, unlike the Golovins, who seek only to forget. Herzen's belief that socialism is most practicable by foreigners is an idealization of displacement, to be sure, but an ideal founded on a profound and profoundly sceptical view that the evils of possessive individualism could ever be cured by communal relations of the nationalist, homogeneous, self-referential sort. Only the knowledge of difference and the experience of displacement can erect a barrier of experience against the appetites of possessive individualism.

In reading Herzen as a writer about our own times in germ, one needs to think about the distinction between liberalism and pluralism. The modern ground rule of identity threatens constantly to restrict personal freedom to cultural practice: your needs are legitimate insofar as they can be identified with what the Mexican community, or elderly Russians, or young black women, *do*. The liberal ideal can be degraded into mere pluralism through a particular application of this rule. Pluralism then becomes simply a matter of defining the borders between communities sharing abutting territories; within each, people live as though they have never left home, as though nothing has happened. Paradoxically, it is the vivid consciousness of oneself as a foreigner that is necessary to defeat this pluralist self-enclosure in ethnicity. Herzen recalls someone in England saying to him, '"In your words," a very worthy man said to me, "one hears an outside spectator speaking." But I did not come to Europe as an outsider, you know. An outsider is what I have become.'[11] And for this same reason, in their recent book *Immigrant America*, Alejandro Portes and Ruben Rumbaut flatly declare, 'Assimilation as the rapid transformation of immigrants into Americans "as everyone else" has never happened.'[12] Their assertion is more than a sociological observation; it is the affirmation of a necessary, enlightened consciousness.

Nostalgia, the opposite danger to amnesia, seems a simpler condition. Indeed, it seemed so to Herzen in Geneva in 1850 just after he had quitted Paris with the other central European refuges. For the first time it dawned on many of them that they were in permanent exile, triggering in them the dangers of nostalgia:

> All *émigrés*, cut off from the living environment to which they have belonged, shut their eyes to avoid seeing bitter truths, and grow more and more acclimatized to a closed, fantastic circle consisting of inert memories and hopes that can never be realized.

And again,

Leaving their native land with concealed anger, with the continual
thought of going back to it once more on the morrow, men do not
move forwards but are continually thrown back upon the past.

From which Herzen concluded that exiles could be enslaved as well by
their own powers of memory, those 'questions, thoughts and memories
which make up an oppressive, binding tradition'.[13]

Fifteen years later, in London, Herzen took up again in his memoirs
the subject of émigré nostalgia, and now it, too, was transformed
by his own transformation in exile. Herzen wrote of his encounters
with Father Vladimir Pecherin in a short portrait worthy of Chekhov.
Pecherin was someone Herzen, like all people of his generation, knew
about. In the mid-1830s, the young Pecherin had taken up the chair of
Greek at Moscow University, and felt himself, in the next few years,
suffocating in his homeland; in Herzen's words, '[R]ound about was
silence and solitude: everything was dumb submission with no hope,
no human dignity, and at the same time extraordinarily, dull, stupid
and petty.'[14] Pecherin, the young classics professor, decided to emigrate,
surprising none of his contemporaries, who were also suffocating in
Mother Russia; Pecherin boarded a boat for England, landed – and
suddenly entered a Jesuit monastery. In this, he did surprise other
young people around him, who could not understand how he could
revolt against one system of authority, only to submit to another.

When Herzen landed in England, he sought out Pecherin, to make
his acquaintance and to ask if some of Pecherin's youthful poems might
be reprinted in Herzen's publication *The Bell*. They met in the Jesuit
monastery of St Mary's Clapham; the two Russians began by speaking
French to each other, then, although Pecherin feared that he could
hardly remember his mother tongue, in Russian. He was avid for news,
doubted the value of his Russian poems, yet was keen for the younger
man's opinion. After their meeting, they began to correspond, the Jesuit
convert writing in French about materialism, science, and faith, writing
with an intensity to this stranger, assuming that no boundaries stood
between their full exposure to one another – as no Frenchman, whether
devout or not, would presume to do.

Herzen tells us all this as preparation for recounting an event he
read about in the newspapers two years later, in 1855. A Jesuit monk,
described in the press as a 'Reverend Father Wladimir Petcherine,
a native of Russia' was on trial for burning a Protestant Bible in a
marketplace in an Irish town. Here is Herzen's digest of what happened
at the trial: 'The proud British judge, taking into consideration the
senselessness of the action and the fact that the accused was a Russian,
and England and Russia were at war [the Crimean War], confined

himself to a paternal exhortation to decent behavior in the streets in future.'[15]

Even more fascinating than the story Herzen recounts is the fact that he had got it all wrong by 1865, when he came to write this part of his memoirs. In fact, Pecherin showed that he had caused some pornographic literature to be burnt, not a Bible, and he was acquitted. The sensation at the time was about a Jesuit taking 'direct action' when discovering smut; the future Prime Minister Gladstone, much interested in the conditions of prostitution in modern England, was, for one, intrigued by this direct action against pornography. There is a reason for Herzen, in recalling it, to alter (I do not suppose with conscious intent to deceive) the story of Pecherin's trial. For to Herzen, this is a story of how those displaced from their homeland can remain prisoners of the past. It makes perfect sense to Herzen: a Russian messenger arrives who will print evidences of Pecherin's past life, the life of a young man passed in Moscow when Tsar Nicholas, abetted by the clergy, had organized police searches in the universities for heretical writings. For Herzen, the point of the story is that Pecherin suffered something like an atavistic seizure. The youthful victim of orthodoxy had become a policeman of heresy.

Pecherin is an exemplary figure of a disaster which Herzen had come to observe with ever greater fear during his years of exile: it is what Freud was later to call the 'return of the repressed'.[16] The return of the repressed is of far greater danger to the foreigner than explicit longing for the past. This return of the repressed befalls those who do not work to transform that part of themselves which lives in memory. The foreigner must confront memories of home; memory must be displaced, refracted, so that he or she is not suddenly seized by the past, acting out the injuries received long ago, now playing instead another role in that old drama. But how is a transformation to occur so that the drama itself is rewritten?

The advice which thus gradually takes form in the pages of Herzen's memoirs about how to behave in the countries where the foreigner lives, is something like this: 'participate, but do not identify'. The admonition, 'participate, but do not identify', is a way for a foreigner to defeat the segregating game of pluralism. The impulse to participate is an assertion that one has rights as a political animal, a *zoon politikon*, wherever one lives. In place of the ancient device, nothing that is human is foreign to me, the device of modern identity could be, nothing that is foreign to me is real. President Nakasone of Japan once asserted: 'Only those who understand one another can make decisions together.'[17] A foreigner's assertion of the right to participate, beyond what pertains to his or her national identity, is one way to force the dominant society to acknowledge that there is, on the contrary, a public sphere beyond the borders of anthropology. It is also the only way to survive being personally imprisoned in a Balkanized, unequal city of differences.

Herzen found a way to create a picture of 'home' so as to make bearable his very yearning for it. In London, he says, suddenly he had become Italian:

> And now I sit in London where chance has flung me – and I stay here because I do not know what to make of myself. An alien race swarms confusedly about me, wrapped in the heavy breath of ocean, a world dissolving into chaos … and that other land – washed by the dark-blue sea under the canopy of a dark-blue sky … it is the one shining region left until the far side of the grave … O Rome, how I love to return to your deceptions, how eagerly I run over day by day the time when I was intoxicated with you![18]

'Home' is not a physical place but a mobile need; wherever one is, home is always to be found somewhere else. As Herzen's life unfolds in England, a sunless land of overly practical, if kindly, people, the home he needs will change countries, from a place of snow to sun, from the intimate village outside Moscow to the languid cafés of Rome. Herzen will always have a home, so long as he can change how it looks. This ironic, slightly bitter, knowledge about his need for 'home' came to Herzen as an older man; he acknowledged that he would never feel complete. Finally, he came to terms with insufficiency; it is permanent, the scar does not heal. And this same power of displacing 'home' was what he hoped for others who did not pack their bags when the borders opened in March of 1848, and who did not return to the beloved world of their childhood, their language, and their soil.

I have perhaps unfairly modulated Herzen's voice, which is that of a man who is more curious than censorious; as a writer, he understood that moral 'points' are best left implicit in the stories of individual lives. Yet, if I have done him this injustice, it is only because in his pages detailing the disastrous schemes of émigré bankers, the rage of Serbian poets reading nearly accurate English translations of their work, the struggle of many political émigrés to prevent the dissolution of socialist ideals in the acid of Slavic pseudo-religiosity – that these portraits of foreigners struggling to create a life abroad which yet does not cut them off from the past seem emblematic lives, just as the assertions of nationalism that took form in the last century are emblematic of the dangers of other racial, sexual, or religious assertions of identity.

The era of the 'universal citizen' celebrated by Kant was an era that could not conceive of mass migration, and that imagined capital as comfortingly stationary when invested in land and estates. The era of the 'universal citizen' in the eighteenth century, which produced constitutional ideas seemingly applicable anywhere – in provincial, self-serious America equally as in the France of a thousand courtesies married to smiling ironies – this era celebrated balance, and its social imagination was of equilibrium. In work of unbalanced material, the need arises, instead, for being-in-place.

The foreigner is the figure who has to cope with the dangers that lurk in this need. Since the foreigner cannot become a universal citizen, cannot throw off the mantle of nationalism, the only way he or she can cope with the heavy baggage of culture is to subject it to certain kinds of displacement that lighten its burdensome weight.

Herzen saw that his displacement from Russia had created a new kind of freedom in his life, a freedom of self apart from place, a freedom he felt strongly, but felt to be so new, so modern, that he could not claim to define it. Indeed, that very inability to say neatly and precisely who he was added to his sense of freedom. In this, he became the first, the emblematic, and, in the very qualities of his introspection and questioning of his condition, perhaps the greatest of foreigners.

Notes

1 Daniel Stern, *Oeuvres*, vol. 6, p. 353.
2 *Ibid.*
3 *Ibid.*, p. 466.
4 Herzen, *My Past and Thoughts*, vol. 3, p. 1024.
5 *Ibid.*
6 *Ibid.*, p. 1025.
7 *Ibid.*, p. 1399.
8 *Ibid.*
9 It is an insight which may bear on a large study of Mexican immigrants and Mexican-Americans which found '… the *higher* the level of acculturation (or 'Americanization') the greater the prevalence of … alcohol and drug abuse or dependance, phobia, and antisocial personality', Alejandro Portes and Ruben Rumbaut, *Immigrant America: A Portrait*, Berkeley, CA: University of California Press, 1990, p. 169.
10 Herzen, *My Past and Thoughts*, vol. 3, p. 1418.
11 *Ibid.*, p. 1065.
12 Portes and Rumbaut, p. 141.
13 Herzen, *My Past and Thoughts*, vol. 2, p. 686.
14 *Ibid.*, p. 1386.

15 *Ibid.*, p. 1397.
16 Cf. Sigmund Freud, *New Introductory Lectures on Psychoanalysis.*
17 An 'off-the-record' remark at the Council on Foreign Relations – but why should it be?
18 Herzen, *My Past and Thoughts*, vol. 2, p. 655.

Chapter 3

The other side of the street: an interview with Stan Cohen*

Laurie Taylor

He has spent his life analysing and opposing injustice and inhumanity. Sociologist Stan Cohen talks to Laurie Taylor about torture, social control and our extraordinary capacity to deny.

The orations that accompany the awarding of an honorary degree are rarely sophisticated studies in personality. There are too many lumpy academic references to get out of the way to leave much time for character insights. And so, when Stan Cohen was recently awarded an honorary doctorate at his old stomping ground, the University of Essex, it wasn't too surprising to find that his proposer, Ken Plummer, used most of the time outlining Stan's major academic achievements: his early work on mods and rockers which introduced the now ubiquitous and much misused concept of 'moral panic'; his Foucauldian exploration of modern systems of social control, which appeared as *Visions of Social Control*; and his most recent work, *States of Denial: Knowing About Atrocities and Suffering*, which won the British Academy Book Prize in 2002.

But after he'd done his formal duties, Plummer paused, as though he knew that none of these details captured anything of the man he'd known for over 30 years. What could he say in the short time that remained that would do proper justice to Cohen's presence in the world? A film came to his aid. 'In the delightful Christmas film by Frank Capra, *It's a Wonderful Life*, the hero, played by James Stewart, is taken back by his guardian angel to see just what life and the world would

*This chapter was first published as an article in *New Humanist* magazine (July/August 2004), and is reproduced with the kind permission of *New Humanist*.

have been like if he had not lived. The angel says: "Each person's life touches so many other lives. If they were not around it would leave an awful hole." So it is with Stan Cohen. It is not just through the big books he has published over the years that change has been effected; it is also in the small acts of kindness, and the little refusals to go along with the crowd's inhumanities.'

It's a well-expressed sentiment even if the phrase 'little refusals' hardly does sufficient justice to the times, particularly during his long stay in Israel, when Stan Cohen risked ostracism from even his most liberal colleagues and friends because of his big refusal to go along with what he saw as their fatally compromised vision.

I'm anxious to talk to him about that time in his life and specifically about the manner in which the work he did there on the torture used by Israeli security agents in the Occupied Territories led to the detailed psychological analysis of denial and self-deceit in his prize-winning *States of Denial*. But these days it's no longer possible to talk to Stan without first checking up on his own state of mind. The last few years have been cruel to him. Seven years ago he was diagnosed with Parkinson's disease. Despite the cocktails of drugs that he consumes, he now finds it increasingly difficult to walk any distance or to sit and write for any length of time. Matters have been further complicated by an extreme back condition that has failed to respond to surgery. The latest blow was the death from cancer of his beloved wife, Ruth. 'You know,' he jokes, after he's waved away my clumsy solicitudes. 'If Glen Hoddle was right, then I must have had a wonderful previous life.'

I take that as a cue to turn to his present incarnation. I know that he grew up in Johannesburg, where he and Ruth were involved in the Zionist youth movement. It was there that he developed his conviction that Israel provided an opportunity to build a good and fair society. At the same time, both of them were student activists in the struggle against apartheid (Zanele Dlamini, now wife of the South African president, Thabo Mbeki, was in Stan's social work class). Stan always looks back to South Africa as the real source of his political ideals. But when he left South Africa for England in 1963, he fully intended to stay for only a couple of years before going off to Israel to resume his Zionist commitment. Somehow or other he ended up living in England for 18 years – 18 years in which any utopian hopes about the type of good society that might be established in Israel were being brutally and systematically dashed.

But it was then, at the very time when even the most fervent supporters of the Israeli cause were beginning to run for cover, that he and Ruth decided to activate their early resolution and move to Israel. Why? 'Well, the quick answer is "madness". The long answer includes the pulls of "being Jewish", what Saul Bellow called "potato love", and then there was the idea of our kids growing up without this connection. I was also acutely aware that our original commitments could never find a home in English politics. I couldn't read about what was happening in South Africa and Israel and then connect with the striking British trades unionists or university Trotskyists. And I was also a sucker at that time for the notion of community, for the sense that there was somewhere where I would be at home. I felt that I had to report in somewhere and do my good things for some recognisable group around me.'

But hadn't he read enough about the realities of Israel in the early 80s to know that it had nothing to do with the Zionist ideals that he'd imbibed in his adolescent days in South Africa? 'For some reason, maybe now I'd call it denial, I didn't really take it in. So strong was the brainwashing that I'd received from the Zionist youth movement that I'd managed to avoid facing the full reality. But I do remember saying to someone who asked me the same question, "No, it is precisely because things are bad now, precisely because there is so much discontent, that people like us with real commitment should be going there".'

What made him feel so confident that he could make a difference? 'I suppose I was still sold on the 60s idea that you could integrate every part of your life: the idea that your self, your soul, your teaching, writing, political activity could all be harmonized into a single whole. I felt that Israel was somehow the place to do this, that there was a ready–made identity for me there. I would slip into this liberal Jewish intellectual identity and tell these brutal people all around me that if they edged a little this way and that, then things would be all right.'

I can personally remember when Stan had been gripped by this set of beliefs. Just before he went to Israel we'd been busy working together on a project, and when I'd heard about his wish to move to Israel I felt almost betrayed. Here was one of my intellectual heroes committing an act of ideological treachery. I did reluctantly visit him a couple of times in Jerusalem, but I spent much of my time there looking for the signs of his disillusionment with the regime. It's only now that I can properly discover how well he was concealing them from me. I ask him if any of his long list of personal and political hopes were realized.

'I have never felt so far from "home" in all my life. I have never been in a place so alien. As for the community of liberal forces, I found their hypocrisies especially repugnant. There was no point in attacking the Right and Centre forces; I had to criticise the people who should have been standing up and weren't. Their attitude to Palestinians was quite unlike the liberalism I knew in South Africa. Nowhere had I met a group of intellectuals who were so sensitive to their country's good image. Many of them adopted a curiously dishonest position. There would be a smell of tear gas coming up from one of the villages near the Hebrew University Mount Scopus campus – and inside the university they would be talking about legality and jurisprudence. Once when I was fund raising for a human rights organisation, I met a well-informed, very progressive American woman who promised that her foundation would provide the grant that we needed for further work. I then casually mentioned that we would need another 2000 dollars to translate the final report on torture from Hebrew into English. "Why into English?" she said. "These are terrible things, but I don't think they should be known to everyone."'

Most readers of this magazine probably have some sort of history of political activism. What made Cohen's radicalism in Israel different was his readiness to go it alone and to improvise. The issue of torture was important itself, but he also chose it to test the liberal threshold of the liberals. He and a colleague spent a year investigating (for an Israeli human rights organisation) the use of torture by Israeli troops in the occupied territories. Their report produced devastating and conclusive evidence that torture was indeed employed systematically against Palestinian detainees. At first, he hoped that the evidence would speak for itself. 'In Israel you can produce that sort of thing. Within the contours of liberal democracy, I could talk openly about the findings and how torture was rationalized and justified.'

But although the findings were indeed made public, they were systematically undermined in the press and elsewhere by a long series of rationalizations and justifications. I asked him if these were similar in kind to those now being invoked to deal with the American torture of terrorist suspects in the jails of Iraq and in Guantánamo Bay. 'George Orwell predicted that democratic societies would use torture. It happened with the French in Algeria, the British in Northern Ireland, the Israelis, and now the Americans. Unlike more totalitarian societies, though, democracies, however flawed, are open to public, and self, scrutiny. So, they have to find a vocabulary to account for abuses. In 1987, an Israeli judicial commission on torture tried to work out a model of how to respond to allegations of torture, a model which was used explicitly in the early days of Guantánamo Bay. To start off with, the Israelis and others realized that one way to deal with the problem was simply to come right out and acknowledge that torture, however reluctantly, had indeed been used, and that all decisions about when it was appropriate were left to the security services. But that was not viable. No Israeli or any other democratic government could abandon all political or legal control over such a practice; that would be the road to fascism.

'The second idea was to deny that it happened at all, to keep on saying, whatever the evidence, that it was prohibited and therefore couldn't exist. Not an easy choice either when the evidence was so compelling. So, we now arrive at the third way: regulation. Yes, it does go on, but it is carefully regulated and supervised by bureaucrats. This third way is now what is actually being called "torture lite". It isn't people hanging from their fingernails, but, in the terminology of the Israeli Commission, "moderate physical pressure". To the French such torture was "an administrative procedure"; to the British, it was "deep interrogation". Each justified what they were doing by reference to the other. Well, after all, this is what the French did in Algeria. Well, after all, this is what the British did in Northern Ireland. A peculiar cosmopolitan circuit.'

And behind this official talk lie the justifications used by those who carried out the actual work? 'Yes, and here you have the classic components of what Kelman called "crimes of obedience": authorization, de-sensitization, and depersonalization. Someone else authorized me to do it: now that I've done it once, I can do it again: I'm only doing it to "others" – people who are our enemy and therefore less than human.

'Then, of course, there is also the justification that torture is only being used now because we are in a completely new situation, in a state of emergency, or a completely different kind of war. And then reality television adds one further component. People actually take photographs to show their participation in torture as though their actions had no ethical status at all. The assumption is that everyone will accept it. This is a normalization of the taboo. On any cheap television show you can find nudity and body exposure. What's the difference here? So Alan Dershowitz, a professor of law at Harvard, can be presented as a "civil libertarian" on the *Larry King Show* and proceed to give concrete examples of approved torture. 'It's as if he's saying: we sit around at Harvard graduate seminars and work this all out. After consultation with doctors, our message is that you can effectively torture someone by putting needles and pins just underneath their fingernails and pressing. Punters can then say, "Well, I saw this liberal professor at Harvard who not only says that torture is okay in special circumstances but actually shows us how to do it." Why should there be any inhibitions after that?'

So what could be done to counteract this sort of moral slippage? Should one stand up and shout out to anyone who would listen that torture was simply wrong and that all these stories about how it wasn't really torture were nothing more than cover–ups?

'I'm not sure about that. A simple denunciation suggests old-fashioned hierarchical moralism. That's now pretty questionable. In some ways we've brought this difficulty on ourselves. A whole lot of ideas floated around in the wonderful, liberatory days of the 60s. But ideas turn around, they are as slippery as eels, and it's easy to lose control of them. You and I wrote books questioning the idea that there could ever be a firm definition of crime, that it was all to do with the definers and the defined. And that led to the idea that it was impossible to make any truth claims at all. This is exactly what happened when my report on torture came out in Israel. One smart-arse group of people who sat around in Tel Aviv cafés and called themselves post-Zionists said I was wasting my time. Why are radicals like you writing such a very orthodox human rights report, full of statistics and deep interviews and photographs, when the government says it didn't happen? Perhaps the government is right. How could anyone ever tell?'

It's not difficult to sense Cohen's disgust with those who employ such rhetorical tactics to deny reality. But this, I suggest to him, was rather a productive disgust because it propelled him into considering not just such abuses of human rights as torture or the justifications of those who did the torturing but also the psychological techniques employed by those who wanted to ignore or dismiss the evidence which lay before them. 'That's right. The sheer accretion of information about things is not enough. Human rights organizations around the world are sustained by this humane Enlightenment philosophy. If only everyone knew how bad things were in Sudan, if only they had the full facts, then they would do something about it. But, of course, people do know and they still don't do anything. This led me back to the same preoccupation that I had dimly sensed in South Africa. This is the question: What happens to all this information about atrocities and suffering? What happens to you as a 30-year old sitting in Montreal or Paris or New York when you read a statement about five children having died in Sudan in the time it has taken you to drink your cappuccino. I want to know what that information does to you. That's now an obsessive part of my life.'

It was an obsession that was to lead to Cohen's most important and subtle book, *States of Denial*. 'It took a psychological turn which I didn't expect. I had initially fixed on the term "denial" to cover the official side of matters, the ways in which a government, for example, could deny that something was torture or a massacre. So I raided the private sector for further visions and versions of denial. It was then that I became so fascinated with the private world of denial: our extraordinary capacity

23

for not seeing and not knowing, for self-deception and bad faith. How can we ignore the evidence of starvation, of suffering? How can we walk past on the other side of the street?'

I suggest to Stan that this sounds almost like a personal cry for attention. Here I am, giving you all these details about human rights abuses and you persistently refuse to pay attention. How do you manage to avoid me and my findings? Did he want to say that there was a link between the ways in which authorities and their minions denied their abuses of human rights and the sort of denial strategies used by people who refused to be stirred by such abuses?

'I'm not saying that one causes the other. But I am saying, I suppose, that one is a metaphor for the other. One of my strongest and friendliest critics was Chomsky. He read the book and wrote to me saying the political stuff was good, but why, he wondered, was a clever bloke spending so much time on people's psychology? Chomsky's position has no psychology. He is not interested in motives or subjective states. Why, he asked, was I spending so much time on degrees of lying and self-deception, why was I bringing in Freud? Why bother about such things? If you are a Vietnamese peasant and a bomb is about to be dropped on you, does it really matter whether the bomb was ordered by someone who is denying the nature of their action? Why should we have all these truth commissions to work out what people said and thought? Why should the state be concerned with whether or not the torturer has real remorse? But I can't stop myself. I am curious about these inner states and their cultural settings. How else do you deal with the curious way we have of knowing and not knowing? There is not a single person who has read the book and come up to me and asked what I mean by "knowing" and "not knowing". Everyone knows what it means.'

This isn't by any means an indulgence which has taken Cohen away from his other work on human rights. Even though the graduate course on human rights which he pioneered at LSE now recruits up to 100 students every year, he is wary of making a whole-hearted subscription to the concept that initially attracts them. 'I am deeply suspicious of the concept of rights and the whole model of strict legality. But both in Israel and South Africa, when you realized that you couldn't just stand by and watch terrible things being done and then being denied, you couldn't just shout about it. You needed exposure in an informed way. And human rights provided that option. No, even more: human rights may now be the last meta-narrative we have left. For better or for worse, it has become an enormously empowering slogan. That's what really draws the students to LSE. If we can no longer rely on religion or politics or trade unionism to provide a meta-narrative, then why not try human rights? But I don't let these students win so easily: my role now is to teach detachment, to go back to the ideas of a pluralist liberal university, to tell them to stop shouting and preaching. An essay or a thesis is not a human rights report.'

It's time to stop. Before I leave, I ask him about the success of *States of Denial*. I'm interested because I regard it as a quite brilliant examination of the human capacity, or incapacity, to handle disaster and tragedy. (Plenty of reviewers agree with me. Anne Karpf in *The Observer* said: 'This is how scholarship should be – zesty, engaged, witty, and always accessible', while the leading American sociologist, Howard Becker, called it 'thoughtful, profound, engaging, disturbing, knowledgeable and comprehensive'. Noam Chomsky found it 'passionate and riveting'.) Stan tells me that he hasn't heard from the publishers for a long time. In a way he'd rather not know. He has quite enough to think about already. It reminds him, though, as do so many other things, of a Jewish joke. 'Remember the classic Jewish telegram. "Start worrying. Details to follow".'

Chapter 4

How we deal with the people we study: 'The Last Seminar' revisited

Howard S. Becker

Stan Cohen's grim fable, 'The Last Seminar' (Cohen 1988: 297–310), is an upsetting story of an ordinary professor in an ordinary British university, someone just like, we can suppose, most of the people who read it when it first appeared. In an unspecified department, probably sociology but maybe social work or criminology, the professor teaches courses in penology, among other subjects. In the story, people of the kind his courses and those of his colleagues deal with – criminals, prisoners, people who are mentally ill, poor people – begin to appear in the classroom and elsewhere on the university grounds and eventually take it over by, it seems, force of arms and other violence, including arson. I suppose I don't overstep any obvious line by assuming that the university is, if not the University of Essex, where Cohen taught at the time he wrote this piece, a place that looks and acts like Essex, its difficulties bearing a family resemblance to those Essex (and many other universities in Britain and elsewhere) went through in the 1960s and 70s.

I had my own personal experience of Essex sometime during the period that provoked the story, having the fortune (good or bad, I leave to readers) to be visiting the campus on the day the police invaded it. Which they did after a lengthy student strike that, as I remember it, was mounted in response to a rise in student fees. My visit took place, I think, in the spring of 1974, when I spent six weeks at the University of Manchester as Lord Simon Visiting Professor.

Those who have visited Essex know that the entire university at that time (and still, I have been told) consisted of a series of connected hollow squares, utterly featureless and indistinguishable from one another. As Stan led me from the car park to the sociology wing, he explained that the corridors and doors were all so similar that he could only find his way by using the names on the doors of people's rooms as landmarks. He found his own room by following directions like these: enter the first building, go up the stairs, turn right at Smith's room, continue down the hall and up the next stairs, turn left at Jones', and so on. God help you when the personnel changed.

The students' strike took advantage of a unique feature of the campus architecture. All motor vehicles entered the campus through one entrance, which ran under the main administration building. No one had been thinking of student uprisings when the campus was planned, but this feature allowed students, by occupying this narrow passage, to make it impossible for any vehicle to enter the campus. Faculty and students could walk in from the parking lot, but no trucks bringing supplies could enter. So there was no food for student dining halls or the faculty dining facilities, nor was there any toilet paper for the bathrooms or any supplies for the offices. On the day I was there, I went to see the site of the occupation, where a student leader was speaking loudly to a crowd of eager and curious listeners, but with so strong a Scots accent that I didn't understand a word.

As we onlookers watched, a large number of police unexpectedly entered the scene, and began clubbing students with their batons. The strike had been going on for a long time and no one knew why the police had chosen that day to strike back, as many had long urged them to do. Standing off to the side and not really feeling part of it – even though I was vaguely in sympathy with student protesters anywhere then, whether I knew the issues or not – I made a number of blurred photographs of the police hitting students, which I never did anything with. But the scene made a great impression on me, especially as I was then taken to deliver my talk – whose subject I don't remember – to the sociologists, faculty and students, most of whom had showed up in spite of the police-caused disorder. Everyone was very upset, I less than the others, and I don't know how they managed to pay attention to whatever I had to say. But they did.

All this had a connection to a question on the minds of people like me and my hosts. At that time, and to this audience, I almost surely would have been talking about the subject then known as 'deviance', what had formerly been called things like 'social disorganization' or 'social problems'. (Although I had switched my main field of work to the sociology of art, people still wanted to hear me talk about deviance and I usually obliged.) The theme of 'The Last Seminar' was much on people's minds. The relation of people like us – researchers in the social sciences – to the people we gathered data on and wrote about was beginning to worry us all. We had left behind the innocence of being

27

happy when we used the tricks we had been taught, and continued to teach to our students, to 'get access' and 'gain rapport'. We rejoiced at our good fortune when people were willing to share their experiences and secrets with us, things they might have preferred the whole world not know about. We were proud of our ability to be 'one of the boys' (or girls).

By the 1970s, we all knew this relation was not so innocent as all that. What were the terms of this one-sided giving of information? Did we give anything back? Was the exchange as unequal as it seemed to be when we took a good look? Were we exploiting our superior educations and class positions to take advantage of innocent people? The answers weren't obvious. Some people said that we gave, in return for data, our undivided attention and our caring acceptance of their lives, however unsavoury those might seem to middle-class people who hadn't achieved our level of 'insider' understanding. Others thought that our research could lead us and others, perhaps people in positions of power who could undertake effective interventions, to an understanding that might improve the lives of the people who gave us our data, and so allow us to pay back their acceptance and even trust.

Still others derided these perhaps self-serving analyses, pointing out that our 'respondents' or 'subjects' – what to call these people, what name would not be condescending, continues to be a problem to the present day – would almost surely continue to be poor, deprived of opportunity, and in no way better off for their kindness to us. The people in power, they thought, who already had the good things of life, would not use our research findings to improve things, but rather to oppress the already oppressed even further. We, on the other hand, even if we shared the privations of the people we studied during our research – ate unhealthy food, slept in unwholesome places, suffered in the cold, ran risks vis-à-vis the law – would waltz off with our precious 'data', and turn it into articles and books from which we would profit by building academic careers of privilege.

That's the crudest version of the opposing positions on this difficult question, to which Stan applied himself often. Many of the essays in *Against Criminology* take it up or allude to it in one way or another.

'The Last Seminar' is a stark analysis of one way the relationship might play out. Fictional, of course, and 'overdrawn', unlikely actually ever to happen just like that. But also quite realistic, exposing in a raw and undisguised form the tensions that might exist in these relations we talk about so easily from the comfort of the senior common room. (Never having been a faculty member at a British university, I have never enjoyed whatever the pleasures of inhabiting such a place might be. It's sort of a mythical creature to me.)

It raises a number of questions about our research practice and experience, and forces us to reconsider (perhaps not always in the direction its author intended) some general problems of social research.

Our people and us

General analyses of conceptual problems are usually coloured by the specific examples the analyst has in mind, though they may never be named. 'The Last Seminar' more or less takes as given that our relations with the people we study are unequal, in the way they would certainly be between, say, prisoners and researchers, or delinquents or (less successful) criminals and researchers. Most discussions of this problem take as a given that we will be studying people poorer than us, less educated, and more at risk of disease and early death, arrest and imprisonment, unemployment and suffering at the hands of unfeeling bureaucrats who administer welfare schemes, and a host of other bad things.

In another direction, discussion of these problems often assumes that we are likely to do harm to those we study, presumably inadvertently, by (in the cant phrases often invoked) 'serving the interests of the powerful'. The question of the harm we do or might do to the people we study deserves more attention than this ideological and typically not empirically based charge, or than the automatic and formulaic 'consideration of the rights of human subjects', which has become a major obstacle to sociological research in universities in North America, without doing much good for the people it is supposed to protect. These safeguards were put into place to protect the research subjects of medical researchers, who did in fact do harm to some of their subjects – injected them with cancer cells, refused to treat their syphilis – and continue to do so where they can get away with it. The safeguards are now applied with plenty of bureaucratic zeal and little comprehension of the situations of research in the social sciences, whose potential for harm is more often asserted than demonstrated.

I'll begin with my own experiences, but I am not the only person whose researches have had this character, and I will mention whole areas of research where the relations between researchers and those studied are quite different from the picture of our subjects evoked in 'The Last Seminar'.

In some of my projects, I studied people who were, in general, just like me (Becker 1963: 79–119). In my first field research, for my master's thesis, I studied musicians of just the kind I was, people who played in bars and clubs or for private parties of various kinds, for not very much money, but (some of us) intent on becoming good jazz players or, at least, competent professionals. I did not and could not take advantage of the people I studied because I had no more power over the conditions of my life than they did over theirs.

You might object that, true as that might have been, the other musicians, the ones I was studying, were stuck with being that and no more, while I, a privileged kid of the middle class, a student at a major university, would eventually leave this life and become the professor/professional my class status made it possible for me to be. Middle-class people who studied factory workers might be criticized in this way. I certainly had the possibility of entering academia and eventually took advantage of it. But so did many of the people who figured in my study. The kind of music I played was almost entirely a part-time job. With few exceptions, the people who did this work had 'day jobs' as well, often quite good ones, though just as often not such good ones either. But 'everyone knew' that it was only prudent to have a day job. I was no more different from them than they were from one another. And within the world of music, we all acted on the understanding that the only status differences that mattered had to do with how you played. The power differentials we considered important were those that put us at the mercy of club owners (often enough small-time hoodlums capable of violence, though it was seldom directed at us), audience members, and others who prevented us from playing what we wanted to play. That privation does not compare with going hungry or being arrested, but, in our world, it was a privation we all suffered.

The only thing all marijuana smokers (another group I studied; see Becker 1963: 41–78) had in common was that they smoked marijuana. And when I studied them, I was just like the people I interviewed in that defining characteristic. Otherwise, we were as various in class origins and positions as it was possible to be. Some were poor, some were from well-to-do families; some were black, some were white; most were men but some were women. Insofar as we were oppressed by virtue of smoking dope, we were all oppressed in just the same way, by being subject to arrest and imprisonment for our indulgence. It is true that some of us were better prepared, because of our class position, to deal with that possibility, but it was equally true that the possibility was remote and that a user who took the simplest precautions had nothing to worry about. (Which is not to say that everyone took those simple precautions; many of us were young and not very thoughtful.)

In neither case did I hide what I was doing from the people I was studying. They typically responded to my requests for information or interviews by trying to be helpful, often because they thought bringing what they regarded as the truth about their activities to public attention would be a helpful thing, or with indifference. I don't remember anyone ever suggesting that I was taking advantage of them. Although an old friend, when I started asking a lot of questions about his experience with marijuana without telling him it was an interview (I ordinarily did tell people that), got angry and shouted, 'You son of a bitch, you're interviewing me!' He was angry because he thought I was taking advantage of our friendship which, indeed, I had unthinkingly done. That's not the same as taking advantage of a powerless person.

In other cases, the people I studied were at least as privileged as I was, and potentially much more so. The medical students I spent three years hanging around with to gather data for *Boys in White* (Becker *et al.* 1961) were on their way, for the most part, to lucrative careers and secure upper-middle-class status (despite the commitment they had all made, because they knew it was something that would help them get admitted to the University of Kansas Medical School, to a life of practising general medicine in a small town in the rural western part of the state, a commitment few of them respected when the time came). They thought what I was doing – sociological research – was 'interesting', but not the most profitable way you could spend your time. Some of them questioned me about how much I earned doing this work and how much I could expect to make at the peak of my career. When they heard the numbers, they nodded sympathetically and soothingly, and made it clear that they felt sorry for me. My only superiority to them (and to the undergraduate college students my colleagues and I wrote about in *Making the Grade* (Becker *et al.* 1968)) was in age, and that didn't count for much.

Physicians and hospital administrators typically treated medical sociologists as a lesser breed, better than nurses perhaps, as was evidenced in the constant jockeying of sociologists in that specialty for a 'better' position vis-à-vis their 'subjects'.

Students of white-collar crime similarly often had an inferior position to those about whom and from whom they got data. When Baker and Faulkner (2003, 2004) interviewed investors in a fraudulent oil-drilling scheme in southern California, they were certainly interviewing people who were dumber than they, since Baker and Faulkner knew better than to invest in such a scam. But they were just as certainly interviewing people who had more money and, probably, a higher class position than they did, people who had the money to put into such a speculation. And when Edwin Sutherland interviewed Broadway Jones (the name of 'Chic Conwell', the author of *The Professional Thief* (Conwell and Sutherland, 1937)), though Jones was later reduced to lecturing to college classes to make some extra change, he had lived very high in his time, and it's not at all clear that he thought (or should have thought) the modest life of even so eminent a college professor as Sutherland preferable to the one he had led, even though he was subject to oppression by the police of a kind Sutherland never risked.

Sociologists of science (e.g., the field study by Bruno Latour reported in Latour and Woolgar 1979) study people who are like us in many ways, often university teachers and researchers themselves, mostly in fields with more prestige than social science, but who often enough don't think that social science is 'real science', though they often charitably cooperate with our (sometimes intrusive) data gathering.

So we are not always better off than the people we study. Sometimes we are more or less equal to them, sometimes we are superior to them, sometimes we are inferior to them, and in each case the problems of relations between us and them will be different.

This immediately raises the question of what scale is being used to calculate these comparative ranks. 'The Last Seminar' seems to use a very conventional scale: money and social rank and legitimacy as sociologists usually measure the latter when they talk about 'deviance', 'oppression', and the like. But it's well attested in the research literature that people use a multitude of different scales to measure rank. In many situations, skill at a particular task outweighs any other consideration. (See the discussion of contradictory status systems in Hughes' essay, 'Dilemmas and Contradictions of Status,' in Hughes 1984: 141–50.) In general, the people we work with use a variety of scales, according to the situation and their interests in it, which cannot simply be deduced from what we think those interests might be, or ought to be.

How does the researcher/researched relation differ when the statuses of the parties differ in these ways? Here are some guesses, informed by my own experiences, reading, and stories others have told me.

People who feel superior to us – in class, in professional status, or otherwise – often patronize us and, feeling sorry for us, give us the data we want from them to help us out. This is the motivation Robert Park told students to rely on when they went out to do the fieldwork he had assigned them. 'Tell them you're a poor student and your teacher wants you to do it; they'll feel sorry for you', and often they did. Sometimes they feel that it's a sort of civic duty to help science out in this way. The schoolteachers I interviewed for my dissertation treated me as a sort of junior teacher who was working on a degree as they once had, or might have done. We can take advantage of such generous motives to get what we want, and that might be a little devious, but it certainly does not constitute taking advantage of powerless folks.

But we can use the knowledge we get in ways people more powerful than us don't like: to take one possibility, to generate publicity that they feel might harm their interests. If they decide that we have injured them in some way, they can and will do something about it, or try. The dean of the medical school we studied was very angry about the first version of *Boys in White* he read, and immediately demanded to see our 'superior'. He meant Everett Hughes, who he mistakenly thought would see things his way. When Hughes didn't agree with him, he threatened to sue us if we didn't change some of the things in the book. We didn't, and he didn't, but the threat was real and more than a little scary. The negotiations that followed, masterfully handled by Hughes (another story for another day), were negotiations between two parties of more or less equal power, this being a surprise to the dean, who was used to being undisputed boss in his own institution and in his relations with non-physicians. He might have pursued the matter, but probably (I never discussed it with him afterward) decided that any kind of legal action would just generate more publicity and be even more harmful than our not likely to be widely known scholarly book.

These possibilities exist in relations with people in other kinds of status relations to us. Getting information from people is always a negotiation. The people we study are not necessarily so powerless in relation to us, so defenceless against our attempts to get what we want from them. In fact, they often tell us they aren't interested, don't want to play our game, and just walk away. That's why questions of 'getting access' occupy so much space in our discussions and in students' nightmares.

Dealing with our equals or peers is a quite different kind of situation. It's not easy for us to take advantage of equals by using a class differential in status or power, since in fact there isn't much differential between 'us' and 'them', as there was not between me and the musicians and marijuana users I wrote about. We can, of course, do harm to them by revealing things we learn, in an apparently confidential relationship, to others who might use it maliciously.

Let's return to 'The Last Seminar'. For all my quibbling about how my own experiences differ from those alluded to as the genesis of the events in the story, it evokes the problem it discusses powerfully and memorably. Could we tell as interesting and compelling stories about a hypothetical future in which our peers or social and political superiors invaded the campuses we work in, and did – well, what would they do? I suppose they would not come and sit in our classes and eye us suspiciously. Nor would they, probably, attack us personally or burn the buildings we worked and taught in. Do we have a story to tell as interesting as the one Stan Cohen tells us? A story that will wake us to something as important ethically and morally? Do we need a sociological imagination as lively and unconventional as Stan's to find the narrative of middle- and upper-class invasion of the university world?

Fortunately – for few of us are as gifted as Stan as thinkers and writers – we don't have to invent these stories. We have only to record what is going on around us. I will speak here only of what I know a little about – the situation in the USA – and not at all of what I know almost nothing about, the situation in Britain and elsewhere.

Are our equals, our peers, present in the university already? Certainly. They are there as students, as the parents of students, etc. They are also there as reporters, who come to reveal the university's secrets to the world. As I write this, my local newspaper, the *San Francisco Chronicle*, has just run a series of stories exposing the outrageously large payments made to top administrators of the university in the guise of reimbursement for all sorts of expenses that others in the university community have to pay for themselves (costs of moving, for example). And that has provoked some other visitors to come: politicians, who will now investigate what was after all not such a big secret in the first place. I'm not sure that 'peer' or 'equal' is the appropriate description of these folks, though they are not really so much more powerful than a university professor, or not for long, or not for many of the things that are important to us.

Have the rich and politically powerful invaded the campus? Of course they have, but 'invasion' is hardly the way to talk about those who come bearing gifts, often very substantial gifts, in the form of endowed university chairs, which some among us will be fortunate enough to sit in; or research centres, in which we can work on our own projects instead of teaching large rooms full of undergraduates; or handsomely equipped libraries with all the obscure journals we might need to pursue our interests; or wonderful concert halls and theatres in which the world's greatest artists will entertain us; or … It is a very long list.

The people and organizations who give these gifts may not be there in person, but their names are everywhere (in American universities, certainly). We can imagine that their influence is there too. We needn't be conspiracy theorists, and imagine that an administrator will lock us out of our rooms and forbid us to enter the campus because we have written something a donor found offensive. But it is not a possibility to dismiss out of hand.

The moral(s)

'The Last Seminar', implicitly and not arguing the point, takes the particular cases of criminals, the mentally ill, and other conventionally despised groups and the people who have studied them as the general situation of researchers and researched. I said to myself, 'That's a good idea, but the specifics don't fit my own research experiences. How would it be if the people I studied occupied the campuses I worked at?'

That's the first moral: to apply general ideas and questions to the full range of cases encompassed by their definitions; in this case, to apply the concern about our relations with those we study to the full range of people sociologists have actually studied, because sociologists have studied people up and down a variety of social scales, and their experiences with those people have not always, and probably not often, been the kind to produce the acts of revenge the story describes. It's possible to imagine people whose lives have been written about in ways they think disrespectful doing those things: ignoring conventional patterns of politeness and civility and disrupting settled professorial routines at first; and then the assaults and fires and all the rest of it, what we can imagine we might want to do if we had been so cavalierly mistreated by researchers.

In fact, no one I studied ever cared very much about what I wrote; they had far more important things to worry about. In the one case where my work created trouble, it was not the people I wrote about who complained. Medical students – the few who read what we wrote – did not find fault with our descriptions. No, it was the school's administrators, for whom our book looked like a potential public relations problem, and they had plenty of weapons available, though in the end they seemed to have decided that any revenge they took would cost more than it was worth.

There's a second moral, though there is no need to preach it to Stan Cohen. He knows and has always practised the simple maxim that it is better to stick close to the nitty-gritty of life than to develop our understanding from general principles. 'The Last Seminar' seems to violate that maxim by indulging in a fiction. The lesson it teaches is that 'nitty-gritty' is just as important as 'what actually happened'. The fiction works because it makes us think about a reality that, though it hasn't happened yet, is recognizable as a reality that could happen. The details prompt our imaginations in a way that abstract concepts seldom do. 'The Last Seminar' gives us details that prompt a serious reconsideration of our relations with people we study.

References

Baker, W.E. and Faulkner, R.R. (2003) 'Diffusion of fraud: intermediate economic crime and investor dynamics', *Criminology*, 41: 1173–1206.

Baker, W.E. and Faulkner, R.R. (2004) 'Social networks and loss of capital', *Social Networks*, 26: 91–111.

Becker, H.S. (1963) *Outsiders: Studies in the Sociology of Deviance*. New York: Free Press.

Becker, H.S., Geer, B. and Hughes, E.C. (1968) *Making the Grade: The Academic Side of College Life*. New York: Wiley.

Becker, H.S., Geer, B., Hughes, E.C. and Strauss, A.L. (1961) *Boys in White: Student Culture in Medical School*. Chicago: University of Chicago Press.

Cohen, S. (1988) *Against Criminology*. New Brunswick, NJ: Transaction.

Conwell, C. and Sutherland, E.H. (1937) *The Professional Thief, by a Professional Thief*. Annotated and interpreted by E.H. Sutherland. Chicago: University of Chicago Press.

Hughes, E.C. (1984) *The Sociological Eye*. New Brunswick, NJ: Transaction.

Latour, B. and Woolgar, S. (1979) *Laboratory Life: The Social Construction of Scientific Fact*. Beverly Hills, CA: Sage Publications.

Part 2
Gradations of Social Control: From Moral Panics to Long-term Imprisonment

Chapter 5

Folk Devils and Moral Panics: an appreciation from North America

Malcolm M. Feeley and Jonathan Simon

We offer here an appreciation of *Folk Devils and Moral Panics: The Creation of Mods and Rockers* ([1972], 1980) Stan Cohen's first and arguably most important – certainly most influential – book, and then assess its influence and explore some of its unanticipated consequences. Like all of Cohen's work, *Folk Devils and Moral Panics* is rooted in the twin concerns of phenomenology and sociology. In this book, as in much of his other writings, Cohen is carrying on a conversation begun by Edmund Husserl, Sigmund Freud, and Émil Durkheim over 100 years ago. Indeed, it is almost as if Cohen's larger project has been to explore each of the several different strands of this tradition that has been so influential in psychiatry, sociology, criminology, and political science throughout the twentieth century.

Folk Devils and Moral Panics is a study of the *reaction* to the rebelliousness of working-class teenagers, the hyped-up creation of deviance that was constructed by the mass media and aligned institutions. As such, it was one of the first sustained and systematic sociological studies to explore the power of the media to construct a deviant group in such a way as to generate sustained social concern and moral outrage. This study is significant for a number of reasons. It certainly set a high standard for analysis in the social problems field. It is rigorously executed, carefully grounded, and modest and measured in its claims. Furthermore, it demonstrates an uncommon eclecticism and openness that is rare among sociologists, drawing as it does on Ed Lemert's social constructionism, Neil Smelser's structural-functionalism, and a great many other theoretical perspectives in between. It is a fine book and ranks with such classics as Howard Becker's *Outsiders*, David Matza's *Becoming Deviant*, Thomas Szaz's *The Myth of Mental*

Illness, Joseph Gusfield's *Symbolic Crusade*, Murray Edelman's *Symbolic Uses of Politics*, and Stuart Scheingold's *The Myth of Rights*, all of which had a significant effect in shaping the agenda for research in criminology, psychiatry, sociology, political science, and cultural studies in the last third of the twentieth century. (This listing no doubt reveals our American bias, but it does seem to us that Cohen's work flows from the mid-twentieth-century American sociology that, in turn, was shaped by late nineteenth-century German phenomenology.)

Indeed, *Folk Devil*s is a foundational text for contemporary studies of the mass media. So far as we know, it was one of the first and certainly one of the finest case studies of the nature of media involvement in the production of social problems. And like all of Cohen's work, it is both elegant and passionate, inspired no doubt by the engaged sociology of C. Wright Mills and Alvin Gouldner. Good company indeed. Finally, it reflects the influence of a number of colleagues who have remained friends and colleagues through long and productive careers. Look at those whose works Cohen repeatedly cites in his footnotes some 35 years ago – David Downes, Stuart Hall, Paul Rock, and Jock Young – and still others he acknowledges in his preface – Ian Taylor and Laurie Taylor (no doubt we have overlooked still others), all of whom have continued to work with and influence Stan and one another over long and distinguished careers. Again, not bad company.

If for no other reason – and as suggested above, there are many others – the book is significant for having introduced a new and enduring concept – *moral panic* – into the lexicon of social sciences. This term has become not only a mainstay in the social sciences and especially mass communications studies, but also a term used in popular political discourse. Although a number of technical terms in psychiatry – *neurosis* is probably the best example – have gained purchase in popular discourse, *moral panic* is one of the few terms in sociology that has achieved this distinction. One measure of the importance and influence of this term is that it is now virtually impossible to diagnose a great many social problems without reference to it. It is as if the term has always been there. Indeed, it has a life of its own that is not rooted in Cohen's work or even attributed to him. Like the term *anomie*, it just is. Since moral panic was first introduced, social scientists have gone back in time to characterize seventeenth-century witchcraft trials as moral panics, and of course they have since used the term to describe successive campaigns in various 'wars on crime' and 'wars on drugs' over the past 35 years. Along with Joseph Gusfield's 'symbolic crusade' and Stuart Scheingold's 'myth of rights,' 'moral panics' has become part of the vocabulary of the social sciences, used by vast numbers who have neither read the books nor even heard of the authors, but have picked up the concept as if by osmosis and through the power of a descriptive title.

Cohen was obviously not the first to call attention to the importance of the media in mass society. Scholars at least since those working in Frankfurt the 1920s and 1930s have been concerned with the relation of the mass media and mass society. But Cohen's work stands out as a singular, early effort to report in detail the role of the media – and other moulders of mass opinion – in the production of deviants and criminal offenders. Other scholars undertaking related studies employing a similar approach had touched on this earlier – Howard Becker, Joseph Gusfield, and Murray Edelman come to mind – but none of them had examined in such detail the nature of the media's involvement in the creation of social problems.

Since the publication of *Folk Devils*, and no doubt in part because of it, there has been a dramatic increase in interest in the production of 'news' and the role of the mass media in shaping attitudes, events, and moral crusades. Indeed, this topic is now probably the single most important concern of those who study the social significance of the mass media. It is also an increasing concern for a great many criminologists and sociologists. But at the time, Cohen's interest was distinctive in criminology and sociology.

Below we want to explore how this field, at least as it has applied to the sociology of law and crime, has evolved, and how it now differs from when Cohen's *Folk Devils* was first published in 1972. In particular, we want to relate it to recent examples of and discussions of the role of the mass media in the production of moral panics that are clearly indebted to Cohen's pioneering analysis. Indeed, as was the case with labelling theory, his concept of moral panics has reached beyond the academy and become a term that is used in popular discourse, as well as by the mass media and policy entrepreneurs.

We begin with what Cohen has to say about 'moral panics':

A condition, episode, person or group of persons, emerges to become defined as a threat to societal values and interests; its nature is presented in a stylized and stereotypical fashion by the mass media; the moral barricades are manned…; socially accredited experts pronounce their diagnoses and solutions; ways of coping are evolved or (more often) resorted to; the condition then disappears, submerges or deteriorates and becomes more visible; … Sometimes the panic passes over and is forgotten, except in folklore or collective memory; at other times it has more serious and long-lasting repercussions and might produce such

changes as those in legal and social policy or even in the way
society conceives of itself (Cohen 1980: 9).

This oft-quoted passage has come to define the idea of moral panics.
Something triggers a threat and if conditions are right, a moral panic
can suddenly appear, only to evaporate as suddenly as it arrived,
though perhaps, at times, leaving in its wake some destroyed lives
but usually few permanent effects. But as Cohen notes, moral panics
can also reappear with some regularity. And while they are usually
short-lived and have ephemeral consequences, at times they can be
'more serious' and 'long-lasting' and even effect 'changes in the way
society conceives of itself'. He returns to emphasize these points in
the extended and thoughtful preface to the second edition of the book,
which we consider later in this chapter.

Inspired as it is by Gustav LeBon's studies of the crowd, Neil Smelser's
functionalist analysis of collective behaviour, and still others concerned
with the dynamics of the responses to natural disasters, Cohen's
developmental scheme envisions recurring and episodic responses
to incidents whose duration and severity are, in Smelser's words,
amplified 'by the *response* of the agencies of social control' (Smelser,
quoted by Cohen 1980: 21; emphasis added). That is, in Cohen's initial
formulation, a moral panic is precipitated by a spontaneous or near
random and unanticipated event or set of events – akin to a natural
disaster – a sudden and unanticipated influx of mods and rockers
in a beach town, or the spontaneous action of a crowd caused by a
concatenation of situational factors. Moral panics ensue when reaction
to this development is amplified by agents of social control.

In the preface to the 1980 edition of his book, Cohen reappraised this
approach and sought greater balance than he thought was present in
the original. The preface begins with an elaboration not of the 'reaction'
that is central to the book's social constructionist framework, but of
'action' – 'structure', 'culture', and 'biography' – in an effort to flesh
out what he suggests was given short shrift in the original. It is an
effort to expand what, in retrospect, he thought was a unidimensional
theory of deviance. In this preface, he examines factors other than the
process of labelling that affect behaviour and social policy. In reflecting
on the fates of the 'actors' and structural factors that have shaped post-
war youth policy and especially social policy in Britain since the 1970s,
Cohen plays down the importance of the 'reactions', that is, the moral
panics that are in fact the focus of the book. In so doing, however,
he remains as level-headed and sceptical about other more recent
formulations as he was with the reappraisal of his own initial account.
Deeply appreciative of the contingencies of history and the importance

of biography, he resists any totalizing theory. There is no magic theoretical bullet, he seems to be saying. Still, he expresses discomfort with the preoccupation with the focus on 'reaction' that characterizes the original edition and the work of others in its wake, and suggests the need for a more grounded and well-rounded theoretical approach.

In his reappraisal, Cohen briefly discusses the work of the Birmingham-produced volume, *Policing the Crisis*. In it, Cohen reminds us, the authors identify a shift in the nature of moral panics. 'Instead of discrete moral panics of the Mods and Rockers types, … the control culture is mobilized in advance, real events being anticipated and taken to confirm and justify the need for gradual ideological repression' (1980: xxiv). Cohen is much too sceptical and too much of a historian to embrace any monocausal explanation, and so, even though he cites this study approvingly, his enthusiasm is less than wholehearted. However, we see this project as significantly expanding Cohen's insights, and, in so doing, pointing to a new and important way that moral panic theory has since been applied with profit. The thesis advanced in *Policing the Crisis* (and other works in this vein) is that social control agents not only have the capacity to take advantage of serendipitous developments that can be used to amplify the significance of incidents and thus create and sustain moral panics, but they also have the means of manufacturing these incidents. If true, this shifts the role of the players in the social constructionist drama from being only 'reactors' to being 'actors' as well, and thus merging what Cohen had sought to distinguish more sharply. This also suggests a marked expansion of the importance of moral panic theory. Moral entrepreneurs are not only able to take advantage of a situation in order to *amplify* its intensity to the point of panic, but they can also manufacture the situation.

There is now a vast body of research that supports this reformulation of Cohen's moral panic thesis. Cohen treats the media and other opinion moulders as largely *reactive* agents; the newer literature treats them as 'actors' who can not only amplify crises but also create the events that precipitate this sense of heightened urgency. Thus, rather than just seizing the moment when disasters occur, they have the capacity to manufacture the disasters from whole cloth and the sense of accompanying moral outrage. This approach goes a long way toward accounting for the nearly continuous 'wars on crime' and 'wars on drugs', at least in the USA, that have been mounted since just about the time Cohen's book was first published

To summarize: policy entrepreneurs have learned not only how to mobilize and amplify moral outrage in order to generate moral panics, but also how to create the conditions that gave rise to it in the first place. Moral panics have become institutionalized, transformed from ad hoc, episodic, and short-lived occurrences into regularly orchestrated campaigns; indeed, into a permanent condition of personal insecurity. The results, at least with respect to crime policy over the past quarter-century, have been more frequent, more intense, and more sustained moral panics. And their consequences have become more substantial.

No doubt, elite interest, state interest, and mass media interest have long coalesced to work in concert to construct and to diagnose social problems, and then to prescribe solutions for them. Further, this dynamic has been particularly acute with respect to the politics of 'law and order'. But, as we have suggested, in the past 40 years or so, students of the mass media have conducted research to show that this process has intensified and accelerated. They point to several factors, including (in the USA at least) the expansion and the consolidation of the mass media, the growth of network television, the dependence of the media on advertising, the increased sophistication of successful marketing strategies, the shift in electoral politics away from appeal to and mobilization of traditional supporters through party organizations to direct appeals through the mass media, and the nationalization of political discourse. Nowhere have such concerns been greater than in the analysis of the rise of the politics of law and order in the USA over the past 40 or so years (Scheingold 1991; Beckett 1997).

In exploring this issue, research questions, methods and theoretical approaches vary widely, but the findings are consistent: 'news' is socially constructed, and framed around a limited number of tropes that either offer soothing palliatives or feed on personal insecurities (Tuchman 1978; Fishman 1980; Edelman 1988). News can be and is strategically manufactured, and increasingly it is produced to advance campaigns toward particular objectives. And savvy policy entrepreneurs make use of such insights; they manufacture crises, and then use the moment to secure permanent changes, thus locking in their policy preferences after the crisis passes. In Cohen's analysis, a natural disaster-like situation emerges, moral entrepreneurs generate a moral panic, and the issue dies down, only to flare up again at some undetermined time in the future. Since then, these same types of moral entrepreneurs have gotten on top of the process.

Consider two examples examined in recent and well-received books. In *Distorting the Law: Politics, Media, and the Litigation Crisis*, William Haltom and Michael McCann (2004) found that, at least when presenting 'news' about torts and tort reform, the media are almost wholly dependent upon industry sources. They write, 'the media have been viewed [by businesses intent on restricting legal liability] as largely passive, porous, and reactive; journalists simply reflect and reproduce the view of those who supply them with content'

(2004: 150). Accordingly, these businesses provide a steady dose of stories, often false or incomplete, that sustain the belief in an out-of-control 'litigation crisis,' and a feeling of outrage. Facts, they report, are regularly distorted beyond recognition or are fabricated altogether. Under such circumstances, crisis is not produced when the functional equivalent of a natural disaster occurs, but the occasion – the man-bites-dog story – is manufactured as needed. A plausible candidate is always present somewhere; the issue is when to transform it into 'news'.

Similarly, in her book, *Making Crime Pay: Law and Order in Contemporary American Politics*, Katherine Beckett (1997) assesses the importance of the media in structuring crime policies. Here, too, she describes a passive, porous, and reactive press. In contrast to tort reform issues, where the primary producer of news is self-interested businesses, however, she found that in crime policy, the government is the primary source of information about crime that is reported by the press. That is, a passive press reproduces stories as presented by self-interested parties. And here, too, in a national media market, there are always enough of the right facts to construct the right story for the right occasion. President George Bush Sr.'s invocation of the black criminal Willie Horton in the presidential debates of 1988 is perhaps the best-known such example. In a country of over 300 million people – or even a state of six million – tragic events unfold with some frequency. They do not make the news so much as news is made as needed.

This work and much more in the same vein reveal how business and government officials in concert with a compliant press can now manufacture crises as a way of mobilizing support for permanent changes, and not simply to garner fleeting publicity. In the 1960s and 1970s, policy entrepreneurs who otherwise had little in common with social scientists seized upon labelling to frame a host of programmes designed to 'divert' people from the criminal process and thus the stigma of the criminal sanction. The result, as Cohen himself has noted, has been wider and deeper nets of social control as policies respond to a generalized sense of personal insecurity and crisis (Cohen 1985). It is almost as if policy entrepreneurs have seized upon the insights of the moral panic literature and learned to manufacture crises, and, in so doing, institutionalize a harsh 'culture of control' (Garland 2001; Feeley 2003; Simon 2007). Whatever the precise case, it is no longer only a matter of seizing the moment for advantage but of establishing the prevailing condition of sensibility as part of a strategy of governance. In the USA, with its weak and fragmented political parties and its tradition of populism, the manufacture of moral panics to affect political objectives has been developed into a high art. Moral panic has been institutionalized.

Institutionalizing the moral panic

At the heart of Cohen's book *Folk Devils and Moral Panics* is a portrait of a social world in which a sense of security is projected as the norm against which episodes of criminal violence are depicted as unacceptable challenges to civil order and governmental power. This allows the powerful analogy that Stan draws with the sociology of disaster. A disaster is unanticipated, comes to pass, and is responded to, but it exists in a series of temporal variations. That sense of variation is not undercut by Cohen's influential account of how the media and law enforcement pick up and enhance moral panics. There is still the sense of a world to which normality can be restored and indeed in which underlying class conflicts driving these panics might be resolved.

The social world of the USA and other societies at the beginning of the twenty-first century is one of a pervasive insecurity that has been described in terms such as 'culture of control', 'culture of fear', and 'governing through crime'. In this social world, moral panics are part of the infrastructure of contemporary society, so much so that the degree of specific episodes of real or imagined violence is of no real salience (Tyler and Boeckmann 1997). The media and law enforcement nodes that Cohen described have expanded and worked to internalize control over the production of insecurity. Moreover, in a social world where crime risk has become a global demand for the attention of responsible governing agents, crime information and methods of security are the subject of powerful consumer demands and are spread throughout the social body.

Consider the following three examples that share much with Cohen's notion of moral panic, but, rather than being episodic (though recurring) as were his examples, now operate on a permanent circuit of knowledge and power concerning crime.

The AMBER Alert System

The AMBER Alert System, as it is called on the US Justice Department website dedicated to informing the public about it, grew out of an initiative of the Dallas Police Department and Dallas-Fort Worth (Texas) area broadcasters (the very sites Cohen would focus on). The target problem was child abduction, spurred on by the abduction and murder of 9-year-old Amber Hagerman (the event which might be said to trigger the moral panic). Should the police become aware of a child abduction in progress, broadcasters would provide an 'early warning system' alerting the general public to the fact of such abduction and providing details useful in identifying the child or the abductor(s).

The police–media partnership is an innovation of the precise sort that Cohen would predict. Linked to the arrival of a Texan in the White House in 2000, the programme received federal attention, including a White House conference in 2002, and the appointment of an AMBER Alert coordinator inside the Department of Justice. But the moral panic did not subside. In 2002, the Congress enacted the AMBER Alert programme and implemented it nationally.

Up to this point, we might see the AMBER Alert System as a textbook example of the kind of moral panic that Cohen described. But we want to point to an important difference that does not so much contradict Cohen's model as highlight changes in the background presumptions of that model. Nobody reading this chapter today would assume that the kidnapping and murder of Amber Hagerman in 1996 – or the kidnapping and murder of Polly Klaas in 1993 or of Megan Kanka in 1994 – shattered a sense of security about children. Indeed, these events came after a decade's campaign against sexual abuse in day-care centres and several highly publicized trials of operators and employees for sexually abusing large numbers of very young children.

At some point, these cases ceased being activities that might profitably be analysed in the moral panics framework, and instead became background norms for understanding concerns of safety and security. In a sense, moral panics analysis has been inverted; the background norm is insecurity and risk, not security and stability. This is the point that David Garland has driven home with typical persuasive force in *The Culture of Control* (2001). The reactive changes in institutions such as law enforcement and the media that Cohen traced have now become part of a permanent cycle of mutual stimulation and amplification between these groups, professional politicians, experts, and consumers of various sorts.

The AMBER Alert System also differs in another way from the kind of institutional innovations in response to moral panics that Cohen observed. The penal code of every modern state includes a large number of new and innovative provisions that give law enforcement officials more leeway in dealing with a variety of threats. What almost all of them share is that they enhance the discretion of police and prosecutors to deal with situations they consider threatening. AMBER Alert and similar systems work differently (but consistently with many other recent innovations we could describe); they restrict rather than expand the discretion of law enforcement officials, compelling rather than permitting the performance of security rituals. Moreover, rather than operating as a tool of police and prosecutors, the AMBER Alert System directly links the public to the action. As it now operates, when an abduction is reported to law enforcement, the AMBER Alert System automatically notifies broadcasters, and this in turn triggers other forms of electronic notification. Special announcements interrupt regular radio and television broadcasts, notices are flashed (in amber) on specially installed electronic highway bulletin boards, text messages are distributed on mobile phones, notices are broadcast over the Internet, and messages are instantly printed on lottery tickets. Panic is institutionalized.

The Jeanne Clery Act

In 1998, Congress passed the Jeanne Clery Disclosure of Campus Security Policy and Campus Crime Statistics Act. This law requires every American college or university receiving federal funds (this is virtually all of them) to disclose reported criminal incidents on or near campuses. The Act is named for a 19-year-old college student who was raped and murdered at Lehigh University (Pennsylvania) in 1986. In conversations with university officials after the incident, her parents were outraged to learn that 38 violent crimes had taken place on or around the Lehigh campus during the three years prior to her death, but that this information had not been provided to students or their parents. Along with other parents and victims' rights supporters, the family lobbied Congress to pass a law requiring colleges to collect and report such information. Such a law was enacted in 1990, and then significantly strengthened in the Jeanne Clery Act of 1998.

As with the AMBER Alert System, here, too, we have the classic pattern of moral panic. A terrible incident followed by amplification and institutional innovations. But also like the AMBER Alert, we have the creation of a system that guarantees the production of more crime information and its mandatory disclosure. Cohen observed that the reaction of law enforcement and media tended to encourage further cycles of publicity as similar incidents were uncovered. But with the Jeanne Clery Act there is much more than a tendency or a kind of elective affinity established between agencies and incidents. Instead, the law creates organizational structures and procedures within colleges and universities to collect and disseminate crime information. This goes beyond the immediate organizations involved (typically campus public safety or police departments) and extends to all campus units (departments, sports teams, dormitories, etc.), which are now required to establish their own procedures to collect reports of crime. In effect, much like a virus, the Jeanne Clery Act turns even ordinary campus units into sites of crime information mobilization and dissemination.

Moreover, the Act also mandates that colleges and universities take steps to disseminate this information to stakeholders. In short, the Jeanne Clery Act is a kind of moral panic automaton, designed to promote and sustain a heightened level of awareness and concern about crime. Here, too, disaster is now established as the norm, and mobilization focuses on how to cope with it.

Dining out/in the gated suburbs

Our third example of inverted moral panic is as follows. Consider a television advertisement for McDonald's from 2000. In it, we follow a father driving an SUV. He is smiling, and we hear his children's voices. Where are they, we wonder – buckled in the back seat of the SUV? Then it is clear; they are even safer – at home, presumably in a well-outfitted suburban house on a quiet cul-de-sac. The father is speaking to them over his cell phone as he pulls in to a McDonald's drive-up ordering station. A happy, clear voice welcomes him to McDonald's and asks for the order. The father picks up the cell phone and extends it toward the ordering station. The kids order for themselves. Their desires appear instantly in written form on a large television screen at the ordering station. A few moments later the father pulls up to a pick-up window, pays for the meal, and is handed a clean white bag, which he stows carefully in the capacious empty seat beside him. As he drives off, we view only the outside of the restaurant, its entranceways and its empty parking lot. It is night and the scene is lit in a vaguely menacing documentary style that suggests that anything could happen to someone who had to move by foot through this environment, without the SUV and the security of a cell phone.

The father featured in the advertisement provides a portrait of the kind of political subjectivity that has been produced by the 30-year war on crime and the kind of citizen that governing through crime both presupposes and serves (Simon 2007). Launched in his lunar landing module-like vehicle, the father can effortlessly reach out in various directions in response to crime, toward those who govern (the police) or toward those he governs (his children). Available safety in an otherwise hostile world.

The advertisement is striking for its suggestion that it is not the food that brings comfort, but the carefully managed and secure environment that invests the food with comfort. The product advertised here is the ability to order and purchase food directly from the safety of one's automobile. The primary theme, although never mentioned, is crime and insecurity – the fear of walking through an empty parking lot at night and entering a near-empty restaurant whose only customers may be some menacing 'others', and the fear of confrontation with a violent criminal bent on robbery or mayhem of some kind. Going into a fast-food restaurant has become fundamentally frightening to people, and those who run them know it. Remarkably, in this advertisement, McDonald's markets its own insecurity by advertising the ease with which customers can access their favourite foods securely.

McDonald's did not invent the crime victim as an ideal political subject (Garland 2001), although, as a firm, it has grown up with and grown wealthy on this subject. This subject is not the product of a pattern of cultural change brought on by the combined effects of transformation of the American family and the emergence of high levels of crime as a condition of late modernity. Instead, the crime victim as the idealized subject is the product of law and a style of lawmaking that in turn has been marketed. In the USA almost steadily since the 1964 presidential election, the 1967 publication of the reports of the President's Commission on Law Enforcement and the Administration of Criminal Justice, and the adoption of the Omnibus Crime Control and Safe Streets Act of 1968, public officials, with the cooperation of the mass media, have offered a steady stream of images and state and federal laws that have identified the crime victim as the subject of concern. In so doing, they have institutionalized the crisis of law and order, and made near-permanent the moral panic about crime. But in doing so, they have turned Cohen's insight on its head. Insecurity is the norm. Moral crusades are mounted not to reinforce comforting symbols of order and security, but as heroic efforts to stem the tide in what appears to be a losing battle. Danger and insecurity are everywhere; the crusade seeks isolated islands of safety and security. AMBER Alerts, SUVs, cell phones, and the like are at best ways to cope in the face of evergrowing threat.

The AMBER Alert and Jeanne Clery Act are not isolated endeavours. Twenty-nine states have amended their constitutions to include victims' 'bills of rights' that create a number of positive claims against the state for crime victims and potential victims, including the right to notice of and opportunity to be heard at any legal proceeding involving the crime against them. Legislatures now routinely name laws enhancing law enforcement powers after victims, most often child victims of violent crime. The most famous is Megan's Law, a package of crime measures aimed at sex offenders, versions of which have been adopted by all the states and the federal government. But there is also the Jacob Wetterling Act (encourages states receiving federal funds to adopt tighter controls on sex offenders), Zachary's Law in Indiana (requires registration of and notification about sex offenders), Ashley's Law in Texas, the Jimmy Rice Law in Florida, Joan's Law in New Jersey (imposes life imprisonment without parole as the mandatory alternative to the death penalty for rape and murder of victims under 14), Elisa's Law in New York (child abuse), the Scotty Trexler Law in Kentucky, the Tyler Jaeger Act in California, the Jeremy Fiedelholtz Safe Day Care Act in Florida, the Thomas Edward Lanni School Bus Safety Act in Florida, the Becca Bill in Washington (gives parents additional authority to seek commitment to custodial care of runaway minors), Courtney's Law in California, Jillian's Law in Rhode Island (enhances penalties for drivers responsible for alcohol-related accidents). The list goes on and on (see Simon 2007).

To be sure, crime is an ancient subject of the law, and crime panics have long functioned to foster social cohesion. But starting with the Omnibus Crime Control and Safe Streets Act of 1968, American lawmakers began a distinctive practice of adopting laws aimed at combating crime and fear of crime as a problem of governance. Subsequent crime legislation is not *just* a symbolic way to signal concern to particular constituents, or an instrument to accomplish particular policy objectives; it is also an influential model of how to make law in a democratic way.

Radiating out from the victim and the offender are metaphoric chains along which the representational security that legislative bodies find in crime legislation can be extended both by repetition and application to other problems in need of governance. The innocent victim of violent crime becomes the paradigmatic example of the citizen who needs government. The vulnerabilities and needs of victims define the appropriate conditions for government intervention. Hence the institutionalization of moral panics.

Conclusion

Moral panics can still be discerned and traced in the terms crafted by Cohen over 35 years ago. Indeed, they can still be profitably analysed and their form and character predicted with Cohen's model. But, we argue, in the era in which social life is enacted against a 'culture of control' and in which institutions increasingly 'govern through crime', moral panics are now part of the manufactured background, a feature of the larger order of knowledge and power that never goes away or recedes, and that must be constantly guarded against.

References

Becker, H. (1963) *Outsiders: Studies in the Sociology of Deviance*. New York: Free Press.

Beckett, K. (1997) *Making Crime Pay: Law and Order in Contemporary American Politics*. New York: Oxford University Press.

Cohen, S. (1980) *Folk Devils and Moral Panics* (2nd ed.). New York: St. Martin's Press.

Cohen, S. (1985) *Visions of Social Control*. London: Polity Press.

Edelman, M. (1964) *The Symbolic Uses of Politics*. Urbana, IL: University of Illinois Press.

Edelman, M. (1988) *Constructing the Political Spectacle*. Chicago: University of Chicago Press.

Feeley, M.M. (2003) 'Crime, social order, and the rise of neo-conservative politics', *Theoretical Criminology*, 7, 111–30.

Fishman, M. (1980) *Manufacturing the News*. Austin, TX: University of Texas Press.

Garland, D. (2001) *The Culture of Control: Crime and Social Order in Contemporary Society*. Chicago: University of Chicago Press.

Gusfield, J. (1963) *Symbolic Crusade: Status Politics and the American Temperance Movement*. Urbana, IL: University of Illinois Press.

Haltom, W. and McCann, M. (2004) *Distorting the Law: Politics, Media, and the Litigation Crisis*. Chicago: University of Chicago Press.

Lemert, E. (1951) *Social Pathology: A Systematic Approach to the Study of Sociopathic Behavior*. New York: McGraw-Hill.

Matza, D. (1969) *Becoming Deviant*. Englewood Cliffs, NJ: Prentice-Hall.

Scheingold, S. (1973) *The Myth of Rights*. New Haven, CT: Yale University Press.

Scheingold, S. (1991) *The Politics of Street Crime: Criminal Process and Cultural Obsession*. Philadelphia: Temple University Press.

Simon, J. (2007) *Governing Through Crime: How the War on Crime Transformed American Democracy and Created a Culture of Fear*. New York: Oxford University Press.

Smelser, N. (1962) *Theory of Collective Behavior*. London: Routledge & Kegan Paul.

Szaz, T. ([1961] 1974) *The Myth of Mental Illness*. New York: Harper & Row.

Tuchman, G. (1978) *Making News: A Study in the Social Construction of Reality*. New York: Free Press.

Tyler, T. and Boeckman, R. (1997) '"Three strikes and you're out, but why?" the psychology of public support for punishing rule breakers', *Law and Society Review*, 31: 237–65.

US Department of Justice (2005) *Report to the Congress on Amber Alert*, July 2005.

Chapter 6

Slipping away – moral panics each side of 'the Golden Age'

Jock Young

The year 2002 marked the publication of the third edition of Stan Cohen's *Folk Devils and Moral Panics*, the thirtieth anniversary of a book first published in 1972. Moral panic is a concept of great theoretical power and resonance. It is one of the few terms coined by sociologists which has entered the language; it is, however, a term often evoked casually and unthinkingly, and as a consequence can easily lose meaning and usefulness. Stan Cohen's classic analysis of moral panic is by far the most sophisticated rendition of the concept, and the study itself and the new edition of *Folk Devils and Moral Panics* remind us of the continued importance of its contribution to deviancy theory. It is a richly analysed text of much greater complexity and subtlety than many of the summaries and studies of moral panics which have followed it, and it reads today with as great impact as it did in the early 1970s.

I want first to briefly situate this work intellectually in the tumultuous world of the late 1960s and early 1970s; then examine the concept itself, attempting to highlight its theoretical purchase and edginess; and, lastly, turn to look at its relevance today.

Eric Hobsbawm, in *Age of Extremes* (1994), describes what he calls the Golden Age of the post-war period in the First World from the 1950s onward. This was a world of constant economic growth, rise in real incomes and full (male) employment where consumer spending increased year after year, and affluence and prosperity became taken for granted. Such economic progress was coupled with social stability in terms of job security, marriage, the family and community, and a sense of shared and relatively uncontested values. The years that followed involved a widespread restructuring of work, the rise of unemployment, uncertainty and insecurity, increased marital breakdown, the decline in community and a wholesale contest of values. The periodisation of this transition into and out of the Golden Age varies with the nation concerned. As Hobsbawm points out, the USA, which had witnessed continued expansion through the war period, sustained economic progress and prosperity that started much earlier than in the war-torn countries of Europe. Indeed, the USA in the 1950s represented to the Europe of reconstruction, regimentation and rationing, very much a shiny contrast: a material utopia of aspiration and desire (see Hebdige 1988). But if the onset of the Golden Age varied, its demise was more of a unity: for from the late 1960s onwards, social commentators talk both of a cultural revolution and of fundamental economic restructuring which transformed the social order of the developed world. The shift into late modernity had begun (see Young 1999). It was at this cusp of change that an extraordinary burst of creativity occurred within sociology and within the sociology of deviance in particular. As Stan Cohen put it, reflecting back some 30 years later: 'After the mid-1960s – well before Foucault made these subjects intellectually respectable and a long way from the Left Bank – our little corner of the human sciences was seized by a *deconstructionist* impulse' (1998: 101). The major site of this intellectual tumult in Britain was the National Deviancy Conference (NDC), which held its first meeting in 1968 and lasted for about ten years (see Cohen 1981; Young 1998). The NDC was deconstructionist, antinomian and eclectic. Its range of topics included anti-psychiatry, gender and sexuality, youth culture, mass media and cultural studies, but its major fulcrum was the sociology of crime and deviance. This is scarcely surprising in that the sociology of deviance (and by implication that of crime) has a privileged position within sociology, in so far as, from its vantage point, power, stigmatisation and the contest of norms are palpably visible. The subject revolves around the point where norms are broken and norms made. It was here that two imports from the American sociology of deviance made their mark. The first was labelling theory and the second the sociology of subcultures.

The deconstructionist impulse commenced in the USA around the work of the labelling theorists: Edwin Lemert, Howard S. Becker, John Kitsuse, Kai Erikson, Edwin Schur and many others. It was revolutionary in its discourse (social control generates deviance rather than deviance necessitates social control); it was relativistic in its analysis (deviance is not an inherent property of an act but a quality bestowed upon an act); and it inverted orthodoxies, lambasted positivism, and defended and celebrated human diversity: it was tremendously *attractive* to the young and to the radical at this time of change. Looking back on it now, it seems only too obvious that these anti-essentialist tales of stereotyping and prejudice were early yet relatively sophisticated accounts of othering. That is, from the depiction of the inception of the moral panic to the denouement of the impact on the deviant in the process of deviancy amplification, we have an analysis of the process of othering.

At the same time as this radical deconstructionist literature was imported to British shores, a second, more cautious and conservative strand became incorporated and transformed within the sociology of deviance. This was American subcultural theory, in particular the work on gangs and delinquency of Cloward and Ohlin (1961) and A.K. Cohen (1955), and the studies on prison subcultures of Gresham Sykes (1958) and Donald Clemmer (1940). A major institutional conduit of this importation of American theory was sociologists working at the London School of Economics, commencing with Herman Mannheim's *Juvenile Delinquency in an English Middletown* (1948), brought to fruition in Terence Morris' *The Criminal Area* (1957) and Terence and Pauline Morris' *Pentonville* (1963), and culminating in the extremely influential *The Delinquent Solution* by David Downes, published in 1966. It is out of this tradition that Stan Cohen's study of mods and rockers emerged as a PhD thesis, as did related studies – for example, my work on drug takers and that of Mike Brake on youth culture (1985).

It was in the debates and presentations which occurred within the NDC that a series of transformations occurred to these two American traditions – labelling and subcultural theory. First of all, the two were brought together in a synthesis. This was facilitated by the logic of their focus, namely, that labelling theory focused on construction downward (the *reaction* against deviance) and subcultural theory in construction upward (the deviant *action*). Secondly, the rather wooden American subcultural theory was given a zest, an energy, a feeling of creativity. Furthermore, the synthesis between the two traditions demanded likewise a sense of passion in the response to deviance. Thirdly, transgression was given a much more positive valuation. It was a sign of resistance, an overcoming, a creative flourish: it was not predominantly a site of failure or simple adaptation. American sociology of deviance became in Britain a sociology of transgression.

Having placed both the thesis and the author in a place and a context, let us now look at how this played out in the book *Folk Devils and Moral Panics*.

The beach

It is 1964 on an English beach at Easter in the small seaside town of Clacton. The weather is cold and wet as usual. Two groups of kids

– mods and rockers – get into a spat, some bikes and scooters roar up and down the front, windows are broken, and some beach huts are wrecked. There was not a great disturbance – the TV footage looks derisory – but there was an extraordinary disturbance in the mass media commentary and among members of the public. 'There was Dad asleep in the deckchair and Mum making sandcastles on the beach,' said *The Daily Express* – one pictures them relaxed, pink in the sun, Dad perhaps with the traditional handkerchief tied around his head, and then suddenly a 'day of terror' with the 'wild ones' who 'beat up the town'. This pattern was reported over a two-year period involving other seaside towns, roaming gangs of mods and rockers 'from London' periodically 'invaded', caused mayhem, displayed their arrogance and new affluence, insulted decent people and were, in a memorable phrase, 'sawdust caesars' puffed up with their own cowardice and aggression.

A common interpretation of moral panic is that of a mistake in understanding, a version of rational choice theory where reason is misled. Thus, one reading of this series of events (and many like it) that is encountered frequently in the literature is that an event occurred (for a reason which is unimportant) that was in itself of little consequence, but it was mistakenly reported and exaggerated by the mass media and consequently generated a feeling of fear and panic in the general public. All of this is, in part, true, but such a simple, liberal, linear model from media down to public scarcely captures the notion of 'moral panic'. What is missing is both the sense of energy and intensity of this happening and that, rather than a one-way process, this is a collective endeavour, for the youth, the media, the moral entrepreneurs, the control agents and the public are, so to speak, accomplices in the action.

Let us look more closely at the constituents of moral panic theory.

Symmetry

Both the subculture and the moral panic have to be explained – that is, both the action and the reaction. Furthermore, they must be explored symmetrically, using the same model of analysis. Thus, both moral panic and subculture are read as narratives where actors attempt to solve problems facing them. For this reason, although in the main body of the book Cohen focuses largely on moral panic, in the fascinating introduction to the second edition, 'Symbols of Trouble', he turns to subculture and finally returns to moral panic in the introduction of the third edition.

Thus, both the folk devils and the moral panickers are endowed with creativity, and both produce narratives, texts to be read. Moral panics, then, tell us something about the moral panickers they are not mere misperceptions engendered like implants from the mass media or the control agencies. Further, there is not one simple text to be read; Cohen is at pains to note how different audiences created different texts (from liberal to reactionary). The depiction of the *Other* thus tells you much about the *Otherer*. And here, of course, there are many parallels in the literature: for example, Edward Said's (2003) famous concept of 'orientalism', the depictions of the 'East' from the vantage point of the 'West', that reveal much of the anxieties and insecurities of the Western world.

Energy

A pulse of energy is introduced at each stage of the process. The kids on the beaches are driven by a creativity and exuberance which generates youth subcultures. They create, but they also thrill, to transgress: to get up people's noses, to annoy, to act out in front of the world's media. Thus Dick Hebdige's surmise in the wonderful *Hiding in the Light*: 'spectacular youth cultures convert the fact of being under surveillance into the pleasure of being watched' (1988: 8). Furthermore, the public watching the skirmishes are not mere passive spectators: they are morally indignant; they cheer the police as they arrest the thugs (Cohen 2002: 134); they are glad that magistrates and police officers reaffirm the boundaries of decency and propriety (as are the magistrates and police officers themselves). They are not merely manipulated recipients of media stereotypes – they *want* those messages, they read the popular papers and watch the telly with gusto, while the media, in turn, have learnt that there is a ready market in winding up audiences – they have institutionalised moral indignation with both enthusiasm and self-righteousness (see Cohen and Young 1973).

Here there is a sense of foregrounding, a phenomenology of transgression and vindictiveness prescient of Jack Katz's *Seductions of Crime* (1988) and the new cultural criminology. And here, one must stress, lies both the fanciful and the visceral. Youth cultures harbour the fanciful: they identify variously with youth in other places, other times, they cross classes, races, sometimes even gender – they conjure up musical tastes across borders, they bricolage styles of dress, demeanour and patois. They can take the commodities sold to them and magically transform their resonance and their meaning. As Dick Hebdige puts it:

57

The mods could be said to be functioning as *bricoleurs* when they appropriated another range of commodities by placing them in a symbolic ensemble which served to erase or subvert their original straight meanings. Thus pills medically prescribed for the treatment of neuroses were used as ends-in-themselves, and the motor scooter, originally an ultra-respectable means of transport, was turned into a menacing symbol of group solidarity. In the same improvisatory manner, metal combs, honed to a razor-like sharpness, turned narcissism into an offensive weapon. Union jacks were emblazoned on the backs of grubby parka anoraks or cut up and converted into smartly tailored jackets. More subtly, the conventional insignia of the business world – the suit, collar and tie, short hair, etc. – were stripped of their original connotations – efficiency, ambition, compliance with authority – and transformed into 'empty' fetishes, objects to be desired, fondled and valued in their own right (1979: 104–5).

Thus, the fanciful begins to edge upon the transgressive, but even more subversive was the core of the lifestyle itself: the attempt to unbalance the *moral equation*, the accepted balance between work and leisure. For the mods, as Stan Cohen put it, 'made a calculated attempt to live in leisure time' (2002: 158). They endeavoured to live a life of excitement, of elegance, and to escape – or, in David Downes' phrase, 'dissociate' – from the world of work. Thus, the bellhop hero of the film *Quadrophenia* (Franc Roddam 1979), based on Pete Townsend's rock opera about the mod experience and set on the beaches, creates a glamorous role at night bridged by the 'alchemy of speed' despite a servile role during the day (see Hebdige 1976).

But let us stress the precariousness of their stance. They are trying to achieve a leisure role, an expressive existence which is constantly in danger of slipping away; indeed, the subculture – from sharp clothes to amphetamines – is in essence an attempt symbolically to shore up a situation which is naggingly undermined by material reality. It is that and it is more – it is also an *accomplishment*, a moment of pleasure, enjoyment, comradeship that they will look back to in later years in their more 'realistic' maturity and reminisce about, and perhaps even feel nostalgically that things were more 'real' and authentic in those days.

But let us turn now to the symmetry, to the panickers, to the public watching the transgressors on the beach. Here, too, energy is being expended. If we listen to Stan Cohen's respondents, we hear the usual litany of vindictiveness: the predilection for the birch, the desire for the return of national service, building roads, digging the Channel Tunnel, detention centres, etc. Such a visceral reaction, heavy with emotional energy, is a key feature of moral panics – a very similar response occurred to hippies and drug users in my own study (Young 1971), which found a general revulsion by police officers and members of the public to images of filth, uncleanliness and degradation. The text of panic is, therefore, a transposition of fear – the very disproportionality and excess of the language, the venom of the stereotype, signifies that something other than direct reporting is up. Listen to the much-quoted *News of the World* (21 September 1969) on the hippie squat in 1969 in an elegant Georgian mansion in Piccadilly:

> HIPPIE DRUGS – THE SORDID TRUTH
> Drug-taking, couples making love while others look on, a heavy mob armed with iron-bars, filth and stench, foul language, that is the scene inside the hippies' fortress in London's Piccadilly. These are not rumours but facts, sordid facts which will shock ordinary decent living people. Drug taking and squalor, sex … and they'll get no state aid etc.

Savour the mixture of fascination and repulsion, attraction and condemnation, in a text which contains fragments of truth, rephrased and contextualised, as they sit there 'lit only by the light of their drugged cigarettes', led by the elusive Dr John, the *nom de guerre* of Phil Cohen, who was later to resurface, in a wicked twist of fate, as a leading theoretician of subculture theory (see commentary in Young 1971; Brake 1985; and especially P. Cohen 1995).

The real problem, the real significance

Cohen is at pains to stress that there is a real problem there and that what is happening is not simply a mere illusion, a misperception. He touches base with Sven Ranulf's (1964) classic discussion of middle-class moral indignation, where such intervention is seen to have a 'disinterested' quality – it is a moral anger about something which does not directly affect their interests. Cohen, quite correctly, doubts that the distinction between interest and disinterest is a viable one (2002: 16), for the hedonism and spontaneity of the new youth culture for the mods *did* threaten the norms and standards of their elders:

> The mods and rockers symbolised something far more important than what they actually did. They reached the delicate and ambivalent nerves through which post-war social change in

Britain was experienced. No-one wanted depressions or austerity but messages about *'never having it so good'* were ambivalent in that some people were having it too good and too quickly. ... Resentment and jealousy were easily directed against the young, if only because of their increased spending power and sexual freedom. When this was combined with a too-open flouting of the work and leisure ethic, with violence and vandalism and drugtaking something more than the image of a peaceful Bank Holiday at the sea was being shattered (2002: 161–2).

You cannot have a moral panic unless there is something morally to panic about, although it may not be the actual object of fear but a displacement of another fear, or, more frequently, a mystification of the true threat of the actual object of dismay. Thus, although it is perfectly possible that the actual object of panic does not exist (e.g. satanic child abuse), the panic is about a moral problem of real dimensions. Further, in the most substantial cases, the objects of panic *do* represent a direct threat to the core values, the strategies of discipline and the justifications of rewards (what I called earlier the moral equation) of those that panic. Only this is a direct threat in a moral and symbolic kind rather in a material sense. Thus, the mods mocked and threatened the work discipline of the decent citizens; the threat, of course, in terms of violence or vandalism, was small and insignificant. As Cohen tellingly puts it, 'Whatever the 'devil' was in the seaside towns it was not in the vandalism' (*ibid.*: 114).

Thus, in these instances, the group panicked about is scarcely arbitrary, and it is not some mere Rorschach blot upon which prejudice is projected. Indeed, the devil, so to speak, exists before the incident which precipitates the moral panic. Read for a moment the marvellous depiction of the folk devil in *Policing the Crisis*:

The Folk Devil – on to whom all our most intense feelings about things going wrong, and all our fears abut what might undermine our fragile securities are projected – is, as Jeremy Seabrook suggested ... a sort of alter ego for Virtue. In one sense, the Folk Devil comes up at us unexpectedly, out of the darkness, out of nowhere. In another sense, he is all too familiar; we know him already, before he appears. He is the reverse image, the alternative to all we know: *the negation*. He is the fear of failure that is secreted at the heart of success, the danger that lurks inside security, the profligate figure by whom Virtue is constantly tempted, the tiny, seductive voice inside inviting us to feed on sweets and honey cakes when we know we must restrict ourselves to iron rations. When things threaten to disintegrate, the Folk Devil not only becomes the bearer of all our social anxieties, but we turn against him the full wrath of our indignation (S. Hall *et al.* 1978: 161).

The three original accounts of moral panics, Stan Cohen's study of mods and rockers (1972) situated in 1964/6, my own study of cannabis and hippies in *The Drugtakers* (1971) situated in 1968, and Stuart Hall and his team's study of the mugging panic in *Policing the Crisis* (1978) situated in 1972, all reflect major structural and value changes in advanced industrial societies as refracted through the prism of youth.

As I argued in *The Exclusive Society* (1999), the post-war period experienced a seismic change in values and structure as we drifted into late modernity. There was a shift from a society which stressed work discipline and deferred gratification to one which emphasised a balance between work and home, a hard-working, hard-consuming Keynesianism, and, then further, a shift from the goal of simple material satisfaction ('the American dream') to one where immediacy, spontaneity and hedonism became ascendant, and where a material success merely became a staging post on the route to self-expression and discovery.

Youth culture prefigured, as always, these social changes, sometimes as a harbinger of the future, sometimes as a grim-faced resistance. Moral panics about the teenage revolution, the hippie, and black youth echoed these changes. The invention of the teenager and the reinvention of teenage by youth themselves was one of the major structural changes of the twentieth century (see Shorter 1977). On its back arose the most extraordinary flourishing of popular culture, no more so than in Britain, albeit late to arrive and looking always over its shoulder to America.

The very austerity of post-war Britain, its rigid demarcations of class, its war-induced sense of sacrifice and discipline, its failed imperial past – all probably added together to make the youth cultures of Britain all the more spectacular when it eventually broke through. What was happening in Clacton; in Brighton; in Margate, of all places; and of course in London was, on the face of it, mysterious, in a Mary Poppins sense of something strange afoot, something about to happen. But change was in the air, even though some of its chief architects and minstrels did not understand at the time the significance of what was happening. But the Stones were playing at the Crawdaddy in Richmond; Rhythm and Blues at, of all places, the Thames Valley; Eric Clapton at Klooks Kleek in Kilburn; and the quintessential mod band, the Who, at Eel Pie Island, launching their gig with 'I Can't Explain' and ending it with the amphetamine stutter: 'Why don't you all f... f... fade away?'

And, of course, the British public half sensed all of this, and in a real way the moral panic over the mods and rockers was a defence of a world that was slipping away – an act of moral resistance if you want. In ten years' time the music would be mainstream, the austerity of self-discipline of the past would be regarded, not with nostalgia, but disdain, and the Mums and Dads themselves would have deserted these windy seaside towns for the warmth and vino of the Costa del Sol and Ibiza.

Late modernity and the permanent moral panic

The concept of moral panic, thus, arose at a particular time of change both in the wider world and in the academy itself. It occurred in a period when society and culture seemed to move rapidly ahead and where sociological theory bustled noisily behind. But this is not to argue that the concept should be locked in time. The most seminal antecedent is Kai Erikson's *Wayward Puritans* (1966), which discussed 'the shapes of the devil' in Puritan New England and, among other things, the witchcraft trials at Salem. From there, it moved to the medieval witchcraft hysteria, and then, via Arthur Miller's *The Crucible*, to McCarthyism and back over the Atlantic to the furies of anti-Semitism. There can be little doubt that these are the unspoken historical antecedents of the concept. But what of today, is there anything special about moral panics in the twenty-first century? There has been a radical shift in society from one which was comparatively stable in terms of work, family and community to one in which all three of these girders of ontological security have become unsteady, less substantial and frequently broken. It is where we have an increasingly insecure middle class and a large underclass of transient, insecure and grossly undervalued labour (see Schulman 2003). If the moral panic upon entering the Golden Age was about a world of austerity and discipline slipping away, the moral panic *this* side of the Golden Age is of prosperity and security slipping away. It is a time of middle-class vertigo, of uncertainty, of a fear of falling (see Young 2007).

In their brilliant updating of the concept in the article 'Rethinking Moral Panics for Multi-mediated Social Worlds' (1995), Angie McRobbie and Sarah Thornton generate some significant pointers.

A major thrust of their argument is that, in a media-saturated world, the division between the media representation and the untouched world beloved of 'effects' research is increasingly unlikely.

Social meanings and social differences are inextricably tied up with representation. Thus when sociologists call for an account which tells how life actually is, and which deals with real issues rather than the spectacular and exaggerated ones, the point is that these accounts of reality are already representations and sets of meanings about what they perceive the 'real' issues to be. These versions of 'reality' would also be impregnated with the mark of media imagery rather than somehow pure and untouched by the all pervasive traces of contemporary communications (McRobbie and Thornton, 1995: 570–1).

Or, as Ferrell and Saunders put it, 'as cultural criminologists we study not only images but images of images, an infinite hall of mediated mirrors' (1995: 14).

Contemporary youth cultures are intensely aware of their image; they grow out of their representation both at the moment and by bricolaging from across the world together with a 'retro' gaze at the past (see Gaines 1998). Moreover, as McRobbie and Thornton point out, they are likely to be intentionally transgressive and to welcome, in a punk fashion, moral panic and adult condemnation. Further, the agencies of control themselves – the police and government spokespersons – exist in a world of press release, spin, and representation and counter-representation. They will be scarcely outsiders in the media circus. Where I would differ from McRobbie and Thornton's analysis is that their notion of a 'multi-mediated world' would suggest a greater diversity of representations than actually occurs. Or, to put it another way, diversity, of course, occurs from speciality magazines to Internet chat circles, but the main thrust of representation hinges around the major media chains and their ever-increasing oligopolisation. Panics and scapegoating would seem to me to focus upon the socially excluded: in particular, the triptych of welfare scrounger, immigrant and drug addict, frequently elided and racialised, and to which, after 9/11, a further refracting mirror has been added: that of actual and imaginary terrorist (see Rothe and Muzatti 2004). In this, I differ also from Stan Cohen; the notion of 'permanent moral panic' may well be something of an oxymoron, but the time of transient panic is long past. Here, in the fibrillating heartlands of the first world, images of the excluded, the immigrant, the drug user and the terrorist visit us daily, the intensity dropping and peaking like tremors, but never vanishing nor presenting temporary relief.

Here we have the extraordinary structural change wherein a sizeable section of the population have become socially excluded and then cast with the stigma of trouble, contamination and danger. Michael Harrington wrote in the 1960s of *The Other America* (1962), a world where the poor had become invisible. Today we have, in contrast, an Othered America (and elsewhere across the industrial world) where the poor are in the searchlight of condemnation, the object of stigmatisation, surveillance and blame. The notion of moral panic delves to the very heart of our social order; its occurrence is potent ammunition in the production of division, and it is subtle rhetoric in the fabric of legitimation. The recent publication of the third edition of *Folk Devils* reminds us of the depth of analysis and continued timeliness of this text; together with a new introduction and the remarkable critique, 'Symbols of Trouble', it remains a must for any student of sociology or any reader seeking to understand the perplexity of the world we now live in.

References

Brake, M. (1984) *Comparative Youth Culture*. London: Routledge and Kegan Paul.

Cloward, R. and Ohlin, L. (1961) *Delinquency and Opportunity*. London: Routledge and Kegan Paul.

Cohen, A.K. (1955) *Delinquent Boys: The Culture of the Gang*. New York: Free Press.

Cohen, P. (1997) *Rethinking the Youth Question*. London: Macmillan.

Cohen, S. (1981) 'Footprints in the sand', in M. Fitzgerald, G. McLennon and J. Pawson (eds) *Crime and Society*. London: Routledge.

Cohen, S. (1998) 'Intellectual scepticism and political commitment: the case of radical criminology', in P. Walton and J. Young (eds) *The New Criminology Revisited*. London: Macmillan.

Cohen, S. (2002) *Folk Devils and Moral Panics* (3rd edn). London: Routledge.

Cohen, S. and Young, J. (1973) *The Manufacture of News*. London: Constable.

Downes, D. (1966) *The Delinquent Solution*. London: Routledge and Kegan Paul.

Erikson, E. (1966) *Wayward Puritans*. New York: Wiley.

Ferrell, J. and Saunders, C. (eds) (1995) *Cultural Criminology*. Boston: Northeastern University Press.

Gaines, D. (1998) *Teenage Wasteland*. Chicago: University of Chicago Press.

Hall, S., Critcher, C., Jefferson, T., Clarke, J. and Roberts, B. (1973) *Policing the Crisis*. London: Macmillan.

Harrington, M. (1962) *The Other America*. New York: Macmillan.

Hebdige, D. (1976) 'The meaning of mod', in S. Hall and T. Jefferson (eds) *Resistance Through Rituals*. London: Hutchinson.

Hebdige, D. (1979) *Subculture: The Meaning of Style*. London: Methuen.

Hebdige, D. (1988) *Hiding in the Light*. London: Routledge.

Hobsbawm, E. (1994) *Age of Extremes*. London: Michael Joseph.

Katz, J. (1988) *The Seductions of Crime*. New York: Basic Books.

McRobbie, A. and Thornton, S. (1995) 'Rethinking "moral panics" for multi-mediated social worlds', *British Journal of Sociology*, 46 (4): 559–74.

Mannheim, H. (1948) *Juvenile Delinquency in an English Middletown*. London: Routledge and Kegan Paul.

Morris, T. (1957) *The Criminal Area*. London: Routledge and Kegan Paul.

Morris, T. and Morris, P. (1963) *Pentonville*. London: Routledge and Kegan Paul.

Quadrophenia (1979) Film directed by Frank Roddam.

Ranulf, S. (19640 *Moral Indignation and Middle Class Psychology*. New York: Schoken Books.

Rothe, D. and Muzatti, S. (2004) 'Enemies everywhere: terrorism, moral panic and US civil society', *Critical Criminology*, 12 (3): 285–308.

Said, E. (2003) *Orientalism*. New York: Vintage Books.

Schulman, B. (2003) *The Betrayal of Work*. New York: The New Press.

Shorter, E. (1997) *The Making of the Modern Family*. New York: Basic Books.

Thornton, S. (1995) *Clubcultures*. Oxford: Polity.

Young, J. (1971) *The Drugtakers*. London: Paladin.

Young, J. (1998) 'Breaking windows: situating the new criminology', in P. Walton and J. Young (eds) *The New Criminology Revisited*. London: Macmillan.

Young, J. (1999) *The Exclusive Society*. London: Sage.

Young, J. (2007) *The Vertigo of Late Modernity*. London: Sage.

Chapter 7

Sexual offenders and the path to a purified domain

Andrew Rutherford

Introduction

> Sensible and humane provisions for the handling of both offenders and victims depend on the public being made aware of the variety and complexity of the problems involved in unlawful sexual behaviour. We have tried to point out the need to avoid reflexive responses of revulsion born of ignorance, to distinguish between behaviour that is a nuisance and behaviour that is truly harmful, to discriminate between remedial inadequacies and wilful violation of the rights of others, to take more account of the needs of victims, and to develop and evaluate improved methods of management and treatment of offenders.
>
> The Howard League for Penal Reform (1985: 166–67)

> The utopian vision has always been homogeneity, conformity, stratification and separation. The point of exclusion is to create purified domains inhabited by just the right groups: not too old and not too young, not too blemished or disabled, not troublesome or noisy, not too poor, not with the wrong-coloured skin.... The 'innocent' scapegoat, the justly punished offender, the members of high-risk groups are all candidates for exclusion.
>
> Stanley Cohen (1985: 234)

During the two decades that followed publication of the passages that open this chapter, the array of controls over offenders in Britain, representing a complex tangle of punishment, surveillance and exclusion, made enormous gains in scope. The prison population of England and

Wales all but doubled over these years, and a legislative roller coaster addressed virtually every aspect of the criminal law and criminal justice process.[1] In particular, the landscape regarding sexual offenders was totally transformed, with three features requiring mention. First, much of this activity treated the sexual offender as a separate and distinct category. Second, as a special category, sexual offenders became regarded as a homogeneous group, not differentiated by offence, risk or individual circumstance. Third, these developments reached beyond extensions of the criminal law and sentencing arrangements (and, indeed, the innovative civil powers bestowed upon the courts) to a myriad activities primarily involving the police and the probation services but also increasingly encompassing agencies that lie beyond the criminal justice process.[2]

This chapter therefore addresses both the formal arrangements of the state as well as localised initiatives, often rather informal, that are instigated by the police, the probation service and other agencies. These activities have given rise to an extensive 'glossary of control talk' and acronyms to be placed alongside the famous appendix, 'On Constructing a Glossary of Control Talk' in *Visions of Social Control*.[3] While press campaigns naming and shaming sex offenders, and indeed judges, are not of immediate concern here, these activities are interwoven into the backcloth of a symbiotic relationship between agencies of the state and the elements of the media.[4]

The consequences of this demonisation by much of the media and the political process has been neatly captured by one of Stan Cohen's fellow sociologists at the London School of Economics. 'Sexual predators, paedophiles, the incorrigibly anti-social are representatives of a new "human kind" – individuals whose very make up as human beings appears somehow faulty or incomplete, and whose very nature thus seems to place them permanently beyond the limits of civility and its demands on subjectivity.'[5] Within a whirlwind of criminal justice policy and practice, the sexual offender may be viewed as a pilot, leading the way, identifying and skirting around obstacles and charting new and sometimes radical ways forward for mechanisms of state control and elimination.[6]

The burgeoning legislative framework

'[S]o fine, and at the same time so indistinct, are the gradations along the continuum, that it is by no means easy to know where the prison ends and the community begins or just where any deviant is to be found at any particular point.'[7] In fact, Cohen's observation provides an acute précis of the extended sentence. Introduced initially in 1998, the extended sentence (as amended by the Criminal Justice Act 2003) provides for an additional eight years post-release licence for sexual offenders (and five additional years for a person convicted of an offence of violence). While the extended sentence not only increases the potential length of a prison sentence, it also serves to blur boundaries between the penal institution and supervision by the probation service. It does this by tightening controls and surveillance over the individual, and by making it more likely that licences will be breached and that any such breach will result in being returned to prison for a period that may be considerably longer than the original 'custodial element' of the sentence.

One consequence of the extended sentence is that the probation service has come to occupy a pivotal role at three stages of the process. First, the judge is likely to be guided by pre-sentence reports recommending an extended period of licence. Second, probation officers are critical to decisions regarding both release and recall. Third, following a recall, members of the probation service also guide decisions about re-release. The reality of the extended sentence is that, once recalled, the individual faces the likelihood of a lengthy period in custody before re-release. Paradoxically, the legislative intent placed emphasis on community supervision, but actual practice has favoured longer periods of confinement. For example, a sex offender who received a one-year sentence of imprisonment for indecent assault and a five-year extended licence spent four and a half years inside prison, having been recalled not for a further offence but for consuming alcohol in a hostel. In this case, notions of proportionality and fairness were quickly overtaken by the risk agenda.[8]

The 'dangerous offender' risk management agenda of the Criminal Justice Act 2003 also increased the tariff periods of life sentences and introduced imprisonment for public protection (IPP). These sentences are mandated for offences subject to sentences of ten years or more on conviction of a sexual (or violent) offence specified in the legislation. The court must impose such a sentence if it is of the opinion that there is a significant risk to members of the public of serious harm occasioned by the commission of further specified offences.[9]

The year 2003 also saw passage of the Sexual Offences Act, through which, as one observer has commented, much was made criminal that previously was not; and most of it is made more severely punishable.[10] The then Home Secretary described the Act as perfectly illustrating his political strategy: 'The whole revision of the sex offences laws [was possible] precisely because I was willing to take on the business of securing confidence. I was on the side of the people, and I knew what I was doing, that I was putting to rest some of the greater fears that people have, and I do believe that that will be the legacy of the time that I have here. Asked to choose what I was most proud of, I could easily have said reductions in crime or the balance on asylum and legal economic migration, but I chose the sex offender legislation to demonstrate that sometimes it takes a very robust and very tough Home Secretary to be able to do the things that others have not done.'[11]

Under this legislation the Sexual Offences Prevention Order (SOPO) replaced the Sex Offender Order that had been introduced alongside (but attracting much less public attention) the Anti-Social Behaviour Order (ASBO). The SOPO may be imposed on an individual who has been convicted of a qualifying offence or following an application from a chief police officer on a person living in the community who has a previous conviction for such an offence.[12] Qualifying offences include violent but non-sexual acts, and there is no requirement that there be a sexual motive.[13]

In making the order, the court has to be satisfied that it is necessary to protect the public or any particular members of the public 'from serious sexual harm'. Matters that trigger the application and finding may have been committed overseas or even have taken place prior to commencement of the Act.[14] The orders must be imposed for a period of at least five years and may be of indefinite duration. Any breach may be punishable as a criminal offence with a maximum sentence of five years' imprisonment. The individual also becomes subject to sex offender registration requirements and MAPP (multi-agency public protection) arrangements. According to Home Office research, in virtually every case the courts granted the application for a Sex Offender Order. Within the first 28 months from becoming available, almost half of all orders were prosecuted for breaches, and 97 per cent of such persons were convicted.[15] Two-thirds of persons dealt with for breach received custodial sentences (usually for less than a year). Of particular significance, a number of police officers reported that they had sought these orders principally in the hope of achieving a criminal conviction on breach when the offender's ability to desist from offending was thought to be particularly weak.[16] The Home Office study also highlighted concerns about the limited information being passed from prisons to the police: 'While there were cases where prisons actively communicated information which went to form the basis of an order on a prisoner's release, the scope for more active dialogue in this area was felt to be considerable.' Some police forces considered that it should be permitted that an application be made in such cases regardless of whether risky behaviour had been exhibited in custody. The agenda was for a further 'joining-up' of the police and prisons, particularly at the level of intelligence units.

Significantly, the study emphasised that the order had to be viewed within the context of a variety of techniques facilitated through the local MAPPA and seen as a last resort, less formal arrangements being regarded as more appropriate. One police force stated that its 'intrusive' monitoring, particularly of offenders after release from prison, had meant that there were few occasions when the order would have been worthwhile. 'This particular force had dedicated prison intelligence officers to work with all the prisons within the force area. Intelligence was collected whilst the offender was in prison and included details on general behaviour, attendance at Sex Offender Treatment Programmes, any visitors and any phone calls made. The prison service would notify the police when a sex offender or dangerous offender was coming out of prison, so a management strategy could be planned. Prior to release, offenders were told that they would be subject to a very intensive level of monitoring. [The orders] were not in this instance viewed as something which would enhance the process of sex offender management.'[17]

In some forces the threat of an order was used as a means of persuading individuals to desist from what was regarded as risky behaviour. Voluntary agreements between the police and the individual, or even more informal approaches, were often preferred. An application for an order risked press publicity as well as a custodial sentence in the event of a breach. As one police officer put it: 'Having an offender in the palm of your hand, being able to control them [sic] without having to go for the legislation … the fact that it is there is enough to be a preventive measure.'[18] Probation officers also welcomed this civil order as a means, if necessary, of continuing to manage the offender after the end of a period of supervision. A probation officer, hinting perhaps at the blurring of police and probation activities, told the researchers: 'We have the ability to operationally make things work in my experience. We have a good blend with the powers that probation has to influence things like parole, licence conditions and police willingness to push the boundaries of tactics to influence managing an offender.'[19]

Localised arrangements

As already indicated, overlaying the range of criminal and civil orders are a variety of localised arrangements intended to enhance public safety. This new administrative landscape, which began to take shape with the Sex Offenders Act 1997 and the creation of a sex offender register, has since been characterised by extraordinary growth. Registration of sex offenders by the police was partly prompted by Megan's Law (a federal statute enacted the previous year in the USA that encouraged states to provide for the registration and public notification of sexual offenders). The 1997 legislation was later amended to extend registration requirements to persons convicted abroad and to reduce the period by which an individual has to inform the police of any change of the notified details from 14 to 3 days. The duration of registration is from a minimum of five years to life.[20] By 2004–5, some 30,000 persons had been registered with estimates that in due course this number would reach 125,000.

Registration requirements apply to a wide range of sexual offences that result in a conviction or, notably, a caution applied by the police.[21] A person regarded as suitable for a police caution must, under Home Office standards, be informed of the implications of agreeing to be cautioned, and in the case of a sexual offender, these include placement on the sex offender register for five years. However, there have been instances of the police failing to alert individuals to the consequence of a caution.[22] There is also a lack of clarity among police officers regarding persons on the register, but no longer subject to a court order, as to the legality of visiting them at their homes. However, early research on registration procedures found that almost all offenders were co-operative in this regard.

> Within the same force, approaches varied. Offenders in one division could be visited by specialist plain-clothes officers with a view to completing detailed questionnaires, taking a Polaroid photograph, a DNA swab or arrange finger-printing, and in another division by officers in uniform, tasked on a one-off basis and without any specific protocol to follow.... Officers conducting visits often cultivated rapport with offenders, assured them that their safety and security were important and encouraged offenders to contact them at any time. This approach was thought to result in offenders being more forthcoming when asked about family history, sexuality and offending behaviour.... Some officers referred the offender to appropriate resources in the community. While this did not look like traditional police work, a sex offender liaison officer commented that such action was in police interests as it helped to keep the offender stable.[23]

Developing alongside registration have been localised arrangements for the more systematic monitoring of sex offenders. These Multi-Agency Public Protection Arrangements (MAPPAs) have developed at an extraordinary pace since 2000.[24] Falling within their auspices are persons required to register with their local police station, violent offenders and those sexual offenders who are not required to register; any other offenders who, because of the offences committed by them (wherever this took place), are considered to pose a risk of serious harm to the public.[25] Of the 45,600 persons within the purview of MAPPAs in 2004–5, the great majority were sex offenders.[26]

Additionally, there has been heightened activity to establish new or reinforced arrangements with respect to the protection of children from abuse. Since 2000, a statutory duty has been placed on the police and probation services to jointly establish arrangements for assessing and managing the risk to children posed by sexual and violent offenders in the community. In the wake of the murder in August 2003 of two young girls in Soham, Cambridgeshire, by a school caretaker (and the subsequent inquiry into the retention and sharing of information by police forces),[27] one commentator concluded that consideration for the human rights of offenders, social exclusion and access to people's criminal records took a significant step backwards. Mike Nash goes on to say that, '[a]ssessing potential dangerousness in the unconvicted therefore raises its head again as society continues to rush towards demands for perfect society'.[28]

Heightened concerns about victims of sexual offences led to a fourth category of persons falling within the purview of MAPPAs. According to guidance issued to the police, police officers and social services personnel are able to take action to reduce the harm posed by 'potentially dangerous persons'. Such persons (generally referred to as PDPs but also as PDOs) have no convictions of either a violent or sexual nature. 'The statutory duties of the police and social services to prevent further serious harm and to protect children allow action to reduce the harm posed by PDPs. For higher risk PDPs, some areas of England and Wales use the framework of the MAPPA to involve relevant agencies and to coordinate risk management plans.'[29] In Shropshire, for example, a protocol was agreed by local agencies that aimed at 'providing protection for the public from known, or suspected, offenders who may present serious threats of a sexual and/or violent nature, to the public in general, or to particular children or adults or targeted groups of children or adults. A key part of the protocol is the identification of PDOs, an assessment of potential risk and arrangements to manage that risk through agreed action plans.'[30]

As two researchers of the development of MAPPAs have stated, 'the key objective of panel work is the constitution and reproduction of networks of surveillance'.[31] Three levels of surveillance have been created, with the most intrusive, level 3, intended to address 'the critical few'.[32] The components of risk management at level 3 include police intelligence, targeted surveillance, access to supervised accommodation, accredited treatment programmes and victim protection.[33] Where there is thought to be a lack of motivation or 'false compliance' on the part of the individual, the 'risk management in such cases is almost entirely about containment in the community, restriction of opportunities to re-offend and protection of known or likely victims'. Surveillance and police intelligence are key components along with rapid recall procedures. There has been variation in referral processes, management of risk levels due to local circumstances and access to services. There was evidence of 'risk inflation' with some cases graded at level 3 instead of at level 2 in order to gain speedier access to resources. Indeed, only 26 of 73 level 3 cases were assessed as clearly meeting the criteria for that level.[34]

Practice at the local level occasionally exceeds lawful powers. As with persons on the sex register, the police have no right of access to an individual's home, and there have been instances where individuals have barred entry and contacted their solicitors. In some parts of the country, there have been, at least implicitly, blanket housing bans on sexual offenders.[35] There have also been instances where MAPPPs have altered licence conditions imposed by the Parole Board.[36] In one area, 'the police and probation worked closely, through MAPPA, where appropriate, in setting any conditions it is felt need to be attached to a licence, share information of the offender's adherence to the licence and ensure that once a decision has been taken to revoke a licence the offender is returned to custody as speedily as possible'.[37] In another area the local Multi-Agency Risk Conference (MARC) placed a licence condition on an offender preventing him from contacting a woman he had been convicted of indecently assaulting. The offender (who had received 20 months' imprisonment) 'was also ordered to sign on the Sex Offender Register for an indefinite period and the officers were able to explain to [the victim] what this meant.'[38]

Elsewhere, a sex offender managed at MAPPA level 3 was released from prison subject to licence conditions, which included a condition of residence at a probation hostel. Other licence conditions included not residing in a household with a child under 18, not working or undertaking voluntary activity with a child under 18 and not entering leisure centres or public parks without the prior approval of a supervising probation officer. In addition, he was not allowed to use computers or photographic equipment without prior permission. As a result of monitoring in the hostel, which included room searches, it was discovered that he had obtained three mobile phones, which included a camera phone. He was recalled to prison for breaching licence conditions. The panel reviewed the information, and the decision was taken that longer-term measures needed to be in place when he was released at the end of his sentence, as he would then not be subject to statutory supervision. The court granted an indefinite SOPO, which included prohibitions on approaching, contacting, communicating, engaging or otherwise associating with any child under 16 years of age or attempting to do any of these whether in any private or public place. 'These prohibitions will be the basis on which he will be monitored and should he breach any of the above then he is liable for prosecution and if convicted could be sentenced to a term of imprisonment for a term not exceeding five years.'[39] Mission creep of this sort by MAPPAs is all too likely given the lack of oversight and structures for public accountability. Indeed, of 12 area protocols examined by researchers, only one specifically addressed issues of accountability.[40]

Within MAPPAs, personnel differed as to how much weight should be attached to the quality of life experienced by sexual offenders, with some practitioners regarding this as being of secondary or incidental importance while, for others, there was awareness of treating people individually, fairly and with respect.[41] Acknowledging that quality of life for sexual offenders cannot be separated from their involvement in the wider community, an inspectorate report concluded that, apart from schemes such as 'circles of support', it was highly unlikely that any involvement of this sort would be encountered.[42]

The emergence of MAPPAs and the accompanying paraphernalia of widely dispersed controls brings to mind Foucault's image of the punitive city. 'This, then, is how one must imagine the punitive city. At the crossroads, in the gardens, at the side of roads being repaired or bridges built, in workshops open to all, in the depths of mines that may be visited, will be hundreds of tiny theatres of punishment.'[43] Cohen's salutary comment on Foucault evokes a powerful resonance in the developments outlined in this chapter. 'This new system of subtle gradations in care, control, punishment and treatment is indeed far from the days of public execution and torture – but it is perhaps not quite as far as Foucault suggests from that early reform vision of the punitive city.'[44] Although in embryonic form, these arrangements reflect a mindset that rejects the sexual offender as a person enjoying inalienable and fundamental human rights. Notions of fairness, proportionality and parsimony have been largely abandoned and few limits or checks are in place. As with Foucault's image of the leper, cut off from all human contact, and underlying projects of exclusion,[45] the sexual offender has become a convenient and expendable pathfinder for a state seeking to extend its apparatus of identification, surveillance and internal exile.

In his prescient novel, *One*, David Karp captures something of where this path might be headed. Mr Lark, of the Department of Internal

Examination, is speaking to a subject of special investigation:

> You know, Professor Burden, that in other times and in other cultures you would have been shot out of hand for disagreeing with the State. I am not mentioning this to make you feel any gratitude. We know such methods are false, that they accomplish nothing, that they postpone the inevitable – that in fact they strengthen the ultimate rebellion – it is the pathetic threat of a threadbare political system. The Department has built its reputation on reason, justice and benevolence.[46]

Notes

1 Of some 50 criminal statutes dealing with criminal justice matters, at least 12 specifically addressed sexual offenders.
2 While Garland (2001: 124–27) refers to developments of this kind as 'governing-at-a-distance', the distance involved may not always be as great as it appears.
3 Cohen (1985: 273–81). Some new acronyms are listed in Nash (2006: ix). Readers of this chapter are provided with a mere taster with references to SOF (Sex Offender Register), VISOR (Violent and Sex Offender Register), MAPPP (Multi Agency Public Protection Panel), MAPPA (Multi Agency Public Protection Arrangements), MARC (Multi Agency Risk Conference), SOTP (Sex Offender Treatment Programme), OASys (Offender Assessment System), RM2000 (Risk Matrix 2000), SOPO (Sexual Offences Protection Order), IPP/DPP (Imprisonment/Detention for Public Protection and PDP/PDO (Potentially Dangerous Persons/Potentially Dangerous Offenders.
4 See, e.g., *The Sun*, 'Sack the softie judge now', 16 June 2006 and 'Sarah's law victory' *The News of the World*, 18 June 2006.
5 Rose (2000: 339).
6 See Rutherford (1997).
7 Cohen (1985: 57).
8 Harding (2006).
9 A 'specified offence' does not have to be a serious offence. By June 2006, there were over 1000 persons in prison serving IPP or DPPs (for persons under the age of 18) compared with about 330 seven months earlier.
10 Spencer (2004, 348).
11 David Blunkett, *The Observer* (7 March 2004), cited in Pollard (2005: 306-7).
12 This approach was first proposed by the new Labour government in November 1997. In its Consultation Paper, the government emphasised that it was considering the *potential* risk to the community as opposed to reliance on evidence that certain acts had been committed (Home Office 1977: 1).

13 As Shute (2004: 425) has commented, there seems to be little logic to a list that includes assaulting an officer on account of his preserving a wreck, hijacking ships and various offences relating to Channel Tunnel trains.

14 This retrospective provision did not exist with respect to Sex Offender Orders that preceded SOPOs. The act also introduced a Risk of Sexual Harm Order. For this order, no offence condition is required. Instead, on at least two previous occasions, the person has to have been engaged in sexually explicit conduct or communication with a child or children (under 16). The defendant's purpose is not at issue, and instead a reasonable person's test is applied. The court has to be satisfied that the order is necessary to protect a child or children from 'harm' from the defendant. These orders are imposed for a minimum of two years and may be of indefinite duration.

15 Knock *et al.* (2002). This study focused on the first 92 orders made (between 1 December 1998 and 31 March 2001).

16 *Ibid.*, 39–40.

17 *Ibid.*, 12.

18 Knock *et al.* (2002: 12–13).

19 *Ibid.*, 19.

20 Five years (caution and non-custodial sentence, including a conditional discharge); seven years (custodial sentence of under six months); ten years (custodial sentence of 6–30 months; indefinite period (custodial sentence of over 30 months). Registration periods for offenders under 18 are half those for adults. Registration is at a local level, although progress has been made in the establishment of a national Violent and Sex Offender Register (VISOR).

21 Registration also applied to persons who, on that date, were in custody, on post-custody licence or under a community penalty supervised by the probation service.

22 Plotnikoff and Woolfson (2000: 26).

23 *Ibid.*, 34–5.

24 MAPPAs, with police and probation as the responsible authorities, were placed on a statutory basis in 2000 under the Criminal Justice Act 2003. The prison service became the third Responsible Authority at this time, and other services with a statutory duty to cooperate with MAPPA include social services departments, housing authorities, health authorities and appropriate victim groups.

25 'If a person is considered by one or more agency to be a danger but does not have a conviction, then local strategy meetings can take place using the MAPPA principles of co-operation to reduce the risk of harm.' Dorset MAPPA Annual Report, 2004/05, 17.

26 Home Office news release, 'Public Protection Arrangements Working to Defend Communities', 17 October 2005. This press statement drew attention to 503 SOPOs granted against persons subject to MAPPA.

27 Bichard (2004).

28 Nash (2006: 145).

29 *Guidance on Investigating Child Abuse and Safeguarding Children* 2005. Centrex 2005: 92.

30 Shropshire MAPPA annual report, 2004-05.

31 Kempshall and Maguire (2003: 192).

32 Maguire *et al.* (2001); level 1 is 'ordinary risk management'; level 2, 'local interagency risk management' that falls short of level 3.

33 These strategies may sometimes be in conflict with each other, particularly so when the media and politicians become closely involved. For example, it was reported that in mid-June 2006 that 'Seventy convicted child sex offenders were unexpectedly moved out of eleven probation hostels close to schools across England and Wales' (*Guardian*, 19 June 2006). Many of these persons were later reported to have been rehoused in bed and breakfast accommodation with minimal supervision.

34 Kemshall *et al.* (2005: 5–15). HM Chief Inspectors of Police and Probation reported that the process for deciding at what MAPPA level a sex offender should be managed varied both within and between areas (HMIP/HMIC 2005, 1.16). Risk assessment tools such as OASys and RM2000 are increasingly evident, although in 2006 their use was far from standard across the country.

35 HMIP/HMIC (2005), 4.21.

36 See, e.g., HMIP (2006) 9.1.23–25.

37 Humberside, MAPPA annual report, 2004–5, 18.

38 Avon and Somerset, Annual Report, 2004/5, 17. This reference to an indefinite period of registration is curious in the light of the reported length of the prison sentence.

39 Devon and Cornwall, Annual MAPPA report, 2004–5.

40 Kempshall *et al.* (2005), 10; local MAPPAs are expected to work within the parameters of *MAPPA Guidance*, Probation Circular 54/2004.

41 HMIP/HMIC (2005, 5.13). There is a dearth of published work on the views and attitudes of sexual offenders themselves. See Hudson (2006) for an academic study, but little has appeared in recent years to match Peter Wildeblood's *Against the Law.* After being charged with homosexual offences, the author recalled: 'That night, a woman spat at me. She was a respectable-looking, middle-aged tweedy person with a sensible felt hat. She was standing on the pavement as the car went by. I saw her suck in her cheeks, and the next moment a big blob of spit was running down the windscreen. This shocked me very much. The woman did not look eccentric or evil; in fact she looked very much like the country gentlewomen with whom my mother used to take coffee when she had finished shopping on Saturday mornings. She looked thoroughly ordinary to me. But what did I look like to her? Evidently, I was a monster. I was quite sure that she had never spat at anyone in her life before. And yet, she had hated me enough to do this' (Wildeblood 1957: 87).

42 HMIP/HMIP (2005, 5.14–5.16); in 2005, three pilot projects involving 'circles of support' were in place in England. However, these schemes may carry net-widening consequences, some advocates viewing them as additions

rather than alternatives to custody. Anne-Marie McAlinden, for example, writes that 'the better approach would be to process formally all but the most minor of sexual offences through the criminal justice system initially. Informal programmes of support and treatment in the community would be available *on release from custody* on the basis of a referral by a statutory criminal-justice agency' (McAlinden 2005: 382).

43 Foucault (1977: 113).
44 Cohen (1979: 362).
45 Foucault (1977: 199).
46 Karp (1969: 108).

References

Bichard, Sir Michael (2004) *The Bichard Inquiry Report*. London: HMSO.

Cohen, S. (1979) 'The punitive city: notes on the dispersal of social control', *Contemporary Crises*, 3 (4): 341–63.

Cohen, S. (1985) *Visions of Social Control, Crime, Punishment and Classification*. Cambridge: Polity Press.

Foucault, M. (1977) *Discipline and Punish, The Birth of the Prison*. London: Allen Lane.

Garland, D. (2001) *The Culture of Control*. Oxford: Oxford University Press.

Harding, J. (2006) 'Some reflections on parole licence and recall procedures for convicted offenders, post the 2003 Criminal Justice Act', *Probation Magazine* (in press).

HMIP/HMIC (2005) M*anaging Sex Offenders in the Community. A Joint Inspection on Sex Offenders*. London: H.M. Inspectorate of Probation and H.M. Inspectorate of Constabulary.

HMIP (2006) *An Independent Review of a Serious Further Offence Case: Anthony Rice*. London: H.M. Inspectorate of Probation.

Home Office (1977) *Community Protection Order: A Consultation Paper*. London: Home Office.

Howard League for Penal Reform (1985) *Unlawful Sex, Report of a Howard League Working Party*. London: Waterlows.

Hudson, K. (2006) *Offending Identities, Sex Offenders' Perspectives on their Treatment and Management*. Cullompton: Willan Publishing.

Karp, D. (1969) *One*. Harmondsworth: Penguin.

Kempshall, H. (2000) *Risk Assessment and Management of Known Sexual and Violent Offenders: A Review of Current Issues*. London: Home Office.

Kempshall, H. and Maguire M. (2003) 'Sex offenders, risk penalty and the problem of disclosure to the community', in A. Matravers (ed.), *Sex Offenders in the Community, Managing and Reducing the Risks*. Cullompton: Willan Publishing.

Kempshall, H. *et al.* (2005) *Strengthening Multi-Agency Public Protection Arrangements (MAPPAs)*. London: Home Office.

Knock, K. *et al.* (2002) *The Police Perspective on Sex Offender Orders: A Preliminary Review of Policy and Practice*. Police Research Series Paper 155. London: Home Office.

Maguire, M. *et al.* (2001) *Risk Management of Sexual and Violent Offenders: The Work of Public Protection Panels*. London: Home Office.

McAlinden, A.-M. (2005) 'The use of "shame" with sexual offenders', *British Journal of Criminology*, 45: 373–94.

Nash, M. (2006) *Public Protection and the Criminal Justice Process*. Oxford: Oxford University Press.

Plotnikoff, J. and Woolfson, R. (2000) *Where Are They Now? An Evaluation of Sex Offender Registration in England and Wales*. Police Research Series Paper 126. London: Home Office.

Pollard, S. (2005) *David Blunkett*. London: Hodder and Staughton.

Rose, N. (2000) 'Government and control', in D. Garland and R. Sparks (eds) *Criminology and Social Policy*. Oxford; Oxford University Press, pp. 183–208.

Rutherford, A. (1997) 'Criminal policy and the eliminative ideal', *Social Policy and Administration*, 31 (5): 116–35.

Shute, S. (2004) 'The Sexual Offences Act 2003, new civil preventative orders', *Criminal Law Review* (May): 417–40.

Spencer, J. (2004) 'The Sexual Offences Act 2003, child and family offences', *Criminal Law Review* (May): 347–60.

Wildeblood, P. (1957) *Against the Law*. Harmondsworth: Penguin.

Chapter 8

Hassles and worse

Harvey Molotch

Sociological thinkers have had difficulty representing felt experience with the same analytic force as they manage in depicting structural phenomena. A strong tendency, unfortunate both politically and intellectually, is to treat individuals' struggles as epiphenomena, useful perhaps as anecdotes of suffering but not as something to be understood and explained. Individual troubles come up as after-effects of the more basic forces. Our tradition, fundamental in Marx but shared by other schools, is to learn the workings of the structures that oppress, note the injustices that result, but do little to show (rather than just assert) the linkage. Attending to the experiences, dilemmas, and *angst* – especially of everyday life – risks descent into psychologism or anecdote. Worse yet, it risks association with naïve self-help aficionados. At whatever their level of sophistication, dwelling upon 'feelings' obscures the need for fundamental change.

There are, of course, both among scholars and political writers, some who manage to keep their eyes on both balls – to be aware of the structural forces as well as cognitive and emotional lives. But I know of no other contemporary who has so managed to situate work and thinking on the cusp of these two realms more fruitfully than Stan Cohen. He does not throw out the personal baby with the sentimental bath water. He thinks about it and it inflects his projects, whether about crime and panic, human rights and suffering, or the tendency of organized social life to grind down capacities for creativity and spontaneity. Some of his projects begin with the felt experiences and work up to structure; in other cases the direction is the reverse. But always, there is attention up and down and how the connections operate.

For reasons I hope will become evident, this appreciation leads me to consider certain programmes in the US health-care system. In their enactment, implementation and consequence on structure, culture and felt experience, they raise issues that resonate with Stan Cohen's preoccupations.

First, let's talk about the Flexible Spending Account (FSA), an oddball among the world's medical arrangements. For the last several years, US taxpayers have had the option to open such a thing. It is one of several mechanisms set up to deal with the country's lack of comprehensive health care. It can decrease 'out of pocket' health-care costs, depending on one's tax bracket and type of private health insurance, by about 40 per cent.[1] It also applies to health-related expenses not usually covered by private insurance such as the full cost of eyewear and dental treatment.

Here's how it works. (Warning: this is going to be a little tedious but that fact is important to my point, so pay attention.) At the beginning of each year, taxpayers declare to their employer how much they want to 'invest' in their FSA. This 'opens' the account. As the year goes by, the employer diverts wages into this account up to the total declared. This amount so deposited is free of all income taxes – state, local and federal. As you incur medical and dental bills beyond what your private insurance covers, your FSA kicks in to pay the rest. It is your own money, of course, but is treated as non-taxable income.

Here's the hitch: any money left in the account at the end of the year (plus a ten-week grace period) is forfeit – it is gone. 'Use it or lose it.'

To work this health plan 'feature' effectively, you have to estimate how sick you will be in the coming year, how much the sickness will cost, and what portion of your bills your insurance will not cover. You can gain wiggle room by electing to have some things that would be nice but not medically necessary. Maybe you could opt for a little orthodontic work, maybe some contact lenses, or banding up those hemorrhoids that are otherwise asymptomatic. These could be added in for an end of the year 'quickie'.

But remember: you must open a new account each year by an amount specified (there is no roll-over of prior requests or dollar amounts). You need to submit (or have submitted on your behalf) the appropriate forms for reimbursements from your private health plan and also keep tabs on the uncovered portion from your FSA to make sure it is spent down in a timely fashion.

Not everyone is equally good at this; not everyone has that sort of talent.

The FSA distributes life chances, making some people better off, some worse off, and leaving some unaffected. It relies on a 'model of man' in which choices are made with a deliberative risk-management orientation. It privileges a certain temperament of cunning, adding a specific dimension to causes of inequality. Among the wealthy, accountants, lawyers, and financial advisers often take care of these things. But for those without the ability to outsource, there are losses – financial and otherwise. I believe such mechanisms of inequality, often hailed by policymakers for their 'creativity', 'partnership' and 'Third Way' attributes, are increasingly being implemented in the USA and other countries. They cumulate in a bad way.

There are other examples besides the FSA from within the health category. In response to the soaring costs of drug prescriptions, the Bush administration implemented a drug benefit programme at the end of 2005 for those enrolled in the federal Medicare system. Medicare covers people over 65 and individuals with permanent disabilities, including those waiting for kidney transplants. Previously, Medicare heavily subsidized doctor and hospital costs, but not prescriptions. In total numbers, about 36 million people became eligible for the new drug benefit – 'Part D' as it is known – as augmenting the prior provisions, A, B, and C, of Medicare.

Profiting from Part D eligibility involves an FSA-type of calculative skill. With one important exception, you must elect to enrol. You must arrange to pay a monthly membership fee to a private drug programme that you select. The amount of drug benefit depends on the specific health-care plan you choose and how it matches up with your prescriptions. Each of the private health-care providers has its own pricing for each medicine and what it charges for a monthly membership fee (its 'formulary' in programme-speak). Plans can make changes in the list of prescriptions they cover and their costs during the year. The net financial outcome depends on each person's own meds mix and how that mix meshes with their chosen drug plan.

The US media were filled, especially in the early months, with accounts of the 'botched' programme. Senior citizen groups across the country voiced concern, with hundreds of organizations going on record as opposed, in part because of the confusion seen as intrinsic to the set-up.[2] The usual sources of medical information to which many turned, physicians and pharmacists, were largely unable to cut through the complexity.

Partly as response, the Medicare website offered a 'cost estimator' to help people figure out the best plan given the specifics of their case. The site asks users first to click on the type of information they are seeking. Then there are about five screens with queries about whether or not they have basic health coverage under various types of private and public schemes. Other screens carry an 'agree to terms' confirmation request and the usual click buttons that allow for 'save', 'prior screen' and so forth.

Simulating the role of a prospective enrollee, I used the website to determine the drug plan that would save me the most.[3] After entering my zip code, I learned there were 47 plans available in my area from which I could choose. To learn the best one, the site asks you to enter the name of your prescriptions, asks you to confirm them, and then assembles them all in a table. Drugs sometimes have long and tricky names, so the computer screen lets you search for your medicines from the alphabet. So if you click on 'A', the drop down gives you everything from 'A/B Otic' to – 350 meds later – 'Azulfidine En-Tabs'. Using this tool, I selected five drugs, which is the number used by a third of US adults and probably is close to what Medicare enrollees average.[4] In honour of Stan Cohen (whose last name has five letters), I proceeded in the following way. I took the first medicine under the letter 'C'. Then I chose 'O' and continued along through to the 'N'. My yield was 'C-Hist SR, O-Cal Prenatal, Halcion, E-Mycin and Nabi-HB' and that spells 'COHEN'.

Here's the finding. I can get a year's worth of COHEN prescriptions for as low as $1253, provided by Humana PDP Standard S 5552-003 Plan. If I opt instead for the SmartHealth RX scheme, my cost would be $3556 – more than double the least-cost option. Near as I can tell, there is no difference, and it would be dumb to join SmartHealth or probably most of the other dozens of plans revealed to lie between the two on the cost spectrum.

To get to my bottom line, I had gone through 23 separate screens, starting with 'Medicare.gov', with many clicks on the right tabs. I had to avoid some pitfalls like clicking on 'Formulary Finder'; the word 'formulary' was not explained, and I only figured it out by searching through other websites. I should also add that in running this experiment several times within the same two-week period, my menu options changed as did the formatting (and information offered) on the final table. My 23-screen count represents the trial in which I made no errors or side explorations; in the earlier efforts, I needed a larger number of moves to find my optimum programme.

Once again, however, there is a hitch. If I should need a different drug mix, either because of adverse reactions, new illnesses, or recoveries from old ones, the right plan can become the wrong plan. For those who suffer from chronic but treatable ailments, the cocktail inevitably has to be altered, and in ways difficult to predict. Again, I have to work the system in multiple ways. I have to be able to click my way through the Medicare menu as just described and I need to anticipate the type of sickness I will be having and the meds available to treat them.

There is still more fine print.[5] The government pays 75 per cent of drug costs between $250 and $2,250. But there is no coverage for drug costs between $2,250 and $5,100 (known as the 'doughnut hole' or 'coverage gap'). After reaching the $5,100 threshold ($3,600 in out-of-pocket spending), beneficiaries reach a 'catastrophic' level of coverage and will be required to pay only the greater of a co-payment ($2 for generic drugs or $5 for brand-name drugs) or co-insurance of 5 per cent. Got it?

These difficulties, whether FSA or Medicare, do not arise in people's lives because of 'bureaucracy'. The complexity comes from the fact that the US government chose to embed welfare within the existing market system, the public-private partnership gambit. It was impolitic to interfere with the pharmaceutical companies by establishing cost controls on drugs. Or to permit public entities, including the universities often responsible for the medical innovation in the first place, to produce drugs. Federal law explicitly forbids the national government to bargain for lower drug prices with providers in order to lower costs. It also does not allow individuals or drug plan providers to purchase and import medicines from other countries, such as Canada, where prices are much lower than in the USA. Needless to say, socialized medicine is off the table.

The federal government's contracts do require the private insurers to answer questions by phone from potential enrollees. But this has been problematic. An arm of Congress, the non-partisan Government Accountability Office (GAO), tested the reliability of the call centres by placing 900 calls to ten of the largest providers. Among other things, callers asked the costs of different programme options. The companies provided complete and accurate responses in only one-third of the calls, with differences between stated costs and actual costs often amounting to thousands of dollars. They were also unable to provide accurate information on such basic issues as whether a beneficiary must stick to a prescribed medicine that is not covered under a plan – or whether they can switch to a similar drug that is (the answer: switching is allowed).

In the aggregate, the result of all the hurdles has been, according to the most recent surveys, that large numbers of people fail to gain benefits despite the federal government's estimated expenditure of $30.5 billion for the programme's first year (2006).[6] Many of the enrollees come from two specific groups. Six million people had previously received drug benefits under Medicaid (as opposed to Medicare); Medicaid is the government's programme for the poor. These people were automatically switched into the new scheme. If they failed to select a programme, they were automatically enrolled in a private plan selected at random. For another seven million enrollees, the new benefits replaced coverage by a prior employer; now government subsidies replace part of the employer's former responsibility. One way or the other, about 27 million get some coverage under the programme, not necessarily 'new coverage' or the best coverage. But that still leaves out about four million people altogether.

Who are these individuals? A survey of eligibles conducted by three economists reveals specific categories of non-enrolment.[7] Probably because of the automatic enrolment for the Medicaid poor, the enrolled seem to differ little in income level from those not enrolled. Low education works against enrolment, even with the automatic Medicaid switching (about two million people fall into this category of low education, non-enrolled). Another segment of the non-enrolled consists of people who do not rely on prescriptions, either because they are healthy, or are sick but do not access doctors for some reason. To pay monthly premiums of $30 or $50 may not make sense to them since they take no drugs. This does mean they are vulnerable should they need an expensive medicine during a non-covered year. A single prescription in the USA can cost $1,000 or more per month; $250 is not an uncommon monthly price. Non-enrolment rates in the low-income segment of this group run especially high, with 38.2 percent uncovered.

For those who did manage to enrol, the experience has not been so good. A different survey (May 2006) found that 42 per cent said they were spending less on prescriptions, 19 per cent were spending more, and 30 per cent were spending the same amount.[8] When the economists' sample of enrollees was asked the question, 'Does your experience with Medicare Part D leave you more satisfied or less satisfied with the Medicare program?,' 58.1 per cent of the 2,027 people responding said that they were less satisfied. To the question, 'Does your experience with Medicare Part D leave you more satisfied or less satisfied with the political process in Washington that produced this program?,' 74.7 per cent of the 2,023 responding said that they were less satisfied. As the researchers observe, 'the responses indicate substantial dissatisfaction with the design and administration of the program.'[9] To explain these findings, these economists – true perhaps to their training and without COHEN-type methodological antidote – remark that 'Consumers are often skeptical about markets and suspicious of their organizers. This seems to be the case for Part D.'

Programmes that change in their specifics, or that require proactive stances among those with few resources, tend toward inaccessibility. Part of the 'success' of Clinton-enacted welfare reform in the USA, which lowered the number of people drawing benefits, rests on just this phenomenon. Each time the welfare rules change, some who are eligible drop away – 'churning' as it is sometimes called. In many cases, requalification is part of the ongoing arrangement (every six months, every year, at school entry, and so forth). In New York, and I presume elsewhere, homeless people must adapt to shifting criteria for shelter, with specific stipulations for single-night access, versus longer temporary accommodation, versus placement in permanent apartments.

At any given time, millions of people are between benefits, some because of shifts in rules. Agencies are unable to 'ramp up' sufficiently to deal with the workload created by new regulations, offerings, and choices. These costs to agencies may be passed on to clients in the form of poorer service or weakened benefits.

Through overzealous enforcement of technical requirements, entitled people can be kept off the rolls, at least for a while. Critics of New York's workfare programme, implemented under the Giuliani administration, point to the fact that of the 25,000 court appeals made by people who were cut off welfare in the city (in 1997), two-thirds went against the city.[10] Even if many of those cut off eventually return to the rolls, the time lapse means less gets spent. And some would-be clients do just disappear, and this further allows politicians to claim 'results' in getting lazy people off the rolls and lowering fiscal burdens.

Whether premeditated or not, harm occurs in the interstices of policy and bureaucracy. No state of denial is explicitly necessary. The harm does not have to be denied because it is rendered invisible in the tedium of administrative detail. In some cases, advocacy groups and political leaders eventually manage to 'repair' the broken policy, but the time lapse is crucial for many people. Indeed, many would-be aid recipients are in critical need for only a short while anyway. If the window of opportunity closes at the crucial moment, serious consequences can follow: an infant lacks prenatal care or an illness becomes fatal.

Much of the debate about inequality turns on what people 'deserve'. At least implicitly, even for the left as well as for the right, whether or not people are getting a raw deal depends on whether or not they display initiative, take charge of their own lives, and act to benefit themselves through opportunities. So the left tries to show that the unfortunate are 'just like you and me' but are not rewarded because 'extraneous' and inappropriate forces intervene – like race or class origin. For the right, the fact of misfortune indicates, given the manifold opportunities in democratic society, the lack of individuals' initiative to exploit them. Both sides, at least implicitly, seem to agree that if people are 'just lazy' they deserve what they get.

Part of the self-help ideal is that people think ahead, manage their affairs in a reasonably systematic way, and pay sufficient attention to the administration of their own existence. They know where things are, keep decent records, and have documents at hand, and a pencil at the ready. They anticipate consequences of their actions; they are cognitive predictors. They are utility maximizers. But some people are not like that or at least it can be said that people vary along this dimension as they do on all the others. Some, at least compared with readers of this book, 'live for the moment'. There is a continuum.

I don't think we really know what makes some people self-starters and others not, some persistent achievers and others only intermittent in fully applying themselves. Among the affluent, there are offspring who become ski bums, hippies, or alcoholics. No amount of schooling, coaching, counselling, or stimulation in the home can bring them 'up to their potential'. Among the poor, as Oscar Lewis famously indicated,[11] there are – from very different modes of inheritance – forces that similarly keep people present-oriented and 'in the moment'. For them as well, efforts designed to break the pattern – whether by teaching 'job skills' or setting up after-school programmes – often fail to meet the characterological goals.

For many, especially in this neo-liberal time of veneration for economic self-reliance, there is special fear of letting loose the spirit of disruption. It is the often remarked upon fear of 'the 1960s' – the mayhem of the unleashed. I think it is also resentment against those who get to enjoy themselves and achieve notoriety, even celebrity, in so doing. George W. Bush appears a case of the resentment that follows on. Enrolled at Yale during the youth rebellions against the Vietnam War and US racism, he was out of it – sticking with the alcohol-based fraternity and secret society system. His campus, like most of the others, was in turmoil. Its leaders and their followers embraced new modes of expressivity (including marijuana rather than booze) and politics instead of sport. Elite class background and capacity to guzzle counted for less; the traditional Big Men on Campus lost panache. I don't think it's too much of a stretch to think of George Bush – and many with whom he conspired in government and industry – as working through their umbrage. Their politics were demeaned, their lifestyles ridiculed, and their entitlements ignored.

Whatever the socio-biographical origins of resentment, the remedy is to move not just back to the culture of the pre-counter-culture, but to some idealized memory of Protestant no-nonsense rectitude. But this time around, at least as evidenced by programmes such as the ones I have sketched out, the bona fide of a moral existence and of social legitimacy is not hard work per se, but the capacity to exploit the interstices of organization and economy. Opportunism, tedious opportunism, reigns as virtue. The greatest good for the greatest number comes from having all noses at that particular grindstone. That the poor seem to do worse at the endeavour certifies them as lacking the pluck that would have made them better off in the first place. That they continue to exhibit incapacity in the face of opportunity is an additional convenience – both for ignoring their plight, but also for seeing the outcome as just desserts. The poor serve as a reservoir of attributes – sloth, hedonism, and a benign passivity – that many prefer not to face in themselves.

But the burden, in objective terms, does fall on particular categories of people. In the case of health plans, old folks are at special risk given their needs for medical support and declining capacities to manipulate data systems. Women, as traditional custodians of compassion and charged with taking care of domestic chores, are the end-users of administrative mayhem (still another aspect of their 'work' that tends to go unrecognized). Class and race likely take their usual toll for the usual reasons, with the extra twist that the poor and people of colour have less informal contact with knowledgeable individuals who could help them navigate the apparatus.

The presence of features like these not only takes a toll on people as individuals but also, at least plausibly, shapes the culture in which they are a part. This is no place to get into a discussion of 'national character', but it is reasonable to assume that institutional contexts shape social psychological tendencies within countries. The types of opportunities and constraints in which people are enmeshed are at least one element in forming them up. It is not so simple a matter as 'training' or discipline; some of it may come from rebellion and resistance. But a degree of fix does set in as people get used to the organizational spaces, iron cages or webs of administrative stipulations, within which they exist.

We see evidence of this in the challenge migrants experience in adapting to strange environments; life under prior arrangements forces a realignment, sometimes challenging, toward the environment in which they are newly located. Some prosper; others fall by the wayside. When contact occurs not through migration, but from imposition – as in historic imperialist adventures to the colonial world – what were once functional modes of thinking and acting become dysfunctional. Those least able to switch codes, not necessarily through a lack of education or economic resources, pay the price.

We are now coming to understand how imposition – and subsequent overturning – of Soviet regimes across Eastern Europe also changed the nature of the elements for success, favouring some personality types and disfavouring others. Being effective in pre-Stalinist Russia involved a different type of praxis than what was needed both before and after. As one snapshot of how life was lived in one country, we have Vaclav Havel's description of how people made their way in communist Czechoslovakia. Havel describes why a grocery shop operator repeatedly puts the government's misleading signs in the shop window. True, he is supposed to do it, but it is not because of any draconian consequences from the authorities. Instead, it is in deference, or at least recognition, of the way things are done among members of the shared collective. If the grocer does not go along, he repudiates the analogous behaviour of friends and neighbours who do acquiesce – people to respect and rely on. So the grocer joins in 'living within the lie', simultaneously imposing a burden on his own consciousness while reinforcing the regime. There is a linkage between 'character and society' as Gerth and Mills termed it, and administrative mechanisms play a role in structuring this linkage.

Whatever comes to be the shared socio-cultural proclivities and through whatever mechanisms, variation nevertheless persists across subgroups and across individuals in adaptive success. And just as some of 'both' are distributed within each otherwise shared culture, they are also distributed within every person. The result is at least ambivalence about just how much utility maximization should guide one's existence. Even the most grinding of calculators make, or at least fantasize, escape attempts.

Sometimes these fantasies are ready to find their outlet in extreme and sadistic ways. Among other examples, I am thinking of the numerous ideologues of 'family values' who turn out themselves to live in the demi-monde. Crusaders for morality are routinely outed as drug-dependent or pathological gamblers. Homophobic politicians later turn out to be homosexual themselves. It may not be a stretch to imagine, in a Cohenesque vision, that such angst underlies moral panics as well as idiosyncratic individual acts that range from the merely inexplicable to the truly heinous.

On the other hand, far from being a problem, those more innocent of life's practical opportunities may be doing very worthwhile things indeed. They may be preoccupied with hobbies or the arts. They may be tending to the needs of friends and family. They may be working through cognitive puzzles that intrigue. Sometimes, ironically enough, they may be laying the groundwork for scientific and business breakthroughs. The memoirs of scientists repeatedly refer to their drive for 'elegance' in solutions and incapacity to back off to attend to the vicissitudes of making a living. Right up to the contemporary era of hackers at MIT and Silicon Valley (but going back much farther in history[12]), the development of mighty industries sprang from people who were just 'into it,' unable to tend to what otherwise would appear the rationalities of material advance. At least some of these pioneers were driven by passion, often with little or no regard for remuneration.[13] And there are even people who devote some or all of their lives to human rights, with strenuous disregard for their own material well-being.

My point in this chapter is to show how policies can embody benefit for one particular version of human attitude as opposed to another. By choosing the cunning, they can ruthlessly ferret out those unfit to make a scheming life. Such a goal can guide any sort of organizational unit, public or private, even those designed to deal with individuals most behind in life's race – indeed, especially, as in welfare administration, those manifestly unable to cope. If would-be clients are found to lack the spirit of capitalism as currently interpreted, they are pariahs. And for those who worked hard and even cunningly but placed the wrong bets in their privatized retirement and pension plans, too bad. That they are losers indicates they may not have had such a good attitude in the first place.

Woe unto us all. There is much damage to be done through this abhorrence of those who do not so plot. We spend resources to detect and expel them. We train people to do the dirty work who otherwise would be considered members of the helping professions, like social workers who look for cheaters rather than sufferers. By so privileging only one dimension of human being, we commit a moral error and let those who do not meet the criteria perish.

Let us return to the FSA and be reminded of what it means when writ large. It is a drag. The calculative mechanism it enshrines belittles meaningful greatness and certainly undermines grace. It is a mechanism of inequality that goes unnoticed and deforms the nature of reform. As it spins through government agencies, schools, and firms it erodes fun – at least for those among us who do not enjoy the green eyeshade and the hunt for the deal. It undermines the generous and caring or just those who don't want to be bored to death.

Notes

1 This is the savings of an individual in the 28 per cent tax bracket.
2 For a list of organizations, see: www.ourfuture.org/docUploads/orgs%20opposing%20medicare%20law.pdf. In support, however, was the highly important American Association for the Advancement of Retired People

(AAARP), which underwent strong internal and external criticism as a result.

3 I did this over the course of several sessions in May 2006.
4 Gardiner Harris, 'Report finds a heavy toll from medication errors', *New York Times*, 21 July 2006: A12.
5 I take this from Dawn M. Gencarelli, 'Overview of the new Medicare prescription drug benefit', National Health Policy Forum, Washington, DC: George Washington University, 21 June 2005.
6 Sarah Lueck, 'Are Medicare estimates too high?', *Wall Street Journal*, 21 April 2006.
7 Florian Heiss, Daniel McFadden, and Joachim Winter, 'Who failed to enroll in Medicare Part D, and why? Early results', *Health Affairs, The Policy Journal of the Health Sphere*, published online 1 August 2006: www.healthaffairs.org.
8 'The drug benefit: a report card', *New York Times*, 5 June 2006: Section A, p. 18.
9 Heiss *et al., op. cit.*
10 Vivian S. Toy, 'Tough workfare rules used as way to cut welfare rolls', *New York Times*, 15 April 1998, p. A.1.
11 Oscar Lewis, *Five Families*.
12 Cyril Stanley Smith, *From Art to Science*, Cambridge, MA: MIT Press, 1980; *A Search for Structure*, Cambridge, MA: MIT Press, 1981.
13 See, for example, R.X. Cringely, *Accidental Empires*; Virginia Postrel, *The Future and Its Enemies*, New York: Free Press, 1998.

Chapter 9

Moral panic, denial, and human rights: scanning the spectrum from overreaction to underreaction

Michael Welch

Introduction

In the late 1970s, I enrolled in a first-year sociology class at a small liberal arts college located in the midwestern USA, named Benedictine College. It was there that I was initially introduced to the work of Stan Cohen. Specifically, it was the concept of moral panic along with folk devils that leapt to the forefront of my understanding of societal overreaction to putative social problems. Since then I have remained regularly guided by Cohen's writings. Indeed, virtually everywhere I turn in my studies of crime, deviance, and human rights, I find articles and books by Cohen, offering tremendous insight into the subject at hand whether it be youth crime, mistreatment of migrants and asylum seekers, or the use of torture as state policy. In this essay, I set out to acknowledge Cohen's wide range of sociological contributions and explain how my research has benefited from them. By doing so, I hope to give credit where credit is due, since Cohen's work is perhaps the single most important influence on my sociological thinking. As demonstrated throughout this essay, almost all of the major research projects that I have developed dating back to the 1980s can be characterized as Cohenesque. Permit me to proceed by first unpacking a collection of studies beginning with those focused on overreaction, most notably manifesting in moral panic. Then I shall travel in the opposite conceptual direction to elaborate on Cohen's exploration of denial, a form of underreaction that turns a blind eye to human rights abuses perpetuated by the state.

Moral panic over flag burning

As a young assistant professor at a large urban university in New York City in the mid-1980s, I became fascinated with the emerging culture wars in the USA, particularly those pitting artists and cultural activists against the religious – and military – rightwing conservatives. At the centre of some of the debates over freedom of expression was whether burning the American flag was a form of free speech protected by the First Amendment. Concerns to protect the flag from desecration reached critical mass in 1988 as the US Supreme Court decided to hear the case *Texas* v. *Johnson*. When the court ruled the following year that flag burning indeed constituted free speech, there was an enormous outcry by citizens and political leaders alike. To many sociologists, those developments marked another chapter in America's civil religion. However, I thought there was something more remarkable in that phenomenon. Amid the growing fury and anger aimed at leftist demonstrators who threatened to burn the flag as a gesture condemning American imperialism, I sensed we were witnessing a classic moral panic. That form of overreaction was producing a criminalization campaign against political protest deemed unpatriotic.

As I wrote in the introduction of *Flag Burning: Moral Panic and the Criminalization of Protest*: 'Exploring moral panic over flag desecration provides a unique opportunity to refine our understanding of adverse reactions to political dissent, especially toward protest considered so offensive that many people believe it ought to be treated as a crime' (2000: 5). Still, I felt it important to emphasize the moral dimension of moral panic given the influence of civil religion shaping the flag protection movement: 'Indeed, a common denominator linking moral panic to civil religion is their shared emphasis on morality, a construct distinguishing right from wrong and good from evil' (2000: 102). With the tools of assessing moral panic at my disposal, I discovered that overreaction to flag burning had conformed to the fundamental criteria: concern, hostility, consensus, disproportionality, and volatility. Among Americans, concern over flag desecration was evident: a *New York Times/CBS News* poll found that 83 per cent of its respondents believed that flag burning should be against the law and 59 per cent of those polled endorsed a constitutional amendment (Greenhouse 1990: B7). Several political commentators expressed their views in harsher tones: conservative columnist Cal Thomas likened the *Johnson* decision to 'protecting pornography' that 'inspires serial killers,' and 'tolerance of marijuana,' which had 'paved the way for crack cocaine,' and even Elvis Presley, who had 'opened the door through which heavy metal and garbage-mouth groups walked' (1989: 55). Hostility to flag burners was palpable as numerous incidents of beatings were reported nationwide. Interestingly, legislators in Pennsylvania introduced a 'beat a flag burner' bill in which a fine of $1 would have replaced the existing penalties of assault and aggravated assault (i.e., a ten-year maximum prison sentence and a fine of $25,000). That proposal marked an attempt by lawmakers to encourage citizens to attack flag burners with relative impunity, thereby creating a unique type of informal social control. Similar measures were proposed in Colorado, Georgia, Illinois, and Tennessee.

In the realm of consensus, public opinion polls serve as persuasive evidence that the vast majority of Americans view flag desecration as a social problem that ought to be remedied by legislation and punishment. Evidence of disproportionality also was difficult to overlook, particularly given the amount of political debate over the issue of flag desecration. During the 12 months between the *Johnson* and *Eichman* decisions (which reaffirmed *Johnson*), Congress was consumed by the debate over flag protection, taking more time than any other issue. Congress devoted more than 100 hours of floor debate and approximately two weeks of public legislative hearings; lawmakers and their staffs spent thousands of hours in meetings deliberating over the fate of the flag. Those activities were entered into the Congressional Record, exceeding more than 400 pages at an average cost of $500 per page; additionally, 1500 pages of hearings also were published by US government printing (1990: S8685).

As Cohen reminds us, moral panic cannot be separated from its volatile nature, especially its rapid decline. Controversy over flag burning was no exception. In the summer of 1989, the flag desecration issue, in the words of a Washington reporter, was 'hot as a magnesium flare' but in less than a year, it had become 'politically lukewarm' (Goldstein 1996: 334). Overall, the flag panic was rooted in a latent fear that American society and culture are ill-fated. That pre-existing anxiety eventually emerged as a pressing 'social problem' as special-interest groups publicly scapegoated flag burners as folk devils. Moral panic theory not only provides a critical lens through which we can view the intricacies of overreaction but, by doing so, it also offers a framework for understanding key cultural transformations including those propelled by politics or religion, or a combination of the two (see Welch, Sassi, and McDonough 2002).

Moral panic over street crime and youth violence

As my career developed, so did my appreciation of Cohen's work that provided numerous conceptual guideposts. Such lessons are recognized in my research on media and the social construction of crime. Drawing inspiration from Cohen and Young's *The Manufacture of News* (1981), I delved into the study of primary definers of crime (i.e., state managers) and their role in stoking moral panic (Welch, Fenwick, and Roberts 1998, 1997). In the course of an extensive content analysis of the leading newspapers in the USA, my associates and I unveiled evidence of alarmist – and stylized – reactions to street crime as part of a larger pattern of moral panic over perceived lawlessness in the early 1990s. We found that statements to the press by politicians and law enforcement officials were particularly demagogic, intended to appeal to citizens' fears for the purpose of advancing a specific agenda (e.g., increased expenditures in the criminal justice system). It was in those studies that we shed light on an often overlooked aspect of moral panic theory that recognizes crime as a bona fide social problem. Aside from its melodramatic symbolism, crime does have material consequences producing social and personal harm. The concept moral panic does not necessarily mean that there is nothing there, but rather that the state-sponsored strategies designed to deal with such problems are fundamentally inappropriate (Cohen 2002). Critics of hard control in criminal justice (e.g., harsher penalties, the proliferation of prisons and expansion of law enforcement) insist that moral panics contribute to the escalating vocabulary of punitive motives used to justify inappropriate strategies of dealing with crime, especially those neglecting the root causes of crime and violence.

My interest in the media as they shape popular views of crime continued into similar realms of constructionism while maintaining a Cohenesque approach. For years, sociologists have turned to the concept of moral panic in their efforts to decipher the emergence of so-called new forms of menace and their impact on public anxiety over social threats. In 1989, while reporting the well-publicized attack on a female jogger in New York City, the media discovered 'wilding', a newly stylized word used to describe sexual violence committed by a group of urban teens. Sociologically, the term 'wilding' became particularly significant due to its racial connotation, perpetuating a stereotype of young black (and Latino) males belonging to a dangerous class. Here my work explored the contours of moral panic over 'wilding' by attending to elements of race, class, and fear of crime, especially as they are manifested in the media. Contrary to the conventional view that moral panic merely breaks out and then vanishes, my research emphasized its lasting effects, namely the criminalization of minority youth. Overall, that study contributes to a critical understanding of youth in society by offering a deeper interpretation of 'wilding', a distinctive form of moral panic that symbolized not only a threat to urban society but also to a political economy that reproduces racial and social disparities (Welch, Price, and Yankey 2004, 2002).

Moral panic over immigrants and asylum seekers

Moral panic theory, particularly because it encourages us to see clearly the marginalization process, is especially useful in studying adverse societal reaction to immigrants, migrants, and asylum seekers. Again Cohen's (2002) writings on the subject prompted me to adopt the moral panic paradigm in studying the phenomenon in the USA when the immigration controversy peaked in the mid-1990s before disappearing from public worries. In *Detained: Immigration Laws and the Expanding I.N.S. Jail Complex* (2002), I closely analysed the language and rhetorical devices used to marginalize so-called illegal aliens, thereby casting them as threats to American society and its predominantly white, Christian culture. As an example of disproportionality, stylized language hyped the immigration issue in ways that fed public anxiety; consequently, immigrants are commonly reduced to an array of stereotypes portraying them as predatory, criminal, lazy, stupid, and diseased. Such hyperbole also manifests in apocalyptic metaphors characteristic of a disaster mentality, giving way to the following catastrophic forecasts:

- 'The United States is not a pile of wealth but a fragile system – a lifeboat. And lifeboats can get overcrowded and sink' (Brimelow 1995: 245).

- 'In effect, by allowing its borders to vanish under this vast whirlwind mass of illegal immigrants, the United States is running on the edge of a demographic buzz saw. One day, it could suddenly look down to find California or Texas cut off' (Brimelow 1995: 35).

As the UK and Continental Europe braced themselves for the most recent wave of migration, I found it fitting to conduct a comparative study on the detention of asylum seekers with the USA. That research project was made all the more possible when Stan suggested that I collaborate with Dr Liza Schuster, then T.H. Marshall Research Fellow in the Department of Sociology at LSE. Our study followed in the path of Cohen's (2002) observations on the social construction of bogus asylum seekers as an emerging threat to British society. Although the prevailing notion of moral panic rests on its noisy features, there are nevertheless constructions that occur under the public radar. In such instances, government officials quietly institute policies and practices that adversely affect a targeted group. Moral panic over so-called bogus asylum seekers in the UK represents a noisy construction whereby claims making is loud and public. In the USA, however, that construction is remarkably quiet and does not resonate openly; still, much like their British counterparts, American officials have resorted to the use of confinement. Our work explored the differences between the UK and the USA in the realm of moral panic over asylum seekers while remaining attentive to their shared consequences, the unjust detention of those fleeing persecution (Welch and Schuster 2005a, 2005b; see Welch 2004).

Denial in a post-9/11 world

In the wake of 11 September 2001, my research on the American war on terror focused not only on overreaction (i.e., ethnic profiling, arbitrary detention, Guantánamo Bay, and the invasion of Iraq) but also on the underreaction to blatant violations of civil liberties and human rights arising in a post-9/11 world. It was in establishing such conceptual balance that I found Cohen's *States of Denial: Knowing About Atrocities and Suffering* tremendously insightful. In formulating a sociology of denial, Cohen examines critically the role of denial in perpetuating long-term social problems, especially those that produce and reproduce human rights violations. More to the point of this analysis, Cohen's framework concentrates on the content of denial manifesting in three forms: literal, interpretive, and implicatory. Literal denial is as blunt as it is blatant (e.g., officials insist 'that atrocity did not occur'), serving as a blanket defence against acknowledging the undisputed facts. Under interpretive denial, however, the facts are not denied but are given a different spin, thus altering the meaning (e.g., officials argue 'what happened is not what you think it is'). By its very nature, reinterpretation is distinctly more intricate than literal denial, typically because it relies on euphemism and legalism. According to Cohen, 'The function of euphemism labels and jargon is to mask, sanitize, and confer respectability. Palliative terms deny or misrepresent cruelty or harm, giving them neutral or respectable status' (2001: 107). Political and military rhetoric is steeped in euphemisms, providing speakers and their audience insulation from the full meaning of harm, injury, and death. Consider the following examples: 'collateral damage' rather than the killing of civilians; 'transfer of population' rather than forced expulsion; 'moderate physical pressure' rather than torture. Legalism also facilitates interpretive denial by employing an infinite array of logical (or illogical) manoeuvres.

> The legal discourse depicts a wholly non-pictorial world. This is a board game with a limited repertoire of fixed moves. One side claims that event X does not fit the appropriate category

(right, law, article, or convention). Yes, this demonstrator was arrested and detained, but this was not a violation of freedom of expression. Yes, it was, comes the counter-move. Event Y may have been a violation of the Fourth Geneva Convention, but the Convention does not apply. Yes, it does. (Cohen 2001: 108)

In the third form of content denial, implicatory denial does not dispute either the facts or their conventional meaning; rather, the psychological, political, or moral consequences are denied, minimized, or muted. By diminishing the significance of the harm of human rights violations and other atrocities, officials evade their responsibility to intervene. Whereas critical criminology is predicated on revealing truths about crime, especially in the social context of inequality and repression, Cohen's paradigm offers additional concepts in analysing the content of official rhetoric. If we apply the sociology of denial to the war on terror, it is clear that literal, interpretive, and implicatory denial contributes to persistent civil liberties and human rights abuses.

In my most recent book, *Scapegoats of September 11th: Hate Crimes and State Crimes in the War on Terror* (2006a), I rely heavily on Cohen's work on human rights (2005, 2001, 1996, 1995) in sorting out the various forms of denial occurring in a post-9/11 world (see also Welch 2006b, 2003). The following segments present some of my findings on the subject.

Literal denial

Along with secrecy, stonewalling, and the knack for making outrageous claims proven to be false, most notably its mantra over Iraq's weapons of mass destruction and Saddam Hussein's links to Al Qaeda, literal denial has become a hallmark of the Bush presidency. Consider the administration's perpetual denial of US involvement in torture. Amid the controversy over 'extraordinary rendition', in which the US government stands accused of transporting terrorist suspects to other countries for purposes of torture, statements of literal denial were emphatic. President Bush, on 27 January 2005, assured the world that 'torture is never acceptable, nor do we hand people to countries that do torture' (Mayer 2005: EV1). Bush's denial is unacceptable to many who know that indeed the USA has rendered – a euphemism for kidnapping – suspects to other nations with the understanding that they will be abused and tortured (Priest and Gellman 2002). Moreover, those renditions are a matter of policy carried out by 'the CIA under broad authority that has allowed it to act without case-by-case approval from the White House or the State or Justice Departments', according to current and former government officials (Jehl 2005: A1).

A case in point is Maher Arar, a Canadian citizen born in Syria. On 26 September 2002, Arar was arrested at John F. Kennedy Airport while changing planes; he had been on vacation with his family in Tunisia and was returning to his home in Canada. American officials said that Arar's name appeared on a watch list of suspected terrorists and detained and questioned him for 13 days, but he was never formally charged with any violation. Then, in handcuffs and leg irons, he was loaded onto an executive jet to Syria, where he was placed in the custody of Syrian interrogators. For a year, Arar was beaten and tortured. It was not until the Canadian government eventually took up his cause that he was released, without charge (Herbert 2005; Mayer 2005; see Greenberg and Dratel 2005). Former government officials say the CIA has flown 100 to 150 suspected terrorists from one foreign country to another, including Egypt, Jordan, Pakistan, Saudi Arabia and Syria (Jehl 2005). Also it is not publicly known how many terrorist suspects are being secretly held by the US government. The CIA is reported to have prisons – so called interrogation centres – in Afghanistan, Diego Garcia, Qatar, and Thailand (Priest and Gellman 2002, Anonymous 2004; Hersh 2004). Incidentally, the Bush team's practice of extraordinary rendition was so secretive that members of the 9/11 Commission were barred from asking questions about it during its investigation.

Interpretive denial

In defending controversial tactics in the war on terror, US government officials also engage in interpretive denial, spinning euphemism and legalism. One such example of relying on soft language, or euphemism, to dampen criticism over harsh measures, is the Justice Department's use of the term 'interview' rather than 'interrogation' in reference to the government's plan to question foreign nationals (holding valid visas) in the months following 9/11. Journalists and political commentators not only detected the euphemism embodied in the term 'interview,' but also ridiculed Attorney-General Ashcroft when he announced, 'We're being as kind and fair and gentle as we can' (Downes 2001: WK2).

Shortly after the attacks of 11 September, Ashcroft also participated in legalism, thereby deepening the government's commitment to interpretive denial in its domestic war on terror. Ashcroft proposed limiting judicial appeals against detention and deportation and setting up a new legal standard for detention that requires only a 'reason to believe' that someone is associated with terrorism (Povich 2001). Under the then newly enacted US Patriot Act, the Justice Department forged ahead with its broad powers, including the government's new rule to listen in on conversations between detainees and their lawyers – in effect suspending the Sixth Amendment right to effective counsel. In both instances, the government's legalistic tactics lend themselves to Cohen's observation on reinterpretation. 'Powerful forms of interpretive denial come from the language of legality itself. Countries with democratic credentials sensitive to their international image now offer legalistic defences, drawn from the accredited human rights discourse' (Cohen 2001: 107). Along with its attempt to rewrite the definition of torture, Bush's invention of the unlawful criminal combatant directive, allowing the US government to detain indefinitely terrorist suspects, demonstrates a high degree of legalism intended to skirt US constitutional law, international law, and the Geneva Convention.

Implicatory denial

Implicatory denial also abounds in the war on terror, particularly given the tendencies for government officials and intelligence operatives to deny the psychological, political, and moral implications of such tactics as ethnic profiling, abusive detention, and even torture. Several of the national security officials interviewed by reporters of the *Washington Post* defended the use of violence against captives as just and necessary. Moreover, they expressed confidence that the American public would back them, especially in light of a new climate encouraging abuse in the wake of 9/11. An unidentified FBI agent told reporters: 'It could get to that spot where we could go to pressure' (Priest and Gellman 2002: A1). While arguing that torture ought not be 'authorized', Robert Litt, a former Justice Department official, suggested it could be used in an 'emergency' (Williams 2001: 11). Similarly, a government operative who has supervised the capture and transfer of accused terrorists remarked: 'If you don't violate someone's human rights some of the time, you probably aren't doing your job. I don't think we want to be promoting a view of zero tolerance on this. That was the whole problem for a long time with the CIA' (Priest and Gellman 2002: A1).

Due in large part to graphic photographs documenting abuse, the Abu Ghraib prison scandal became a worldwide embarrassment for the USA. Promptly, the Bush team set out to control the blaming process, unleashing the standard 'bad apples' explanation to counter suspicion that the use of torture was systemic, and a matter of counter-terrorism policy in a post-9/11 world (Hersh 2004; Harbury 2005). Strangely, however, some members of Congress swam against the tide of international condemnation by suggesting that their ill treatment was somehow deserved. Senator James Inhofe, a Republican from Oklahoma and member of the Senate Armed Services Committee, insisted: 'These prisoners . . . you know they're not there for traffic violations. If they're in Cellblock 1-A or 1-B, these prisoners, they're murderers, they're terrorists, they're insurgents. Many of them probably have American blood on their hands, and here we're so concerned about the treatment of those individuals' (Sontag 2004: 42; see Rich 2004).

In a parallel vein, former Senate majority leader Trent Lott defended the interrogation techniques, commenting: 'Most people in Mississippi came up to me and said: "Thank Goodness. America comes first." Interrogation is not a Sunday-school class. You don't get information that will save American lives by withholding pancakes' (Solomon 2004: 15). Journalist Deborah Solomon confronted Lott, pointing out that unleashing killer dogs on naked prisoners is not the same as withholding pancakes. Lott responded: 'I was amazed that people reacted like that. Did the dogs bite them? Did the dogs assault them? How are you going to get people to give information that will lead to the saving of lives?' (Solomon 2004: 15). Contributing to the wave of implicatory denial, Secretary of Defense Rumsfeld, who insisted that Iraqi prisoners, as unlawful combatants, do not have any rights under the Geneva Convention, mocked restrictions on stress and duress positions (like standing) to a maximum of four hours: 'I stand for 8–10 hours a day. Why is standing limited to 4 hours?' (Jehl 2004: A10). Each of these forms of denial – literal, interpretive, and implicatory – serves the US government's wider interest in averting blame and refusing to take responsibility for its policies and actions. Taken together, they contribute to the dynamic of passing the hot potato that would otherwise force government officials to be held accountable for its trampling of civil liberties and human rights, activities that have become a defining emblem on the war on terror while contributing to denial emerging at a broader cultural level.

Conclusion

For decades, the writings of Stan Cohen have echoed around the globe, motivating yet another generation of scholars eager to explore further the potential of his concepts and theories. This essay offers an overview describing how Cohen's understanding of the overreaction to putative social problems, most evident in moral panic, is balanced by his keen observation on the underreaction in which knowledge of human rights violations is concealed and denied. Throughout this work, I refer to key developments in my own research (e.g., criminalization of protest, youth crime, detention of undocumented immigrants and asylum seekers, and a host of human rights abuses in the war on terror) to demonstrate the force and impact of Cohen's influence on young scholars interested in confronting both polarities of the overreaction/underreaction spectrum. The essay sheds light on how together both forms of societal reaction perpetuate human rights violations while simultaneously repressing public and political awareness that would otherwise acknowledge such injustice and suffering. In closing, it is difficult to imagine that I would have reached my conceptual and theoretical findings concerning underreaction and overreaction without Cohen's work serving as guideposts along the way. Speaking on behalf of perhaps all of the Cohenesque thinkers, I am grateful for his genuine inspiration and for making a significant imprint on contemporary sociology that promises to endure well into the future.

References

Anonymous (2004) *Imperial Hubris: Why the West is Losing the War on Terror.* Washington, DC: Brassey's.

Brimelow, P. (1995) *Alien Nation: Common Sense About America's Immigration Disaster.* New York: Random House.

Cohen, S. (1979) 'The punitive city: notes on the dispersal of social control', *Contemporary Crisis,* 3, 339–63.

Cohen, S. (1985) *Visions of Social Control.* Cambridge: Polity Press.

Cohen, S. (1988) *Against Criminology.* New Brunswick, NJ: Transaction.

Cohen, S. (1995) 'State crimes of previous regimes: knowledge, accountability, and the policing of the past', *Law and Social Inquiry,* 20: 7–50.

Cohen, S. (1996) 'Government responses to human rights reports: claims, denials, and counterclaims', *Human Rights Quarterly,* 18: 517–43.

Cohen, S. (2001) *States of Denial: Knowing about Atrocities and Suffering.* Cambridge: Polity.

Cohen, S. (2002) *Folk Devils and Moral Panics: The Creation of the Mods and Rockers* (3rd edn). London: Routledge.

Cohen, S. (2005) 'Post-democratic torture', *Index on Censorship,* 34, 1.

Cohen, S. and Young, J. (1981) *The Manufacture of News.* Beverly Hills, CA: Sage.

Congressional Record (1990) Washington, DC: US Government Printing.

Downes, L. (2001) 'Hope you can come!' *New York Times,* 2 December: WK2.

Goldstein, R.J. (1996) *Burning the Flag: The Great 1989–1990 American Flag Desecration Controversy.* Kent, OH: Kent State University Press.

Greenberg, K.J. and Dratel, J.L. (2005). *The Torture Papers: The Road to Abu Ghraib.* Cambridge: Cambridge University Press.

Greenhouse, L. (1990) 'Supreme Court voids flag law', *New York Times,* 12 June: A1, B7.

Harbury, J. (2005) *Truth, Torture, and the American Way: The History and Consequences of U.S. Involvement in Torture.* Boston: Beacon Press.

Herbert, B. (2005) Torture, American style. *New York Times*, 11 February: A25.

Hersh, S.M. (2004) *Chain of Command: The Road from 9/11 to Abu Ghraib*. New York: HarperCollins.

Jehl, D. (2004) 'Files show Rumsfeld rejected some efforts to toughen prison rules', *New York Times*, 23 July; A10.

Jehl, D. (2005) 'Questions left by C.I.A. chief on torture use: Goss vouches only for current practices', *New York Times*, 18 March: A1, A11.

Mayer, J. (2005) 'Outsourcing torture', *New Yorker*, 21 February: EV1–14.

Povich, E.S. (2001) 'Ashcroft seeks broad laws', *New York Newsday*, 20 September: EV1–3.

Priest, D. and Gellman, B. (2002) 'U.S. decries abuse but defends interrogations "stress and duress" tactics used on terrorism suspects held in secret overseas facilities', *Washington Post*, 26 December: A1.

Rich, F. (2004) 'It was the porn that made them do it', *New York Times*, 30 May: Section 2, 1, 16.

Solomon, A. (2004) 'Questions for Trent Lott', *New York Times Magazine*, 20 June: 15.

Sontag, S. (2004) 'The photographs *are* us', *New York Times Magazine*, 23 May: 24–9, 42.

Thomas, C. (1989) 'Comments', *New York Daily News*, 12 August: 55.

Welch, M. (2000) *Flag Burning: Moral Panic and the Criminalization of Protest*. New York: de Gruyter.

Welch, M. (2002) *Detained: Immigration Laws and the Expanding I.N.S. Jail Complex*. Philadelphia: Temple University Press.

Welch, M. (2003) 'Trampling of human rights in the war on terror: implications to the sociology of denial', *Critical Criminology: An International Journal*, 12: 1–20.

Welch, M. (2004) 'Quiet constructions in the war on terror: subjecting asylum seekers to unnecessary detention', *Social Justice: A Journal of Crime, Conflict and World Order*, 31: 113–29.

Welch, M. (2006a) *Scapegoats of September 11th: Hate Crimes and State Crimes in the War on Terror*. New Brunswick, NJ: Rutgers University Press.

Welch, M. (2006b) 'Torture in a post 9/11 world: exploring the forces and sources of a culture of impunity', *Interdisciplinary Academic Conference on Human Rights Crossing the Boundaries: The Place of Human Rights in Contemporary Scholarship*, Centre for the Study of Human Rights, London School of Economics, 24 March.

Welch, M. (2006c) 'Immigration, criminalization, and counter-law: a Foucauldian analysis of laws against law', *Merging Immigration and Crime Control: An Interdisciplinary Workshop*, Baldy Center for Law and Social Policy, University at Buffalo Law School, Buffalo, New York, 28–29 April.

Welch, M., Fenwick, M. and Roberts, M. (1997) 'Primary definitions of crime and moral panic: a content analysis of experts' quotes in feature newspaper articles on crime', *Journal of Research in Crime and Delinquency*, 34: 474–94.

Welch, M., Fenwick, M. and Roberts, M. (1998) 'State managers, intellectuals, and the media: a content analysis of ideology in experts' quotes in featured newspaper articles on crime', *Justice Quarterly*, 15: 219–41.

Welch, M., Price, E. and Yankey, N. (2004) 'Youth violence and race in the media: the emergence of *wilding* as an invention of the press', *Race, Gender and Class*, 11: 36–48.

Welch, M., Price, E. and Yankey, N. (2002) 'Moral panic over youth violence: *wilding* and the manufacture of menace in the media', *Youth and Society*, 34: 3–30.

Welch, M., Sassi, J. and McDonough, A. (2002) 'Advances in critical cultural criminology: an analysis of reactions to avant-garde flag art', *Critical Criminology: An International Journal*, 11: 1–20.

Welch, M. and Schuster, L. (2005a) 'Detention of asylum seekers in the UK and US: deciphering noisy and quiet constructions', *Punishment and Society: An International Journal of Penology*, 7: 397–417.

Welch, M. and Schuster, L. (2005b) 'Detention of asylum seekers in the US, UK, France, Germany, and Italy: a critical view of the globalizing culture of control', *Criminal Justice: The International Journal of Policy and Practice*, 5(4): 331–55.

Williams, P.J. (2001) 'By any means necessary', *The Nation*, 26 November: 11.

Part 3
Extremities of Control:
Torture and the Death Penalty

Chapter 10

The power to classify: avenues into a supermax prison

Sharon Shalev

> The real significance of classification lies in the form, not the content, the enterprise itself and not its end-results. The power to classify is the purest of all deposits of professionalism.
>
> (Cohen 1985: 246)

Once prisoners are sentenced by the courts to a custodial sentence, the 'administration of their penalty' is handed over to prison authorities: 'although the principle of penalty was certainly a legal decision, its administration, its quality and its rigours must belong to an autonomous mechanism that supervises the effects of punishment within the very apparatus that produces them' (Foucault 1977: 246). The prisoner security classification process is the main mechanism through which the 'quality and rigour' of prisoners' confinement are determined: once prisoners are classified to a certain security category, their institutional placement, provisions, entitlement to 'privileges', access to programmes and entire experience of the prison system are predetermined to a very large extent.

This chapter illustrates Stan Cohen's observation on the 'power to classify' by examining how, and which, prisoners are selected for placement in the highest security prisons in the USA, generically known as 'supermaxes'. These are large prisons dedicated to holding prisoners in strict and prolonged separation from one another, from prison staff and from the outside world. Prisoners in these prisons are typically held in small, windowless cells, where they eat, sleep, and spend up to 24 hours a day with no access to vocational, educational or recreational activities. Daily routines are highly structured and strictly timetabled, and prisoners are subjected to constant surveillance, inspection and monitoring. In most units, prisoners are only allowed out of their cells, individually, to exercise in a small barren exercise yard for one hour four times a week, for a 15-minute-long shower three times a week, and for one-hour-long, no-contact family visits infrequently. On the rare occasions that prisoners leave their housing units to go to other parts of the building – for example, to see a doctor – they are put in hand, leg and body restraints and escorted by a minimum of two guards. Reviewing conditions in one supermax unit in California, a federal district court concluded that these 'may press the outer bounds of what most humans can psychologically tolerate' (*Madrid* v. *Gomez* 1995).

Supermax prisons are built as an addition to, not a replacement of, the segregation units which can be found in most prisons and jails, where prisoners are typically segregated for relatively short periods of time. Further, in contrast to 'regular' segregation units, supermax prisons are designed to hold hundreds, rather than dozens, of prisoners. The percentages of prisoners classified as requiring long-term isolation in a supermax vary significantly from state to state, reflecting sentencing policies, 'law and order' politics, bed availability, and the classification tools used in the process. California holds around 2.5 per cent of its prisoners in supermax units. Florida and Iowa reported that 3 per cent of their prisoners require supermax custody. Louisiana and Washington hold 6 per cent of their prisoners in a supermax. Ohio, Wyoming, Maryland and Michigan require supermax housing for 1 per cent of their prisoner population, while Mississippi holds as many as 20 per cent of its male, adult prisoners in a supermax (National Institute of Corrections 1997: 4–6). Nationwide, in 2005, an estimated two per cent of the total US prison population of 1.44 million people were held in supermax confinement.[1]

Officially, supermax prisons are designated for the 'worst of the worst', the most dangerous, and predatory prisoners, 'the baddest of the bad – the most violent, the murderers, rapists, terrorists, bombers – those who cannot be managed anywhere else … the meanest, nastiest, most intransigent criminals in the country, the ones upon whom everyone else has given up' (Molden N.D.). But who are these 'worst of the worst' who supposedly cannot be controlled in less restrictive environments, and how are the generalised concepts of 'risk' and 'dangerousness' translated into operational bureaucratic principles? Most importantly, who decides?

Below, I briefly discuss these issues drawing on California's Pelican Bay Security Housing Unit (SHU) and on California Department of Corrections (CDC) prisoner classification instruments. The SHU is one of the first supermaxes in the USA, and the prototype for many other such units. It is an X-shaped free-standing building with 1,056 self-contained cells, located on the site of Pelican Bay Prison, a maximum security (level IV) facility.

The 'special security' category: avenues into a supermax

> The magic wand of classification has long been held out as the key to a successful system…. All that has changed over the last century is the basis of the binary classification. It used to be 'moral character'; sometimes it was 'treatability' or 'security risk', now it tends to be 'dangerousness'.
>
> (Cohen 1985: 194–5)

Supermax prisons are by far the most powerful weapon in the arsenal of penalties and control measures available to prison administrators. Prisoners' life in isolation is tightly controlled and potentially very damaging. In theory, the tool of the supermax is used only for those who have been identified as 'predatory' and 'dangerous' by objective classification criteria. In practice, as the discussion below demonstrates, definitions of 'predatory' and 'dangerous' are wide and potentially all-encompassing, and those placed in supermaxes are often petty offenders who pose a management problem rather than those who are really a threat.

The specific composition of official groupings of 'difficult-to-control' prisoners differs slightly from one jurisdiction to another, but most states house in their supermax prisons a combination of prisoners who have committed a serious offence in prison, mentally ill prisoners, gang members and death-row prisoners. Arizona, Colorado, Oklahoma, Utah and Maryland, among others, hold their death-row prisoners in supermax prisons regardless of their disciplinary record, while California holds them in segregation wings in high-security prisons, but not in supermax units. Some jurisdictions, including Oklahoma, Indiana, Ohio, Texas and Illinois, hold mentally ill offenders in their supermaxes, although courts increasingly intervene and order that mentally ill prisoners be removed to specialist facilities, as was the case with California (*Madrid* v. *Gomez* 1995). The overrepresentation of racial minorities in prisons and jails, which is prevalent across the USA, is even more acute in supermax prisons. Hispanics, for example, make up only 17 per cent of California residents, yet they make up 35 per cent of the CDC adult male prisoner population, and a staggering 68 per cent of prisoners at Pelican Bay SHU.

According to official directives, the main groups of prisoners who may be placed in a SHU in California include 'serious rule violators', gang members, and prisoners who were paroled from the SHU and returned to custody following a violation of their parole terms or to serve a new prison sentence. There is also an open-ended provision for cases where 'the inmate's continued presence in general population would severely endanger lives of inmates or staff, the security of the institution or the integrity of an investigation into suspected criminal activity' (CDC Operations Manual, section 62050.13.2). Prior to placement at the SHU, prisoners appear before Pelican Bay Prison's institutional classification committee (ICC), which is chaired by the warden or chief deputy warden and includes prison staff and a psychiatrist or physician. Placement in a SHU requires further approval by a classification staff representative (CSR) at headquarters level. Although, once at the SHU, all categories of prisoners are subjected to the same conditions and provisions, different rules and regulations govern serious rule violators, gang members and parole violators. These are briefly examined below.

Serious rule violators

A prisoner found by a disciplinary hearing to be guilty of a serious prison offence may be referred to the ICC to be reclassified and assigned to a SHU for a determinate time. The length of 'SHU term' is regulated by administrative rules, and calculated according to the 'SHU term assessment chart', which lays out the minimum and maximum SHU time that may be given for listed offences. The maximum determinate SHU term is five years. Misconduct is classified as 'serious' if it involves one or more of the following: the use of force or violence against another person, a breach of or hazard to facility security, a serious disruption of facility operations, the introduction or possession of a controlled substance *or an attempt or threat to commit any of the above*, coupled with the ability to carry out the threat (California Code of Regulations, Title 15, section 3315 (hereafter 'Title 15). A non-exhaustive list of 23 'serious rule violations' includes some of the following offences:

[B] Theft, destruction, misuse, alteration, damage, unauthorized acquisition or exchange of personal or state property amounting to more than $50; [D] Tattooing or possession of tattoo paraphernalia; [G] Possession of $5 or more without authorization; [H] Acts of disobedience or disrespect which by reason of their intensity or context create potential for violence or mass disruptive conduct; [J] Refusal to perform work or participate in a program as ordered or assigned; [O] Harassment of another person, group or entity either directly or indirectly through the use of the mail or other means; [P] Throwing any liquid or solid substance on a non-prisoner; [S] Participation in gambling; [U] Unauthorized possession of materials or substances which have been diverted or altered from the original manufactured state or purpose with the potential to be made into a weapon, explosive, poison, caustic substance, any destructive device; (V) Self mutilation or attempted suicide for the purpose of manipulation; and (W) Involvement in a conspiracy or attempt to do any of the above (Title 15, section 3315).

As noted above, the length of the SHU term is determined according to the SHU term assessment chart, which sets out the range of typical terms for 20 listed offences. Beyond the prescribed maximum and minimum terms, classification staff retain wide discretion. The SHU term for homicide, for example, is 36–60 months. Assaults result in varying terms, depending on the nature of the assault, and on whether it was committed against a prisoner or against a 'non-inmate'. An assault on a prisoner with a weapon or physical force capable of causing mortal or serious injury, for example, results in a SHU term of 6–24 months. The same offence against a non-prisoner results in a SHU term of 9–48 months. *Attempts* to commit listed offences result in half of the specified term. An inmate who *conspires* to commit any of these offences is placed in the SHU for the full specified SHU term.

Since supermaxes are intended for the 'worst of the worst', the list of serious rule violations appears somewhat insubstantial. Further, not only actual acts but also attempts, threats, and even alleged *intentions* are sufficient grounds for allocation to one of the most restrictive environments in the prison estate. Nonetheless, the practice of 'isolating risk', as the author of a National Institute of Corrections (Riveland 1999) report on supermax prisons put it, is widespread across the USA. Moreover, some of the listed offences are specific to prison environments and have come to be defined as 'serious' as a result of internal pressures and the bargaining power of prison staff and their representatives, and not necessarily because they pose a legitimate security concern. One good example of this is item (P) ('throwing any liquid or solid substance on a non-prisoner'), or 'gassing', as it is termed internally, which has been classified in 1998 as aggravated battery, punishable by two to six years in segregation.

Alleged gang members

The problem of gang activity in California's prisons is perceived to be a serious one, and isolating gang leaders is one of the strategies for breaking up gang activity. Identifying prisons as independent entities which require protection, Title 15 states that 'Gangs present a serious threat to the safety and security of California prisons' (subsection 3023) and sets the criteria for determining gang membership, including:

> Self admission; Tattoos and symbols ('Body markings, hand signs, distinctive clothing, graffiti and so on, which have been identified by gang coordinators/investigators as being used by and distinctive to specific gangs'); Written materials ('membership or enemy lists, organizational structures, codes, training material') of specific gangs; Photographs; Staff information; Information from other agencies; Association ('information related to the inmate/parolee's association with validated gang affiliates'); Informants; Visitors ('visits from persons who are documented as gang 'runners' or community affiliates'); Communications ('documentation of telephone conversations, mail, notes, or other communication, including coded messages evidencing gang affiliation'); Debriefing reports.

The all-encompassing nature of the criteria means that almost anyone can be defined as a gang member. Prisoners testified that talking to someone they know in the exercise yard who is an alleged gang member, or being reported as a gang member by another prisoner who had a personal score to settle with them, constituted enough evidence to validate them as gang associates. In fact, based on these criteria it may be difficult for prisoners from certain socio-economic and racial backgrounds *not* to be labelled as gang members.

Prisoners assigned to a SHU due to gang membership will be placed there for an indeterminate time.

Parole violators

Returning parolees who have paroled from the SHU and have either violated the terms of their parole or were returned to prison with a new prison term may be directly placed in a SHU regardless of the nature of their original or new offence.

Assignment to custody, programme, privilege and incentive groups

Once classified as requiring 'special security', prisoners are assigned by the ICC to an appropriate housing unit. The ICC then assigns the prisoner to educational, vocational, therapeutic or other institutional programmes, arranged in categories from Work Group A-1 to Work

Group D-2. Each group is entitled to different good-time credits and privileges. Although this segment of the classification process is supposed to be individually tailored and separate from the security classification, in practice prisoners' housing assignment determines their access to work and education. Prisoners who are assigned to a SHU are automatically classified as Work Group D-2, and hence are not entitled to any good-time credits. Previously, the regulations made a distinction between inmates serving indeterminate SHU terms (mainly alleged gang members), who were entitled to one-day credit for each two days served, those serving and determinate SHU terms (mainly 'serious rule violators'), who were not entitled to any good-time credits. In February 2000, the CDC changed its regulations so as to preclude all SHU prisoners from entitlement to any good-time credits. The rationale was laid out in the explanatory notes accompanying the new regulations:

> Conforming behavior in SHU is not equivalent to conforming behavior in a general population setting … periods spent by the inmate in maximum custody do not provide the same type of freedom and risks presented in periods of close custody…. The purposes of SHU are the protection of staff and other inmates and the security of the facility. SHU is not intended to provide an opportunity to observe inmate success in good behavior and programming (Title 15, article 3.5 Feb. 2000 amendments).

In other words, since there are few opportunities to offend in the SHU, prisoners cannot demonstrate good behaviour that would earn them good-time credits and therefore should not be entitled to any. This Alice in Wonderland logic leaves SHU prisoners with little to lose, and prison administrations with even more control over all aspects of prisoners' lives than usual in the prison setting.

Privileges constitute an administrative tool which can be, and originally was, used as an incentive for prisoners to demonstrate good behaviour. But alongside the wider shift in the 1980s toward the managerial approach to corrections and the growing emphasis on standardisation, administrative discretion in the use of privileges was gradually reduced, and regulations regarding their distribution established. Currently, all prisoners assigned to a SHU are entitled only to the minimal level of privileges, as required by law and by court orders, and are automatically placed in Privilege Group D, which includes:

- one-quarter of the maximum monthly canteen draw
- telephone calls on an emergency basis only

- limited yard access; no access to any other recreational or entertainment activities
- one annual package
- one-off special purchase of a TV/radio.

All prisoners assigned to a SHU, then, are automatically excluded from association with other prisoners, from participation in any programmes which might enhance their personal development or earn them credits toward parole, and from receiving any provisions beyond the basic minimum required by law as stipulated above. They also 'earn' a label that cannot be easily revoked later, as the housing assignment is noted in the prisoner's file and will follow him for the rest of his life.

Avenues out of supermax

Classification, according to official directives, 'shall be an ongoing process of evaluating the inmate's needs, interests and desires, keeping in mind individual, security and public safety' (CDC Operations Manual, section 62010.4). The reclassification or review process is theoretically intended to re-evaluate and fine-tune initial decisions according to the prisoner's actual (rather than predicted) behaviour at the assigned prison. In practice, however, the process is essentially formalistic, pays little attention to individual needs and focuses mainly on issues of institutional security.

The body charged with reviewing prisoners' classification score in California is the unit classification committee (UCC), which is chaired by the SHU's captain and includes 5–7 other SHU staff members. Regulations require that prisoners serving determinate SHU terms appear before a UCC at least once a year, whereas those serving indeterminate SHU terms will be reviewed by the UCC at least once every 180 days.

In these hearings, prisoners' classification scores are examined in light of 'favourable' and 'unfavourable' behaviour since the last classification hearing. The definitions of 'unfavourable behaviour' are the ones used when the prisoner was initially classified to the special security category, including (Title 15, section 3375.4):

(a) **Unfavorable behavior** serious rule violation during 6 months period (6 points for each violation); escape (8 points); physical assault or attempted assault on staff (8 points); physical serious assault on another prisoner (4 points);

(b) **Favorable behavior** since last review (no rule violation, 2 credits).

Average hearings last 5–25 minutes and take place inside the SHU building in a setting that discourages individual and positive interaction with the prisoner. The body charged with making the final decision in the case of disputes is the departmental review board (DRB) at CDC headquarters level, which only reviews decisions that are referred to it by the ICU, an internal body whose decision is challenged in the first place, and whose main consideration is 'institutional security' as represented by staff reports.

A 1996 CDC internal audit report found that up to 60 per cent of annual reviews result in no change to the prisoner's programme assignment or custody level (California Department of Finance 1996: 48). As good conduct is meagrely awarded with two credits and misconduct is widely defined and heavily penalised, prisoners have few avenues for leaving the SHU before their minimum eligibility release date (MERD) from prison. Indeed, prisoners are more likely than not to commit minor breaches of the strict rules and regulations that govern their lives, thus reaffirming their label and feeding into the classification system's self-fulfilling prophecies. Prisoners who are allocated to the SHU for a determinate time undergo a fairly straightforward process. Unless they have breached SHU rules and regulations (in which case they will stay in the SHU for an additional time), they will remain in the SHU until they have finished serving their assigned SHU term.

Prisoners who were placed in the SHU on gang-related grounds remain there for an indeterminate time. The only avenues they have for leaving the SHU are limited to what is colloquially known as 'snitching, paroling, or dying'. Death and parole are self-explanatory. 'Snitching', or 'debriefing' in official language, involves the prisoner providing prison authorities with a detailed report of his gang-related activities, names of other people involved and any other pertinent information (a 'biography' as prisoners call it). The process of debriefing brings to mind the Roman Catholic confession, but its function is perhaps closer to the brainwashing in communist Russia and China of political dissenters, where, after a period in isolation, the prisoner 'was forced to prove his sincerity by making irrevocable behavioural commitments, such as denouncing and implicating his friends and relatives in his own newly recognised crimes. Once he had done this he became further alienated from his former self, even in his own eyes' (Schein 1960: 155).

Renouncing a gang is not a simple or an easy option for prisoners. In the prison setting, gang membership provides prisoners with protection, a sense of belonging and sometimes simply a group of familiar faces.

As one senior Pelican Bay official put it in an interview, for many prisoners, the 'gang' is synonymous with 'family':

> Most of these guys didn't just come to prison and decide, 'Gee, I think I'm going to be a gang member' and they go out and join a gang. Most of them had been associated with gang activities, many of them, since pre-teen. For many of them it was a family lifestyle – their fathers, their mothers, their brothers, sisters, aunts, uncles – the whole family network was associated with gang activity.

This understanding of the dynamics of inner-city poor and racially segregated communities is not an empathetic one, but part of the social distancing between 'us' and 'them'. Such statements are also deterministic in the sense that they imply that SHU prisoners cannot change.

Prisoners who do wish to debrief have to complete a detailed 'debriefing' report, which is sent to the CDC headquarters for evaluation. If the prisoner provides what gang investigators consider to be an 'unreliable' or 'insufficient' amount of information, the debriefing report may be rejected, and the prisoner will remain in the SHU. If the report is accepted, the prisoner will appear before the ICC to be reclassified and allocated to a 'transitional housing unit' (THU), where he will be housed with others who have debriefed. This time, the purpose of the 'special placement' in a THU is to protect the prisoner, and to test his good faith and willingness to disassociate himself from gang activity. At the THU, members of opposing gangs are expected to demonstrate their 'sincere' intentions by getting along with each other. Prisoners may be put two to a cell and asked to sign a 'marriage contract', as it is colloquially known, vowing not to engage in any hostile acts toward each other.

Some of the prisoners labelled as gang members reject the very label, contest any involvement in gang activities and say that they cannot debrief, since they have no knowledge of gang activities. These individuals find themselves in an impossible situation: they will not be released from the SHU unless they debrief, but since they are not gang members, they cannot provide any information on gang activities and therefore are unable to debrief. Another group of prisoners who find themselves in a difficult position are those who were gang members when they were first placed in a SHU, but have been isolated for so long that any information they might have had in the past is outdated and irrelevant. Following court interventions and a growing demand for SHU beds, in April 2000, over a decade after Pelican Bay SHU was opened, the CDC introduced a new category, 'inactive gang members'. This new category is designed as an alternative to 'debriefing' for prisoners who have not been involved in gang activity for a minimum of six years. The process is highly subjective and discretionary. Prisoners may (but do not have a right to) be reclassified by the departmental review board (DRB) as inactive gang members. Regulations stipulate that the decision made by the DRB will be reviewed *no more* than once every two years. Inactive gang members who are selected by the DRB for release from the SHU have to 'pass' another test. They are allocated to the general population of a level IV facility (maximum security) for a period of observation, which may last up to 12 months, and upon its completion they are housed in a facility consistent with their (initial) classification score. It is sufficient for one 'reliable source item' to identify the prisoner as being involved in gang activity during this period for the prisoner to be returned to the SHU. The DRB may also decide that although a prisoner is an inactive gang member he should be retained in the SHU. In short, the number of prisoners that can be included in the 'inactive' category is very small to begin with, and the CDC retains complete discretion in releasing or retaining these prisoners in the SHU.

The dry process of classification, then, has the most profound consequences for many caught up in the prison system. Through its own perverse, internal logic, the bureaucracy of classification may push a relatively minor offender deeper into a Kafkaesque nightmare that ends in solitary confinement in a supermax prison with no route out. Classificatory decisions are made by prison staff and, other than where the courts are involved, are not subjected to external scrutiny. Despite its serious implications for prisoners, in California, a relatively low-level body, the ICC, is charged with allocating prisoners to a SHU. A US national survey of supermax confinement (National Institute of Corrections 1997) found that this was the case elsewhere. Of the 34 departments of corrections that responded and operated a supermax facility at the time, half reported that placement and removal of prisoners from supermax are decided at the institutional level, while the other half reported that the decision is made at central office level, by the DOC director or deputy director. None of the jurisdictions had mechanisms for external scrutiny of allocation and release processes (National Institute of Corrections 1997: 3).

Conclusions

Prisoner classification dictates the physical conditions in which prisoners are held, and their access to vocational, educational and recreational programmes and other privileges that encompass most aspects of their daily lives. Through the use of classification factors in parole hearings designed to assess prisoners' risk to the community, and through the administration of good-time credits, classification also affects prisoners' chances of parole. The classification process is a circular one, as prison systems use their own definitions, regulations and database of prior institutional behaviour to reinforce their own predictions. These self-fulfilling prophecies become set in stone, quite literally, since projections of future prison construction needs are based on current classification groupings. Since the early 1990s, these have consisted of growing numbers of maximum and special security prisoners.

Current trends do not indicate a reduction in the number of prisoners assigned to high-security categories. Most prison systems in the USA are, in fact, seeing an increase in the construction of supermax prisons, an increase in the number of prisoners categorised as requiring this type of housing, and a reduction in avenues for leaving the category of 'special security'. Inside these prisons, we see the creation of subcategories of 'dangerousness' for prisoners who are claimed to require even more control inside supermax prisons. The threshold of 'dangerousness' is lowered as a new subcategory is created among those classified as the 'most dangerous' – the most dangerous among the most dangerous. Adopting such tactics, some supermax facilities now have a 'violence control unit' for prisoners who commit violent offences while in isolation. Prisoners who 'gas' guards have their cell doors covered with Plexiglas, further isolating them. Repeat 'gassers' will be identified as such in their personal file, and will be unable to leave the SHU, since gassing is now classified as a serious offence. This process brings to mind what Messinger (1969) termed the 'complicated Chinese box effect' when, in the 1960s, California developed special segregation units within existing segregation units as a tool for managing 'difficult' prisoners who were already segregated. This resulted in 'inmates in the innermost box ideally required to traverse each enclosing one on the way to relative freedom'.[2]

Some of the offences which are considered as serious enough to merit placement in a supermax are minor at best. But if allocation to a supermax is a managerial tool for incapacitating and controlling certain segments of the prison population, then the definition of the category of 'special security' is flexible enough to include in it anyone whom prison authorities wish to include, according to either penal policies or administrative convenience. The so-called objective nature of classification instruments and processes, and the rules and procedures guiding their application, are flagged-up by officials as 'proof' of the authenticity of the results of the process, making it difficult for prisoners to challenge classificatory decisions in the courts.

Those less familiar with the ins and outs of prison systems may be satisfied by official narratives regarding the assignment of prisoners to solitary confinement, and may be reassured by the promise that it keeps the most dangerous predators securely under lock and key. Those more familiar with prisoner classification repeatedly comment on the components and structure of the classification process, but few have taken the more radical step of questioning the utility of its principles. As Cohen observed, 'the 'failure' of a classification system rarely evokes troublesome ideological questions and never threatens professional interests. It simply calls for more and better classification, an agenda which can be followed with total agreement from everyone' (Cohen 1985: 193).

Notes

1   In addition to those held in 'regular' segregation units in general population prisons and jails. In 2005, the total prison and jail population in the USA was well over two million.
2   S. Messinger, *Strategies of Control* (Center for the Study of Law and Society, University of California, Berkley, 1969), cited in Cohen and Taylor (1981: 201).

References

California Department of Corrections, Regulations and Policies manuals. Sacramento, CA.
California Department of Corrections, Notice of Change to the Director's Rules, 27 March 2000.
California Department of Finance, Performance Review Unit (1996) *California Department of Corrections, A Performance Review*. Sacramento, CA.
Cohen, S. (1985) *Visions of Social Control*. Cambridge: Polity Press.
Cohen, S. and Taylor, L. ([1972] 1981) *Psychological Survival: The Experience of Long-Term Imprisonment* (2nd edn). Harmondsworth: Penguin Books.
Foucault, M. (1977) *Discipline and Punish: The Birth of the Prison*. Harmondsworth: Penguin Books.
Madrid v. *Gomez*, 889 F.Supp. 1146, 1249 (N.D. Cal. 1995).
Molden, J. (N.D.) FLO: The Big One. *Correctional Technology Magazine* (CTM). Available from: <http://infobase.thirdcoast.net>.
National Institute of Corrections, US Department of Justice (March 1997) *Supermax Housing: A Survey of Current Practice*. Special Issues in Corrections. Longmont, CO: NIC Information Center.
Riveland, C. (1999) *Supermax Prisons: Overview and General Considerations*. Washington, DC: US Department of Justice, National Institute of Corrections.
Schein, E., (1960) Interpersonal communication, group solidarity, and social Influence. *Sociometry*, 23(2): 148–161.

Chapter 11

The torture debate: Israel and beyond

David Kretzmer

Introduction

In 1991, B'Tselem – the Israeli Information Center for Human Rights in the Occupied Territories – published a report on the interrogation of Palestinians by the Israeli General Security Service (GSS).[1] The report, written by Stan Cohen and Daphna Golan-Agnon, should serve as a model for an NGO report on human rights violations. On the basis of careful and thorough research that included in-depth interviews with 41 former detainees, Cohen and Golan-Agnon were able to establish patterns in interrogation of detainees that revealed systematic use of force and other methods of physical and psychological pressure. They also revealed that in most cases in which these methods of interrogation were used the detainee was eventually released without charge, or was charged with minor offences. While Cohen and Golan-Agnon did not mince their words and stated plainly that the methods of interrogation being used, particularly when used together, amounted to torture, they were also careful not to overstate the case.[2]

The B'Tselem report brought the issue of torture in Israel to the surface. In a follow-up report prepared by Cohen and Golan-Agnon a year later, the authors described the reaction to the original report, both in the press and in the political arena.[3] While the report had not led to termination of the interrogation practices it described, it had opened up a debate in Israel and forced the authorities to relate to the serious allegations. Both the press and a number of politicians demanded proper investigation of the findings and a number of official investigations had been initiated. The matter also reached the Supreme Court of Israel.

The exposure of the interrogation practices of the GSS, and the attempts of the Israeli authorities to defend these practices, while hotly denying that they amounted to torture, meant that for a long time Israel was regarded as the lone state that actually attempted to legalize and legitimize use of force and other forms of interrogation that could be regarded as torture. True, while most states had ratified the Convention Against Torture and other human rights treaties that prohibit torture, torture remained prevalent in a depressingly large number of states.[4] But all these states denied engaging in torture, or anything that approached it, and when faced with individual cases in which use of torture was exposed, routinely claimed that these cases were exceptions, carried out by deviant officials, who would be punished for their acts.

And then came 9/11. The debate changed. Rather than a discussion of the means of narrowing the gap between law and practice, the very prohibition itself began to be questioned. Not that anyone started advocating a return to the torture chambers of the Inquisition, or to wide-scale use of torture. Torture as a form of punishment or control, or as a means of eliciting a confession from a prisoner, was still regarded as a no-no. Rather the emphasis was placed on what has been termed 'preventive investigational torture',[5] i.e., torture as a means of obtaining crucial information needed to thwart terrorist attacks. Attempts were made to unravel the international definition of torture, so as to open the path for use of methods of interrogation that are clearly covered by this definition.[6] One realist argued that, whether we like it or not, authorities are going to use torture in extreme circumstances, and we should therefore adopt a system of judicial 'torture warrants'.[7] An academic journal carried an article by two law professors who openly argue that the absolute prohibition cannot be defended, and that a space for 'lawful torture' should be created.[8] A vast number of publications discussed the use of torture or other coercive techniques in interrogation of suspected terrorists.[9] The issue was widely discussed in the press too.[10]

For an Israeli lawyer, these arguments are not really new. They all appeared in one form or another in the debate in Israel surrounding the interrogation practices of the GSS that Stan Cohen had exposed. As a tribute to Stan, in this chapter I intend reviewing the experience with the issue in Israel and discussing what conclusions can be drawn regarding the legal aspects of 'preventive investigational torture'. Before doing so, I shall comment on the contours of the present discussion on this type of torture and what is perceived by some as the unyielding stance of international law.

The absolute prohibition of torture

The prohibition of torture in international law is clear and absolute. 'No exceptional circumstances whatsoever … may be invoked as a justification of torture' (Article 2 of UN Convention Against Torture and Other Forms of Cruel, Inhuman and Degrading Treatment or Punishment (CAT)). A total of 144 states are a party to CAT and are bound by this prohibition. Furthermore, the prohibition is a part of customary international law that binds all states, whether they are party to CAT or not; in fact, the prohibition is widely regarded as *ius cogens*, a peremptory norm that may not be changed by states.[11] Not only are states themselves required to refrain from torture and to take effective measures to prevent torture in any territory under their jurisdiction; under article 3 of CAT, they are strictly forbidden to expel, return or extradite people to another state where there are substantial grounds for believing that they would be in danger of torture.

The prohibition against torture also figures in the International Covenant on Civil and Political Rights (ICCPR) and in regional human rights treaties. The prohibition is absolute and non-derogable, meaning that even in a state of emergency states may not derogate from their obligation not to torture, notwithstanding the claim that relaxing the prohibition is strictly required by the exigencies of the situation.

There is an important difference between CAT and the other human rights conventions that prohibit torture. The absolute prohibition in CAT refers only to torture itself, defined as 'any act by which severe pain or suffering, whether physical or mental, is intentionally inflicted on a person for such purposes as obtaining from him or a third person information or a confession … when such pain or suffering is inflicted by or at the instigation of or with the consent or acquiescence of a public official or other person acting in an official capacity'. While CAT also prohibits other forms of cruel, inhuman or degrading treatment or punishment, this prohibition does not appear as absolute as the prohibition on torture, thus leaving room for states to argue that the prohibition does not apply to the interrogation methods they use. The general conventions, on the other hand, such as the ICCPR, do not define 'torture', but they include both torture and other forms of cruel, inhuman or degrading treatment or punishment in the same absolute and underogable prohibition. Thus, even if a state that is a party both to CAT and ICCPR could conceivably escape liability under CAT for an interrogation that constitutes cruel or inhuman treatment, rather than torture, it would incur liability under the ICCPR.

The absolute prohibition and the ticking bomb

The present debate on the limits of the prohibition on torture inevitably begins from the ticking bomb scenario.[12] The main function of this scenario is to force one to concede, at least on moral grounds, that the prohibition of torture cannot be as absolute as the legal norms imply.[13] Apart from a few orthodox Kantians, there is hardly a soul who would not have to concede that in an extreme enough situation, in which hundreds of lives could be saved by using force to extricate the information needed to find and defuse a ticking bomb from the person responsible for placing it, if no other means were available, severe force could, and possibly even should, be used to extract the information.[14] The real question is not whether in such an extreme situation torture could be morally justified, but what relevance this has when considering the absolute nature of the legal prohibition on torture.

A number of answers have been suggested to this question. I do not intend canvassing all of them here. Rather my intention is to show what the Israeli experience can teach us about one possible answer: creating a legal loophole to the prohibition, so as to cater for ticking-bomb cases. Before discussing this experience, however, I do wish to relate to two possible answers, which I find neither convincing nor helpful in discussing the issue.

One argument is simply to deny that the scenario of a ticking bomb is a realistic case. As one writer has put it: 'The idea that the authorities might get a dangerous terrorist into their custody, after he has planned an attack but before he has executed it, is a utopian fantasy.'[15] While the real 'ticking-bomb' situation described in the literature may be extremely rare,[16] there is in my mind nothing to suggest that it is a 'utopian fantasy'. More importantly, it seems to me that the argument begs the issue. What does the (not unreal) assumption that there may indeed be a real ticking-bomb case teach us about the legal rules that should apply to interrogations? Does the possibility of such a rare case justify departure from the absolute legal prohibition?

A second unhelpful line of argument is that torture is ineffective, and often leads to wrong information. There is therefore no point in relaxing the standards, even in the case of a ticking bomb.

It may very well be true that, as a method of criminal investigation, torture is not likely to be an efficient method of interrogation. Detainees may often tell interrogators what they want to hear, rather than what actually happened. However, in the particular context of 'preventive investigational torture', this argument is not really relevant. In this context, the information sought by the authorities does not relate to what happened in the past, but to what is happening in the present,

123

or is about to happen in the near future, and the very point of seeking that information is to verify it. If the detainee reveals where explosives are hidden, or where a terrorist cell is hiding, the authorities will know very soon whether that information is accurate or not. Thus, depressing as that conclusion may be, our working assumption in this case has to be that torture may very well be effective.

The problem with the ticking-bomb scenario is not then that it is totally unrealistic, nor that torture will never be an effective way of extracting information, but that it misrepresents the argument for an absolute prohibition on torture. That argument does not rest on the notion that there could never possibly be a case in which torture could be morally justifiable, but on the sad human experience with the use of torture and the fear that *any* relaxation of the prohibition will inevitably lead to use of torture in a wide range of situations that could not, on any stretch of the imagination, be regarded as ticking-bomb ones. It is in relation to this argument that the Israeli experience is most telling.

The Israeli experience

Stage 1: denial

Soon after the occupation of the West Bank and Gaza began in 1967, serious allegations regarding the interrogation of Palestinian detainees by Israel's security services were raised. In June 1977, especially serious allegations of the use of torture in interrogations were published in the London *Sunday Times*.[17] These allegations were categorically denied by the authorities.[18]

The event that eventually led to exposure of use of force in interrogations involved the conviction for security offences of an Israeli army officer who belonged to the small Circassian community. The officer claimed that force had been used to extract a confession from him. While this was rejected by the military court which tried him, it later transpired that his allegations were well founded. The military prosecutor agreed to reversal of the conviction on appeal, and the cabinet decided to appoint a commission of inquiry to examine the methods of interrogation of the GSS and to recommend methods and guidelines for interrogations, 'taking into consideration the special needs of the struggle against hostile terrorist activities'.

Stage 2: the Landau Commission

The Commission of Inquiry, chaired by the former president of the Supreme Court, Justice Moshe Landau, found that since the early 1970s the GSS had indeed used force in interrogations and had systematically lied when challenged in court. The commission strongly condemned the behaviour of the GSS. Nevertheless, the GSS managed to convince the commission that limiting methods of interrogation to accepted police practice would mean that 'effective interrogation would be inconceivable'; interrogators would be unable to obtain the information needed to thwart planned terrorist acts.

In setting principles and guidelines for future interrogations, the commission considered three possible approaches:

1 rejecting use of force in all cases, however crucial it was to obtain information relating to planned terrorist attacks;

2 maintaining the position that the law prohibits all use of force while accepting that law enforcement authorities would turn a blind eye when the interrogators acted outside the law;

3 establishing guidelines for use of 'special interrogation methods' where essential in order to extract information that could lead to frustration of planned acts of terror.

The commission was convinced that, in light of Israel's security situation, the price to be paid for adopting the first approach would be too high. It rejected the second approach as hypocritical. It therefore opted for the third approach, according to which, when other forms of pressure were not efficacious in obtaining crucial information from suspected terrorists, special interrogation methods could be used, including non-violent psychological pressure and even a moderate degree of physical pressure.

It is important to understand the assumptions on which the Landau Commission based its recommendations. In the first place, it declared that torture could never be used. Relying largely on the decision of the European Court of Human Rights that had held that the interrogation practices of the British authorities in Northern Ireland did not amount to torture,[19] the commission took the view that the kind of methods it was prepared to condone would not constitute torture. Second, the commission was convinced that it may not be possible in some cases to obtain information necessary to thwart terrorist attacks by accepted methods of interrogation, and that in such cases departure from accepted practices would be justified. Third, rather than leaving the types of methods that could be used to the investigation authorities themselves, the commission laid down guidelines. It seems that its assumption was that in this way it could contain the methods and lessen the chances that they would amount to what the commission itself regarded as torture.[20] In the parlance later adopted, the commission assumed that if the authorities were allowed to use coercive methods of interrogation that may involve cruel, inhuman or degrading treatment, or what has recently been termed 'torture lite',[21] they would refrain from 'hardcore torture'.

The commission attempted to base legal justification for the use of moderate physical force in interrogations on the defence of necessity in criminal law. The argument was that if an interrogator used moderate physical pressure against a suspect in order to prevent the greater harm likely to be caused to innocent persons by a terrorist act, he would not be criminally liable. The commission did not address the issue of the legal authorization required under Israeli law for any interference with the liberty of the individual, and assumed that a defence against criminal liability would be adequate.

The commission divided its report into two parts. In the first part, which was published, it laid out the general issue and its principled recommendations.[22] In the second part, which has never been published, it laid out guidelines and constraints for the GSS regarding interrogation methods. It recommended that these guidelines be reviewed periodically by a ministerial committee.

The commission's recommendations were severely criticized in many quarters.[23] Critics argued that while the commission had expressly stated that methods amounting to torture were never to be allowed, it had in fact licensed torture. Lawyers also argued that in the light of an express provision criminalizing use of force in interrogations, the defence of necessity does not apply to interrogations. If a defence against criminal liability for use of force in interrogation could ever be available, it would be that of self-defence, rather than necessity.[24] Furthermore, a defence against criminal liability, which by its very nature must be examined ex post facto within the individual circumstances of a specific case, cannot provide a basis for governmental power to violate individual rights and freedoms.

Notwithstanding the criticism, the government decided to adopt the commission's recommendations. The commission's unpublished guidelines provided the basis for the interrogation practices of the GSS.

Stage 3: Landau Commission guidelines

Fate would have it that the first intifada began a short time after publication of the Landau Report. Three years later, the B'Tselem report of Cohen and Golan-Agnon was published. This report showed that not only had the Landau report not put a stop to use of force in interrogations, but it had, in fact, provided legitimization for interrogation methods that could fairly be described as torture. These methods were certainly not restricted to 'ticking-bomb' situations, but had become widespread in interrogation of Palestinian detainees.[25]

Several attempts were made to challenge both the legality of various interrogation methods used by the security services and the Landau Commission's legal theory on the basis of which the authorities sought to justify these methods.[26] In many of the petitions, counsel applied not only for rulings on the legality of the interrogation methods allegedly being used against their clients, but for interim injunctions against use of these methods until the case had been decided. In most of these cases, the authorities claimed that they had no intention of using the methods or that the interrogation had ended. The court therefore stated that there was no need to issue an interim injunction.[27] However, in a few cases, the authorities objected to interim injunctions against use of force, and in some cases even applied for revocation of an injunction that had been issued.[28] After being shown privileged evidence, the court in these cases either refused to grant the injunction or revoked an existing injunction, thus intimating that use of force was not necessarily unlawful in all circumstances. The court did indeed state that failure to grant an injunction did not imply that the authorities could act unlawfully, but this caveat was meaningless when the very question before the court was whether the approach and guidelines of the Landau Commission on which the authorities relied were compatible with domestic and international legal norms.

After the interim injunctions were refused or revoked, the petitions in the above cases were left pending. A significant number of additional petitions by interrogatees were submitted. These were joined by petitions submitted by human rights NGOs that tried once again to challenge the legal theory on which the Landau Commission based its justification of 'special' methods of interrogation, including use of moderate physical force.

Some of the petitions were submitted in 1994, 1995 and 1996. The court held a number of hearings on these petitions but dragged its feet and refrained from finalizing the hearings and delivering judgment. In the intermediate period, both the state of Israel and the Supreme Court itself were subject to severe criticism by domestic and international NGOs and by international forums for the methods used in interrogation.[29] Eventually, in September 1999, an expanded bench of nine justices, headed by the court's president, Justice Aharon Barak, delivered its opinion, which must be regarded as one of the most courageous ever delivered by the court.[30]

In its decision, the court mentioned the difficult situation the state of Israel faces in having to contain terror, and the authorities' claim that information extracted from some of the individual interrogatees had led to prevention of terrorist attacks. However, it accepted the legal arguments against use of force and other methods of pressure in interrogations. The court held that while necessity could conceivably serve as a defence in a specific criminal case, it does not arm the investigating authorities with the power needed to use 'special' methods of interrogation. As there was no other legal basis for such power, neither the government nor the GSS had the authority to 'lay down guidelines, rules or permits for use of physical means in the course of investigating those suspected of hostile terrorist activity'.

While the court ruled that specified interrogation practices of the GSS were illegal, it based its decision on formal grounds of the domestic legal system, namely that the interrogators had not been given statutory authority to depart from the usual rules of fair interrogation. The court mentioned standards of conventional international law, according to which all forms of torture and cruel, inhuman and degrading treatment or punishment are prohibited without exception, but refrained from stating whether all, or any, of the methods used by the authorities were covered by this prohibition. It specifically left open the possibility that the law would be changed by the Knesset, which could decide that the special security difficulties of the state justify legislation empowering use of physical force in interrogations, provided such legislation meets the demands of the Basic Law: Human Dignity and Liberty.[31]

More significantly, although it ruled that the necessity defence could not serve as legal authority for the interrogation methods used by the GSS, the court did not exclude the possibility that were unlawful interrogation methods to be used, in certain circumstances the interrogators could raise this defence against criminal liability. The court went even further and stated that its decision:

> does not negate the possibility that the 'necessity defense' will be available to GSS investigators – either in the choice made by the Attorney-General in deciding whether to prosecute, or according to the discretion of the court if criminal charges are brought.

Furthermore, the court stated that the Attorney-General could establish guidelines describing circumstances in which he would refrain from initiating criminal proceedings, when interrogators claimed to have acted from 'necessity'.

Stage 4: necessity guidelines

Initially, the Supreme Court's decision had an immediate and dramatic effect on interrogation practices. Some of the practices which the court had expressly ruled to be unlawful – 'shaking' the interrogatee or tying him to a low chair and playing loud noise – were abandoned.[32] However, based on the statement in the court's decision the Attorney-General issued guidelines, under which investigators would not face criminal prosecution if they used some forms of physical force in certain kinds of interrogations. The Attorney-General put the matter as follows:

> As long as the legal situation – following the High Court ruling – remains unchanged, the powers of the GSS investigators are those of police. They have no legal power or authority over and above those that a policeman may use in the course of a regular police interrogation....
>
> In cases in which, during an interrogation, an interrogator has used means of interrogation that were needed immediately in order to gain essential information for the purpose of preventing a concrete danger of severe harm to state security, human life, liberty or bodily integrity, where there was no other reasonable way in the circumstances of immediately obtaining the information, and where the means of interrogation used were reasonable in the circumstances to prevent the harm, the Attorney General will consider not opening criminal proceedings. The decision of the Attorney General will be given in each case on its merits, after examining all the above elements, namely, proportionality, the severity concreteness of the danger and the harm that was prevented, the alternatives and the proportionality of the means, including the perception of the interrogator at the time of the interrogation, the rank of the people who authorized the action, their involvement in the decision and their discretion when it was carried out, as well as the conditions of carrying out the act, the supervision over it and its documentation. The above shall not apply to any method of interrogation which amounts to 'torture', as defined in the Convention against Torture.[33]

As can be seen, this was obviously an attempt to have one's cake and eat it. There was, on the one hand, no legal authority to use force in interrogations; on the other hand, no sanction if an interrogator exceeded his authority and used force in some circumstances. There was a clear statement that methods that constitute 'torture' under

CAT are unacceptable in all circumstances, but, unlike the Landau Commission guidelines, no attempt to clarify the implications of this statement, vis-à-vis methods of interrogation used by the GSS. The matter is apparently left for the GSS to decide, with the possibility that ex post facto the Attorney-General will not accept their approach. It is therefore not surprising that despite the ruling (repeated by the Attorney-General) that the necessity defence could not serve as legal authorization to employ force in interrogations, in effect, the Attorney-General's guidelines on this defence serve as exactly that. Thus, a new concept, 'necessity interrogations', was born.

The second intifada started one year after the Supreme Court decision and with the general rise in violence and terror attacks on Israelis in Israel and the Occupied Territories, use of force in interrogations soon became prevalent again. In July 2002, the GSS admitted that it had employed 'necessity interrogations' in 90 cases which it regarded as 'ticking-bomb' cases.[34] An NGO report which examined the situation from September 2001 to April 2003 concluded that physical force, shackling the detainee, sleep deprivation and other forms of abuse had become common.[35] The Attorney-General had not opened criminal proceedings in any cases.[36] The Supreme Court has so far resisted all attempts to subject the legality of these practices to judicial review.

Some general conclusions

Where does this lead us? If we are serious about preventing torture, the absolute prohibition on its use must be maintained. Any other solution, meant only for the most extreme 'ticking-bomb' situations, will inevitably undermine the core of the prohibition and pave the way for use of force and other forms of physical and mental abuse that could constitute torture in a large number of cases that cannot possibly all be ticking-bomb situations. The legal situation has to be clear and it has to be approached from two angles:

1 Interrogators do not have the legal authority to use force or other forms of physical or psychological abuse that constitute torture or cruel, inhuman or degrading treatment.

2 Use of force in interrogations incurs criminal liability and interrogators who use force will be subject to the criminal process.

The idea that one can avoid this situation by claiming that interrogators do not have authority to use force, but will be protected from criminal prosecution if they do so in 'appropriate cases', also seems doomed to failure and will probably lead to the criminal liability escape clause becoming the de facto grounds for legal authority to use force. This is especially so in a society in which the threat of terrorist attacks is quite real, and the tendency of the prosecuting authorities to 'display understanding' for the difficult situation of those responsible for protecting the public is to be expected.

But what of the real 'ticking-bomb' situation? Do the above rules hold there too?

There is no 'legal' way to resolve this question. One could, of course, argue that interrogators must stick to the prohibition, even in a real ticking-bomb situation (however rare that may be). According to this view, even in such a situation the authorities should refrain from any irregular interrogation practices that may cause severe pain or suffering to the captured terrorist who refuses to divulge the information necessary to find and neutralize the bomb. It must be appreciated, however, that the implications of such an approach are twofold:

1 that if asked in real time for instructions for how to act in a concrete ticking-bomb situation, the answer has to be: refrain from any use of force and if the bomb goes off – so be it

2 that if unlawful force is used, those responsible will be prosecuted and punished *even if they were successful in obtaining the information necessary to neutralize the bomb.*

If we exclude the second possibility we are necessarily undermining the force of the absolute prohibition.

Given the reluctance of most commentators to accept the implications of maintaining the moral prohibition even in a real ticking-bomb situation, there are only two other possibilities. One is to try to regulate use of force so as to allow for a ticking-bomb exception. It seems to me that the Israeli experience reveals the dangers of such a solution. The term 'ticking bomb' will no longer be taken to refer to an extremely rare scenario which, while possible, is highly improbable, but will become the code word for those situations in which the authorities believe that it is important to obtain information immediately. The exception designed for the extremely rare case will be extended, until it becomes the rule in a wide range of interrogations.

We are therefore left with the final, and imperfect, solution. It is the one suggested by Henry Shue:

An act of torture ought to remain illegal so that anyone who sincerely believes such an act to be the least available evil is placed in the position of needing to justify his or her act morally in order to defend himself or herself legally. The torturer should be in roughly the same position as someone who commits civil disobedience. Anyone who thinks an act of torture is justified should have no alternative but to convince a group of peers in a public trial that all necessary conditions for a morally permissible act were indeed satisfied. If it is reasonable to put someone through torture, it is reasonable to put someone else through a careful explanation of why. If the solution approximates those in the imaginary examples in which torture seems possible to justify, a judge can surely be expected to suspend the sentence. Meanwhile, there is little need to be concerned about possible injustice to torturers and great need to find means to restrain totally unjustified torture.[37]

Notes

1 See B'Tselem, The Israeli Information Center for Human Rights in the Occupied Territories, *The Interrogation of Palestinians During the Intifada: Ill-Treatment, 'Moderate Physical Pressure' or Torture*? (March 1991) available at www.btselem.org/Download/199103_Torture_Eng.doc (visited 22 June 2006).

2 Thus, for example, while finding that in most cases detainees subjected to harsh interrogation (in their estimate about 20 per cent of the detainees who were not released within 18 days of their arrest) were subjected to beatings, they found no 'evidence, of special implements or machinery for inflicting pain' (*ibid*.: 86).

3 See B'Tselem, The Israeli Information Center for Human Rights in the Occupied Territories, *The Interrogation of Palestinians During the Intifada: Follow-up to March 1991 B'Tselem Report*, Jerusalem, March 1992.

4 See, for example, Amnesty International, *Annual Report for 1996*, (available at www.amnesty.org/ailib/aireport/ar97/introsum.html), in which the organization reported that it had recorded cases of torture or ill-treatment in at least 124 countries, although it believed the real figures to be much higher.

5 See Oren Gross, 'The prohibition on torture and the limits of law', in Sanford Levinson (ed.) (2004) *Torture, A Collection*, Oxford: Oxford University Press, p. 232.

6 See US Department of Justice, Office of Legal Counsel, Memo *Re: Standards of Conduct for Interrogation* (otherwise known as the 'Torture Memo'), 1 August 2002, available at www.washingtonpost.com/wp-srv/nation/documents/dojinterrogationmemo20020801.pdf (visited 22 June 2006). For

a devastating critique of this memo, see Jose Alvarez, 'Torturing the law', *Case Western Journal of International Law* (2006) 37: 175. The original memo was withdrawn in December 2004: see US Department of Justice, Office of Legal Counsel, Memo *Re: Legal Standards Applicable Under 18 U.S.C. §§2340-2340A* (otherwise known as the 'Levin Memo'), 30 December 2004 available www.usdoj.gov/olc/dagmemo.pdf (visited 22 June 2006).

7 See Alan M. Dershowitz, *Why Terrorism Works: Understanding the Threat, Responding to the Challenge*, New Haven, CT: Yale University Press, 2002.

8 See Mirko Bagaric and Julie Clarke, 'Not enough official torture in the world? the circumstances in which torture is morally justifiable', *University of San Francisco Law Review*, (2005) 39: 581.

9 See, e.g., *Torture, A Collection*, note 5, *supra*; Karen J. Greenberg (ed.), *The Torture Debate in America*, Cambridge University Press, 2006; Kenneth Roth and Minky Worden (eds), *Torture. Does It Make Us Safer? Is It Ever OK? A Human Rights Perspective*, New York: Human Rights Watch, 2006.

10 See, e.g., 'Editorial: legalizing torture', *Washington Post*, 9 June 2004; Joseph Lelyveld, 'Interrogating ourselves', *New York Times Sunday Magazine*, 12 June 2005; Evan Thomas and Michael Hirsch, 'The debate over torture', *Newsweek*, 21 November 2005; Clive Coleman, 'Why ticking-bomb torture stinks', *The Times*, 5 January 2006.

11 See *Regina v. Bartle and the Commissioner of Police for the Metropolis and Others* (*ex parte Pinochet*) [1999] 2 W.L.R. 827.

12 The best discussion of this argument may be found in Daniel Statman, 'The question of the absoluteness of the moral prohibition on torture', *Mishpat Umimshal* (1997) 4: 161 (in Hebrew).

13 See David Luban, 'Liberalism, torture, and the ticking bomb', (2005) 91 *Virginia Law Review* 1495, reprinted in Karen J. Greenberg (ed.), *The Torture Debate in America*, Cambridge University Press, 2006, p. 35.

14 See the essays of Henry Shue, Michael Walzer, Jean Bethke Elshtain and Elaine Scarry in *Torture: A Collection*, note 5, *supra*.

15 See Stephen Holmes, 'Is defiance of law a proof of success? Magical thinking in the war on terror', in *The Torture Debate in America*, p. 118, at pp. 127–8. Also see Coleman, note 10, *supra*.

16 A lot depends, of course, on how one defines the real 'ticking-bomb' case. In his article (note 12, *supra*) Daniel Statman argues that there could be a case that torture is morally acceptable only when we are certain that: 1. there is indeed a ticking bomb that will explode if we do not defuse it; 2. that the person in our hands was responsible for laying it; 3. that if that person provides us with the required information we will be able to defuse the bomb; 4. that using torture will indeed induce him to provide us with that information; 5. that other methods of interrogation will not be successful; and 6. that there is no other way of finding and defusing the bomb.

17 See 'Israel and torture: an insight inquiry', *Sunday Times*, 19 June 1977.

18 See Roy Reed, 'Israelis deny a London paper's charges of torture', *New York Times*, 2 July 1977, p. 3.

19 See *Ireland v. U.K.* (1978) 2 EHHR 25.

20 See Eyal Benvenisti, 'The role of national courts in preventing torture of suspected terrorists', *European Journal of International Law*, (1997) 8: 596.

21 See Mark Bowden, 'The dark art of interrogation', *Atlantic Monthly*, October 2003.

22 See Report of Commission of Inquiry into the Methods of Investigation of the GSS Regarding Hostile Terrorist Activities (the Landau Report), Jerusalem, October 1987. Parts of the Report were published in *Israel Law Review* (1989), 23: 146 *et seq*.

23 For a series of articles criticizing the Landau Report, see *Israel Law Review* (1989), 23: 192–406.

24 See Arnold Enker, 'The use of physical force in interrogations and the necessity defence', in Center for Human Rights, Hebrew University of Jerusalem, *Symposium on Israel and International Human Rights Law: The Issue of Torture* (1995), available at http://humrts.huji.ac.il/rodley.htm at p.6. This view was later developed by Miriam Gur-Arye, 'Can the war on terror justify the use of force in interrogations? Reflections in light of the Israeli experience', in *Torture: A Collection*, note 5, *supra* p. 183. This is not a mere technical difference. The necessity defence could possibly be raised even if force were used against a person who was not responsible for the impending explosion/attack; self-defence would be restricted to action against the person who had created the danger.

25 *The Interrogation of Palestinians During the Intifada*, note 1, *supra*.

26 In *Salkhaht* v. *Government of Israel* (1991) 47 PD IV 837, the court dismissed a petition challenging the legality of the Landau Commission guidelines on the grounds that the issue could not be decided in the framework of a general petition, but would have to be resolved in a case challenging validity of a confession extracted by use of the 'special' interrogation methods, or one in which a member of the security services was charged with acting illegally. This decision was a way of avoiding the issue. The court's reasoning was totally removed from reality. Once the Landau Commission had let the cat out of the bag, the authorities would not use confessions extracted by force in criminal proceedings. If an interrogator acted on the basis of the guidelines, he would not be charged.

27 See, e.g., *Hassan* v. *General Security Service* (1995) 42 Dinim-Elyon 83; *Kamal* v. *Minister of Defense* (1997), unreported decision of 23 June 1997 in H.C.3802/97; *Korahn* v. *Minister of Defense* (1997), unreported decision of 8 January 1998 in H.C. 7628/97 (the last two decisions may be found on the home page of the Supreme Court: www.court.gov.il). In the last case, the authorities declared that they were not using the methods mentioned by the petitioner 'at this stage'. And see Kremnitzer and Segev, 'Using force during interrogations', *Mishpat Umimshal*, (1998) 4: 667, 671–5.

28 See *Balebisi* v. *General Security Service*, 1995 (1) Takdin-Elyon 1634; *Khamdan* v. *General Security Service*, 1996 (3) Takdin-Elyon 1018; *Mubarak* v. *General Security Service*, 1996 (3) Takdin-Elyon 1013.

29 See, for example, the *Report of the UN Special Rapporteur on Torture*, E/CN.4/1999/61, para. 394, in which the special rapporteur refers to the court's positions and states that he 'is also bound to note that administration

of justice in these formally authorized practices can only tend to corrode the integrity of those organs, whose traditional commitment to the rule of law and human rights have in the past been internationally respected'. Also see *Conclusions and Recommendations of the Committee against Torture*, A/53/44, paras. 232–42; *Concluding Observations of the Human Rights Committee*, CCPR/C/79/Add. 93, para. 19.

30 See *Public Committee Against Torture in Israel* v. *Government of Israel* (1999), English translation available at http://elyon1.court.gov.il/files_ eng/94/000/051/a09/94051000.a09.pdf. The decision deals with two petitions submitted by the NGOs and five petitions submitted by individual interrogatees.

31 Given the reasoning of the court and the prohibition of torture in international law, it seems highly unlikely that Knesset legislation that sanctioned torture or cruel or inhuman treatment would stand up to judicial review. An internal committee was established by the government to examine the possibility of proposing legislation, but there was fierce opposition to such legislation in the Ministry of Justice and no legislation was proposed.

32 See Public Committee Against Torture in Israel, *Flawed Defense: Torture and Ill-Treatment in GSS Interrogations Following the Supreme Court Ruling, 6 September 1999 – 6 September 2001* (Jerusalem, September 2001) available at www.stoptorture.org.il//eng/images/uploaded/publications/13.doc.

33 Attorney-General, 'Investigations by the GSS and the defence of necessity – framework for discretion of the Attorney General (following High Court judgement)', Jerusalem, 28 October 1999 (on file with the author).

34 See Public Committee Against Torture in Israel, *Back to a Routine of Torture: Torture and Ill-Treatment of Palestinian Detainees During Arrest, Detention and Interrogation September 2001 – April 2003*, p. 9–10, available at www. stoptorture.org.il//eng/images/uploaded/publications/58.pdf.

35 *Ibid.*

36 *Ibid.*

37 Henry Shue, *Torture: A Collection*, note 5, *supra*, pp. 58–9. For an attempt to place this argument in a legal framework see Oren Gross, 'Are torture warrants warranted? Pragmatic absolutism and official disobedience', *Minnesota Law Review*, (2004) 88: 1481.

Chapter 12

Death, denial, discourse: on the forms and functions of American capital punishment

David Garland

The death penalty in America today is a peculiar institution for which we lack an adequate sociological account. The institutional arrangements that have grown up there over the last 40 years appear to put the state, law and lethal violence into a new and strange relation. Yet, our standard explanations are borrowed from historical accounts that were generated to explain the role of capital punishment several centuries ago. We have not yet developed analyses that can explain the distinctive forms and functions that define the contemporary institution.

The theoretical frameworks that predominate in the sociology of punishment have little to tell us about the particulars of contemporary capital punishment. When sociologists write about capital punishment, they mostly draw on the work of historians such as Vic Gatrell (1994) or Douglas Hay (1975), who write about the eighteenth and nineteenth centuries, or else upon the theoretical ideas of Émile Durkheim (1983), which associate capital punishment with pre-modern penal regimes. Above all, they draw upon the work of Michel Foucault (1977), which, as I will argue, is singularly ill-fitted to understanding the modern American institution.

The effect of this theoretical orientation is to produce an implicit conception of contemporary capital punishment (where it still exists in the developed world) as a vestigial phenomenon. The modern death penalty is regarded as a relic of an earlier age, a near-extinct practice, badly adapted to its environment, teetering on the edge of extinction. For some American commentators, this anachronistic, residual, status is what accounts for the apparent dysfunctions and irrationalities of the institution (Laqueur 2000). If capital punishment persists in a few modern democratic societies, it does so as a result of some kind of inertia or lag effect. It is a product of the past, not the present, and its destiny is soon to disappear. That this view fits comfortably with the normative sentiments of most sociologists ensures that its underlying assumptions are not too often questioned. The consequence of this neglect is that a number of explanatory puzzles await our attention.

Look, for example, at the 'violence' of American capital punishment. It is real enough, and lethal. Individuals are put to death, killed by judicial order. An execution must count as a pretty serious form of violence. But the death penalty's form, its techniques, and its performative characteristics tend to work against that connotation. The death penalty is administered in ways that seek to deny its violence, to disguise its force, and to efface its physicality. Executions are represented as painless medical procedures. Their bodily aspects are minimized, their intrinsic violence obscured.

But even if we insist, against the grain of the institution, on exposing the execution's violence (and opponents insist that even the lethal injection entails severe physical pain which is all the worse for being invisible – see *Hill* v. *McDonough* 2006), we have to admit that this violence is actually a minor part of what one might call the practice of capital punishment. For the most part, American capital punishment is not about executions (which are now relatively rare – more Americans are killed each year by lightning). It is about mounting campaigns, taking polls, passing laws, bringing charges, bargaining pleas, imposing sentences, and rehearing cases. It is about threats rather than deeds, anticipated deaths rather than actual executions. What gets performed, for the most part, is discourse and debate. From the point of view of the system, the discreet violence of the execution is a necessary underpinning, but not the thing itself. Capital punishment is like a credit system with a high volume of circulating value underwritten by a gold standard that is only occasionally cashed out.

Look, as well, at 'the state' in the capital punishment process. This is another defining element that is somehow hidden beneath the surface of things. If one attends to events, to spoken and written discourse, even to symbols and rhetoric, it turns out that 'the state' (in the proper, European sense of the term) is virtually absent. One sees, instead, the repeated invocation of 'the law' and of 'the people'. Capital punishment is all about the law, the Constitution and the jury, or else it is about the electorate, public opinion, and democracy. When it comes to judicial executions, America's killing state is nowhere to be seen.

And what about the institution's social function? Can we suppose that the American death penalty is undertaken as an instrument of crime control and social ordering? Is it a means of reducing crime, upholding law, and keeping Americans orderly? That seems unlikely.

Even if one were to accept, for the sake of argument, that penal institutions play a substantial role in the reproduction of social order, it is hard to believe that a penalty which affects so few people could have a major structural impact of that kind. Only a tiny minority of homicide defendants ever face capital charges and only about 120 are now sentenced to death each year. Compared to the tens of millions of offenders who are sentenced to imprisonment or penal supervision each year (Garland 2001a; Western 2006), capital punishment's impact on social order is liable to be vanishingly small.

These, it seems to me, are paradoxes that should invite sociological attention.

Peculiarities of form and function

Let me begin by highlighting more systematically some of the specific characteristics of the American system that stand in need of explanation.

Notice that I define my object of study not as 'the death penalty' or 'executions' but as the 'capital punishment complex' – by which I mean the whole set of discursive and non-discursive practices through which capital punishment is enacted and experienced, both within criminal justice and in society more generally. And the question I pose is not, 'why is the death penalty retained in America?' (for a critique of this approach, see Garland 2005a), but 'How does today's capital punishment come to be enacted through these specific forms and concrete practices with these particular meanings?'

The anomalous nature of American retention

Even if we put aside all notions of 'exceptionalism' and studiously avoid the idea that Europe's experience should be regarded as some kind of historical norm, it remains puzzling that America – the supposed home of democracy, due process, limited government and individual freedom – should persist in retaining a 'killing state' in a context of widespread abolitionism. The anomaly of American capital punishment in the twenty-first century is as much an internal one as a comparative one.

The labyrinthine legal structures

The capital punishment process is now overlaid by a set of rules and procedures that is more complex and elaborate than any other in the American legal order (or in any other legal order for that matter). This dense maze of procedural requirements ensures that any particular case will be constantly delayed and deferred so that an average of 12 years will elapse between sentence and execution.[1] The same complex laws – together with competent legal counsel who arrive, if they arrive at all, rather late in the process – ensure that, in the end, 66 per cent of all capital sentences will eventually be reversed prior to execution (Liebman 2000). As a consequence, completed death sentences – i.e., executions – are very rare. In recent years, only 50 or 60 executions occur in the USA annually – this, in a nation where more than 3,400 inmates sit on death row and 12,000 death-penalty-liable homicides occur every year.

Varieties of capital punishment

What we call 'capital punishment' exists in a variety of ontological forms – as a law on the books, as a sentencing practice, and as a practice of judicial execution. States like New Hampshire have the law on the books but do not impose death sentences; states like New Jersey impose sentences but have not carried out an execution since the 1960s; states like California impose many death sentences but execute only a few of them; and states like Texas, Oklahoma and Virginia have the law, impose sentences, and carry out frequent executions. Then there are the 12 states in which capital punishment does not exist.

Geographies of capital punishment

The ontology of capital punishment maps onto a specific geography (Harries and Cheatwood 1997). Abolitionist states are concentrated in the northern tier of the country, mixed states in the middle tier, and execution states are heavily concentrated in the South. Since the reintroduction of capital punishment in 1976, Southern states have carried out more than 70 per cent of all American executions. Texas alone accounts for more than one-third of the 1,000 executions that have taken place in that period.

Jury sentencing

The decision to impose death – which is quite separate from the decision to convict the defendant of capital murder – is made not by a judge, or even by the application of a legal rule, but by a jury of laypeople who are given discretion to decide thumbs up or thumbs down. The composition of the jury, the prejudices of the jurors, and the narrative skills of defence counsel, therefore, become crucial determinants of the outcome.

Victim involvement

Since the Supreme Court's decision in *Payne* v. *Tennessee* in 1991, murder victims' relatives have been entitled to present 'victim impact statements' to the jury as part of the penalty-phase proceedings. Typically, these statements present an emotionally wrenching account of the personal suffering and private grief produced by the crime.

Racial disparities

In the modern American legal system, laws are facially race neutral and race discrimination is strictly prohibited. Nevertheless, racial disparities are routinely produced by the death-penalty process. Research consistently shows that race, social class and the quality of legal counsel are the chief factors that structure outcomes, with the result that poorly represented blacks, convicted of atrocious crimes, against white victims, are the group most likely to be executed (Ogletree and Sarat 2006).

Peculiarities of the execution protocol

The staging of the event
In the rare cases when a sentence is actually executed, these executions are low-visibility events, hidden from the public, usually in a special death chamber deep in a state prison.

The execution technology
The actual execution is carefully arranged to ensure the minimum possible physical suffering: a zero degree of explicit violence. Any visible signs of pain are regarded as a failure. Instead of torture and bodily torments, there is medical solicitude and sedation.

The performative aspects
The event itself is organized not as a public ceremony but as a bureaucratically managed procedure emphasizing speed and no-nonsense efficiency. It is anti-theatrical, lacking much in the way of ritual, ceremonial, or deliberate symbolism. Communication is suppressed, photographs are prohibited, and the event is minimally reported – unless something goes wrong, in which case the state authorities are the subject of criticism. In the physical process of killing, the authorities seek to avoid any spectacle, but to the extent that some display is inevitable, they aim to display restraint rather than excess, bureaucratic efficiency rather than unseemly violence (Trombley 1993; Johnson 1997; Sarat 2001).

Capital punishment as discourse

Finally, and to return to a point hinted at earlier, there is a striking imbalance between the amount of capital punishment talk and the amount of capital punishment action. The 'death penalty' is invoked in political discourse, legal discourse, and moral discourse to an extent that is quite out of keeping with its practical importance. And, of course, talk about and images of capital punishment are prominent features of the mass media and the entertainment zone of modern culture.

How should we think about these peculiar forms and characteristics? As I stated at the beginning, sociologists have yet to produce a developed, grounded account of modern capital punishment and its peculiar forms. But in the absence of anything better, one of the accounts that is repeatedly invoked is that of Michel Foucault, so I begin by discussing the Foucauldian interpretation.

Foucault on sovereign power and the spectacle of the scaffold

In his famous account of the execution of Robert Damiens in 1757, Foucault (1977) offers us a powerful model of capital punishment – an archetypal image that has shaped much thinking about the subject ever since. Here is the passage that opens *Discipline and Punish*:

> On 2 March 1757 Damiens the regicide was condemned to 'make the *amende honorable* before the main door of the Church of Paris', where he was to be 'taken and conveyed in a cart, wearing nothing but a shirt, holding a torch of burning wax weighing more than two pounds'; then, 'in the said cart, to the Place de Grève where, on a scaffold that will be erected there, the flesh will be torn from his breasts, arms, thighs and calves with red-hot pincers, his right hand, holding the knife with which he committed the said parricide, burnt with sulphur, and, on those places where the flesh will be torn away, poured molten lead, boiling oil, burning resin, wax and sulphur melted together and then his body drawn and quartered by four horses and his limbs and body consumed by fire, reduced to ashes and his ashes drawn to the winds (Foucault 1977: 3).

I could go on, but I suspect there is no need. Everyone knows this passage. It is fixed in the theoretical imagination. In this account of Damien's destruction, Foucault theorizes capital punishment as a ritual of 'sovereign state power' – a public ceremony in which state actors utilize spectacular violence and an offender's body to display the force and majesty of state power. Capital punishment is a means whereby the sovereign seeks to create submission, obedience and social order. It is an exemplary act that asserts a monopoly claim over violence.

Foucault puts it thus:

> The public execution is to be understood not only as a judicial, but also as a political ritual. It belongs, even in minor cases, to the ceremonies by which power is manifested (Foucault 1977: 47).

> The right to punish ... is an aspect of the sovereign's right to make war on his enemies (Foucault 1977: 48).

> The public execution ... has a juridico-political function. It is a ceremonial by which a momentarily injured sovereignty is reconstituted. It restores that sovereignty by manifesting it at its most spectacular. The public execution, however hasty and everyday, belongs to a whole series of great rituals in which power is eclipsed and restored (Foucault 1977: 48–9).

We should note that, for Foucault, the sovereign state is the principal actor in this scene. It is the unmoved mover, provoked by the insult of the criminal's offence, but obedient to no one outside of itself. It follows that 'the people' have merely an auxiliary part in this drama, as onlookers and consumers. They may be supporters, but they are in no way essential.

> Here is what he says: 'The people also had a right to take part ... The vengeance of the people was called upon to become an unobtrusive part of the vengeance of the sovereign. Not that it was in any way fundamental, or that the king had to express in his own way the people's revenge; it was rather that the people had to bring its assistance to the king' (Foucault 1977: 59).

Foucault on modern capital punishment

Foucault does not address the modern American death penalty of course, but France continued to decapitate offenders by guillotine right up to 1977 and in a variety of interviews, in *Discipline and Punish*, and in *The History of Sexuality: Volume I*, Foucault offered analyses of the changing form of capital punishment as it evolved in modern France.

As we will see, many of Foucault's descriptive observations fit well with today's American system and illuminate it to some degree. But I will argue that his theoretical insistence on seeing capital punishment as an act of state sovereignty severely limits the value of his analysis when applied to the present. First, the descriptive account:

Foucault describes a shift from the imposition of death to the deprivation of life. He stresses the new way in which this measure is now carried out, the shift from a painful, atrocious death to a simple extinguishing of life:

'The guillotine takes life almost without touching the body' (Foucault 1977:13).[2] He emphasizes what he calls 'judicial reticence' and the avoidance of pain: 'When the moment of execution approaches, the patients are injected with tranquillizers. A utopia of judicial reticence: take away life, but prevent the patient from feeling it; deprive the prisoner of all rights, but do not inflict pain' (Foucault 1977: 11).

Finally, he notes a shift from spectacle to secret procedure:

In the end, the guillotine had to be placed within prison walls and made inaccessible to the public ... the scaffold was hidden ... Witnesses who described the scene could ... be prosecuted, thereby ensuring that the execution should cease to be a spectacle and remain a strange secret between the law and those it condemns (p. 15).

The modern rituals of execution attest to this double process: the disappearance of the spectacle and the elimination of pain (Foucault 1977: 11).

Later, in the *History of Sexuality: Volume I*, he returns to this phenomenon and offers an explanation of sorts. He explains the changes in the penalty's form by reference to the conflict between the 'sovereign' form of rule and the 'bio-politics' of the twentieth-century welfare state:

As soon as power gave itself the function of administering life, its reason for being and the logic of its exercise – and not the awakening of humanitarian feelings – made it more and more difficult to apply the death penalty (Foucault 1978: 138).

For such a power (bio-power, welfarism) execution was at the same time a limit, a scandal and a contradiction. Hence capital punishment could not be maintained except by invoking less the enormity of the crime itself than the monstrosity of the criminal, his incorrigibility ... [In a bio-power regime] one had the right to kill those who represented a kind of biological threat to others (Foucault 1978: 138).

So the death penalty changes its form, changes its rationale, and is used less frequently. But none of this causes Foucault to doubt his axiomatic premise that the death penalty is to be understood as an exemplification of sovereign state power.

My final quotation is taken from an article he wrote in 1981, on the occasion of capital punishment's abolition in France: 'If death figured at the apex of the criminal justice system for so many centuries, this was not because the lawmakers and judges were especially sanguinary people. The reason was that justice was the exercise of sovereignty' (Foucault 2001: 459).

For Foucault, the modern twentieth-century death penalty is, as it ever was, an act of sovereign power, though one that is restrained and subdued by its new context of operation. From beginning to end, his view on this is consistent.

Foucault, sovereignty, and the American polity

Let us try to conceptualize the American death penalty using Foucault's model. Capital punishment in twenty-first-century America is an entirely state-administered process, conducted in strict accordance with state and federal law, and carried out by state functionaries. The authority of state law and the force of state power is what guarantees the sanction. In that formal-legal sense, it fits the Foucauldian model.

And Foucault makes many observations about modern capital punishment that are exactly right as descriptive claims – the embarrassment about violence, the avoidance of the body, the 'reticence' of the judges, the dangerousness of the criminal, and so on.

But these are descriptive observations without any theoretical underpinning. Foucault does not tell us why, if judges and state officials are so embarrassed, they nevertheless persist in using capital punishment. Unlike Émile Durkheim (1984), he does not have any theory of the social and psychic forces that push legislatures and courts to enact and apply capital punishment despite their apparent 'reticence'. He does not offer any analysis of sovereign power in a democratic state. His only explanation of why the death penalty persists within a modern 'politics of life' is that 'sovereignty' somehow demands capital punishment – though there are large numbers of nation states in the world that somehow do without it, as has the French state since 1981.

Nor does this 'sovereignty theory' have an easy relation to American practices and institutions. The American death penalty is never a straightforward assertion of untrammelled concentrated sovereign power – there is no such power in the USA. The process of producing an execution is always conflicted, with competing authorities pressing against one another. Sovereignty is not 'expressed' in these processes; it is asserted, contested and divided.

In these matters at least, the American state is not just a divided, pluralistic state. It is also a self-effacing state – it prefers to disappear into the concepts of 'the people' and 'the law'. In administering the death penalty, it always points to the jury, the victims, the public, the electorate, the people, as the real principals of the action. It is merely their dutiful agent. It does their bidding, taking care to observe the rules and due process of law. The state authorities represent themselves as the people's servants, dutifully carrying out a democratic legal mandate.[3]

Here I want to draw a distinction between form and substance that may prove useful for our understanding. American state officials, in dialogue with courts of law (and in alliance with cultural elites) can shape the *form* of capital punishment – its execution protocols, its killing techniques, the legal procedures that lead up to it, its official representation, etc. These forms and processes are within their control. And they have shaped these forms in ways that are familiar to any observer of the modern history of death penalty reform, rendering it more refined, more restrained, and more tightly controlled – that is to say, more compatible with a liberal democratic society in which state violence is problematized and the individual person is deemed sacrosanct.

But these politico-legal elites have not controlled the *substance* and *incidence* of capital punishment: the decision whether to have it or not and the pattern of its imposition and distribution. These decisions they share with their constituencies and with the other political actors in electoral competition. They are therefore shaped, in large part, by the distinctive structures of political competition, of party organization, of judicial accountability, of criminal justice politics, and of elite/popular relations that prevail in the USA (Savelsberg 1994; King 1997; Pildes 2004).

In modern America, it is a mistake to view capital punishment as a relationship between a sovereign state and a disobedient subject,[4] or even between a penal state and a subordinate class. If we think of capital punishment as a sovereign act of state, we lose any sense of the political competition and the popular forces that drive decision-making. We lose sight of the political outcomes that reflect group conflicts and racial hierarchies. And we neglect the energy, the passions, the values and the pleasures that popular sentiment injects into the politics of capital punishment. Foucault has no theory of any of this. His framework leads us away from where most of the action is.

Let us look, instead, at a different historical image.

Public torture lynchings and the people's justice

Here is an eyewitness account of the lynching of Henry Smith that took place in Texas in 1893. Smith was a black man alleged to have raped and murdered a white female child.

> Arriving here [Paris, Texas] at 12 o'clock, the train was met by a surging mass of humanity 10,000 strong. The Negro was placed upon a carnival float in mockery of a king upon his throne, and, followed by an immense crowd, was escorted through the city so that all might see the most inhuman monster known in current history … His clothes were torn off piecemeal and scattered in the crowd, people catching the shreds and putting them away as mementos. The child's father, her brother, and two uncles then gathered about the Negro as he lay fastened to the torture platform and thrust hot irons into his quivering flesh. It was horrible – the man dying by torture in the midst of smoke from his own burning flesh. Every groan from the fiend, every contortion of his body was cheered by the thickly packed crowd of 10,000 persons, the mass of beings 600 yards in diameter, the scaffold being the center. After burning the feet and legs, the hot irons … were rolled up and down Smith's stomach, back and arms. Then the eyes were burned out and irons were thrust down his throat. The men of the [child's] family having wreaked vengeance, the crowd piled all kinds of combustible stuff around the scaffold, poured oil on it, and set it alight (quoted in Paterson 1999: 193).

The public torture lynching of Henry Smith was by no means a unique event. There were between three and four hundred such events in the South between 1890 and 1940, and several thousand other lynchings that proceeded with less cruelty, crowds and ceremony (Brundage 1993; Pfeiffer 2004; Garland 2005b).

These modern, medieval-style lynchings were not undertaken for the lack of a functioning criminal justice system. Public torture lynchings were a preferred alternative to 'official' justice, not a necessary substitute for it. All of the 'crimes' (they were, of course, merely *alleged* crimes) that were 'punished' this way were interracial atrocities. They were, in every case, crimes that would have been subject to the death penalty had the accused been tried and convicted within the official criminal process.

But for Southern lynch mobs, regular hangings were too good for these 'offenders', regular justice too respectful and too dignified. By reviving the ancient penalties – of torture, burning, dismemberment – the lynchers created an aggravated form of capital punishment, more terrible than official justice, and more nearly proportionate to the outrage produced by the black man's 'crimes'. The public torture lynching was invented, at the turn of the twentieth century, to communicate impassioned sentiments that could no longer be expressed in the official idiom of the criminal law, and to inflict a level of suffering that had long since been officially disavowed. The penal excess of these lynchings was not an accidental effect of a crowd getting carried away – it was at the very core of the event's penal purpose and political meaning. Let us pause to note some characteristics of these lynchings:[5]

1 They were enjoyed as good days out, as entertainments, both by the crowds who attended and by the consumers of photographic images and newspaper reports. The modern media was drawn to them immediately. Professional photographers set up shop at the scene of these lynchings and did a brisk business selling photo-souvenirs of the event. Newspaper reports appeared all across the country.

2 They gave a prominent role to the white victim of the alleged crime, and his or her kin and supporters. The offence involved in the criminal act remained personal, a private wrong to be avenged, not a legal violation to be sanctioned.

3 The object of punishment was an 'inhuman monster', not a disobedient subject or a political enemy. The lynch victim was outside the law, not a violator of it.

4 The atrocious, interracial crimes that the lynchings avenged provided good occasions for political mobilization. They helped forge alliances – between race radicals and lower-class whites. They created ideological associations – linking black males and violent crime. They legitimated racial violence by representing it as criminal punishment. They empowered some groups vis-à-vis others within the white community. They were political opportunities, not just for white against black, but for white against white.

5 In these lynchings we do not see a strong state asserting its power, but rather a group of people defying it. It is not a story of

sovereignty affirmed but rather sovereignty contested. The force being displayed is not the state's law but the mob's rule. If there is a 'sovereignty' being imagined and enacted here, it belongs to (groups of) the people, and not to the state.

6 The public torture lynching is a practical critique of official criminal justice. By their actions, and in the subsequent statements of their apologists, the mobs made clear their demand for harsher treatment for these particular 'criminals' and for these specific 'crimes'. The state's criminal justice was deemed too lenient, too slow, too uncertain, and altogether too respectful of the 'criminal' and his 'rights'.

7 The event is not an official ceremony but instead a popular carnival. It takes place not in the centres of national power but in the rural counties of the South far from the seat of central government.

8 The lynchings were explicitly violent and self-consciously uncivilized – the mob insisted on punishments that were widely regarded at the time as anachronistic and barbaric. That they scandalized liberal and elite opinion elsewhere was a large part of their local appeal.

9 They were openly and unashamedly racialized: they utterly rejected the law's commitments to equality and emphatically affirmed local norms of caste superiority.

10 They were open, public, communicative – what we would now call 'media events'. They invited crowds, encouraged photographs, generated postcards, supplied graphic material for newspaper reports and personal narratives. They put death into discourse and invested criminal punishment with drama and entertainment value.

Modern capital punishment and its relation to lynching

To return now, to contemporary capital punishment. Am I implying that capital punishment in modern America is, in fact, some kind of lynching? Not at all. Just the opposite. Capital punishment today is not a 'modern lynching': that would be another version of the vestigial theory.[6] Nor is it an instance of a sovereign state exercising its power. Neither one of these images captures the truth of the matter. But if we think of today's system in its relation to these two exemplars, we can see more clearly some of the tensions that structure it, giving rise to its peculiar forms and its specific functions.

The conflicts between national and local powers; between representatives and constituents; between social classes and racial groups; between North and South; between federal law and popular democracy; between personalistic power and bureaucratic authority – these are the tensions that have shaped the system over time and continue to structure the system today.

If we think of the capital punishment system in relation to these heuristic models, we notice that, in virtually every respect, the formal aspects of state-controlled capital punishment are the inverse of those we see in the lynchings – whether we consider staging, technology, performance, participation or communication.

Considered in *formal* terms, today's death penalty is a mirror image of a public torture lynching – an inverse institution, a disavowal, calculated to resist and deny any such association. But, *substantively*, many of the same social forces that previously prompted lynchings nowadays prompt capital punishment; many of the same social functions performed by lynching then are performed by capital punishment now; and much the same political structures that permitted lynchings then enable capital punishment now.

The inverse of the lynching

Today's capital punishment process is heavily proceduralized, legally regulated and federally controlled. The defendant's constitutional rights of due process are fastidiously upheld. Executions, where they occur, take place, in private, at a great distance from the crime in time and space. They are explicitly 'non-violent', solicitous, dispassionate, careful to avoid humiliation and degradation. Bureaucratic protocols ensure that crowds, cruelty and ceremony are reduced to a minimum.

The negative symmetry of this 'mirror-image' might lead one to suppose that the modern death penalty has been *designed* to be an anti-lynching – and there is some validity in this view. The modern American death penalty law has been forged over time by a series of struggles between the federal courts and the Southern states, whose too-summary, too-arbitrary and too-racist processes became the subject of constitutional litigation. The modern system's contours were marked by an effort to eliminate Southern practices of open racial violence and legal defiance.

Over the last 75 years, in one case after another, the federal courts have intervened in Southern state cases where black defendants have been sentenced to death for interracial crimes. From the Scottsboro Boys case of the 1930s (*Powell* v. *Alabama, Norris* v. *Alabama,* and *Patterson* v. *Alabama*) to Justice Goldberg's landmark dissent in *Rudolph* v. *Alabama* in 1963, to *Furman* v. *Georgia*, *Gregg* v. *Georgia*, and *Coker* v. *Georgia* in the 1970s and *McCleskey v. Kemp* in the 1980s – the constitutional history of twentieth-century capital punishment has been one of civil rights litigation alleging that Southern courts engaged in mob-dominated, racist, cruel and unusual practices. In the face of these constitutional claims, the federal courts responded (some of the time) by insisting upon procedural reforms and due process requirements.[7] For the most part, the states have folded these requirements into their process while continuing, nevertheless, to enact, impose and execute death penalties.

As a result of this struggle, the death penalty has been purged of its more egregious defects and cruelties. It has been domesticated, bureaucratized, sanitized and, above all, legalized. And yet it has not been abolished. It survives in 38 states and the federal government, and, in the period after 1976 – in the context of a new 'culture of control' – it has enjoyed a practical expansion and a political revival.

A detailed examination of the system reveals that it continues to have many substantive and distributive features in common with those lynchings that it does its best to disavow. It continues to be concentrated in the South – indeed, as Zimring (2003) and others have observed, the states that exhibited most lynching 100 years ago are the same ones that now have the most executions. It continues to be driven by local politics and populist politicians. It is imposed by juries, not judges, and to that extent remains a 'popular' punishment. It gives a special place to victims and 'victim impact statements', implicitly concerning itself with private vengeance as well as public order. Racial hatreds and caste distinctions, together with the passions aroused by atrocious crimes, still provide much of its energy. Its supporters still insist that regular punishment is too good for 'the worst of the worst' and that only death can sufficiently mark the enormity of their crimes. And, of course, it continues to produce false accusations (look at the faces of the exonerated) and racialized outcomes (Ogletree and Sarat 2006).

Moreover, the collective killing of hated criminals (or merely the assertion of the right to do so) remains one of the ways in which groups of people express their autonomy, invoke traditional values, and assert their local identity. The death of demonized others – and the discourse and drama that it permits – also makes news, gives pleasure, and functions in a variety of practical contexts.

Conclusion

With respect to America at least, we should not view capital punishment as a relationship between a sovereign state and a disobedient subject, or even between a penal state and a subordinate class. We need to view it, as well, as a matter of group relations (involving conflicts of race, class, region and religion), of popular pressures on state actors, of contests over sovereignty, and of strategic choices by political actors – all of which are structured by definite political processes and specific institutional arrangements.

We need an account that attends to the tensions between the popular demand for *penal excess* (with all of its political uses) and the governmental commitment to *penal restraint* (which allows state violence to appear restrained, rule-governed, and above all, 'legitimate').

These tensions – which are generic features of any democratic society – are played out today within the distinctive structures of the American polity and contain within themselves the peculiar history of America's group relations, its laws and its patterns of violence.

Viewed from the outside, from the perspective of other nations, America is a military, economic and political superpower, the strongest nation state in world history. But viewed as a domestic power, the American state is weak, divided, contested at every level, often incapable of effective, concentrated, action. Spread across a whole continent, the central government's writ does not always run. Peripheries and localities remain powerful. As a violent, killing state – and as a *penal state* – the USA is unmatched in its power; as a *social state*, it is weaker and more contested than most.

This is partly the story of America's founding and its Constitution. The American nation state was designed to be weak so that the local powers, including Southern slave-owning powers, could be strong. Government has been restrained and limited so that popular power could prevail. This restricted state formation has had effects right from the start, notably in failing to completely disarm and pacify the population, and failing to develop effective social institutions or forms of solidarity (Mennell forthcoming). A history of violence and insecurity has been one result. Another has been the fact that groups (above all, African-Americans) have been incompletely integrated, and social, regional, and religious divisions have been incompletely resolved by national policies. The long-term commitment to market individualism and minimal welfare has further weakened the ties that bind, and has established inequalities that are more pronounced than in comparable nations elsewhere.

The resort to violence (and, nowadays, to penal power) to resolve social problems is therefore somewhat over-determined – it is the strongest instrument readily available to the state (without need of coordination or cooperation), and it is often powerfully demanded by popular majorities, especially in situations where criminal violence causes insecurity or when a dominant group feels threatened by a subordinate one.

I have discussed some of the dynamics of capital punishment as a form of state violence. In particular, I have drawn attention to the representation of the state in this enactment of this violence (a representation that displaces the state and substitutes 'the law' and 'the people'). I have discussed the performative aspects of judicial killing (which are undertaken as an anti-performance, an effacement, a disappearing act). One thing I have not discussed is the *constitutive* effects of capital punishment. What does capital punishment create? What is the death penalty's productivity? What value does it produce and for whom? This is a properly Foucauldian question (to give a great thinker his due) and one that would take us into the uses of death penalty discourse in politics, in law, and above all, in the entertainment zone of the mass media and popular culture. But to answer that question would require a different chapter, one that might be titled 'Putting death into discourse – for power, pleasure, and profit'.

Notes

1 Unless otherwise noted, the Death Penalty Information Center website is the source for my factual claims about the American death penalty. See www.deathpenaltyinfo.org/.
2 'almost without touching the body' seems a very French perception. Anglo-American viewers might notice that decapitations cause blood to spurt and heads to roll. The lethal injection is a better illustration of Foucault's claim.
3 Hood (2002: 67) provides a good illustration of this when he quotes the US government response to the UN 6th Quinquennial. Survey in 2000: 'We believe that in democratic societies the criminal justice system – including the punishment for the most serious and aggravated crimes – should reflect the will of the people freely expressed and appropriately implemented through their elected representatives.'
4 My claim is not that sovereignty and capital punishment are unrelated. There is a deep historical association – dating from the formation of the first nation states – between the claim of sovereignty and the power to impose a penalty of death. And in situations where an uncertain sovereignty is being asserted – for example, in relations between post-colonial nations and former imperial powers – the death penalty can function as a demonstrative marker of sovereign power: the current debates about capital punishment in the Caribbean are an example of this. And when Supreme Court Justice Sandra Day O'Connor discussed the court's non-recognition of international norms rejecting the death penalty, she invoked America's 'national sovereignty interests' as the basis for the court's decision. But

where claims to sovereignty are not in doubt, as, for instance, in the French Republic in 1981, the death penalty can be abolished without prompting anxieties in this respect. An interesting case is the European Union, where new member nations who wish to 'pool' their sovereignty in the larger union must establish their eligibility by meeting certain preconditions, one of which is the abolition of capital punishment (Hood 2002: 67).

5 For a detailed discussion of these points, and reference to primary source evidence, see Garland 2005b.

6 For different accounts of the relationship between lynchings and contemporary capital punishment, see Jackson *et al.* (2001), Kaufman-Osborn (2006) and Vandiver (2006).

7 The court required that all capital defendants receive the meaningful assistance of counsel at trial, that the defendant's guilt be judged by a jury composed in a non-discriminatory fashion and that evidence of the defendant's guilt be reliable and not obtained through torture or the threat of lynching. In these cases, the court also established its ability, through the writ of *habeas corpus*, to review the judgements of state courts for any constitutional error (Klarman 2004; Murell 2006).

References

Brundage, W.F. (1993) *Lynching in the New South*. Chicago: University of Illinois Press.

Durkheim, E. (1983) 'Two laws of penal evolution', in S. Lukes and A. Scull (eds) *Durkheim and the Law*. Oxford: Martin Robertson.

Durkheim, E. (1984) *The Division of Labour in Society*. London: MacMillan.

Foucault, M. (1977) *Discipline and Punish*. London: Allen Lane.

Foucault, M. (1978) *The History of Sexuality Volume 1*. New York: Vintage.

Foucault, M. (2001) *Power: The Essential Works of Michel Foucault Volume 3* (ed.) J. Faubion *et al.* New York: New Press.

Garland, D. (ed) (2001a) *Mass Imprisonment: Social Causes and Consequences*. London: Sage.

Garland, D. (2001b) *The Culture of Control*. Oxford: Oxford University Press.

Garland, D. (2005a) 'Capital punishment and American culture', *Punishment and Society*, 7 (4): 347–76.

Garland, D. (2005b) 'Penal excess and surplus meaning: public torture lynchings in 20th century America', *Law and Society Review*, 39.

Gatrell, V. (1994) *The Hanging Tree: Execution and the English People 1770–1868*. Oxford: Oxford University Press.

Harries, K. and Cheatwood, D. (1997) *The Geography of Execution*. New York: Rowman and Littlefield.

Hay, D. (1975) 'Property, authority and the criminal law', in D. Hay *et al.* (eds) *Albion's Fatal Tree*. Harmondsworth: Penguin Books.

Jackson, J. Sr, Jackson, J. Jr, and Shapiro, B. (2001) *Legal Lynching: The Death Penalty and America's Future*. New York: New Press.

Johnson, R. (1997) *Death Work: A Study of the Modern Execution Process* (2nd edn). New York: Wadsworth.

Kaufman-Osborn, T. (2006) 'Capital punishment as legal lynching', in C. Ogletree and A. Sarat (eds) *From Lynch Mobs to the Killing State*. New York: NYU Press.

King, A. (1997) *Running Scared: Why America's Politicians Campaign Too Much and Govern Too Little*. New York: Free Press.

Klarman, M. (2004) *From Jim Crow to Civil Rights*. New York: Oxford University Press.

Laqueur, T. (2000) 'Festival of punishment', *London Review of Books*, 22 (19): 5 October.

Liebman, J. (2000) 'The overproduction of death', *Columbia Law Review*, 100: 2030–2156.

Mennell, S. (forthcoming) *The American Civilizing Process*. Oxford: Polity.

Murell, C. (2006) 'The dialogue about death' (unpublished class paper, on file with the author).

Ogletree, C.J. and Sarat, A. (eds) (2006) *From Lynch Mobs to the Killing State: Race and the Death Penalty in America*. New York: NYU Press.

Paterson, O. (1999) *Rituals of Blood: Consequences of Slavery in Two American Centuries*. Washington, DC: Counterpoint.

Pfeiffer, M. (2004) *Rough Justice: Lynching and American Society 1874–1947*. Chicago: University of Illinois Press.

Pildes, R. (2004) 'The constitutionalization of democratic politics', *Harvard Law Review*, 118: 29.

Sarat, A. (2001) *When the State Kills*. Princeton, NJ: Princeton University Press.

Savelsberg, J.J. (1994) 'Knowledge, domination, and criminal punishment', *American Journal of Sociology*, 99: 911–43.

Trombley, S. (1993) *The Execution Protocol*. New York: Anchor Books.

Vandiver, M. (2006) *Lethal Punishment: Lynchings and Legal Executions in the South*. New Brunswick, NJ: Rutgers University Press.

Western, B. (2006) *Punishment and Inequality*. New York: Russell Sage.

Zimring, F.E. (2003) *Contradictions of American Capital Punishment*. New York: Oxford University Press.

Cases cited

Coker v. *Georgia* 433 US 584 (1977)
Furman v. *Georgia* 408 US 238 (1972)
Gregg v. *Georgia* 428 US 153 (1976)
Hill v. *McDonough* 547 US (2006) No 05–8794
McCleskey v. *Kemp* 481 US 279 (1987)
Norris v. *Alabama* 294 US 587 (1935)
Patterson v. *Alabama* 357 US 449 (1958)
Payne v. *Tennessee* 501 US 808 (1991)
Powell v. *Alabama* 287 US 45 (1932)
Rudolph v. *Alabama* 375 US 889 (1963)

Part 4
Visions of Social Control

Chapter 13

Pathologies of markets and states

Steven Lukes

In what follows I want to ask: when markets do harm, what distinctive harms do they do? And, similarly, when states do harm, what distinctive harms do they do? In asking these questions, I am not interested in market or state failure, but in the harms which, when they occur, are consequent upon their success. That is, I will not be concerned with what economists call market failure and political scientists call weak or failed states, but rather with what harms can be attributed to markets and states when they function as their advocates recommend – when they function well in the ways that they are supposed to function. So I shall have little to say about the well-known virtues of market exchange and state planning, but focus instead on the evils or undesirable or unacceptable consequences that have been held to result from the successful functioning of these twin and often contrasted modes of coordination and allocation. Quite often, these are not only contrasted but also seen as alternatives. The strongest version of this thought is that they are to be seen as mutually exclusive and even jointly exhaustive modes. Fundamentalists on either side of the debate claim that the one is the panacea for all the ills caused by the other. In recent times, market fundamentalists have been in the ascendant, advocating the encroachment of the market in successive and hitherto market-free spheres of social activity. In previous times, advocates of state planning sought severely to restrict, or even eventually to abolish, market exchange. Those less extreme advocate various forms of mixed economy, differently configured combinations of market exchange and state planning. I shall conclude by questioning two assumptions very commonly made: that the defects of each are genuinely *distinctive* of markets and states respectively; and consequently that each is best thought of as always the appropriate remedy for the defects of the other.

First, some definitional ground-clearing. Of course, there are many different kinds of markets, but for shorthand I shall here refer to 'the market' to mean a process by which the buyers and sellers of a good interact to determine its price and quantity. Marketing is trading through enforceable contracts where, unlike gift giving, the giving is conditional upon payment in return: in markets the operating rule is *quid pro quo*. And, following Max Weber, I shall take 'the state' to mean 'a human community that (successfully) claims the monopoly of the legitimate use of physical force within a given territory' (Weber 1948: 78), and add the need for a legitimating constitution (formal or informal) and a minimum range of legitimated and functioning institutions.

Market failure occurs when reality fails to live up to theoretical requirements. Real markets fail because they are imperfect: they fail to exhibit the idealized conditions under which they would otherwise succeed. When economists apply their theory to real-world markets, it soon becomes evident that the typical causes of market failure – negative externalities, asymmetrical information, natural monopolies and monopoly power in general, non-zero transaction costs, economies of scale, outright coercion and social norms incompatible with efficiency – are widely prevalent. One response on the part of pro-market economists is 'to present the reality of imperfect competition as coming close to the ideal of allocative efficiency and all-round welfare maximization' (Hirschman 1986: 123), sometimes with greater, sometimes with lesser plausibility. Another response, ever more significant at the present time, is for market actors and policymakers to transform that reality by *marketizing* it, by converting areas of social life that are insufficiently marketized into markets or pseudo-markets. Marketization means reconfiguring goods and services so that they can be priced and sold, inducing people to want to buy them and redirecting the motivation of workers who produce or provide them from collective aims and a service ethic to profit seeking and market discipline.

State failure results from inadequate institutional capacity. Typically, this is the problem of industrializing states: the problem of inadequate fiscal capacity needed for funding development projects, and of inadequate capacity to coordinate the investment strategies of firms, to monitor their performance and ensure their compliance, and to acquire, process and apply the information required to perform these functions. The prerequisites for avoiding such failure are a rational, well-oiled bureaucracy, a central coordinating agency with real authority and a high degree of embeddedness in the economy, with dense ties to the industrial sector (see Chibber 2003). These are the problems of industrializing states, but we need to consider state failure in advanced industrialized states. There the problem is not inadequate but *inhibited* state capacity that results from the implementation of currently prevalent beliefs – that the state, whether in practice or in principle, lacks the capacity for planning the economy and other areas of social life, and that the market should replace it, or, more simply, that those from the business world always know and do better than state bureaucrats.

I

The virtues of the market system have been proclaimed for some three centuries, beginning with French and Scottish Enlightenment thinkers. The French deemed it socially beneficent, writing of *le doux commerce*. According to Montesquieu, 'wherever manners are gentle there is commerce; and wherever there is commerce, manners are gentle' (Montesquieu 1748: 8). Condorcet wrote of 'the spirit of commerce and industry, those enemies of the violence and turmoil which cause wealth to flee' (Condorcet 1795: 238), and Voltaire praised the London Stock Exchange as a place where 'you will see representatives from all nations gathered together for the utility of men. Here Jew, Mohammedan and Christian deal with each other as though they were all of the same faith, and only apply the word infidel to people who go bankrupt' (Voltaire 1733: 41). As for the Scots, David Hume was praised by Adam Smith for showing in his *History of England* how commerce and manufactures gradually introduced order and good government, and with them, the liberty and security of individuals, to succeed a previous continual state of war and hierarchical dependency. And it was, of course, Smith who developed the classical economic defence of the market: the market system accounted for 'the wealth of nations', maximizing allocative efficiency through mutual adjustment rendering incentives compatible, and, as wants multiply, enabling self-sustained growth and development.

In general, we can say that the case for the market's beneficence, as it stands today, is partly economic and partly social and political. On the one hand, markets coordinate economic activity, by communicating through prices information unavailable through any other mechanism, and provide incentives for people to train themselves and to innovate. In consequence, markets exhibit dynamism, the capacity for innovation and long-term growth. And markets are, under ideal conditions (which, as indicated, mostly do not exist), Pareto-efficient, leading to an equilibrium in which no one can be better off over time without someone else becoming worse off. On the other hand, again ideally, they secure liberty, enabling autonomous preference-formation on the basis of adequate knowledge, and voluntary exchange expressing consent and cooperation in the face of divergent values. And they promote certain kinds of equality, enabling unforeseen relations between strangers and dissolving hierarchies, with a formal right of exit.

So what harms do markets do? Here we need to go back to the nineteenth century and the heritage of German romanticism. Deploring 'the brutish godforgetting Profit-and-Loss Philosophy', Carlyle protested that 'Cash-payment is not the sole nexus of man with man' (Carlyle (1977 [1843]): 187). Five years later Marx and Engels took up the very phrase in *The Communist Manifesto,* writing that, as 'the constantly expanding market' spreads over the surface of the globe, pitilessly tearing 'asunder' the motley feudal ties that bound man to his 'natural superiors', all that survives is 'callous "cash payment"': men are drowned in the 'icy waters of egotistical calculation' (Marx and Engels 1848: 51–3). Neo-Marxists, such as Lukács, developed this theme, writing of commodity fetishism and reification and the Frankfurt School of the colonization of the life-world, but critiques of the market extend across the left–right spectrum and beyond. Policy-oriented social democrats like Richard Titmuss (Titmuss 1970) and cooperative socialists like Marcel Mauss (1925) speak of the market driving out altruism and reciprocity. Communitarians speak of 'the morality of the bazaar' (Walzer 1983: 109) and republicans of the erosion of public institutions and the corrosion of civic virtues. Feminists see the market in gestational surrogacy as degrading to women and argue about whether prostitution oppresses and entraps women or expresses their economic freedom. Tradition-minded right-wingers resent the way in which markets disrupt hierarchies and anti-immigration movements oppose open labour markets. And beyond the left–right continuum, supporters of green politics defend protecting the environment against the anthropocentric view of well-being as maximizing, through markets, merely human preference satisfaction.

I suggest that there are basically three broadly plausible ways of viewing markets as harmful – and that the first, on inspection, mostly dissolves into the second and third. The first is summed up by the term *commodification* – a highly normative notion. As generally used, to commodify something or someone is to treat as a commodity what should not be so treated. Let us look more closely at what this can mean.

Margaret Radin has most helpfully dissected the notion of commodification into four component processes. Goods or services are, she suggests, commodified when they exhibit the following features:

1 *objectification*: treating persons and things instrumentally, as manipulable at will
2 *fungibility*: when they are fully interchangeable with no effect on their value to the holder
3 *commensurability*: when their values can be arrayed as a function of one continuous variable or can be linearly ranked
4 *money equivalence*: where the continuous variable in terms of which they can be ranked is monetary value (Radin 1996: 118).

When all of these features are present, commodification is fully at work. So what is the harm that is held to flow from them? I suggest the answer is twofold. First, certain goods and services are said to be debased or distorted by being commodified, that is, treated as marketable. Call this the *corruption argument.* By 'corruption', I mean to adduce the idea of *pathology*: the thought that the impact of the market is to impair or degrade otherwise well-functioning and potentially flourishing activities and relationships. So, for example, in his book *Everything for Sale*, Robert Kuttner writes that 'advertiser dominance debases journalism into entertainment', that religious and then secular holidays have been 'debased into three-day shopping weekends', and that making 'free libraries more market-like would destroy their essence' (Kuttner 1997: 57, 58, 63). But, second, the corruption can spread: once the process begins in respect of one such good, others are infected and the contamination spreads, across persons and across goods. Call this the *contamination argument.* So Richard Titmuss argues for both corruption and contamination, claiming that selling blood crowds out altruism, diminishing the scope for giving it and also other worthwhile things in society. As he famously put it, 'private market systems in the United States and other countries … deprive men of their freedom to choose to give or not to give'; the commercialization of blood has the effect of 'discouraging and downgrading the voluntary principle. Both the sense of community and the expression of altruism are being silenced' (Titmuss 1970: 239, 157). And Margaret Radin speculates that full and open commodification of sexual services (advertised, for instance, as automobiles are) would 'be reflected in everyone's discourse about sex, and in particular about women's sexuality' and with this 'would come a change in everyone's experience, because experience is discourse-dependent' (Radin 1996: 133).

To some ears, there is more than a hint of paternalism, primness, prissiness, cultural elitism or else communitarian nostalgia about such arguments, so here is a more robust claim. I refer to the economist William Baumol's idea that there are services 'in which the human touch is crucial, and are thus resistant to labour productivity growth':

they resist standardization because 'treatment must be tailored to the individual case', and 'quality is, or is at least believed to be, inescapably correlated with the amount of human labour devoted to their production' (Baumol 1997: 513). Baumol's original examples were the performing arts but he then extended them to other services, such as teaching, doctoring and policing. But, as Colin Leys has argued, Baumol

> underestimated the constant resourcefulness that capital displays in its efforts to resolve the problems it confronts – including its ability to wean consumers from services on to consuming material goods and providing the labour component themselves [and] finally, consigning any small residue to 'high-end' markets, or leaving them to (increasingly beleaguered) state provision (Leys 2001: 94, 95).

The question is: what exactly is objectionable here? In Britain the commodification of medical services has involved the splitting up of different services, not all of which are Baumol-like in resisting productivity increases, while enlisting patients in the provision of the service is not obviously a bad idea. On the other hand, the growing consumption of drugs and painkillers, the speeding-up of the examination of patients and the very fragmentation of services points in the other direction. More generally, the very idea of *care* (as in health care and childcare) implies uninhibited responsiveness and flexibility, and that is precisely what is threatened by the demand for efficiency and contractual arrangements. But note that these are not unique to the market; both profit-driven markets and taxpayer-driven bureaucracies impose these managerial constraints on care-giving – a point to which I will return.

   The central thought behind the corruption and contagion arguments is that certain goods and services are too morally important to be bought and sold. Michael Sandel writes that in 'the cases of surrogacy, baby-selling, and sperm-selling, the ideals at stake are bound up with the meaning of motherhood, fatherhood and the nurturing of children' (Sandel 1998: 125). Elizabeth Anderson suggests that market allocation is only suitable for 'pure economic goods' that are merely means to other individual ends and are 'traded with equanimity for any other commodity at some price' and that it is inappropriate for goods that are 'higher, personal or shared' (Anderson 1995: 143–7). So, recalling Radin's component elements of commodification, we deny or neglect the meaning of such goods by treating them as objects, as exchangeable, as commensurable and as having prices.

Is this convincing? Is Titmuss right that selling blood crowds out altruism or was Kenneth Arrow right in criticizing him for failing to provide either a theoretical analysis of why it should or any real evidence that it does? (Arrow 1972). Is Radin right that commodifying sex changes everyone's experience or is Ann Lucas right that

> Both reasoning and evidence suggest that commodified and noncommodified sexuality coexist without diminishing human flourishing. Indeed this diversity and coexistence may actually *enhance* flourishing in other areas of life? (Lucas 2005: 264).

Do not people endlessly contain contradictions and exhibit ambivalence? Is it really true that treating others as means to individual ends and seeing the world in impersonal and quantifiable terms are incompatible with altruism, reciprocity and the realization of values that are 'higher, personal and shared'? Mary Douglas has persuasively argued that goods are to be seen as 'ritual adjuncts' and their consumption as a 'ritual activity' which uses goods to make 'firm and visible a particular set of judgments in the fluid process of classifying persons and events' (Douglas 1979: 45).

Are there not many contexts in which instrumental relationships and seeing the world in anonymous and commensurable terms is much to be valued, indeed an essential precondition for, and counterpoint to, mutual relationships in more intimate settings? Moreover, this very opposition between the market and intimate settings can be questioned, as Williams and Zelizer do when they write that 'what appear to be self-contained market transactions always involve meaningful, negotiated interpersonal relations, such as transfers of money, that, far from predetermining an impersonal gray quality to the social relations involved, instead take their meaning from the interpersonal setting in which they occur' (Williams and Zelizer 2005: 368). Is it even obvious that treating people as objects and as a means to some end is always a bad idea? (Kant's famous categorical imperative enjoins us to treat persons *never simply* as a means.) Surely it must depend on the end and on who is doing what in pursuing it. According to his biographer, Beethoven was 'filled with a deep conviction as to the significance of his work and his art' and in 1801 he referred to two of his friends as 'merely instruments on which to play when I feel inclined ... I value them merely for what they do for me' (Solomon: 1977: 86). As for commensurability and pricing, why assume that we cannot both know the price of something and that it is priceless? I believe we do this all the time. We adhere to the Christian and Kantian idea that the individual is sacred, while we make insurance decisions and pay medical administrators and planners to allocate resources and plan the siting of roads and airports on the basis that all the options involve the statistical certainty of a certain number of deaths and injuries that we expect to be costed on a rational and systematic basis that puts a (regularly updated and commercially based) value on human lives.

Marketing and marketizing goods and services do in some cases distort or debase their nature (for instance, in the contracting out of hospital services, from nursing to cleaning), and the harm may be amplified through contagion (throughout the health-care system and beyond). But I believe that when we think of markets as harmful we mainly have either of two further major concerns in mind and that much of the animus against corruption and contagion really focuses on these.

The first of these concerns is with *inequality*. Markets reproduce and amplify inequalities of class, gender and race. How many people would sell their kidneys and how many women would sell their reproductive capacity under conditions of greater equality of condition? (Is the case against prostitution parallel? Is the primary objection commodification or inequality?) The inequality worry is essentially the thought that in real-world markets sellers are pressured into selling and buyers are unable to afford the good things of life – leading at the extreme to what Walzer calls 'desperate exchanges' (Walzer 1983: 121). In the transnational market for organs, kidneys sell for $10,000 to $15,000 in Egypt and for $1,500 in India, where a cornea fetches $4,000; and in the baby market black babies cost less than white babies (Williams and Zelizer 372).

The general point here is that markets reproduce pre-existing unequal distributions of assets – capital assets and the rights to these, and personal assets, such as brain, brawn and education, across individuals, classes, regions and countries. They also generate inequalities of income and status because markets as such entail insecurity and risk. As Lindblom writes,

> Employed today, one may lose one's job tomorrow, shortly then lose one's savings, home and even status in the community. Business fluctuation, recession, and depression evict people from their jobs and cut off their claims to income from their labour. Illness and temporary disability put a stop to one's market claims, and old age often promises a termination to all market claims (Lindblom 2001: 121).

Neo-liberals put their faith in private ownership of all assets, unfettered markets and minimal redistribution through taxation. Their goal is efficiency, not equality, and at best relieving extreme poverty, relying on market mechanisms to alleviate this and negative externalities, such as pollution. Socialists have sought both to equalize the pre-existing inequalities of assets and property rights and to provide social security and redistribution through the welfare system and taxation. Social democrats have focused exclusively on the latter, leaving the ownership of capital private and very unequal. In Scandinavia and elsewhere, they have achieved dramatic successes which survive. One big question is whether this success requires citizen homogeneity as its precondition.

Which leads me to the other major way in which markets are harmful: namely, that, when unchecked, they undermine the bases of *citizenship*. T.H. Marshall's story of the cumulative development of citizens' rights from civic through political to social rights (Marshall 1950) culminated in the stabilization of a significant range of these in various European welfare regimes after the Second World War: the universal provision of education to ever higher levels; health care; financial support in case of unemployment, injury, ill-health and old age, and, in some fortunate places, housing, legal aid, citizens' advice, access to public spaces, public libraries and so on (see Crouch 2003). These can all be seen as supplying the preconditions for core citizenship by enabling citizens to acquire and maintain the capacities needed for its equal exercise. In these ways, the market's reach was resisted by an ethos, whether based on social democratic or Christian ideals of welfare, publicly funded and publicly provided. But in the 1970s, the mid-century citizenship package started to unravel as capitalist firms have resorted to the service sector in pursuit of profit. With the worldwide spread of neo-liberal ideology, abetted by governments of the centre-left in pursuit of economic efficiency, health services, education, public utilities, transport and broadcasting have been opened up to marketization and privatization. So what harms can be attributed to these invasions by the market of the domain of citizenship?

Two are worth stressing here. One is the severing of the link between representative (national or local) and citizen and elector (who becomes a customer and consumer). Marketization and public–private partnerships enable politicians to divest themselves of responsibility and, crucially, of accountability for the provision of public services. The government contracts with the supplier, but citizens can no longer hold their representatives accountable for service delivery, which is rendered faceless by being consigned to the anonymous forces of the market. Meanwhile governmental agencies, such as local education offices in the UK and the Federal Emergency Management Association in the USA become hollowed out and marginalized. The other harm concerns not merely the preconditions of citizenship but those of *good* citizenship – namely, the services that generate and sustain people's capacity to function as good citizens. There is no reason to think that these will be provided by market forces alone to a sufficient extent and in adequate breadth and depth. In particular, when markets invade the spheres of educational provision and public broadcasting, some of the capacities – notably the cognitive capacity to process information and achieve a rational understanding of one's world – are, to say the least, not encouraged. Public broadcasting is a crucial and endangered area here. The point goes far beyond Kuttner's complaint that advertising debases journalism into mere entertainment. It is that, as US experience abundantly shows, where public broadcasting is only marginally present in a predominantly commercial environment, there are no countervailing mechanisms to resist the descent into trivialization and fragmentation. That is why the glorious BBC is the citadel to be defended to the last against market forces, and not just for the sake of British citizens. Just compare the state of radio in the USA and Britain. Moreover, in a market environment, truthfulness is not at a premium. If consumers do not value truth very much, market competition will tend to ensure that they do not get very much of it as compared with other goods they do value. In general, market dominance means subservience to corporate media power and (as we have seen in the context of the Iraq war) to the dictates of the White House and the Pentagon.

II

States are the source of citizenship and the natural framework of the public sphere, but they are also collective actors. So, when they act, what harm do they do? The best-known answer to this constitutes one of the pillars of neo-liberal ideology and is of Austrian provenance. It says: 'Beware the state as an agency of central planning, above all when in pursuit of social justice!' The arguments for this view of the interventionist state's maleficence were formulated by von Mises and developed by Hayek. The Hayek version (which achieved fame in his book *The Road to Serfdom*) was formulated in the 1930s in answer to Beveridge's and Mannheim's arguments that fascism is a natural outgrowth of capitalism and that only through planning could totalitarianism of the Left or the Right be avoided. In 1939, Hayek asked:

Is it a mere accident that the continuous expansion of the powers of the state, which they had welcomed as an instrument to bring about greater social justice, has in so many countries brought the disappearance of all personal freedom and the end of all justice? (Hayek 1997 [1939]: 190; see Caldwell 2004).

He obviously thought it was no accident: a state engaged in central planning and redistribution was *necessarily* the enemy of freedom and justice. Hayek's key and best argument was epistemic and amounted to an impossibility theorem. For Hayek, the fundamental economic problem was

> the fact that the knowledge of the circumstances of which we must make use never exists in concentrated or integrated form but solely as the dispersed bits of incomplete and frequently contradictory knowledge which all the separate individuals possess ... It is rather a problem of how to secure the best use of the resources known to any of the members of society, for ends whose relative importance only those individuals know. Or, to put it briefly, it is a problem of the utilization of knowledge which is not given to anyone in its totality (Hayek 1945: 77–8).

The argument is against the very possibility of 'social engineering':

> [n]either the 'available' resources nor the 'existing' needs are objective facts in the sense of those with which the engineer deals in his limited field; they can never be known in all relevant detail to a single planning body (Hayek 1952: 176).

A central authority can only rely on statistical aggregates, which 'are always arrived at by a deliberate disregard of the peculiar circumstances of time and place' (Hayek 1952: 176). And Hayek concluded that a 'successful solution' can only be based on 'a method of utilizing the knowledge dispersed among all members of society, knowledge of which in any particular instance the central authority will know neither who possesses it nor whether it exists at all' (Hayek 1952: 176). This can only be done through 'some mechanism which will delegate the particular decisions to those who possess it, and for that purpose supply them with such information about the general situation as will enable them to make the best use of the particular circumstances of which only they know' (Hayek 1952: 172). That mechanism, unsurprisingly, is the market.

From this argument, Hayek drew wildly extravagant conclusions, employing what Albert Hirschman calls 'the rhetoric of reaction' (Hirschman 1991). Start central planning and redistributing income in pursuit of 'the mirage' of social justice anywhere and you are on the slippery slope to full-scale disaster, imposing one group's values on all and breaking the fetters of democratic procedure. Moreover, whatever you do will be massively counterproductive. It will also be futile. It will also, in the name of advancing equality, destroy your citizens' liberty. Hayek assumed that the 'competitive market' is the 'natural spontaneous order' of human society. He has nothing to say about the realities of monopolistic and oligopolistic markets and of massive corporate power. And yet Hayek, who after all won the socialist calculation debate, was right about the indispensability of market signals for the relaying of inherently dispersed and local knowledge, and he was right about the limits that this knowledge, embodied in local practices, sets to projects of state-led social engineering.

This last theme has been graphically portrayed in James Scott's book, *Seeing Like a State* (Scott 1998), which explores the ways in which modern state-led projects of social engineering extinguish practical knowledge that is local, dispersed and contextually specific. In fact, Scott scarcely refers to Hayek and his inspiration is anarchist and not market-liberal. Where Hayek offers a deductive argument, concerning the indispensability of the market for the provision of knowledge, Scott's work exemplifies and illustrates a hypothesis. Unlike Hayek, he does not offer an impossibility thesis but rather three compelling case studies of successful state enterprises that are human disasters: the designing, planning and building of Brasilia, Soviet collectivization and compulsory villagization in Tanzania – three 'extreme instances of massive, state-imposed social engineering'. His claim is that they exemplify 'high modernist faith', found 'among those who wanted to use state power to bring about huge utopian changes in people's work habits, living patterns, moral conduct and worldview' – a faith typical of 'planners, engineers, architects, scientists and technicians'. Their projects prevail under certain conditions: when

> the legibility of a society provides the capacity for large-scale social engineering, high-modernist ideology provides the desire, the authoritarian state provides the determination to act on that desire, and an incapacitated civil society provides the leveled social terrain on which to build (Scott 1998: 5).

Scott's three cases illustrate that the

> necessarily thin, schematic model of social organization and production animating the planning was inadequate as a set of instructions for creating a successful social order. By themselves

the simplified rules can never generate a functioning community, city or economy. Formal order, to be more explicit, is always and to some considerable degree parasitic on informal processes which the formal scheme does not recognize, without which it could not exist, and which it alone cannot create or maintain (Scott 1998: 310).

Scott thinks of these processes (rather in the spirit of Michael Oakeshott) as *practical knowledge* – a wide array of practical skills and acquired intelligence in responding to a constantly changing natural and human environment – local, situated knowledge which contrasts with the central state's necessarily crude general understandings.

Scott attributes three distinct but related harms to the state's lack of local, practical knowledge. First, it leads to mistaken policies, ranging from blunders to catastrophic errors – mistaken calculations of demand, misallocation of resources and people, suboptimal or counterproductive policy choices, failures to perceive and seize opportunities, and so on. All this, of course, was central to the Austrians' concerns and fully illustrated in the record of economic polices under actually existing socialism. Second, it leads to bureaucratic rigidity, unresponsive to local conditions and the particular needs of individuals and groups, to inflexible laws and rules, suppressing diversity and exhibiting the logic of uniformity and regimentation. (So Scott sides with Jane Jacobs against Le Corbusier and with Aleksandra Kollontai against Lenin. His book juxtaposes images of homely-looking, higgledy-piggledy townscapes and quaint old maps with those of lonely inhuman streets and squares and austere geometric plans.) And third, the state's lack of local knowledge systematically distorts people's lives by imposing technocratic dreams upon them, irrespective of their own dreams and values. As Scott puts it, his case is that 'certain kinds of states, driven by utopian plans and an authoritarian disregard for the values, desires and objections of their subjects are indeed a moral threat to human well-being' (Scott 1998: 7).

Like Hayek, Scott exaggerates and he focuses on extreme, worst-case scenarios of state planning (Yes, Brasilia, but what about St Petersburg and Haussmann's Paris? What about the New Deal, Scandinavian social democracy, the US interstate highway system, public health successes such as the eradication of yellow fever, cholera and polio? See Sunstein 1998.) Yet he suggests (and certainly his title suggests) that all states are disposed to 'seeing like a state' and thereby threaten the indicated harms to human well-being.

III

I now want to conclude with two observations about the respective pathologies of the market and the state.

First, the harms each has been held to cause are not distinctive of either. So market actors can certainly see like a state and states can commodify and behave or seek to behave like market actors. Corporations employ ever more sophisticated ways of rendering their markets and potential markets 'legible' and of monitoring their own operations, and they certainly exhibit the logic of uniformity and regimentation. Here are two examples. In its relentless pursuit of low prices, Wal-Mart has become 'arguably the world's most important privately controlled economic institution': its 'scale allows it to constantly and quickly extend the area it controls deeper into the factories and offices and decisions of the chain of companies that feed it, across new lines of business, and across wider and wider geographies' (Fishman 2006: 20). Wal-Mart is increasingly in control of its own ecosystem. Moreover, it 'keeps track of the number of items per hour each of its checkouts scans at every cash register, at every store, in every state, for every shift as a means of measuring their productivity' and 'measures sales per running foot of shelf space for every item and category to make sure stores and individual products are productive and to compare their profitability' (Fishman 2006: 12–13). As it swallows up competing retailers and dragoons its suppliers, its impact on local practices and the knowledge they embody is notorious: its arrival in small towns coincides with a swath of destruction of local retail businesses, while its car parks swallow up the landscape. And a second example: giant pharmaceutical companies are increasingly adept at monitoring and, in turn, influencing the prescribing practices of doctors. In both cases, demand is investigated, monitored and shaped, on a global scale and in ever greater depth (Lakoff 2005). And, as these two examples show, the seeing like a state is intimately bound up with commodification – with instrumental relationships (not least in Wal-Mart's management practices), with measurement and with pricing.

Conversely, since Max Weber, it is surely not news that such practices, typical of bureaucracies, are characteristic of the way states behave, and all the more so these days, under the pressures of auditing and cost-cutting in the context of globalized market conditions. Consider the ways this works, for example, in the assessment of teaching and research in public educational institutions funded by the state (and it is curious that in the real academic market, in the USA, the commodification – at least the obsession with quantitative measurement of productivity and rewarding it with money – is significantly less developed, although it is on the way). Moreover, states are, more and more, behaving as market actors, as partners of market actors and as seeking to simulate real markets in the absence of private ownership and even private provision, as when public authorities seek to allocate collectively owned resources by market pricing (as Colin Crouch suggests (Crouch 2003), these should perhaps be better described as cases of oligopolistic providers making deals with monopsonist customers).

What bearing do states have on the other harms I referred to as consequent upon markets: the reproduction and aggravation of inequalities and the undermining of citizenship? Obviously, states can contribute to these harms by favouring markets and by partnering or simulating market actors. But now we may ask another question. To what extent is it feasible, through state policies, to reduce these harms? Consider first inequalities of assets, whether property and property rights or marketable skills, and, alternatively, inequalities of income and other benefits that accrue to individuals. More specifically, to what extent is this feasible in the case of competitively democratic states? (I assume that it is states, and these states in particular, that are, for the foreseeable future the only plausible agents of such equalization, as compared with local, regional or supranational bodies.) Clearly, the former, socialist policy of asset equalization – of equalizing property rights and marketable skills – is the less feasible. Here, doubtless, an equalizing educational policy is the most promising. As for the latter, the social-democratic policy of equalizing flows of income and other benefits through fiscal redistribution and social insurance, as in the welfare states of northern Europe, especially the five Nordic countries, has demonstrated remarkable successes. Despite the predictions of some that the welfare state is moribund, that is not so. These welfare states are changing at the edges, largely because of changing demographies and immigration, but they are not disappearing.

But herein lies the other harm we have been considering: the undermining of citizenship rights. For, if, as I suggested before, the success of these social democratic welfare states has relied upon the precondition of citizen homogeneity, then they may not be generalizable or indeed sustainable in the longer term. For it is the market, in this case the international labour market, which enables and encourages these changing demographies and immigration. It is an open and increasingly urgent question within Europe and elsewhere to what extent states can or should limit immigration in the interests of preserving citizens' rights.

My second and concluding observation is simply a worry about the very topic I have been addressing. Perhaps we should question the bipolar disorder that leads us to think in an 'either-or' way about markets and states. In this chapter, I have focused on the harms attributable to markets and to states. I suggested the ways in which markets commodify, aggravate inequality and undermine citizenship rights, and that states disregard and extinguish local knowledge. I further suggested that these harms are perpetrated by both states and markets. Finally, I indicated that markets, as repositories and distributors of knowledge, are indispensable to states and that states, as agents of social insurance, social services and redistribution, are an indispensable corrective to markets. And so, we may conclude, neither is the panacea for the ills of the other.

References

Anderson, E. (1995) *Value in Ethics and Economics*. Cambridge, MA: Harvard University Press.

Arrow, K. (1972) 'Gifts and exchanges', *Philosophy and Public Affairs*, 1 (4): 343–62.

Baumol, W. (1997) 'Health care, education and the cost disease', in R. Towse (ed.) *Baumol's Cost Disease: The Arts and Other Victims*. London: Edward Elgar.

Caldwell, B. (2004) *Hayek's Challenge: An Intellectual Biography of F.A. Hayek*. Chicago: Chicago University Press.

Carlyle, T. (1977 [1843]) *Past and Present*. New York: New York University Press.

Chibber, V. (2003) *Locked in Place: State-Building and Late Industrialization in India*. Princeton, NJ: Princeton University Press.

Condorcet, Marquis de (1795) *Esquisse d'un Tableau Historique du Progrès de l'Esprit Humain*. Paris: Agasse.

Crouch, C. (2003) *Commercialization and Citizenship: Educational Policy and the Future of Public Services*. London: Fabian Society.

Douglas, M. (1979) *The World of Goods* reprinted as *Collected Works*, vol. VI. New York: London: Routledge.

Ertman, M.A. and Williams, J.C. (eds) (2005) *Rethinking Commodification: Cases and Readings in Law and Culture*. New York: New York University Press.

Fishman, C. (2006) *The Wal-Mart Effect*. New York: Penguin Press.

Gold, N. (2006) 'Markets, motivations and frame crowding', *Archives européennes de sociologie (European Journal of Sociology)*, 47: in press.

Hayek, F.A. (1997 [1939]) 'Freedom and the economic system', in B. Caldwell (ed.) *Socialism and War: Essays, Documents and Reviews* (vol. 10 of *The Collected Works of F.A. Hayek*). Chicago: Chicago University Press, pp. 189–211.

Hayek, F.A. (1945) 'The use of knowledge in society', reprinted in F.A. Hayek, *Individualism and Economic Order*. Chicago: Chicago University Press.

Hayek, F.A. (1948) *Individualism and Economic Order*. Chicago: University of Chicago Press.

Hayek, F.A. (1979 [1952]) *The Counter-Revolution of Science* (2nd edn reprinted). Minneapolis, MN: Liberty Fund.

Hirschman, A.O (1977) *The Passions and the Interests: Political Arguments for Capitalism before its Triumph*. Princeton, NJ: Princeton University Press.

Hirschman, A.O. (1986) *Rival Views of Market Society*. New York: Elizabeth Sifton Books, Viking Penguin.

Hirschman, A.O. (1991) *The Rhetoric of Reaction: Perversity, Futility, Jeopardy*. Cambridge, MA: The Belknap Press.

Kuttner, R. (1999 [1997]) *Everything for Sale: The Virtues and Limits of Markets*. Chicago: Chicago University Press.

Lakoff, A. (2005) *Pharmaceutical Reason: Knowledge and Value in Global Psychiatry*. Cambridge: Cambridge University Press.

Leys, C. (2001) *Market-driven Politics: Neoliberal Democracy and the Public Interest*. London: Verso.

Lindblom, C.E. (2001) *The Market System: What It Is, How It works, and What to Make of It*. New Haven and London: Yale University Press.

Lucas, A. (2005) 'The currency of sex: prostitution, law and commodification', in Ertman and Williams, pp. 248–270.

Marshall, T.H. (1992 [1950]) *Citizenship and Social Class*, reprinted in T.H. Marshall and T.B. Bottomore, *Citizenship and Social Class*. London: Pluto.

Marx, K. and Engels, F. (1957 [1848]) *The Communist Manifesto*. Moscow: Foreign Languages Publishing House.

Montesquieu, C.L. (1748) *De l'Esprit des Lois*. Paris: Garnier.

Sandel, M. (2005 [1998]) 'What money can't buy: the moral limits of markets', reprinted in Ertman and Williams, pp. 122–7.

Scott, J.C. (1998) *Seeing Like a State: How Certain Schemes to Improve the Human Condition Have Failed*. New Haven, CT: Yale University Press.

Solomon, M. (1977) *The Life of Beethoven*. New York: Schirmer Books.

Sunstein, C. (1998) Review of Scott 1998, *The New Republic*, 18 May.

Titmuss, R. (1970) *The Gift Relationship: From Human Blood to Social Policy*. London: Allen and Unwin.

Voltaire (François-Marie Arouet) (1733) *Letters on England* translated with an introduction by L. Tancock. Harmondsworth: Penguin.

Walzer, M. (1983) *Spheres of Justice: A Defense of Pluralism and Equality*. New York: Basic Books.

Weber, M. (1948) *From Max Weber: Essays in Sociology* translated, edited and with an introduction by H.H. Gerth and C.W. Mills. London: Routledge.

Williams, J.C. and Zelizer, V.A. (2005) 'To commodify or not to commodify: that is NOT the question', in Ertman and Williams, pp. 362–82.

Chapter 14

Visions of Social Control revisited

Thomas G. Blomberg and Carter Hay

Introduction

Stanley Cohen's (1985) book, *Visions of Social Control*, is a classic that to this day remains remarkable in several respects. In terms of scope, it provided a sweeping analysis not just of the historic growth of Western systems of social control, but of the key features of those systems in Cohen's present day and the pathways that they would take in the future. Also notable was Cohen's ability to discuss the past, present, and future of social control in a way that incorporated the role of ideology while still staying above the fray of the divisive ideological battles that surround the dialogue on trends in social control. Indeed, *Visions of Social Control* is impermeable to standard ideological categorization. It also is remarkable for its sense of nuance. Cohen showed a willingness to acknowledge and even dwell upon inconvenient facts that contradicted the obvious prevailing patterns. Thus, far from presenting a uniform, tidy discussion in clear black-and-white terms, *Visions of Social Control* gave us a view of social control marked by all the various shades of grey that capture the issue as it really exists. In the words of James F. Short (1986: 242), who reviewed the book shortly after its publication, *Visions of Social Control* will be of little use 'for those who require unambiguous conclusions'. For others, however, 'it is a model worthy of emulation and a challenge to all, regardless of theoretical, methodological, or ideological persuasion'.

After more than two decades since its publication, this chapter revisits and assesses *Visions of Social Control* with particular attention to Cohen's predictions regarding the future of social control efforts in Western societies. We describe these predictions in greater detail in the next section, but for now, it can be emphasized that while Cohen tried to eschew the dreary pessimism that often dominates the discussion of social control trends, and while he insisted that unintended consequences could sometimes be beneficial, he nevertheless presented a view of the future that was bleakly Orwellian. Central to this was his prediction of a 'decisive and deepening bifurcation' (Cohen 1985: 232) of social control that would include an expansion of both inclusionary and exclusionary strategies. As we describe below, Cohen saw these developments in terms of the cultural changes that would facilitate them – expanding social control would not be imposed upon an unwilling citizenry, but instead would be in many respects embraced by the masses.

Our central question is this: was Cohen correct in these predictions? In approaching this question, we first describe the central arguments put forth in *Visions of Social Control*, including his vision of the future of social control. We then consider the accuracy of Cohen's predictions, focusing in large part on the emergent social control trends taking place in the state of Florida from 1985 to the present, as well as related changes occurring throughout the USA. We then conclude by elaborating on some of the key patterns that emerge, and considering a question that was central to *Visions of Social Control:* where do we go from here?

Cohen's *Visions of Social Control*

Among the significant contributions of *Visions of Social Control* was its discussion of master patterns – the historic transformations that had occurred and were occurring in the use of social control. Cohen began by describing four key transformations that took place between roughly 1800 and the 1960s. First, the state became increasingly involved in the business of social control. Rather than social control being dominated by traditionally employed informal practices, it became the domain of an explicit 'centralized, rationalized and bureaucratic apparatus' (Cohen 1985: 12). Second, there emerged a greater differentiation and classification of deviant groups into separate types and categories, each of which required 'its own body of "scientific" knowledge and its own recognized and accredited experts'. Third, there was greater emphasis upon the segregation of deviants into asylums of different types, including prisons, almshouses, mental hospitals, and reformatories. Overall, this period involved the emergence of the idea that closed, exclusionary institutions were essential to the punishment and reformation of deviants of all kinds. Fourth, this period saw a shift from punishments that emphasized public infliction of bodily harm to those emphasizing the alteration of the offender's internal or mental states. Thus, sentences to galley-ship slavery or to public whippings were replaced with efforts directed at the mind – efforts that might lead offenders to reflect on their transgressions and seek an alternative future course of behaviour.

Cohen identifies and assesses several different interpretations for why these changes occurred and whether they were desirable. One view took an optimistic, functionalist view, arguing that the reforms were motivated by benevolence, and that while translating good intentions into real progress is difficult (and mistakes will be inevitable), the overall direction of change was toward a wiser and more humane application of social control. Another account of these changes took a less favourable view, with Cohen suggesting that this might be described as the 'we blew it' account of social control history. This view – best illustrated by Rothman's (1971) *The Discovery of the Asylum* – emphasized that while the reformers may have had good intentions, the imperfect expertise, information, and resources with which they worked produced disastrous consequences. Most notably, the exclusionary institutions heralded by the reformers were soon revealed as overcrowded, corrupt, and inhumane, and therefore inadequate for the task of rehabilitating offenders. The other and most radical account of these changes was both unfavourable and suspicious. This view – best illustrated in the work of Foucault (1977) and Rusche and Kircheimer (1939) – perceived the changes in social control as driven by the demands of a capitalist economy for an obedient, docile working class. From this standpoint, the rise of overcrowded, poorly funded, and inhumane closed institutions was successful for its intended goal – to provide 'continual repression of recalcitrant members of the working class' (p. 22).

As these accounts indicate, the major transformations in social control met some degree of resistance. Indeed, the 1960s and 1970s would see a fundamental shift, at least in terms of rhetoric. Cohen saw this as the second major social control transformation, and he referred to it as the destructuring movement. The reformers of this period sought to do away with many of the changes that had occurred. Specifically, Cohen saw four major goals sought by the proponents of the destructuring movement. The first was decentralization, whereby the state would divest itself of certain control functions so that community-based agencies could thrive and innovate. Second, they called for deprofessionalization – a decrease in reliance on the professional and expert diagnoses that had come to monopolize social control efforts. Third, critics called for decarcaration – a movement away from the exclusionary institutions that had fared so poorly. This was replaced with a renewed interest in inclusionary, community-based alternatives that would allow offenders to be more easily reintegrated into the community of law-abiding citizens. And fourth, the new reformers sought to get 'back to justice' (p. 31) – to de-emphasize an individual-based, medicalized approach to 'treating' deviants, and replace it with efforts that focus on the act (not the actor).

As Cohen points out, these critiques – especially the attacks on exclusionary institutions – were widespread and they seemed to portend significant change to the system of formal social control. Moreover, it was expected that the overall effect of any change would be to decrease the system's reach and intensity. As Cohen concludes, however, destructuring of the system simply never occurred: 'Instead of any destructuring … the original structures have become stronger' (p. 37). Of greatest relevance is that the historic reliance upon exclusionary prisons never decreased. On the contrary, the late 1970s marked the beginning of the most precipitous increases in the incarceration rate in US history. Inclusionary community-based sanctions greatly expanded as well, but largely as a supplement rather than an alternative to imprisonment. Cohen responded to this with the bleak observation that 'the system enlarges itself and becomes more intrusive, subjecting more and newer groups of deviants to the power of the state and increasing the intensity of control' (p. 38).

It is within this context that Cohen offers a vision of what form social control efforts will take in the decades to come. Cohen (p. 232) described this future in terms of a 'decisive and deepening bifurcation' in which control would expand and become more intense, but in different ways for 'soft' and 'hard' deviance. For soft deviance (minor crime and delinquency), Cohen foresaw a continuing expansion of inclusionary practices that would be invisible and normal, and that would integrate and absorb offenders rather than isolate them. This inclusionary control would be directed at both our inner space and our social space. Regarding the former, it would – for both deviants and those at-risk of deviance – make use of new therapies, scientific specialties, and cultural movements that lead us to embrace new control over every realm of our existence (leisure, family, child rearing, and so on) – 'the goal is to discourage anything from being casual' (p. 232). The control directed toward our social space, on the other hand, would be centred on the idea of surveillance. This, too, would be both reactive (for offenders) and preemptive (for those at risk of deviance), and it would make use of a full range of possibilities, including data banks, crime prevention through environmental design, electronic monitoring, and even secret agents, informers, and decoys (p. 221).

For 'hard' deviance (serious criminality), Cohen foresaw continued domination of exclusionary controls that segregate and isolate offenders into closed institutions. Such practices provide the public with what it demands in the wake of serious acts of crime: the creation of scapegoats, the clarification of moral boundaries, and the reinforcement of social solidarity. For these purposes, exclusionary practices are simply much richer than inclusionary practices: 'stigma and status degradation are sharper, deviants are clearly seen as different than non-deviants and, above all, there is the promise that they [deviants] will ... not just keep coming back to be "reintegrated".' Thus, Cohen envisioned increasingly more rigid exclusion for those on the extreme end of hard deviance, and this would include longer, determinate sentences 'in tougher prisons', as well as selective incapacitation and greater use of the death penalty (p. 234).

Cohen emphasizes that there is a logical connection between this expanded use of both inclusionary and exclusionary control. Both will satisfy an increasing desire of control among the citizenry in response to risks that are perceived as inherent results of the fast pace of economic, demographic, and technological change. In short, Western societies will come to be characterized by a cultural ethos that 'there is never the fear of too much control'; the fear is, instead, only 'of too much chaos' (p. 235). This desire for greater control will lead individuals to voluntarily submit to all sorts of inclusionary controls, including surveillance and thought control. As compensation for accepting widespread inclusionary control, 'the ordinary citizen will want to be ensured that the state means business' when it sets out to control hard deviance – he or she wants to be certain that 'the exclusionary lines are properly and firmly drawn' (p. 234).

For Cohen (p. 234), these patterns suggest a vision 'not too far from Orwell's' – he foresaw the pursuit of a utopian city in which social control increasingly spirals to greater levels. Our entire cognitive and social existence will be subject to greater inclusionary controls and in those cases where deviance persists nonetheless, the system would be provoked into using an increasingly more punitive and rigid set of exclusionary controls.

Was Cohen correct? Tracing social control changes and practices (1985–present)

In considering the question of whether Cohen's vision for the future of social control was correct, we consider four key predictions for the period from roughly 1985 through the present. First, there should have been a continued expansion in the use of exclusionary practices such as imprisonment and the death penalty for serious offenders. Second, this greater emphasis on exclusion should not have come as a substitute for inclusionary practices, because use of the latter should have expanded as well. This is the essence of the bifurcation of social control – citizens and governments will cease to choose between inclusion and exclusion, but instead will seek both. Third, there should have been a significant expansion of inclusionary controls that are pre-emptive in nature. These controls will be devoted to the widespread surveillance of space, actions, and individuals that pose a risk of crime or deviance. Fourth, this expansion of control – this greater intrusion into the lives of citizens (both deviant and conforming) – should have been in large part welcomed by the public.

In assessing these predictions, we focus on the state of Florida. Florida is the fourth most-populated state in the USA and it continues to grow rapidly, its population increasing by nearly 25 per cent between 1990 and 2000 (US Census Bureau 2001). Moreover, Florida is distinct from other states of the USA with respect to issues of crime and justice. Its rate of serious violent crime often is the highest in the nation (Federal Bureau of Investigations 2004), and its correctional system is among the largest in the USA as well. Indeed, Clear, Cole, and Reisig (2006) designate Florida (along with California, New York and Texas) as one of the 'big four' – states that dominate the U.S. correctional scene by together accounting for nearly 40 per cent of offenders under correctional supervision.

The expansion of exclusionary control

Cohen's prediction that the system of exclusionary control would become greater in its reach and intensity accurately captures the circumstances of Florida, especially with respect to imprisonment. In 1985, when Cohen published *Visions of Social Control*, prisons were returning to the forefront of the corrections system following several decades of experiments with alternative, community-based inclusionary control strategies. Many mechanisms contributed to this re-emergence of the prison. The first involved a shift from indeterminant to determinant sentencing that occurred both in Florida and in other states. Florida enacted its first set of sentencing guidelines during this period and heralded them as 'Truth in Sentencing'. However, Florida did not have sufficient prison space to fully implement these guidelines. As a result, and to control prison overcrowding, a series of gain-time incentives and early-release mechanisms were employed that allowed inmates to substantially reduce their actual time served in prison. By 1987, and despite various gain-time and early-release practices, Florida's prisons approached their court-ordered inmate capacities. In response, the state enacted an early prison release law to keep the prison population below lawful limits. Between 1987 and 1994, various early prison release mechanisms were in place in Florida. However, in 1995, a new set of strict sentencing guidelines were enacted that brought the state close to determinant sentencing. The new guidelines required prison inmates to serve a minimum of 85 per cent of their actual sentences. This sentencing policy of a minimum of 85 per cent of sentence served remains in practice today.

A related mechanism involves the mandatory minimum sentences required by policies like the 10–20–life legislation passed in Florida in 1999. This law mandates that felons who use a gun during the commission of a crime receive at least a 10-year sentence in state prison. If the gun is discharged, the mandatory sentence moves to 20 years; if someone is shot, the sentence becomes 25 years to life. This law also created a new mandatory three-year prison sentence for any convicted felon who even possesses a gun. In the first five years of its use, more than 4,000 offenders were sentenced under this law, with more than 600 inmates receiving a sentence of 20 years or more (Florida Department of Corrections 2006).

Not surprisingly, these changes have produced extraordinary increases in the use of imprisonment in Florida. In 1985, Florida's total prison population stood at 28,310 inmates or 251 inmates per 100,000 resident population. Five years later, the prison population had increased to 42,733, for a rate of 325. This substantial five-year increase in inmate population led to the construction of new prisons as well as increasing reliance upon private providers to operate prisons throughout the state. Between 1990 and 1995, the inmate population increased to 61,992, for a rate of 438 per 100,000 members of the population. In 1995, Florida enacted the 85 per cent time-served requirement, and from 1995, Florida's inmate population exploded to 87,659 in 2005. In line with these changes, from 1985 to 2005, the number of prisons in Florida increased from 58 to 128 and the overall corrections budget increased a startling 470 per cent, from roughly $340 million in 1985 to nearly $2 billion in 2005.

Not only did Florida expand its use of incarceration, but it made prisons tougher, more punitive places. For example, in Florida and elsewhere, recent decades have seen a significant expansion of 'supermax' prisons – prisons in which inmates are relegated to solitary confinement in a cell for 23 hours a day and are provided few if any services (Mears and Watson 2006). Moreover, beginning in the 1980s, most of Florida's prisons began to shift from an individual treatment focus to what became termed 'structured treatment', which centred upon institutional order rather than individual inmate treatment. Maintaining order in prison became an increasingly important mandate given both the escalating numbers of inmates that required management and the growing number of large prisons. With the increased focus upon structured treatment or inmate management came a corresponding decline in the number of educational and vocational prison programmes and drug treatment services. For example, today out of all Florida prisoners diagnosed to be in need of drug treatment, less than 20 per cent receive treatment because of the limited number of available drug treatment programmes and capacities (Florida Department of Corrections 2006b).

The death penalty is an additional exclusionary punishment that Cohen emphasized. For this sanction, however, there is little evidence of expansion. Figure 14.1 provides data on death sentences and actual executions in Florida between 1985 and 2005. For death sentences, there was an average of 26 per year and an apparent increase in the late 1980s and early 1990s (peaking at 45 in 1991). A steady drop occurred shortly thereafter, however, falling to between 10 and 15 in recent years. For executions, there is no clear pattern over time (Death Penalty Information Center 2006a). There has been an average of two executions per year over the time period, with the number ranging from a high of six (in 2000) to a low of one (in five separate years, including four of the last nine years) (Death Penalty Information Center 2006b).

What explains Florida's stable (or even declining) appetite for the death penalty? This pattern almost certainly is linked to a similar pattern occurring for the USA as a whole. The last decade has seen growing concern about the fairness of the death penalty. Most notable is the concern that poor legal representation of defendants and overzealous

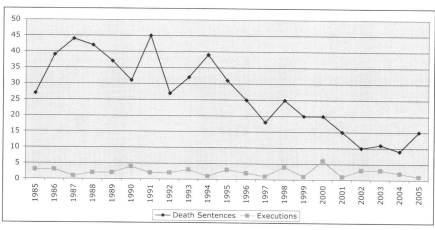

Figure 14.1 Death sentence and executions in Florida, 1985–2005

prosecution has created a system in which justice is arbitrary and innocent defendants may be sentenced to death or executed. This concern likely has been fuelled by widespread media coverage of mistakes that have been made in death penalty cases. Since 1973, an average of three death row inmates per year have been exonerated and released because of clear evidence of innocence or severe constitutional problems with their conviction, and this rate has doubled for the years since 1998. (By itself, Florida accounts for nearly 20 per cent of these exonerations.) These circumstances are thought to have contributed to a decline in executions in the USA as a whole, with the number of executions peaking in 1999 at 98 but declining to around 60 in more recent years (Death Penalty Information Center 2006b).

The expansion of inclusionary control

While the destructuring rhetoric of the 1960s and 1970s often treated inclusionary and exclusionary control as opposing strategies, Cohen emphasized that for a culture seeking maximum control, the two are complementary. Thus, in looking to the future, Cohen predicted that inclusionary control should continue to expand, along with the expansion of exclusionary control offered by such things as prisons.

This prediction closely (but not perfectly) matches the events in Florida in recent decades, particularly in reference to the expanded use of community-based supervision of offenders, including such practices as felony probation, home confinement with and without electronic surveillance, administrative probation, drug offender probation, sex offender probation, pretrial intervention and drug offender pretrial intervention. From 1985 to 2005, the number of offenders receiving these forms of community supervision nearly doubled from 73,866 in 1985 to 141,471 in 2005 (Florida Department of Corrections 1985 and 2005). Importantly, expanded use of these sanctions (and incarceration as well) cannot be explained by an expanded pool of offenders – between 1985 and 2004, Florida's rate of index crime declined by 38 per cent (Florida Department of Law Enforcement 2006).

One of the most notable trends in this area of inclusionary control involves the expansion of home confinement. Prior to the mid-1980s, Florida's community alternatives to prison consisted solely of felony probation. In 1983, Florida began implementation of both new sentencing guidelines and a home confinement programme. Florida's home confinement programme was officially promoted as a way to divert adult offenders from Florida's prisons, which were experiencing unprecedented growth and associated conditions of overcrowding. The home confinement programme involved intensive 24-hour supervision of offenders in their homes normally for a two-year sentence. Home confinement officers were mandated by statute to a maximum caseload of 20 offenders.

The specific offender requirements of the programme included:

1 Report to a home confinement officer at least four times per week or if employed, report daily;

2 Perform at least 140 hours of community service without pay;

3 Remain confined to home except for approved employment;

4 Make restitution payments for a specific dollar amount;

5 Submit to and pay for any required urinalysis, breathalyser, or blood specimen tests as requested by the home confinement officer;

6 Maintain an hourly account of all activities on a daily log which, upon request, is to be submitted to the home confinement officer for review;

7 Participate in self-improvement programmes as determined by the Home Confinement officer;

8 Answer truthfully any enquiries of the home confinement officer and allow the officer to visit home and place of employment and employer;

9 For sex offenders, as a special condition of home confinement, agree to the release of treatment information to the home confinement officer or court.

Four groups of offenders were targeted for home confinement. These included:

1 Probation violators with either technical or misdemeanour violations;

2 Parole violators with technical or misdemeanour violations;

3 Offenders found guilty of non-forcible felonies;

4 Miscellaneous 'other' offenders deemed appropriate by the sentencing judge. The 'other' offender category was included as a result of strong lobbying by the state's judges. In effect, to avoid opposition from the judges, the open-ended 'other' offenders group was added to home confinement's eligible list of targeted offenders.

Beginning in 1987, Florida implemented electronic monitoring for the higher-risk offenders on home confinement. This early system of electronic monitoring involved a radio-frequency (RF) system. Offenders were required to wear an electric security device that was hooked up to the home telephone to maintain continuous contact. As long as the offender did not go beyond a certain distance from the home telephone line, the frequency remained intact. Florida employed 'active' tamper-alert devices with these systems. Florida's Department of Corrections maintains a centralized computer that receives the information regarding the movements within their homes of those offenders wearing the RF devices. Should the offender be allowed to leave his/her home for employment, the information received is compared to the offender's work schedule. As a result, when the offender is away from home, RF cannot be employed to monitor the offender's whereabouts.

In 1998, and associated with the continuous advances in electronic surveillance technology, Florida added global positioning system (GPS) monitoring to track more serious offenders in near real time and provide mapping of these offenders' movements for retrieval upon request. This new technology enables 24-hour surveillance as compared with home-only surveillance with the RF system. Another feature of active GPS surveillance is that it can notify the home confinement officer immediately of any violations of sentencing requirements. For example, in a number of cases involving paedophiles or other sex offenders, a series of explicit geographic boundaries are set, and if offenders violate any of these boundaries, their home confinement officers are notified. These various forms of home confinement have provided Florida with a continuum of supervision and surveillance presumably based upon offender danger or risk to the community.

A key consideration – and one that is relevant to Cohen's predictions – is whether these new forms of surveillance were targeted to those who normally would have gone to prison. Despite the professed intentions of using new inclusionary sanctions as a substitute for prisons, the pattern has been that these sanctions largely draw from the pool of offenders who would have avoided legal sanctions altogether or received only probation (Blomberg and Lucken 1993). In the case of Florida, there is little reason to suggest that the rising use of community supervision significantly reduced the prison population. After all, the prison population has grown by 209 per cent in recent decades. There is recent evidence, however, that GPS and RF home confinement in particular are disproportionately drawing cases from a pool of more serious offenders. In the largest and most comprehensive study of electronic monitoring to date, Padgett, Bales and Blomberg (2006) found that offenders receiving either RF or GPS monitoring have a greater likelihood of a prison sentence than offenders on home confinement without electronic monitoring. Thus, the addition of these technologically enhanced forms of home confinement appear to be actually serving as an alternative to prison rather than as a net-widening supplement to it.

An additional finding by Padgett, Bales, and Blomberg (2006) is worth emphasizing: RF and GPS monitoring significantly reduced the likelihood of offenders committing a new offence or absconding from supervision. Moreover, this was true for all types of offenders considered, including violent, property, and drug offenders.

The expansion of pre-emptive inclusionary controls

The discussion to this point has emphasized legal reactions to those caught committing a crime. Of central importance to Cohen (1985), however, was the possibility of new pre-emptive controls designed for surveillance of space, actions, and individuals that pose any risk of crime or deviance. While quantitative assessments of these types of surveillance are not available, it nevertheless is safe to conclude that recent decades have seen an explosion in these forms of control. The trends in Florida would appear to be no different than those occurring in the USA as a whole and in other industrialized nations. Central to these trends is the expansion of closed-circuit television (CCTV) to provide round-the-clock video surveillance of banks and other offices, retail outlets, neighbourhood and apartment entrances, and crime 'hot spots' (Welsh and Farrington 2004). Other examples include the greater use of technological systems to monitor and track access to certain locations, including offices and schools. For example, Schuck (2005) describes the growing use of biometric techniques (including facial recognition, iris scanning, retinal scanning, and voice recognition), and notes the introduction of iris scanning technology in New Jersey schools in a programme sponsored by the US Department of Justice. Also central to this growing use of pre-emptive controls is the trend toward mandatory drug testing in the workplace (Tunnell 2004).

In commenting on how rapidly these and other controls have proliferated, Marx (2005: 385) recently drew attention to the concept of 'surveillance creep', which occurs 'when a tool introduced for a specific purpose comes to be used for other purposes ... [because] those with the technology realize its potential, and ask "why not?"' The US use of social security numbers is cited as a key example. This programme initially was developed only to track employment earnings and contributions to the social security programme, but the number itself has evolved into a 'general purpose universal identification number' that can be used to track loans and consumer purchases, involvement in certain legal proceedings, and changes in residence, among other things (p. 386). A similar example involves the history of the bar code.

It originally was developed to scan items purchased in a store to control shoplifting and monitor inventories. Ever more sophisticated bar-code designs, however, now allow them to be encoded with vastly greater information, including biometric and health information. These bar codes can then be attached to various pieces of identification (such as a driver's licence) that are needed to access different locations, products, or services.

These are precisely the sort of developments that Cohen (1985) predicted in *Visions of Social Control*. Importantly, however, what Cohen could not foresee was the occurrence of the 9/11 attacks and the implications they would have for social control. These events have spurred urgent growth of new and more far-reaching social control methods and practices throughout US communities in the official war on terrorism. These post-9/11 efforts include the US Department of Justice and Homeland Security providing over half a billion dollars to expand local and state police intelligence capacities for such different groups as suspected terrorists, biker gangs and even environmentalists. In addition, these funds are being used for the accelerated growth and development in local and state police computing and data integration. Various police and intelligence reports and numerous public records are being integrated into large databases for quick access by more than 700,000 state and local police agencies throughout the USA. The emergence of what are termed 'fusion centres' has accompanied this intelligence and computing movement. These centres now exist in 31 states, and many other states are now moving to develop them as well. Fusion centres pool information from multiple jurisdictions concerning all matters involving potential criminal activity including fraud, racketeering, and computer hacking without any clear guidelines or restrictions as to exactly what constitutes homeland security-related threats (*U.S. News and World Report* 2006).

What is emerging, as predicted by Cohen, is an ever more inclusive and technologically driven system of control that is merely a computer click away. For example, the Multi-State Anti-Terrorism Information Exchange (MATRIX) system employs 'data-mining' technology to gather data from a broad range of private and public sources (including data on criminal records, marriages and divorces, property ownership, and personal finances) to create instant dossiers for individuals (Schuck 2005). While the MATRIX system is no longer funded, in part because of public outcries over privacy concerns, other systems similar to MATRIX are now being employed throughout the country, including RISS.NET (the Regional Information Sharing Systems Network), a data-sharing collaboration between the Federal Bureau of Investigation, the Department of Defense, and the Department of Homeland Security.

Additionally, recent news reports indicate that shortly after 9/11, the National Security Agency (NSA) began working with three major US telecommunications companies (BellSouth, AT&T, and Verizon) to amass and examine the domestic call records of tens of millions of US households and businesses who are not suspected of any wrongdoing (*Washington Post* 2006). Similarly, it is now clear that the Bush administration has used broad administrative subpoenas – rather than court-approved warrants – to gain access to records for millions of international bank transactions (Lichtblau and Risen 2006). Clearly, the line between suspected terrorists and other citizens considered to be potential threats is ambiguous, and perhaps even becoming largely irrelevant. Moreover, as technology continues to develop, it can be expected that more far-reaching monitoring and surveillance will occur. In Marx's (2005: 385) words, 'the surveillance appetite once aroused can be insatiable'. The emergence of a surveillance society is upon us with Cohen's vision of social control being clearly realized.

Expanded control will be widely supported by the public

A key part of Cohen's view of the future was that the capacity for official social control would be increased not simply by the development of new technologies, but also by the public's willingness to accept such control. With scattered exceptions, this prediction largely appears to be supported for the USA as a whole, and there is little reason to suspect that Florida diverges from this pattern. This pattern is most evident in the public opinion research indicating that new forms of control are widely supported by the public. For example, while the USA has more severe criminal penalties than virtually any other industrialized nation, public opinion surveys continue to show that more than two-thirds of Americans believe that the courts in their local area do not deal harshly enough with offenders (Sourcebook of Criminal Justice Statistics 2003: Table 2.47). Moreover, most surveys show that about two-thirds of the public continues to support the use of the death penalty for those convicted of murder (Sourcebook of Criminal Justice Statistics 2003: Table 2.50). In some surveys, support for the death penalty is decreased when respondents are offered an alternative sanction for those convicted of murder (Death Penalty Information Center 2006b), but the alternative (life imprisonment without any chance of parole) is itself an imposition of control that exceeds what actually is delivered for the typical murder conviction.

Figures such as these often are cited as evidence for American support for punitive, exclusionary punishments. Importantly, however, Americans also appear to be highly supportive of a broad range of intermediate and rehabilitative reactions to crime; that is, Americans also support the *inclusionary* punishments that *Visions of Social Control* emphasized. For example, in studying a national sample of US adults, Cohen, Rust, and Steen (2002) found that inclusionary social services involving drug treatment or prevention were the most supported options when respondents were asked how additional crime control funding should be spent. Similarly, Moon *et al.* (2000) found high public support for a wide range of community corrections options. For a sample of Tennessee residents, at least 60 per cent of respondents selected the strongest level of support offered by the survey for a wide range of community sanctions, including family counselling, drug and alcohol treatment, educational and vocational training, and community service.

The public also has been fairly supportive of the new pre-emptive controls that emerged in the wake of 9/11, even those directed to the mass public, rather than just those thought to have ties to terrorism. A good example of this is the public reaction to the revelation that the NSA and major US telecommunications firms were collaborating – without a court order – to track telephone calls made by millions of Americans who have no known ties to terrorism. The media, policymakers, and social commentators generally treated this programme as highly controversial – up to that point, the Bush administration had intimated that the NSA's monitoring of telephone calls was limited to international calls of those suspected of terrorism. The public's reaction to this programme was quite muted, however. Although the polling results on this issue are not conclusive and they vary based on the exact wording of questions, as much as half of US adults are not concerned that their calling patterns are being amassed and analysed by the NSA (Pollingreport.com 2006). Moreover, in response to generic questions about the balance between expanding controls to prevent terrorism and protecting individual civil liberties, a significant portion of Americans (at least 40 per cent, but sometimes as much as 60 per cent) state a preference for erring on the side of expanded governmental control (Pollingreport.com 2006).

These patterns provide strong evidence for Cohen's prediction that expansions in official social control would be achieved more easily than one might initially suspect. In a society in which a fear of chaos and the evil motives of others is paramount, the majority of citizens will accept expanded governmental control, and perhaps even unequivocally embrace it. Drawing from Staples (1997), Blomberg and Lucken (2000: 228) conclude that 'there is no "Big Brother" ... instead, we, the citizenry, are behind the culture of control'.

Conclusion

Since the 1985 publication of *Visions of Social Control*, a number of arguments have been proposed concerning the continuous changes and resulting expansions in social control resulting from various crime control initiatives. This includes the use of such metaphors and theoretical abstractions as net-widening, dispersal of discipline, transcarceration, carceral society, maximum security society, the new penology, and the culture of control. Among the concerns addressed by these metaphors and theoretical interpretations has been the repeated disparity between the ideas and practices of different social control strategies and reforms and the resulting pattern of expanding social control. These metaphors and theoretical interpretations have been useful in helping account for the unintended and negative consequences of various social control reforms and related initiatives. However, the question of what can be done to change or alter these expanding social control trends remains unanswered.

As Cohen predicted, while there has been a proliferation of social control with a number of negative outcomes resulting from different crime control efforts, there have also been other intended and positive outcomes, as shown in the case of Florida's use of electronic monitoring. To elaborate, electronic monitoring can be seen as intrusive and expansive when used with less serious offenders who would not have been subject to prison in the absence of electronic monitoring. Alternatively, electronic monitoring can be viewed as liberating when applied to the more serious and violent offenders, thereby providing an alternative to prison while simultaneously providing more refined and effective methods of control or what Cohen referred to as 'technicism'. As Cohen suggested, this technicism could actually lead to a loss in interest in crime causation altogether in the endless pursuit of what works best.

Certainly, technology makes it possible to control subjects more completely and to control subjects in more discerning ways. Stated differently, emerging technologies need not always result in more control and other unintended and negative consequences. These technologies are capable of producing more refined and liberating control as well. However, such social control arguments as transcarceration, new penology, and culture of control generally lump these strategies together, including electronic monitoring as resulting only in net-widening and ineffective intrusions into basic individual rights and liberties. Clearly, there is much to be concerned about regarding the future of social control, and that includes a number of important public policy issues. For example, Downes (2006) suggests that there is a fundamental value issue of how far an already criminogenic society may go in ceasing to care about what motivates offenders if these offenders can be controlled ever more effectively and cheaply. However, if as a result of more complete and effective crime control, crime ceases to be the potential solution or best response for whatever motivates individual criminal offenders, perhaps some offenders will seek other more democratic, political and legal courses of action. But this, of course, is speculative. What is not speculative is that the vision of social control provided by Cohen more than two decades ago has indeed been realized. As he summarized:

> The study of social control shows a wide gap between our private sense of what is going on around us and our professional writings about the social world. This private terrain is inhabited by premonitions of *Nineteen Eighty-Four*, *Clockwork Orange* and *Brave New World*, by fears about new technologies of mind control, by dark thoughts about the increasing intrusion of the state into family and private lives, by a general unease that more of our actions and thoughts are under surveillance and subject to record and manipulation. Social control has become Kafka-land, a paranoid landscape in which things are done to us, without our knowing when, why, or by whom, or even that they are being done. We live inside Burroughs' 'soft machine,' an existence all the more perplexing because those who control us seem to have the most benevolent of intentions. Indeed we ourselves appear as the controllers as well as the controlled. Suspending all critical judgment, we accept readily – almost with masochistic pleasure – the notion that *Nineteen Eighty-Four* has literally arrived (Cohen 1985; 6–7).

As mentioned previously, what is particularly notable about the accuracy of Cohen's 1985 social control characterizations and predictions is that they were made well before 9/11. The post-9/11 terrorism threat significantly elevated the quest for ever greater control. Moreover, and consistent with Cohen's social control vision, is the culture that is associated with this ever-expanding technology, surveillance and control that now pervades our everyday lives. Whether driving through intersections, entering public restrooms, shopping, banking, eating at restaurants, travelling, or conducting other routine and everyday activities, the level of surveillance, monitoring and recording of these activities is continuous and generally unquestioned by the public. It is as if we have little choice other than to accept the cameras, surveillance and monitoring. Moreover, our children are accustomed to computers, videos, PlayStations and a host of other quickly changing technologies. It was reported in a recent research study that eight out of ten US children up to age six watch television, play video games or use the computer at least two hours per day (Kaiser Family Foundation 2006). The study found that most parents view the frequent use of media by their children as positive educational experiences. Indeed, this is our evolving culture and it extends throughout our daily lives, experiences and perceptions of normalcy.

Undoubtedly, we have reached Cohen's social control predictions. Further, the future promises even more integrated and technologically driven social control. This ever-escalating inclusive and exclusive social control is being facilitated by a responsive culture that both supports and considers these changes in social control as largely necessary, utilitarian, and inevitable. Social control changes are being promoted and understood as responsive and necessary given the challenges of crime, and the challenges associated with globalization and related threats of terrorism.

But several questions warrant thoughtful consideration, including the following: Is this ever-escalating pattern of social control necessary, and is there something scholars can do to address more effectively these patterns and associated policy questions? What is occurring now in both sociology and criminology is an unprecedented recognition and associated effort to directly address timely public policy issues with more accessible empirical and theoretical study. While not all scholars agree that they should assume any sort of public policy role, it appears that it is becoming clear to a growing number of scholars and disciplines like sociology and criminology that a more committed and active public policy role is necessary in the future (for example, see Clear and Frost 2001 and Burawoy 2005).

Stanley Cohen provided us with a very telling and precise analysis and prediction of social control. His forecast has been realized and the future of social control looks to offer more of the same. Clearly, the traditional divide between social control scholarship and public policy needs to be seriously questioned if we are to help guide, temper, and, very importantly, understand what now appears to be a very ominous future for democratic principles, individual rights and social justice. The question need not only be what works in social control but also, what kind of future do we seek and at what price? Moreover, is now the time for social control scholars to move beyond negative analyses and ominous forecasts and instead toward a more public purpose? Throughout his career in the study of crime and deviance and human rights, Cohen successfully demonstrated the role of committed and activist scholar with important clarifications.

In relation to these role clarifications, Cohen (2006) recently wrote that there is a tension for scholars between being accessible and dealing with the immediate issues of today's headlines, journalists' questions, and urgent e-mail enquiries while simultaneously being complete, reflexive and theoretical. He elaborates that theoretical complexity requires scholarly work to be more dense and often impenetrable to the larger public. Cohen illustrates this issue by comparing academic sociology with human rights reports. Both share a guiding commitment to honesty, accuracy, and reliability without damaging the study's subjects while simultaneously facing the temptation of becoming focused upon confessions, subjectivity and authenticity. But human rights reports that communicate the voices of victims, perpetrators and bystanders do not add up to the 'story' of an atrocity which is the very task of sociological scholarship.

Moreover, and beyond immediacy and accessibility are the issues of commitment and values. Cohen asserts that Howard Becker's (1967) famous question, 'Whose side are we on?', now appears to be little more than an unconvincing mission statement. He points out that conventional answers to this question would be, 'You are not always on the side of whomever you are studying' (a very strange idea!), nor that of 'the underdog' (who soon becomes the top dog), or that of 'those who can reach the levers of power'. Rather, committed scholarship involves a delicate balance even when scholars believe they know the 'inside' of the situation. It is not so much a matter of committed scholars becoming embroiled in public debates by supporting a particular policy over another as of their identifying and explaining what choices and likely consequences are involved in particular decisions. Careful and objective analysis should never be trumped by advocacy or the 'taking of sides' for some specific policy.

Today, the question of what is the appropriate public role for sociological and criminological scholars is generating considerable dialogue, reflection and associated disciplinary changes. For example, in sociology, Burawoy (2005) explains there has been a traditional division in sociological labour that produces four different types of knowledge, namely, professional, critical, policy and public. While these four divisions have experienced different degrees of exclusion and subordination within the discipline, they share the common thread of contributing to civil society in the effort to make the world better. Efforts aimed at forging new relationships between these four areas of sociology have culminated in the emergence of what is now called 'public sociology'. Associated developments in 'public sociology' include publication of the magazine *Contexts* and the American Sociological Association's organized efforts at lobbying and outreach through regular congressional briefings and news releases. Similarly, the American Society of Criminology began publishing the journal *Criminology and Public Policy* in 2001. This journal is aimed at bridging the traditional divide between criminological scholarship and public policy by disseminating state-of-the-art research to a larger audience of academics and policy-related personnel. While debate and dialogue will go on over the appropriateness and value of a more public role and purpose for sociologists and criminologists, it appears likely that this role will continue to be clarified, refined and advanced in the future in response to such increasing public dilemmas as the ever-increasing patterns of social control.

References

Becker, H.S. (1967) 'Whose side are we on?', *Social Problems*, 3: 239–47.

Blomberg, T.G. and Lucken, K. (1993) 'Intermediate punishment and the piling up of sanctions', in G.F. Cole (ed.) *Criminal Justice: Law and Politics*. Belmont, CA: Wadworth.

Blomberg, T.G. and Lucken, K. (2000) *American Penology: A History of Control*. Hawthorne, NY: Aldine de Gruyter.

Burawoy, M. (2005) 2004 ASA Presidential Address: 'For public sociology', *American Sociological Review*, 70: 4–28.

Clear, T.R. and Frost, N.A. (2001) '*Criminology and Public Policy*: a new journal of the American Society of Criminology', *Criminology and Public Policy*, 1: 1–3.

Clear, T.R., Cole, G.F. and Reisig, M.D. (2006) *American Corrections*. Belmont, CA: Thomson Wadsworth.

Cohen, S. (1985) *Visions of Social Control: Crime, Punishment, and Classification*. Cambridge, UK: Polity Press.

Cohen, S. (2006). Personal correspondence.

Cohen, M.A., Rust, R.T. and Steen, S. (2002) *Measuring Public Perceptions of Appropriate Prison Sentences*. Washington, DC: US Department of Justice.

Death Penalty Information Center (2006a) *Death Sentences in the United States from 1977 to 2005*. Accessed at www.deathpenaltyinfo.org/article. php?scid=9&did=847.

Death Penalty Information Center (2006b) *Searchable Database of Executions*. Accessed at www.deathpenaltyinfo.org/executions.php.

Death Penalty Information Center (2006c) *News and Developments: Public Opinion*. Accessed at www.deathpenaltyinfo.org/newsanddev.php?scid=23.

Downes, D. (2006) Personal correspondence.

Federal Bureau of Investigations (2004) *Crime in the United States 2004*. Accessed at www.fbi.gov/ucr/cius_04/.

Florida Department of Corrections (1985) *Florida Department of Corrections 1984–85 Annual Report*.

Florida Department of Corrections (2005) *Florida Department of Corrections 2004–05 Annual Report*.

Florida Department of Corrections (2005) *10–20–Life Felons Admitted to Prison*. Accessed at www.dc.state.fl.us/pub/10-20-life/.

Florida Department of Corrections, Bureau of Research and Data Analysis (2006) Unpublished data.

Florida Department of Law Enforcement, Florida Statistical Analysis Center (2005) *Florida Uniform Crime Report, 1960–2004*. Accessed at www.fdle.state.fl.us/fsac/Crime_Trends/total_Index/total_crime.asp.

Foucault, M. (1977) *Discipline and Punish: The Birth of the Prison*. New York: Pantheon.

Lichtblau, E. and Risen, J. (2006) 'Bank data is sifted by US in secret to block terror', *The New York Times*, 23 June.

Marx, G.T. (2005) 'Seeing hazily (but not darkly) through the lens: some recent empirical studies of surveillance technologies', *Law & Social Inquiry*, 30: 339–99.

Mears, D.P. and Watson, J. (2006) 'Towards a fair and balanced assessment of supermax prisons', *Justice Quarterly*, 23: 232–70.

Moon, M.M., Sundt, J.L., Cullen, F.T. and Wright, J.P. (2000) 'Is child saving dead? Public support for juvenile rehabilitation', *Crime and Delinquency*, 46: 38–60.

Padgett, K.G., Bales, W.D. and Blomberg, T.G. (2006) 'Under surveillance: an empirical test of the effectiveness and consequences of electronic monitoring', *Criminology and Public Policy*, 5: 61–92.

Pollingreport.com (2006) Information retrieved from http://pollingreport.com/terror.htm.

Rothman, D.J. (1971) *The Discovery of the Asylum: Social Order and Disorder in the New Republic*. Boston: Little, Brown.

Rusche, G. and Kircheimer, O. (1939) *Punishment and Social Structure*. New York: Columbia University.

Schuck, A.M. (2005) 'American crime prevention: trends and new frontiers', *Canadian Journal of Criminology and Criminal Justice*, 47: 447–62.

Short, J.F. (1986) Book review: *Visions of Social Control: Crime, Punishment, and Classification. American Journal of Sociology*, 92: 240–2.

Sourcebook of Criminal Justice Statistics (2003) Tables 2.47 and 2.50 retrieved from www.albany.edu/sourcebook/tost_2.html#2_u.

Staples, W.G. (1997) *The Culture of Surveillance: Discipline and Social Control in the United States*. New York: St Martin's Press.

Tunnell, K. (2004) *Pissing on Demand*. New York: New York University Press.

US Census Bureau (2001) Census 2000 PHC-T-2. Ranking Tables for States: 1990 and 2000. Accessed from www.census.gov/population/www/cen2000/phc-t2.html.

Washington Post (2006) *NSA: Spying at Home*. Special report accessed at www.washingtonpost.com/wp-dyn/content/politics/special/index.html.

Welsh, B.C. and Farrington, D.P. (2004) 'Surveillance for crime prevention in public space: results and policy choices in Britain and America', *Criminology and Public Policy*, 3: 497–526.

Chapter 15

Governing security: the rise of the privatized military

Tim Newburn[1]

The globalisation of information systems, the standardisation of the mass media and the loss of a 'sense of place' – all of which happen despite the resurgence of separatism and nationalism – facilitate the export of control methods which offer a quick solution to growing problems of street crime. Private security systems, for example, have an obvious attraction. And now that Disneyland has been exported from California to France, the next stage might be Poland – reproducing not just the spectacle, but its distinctive system of proactive social control.

(Cohen 1994: 84)

Introducing security

In this chapter, I want to pick up Stan Cohen's observation about the globalization of control methods and the spread of privatized security. In doing so, I will focus not on the attractiveness of private security as a response to street crime, but on its growing role in international security. In doing so, I also pick up on a number of by now quite well-established arguments in this field. The first is that we are witnessing the blurring of the boundary between international security and domestic concerns of order maintenance. Criminologists are taking increasing note of international affairs at the same time that international relations scholars are more and more preoccupied with domestic issues (Zedner 2003). There are a number of reasons for this. First, there are various ways in which the connections between the local and the global, the national and the international, are becoming increasingly visible. The spread of complex, transnational criminal networks and the nature of international terrorism would be two of the more obvious examples (Crotty 2004; Nordstrom 2004).

Second, and linked with this, events such as the terrorist attacks of 11 September 2001 in the USA, and those subsequently in Madrid and London in particular, have begun to reconfigure the governance of security both across locations, and in ways, that speak to the traditional concerns of both political scientists and criminologists. In the USA in particular, but also in a number of other Western democracies, not least the UK, 'new' security concerns have led to further militarization of domestic policing (Dunlap 2001), and to the intensification of surveillance of citizens (Lyon 2003; Parenti 2003) – much of which is undertaken by privatized security agencies. There has also been something of a blurring of the boundaries between policing and national (homeland) security bodies and, linked with this, a further increase in the securitization of policing – particularly in connection with issues of immigration, asylum and terrorism (Welch and Schuster 2005).

Third, it is increasingly clear that much of what criminologists have had to say about the governance of security in the domestic arena is increasingly applicable to the subject of international security. Thus, within criminology, we are now very used to observing that plurality of provision means that it is no longer possible simply to focus on the police when talking about policing. Robert Reiner put this most succinctly when he wrote that 'policing now reflects the processes of pluralism and fragmentation which have been the hallmarks of the postmodern' (Reiner 1992: 780). The same globalizing, postmodernizing processes that are transforming policing are also transforming the field of international security. Just as we can no longer understand policing by focusing on the police so, too, we can no longer understand wars and the playing out of international conflict through a focus on the military (Kaldor 1999).

A large body of criminological work has documented in the course of the second half of the twentieth century the emergence of a series of complex, overlapping networks of agents and institutions responsible for policy formulation, finance and delivery in relation to security (Shearing and Stenning 1983; Jones and Newburn 1998; Crawford 2003; Johnston 2006). This new landscape is described variously as 'pluralized' or, more recently, by Bayley and Shearing (2001) as 'multilateralized'. Though they do not spell out precisely why this is their preferred term, they suggest that there are four crucial sets of changed circumstances. First, we no longer operate under a system in which governments have primary responsibility for providing security (though this seems pretty debatable). Second, there is now a greater split between the 'auspices' and the providers of security. Third, people now tend to spend more time in spaces where security is provided by nongovernmental groups rather than by governmental agencies. Fourth, this reconstruction is occurring worldwide and is not restricted to particular economic or political systems.

This is so substantial a shift away from the traditional state-centred view of policing that a number of authors – most notably Clifford Shearing – have argued that we should now be talking about the 'governance of security' rather than policing (Shearing 1995; Johnston and Shearing 2003). Irrespective of the plausibility of this argument, one of the most surprising and notable features of this developing literature is its preoccupation with the nature, delivery and control of low-level policing and order maintenance. Thus, despite the avowed preference for the terms 'governance' and 'security' rather than 'policing', such work has tended to focus on matters that are very similar to those that have preoccupied sociologists of policing for the last three or four decades, while largely ignoring matters that might generally fall under the rubric of '(inter)national security'. Though not, strictly speaking, precisely what Brodeur (1983) meant by the use of these terms, one might characterize the 'governing security' literature as tending to focus on 'low' rather than 'high' policing, whether this is done by security agencies or law enforcement bodies (but see Manning 2006). This is intriguing, for it is perhaps in this field that many aspects of the role of non-state actors that Shearing and others identify are developing most swiftly and, arguably, where concerns about the means of governing security are most pressing. I return to this below.

Much of what has been happening to security provision in the domestic arena is already well researched and described (Jones and Newburn 2006; Johnston 1992). Indeed, even the area of transnational policing and security has been receiving increasing attention (Edwards and Gill 2003; Sheptycki 2000). However, the arena that has perhaps received less attention from criminologists – though that will no doubt change – is the very rapid emergence of a privatized military industry (for exceptions see Whyte 2003; Jamieson and McEvoy 2004; Walker and Whyte 2005; O'Reilly and Ellison 2006). What I want to do in the remainder of this chapter is review briefly some of the recent history and developments in the privatized military arena and then finish with a few observations about governing security in this context and on the continuing importance of human rights discourses in that regard.

Privatizing security

Now, of course, there is a long history of private contracting of military services even during the nation state era. Much of this, in recent times, is a murky history of mercenary activity. However, in the last decade and a half or so, a vast international network of privatized military operators has emerged to become an established part of (late) modern warfare. Though some continue to characterize those operating in this industry straightforwardly as 'mercenaries' (Brayton 2002; Whyte 2003), and there can be little doubt that something like old-fashioned mercenaries continue to operate around the world (Spicer 1999; Vines 1999), the new private military industry is largely made up of a complex web of large corporate providers, many working in direct partnership with established military forces to provide both the goods and the services of war (Avant 2004). As such, Singer's (2005) argument that this industry represents 'the corporate evolution of the age-old profession of mercenaries' seems apposite.

Before considering what this industry does, a word or two about why it has developed. The obvious starting point is the end of the Cold War and the removal of any immediate threat of war between East and West. This led many states to reduce the size of their standing armies, navies and air forces (though not necessarily their overall military expenditure) and had two important consequences. First, it reduced state military capacity. Second, it produced an enormous supply of often highly trained personnel looking for employment. Third, despite the downsizing of professional armies in the post-Cold War period, there were other developments that had the effect of actually increasing the demand for more troops. Crucial among these was growing global instability and the emergence of a series of bloody conflicts in Africa and Eastern Europe in particular. These conflicts are unlike the wars of previous eras. They involve few battles. The bulk of violence is directed toward civilians. Participation is low relative to populations and it is frequently difficult to identify with any certainty precisely whom the conflict is between. These distinctive characteristics have led authors like Mary Kaldor (1999) to describe them as the 'new wars', Mark Duffield (2005) as 'network wars', and Ulrich Beck (2005) as 'post-national wars'. These conflicts are 'post-national' in that they are not waged in the national interest; they do not result from established rivalries between hostile nation states; and, frequently, they are the *result* of the weakening or weak*ness* of particular nation states.

This specific character of modern conflict is the third factor behind the rise of the private military industry. The messiness of the 'new wars' has meant that Western powers have become increasingly reluctant to intervene, producing situations in which transnational bodies such as the UN, non-state actors such as NGOs and, increasingly, private corporations are involved. Indeed, every multilateral peace operation conducted by the UN since the 1990s, including some that would be considered to be among the more successful, has included private security companies (Avant 2005). And, where the advanced militaries have been involved in peacekeeping or other frontline operations, more and more often it was the case that they acted with the support of, or in partnership with, private military suppliers in various forms. Finally, there are two other major imperatives we might identify. The first concerns technological changes that have led to a very rapid increase in the sophistication of equipment required by the military, with a parallel expansion of the number of civilian specialists required. The other crucial element has of course been the increasing influence of neoliberalism in most if not all areas of public administration and government business (Harvey 2005), which has led to a restructuring of the delivery of most services, including the military.

Examining security

So, to the industry itself. According to Singer (2003) and others, it consists of three main sectors. First, there are *military support firms,* which provide logistical and intelligence services. Second, there are *military consulting firms*, which provide strategic advice and training. The third sector consists of *military provider firms*, which offer tactical military assistance, including the defence of key installations and individuals together with combat services. This latter sector is sometimes referred to as 'private security', though much of what they undertake has little in common with what one might observe in any city centre on a Saturday night.

One can get an indication of the speed, the size and the spread of the privatized military, and some of the reasons behind its development, by looking briefly at the UK example. As in other areas of public policy in the UK, the move toward privatization began in the early 1980s with the increasing emphasis across government on 'new public management'. In 1983, the Ministry of Defence (MoD) introduced a new competitive procurement policy in which competition to provide equipment and support services was encouraged. From this point onward, it was official policy to outsource in these areas if economic gains could be demonstrated while operational capability remained undiminished. By 1991, contractors were being used in areas such as cleaning, catering, security guarding and maintenance, training/instruction, and target simulation and electronic warfare training (Hartley 2002). Outsourcing policy was extended in 1992 with in-house services progressively being market tested and contracted out.

Although New Labour had been critical of elements of existing privatization policies, governments since 1997 have both extended the range and increased the pace of such changes in recent years. Following the Strategic Defence Review, official MoD policy became 'where appropriate... [to] consider the use of contractors to assist with logistic support' (Uttley 2004), and under the government's Better Quality Services initiative since 1998, and under the general banners of *modernization* and subsequently *public sector reform*, there has been 'a systematic expansion of contractor involvement in non-deployed defence support services'. By 2001, a total of 36 PFI contracts had been signed by the MoD to a value of just under £2 billion, with a further 70 projects worth £10 billion under consideration. The largest PFI deal to date has been for the Skynet 5 project – a satellite communications system – contracted to Paradigm Secure Communications in 2003 for £2.5 billion (Kershaw 2004).

After the privatization of a significant element of support services, the next logical step was to shift the focus from non-deployable support services to the contracting out of services closer to the front line of deployed military operations. In 2003, MoD directives sought to 'maximise the use of contractors' during operations in Iraq, and recent estimates suggest that approximately £11 billion of the annual £24 billion defence budget is spent with industry on the provision, operation and maintenance of equipment, with a further £2.5 billion on the provision and operation of services.

Indeed, Iraq is the site of the largest deployment of private military firms (PMFs) ever. There are currently over 60 firms employing over 20,000 private personnel engaged in military activities in Iraq (and thousands more providing non-military services). As Peter Singer (2003) has only half-jokingly put it, 'this is less *the coalition of the willing* than the *coalition of the billing*!' The UK Foreign Office confirmed that it alone had paid £20 million during 2004 to private security companies working in Iraq. Armor, a private security company listed in London, chaired by Sir Malcolm Rifkind (ex-Foreign Secretary), is estimated to have earned over £50 million during 2004 alone – almost half its total revenue – through its guarding activities in Iraq (*Evening Standard*, 24 January 2005). It currently employs around 1300 people in Iraq. The largest private security contract went to another London-based company, Aegis Defence Services, headed by Col. Tim Spicer, whose previous company, Sandline, was involved in breaking the UN arms embargo in its private military work in Sierra Leone in 1998 (*Independent*, 5 January 2005).

All three major forms of PMF activity can be found in plentiful supply in post-war Iraq. The American company Halliburton, for example, is reckoned to have undertaken at least $6 billion worth of business providing military logistical support activity (Singer 2004). Similarly, a number of companies have secured large contracts to provide military consulting services such as creating the new Iraqi police force and army. Among these, the major player is DynCorp, whose contract for police training is estimated potentially to rise close to £800 million. Another company, Erinys, won a $40 million contract to establish a paramilitary guard to protect Iraq's oilfields, employing a number of ex-soldiers and police officers from the former South African apartheid regime for the purpose (Rosen 2005). Private corporations have been involved in taking over the guarding of buildings initially protected by US soldiers in Iraq (*Financial Times*, 30 September 2003), and the Iraqi army has been trained by Vinnel, a subsidiary of Northrop Grummar, with the bill potentially rising to £2 billion.

But, as Peter Singer (2004) notes, 'the most dramatic and controversial expansion of PMF involvement is in the combat realm' through tactical PMFs like Blackwater and the wonderfully named Custer Battles and Control Risks. Prior to the election in Iraq, Blackwater, for example, provided protection and transport to the chief of the Coalition Provisional Authority, Paul Bremer (this contract alone was worth $21 million), and guarded 15 regional authority headquarters and the 'green zone' in downtown Baghdad. Far from the everyday image of private security, these corporations are engaging in activity that is very similar to that of, and undoubtedly carries the same risks as, the military. One account noted that:

> Blackwater, the firm that lost the four men in Fallujah, just days later defended the CPA [Coalition Provisional Authority] headquarters in Najaf from being overrun by radical Shiite militia. The firefight lasted several hours, with thousands of rounds of ammunition fired, and Blackwater even sent in its own helicopters twice to resupply its commandos with ammunition and to ferry out a wounded U.S. Marine (Singer 2004).

A clear indication of the philosophy underpinning much tactical PMF activity, and much of its approach to its work, can be found in the corporate promotional literature. Let me quote at length from the home page of the website of the PMF Custer Battles. In a revealing puff for the company, the full description on the Custer Battles website offers the clearest insight into the risk-oriented, market mentality that underpins the modern PMF (see also Rosen 2005). Under the banner, 'Turning

Risk into Opportunity', it describes Iraq as 'a nation and marketplace wrought with challenges, obstacles, and malevolent actors'. It goes on,

> However, Iraq offers contractors, traders, entrepreneurs as well as multi-national enterprises an unprecedented market opportunity. The ability to identify, quantify, and mitigate this myriad of risks allows successful organizations to transform risk into opportunity. Terrorist, sophisticated criminal enterprises, political and tribal turmoil, and a lack of modern infrastructure present formidable challenges to companies operating in all areas of Iraq. Organizations that have a comprehensive understanding of the threats facing their efforts, combined with a flexible strategy for overcoming these obstacles, will have a far greater chance of success. Risk management is not just about identifying hazards and implementing control measures to keep people safe. The Custer Battles approach to risk is about seeking opportunities, and designing solutions to enable these opportunities to be exploited. The greatest threat to success is failure to manage risk (http://www.custerbattles.com/iraq/index.html; accessed 28 September 2006).

The Iraq War illustrates just how quickly and fruitfully this market has been exploited by the private military industry. Indeed, it is not just the war and its aftermath within Iraq itself. The entire conflict has been bookended by the activities of the private military. The invasion of Iraq was launched from Camp Doha, built, operated and guarded by a number of private corporations led by a consortium called Combat Support Associates. Since the end of the main phase of the conflict, detainees have been held in camps and prisons similarly built and often run by private corporations including, infamously, both Abu Ghraib and Guantánamo Bay military prison – the latter built by the Kellogg, Brown and Root division of Halliburton at a cost of $45 million (Singer 2003). The conflict has meant that opportunities for private corporations have continued to expand, and the Private Security Company Association of Iraq (http://www.pscai.org/), a non-profit organization representing such interests, now has over 40 corporate members employing, it has been estimated, 35,000 people.

Concerning security

Clearly, the multilateralizing influences that criminologists have identified in relation to private security in our towns and cities are also increasingly coming to shape the international military and security field. Should we be concerned about such developments? The question, of course, is rhetorical and, indeed, the answer is an old one. Over 50 years ago, in his final speech as president, Dwight Eisenhower said[2]:

> In the councils of government, we must guard against the acquisition of unwarranted influence, whether sought or unsought, by the military-industrial complex. The potential for the disastrous rise of misplaced power exists and will persist.
>
> We must never let the weight of this combination endanger our liberties or democratic processes. We should take nothing for granted. Only an alert and knowledgeable citizenry can compel the proper meshing of the huge industrial and military machinery of defense with our peaceful methods and goals, so that security and liberty may prosper together.

Recent events in Iraq, which is what I want to turn to next, have reinforced such concerns. There has been no shortage of stories of human rights abuses emerging during the 'war on terror'. Among them, the allegations of the mistreatment of prisoners – including the widespread publication of photographic evidence – have become one of the best known. A brief look at the Abu Ghraib scandal illustrates some of the difficulties and dangers involved when private security becomes involved in war. Abu Ghraib, a notorious Iraqi prison, was selected by the Coalition Provisional Authority for use as a detention facility in the Iraq War in May 2003 and began receiving prisoners in June that year. In October 2003, civilian personnel from two corporations, Titan and CACI, arrived to join the military police and military intelligence staff already there.

The Taguba Report into the allegations of torture and abuse at Abu Ghraib found that 'In general, US civilian contract personnel (Titan Corporation, CACI, etc), third country nationals, and local contractors do not appear to be properly supervised within the detention facility at Abu Ghraib' (cited in Greenberg and Dratel 2005: 424). The report went on to make the following recommendations:

11.(U) That **Mr. Steven Stephanowicz, Contract US Civilian Interrogator, CACI, 205ᵗʰ Military Intelligence Brigade**, be given an Official Reprimand to be placed in his employment file, termination of employment, and generation of a derogatory report to revoke his security clearance for the following acts…

- Made a false statement to the investigation team regarding the locations of his interrogations, the activities during the interrogations, and his knowledge of abuses.

- Allowed and/or instructed MPs, who were not trained in interrogation techniques, to facilitate interrogations by 'setting conditions' which were neither authorized and in accordance with applicable regulations/policy. He clearly knew his instructions equated to physical abuse.

The report concluded that Stephanowicz, along with two other employees of private contractors, 'were either directly or indirectly responsible for the abuses at Abu Ghraib' (cited in Greenberg and Dratel 2005: 442–3). The subsequent Schlesinger and Fay–Jones Reports into US Department of Defense detention operations in Iraq confirmed the problems with civilian contractors. Schlesinger observed that as a result of the shrinking of the US Army's intelligence capability after the end of the Cold War it had been necessary to employ private contractors to undertake interrogation in the Abu Ghraib detention facility. These contractors, it reported, 'were a particular problem'. The Army inspector general found that 35 per cent of the private contractors employed in the prison neither had nor received formal training in military interrogation techniques, and, it would appear, were not aware that they were subject to the requirements of the Geneva Conventions (*ibid.*: 1055). Moreover, and damningly, 'Oversight of contractor personnel and activities was not sufficient to ensure intelligence operations fell within the law and the authorized chain of command' (*ibid.*: 942). This was reinforced by a further investigation conducted by Lieutenant General Anthony Jones and Major General George Fay in August 2004, which observed, 'There was at least the perception, and perhaps the reality, that non-DOD [Department of Defense] agencies had different rules regarding interrogation and detention operations. Such a perception encouraged soldiers to deviate from prescribed techniques' (*ibid.*: 1007). Despite the problems, and the general absence of accountability structures for non-military personnel, the Schlesinger Report concluded 'that some use of contractors in detention operations must continue into the foreseeable future' (*ibid.*: 952).

The experience of the Iraq War, and of that in Afghanistan also, reinforces the reasons for concern. From accusations of profiteering made against Halliburton and other major corporations – none of which has resulted in any downturn in business for such contractors – to the abuses that have been committed by private military personnel at Abu Ghraib and in eastern Afghanistan, the case for increased regulation seems clear. According to Amnesty International USA (2006), there have been at least four deaths in custody involving civilian contractors. In practice, it is impossible to know the scale of human rights abuses committed by employees of private corporations. In the USA, until recently, only the Department of Defense (DoD) was required to develop regulations for contractors. Many contracts, however, were let via the CIA, the State Department, the Department of the Interior and the US Agency for International Development, where no such regulations existed or applied. Even under new DoD regulations, the discipline of contractor personnel remains the responsibility of the contractor (already identified as having been a particular problem at Abu Ghraib) (Amnesty International USA 2006). To date, in only one case, that involving a CIA contractor, have any charges been brought.

Governing security

There is a broad range of potential and actual problems associated with the rise and spread of the privatized military, including whether private interests and public goods match up; to what extent appropriate command and control mechanisms exist for managing the work of such contractors; the limitations of existing systems of legal controls on such activity; the lack of regulation of employment practices in the sector; the perils facing their employees; the relative absence of restrictions on the customers of such businesses; the economic inefficiencies in such activity (as against one of its primary justifications); its impact on the capability of public bodies; and the opportunities created for governments to avoid normal approval procedures and restrictions of their activities. I will limit my final comments to this last concern.

Politicians, by virtue of their position, stand on the 'invitational edge' (Manning and Redlinger 1977) of state crimes. The 'war on terror', with its gradual replacement of due process with security concerns (Gearty 2006), has seen some profound moves to circumvent both domestic and international human rights obligations, to reduce democratic accountability and to redefine the boundaries of acceptable conduct. In this regard, national security has become the 'trump of trumps, carrying all before it' (Gearty 2003: 205). In its name, supposedly liberal democratic regimes have sought to sanction and legitimize the use of torture (Danner 2005) and other egregious human rights abuses. In this context, private military companies, whose operations are poorly regulated, and whose activities are often relatively invisible, can be a seductive option for governments.

It is undoubtedly the case that the 'market for force' has grown in part because of the operational difficulties faced by multilateral security bodies (Avant 2005). However, the growth of this sector is not just a functional consequence of the difficulties faced by the UN and others. Quite clearly, the use of private providers sits neatly with the broader neoliberal economic agenda that has come to dominate polities like the USA and the UK where the private military industry has developed most strongly. Part of the attractiveness of using private contractors also lies in the fact that it helps facilitate the appearance that state capacity is shrinking while it is actually increasing (Walker and Whyte 2005). Finally, and most importantly for our purposes here, though one should not overplay this argument, the other draw of the private sector is its potential for placing distance between the state and state crimes, in enabling 'denial' (Cohen 2003) or 'othering' (Jamieson and McEvoy 2005). Crudely, the private sector enables the state to do things – at a distance – that would be more difficult for it to achieve directly.

Now, of course it would be quite misleading to imply that the problems discussed are in some way confined to private contractors, as the abuses at Abu Ghraib make clear (Cohen 2005). The real issue relates to the relative absence of systems for control and for redress in relation to the private sector (War on Want 2006). However inadequate the systems may be in some respects, the military are at least subject to relatively clear rules and regulations. Therefore, the most obvious question raised by the fragmentation of authority that appears to be occurring, is how can effective systems for the governance of security be constructed? Now, this is far from virgin territory (Johnston and Shearing 2003). One influential model that has been developed in recent years, associated primarily with the work of Clifford Shearing and colleagues (Shearing and Wood 2000), is that of 'nodal governance'. This approach urges the replacement of a traditional boundary-based model of governance, centred on the nation state, with a network-based model in which no single 'node', including the state, is given priority. However, in the context of a search for new approaches to effective governance, the network-based approach may have greater analytical than diagnostic power. In refocusing attention away from the nation state toward the plurality of auspices and providers that are increasingly characteristic of contemporary arrangements, the nodal governance model undoubtedly aids empirical enquiry. Where its utility is less clear is in providing guidance – both normative and practical – as to what systems for the governance of democratic security might look like.

By contrast, the area that has recently stimulated a significant debate relevant to such questions is precisely that of global security. The changing nature and role of the nation state, the emergence of global markets and problems, and the changing character of conflict, have predictably raised the question of what new systems of global governance might look like. It is in this context that ideas of 'cosmopolitanism' have once again come to the fore. At the heart of the concept lies the idea of citizenship beyond the state – a citizen of the world. In recent work, the notion has had a number of underlying assumptions: that individuals, not states, are the core units of moral concern; that this status of equal worth should be acknowledged by all; and that all individuals should enjoy the impartial treatment of their claims. These principles, and others, are used by a growing body of advocates as the basis for outlining generalized political projects such as global social democracy together with more specific considerations such as peacekeeping in weak states. What cosmopolitanism seeks to do is to begin to outline and apply international humanitarian standards to the goal of governing security. At the heart of cosmopolitanism, according to Ulrich Beck (2000) and others, is a shift toward the prioritization of human rights. At least part of the attraction of such an approach, therefore, is that it requires attention to be turned directly to the question of 'values'.

Models advanced by David Held (2004) and others also have the other attraction in this context of requiring a reframing or restructuring of the market itself as part of the process of constructing new forms of governance. The rise of the private military industry provides one of the more pressing examples of the importance of developing governance models which focus on the necessity of market regulation and which prioritize values that seek to redistribute risks in ways that promote greater equality. In essence, what is required by cosmopolitan governance projects is the linking of (social) justice with security. Domestically or internationally, it is in such cosmopolitan human rights protocols that we can look, as Stan Cohen (2006: 317) so aptly put it, 'for the rule of law rather than the rule by law'.

Notes

1 I am grateful to David Downes and Michael Welch for comments on an earlier version of this paper.
2 *Public Papers of the Presidents*, Dwight D. Eisenhower, 1960, pp. 1035–40.

References

Amnesty International USA (2006) *Annual Report*. Available at: www.amnestyusa. org/annualreport/index.html.
Avant, D. (2004) 'Mercenaries', *Foreign Policy*, August: 20–8.
Avant, D. (2005) *The Market for Force: The Consequences of Privatizing Security*. New York: Cambridge University Press.
Bayley, D. and Shearing, C. (1996) 'The future of policing', *Law and Society Review*, 30: 583–606.

Bayley, D. and Shearing, C. (2001) *The New Structure of Policing: Conceptualization and Research Agenda*. Washington, DC: National Institute of Justice.

Beck, U. (2000) 'The cosmopolitan perspective: sociology of the second age of modernity', *British Journal of Sociology*, 51: 79–105.

Beck, U. (2005) 'War is peace: On post-national war', *Security Dialogue,* 36: 5–26.

Brayton, S. (2002) 'Outsourcing war: Mercenaries and the privatization of peacekeeping', *Journal of International Affairs,* 55: 303–29.

Brodeur, J.-P. (1983) 'High policing and low policing: remarks about the policing of political activities', *Social Problems*, 30: 507–20.

Buzan, B., Waever, O. and de Wilde, J. (1998) *Security: A New Framework for Analysis*. Boulder, CO: Lynne Rienner Publishers.

Cohen, S. (1994) 'Social control and the politics of reconstruction', in D. Nelken (ed.) *The Futures of Criminology*. London: Sage.

Cohen, S. (2003) *States of Denial: Knowing about Atrocities and Suffering*. Cambridge: Polity.

Cohen, S. (2005) 'Post-moral torture', *Index on Censorship,* 34: 24–30.

Cohen, S. (2006) 'Neither honesty nor hypocrisy: the legal reconstruction of torture', in T. Newburn and P. Rock (eds) *The Politics of Crime Control: Essays in Honour of David Downes*. Oxford: Clarendon Press.

Crawford, A. (2003) 'Policing beyond the police', in T. Newburn (ed.) *Handbook of Policing*. Cullompton: Willan.

Crotty, W. (2004) (ed.) *The Politics of Terror: The U.S. Response to 9/11*. Boston: Northeastern University Press.

Danner, M. (2005) *Torture and Truth: America, Abu Ghraib and the War on Terror*. London: Granta.

Duffield, M. (2005) *Global Governance and the New Wars*. London: Zed Books.

Dunlap, C.J. Jr. (2001) 'The thick green line: the growing involvement of military forces in domestic law enforcement', in P. Kraska (ed.) *Militarizing the American Criminal Justice System*. Boston, MA: Northeastern University Press.

Edwards, A. and Gill, P. (2003) *Transnational Organised Crime*. London: Routledge.

Gearty, C. (2003) 'Reflections on civil liberties in an age of counterterrorism', *Osgoode Hall Law Journal*, 41: 185–210.

Gearty, C. (2006) *Can Human Rights Survive?* Cambridge: Cambridge University Press.

Gordon, A.F. (2006) 'Abu Ghraib: imprisonment and the war on terror', *Race and Class*, 48: 42–59.

Greenberg, K.J. and Dratel, J.L. (2005) *The Torture Papers: The Road to Abu Ghraib*. New York: Cambridge University Press.

Hartley, K. (2002) 'The economics of military outsourcing', *Public Procurement Law Review,* 5: 287–97.

Harvey, D. (2005) *A Brief History of Neoliberalism*. New York: Oxford University Press.

Held, D. (2004) *Global Covenant*. Cambridge: Polity Press.

Jamieson, R. and McEvoy, K. (2005) 'State crime by proxy and juridical othering', *British Journal of Criminology*, 45: 504–27.

Johnston, L. (1992) *The Rebirth of Private Policing*. London: Routledge.

Johnston, L. (2000) 'Transnational private policing: the impact of global commercial security', in J. Sheptycki (ed.) *Issues in Transnational Policing*. London: Routledge.

Johnston, L. (2006) 'Transnational security governance', in J. Wood and B. Dupont (eds) *Democracy, Society and the Governance of Security*. Cambridge: Cambridge University Press.

Johnston, L. and Shearing, C. (2003) *Governing Security*. London: Routledge.

Jones, T. and Newburn, T. (1998) *Private Security and Public Policing*. Oxford: Clarendon Press.

Jones, T. and Newburn, T. (2006) *Plural Policing: A Comparative Perspective*. London: Routledge.

Kaldor, M. (1999) *New and Old Wars: Organised Violence in a Global Era*. Cambridge: Polity.

Kershaw, S. (2004) 'Private finance for Skynet 5', *RUSI Defence Systems*, Summer: 102–3.

Kraska, P.B. (2001) *Militarizing the American Criminal Justice System: The Changing Roles of the Armed Forces and the Police*. Boston: Northeastern University Press.

Lyon, D. (2003) *Surveillance After September 11*. Oxford: Polity.

Manning, P.K. (2006) 'Two case studies of American anti-terrorism', in J. Wood and M. Kempa (eds) *Democracy, Society and the Governance of Security*. Cambridge: Cambridge University Press.

Manning, P.K. and Redlinger, L.J. (1977) 'Invitational edges of corruption: some consequences of narcotics law enforcement', in P. Rock (ed.) *Drugs and Politics*. Rutgers, NJ: Transaction.

Nordstrom, C. (2004) *Shadows of War: Violence, Power and International Profiteering in the Twenty-first Century*. Berkeley, CA: University of California Press.

O'Reilly, C. and Ellison, G. (2006) '"Eye Spy Private High": re-conceptualizing high policing theory', *British Journal of Criminology*, 46: 641–60.

Parenti, C. (2003) *The Soft Cage: Surveillance in America*. New York: Basic Books.

Pelton, R.Y. (2006) *Licensed to Kill: Hired Guns in the War on Terror*. New York: Crown Publishers.

Reiner, R. (1992) 'Policing a postmodern society', *Modern Law Review*, 55: 761–81.

Rosen, F. 2005) *Contract Warriors: How Mercenaries Changed History and the War on Terrorism*. New York: Alpha Books.

Schumacher, G. (2006) *A Bloody Business: America's War Zone Contractors and the Occupation of Iraq*, St. Paul, MN: Zenith Press.

Shearing, C. (1995) 'Reinventing policing: policing as governance', in O. Marenin (ed.) *Policing Change Changing Police*. New York: Garland Press.

Shearing, C. (2006) 'Reflections on the refusal to acknowledge private governments', in J. Wood and B. Dupont (eds) *Democracy, Society and the Governance of Security*. Cambridge: Cambridge University Press.

Shearing, C. and Stenning, P.(1983) 'Private security: implications for social control', *Social Problems*, 30: 493–506.

Shearing, C. and Wood, J. (2000) 'Reflections on the governance of security: a normative inquiry', *Police Research and Practice*, 1: 457–76.

Sheptycki, J. (ed.) (2000a) *Issues in Transnational Policing.* London: Routledge.

Singer, P.W. (2003) *Corporate Warriors, The Rise of the Privatized Military Industry.* Itaca: Cornell University Press.

Singer, P.W. (2004) 'Warriors for hire in Iraq', Salon.Com, 15 April.

Singer, P.W. (2005) 'Outsourcing war', *Foreign Affairs*, March/April.

Spicer, T. (1999) *An Unorthodox Soldier.* London: Mainstream.

Uttley, M.R.H. (2004) 'Private contractors on deployed operations: the UK experience', *Defence Studies*, 4: 145–65.

Vines, A. (1999) 'Mercenaries and the privatization of security in Africa in the 1990s', in G. Mills and J. Stremlau (eds) *The Privatization of Security in Africa.* Johannesburg: South African Institute of International Affairs.

Walker, C. and Whyte, D. (2005) 'Contracting out war? Private military companies, law and regulation in the United Kingdom', *International Comparative Law Quarterly*, 54: 651–90.

War on Want (2006) *Private Military: The Threat of Private Military and Security Companies.* London: War on Want.

Welch, M. and Schuster, L. (2005) 'Detention of asylum seekers in the US, UK, France, Germany, and Italy: a critical view of the globalizing culture of control', *Criminal Justice*, 5: 331–55.

Whyte, D. (2003) 'Lethal regulation: state-corporate crime and the United Kingdom Government's new mercenaries', *Journal of Law and Society*, 30: 575–600.

Zedner, L. (2003) 'The concept of security: an agenda for comparative analysis', *Legal Studies*, 23: 153–76.

Chapter 16

The free movement of people: ethical debates before and after 9/11[1]

Robin Cohen

With the collapse of communism in the Soviet Union and the other countries of the Warsaw Pact, *emigration* control effectively ended in all but one or two of the world's 191 UN-recognised states. By contrast, *immigration* control has been strengthened everywhere in response both to security concerns arising from the terrorist outrages of recent years and to public concern about the level of immigration. In the wake of 9/11, 11M and 7/7 (the atrocities in New York, Madrid and London), the ethical case for the free migration of people has been effectively silenced and restrictionist policies have become near universal.[2] But how effective are such measures? Increased global mobility, regional free movement zones, dual citizenship, the growth of student and tourist mobility, the demographic and economic needs of rich countries, weak state structures in some developing countries and irregular migration (to name just the major factors) have made it more difficult to police national frontiers. How these contradictory pressures will be resolved remains uncertain. In this contribution I focus on the theoretical, ethical and rhetorical basis for state regulation of the flows of people. Precisely because the case for control seems self-evident, it is timely to review the arguments made for the free movement of people, their own self-limiting conditions and the extent to which the contemporary political pressures for further restrictions can be justified by reference to general concepts of social justice and the public good.

Free movement: Kant and Carens

The long-standing ethical argument for the free movement of migrants is often traced back to Kant's essay *Toward Perpetual Peace* (1795), in which he maintains that the peoples of the earth (*not* rulers or states) own the earth and therefore they must be free to travel anywhere on its surface. It is unjustifiable, therefore, for states to section off this or that bit of the planet. However, as Bauböck (1994: 321–2) argues, Kant is effectively maintaining that anybody should be free to *travel* both in respect of conducting peaceful trade and 'to *offer* themselves for social contact with established inhabitants of any territory' (emphasis added). The host society, in Kant's view, is bound to proffer hospitality.

Even in this generous formulation of free mobility, there are clear limitations imposed by Kant himself and some that we may infer. Migration for the purposes of colonization can only be undertaken to 'bring culture to uncivilised peoples' (Kant betrays his 'Occidental' attitudes here), and only in a way that avoids the plunder, subjugation and extermination of conquered peoples (Fine and Cohen 2002: 143). As to limits we might infer, note that free migration for *peaceful trade* is defended – not a trade in arms, biological agents or drugs. Equally, there seems to be a necessary moment of *consent* by the current residents if travellers have to 'offer' themselves for social acceptance. Proffering hospitality is prior to and not the same thing as conferring social membership.

If we now turn to twentieth-century political philosophers, probably the most widely cited discussion of the ethics of migration was initiated by Joseph Carens (1987: 251–73). Drawing on Rawlsian ideas (Rawls 1971), which are predicated on a single society with a bounded social membership, Carens suggested that the principles of 'fair opportunity' and 'equal liberty' could be extended across societies (not merely within one) to cover such issues as trade and migration. With respect to migration, a Rawlsian principle that all people within a society are equal moral persons could not, by extension, be denied to people of other origins. If we hold it right that people should be free to migrate within a country to better themselves, find a loved one, join their co-religionists or extend their cultural horizons, a similar principle could be applied across borders (p. 258). Carens derived from Nozick (1974) the argument that the state has no basis for compelling someone to treat an alien or a citizen either differently or similarly.

To use the language of market economics, Carens proposed that there is a good philosophical basis for unimpeded human mobility within and between nations. However, he (1987: 251) allowed a crucial limitation to his own case, distinguishing, in effect, between the 'good' migrant and the 'bad' migrant. The former were cast in somewhat journalistic terms – Haitians in leaky boats, Salvadorians dying from heat in the Arizonian desert and Guatemalans crawling through rat-infested sewer pipes from Mexico to California ('ordinary peaceful people, seeking only the opportunity to build secure lives for themselves and their families'). The latter were 'criminals, subversives or armed invaders'. The bad migrants clearly could not have rights of free entry.

The free movement of migrants: discussion after 9/11

It is surprising to find that the philosophical proponents of the free movement of migrants were so self-limiting and so timid in their claims. This weak advocacy opened them to at least four countermoves that were given additional impetus in the period after 9/11. First, border controls were naturalised so that opposition to excessive (and, as we will see later, expensive and ineffective) enforcement measures was deemed incredible or even treasonous. The expressed need for 'homeland security' has been invoked to the point that the historical rights and liberties of the settled populations are being undermined with little political resistance. Second, while in the wake of 9/11 liberal political theorists have articulated a modest defence of migrant rights, these have remained firmly constrained by their acceptance of the primacy of national sovereignty and the need for 'realism'. Third, surveillance measures have been instituted that increasingly overlap with other forms of social control. Finally, checks on immigration have provided the occasion for a reaffirmation of singular national, monochromatic identities and an attack on multiculturalism, diversity and immigration 'of the wrong sort'.

Border controls and the erosion of domestic rights

Passport controls are a much later manifestation of state power than has sometimes been supposed (Cohen 2006: Chapter 3). It is also a useful corrective to remember that even by 2005 only 20 per cent of US citizens had passports, a percentage that is barely exceeded by members of the US Congress. Despite the need for recognition of the fact that many do not travel outside their countries of origin, and that passport regimes are not universal, for the bulk of conventional travellers, whose numbers exceeded 700 million in 2004, enhanced border controls have become a tedious reality. Air travellers have to accept extended check-in times and long lines at arrival gates. The security concerns of the USA have been gradually extended to the rest of the world. Border checks have been augmented by biometric data (fingerprinting, digital photographs and iris recognition). Even travellers from those countries with visa waiver arrangements with the USA are forced to submit to biometric checks on entry and exit.

The increased surveillance of the US border commenced virtually immediately after the events of 9/11, but the commission established in its aftermath notably hardened its border controls in its final report, issued in July 2004. In summarising that report, Cooper (2004) explains that it called for the integration of the border security system with screening networks used in the transport system and in the protection of sensitive facilities like nuclear plants. A comprehensive screening system at *external* points of entry had to be paralleled with a standardisation of *internal* identity documents, in particular driving licences and birth certificates. Foreign governments, private corporations and the 15 [*sic*] national intelligence agencies had to be encouraged or induced to cooperate and coordinate their security efforts.

The commission also recommended drawing citizens of the USA itself and adjacent countries (like Canada) into the net with compulsory biometric passports. In response to this recommendation, in April 2005 the US administration announced that US nationals will need passports to re-enter the USA from Canada, Mexico, Panama and Bermuda by 2008 in view of the need to protect the USA against a terrorist threat. Similarly, Canadians will also have to present a passport to enter the USA.

Surveillance and Cohen's punitive city

These developments indicate that various types of security, which have been historically separated, are rapidly converging. This development was anticipated by Stanley Cohen (1979, 1985) in the case of crime control. As he foresaw, 'The resultant forms of control will be less noteworthy for their effects on crime than their intrusive side effects on ordinary citizens: a retreat into fortress living; streets abandoned to outlaws; inconvenience and erosion of civil liberty as a result of continual security checks and surveillance systems' (1985: 201). At the level of street security, shoppers and residents have long had to accept both visible and covert surveillance of their movements. In shopping centres, cameras are pervasive. So many of them have now been installed that there is said to be, in number, one camera for every street in Britain. Government-authorised telephone tapping has been massively enhanced, and there are many devices for eavesdropping that are available on the market and used illegitimately by private security agencies. The interception, scanning and reading of post and email is now routinely undertaken. At airports (and now increasingly at railway, underground and bus stations), identity and luggage checks are increasingly frequent and pervasive. Body searches, X-rays and invasive cameras are either current or planned. Biometric data are now embedded in passports, credit cards and other ID documents. These and other measures amount to a historically unprecedented intrusion into the private lives of citizens.[3]

Stanley Cohen (1985: 226–7) also notably focused on the contemporary city as a metaphor for social breakdown and the resultant attempts at social control. Using a succession of 'visions of social control', he sets out the various models of inclusion and exclusion of the 'dangerous classes'. The 'purified city' divided the city by the moral attributes of its inhabitants; the 'sandbox city' provides a placebo for the poor and excluded (while the middle classes decamped to the suburbs); 'the city as reservation' treated the unwanted, deviant and poor as Native Americans and those who managed their welfare as colonial bureaucrats; 'the pariah city' institutionalised containment and care as municipal bureaucracies, professional minders, landlords and shopkeepers become dependent on their functions. To these visions we must now add another. The 'terrorist city' is the contemporary global, multicultural entrepôt where all pursue their hedonistic pleasures and material well-being, but none can finally tell friend from foe, Muslim from Hindu, Brazilian from other 'olive-skinned' people. The punitive city of Stanley Cohen's vision has taken a new turn; soft power and the 'iron cage of bureaucracy' have been supplemented by armed and dangerous officers of the law – there to protect us from the global terrorist.

A defence of migrant rights

Can we defend migrant rights in such an atmosphere of control and exclusion? In an important contribution to the post-9/11 debate, Ruhs and Chang (2004: 70) argue that what is distinctive about international labour migration (in contrast to trade and capital flows) is that migrants 'lay claim to certain rights vis-à-vis the host state and their fellow residents'. Despite an acceptance of the language of 'rights', they continue, the participants in the debate show a marked inability to discuss the ethical assumptions underpinning their arguments. Inward migration is discussed in terms of skill and utility, rather than the rights that are to be conferred, however minimal, after admission. Rights like job mobility, access to the courts, welfare services, health benefits and the right to vote are rarely made explicit. In some countries, temporary workers can become permanent residents – a route that is prohibited in other countries. As Ruhs and Chang (2004) argue, the variation in the conferral of rights like these lead to quite different outcomes. For example, if migrant workers are permitted to change jobs, the preferential access of nationals to the internal labour market is thereby challenged.

215

Variations in accorded rights also, they argue (pp. 83–5), depend on the 'moral standing' accorded to nationals, migrants and the citizens of the sending counties, who may not themselves be migrants but may be affected by migration. The moral standing of the different participants in turn relates to where the social actors and decision makers locate themselves on a cosmopolitan–nationalist spectrum. Here Ruhs and Chang (2004: 91 *et seq.*) are drawn back to the realistic–idealistic dyad enunciated by Carens and discussed earlier. Rights-based and cosmopolitan views of migrants may be held by international organisations like the International Labour Organisation and NGOs ('idealists'), but it is hardly surprising that national policymakers have to yield to the pressures that elevate the moral standing of nationals above that of migrants ('realists'). So far, so predictable. However, Ruhs and Chang provide an unexpected twist to the argument. Because migrants are more productive, have lower claims on welfare and other benefits, and are less likely to be criminals than the long-standing population (despite many myths to the contrary), there may be a material stake in protecting and furthering the interests of migrants. It is also the case that most countries both send and receive migrants, so according a degree of recognition and respect to a migrant may be necessary to advance a moral claim to protect a country's own nationals abroad.

In combining realistic and idealistic perspectives, Ruhs and Chang (2004) enunciate a balanced set of prescriptions, avoiding general declarations of human rights as applied to all migrants in favour of more targeted core rights that are carefully monitored, transparent and effectively enforced. Again, they deem programmes for temporary work (and enforced departure) legitimate so long as some pathways for permanent settlement are established in return for a largely unspecified set of positive 'ticks' against the temporary migrant. It is not too difficult to see what such an evaluation might comprise. Such tests might include good conduct (denoted by the absence of a criminal record), a valued economic contribution, a high degree of familiarity with the majority population's language and way of life, a loyalty test, a limited number of dependants or a clean bill of health.

While I have considerable sympathy with many of the ethical dilemmas raised by Ruhs and Chang and some admiration for their detailed reasoning, it is nonetheless clear that liberal political philosophy on the ethics of immigration policy has been severely circumscribed by a self-denying ordinance arising from past tentativeness and a present atmosphere of immigration restrictions. On the one hand, this line of reasoning recognises the economic contribution of migrants and the need to protect minimal standards of decency and universality. On the other, the sovereignty of state power is left intact and it is acknowledged that politicians will find it impossible not to elevate the moral standing of the national over the migrant.

The attack on diversity and the question of immigration restriction

The neo-conservative and conservative Right in the USA and Europe has seized the political moment afforded by the terrorist threat to question both the extent of migration and the degree of recognition afforded to migrants' home cultures, religions, languages and social practices. The attack on diversity and difference has been particularly fierce in the USA. Perhaps the most powerful academic voice on this question has been that of Samuel P. Huntington (2004: 142–43), professor of politics at Harvard and the director of security planning for the National Security Council in the Carter administration. In his *cri de coeur* titled *Who Are We?*, he angrily denounces those in the USA who had discarded earlier notions that the USA is a 'melting pot' or 'tomato soup' and proposed instead that it is more like a 'mosaic' or 'salad bowl' of diverse peoples. He insists on the primacy of the English-speaking, Protestant, eastern seaboard and deplores the 'deconstructionists' who sought to 'enhance the status and influence of subnational racial, ethnic, and cultural groups', an advocacy that, he claims, had deleterious effects on democratic values and liberties:

> They downgraded the centrality of English in American life and pushed bilingual education and linguistic diversity. They advocated legal recognition of group rights and racial preferences over the individual rights central to the American Creed. They justified their actions by theories of multiculturalism and the idea that diversity rather than unity or community should be America's overriding value. The combined effect of these efforts was to promote the deconstruction of the American identity that had been gradually created over three centuries (2004: 142).

The main implication of this argument for the free movement of migration is that freedom can be curtailed for the sake of freedom. This Rawlsian principle[4] could be used to discountenance both (a) 'unlimited immigration' and (b) the immigration of 'dangerous' people. Let us immediately concede a limited list in the (b) category. It is generally not a good idea to roll out the red carpet for psychopaths, gangsters, drug dealers or terrorists. Category (a) is more ambiguous. Does large-scale immigration really pose a threat to public order, economic prosperity, social well-being or cultural cohesion? This is by no means an invariable outcome. In circumstances of underpopulation and demoralisation, a large, culturally cognate cohort of immigrants with skills and capital will generally be welcomed. In circumstances where the settled population is under threat or perceives a threat (of job loss, housing shortage or welfare rationing), the arrival of a large, culturally dissimilar group may well be resisted even if the long-term effects may be benign. It is certainly more than possible that an ambitious politician will fan the flames of xenophobia.

Is it justifiable to reduce the risk of this last negative reaction, thereby generating a moral purpose for immigration restriction? I would argue that defending a settled population's rights must mean there is something worth defending – for example, hard-fought civil liberties, a tradition of toleration for unpopular minorities, the production of imaginative works of art and literature, or a broad-minded education system. For immigration restrictions to have an ethical rationale, it should be clear which freedom or freedoms are being protected, which are being threatened, why such a threat is real and how a restriction will help to retain a particular freedom. Perhaps it is easier to construe this argument in the opposite direction. Restricting inward migration (or appearing to advocate this position) to win an election, while pretending a more noble purpose is at stake, is clearly reprehensible.

In this respect it could be instructive to contrast the immigration policies of recent governments of Canada and Australia with the immigration practices of France and the UK. Whereas the former pair has entered into an open dialogue with its settled population on appropriate numbers and criteria for exclusion, governments in France and the UK have on the whole remained secretive and patrician in the implementation of their policies, now recognising the claims of the gangmasters for cheap agricultural labour, later throwing sops to the right-wing newspapers and political parties. If they are to be legitimate at all, restrictions have to be open, consensual and clearly used to defend an existing freedom that would otherwise be in jeopardy. Restrictions, in this moral universe we are constructing, cannot be used for a concealed purpose, especially if that purpose is unworthy.

The practical and political limits of restriction

There remains the important task of assessing the practical and political limits of restrictionist policies and considering what consequences, intended and unintended, might arise from such constraints. Here I consider three questions:

1 Can 'good' migrants be separated from 'bad' migrants?
2 Are restrictive measures likely to be affordable and effective?
3 Are politicians in a strong position to judge the potential threat posed by free movement?

Can 'good' migrants be separated from 'bad' migrants?

I have already alluded to Carens's somewhat cardboard characterisations of migrants. However, immigrants do not arrive at Heathrow or Charles de Gaulle airports sporting devils' tails or angels' wings. Many immigrants are young or bring impressionable young families. It would be absurd to demand an oath of loyalty of a four-year-old or to interrogate such a child about ritual slaughter, nude sculptures, alcohol abuse, religious education or the wearing of veils. Perhaps it would not be so absurd to ask his or her parents about these things. What, however, would be the purpose of such an interrogation? It seems to imply a non-questionable assumption that indigenous practices are self-evidently superior.

Let me provide two examples to question this view. Family values are strongly articulated and defended by Indian and Chinese immigrants, who characteristically show low rates of teenage pregnancy and juvenile delinquency, have fewer single-headed households, and rarely neglect old people. Again abstinence or restraint in the consumption of alcohol (which results in so many needless deaths and injury) might also be a lesson usefully learned from some immigrants. I appreciate that crucial normative considerations are introduced by these examples, which require further defence. However, my primary argument is that it is not apparent on *prima facie* grounds that an imported culture is inferior to a host culture or will not offer positive alternatives to local social practices.

Consider a related question. There is nothing to stop migrants lying to the immigration authorities about their ideological convictions or preferred social attitudes, especially if these are not illegal. Despite this, it seems to be a reasonable expectation on the part of the host society that immigrants should not be deceitful and intend to obey the laws of the country that they are entering. Likewise, there is nothing in principle offensive about a loyalty ceremony associated with citizenship (long held in Canada, recently initiated in Britain). The principle is not unlike that first enunciated by Kant – a (legal) immigrant may *offer* herself or himself for social membership; a citizenship ceremony would confer it in a public arena.

This is not an identical argument to the one made by Walzer (1983: 61) that states are like (private) clubs – the existing membership is free to exclude whomsoever it pleases, subject to the rules of the club. Carens's (1987: 265–70) rebuttal of Walzer's conflation of a club and a state is persuasive on a number of grounds, the most obvious being that there is a legal and moral distinction between a private and public act of exclusion. In the former setting, freedom of association is the paramount virtue; in the latter, equal treatment between all is the major ethical consideration. To repeat – it may be legitimate to ask of intending adult immigrants (of sound mind) whether they intend to obey the laws of the land and and ascertain that they do not harbour a sinister intent directed against the life, liberty and well-being of the inhabitants of the country whose citizenship they aspire to. This creates a moral equivalence between a politician's demand for exclusion and an immigrant's claim for inclusion. And lest this appears too naive, it may be useful to note that current immigration laws permit deportation on the grounds that an immigrant's statements to a responsible authority were shown to be intentionally misleading.

Are control measures affordable and effective?

In a 2003 report by the International Organisation of Migration (cited by Pécoud and Guchteneire 2005: 4), the cost of enforcing immigration restrictions was calculated at US$ 25–30 billion each year. This covers not only border controls, but also the issuing of visas and passports; the apprehension, detention, prosecution and deportation of unwanted migrants; inspections of labour conditions; the processing of asylum seekers' claims; and the resettlement of refugees. To get some sense of scale, this sum is only about 1/16th of the 2004 US defence budget. However, the sum would pay for three years of clean water for all the world's 6.1 billion people.

At any event, the costs of policing the frontiers are certainly not inconsiderable. And given that, it is legitimate to ask whether the measures undertaken are effective. A considerable weight of evidence has now built up to suggest that sophisticated control measures are met with more sophisticated methods of evasion. People trafficking is now highly profitable and professionally organised. Moreover, once a culture of emigration is established in a labour-exporting zone and networks of migrants are in place, it is extremely difficult to stop the movement of determined migrants (see Pécoud and Guchteneire 2005: 4).

These general observations have been contradicted by those who believe that the extensive use of digital technology and a more determined and costly regime can finally control unwanted movement. Koslowski (2004, 2005), who has studied the implementation of the current US policies, casts considerable doubt on their effectiveness. The magnitude of the task is considerable. Take the USA in the year after 9/11, remembering that there are 326 legitimate ports of entry, 2,000 miles along the Rio Grande and 5,500 miles separating Canada and the USA. Recorded entries for 2002 were 440 million (down from 500 million in 2001) and exits were not effectively recorded. As Koslowski (2004: 9) argues, lost forms, incomplete data entry and exit from the lightly policed land frontiers meant that there was no way that overstayers could be detected and deported with certainty. Indeed, several of the 9/11 terrorists had overstayed their visas.

The land borders with the USA (Canada and Mexico) presented special problems. The Ambassador Bridge, linking Windsor to Detroit, carried motor-car parts for 'just-in-time' production to the three major automobile manufacturers in Michigan. Up to ten million vehicles crossed the Ambassador Bridge each year – inspecting them on the basis of current infrastructure and technology would be impossible without halting production in a key manufacturing state. Nor should one forget that if the stakes are high enough, identity theft and the forging of passports will become more commonplace. According to Koslowski (2005), in 2004 there were 12,404 fraudulent claims to US citizenship detected and 79,273 fraudulent passports intercepted at all ports of entry. One can reasonably surmise that the number detected and intercepted was only a fraction of the total.

There is one other element to this story that needs mention. Much of the data capture and processing of the hundreds of millions of records needed to operate the US-VISIT system have been subcontracted to companies that have inadequate security measures and sometimes are located in countries, like Pakistan, with strong links to terrorism. A major security breach was also reported in April 2005 (*Guardian*, 13 April 2005: 21) when Reed Elsevier allowed access to the personal details of as many as 310,000 US citizens. Information that might have been accessed (and which could now be on the market for sale) includes names, addresses, and social security and driver's licence numbers, the precise building blocks for identity theft and illegal documentation. What is even more damaging is that those who operate the system are often victims of 'the technological fallacy'. Believing the system is secure when it is not leads to more serious errors in control systems (just as believing that wars can be won by guided missiles alone leads to more 'Vietnams' and 'Iraqs').

Can politicians effectively assess a potential threat?

In public discussions about the legitimacy of the war in Iraq, we have all been saturated with discussions of 'the precautionary principle'. It was said that even if Saddam Hussain did not possess weapons of mass destruction, he had *programmes* to produce them and the stated intention to use them. It is worth noting that if Bush and Blair believed Saddam Hussain's proclamations, they have a higher estimation of the candour of politicians than most of the rest of us share. If, however, they were relying on intelligence reports (erroneous or not), they could validly argue that the precautionary principle dictated that they act decisively and overwhelmingly to disarm Saddam Hussain or overthrow his regime.

The burden of proof demanded is of course much lower than that demanded in a criminal court, where both the intention to act and the act itself must be attributed to the perpetrator without reasonable doubt. In the US constitutional tradition, the president can also act on a less severe burden of proof – namely, if there is 'a clear and present danger' to the country. But how clear and how present? Supposing an armed secret agent of the Spanish government observed a known member of a terrorist network about to push the keys on his mobile telephone that would trigger a bomb that would certainly kill many civilians. In such a circumstance, that agent would, without doubt, seek to kill the terrorist and would, again without doubt, be supported in this act by the majority of public opinion.

Now consider migrants. If they present a threat at all, it would be a far more diffuse, uncertain and long-term threat. Echoing Carens, most migrants seek a peaceful and secure life. What they bring with them (in terms of skills, cultural practices and financial capital) and what they contribute may be wholly benign. There will be room for disagreement in making any cost/benefit assessment. Equally, there might be short-term tensions, but long-term gains, in the admission of a particular cohort of migrants.

In short, assessing a potential threat arising from the movement of migrants is a matter of human judgement and, therefore, human error. Unfortunately, the political leaders of many countries have three grave disadvantages in exercising wise judgements: (a) they are largely unskilled in philosophical reasoning or social scientific knowledge; (b) they are often in the hands of narrow ideologues or special interest groups; and (c) they are sometimes untrustworthy and often thought to be untrustworthy. What we saw on the streets on Spain after 11M was a populace angry that it was compelled to place life-and-death judgements in the hands of people incapable of making them without considering their own political advantage.

Conclusion

Even interrogating proponents' views of the free movement of persons reveals considerable self-doubt and a number of limiting conditions. When one adds to these old arguments the pressures derived from contemporary security concerns, it is clear that the restrictionists have won the argument. But, as I have suggested, the debate about free movement cannot stop there. In imposing restrictions, one has to bear in mind the justification for such limits and the dangers to our own freedoms in abnegating too much and too many of our hard-won freedoms.

The common thread underlying these measures is fear and the politicians' manipulation of fear. The mesh of surveillance that characterised Stanley Cohen's 'punitive city' has escalated with the rising level of public concern for safety and security. The connection to the movement of migrants is that there are either proven or alleged causal links between unregulated mobility, and security and criminal concerns. Those who have worked in the field of ethnic relations are long used to the tendency of local populations to blame immigrants for anything that goes wrong – but in particular for street violence, criminal activity and drugs dealing. The nihilist terrorist, who sadly is not merely a phantom of the imagination, simply adds to the cast of 'folk devils'. There are at least three grounds for concern at this development:

- The first is that the more affluent sections of the population will become so preoccupied by personal security that, as Stanley Cohen (1985) suggested, they will retreat to gated communities, leaving the streets and public spaces to a condition previously depicted only in science fiction.

- The second is that the mesh that is used to filter out the dangerous alien will become finer and finer. In this respect there will be an intractable escalator as the 'bad guys' (Bush's term) get smarter and the 'good guys' have to try harder and harder to catch them.

- The third is that there are simply no serious mechanisms in place to restrain the security agencies from undertaking further and more far-reaching forms of surveillance. Particular measures may either be ineffective, inappropriate or disproportionate, yet we (the public) have no means to stop the escalator. People who have questioned security measures on grounds of civil liberties are largely ignored or derided.

Fear, it is rightly said, is contagious, and with this primordial response irrationality and poorly considered responses become common. Migrants who generate jobs, wealth, and creative cultural and social alternatives are important means of preventing economic stagnation, and counteracting cultural stasis and social decay. However, it is extremely difficult to tell the difference between benign and malign mobility. Consequentially, there are necessarily difficult questions in implementing a system of control, restriction, sorting and surveillance.

What values and freedoms do we wish to defend? Can we explicitly define them? Who is challenging our cherished freedoms and how are they doing so? Can we act in advance of a clear and present danger and how long in advance, at what level of threat and on what grounds? Have we honestly assessed the values and norms brought by migrants in an informed and open-minded way? Who is permitted to operate our systems of surveillance and restriction? Are they adequately trained and informed? Are their motives pure and untainted by personal interest or undisclosed influences? Are the measures we effect proportionate, appropriate, effective and legal? Who will police our police? These questions are not fully answered here, but despite the current climate of xenophobia, fear and anger, we need at least to ask them.

Notes

1 This chapter is partly derived from Chapter 9 in my book *Migration and Its Enemies* (2006), in which I also consider the parallel issue of the free movement of money. Perhaps it concedes too much to a USA-centric view of the world to use the expression '9/11' in the title to this chapter. I simply intend it to refer to the Islamicist-inspired terrorist outrages of recent years.

2 I mention New York, Madrid and London as the primary examples of international (non-state) terror in recent years partly because of the scale of human destruction and because the debates I consider are centred in Europe and North America. However, one must not forget that Islamicist extremists have been responsible for other incidents – 29 December 1992, when a bomb in Aden killed two tourists; 7 August 1998 in East Africa, when bombs directed at US embassies killed 224 and injured 5,000 (nearly all locals); 11 April 2002 in Tunisia, when 20 tourists were killed; 8 May 2002 in Karachi when 11 French naval officers and three Pakistanis were killed; 14 June 2002, again in Karachi, with 12 killed and 45 injured in a car bomb directed at the US consulate; and 23 July 2005 in Sharm el-Sheikh (an Egyptian resort on the Red Sea) with 83 dead and over 200 injured. Chechnyian and Palestinian groups perpetrating atrocities are probably better considered as armed sections of national uprisings, though the Israeli and Russian governments seek to link their responses to these acts to the US-led 'war on terror'.

3 An innovative online journal, *Surveillance and Society*, can usefully be consulted to extend this discussion (see www.surveillance-and-society.org).
4 Rawls uses 'liberty', not 'freedom'. I appreciate that much can be made of the distinction, but that debate is not salient here.

References

Bauböck, R. (1994) *Transnational Citizenship: Membership and Rights in International Migration*. Cheltenham: Edward Elgar.

Carens, J. (1987) 'Aliens and citizens: the case for open borders', *Review of Politics*, 49: 251–73.

Cohen, R. (2006) *Migration and Its Enemies*. Aldershot: Ashgate.

Cohen, S. (1979) 'The Punitive City: notes on the dispersal of social control', *Contemporary Crises*, 3: 339–63.

Cohen, S. (1985) *Visions of Social Control: Crime, Punishment and Classification*. Cambridge: Polity.

Cooper, B. (2004) *9/11 Commission Urges Immigration and Border Reform*. Washington, DC: Migration Policy Institute. At www.migrationinformation. org/feature/display.cfm?ID=243.

Fine, R. and Cohen, R. (2002) 'Four cosmopolitan moments', in S. Vertovec and R. Cohen (eds) *Conceiving Cosmopolitanism: Theory, Context and Practice*. Oxford: Oxford University Press, pp. 137–62.

Huntington, S.P. (2004) *Who Are We? America's Great Debate*. London: Simon and Schuster.

Kant, I. (1957 [1795]) *Perpetual Peace*, edited and with an introduction by L.W. Beck. Indianapolis, IN: Bobbs-Merrill.

Koslowski, R. (2004) 'Intersections of information technology and human mobility: globalization vs. homeland security Position Paper prepared for the ESRC/SSRC Money and Migration after Globalization Colloquium', University of Oxford, 25–28 March.

Koslowski, R. (2005) 'Virtual border and e-borders', Lecture to the Centre on Migration Policy and Society, University of Oxford, April.

Nozick, R. (1974) *Anarchy, State and Utopia*. New York: Basic Books.

Parker, O. and Brassnet, J. (2005) 'Contingent borders, ambiguous ethics: migrants in (international) political theory', *International Studies Quarterly*, 49: 233–53.

Pécoud A. and de Guchteneire, P. (2005) *Migration Without Borders: An Investigation into the Free Movement of People*. Global Migration Perspectives, Working Paper, Global Commission on International Migration, No. 276, April, Geneva (www.gcim.org).

Rawls, J. (1971) *A Theory of Justice*. Cambridge, MA: Harvard University Press.

Ruhs, M. and Chang, H.-J. (2004) 'The ethics of labour immigration policy', *International Organization*, 58: 69–102.

Walzer, M. (1983) *Spheres of Justice*. Oxford: Blackwell.

Chapter 17

Detain – restrain – control: sliding scale or slippery slope?

Jill Peay

> There is never the fear of too much control, but of too much chaos.
> If we feel we are losing control, we must try to take control.
>
> (Cohen 1985: 235)

In the 1980s, Stan Cohen's work on the dispersal of discipline (1979, 1985) helped us properly to understand the process by which the burgeoning forms of control in the community had ebbed out from more confined, and largely institutional settings (see also Lowman *et al.* 1985). As these methods of control dispersed, partially magnified by the influence of new technologies, they mutated, and progressively more people became involved in the servicing of that control. Which constituted the driving mechanism, controllers or controlled, or whether the process is symbiotic, is unclear; but the result has been that more individuals and more marginal groups have been drawn into the network of control, extending its remit from the manifestly criminal and deviant, and from those who were seriously disordered, to those who were merely delinquent, transitionally problematic or socially inept. That Cohen's vision has come to fruition with the force that it has, with supervision and surveillance the norm, and community treatment the goal, testifies to the power of the original thesis.

Yet, underpinning all of this expansion of state control, there is believed to be some legal regulation of the state's power. This may be a quaint notion, given that so much control is exercised coercively and in the shadow of the law, rather than overtly, with all of the safeguards and constraints that such overt use of law requires. Nonetheless, what I want to do in this chapter is briefly to examine the operation of some of these concepts of control, with particular emphasis on their application in the field of mental health. This may provide a useful analytical tool both because what separates control, restraint and detention in mental health law has recently been the subject of discussion in the European Court of Human Rights (ECtHR) and because people with less than full capacity, for whatever reason, are peculiarly vulnerable to being seen as the proper objects of control, while being imperfectly subject to it.

The chapter looks first from the legal perspective at the expectations for a graded response to increasing levels of control; secondly, it reflects on a real-world application, namely, that of the anti-social behaviour orders (ASBO) (see, generally, Burney 2005), where the relationship between restraint and detention is much more slippery. The linkage between these two fields, both of which serve to exclude those perceived as problematic either from view or from full social participation, derives partly from the application or threat of detention and partly from the difficulties of resorting to such mechanisms where their exclusionary potential may not be fully understood by those to whom they are applied. The chapter also addresses, when determining what constitutes different levels of control, whether the relevant perspective should be objective or subjective: that of the controller or, more problematically, from the perspective of the person – maybe that of a child or mentally disabled person – who is controlled? It also questions the process whereby a precautionary preventive measure can be transformed into a punitive intervention; in such circumstances, does there need to be a graded legal response? In essence, in propelling individuals from control, through restraint to detention, should there be an effective requirement to pass legal GO?

Sliding scale?

HL v. *UK* (2004) will be very familiar to mental health lawyers, but perhaps not so to those outside the field. It concerns the case in 1997 of a severely autistic man admitted to, and treated thereafter in, a psychiatric hospital. Although incapable of consenting to admission, he was dealt with on the basis of his passive assent without further ado. In this country, the case went right through the judicial process to the House of Lords, where his admission was held to be lawful under the common law; but subsequently, at the ECtHR, admission on the basis of his passive assent was found not to be in compliance with Article 5.1 or 5.4 of the Convention; in essence, the law required that where individuals are deprived of their liberty certain procedural standards and safeguards need to be met. In this case they were not, because the professionals had acted on the belief that the authority of the common law, which embodies no such procedural safeguards, was sufficient. The government's intention is now to amend the Mental Capacity Act 2005 in order to bring domestic legislation into compliance with the ECtHR (Hansard 2006a).

What is of interest here is the ECtHR's observations in respect of the dividing line between what constitutes the restriction of liberty (restraint) and the deprivation of liberty (detention). The former would have been in compliance with Article 5 and the latter not. To be lawful, detention required procedural safeguards. It is important to stress at this juncture that detention is not a matter of merely keeping people behind locked doors. Indeed, in an earlier case (*Ashingdane v. UK* 1979), a patient was held to be deprived of his liberty even though he was on an unlocked unit at a hospital and was free to leave during the day: however, since this freedom could be revoked by the hospital he was found to be 'detained'. In respect of *HL*, the ECtHR was clear that his detention was established on the basis that the health professionals treating and managing him 'exercised complete and effective control over his care and movements' and that he was 'under continuous supervision and control' (para 91); had he tried to leave (which he did not), they would have stopped him and imposed statutory detention under the Mental Health Act 1983. Yet, it was not clear at what point detention merges into mere restraint (and thus at what point the procedural safeguards became legally superfluous) since the distinction between the two was one of 'degree or intensity, not one of nature or substance' (para. 89). Specific factors would provide the necessary degree or intensity: but what might these be? The court identified the 'type, duration, effects and manner of implementation of the measure in question' as relevant (para 89), but could, for example, the administration of medication that made a patient quiescent and thereby unlikely to challenge the status quo convert restraint into detention?

So, even though the ECtHR had difficulty in delineating restraint from detention, the ends of the spectrum were clear, and these contrasting situations required different consequences. Detention engaged Article 5 and required certainty with regard to the procedures for admission: for how long was the detention to last, what were its objectives and what limits were there to what could be done with patients who were admitted? Indeed, detention also required regular review by a quasi-judicial body, in order to determine that the conditions justifying detention still pertained. Restraint, on the other hand, required a much less robust response: where actions were taken in respect of those lacking capacity, proportionality of the response to the likelihood and seriousness of the harm to be prevented was a prerequisite, and any action taken had to be in the individual's best interests. But beyond this, professionals had a much freer rein.

What this implies is that where the state deprives someone of their liberty specific consequences must follow if the state is to act lawfully; thus, there is, as it were, a sliding scale of responses. At one end of the scale, where detention is involved, the parallel requirements are clear and certain: further along, where restraint is involved, while proportionality is a given, there can be greater disagreement about whether an action is indeed a proportionate response or not. And at the other end of the scale, where control or mere coercion is entailed, even the nominated response may evade clear definition. So, from the perspective of the law, there is a clearly graded response required; but, are these graded responses as clearly delineated from the perspective of the person on whom detention, restraint or control is imposed?

Slippery slope?

Anti-social behaviour orders (ASBOs) were introduced by the Crime and Disorder Act 1998 (as amended by the Police Reform Act 2002 and the Anti-Social Behaviour Act 2003). Their intentions were honourable, albeit draconian, in that they were designed to tackle low-level but repetitive disorder by individuals, disorder which was blighting the lives of others, largely in communities that were already seriously disadvantaged. The archetypal recipient would have been a young person, out of or beyond parental control, who engaged in threatening, abusive or frightening behaviour, but where that behaviour fell short of actual criminality. Additionally, while some of this behaviour could be caught by the criminal law (criminal damage, burglary, drug offences, etc.), proving cases in court to the criminal standard of beyond reasonable doubt had proved sufficiently problematic for a civil response, with its lower proof requirements, to be preferred. ASBOs could be granted by the civil courts on the basis that the person concerned had acted 'in a manner that caused or was likely to cause harassment, alarm or distress' (s.1(1)(a)) and that the order was necessary to protect others from further anti-social acts by the perpetrator (s.1(6)). The magistrates' court could make an order prohibiting the perpetrator 'from doing anything described in the order' (s.1(4)). Any order made will last for a minimum of two years, and breach of the conditions constitutes a criminal offence, which, on indictment, can attract a maximum penalty of five years' imprisonment. As a response to anti-social behaviour, ASBOs need to be appropriate, proportionate and effective; but the nature of the conditions imposed thereafter is limited only by the imaginations of the magistrates in respect of what is deemed 'necessary for the purpose of protecting [others] from further anti-social acts' (s.1(6)). For example, curfew orders, orders banning someone from particular neighbourhoods or streets, or orders preventing someone from using abusive language, wearing particular items of clothing or associating with named others were commonplace.

Thus, ASBOs aim to control the behaviour of those engaging in anti-social acts in the community; these acts may fall short of criminal conduct and yet may thereafter attract the criminal penalty of imprisonment if the terms of the order (whatever these might be) are breached. While the House of Lords in *Clingham and McCann* (2003) has been alive to the problems of permitting civil adjudication to lead to criminal penalties, and has concluded that the civil standard of proof should be applied with a degree of rigour sensitive to the potential consequences (thus arguably importing the criminal beyond reasonable doubt standard), many of the orders made have contained terms to which it will be difficult for the perpetrators to adhere. This can derive either from the nature of the behaviour that is being 'banned' or because of the nature of the person on whom the order is being imposed. They have, for example, been widely used to regulate prostitution and begging, and have been applied to those with mental and behavioural disorders. Ashworth (2004: 291) has argued cogently that such preventive orders are not undesirable in themselves, but that they should 'be subjected to proper procedural scrutiny in order to ensure that declared rights are not undermined'. In respect of the government's policies to combat anti-social behaviour generally, Ashworth (2004: 287) asserts that they are 'incoherent, potentially oppressive, and contrary to both the spirit and letter of the European Convention on Human Rights'; and he specifically questions, in respect of ASBOs, whether the conversion of a civil order by 'sleight-of-hand' into a criminal penalty amounts to 'a subversion of fundamental legal values?' (2004: 288).

The evidence to date raises concerns that resort to ASBOs may be all too easy and that conditions are being imposed that are all too readily and inevitably breached, propelling offenders into custody. Thus, a total of 6,497 ASBOs were issued between April 1999 and June 2005 for England and Wales (see www.crimereduction.gov.uk). And, by the summer of 2005, 42 per cent of all ASBOs were being breached (Hansard 2005b). The figures on the penalties imposed are less comprehensive, but for Greater London they indicate that of those breaches that resulted in criminal convictions, in 62 per cent custody was the penalty (Hansard 2006c: 116 breaches during the period June 2000 to 31 December 2003). The figures are a little difficult to disentangle, a feature exacerbated by the ability since 2003 for the criminal courts to add an ASBO to a sentence for established criminal conduct, making any subsequent custodial sentence less extraordinary. But it remains the case that some ASBOs do lead to criminal convictions where no true, or sufficiently, criminal conduct has been engaged in; and that those convictions are then used to justify custody. This indeed is a slippery slope.

It is also important to appreciate that the initial impulse behind ASBOs was clearly exclusionary and not in any sense rehabilitative. While this has been tempered by the introduction in May 2004 of individual support orders, designed to address the underlying causes of anti-social behaviour among 10–17-year-olds, for the bulk of the ASBO operation the emphasis has been on exclusion and control. Here is not the place for an exploration of the vulnerability and alienation of young people; suffice it to say there is an alternative view to that propounded by a government promoting policies of exclusion and control (see, for example, Howard League for Penal Reform 2005). Whatever view one might hold about the recipients of ASBOs, it would be a rational strategy, if effectiveness were an objective, to attempt to understand, or at the least consider, the way in which ASBOs are perceived by those on whom they are imposed. For some, they may be regarded as a badge of honour. For others, their import may just not be understood. And, without such a common understanding, it is arguable that the impact of an ASBO cannot be proportionate since any bargain is one-sided. Thus, the individual is perched at the top of the slippery slope, without any proper understanding of the consequences that will follow should their balance be lost. Of ASBOs used to date, well over 40 per cent have entailed people between 10 and 18; thus, the issue of understanding consequences is highly pertinent. Moreover, whatever problems there might be in respect of inappropriate application with this group of young people, the problems are magnified where the recipients of the orders are mentally ill, brain damaged or learning impaired.

Preliminary results from a survey of Youth Offending Teams conducted by the British Institute for Brain-Injured Children (BIBIC 2005) indicated that of ASBOs imposed on those under 17 from April 2004, 35 per cent involved children with a diagnosed mental health disorder or an accepted learning difficulty; and the vast proportion of these had already failed to maintain the conditions of an Acceptable Behaviour Contract, a less draconian measure than an ASBO. The likelihood of unblemished success when imposing the ASBO did not therefore bode well. Two examples will suffice from the survey. First, the case of a 14-year-old child with the cognitive ability of a 7-year-old, learning difficulties, a language impairment and suspected attention deficit hyperactivity disorder. He had a nine o'clock curfew imposed on him, yet he could not tell the time. Not surprisingly, he repeatedly breached the curfew and had spent 13 of the previous 24 months in custody for breach. Yet, during this period, he committed no other criminal offence. Secondly, the case of another young man with learning difficulties whose ASBO banned him from a particular street: on questioning, he said that it was ok if he ran down the street because he was not stopping. Whether this is the interpretation of a budding lawyer, or a simple misunderstanding, the potential for breach is obvious.

It is also important to recognise that this is a very steep slope. Under the Criminal Justice Act 2003, crossing the custody threshold requires sentencers to be satisfied that the offence committed is so serious that neither a fine nor a community sentence is justified. Yet, for breach of an ASBO, it is the breach itself that seemingly determines seriousness, almost as if this were a more serious activity because it showed some contempt or defiance in the face of the civil-court-imposed ASBO. But a finding of contempt of court as a result of breaching other civil orders would not attract a maximum penalty of the magnitude of anything like five years. And for ASBOs, the breaching behaviour may not be criminal *per se*: for example, Payne (2006) reports the case of two 12-year- old twin brothers who had terrorised their local community. The boys were already at a special needs school, and the ASBO imposed prevents them from being together outside their home unaccompanied by a responsible adult. So, mere association on their part over the next two years could result in a custodial sentence. But it seems so inconceivable that by the time these twins were 14 they would *not* have spent time alone together, that the court can only be described as condemning them to failure and criminality.

But is this too bleak a portrayal? As ever, things need not be quite what they seem. Until March 2006, these orders were associated, in my mind at least, with the very target group to whom the government intended they should be applied: namely, representatives from some socially threatening underclass of largely young people who terrorised their neighbourhoods and made respectable residents wail at the passing of some mythical golden era. But then I, and probably many others, had a 'road to Damascus' moment, for a report appeared in the *Guardian* (Laville 2006) of an attempt by residents in the Elcombe Valley to seek ASBOs against members of the Cotswold Hunt, on the basis that they had allowed the tools of their trade, namely, their hounds, to trespass on private land and frighten domestic animals and other livestock. The residents, who undoubtedly had suffered sudden fright, argued that they had been caused 'harassment, alarm or distress'. Two features of this report are noteworthy: first, rather than making the application for ASBOs on the basis of the reported behaviour, the anti-social behaviour coordinator for Stroud District Council offered a warning, allegedly under the Anti-Social Behaviour Act 2003, to those engaging in the anti-social behaviour that, if they persisted, ASBOs would be pursued. Secondly, the senior master of the hunt responded by saying that the hunt had never broken the law. At one level it is comforting to know that the law is widely misunderstood even by those not lacking an education or mental capacity. For, of course, ASBOs apply in a civil context and they do not require criminal law breaking. Indeed, the very vagueness of what constitutes 'anti-social behaviour' is problematic and contrary to the law's desire for certainty. As Poole (2006) has so ably demonstrated, what is anti-social gets defined not by what people do, but by how others respond; combined with a broad definition, 'anti-social behaviour' can certainly capture the hunt members' activities, even if it would not be in accordance with their expectations about certainty in the criminal law. What this vignette reveals, on one interpretation at least, is that the first steps had been taken down a route not previously envisaged, by me at least, for ASBOs; suddenly, the potentially extensive and socially *inclusive* nature of these orders had been made manifest. Will champagne drinkers in Henley and Ascot join the ranks of lager louts at Highbury and Anfield as being 'at risk' for their anti-social conduct?

But there is another, more subtle, interpretation. Having been intrigued by the notion of issuing a pre-ASBO warning, a concept with which I was not familiar and for which I could find no obvious authority in the Act, I contacted the relevant officer. In discussion (Peake: personal communication, 30 March 2006), it emerged that there was indeed no power *per se* to do what had been done. Rather, the officer had taken the initiative to engage in what, to a criminologist's eye, looks more like a form of restorative justice. He had gathered together around a table some members of the local hunt, and some of the objectors; in so doing, it became evident that the hunt members were aware that they had repeatedly engaged in behaviour that they knew the objectors found frightening. An ASBO could have been imposed, but the officer took the view that he might not have the ratepayers' support for it; similarly, a civil injunction could have been pursued, but that would have been costly for all involved. Instead, he proposed a course of action that (in his mind at least) equated to a caution. He wrote a tailor-made warning letter to the hunt members explaining that if the behaviour were repeated, evidence of the letter would be put before the court. Everybody seemed content with this. Of course, whether these actions represent those of an officer acting *ultra vires* and using coercion to achieve a desired objective or an imaginative, innovative, problem-solving, cost-saving approach depends very much upon one's perspective of the proper relationship between the state, the exercise of control and citizens.

But this was not the only innovative use of ASBOs. This officer also used them as a way of bringing to the attention of the authorities, and thereby gaining access to services, people who had evidently fallen through the net of community care and had become a source of irritation, annoyance or fear to their neighbours. Typically, these would be isolated, mentally ill individuals, about whom there had been complaints because of their unacceptable or bizarre behaviour. Again such use of the law as a route to accessing scare resources is not uncommon (James *et al.* 2002). So, a complex nexus of carrot and stick, coercion and control emerged, but not necessarily with any of the procedural safeguards or necessary proportionality associated with detention or restraint.

Taking liberties?

So, the question becomes, do any of the conditions imposed by ASBOs constitute detention? In the case of *Clingham and McCann* (2003), the House of Lords justified the restrictions on freedom ASBOs entailed on the basis of their preventive rationale; these preventive purposes justified restrictions on liberty, but not deprivation of it (see Lord Hope at para. 76). But *HL* (above), when considering the issue of deprivation of liberty in a mental health context, asserts that detention and restraint are separated only by degree and intensity, not nature or substance. Thus, might curfews combined with comprehensive or systematic surveillance to detect breach begin to look like exercising complete and effective control? Moreover, from the perspective of those on whom they are imposed, control *is* achieved through the coercive threat of imprisonment. And it should be recalled that one of the factors referred to in *HL* was the acceptance by the clinical staff that they would have detained the patient if he had tried to leave. Thus, what might be the difference between controlling someone's behaviour through the threat of a certain deterrent and the intention to detain should someone's behaviour, unbeknownst to them, raise the necessity for control in the minds of clinical staff? Similarly, what is the relationship between controlling motivation through medication, and controlling it through fear of consequences? From the perspective of the person being controlled, acceptable restraint could slip seamlessly into unjustifiable detention.

The extent to which general surveillance has become commonplace is widely acknowledged. However, individualised supervision is now also routinely part of criminal sentences: the ability of the supervisors to do this with any degree of effectiveness is not the critical question. What is critical is the seeming desire to maintain control. In the field of mental health, one of the government's key objectives in reform of the 1983 Mental Health Act has been to achieve new community treatment orders (compulsory treatment can only currently be given to those detained in hospital). And even though the Draft Mental Health Bill 2004 has now been abandoned in the face of professional opposition and spiralling costs, the commitment to community treatment orders remains on the government's agenda in respect of its intentions to amend the current act (Hansard 2006a). Notably, these orders were characterised by the Mental Health Act Commission in evidence to the Joint Scrutiny Committee (2005: para. 194) as having the potential to become 'ASBOs' for the mentally disordered. Yet, it would be perverse to suggest that coerced treatment in the community does not already take place: thus, patients on conditional discharge from a restriction order may 'agree' to take medication in the community when offered a choice between this and recall to hospital. And, of course, people face hard choices all of the time in their lives; we are all coerced to a greater or lesser extent in our freedom of action. But, is coercion acceptable to achieve some kinds of aims, but not others, where procedural safeguards are critical? Is taking anti-psychotic medication one such example where the intrusive nature of the intervention and the heightened risks and benefits require some external validation?

There are undoubtedly both increasing forms of control in the community and increasingly legally regulated forms of control: to name but a few, supervision orders, sex offender orders, parenting orders, curfew orders, licence terms for those released from custody, home detention curfew, control zones and control orders. Then there is the work of the various agencies involved in control and the cross-cutting interagency activities of such new bodies as the multiagency public protection panels. While real control may be ephemeral, breach of preordained terms can be draconian. And although the courts have recently upheld a challenge to the blanket use of curfews on unaccompanied children in a designated area (*R (W)* v. *Commissioner of Police for the Metropolis* 2005), made under s.30(6) of the Anti-Social Behaviour Act 2003, on the basis that it was not clear that Parliament had intended thereby to provide for the forcible removal of a child, such a robust response to the mushrooming legislative provisions in this field has not been typical. So is it likely that the regulation of these new forms of control will be subject to the finely tuned procedural protections that *HL v. UK* seemingly demands with its sliding scale? Or rather that they will be used imaginatively, or coercively, by those with objectives not necessarily predicted or shared by the legislature?

Or is the merging of forms of control more akin to a slippery slope where the trajectory of failure can propel those who cannot or will not be controlled into detention, whether it be custodial or therapeutic? The resolution and conclusion of these developments is, on balance, bleak. And while more control in the community might have been a price worth paying if it meant less control in custodial institutions, the evidence is that prison populations have increased dramatically since the 1980s, and that there has been a significant increase in the use of compulsion under the Mental Health Act 1983. For example, on 30 June 1980, the prison population was 42,300; on 31 March 2006, it was 77,035 with a further 3,086 people under Home Detention Curfew (see, respectively, Hansard 2003, and National Offender Management Service 2006); in 1989–90, there were 16,297 compulsory psychiatric admissions, a number increasing to 26,235 by 2003-4 (see, generally, Hotopf *et al.* 2000, and the annual Department of Health figures for 2000 and 2005). But, of course, Stan Cohen had already warned us of this. And while many more of the key features of his thesis have also come to fruition, reflecting considerable prescience of mind on his part, it is almost certainly a situation for which he would want little credit and is one which he almost certainly laments.

References

Ashingdane v *UK* (1979) 2 EHRR 387.

Ashworth, A. (2004) 'Social control and "anti-social behaviour": the subversion of human rights?', *Law Quarterly Review*, 120: 263–91.

British Institute for Brain Injured Children (2005) *Ain't Misbehaving: Young People with Learning and Communication Difficulties and Anti-Social Behaviour.* A report prepared by BIBIC. Campaign Update. www.bibic.org.uk.

Burney, E. (2005) *Making People Behave: Anti-social Behaviour, Politics and Policy.* Cullompton: Willan.

Clingham v *Kensington and Chelsea Royal L.B.C.; R (McCann)* v *Crown Court at Manchester* [2003] 1 AC 787.

Cohen, S. (1979) 'The punitive city: notes on the dispersal of social control', *Contemporary Crises*, 3: 4, 341–63.

Cohen, S. (1985) *Visions of Social Control.* Cambridge: Polity Press.

Department of Health (2000 and 2005) 'In-patients formally detained in hospital under the Mental Health Act 1983, and other legislation England 1989–1990 to 1999–2000.' London: Department of Health.

Hansard (2003) *Hilary Benn, Secretary of State for the Home Department in Answer to Ministerial Questions.* HoC, 13 Feb 2003 Col 913W.

Hansard (2006a) *Written Ministerial Statement: Mental Health Bill.* HoC Vol 444 Part 131 Col 29-30 WS.

Hansard (2006b) *Written Ministerial Statement by Hazel Blears,* 1 March 2005.

Hansard (2006c) *Fiona MacTaggert in Response to Questions.* HoC, 7 March 2006 col 1322W.

HL v *UK* (2004) Application no 45508/99, judgement 5 October 2004.

Hotopf, M., Wall S., Buchanan, A., Wessely, S. and Churchill, R. (2000) 'Changing patterns in the use of the Mental Health Act 1983 in England, 1984-1996', *British Journal of Psychiatry,* 176: 479–84.

Howard League for Penal Reform (2005) *Once Upon a Time in the West: Social Deprivation and Rural Youth Crime.* London: Howard League for Penal Reform.

James, D., Farnham, F., Moorey, H., Lloyd, H., Blizard, R. and Barnes, T. (2002) *Outcome of psychiatric admission through the courts.* Home Office: RDS Occasional Paper no. 79.

Joint Committee on the Draft Mental Health Bill. (2005) *First Report.* House of Lords and House of Commons 9 March 2005. Also available from Parliament website.

Laville, S. (2006) 'Hunt receives ASBO warning after CPS rules out action', *Guardian,* 25 March.

Lowman, J., Menzies, R.J. and Palys, T.S. (eds) (1985) *Transcarceration: Essays in the Sociology of Social Control.* Aldershot: Gower.

National Offender Management Service (2006) *Prison Population and Accommodation Briefing for 31 March 2006.* Prison Service: Estate Planning and Development Unit.

Payne, S. (2006) 'ASBO bans tearaway twins, 12, from being together in public', *Daily Telegraph,* 28 March 2006.

Poole, S. (2006) *Unspeak.* London: Little, Brown and Company.

R (W) v *Commissioner of Police for the Metropolis* [2005] EWCA Crim 20 July 2005.

Chapter 18

Social control talk/talking about social control: encounters with Stan Cohen and his work

Andrew Scull

Stan Cohen and I first became friends at a relatively early stage in our respective academic careers. In graduate school, as I became acquainted with the literature on deviance and social control, I came across the collection of essays Stan edited for Penguin on *Images of Deviance*,[1] and shortly thereafter, I read his classic *Folk Devils and Moral Panics*.[2] My relocation to London for the 1976–77 academic year coincided with the appearance of my first book, *Decarceration*,[3] and our shared intellectual interests soon led me to meet Stan, as well as Paul Rock and David Downes, at the London School of Economics.

Stan and I, in particular, found that we shared a developing concern with the relations of state power and social control and, notwithstanding the geographical separation which then ensued, we stayed in touch, eventually deciding to collaborate on a book bringing together some of the best young sociologists and historians working in this emerging area. That book, *Social Control and the State*,[4] together with another collection edited by David Garland and Peter Young that appeared almost simultaneously (and to which Stan and I both contributed),[5] helped to establish the research agenda in the field for the next decade and more. It materialized despite Stan's decision to relocate to Israel – a further geographical separation that greatly complicated, in that pre-Internet era, the sheer physical difficulty of our collaboration, and reduced us, on more than one occasion, to working together in hotel lounges not far from Heathrow Airport, when our travel schedules temporarily allowed us some brief face-to-face contact.

In important ways, naturally enough, the field has moved on from the preoccupations that were so evident among the contributions to these two seminal volumes. If the preoccupations of the field have changed, so too have those of the contributors, most of whom, two decades ago, were still nearer the beginning than the end of their academic careers. And yet, on another level, I suspect that the fundamental problematics that engaged the otherwise diverse group of us who wrote for those two collections continue to fascinate us all: the common concerns with, as David Garland's and Peter Young's title proclaimed, power and punishment; the underlying fascination with understanding the bases of social order and the containment of challenges to it; the shared commitment to endeavouring to explain as well as describe shifts in social control styles and practices; and (in varying degrees, to be sure – though that was as true in 1983 as now), the consciousness of the political dimensions of our own scholarship, associated as that has necessarily been, with an interest in reflecting upon the possible connections between our ivory-tower analyses and the larger social universe within which we find ourselves embedded.

The two books were influential, of course, in substantial measure because they brought together authors who had something significant to say, and did so at a moment when the critical analysis of penality had become an increasingly fashionable topic in social theory. During the 1970s, in Britain, France, and North America, the analysis of social control had been reconnected to the study of power and the political order. Revisionist scholars in history, criminology, socio-legal studies, and sociology were seizing upon crime and punishment, madness and its confinement, poverty and its management as intellectually exciting topics, worthy of examining as something more than a problem of administration or a tale of linear progress.

My own intellectual interest in power and punishment had emerged only indirectly. Interested when I entered graduate school in joining together sociological and historical analysis, and combining those interests with a deep concern with issues of political power and process, I became fascinated with one aspect of what is surely the central question for sociologists, the problem of social order. Specifically, and it must be said largely serendipitously at the outset, I found myself increasingly drawn to the question of the changing structures and techniques of social control in the era of the Great Transformation, seeking both to grasp what the central characteristics of those changes had been, and to begin to account for their unfolding development.

In principle, these concerns might have led me in a variety of directions. I might have examined, for example, as Michael Ignatieff proceeded to do at just that time, the nexus of crime and punishment.[6] Or I might have focused on the crucial issue of poverty and its containment, as Frances Piven and Richard Cloward had begun to do a few years earlier.[7] Revisionist studies of schools as vehicles for the control of children had begun to appear,[8] as had studies of emerging systems for controlling children already gone bad,[9] and perhaps I could have added to their number. Here, too, there would have been a clearer path forward to a concern with modern penality.

Instead, I elected first to focus upon the issues surrounding craziness and its treatment. It was the nineteenth-century asylums, those monuments of moral architecture I was to dub 'museums of madness', and the proto-professionals who ran them, the variously titled mad-doctors/alienists/psychiatrists that first attracted my gaze, and to which and to whom I devoted much of the first decade of my career as scholar – more than that, it would turn out, but that is a topic to which I shall return later in this chapter. This intellectual focus on the management of the mad in part reflected some of my reading at that time: Michel Foucault's *Madness and Civilization*,[10] David Rothman's *Discovery of the Asylum*,[11] and Erving Goffman's *Asylums*.[12] But it also derived from my conviction that the empire of asylumdom and its nominal rulers were a strategically crucial site for investigating larger themes.

As I saw and still see it, there were a number of key elements distinguishing deviance and its control in modern societies from the shapes which such phenomena assume elsewhere. In British (and to some extent American) society, from the eighteenth century forward, one observed a substantial and growing involvement of the state, and the emergence of a highly rationalized, and centrally administered and directed social control apparatus; in increasing measure, the treatment of many types of deviance in institutions providing a large measure of segregation from the surrounding community; the steady differentiation of different sorts of deviance, and the consignment of each variety to its own set of institutions; and, as a corollary of this process of differentiation (and in part produced by it), the parallel emergence of professional and semi-professional occupations laying claim to expertise in the management of crime, delinquency, poverty, craziness, mental handicap, and so forth. From this perspective, the differentiation of the insane, the rise of a state-supported asylum system, and the emergence of the psychiatric profession can be seen to represent no more than a particular, though very important, example of this much more general series of changes in the social organization of deviance – interesting, not least, because even though psychiatry for much of its history has been an isolated and stigmatized branch of the medical profession, its claims to ground its expertise in the neutral, value-free foundation of 'science' have nonetheless been accorded more credibility and respect than less-developed claims by those operating in other sectors of the social control apparatus. The dramatic and radical changes in the typical societal responses to the deranged between 1750 and 1850 were thus the focus of my first major scholarly research, which examined the metamorphosis at the level of both ideas and social practices.

The discovery of the asylum

Whereas in the eighteenth century, only the violent and destructive among those now labelled insane would have been segregated and confined apart from the rest of the community, with the achievement of what was widely portrayed as a major social reform, symbolized by the passage of the Asylums Act in 1845, the asylum was endorsed as the sole officially approved response to the problems posed by mental illness. In the process, and equally as important, the boundaries of who was to be classified as mad, and thus to be liable to incarceration, were themselves transformed. One needs to understand how, then, over the course of a century and more, the crystallization of this new ensemble of social practices and moral meanings came about, and to make sense of their striking and significant embodiment in new physical forms that constitute such a notable example of the moral architecture of the nineteenth century. And in analysing these developments, it is vital simultaneously to attend to the reciprocal constitution of new forms of expertise and knowledge alongside and in intimate relationship with this new institutional apparatus, to pay attention to the development of new theoretical codes and technologies of intervention, and to delineate the redrawing of the boundaries between the normal and the pathological that accompanied the shutting away of the mad in what was pronounced to be a therapeutic isolation. Institutions and knowledge, theory and practice, and the constitution and the capture of particular sorts of problem populations do not develop in some linear, sequential fashion, with one side of these equations preceding and producing the other. They are, on the contrary, mutually reinforcing and deeply interdependent, the development of the one deriving from and simultaneously advancing the maturation of the other.

My work on 'lunacy reform' in nineteenth-century Britain in one important respect paralleled the influential reinterpretation of the rise of the asylum in the USA that David Rothman had offered a few years earlier, for Rothman, too, interpreted the rise of segregative responses to insanity through the lens of social control. But Rothman's perspective was in most respects very different from mine. His vision of society and its dynamics; his relative lack of interest in trying to tease out connections between changing social and political structures and the rise of asylums; and his treatment of developments in the

USA in isolation from parallel changes elsewhere, all combined to produce a very different portrait of the *sources* of institutional change, even if both of us took sharp issue with the Whiggish histories that had hitherto dominated the field and concurred, for the most part, in our assessments of the *outcome* of 'reform'.[13] We did share, however, one other point of theoretical convergence: heavily influenced by his reading of Goffman, as his use of the term 'asylum' as a synonym for 'total institution' made clear to any sociologist encountering his work, Rothman saw the rise of the lunatic asylum as co-extensive with, and only understandable within the context of, a broader shift toward institutionally based modes of responding to deviance, just as he argued that the subsequent history of penitentiaries, poorhouses, and asylums displayed some fundamental similarities.[14]

This was a position with which I had considerable, indeed, perhaps at that time too much, sympathy, for I have subsequently come to feel that one must be careful about the analytic dangers that flow from eliding the distinctiveness of institutions directed at crime, poverty, madness, and so forth. That is not to suggest that there are no points of convergence or structural similarity, or to deny that, to some degree, changes in all these sectors may respond to a similar underlying set of factors. But it is to acknowledge that there are risks and dangers in neglecting the distinctiveness of each of these realms, and the separate logics that may and frequently do inform developments in each of them. This is a point David Garland has also forcibly made in his critique of Foucault's work on the penal system: 'When [Foucault] says that the prison is "just like" the factory, or the school, or the monastery [or, we might add, the asylum], he is referring only to its internal practices, and not to the social meanings through which it is publicly understood. And while there are clear technical homologies linking what is done within these various institutions, their social usage and significance are altogether different.'[15]

Alongside my continuing interest in the empire of asylumdom, in the mid-1970s, I had become interested in the contemporary drive toward deinstitutionalization, and had begun the research that led to the publication of my book, *Decarceration*.[16] In many respects, that period represented the high tide of the deinstitutionalization movement, at least on the ideological level. The drive toward community corrections for both adult and juvenile offenders was widely portrayed as a far-reaching reform, as was the contemporaneous effort to replace the traditional mental hospital with a community-based mental health system. Moreover, the ideology that underpinned the changes, or apparent changes in all these sectors, shared much in common, being premised on a shared assumption that the rise of the penitentiary, the reformatory, and the lunatic asylum had formed part of a common Enlightenment project that had proved to be a colossal mistake.

Gary Wills vividly made the case for the bankruptcy of the traditional reliance on the prison. The penitentiary was, he asserted, a classic 'failed experiment' that had somehow lingered on for almost two centuries, 'the most disastrous survivor of the Enlightenment still grasping at a death-like life. [In] our culture's human sewer, clogged and unworkable with human waste ... the criminal is sequestered with other criminals, in conditions exacerbating the lowest drives of lonely and stranded men, men deprived of loved ones, of dignifying work, of pacifying amenities.... Smuggling, bullying, theft, drug traffic, homosexual menace, are ways of life. Guards, themselves brutalized by the experience of prison, have to ignore most of the crimes inflicted on inmates, even when they do not connive at them, or incite them. [As a result,] prisons teach crime, instill crime, inure men to it, trap men in it as a way of life.'[17] Studies of the mental hospital echoed the theme. American psychiatrists expressed the fear that 'the patients are infantile...because we infantilize them'.[18] British psychiatrists wrote of the dangers of 'institutionalism', and one of their number coined a new diagnostic category for this iatrogenic disorder: 'institutional neurosis.'[19] Sociologists were still fiercer in their criticisms. One could not help concluding, one of them suggested, that 'in the long run the abandonment of the state hospitals might be one of the greatest humanitarian reforms and the greatest financial economy ever achieved'.[20] The bins we had inherited from the Victorian age were, in Erving Goffman's words, 'hopeless storage dumps trimmed in psychiatric paper. They have served to remove the patient from the scene of his symptomatic behavior ... but this function has been performed by fences, not doctors. And the price that the patient has had to pay for this service has been considerable: dislocation from civil life, alienation from loved ones who arranged the commitment, mortification due to hospital regimentation and surveillance, permanent post-hospital stigmatization. This has not merely been a bad deal; it has been a grotesque one.'[21]

Sociological critics of the total institution were for a time convinced that prisons, reformatories, and mental hospitals deformed and destroyed the human raw materials they processed for fundamentally similar structural reasons. In the 1970s, their account of the virtues of their preferred alternative: community care or community corrections, used the same rhetoric and arguments about these two very different domains. Just as David Rothman's nineteenth-century reformers had touted the nineteenth-century asylum as a model of sociability for the larger society, so their contemporary equivalents boasted of the larger value of their chosen panacea: 'the destination is a degree of community

243

participation and effectiveness which has all but departed our lives as people living together. Part of the powerlessness and frustration which some may sense at this juncture will be resolved in this trend, to the benefit not only of inmates or clients or patients or criminals now in institutions – but of the community as a whole.'[22]

Living in a country that boasts one of the highest rates of imprisonment in the world, and in a state whose prison system was alone spared the budgetary axe in the midst of desperate maneuvering to paper over a $35 billion dollar deficit, I find it difficult to recall how different the picture looked in the mid-1970s, when for a decade state and federal prison populations had been static or declining, albeit slowly, and where a state like Massachusetts had just, with much fanfare, shut its juvenile reformatories.[23] In an era of three-strikes laws, moral panics about juvenile crime, and popular pressure to try children as adults, the notion of a stable, let alone a declining, prison population seems a pipedream. Yet the apparent match of rhetoric and reality in the penal sector in 1975, and the even sharper fall-off in mental hospital censuses, made it all too easy to conclude that the changes that were under way were fundamentally similar in character across this whole array of institutions. The Goffmanian vision, which lumped together prisons, reformatories, nunneries, boot camps, concentration camps, and mental hospitals, seemed to have been embraced by politicians and policymakers, and the flight seemed to be on from these disabling, custodial institutions.

But only *seemed* to be so, and for a very few years at that. To be sure, the abandonment of the asylum has continued apace. The brooding presence of the barracks asylum, which for so many years dominated both the physical and the symbolic landscape of madness, has largely been superseded by the sidewalk psychotics who are now so familiar a feature of our urban landscape. But matters are far different with respect to crime and punishment, for the penal apparatus has remained heavily wedded to imprisonment as a dominant response to the criminal. Ideologically, even in the 1970s, there was a strong conservative backlash against anything smacking of leniency toward crime and criminals, and where mental hospital populations have declined remorselessly and at an accelerating pace, the opposite has been true for the penitentiary. If 'community treatment' of the mentally ill has in reality mostly corresponded to a policy of neglect and abandonment of the chronically crazy, 'community corrections' in its various manifestations has more commonly consisted of a widening of the net of social control, what Stan Cohen early on identified as a substantial growth of the crime-control apparatus.[24] Criminals and delinquents, as Chan and Ericson would have it, 'are not diverted *from*, but *into* and within the system'.[25]

Social control and the net-widening thesis

To study social control is, as we all must have reflected from time to time, and as Stan Cohen has so eloquently documented,[26] to enter a Kafkaesque universe rife with ironies. Here is one of them: the very fact that the measures designed to dispose of the disoriented and the senile are ostensibly undertaken from a benevolent and humanitarian concern for their welfare has facilitated their casual dumping. If it is concluded that traditional approaches to the management of the gravely mentally ill, centred on their confinement in large asylums, are destructive and anti-therapeutic, then non-intervention, dressed up as community treatment, and promoted in the name of the very virtues once attributed to the asylum, can be advocated on the grounds of its advantages to the client. If this is coupled with the claim that a revolutionary breakthrough has occurred in the technological capacities of the professionals to whose charge they are entrusted in the form of the miracle of modern psychopharmacology, and the fact that many of the chronically disturbed can be isolated and contained while being neglected (their very infirmity limiting the threat they pose), one understands why, in the words of Sir Roy Griffiths, a skeletonized community care can persist like the proverbial pernicious 'poor relation: everybody's distant relative, but nobody's baby'.[27]

By contrast, as David Garland has emphasized, 'The punitive, condemnatory sign throws a long shadow over everything the penal system does'.[28] Foucault famously sought to assimilate penal practices and the rationalities they employ to the administrative normalization of modern societies, claiming to trace the transformation of punishment 'from being a morally-charged and emotive set of ritual practices into an increasingly passionless and professionalized instrumental process'.[29] Such assertions capture important dimensions of the evolution of the power to punish, but as Garland rightly contends, as a global portrait of modern penality, they are clearly inadequate, for they neglect the persistent presence of passionate moral condemnation and of retributive sentiments in the criminal justice arena, those vengeful emotions that Durkheim insisted continue to lie at the heart of our collective response to crime.[30]

'Radical non-interventionism' thus had few supporters beyond the professoriate as a crime-control strategy. On the contrary, the fear of crime is a political issue capable of mobilizing powerful if somewhat confused pressures for 'action' among an otherwise fractured and fragmented public. As James Jacobs suggested two decades ago, and as the popularity of California's misguided, fiscally irrational, and yet immensely popular three-strikes law has more recently confirmed, here

245

is an issue that transcends standard ideological divisions to provide 'strong support for a fundamental change in punishment policy – one that pushes toward greater severity and more frequent use of incarceration'.[31]

Neglect has still other disadvantages as a response to crime and many forms of delinquency. To the extent that crime represents a 'rational' form of activity, the erosion of sanctions threatens to elicit more of it. If criminals are able to violate the law with something approaching impunity, the incentives to conform are significantly weakened, and public outrage is all but certain. And a social and political order that permits such developments will suffer an insidious but powerful loss of legitimacy. It should thus come as no surprise to learn that, quite apart from the striking increases in prison populations I have already referred to, there is substantial evidence that the development of so-called 'diversionary' programmes leads instead to 'a more voracious processing of deviant populations, albeit in new settings and by professionals with different names'.[32]

Adding still further weight to these pressures to broaden the scope of the crime-control apparatus, the fate of the crime-control bureaucracy, unlike that of the profession of psychiatry, is inextricably bound up with the state sector. Police and prison officers operate in a severely restricted market, and the sorts of professional 'convenience' that David Rothman identified as serving to shape the character of such Progressive Era reforms as the introduction of probation and parole[33] add yet a further layer of pressure toward a policy of greater intervention and further expansion of their own empires. In California, for instance, the three-strikes law, the massive expansion of the prison system, and the inexorable rise in spending on incarceration owe much to the carefully calculated financial contributions of the prison officers' union, and to the pressing need of our politicians, from the governor down, to secure the money they need for their campaigns and the politically potent endorsements that signal that they are 'tough on crime and criminals'. In 2006–7, the California correctional budget will amount to more than $8 billion, and the number imprisoned will exceed 170,000, compared with only 25,000 a quarter century earlier. And still there is a clamour for yet more new prisons and yet further increases in expenditures.[34]

Atrocities and denials

The penal archipelago, like the nearly defunct network of Victorian bins for the confinement of the crazy, continues to be rife with violence, brutality, inhumanity – a reality we mostly manage to ignore.

Remarkably, we have likewise learned to live with the sidewalk psychotic in our midst, and to pretend that the mentally ill now reside in the 'communities' that exist only in the land of myth. Locked away or lying in plain sight, the spectacle of suffering and the manifest and manifold failures of the entire system to achieve its ostensible and official goals for the most part remain safely obscured or ignored. If occasionally they surface in the media scandal of the day, such unpleasant features of the social control apparatus and of those caught up in its coils are swiftly pushed back out of sight. Denial rules.

When Stan and I began to work in the field, three or even four decades ago, a different kind of denial characterized much of the extant scholarship. Mental illness, so a well-known renegade psychiatrist would have it, was a myth. Or, as my sociological colleagues preferred, madness, like criminality, was the product of stigma and labelling. All was relative, and deviance lay only in the eye of the beholder. The mental patient was the victim of 'contingencies', the criminal of the misfortune of having been caught, and both were stabilized in their deviant roles by public denunciation and stigmatization, and by the pernicious effects of being processed through malevolent total institutions. It is one of Stan Cohen's signal virtues that his intellectual pragmatism early on led him to recoil from the romantic excesses of societal reaction theory, and still more from the radical relativism of the postmodernists, though without falling back into the trap of embracing the simplicities of an earlier positivism.

As Stan clearly saw, such romantic notions made for as one-sided a view of deviance as those they replaced. For though social control may have its irrational and arbitrary qualities, and all-too-often its own peculiar perversities and horrors,[35] it must also in substantial measure be seen as a response to threat, to disruption, on occasion – dare one say it – to evil. To neglect this side of the equation is to engage in avoidance and evasion of disturbing and uncomfortable realities. And it is to leave us without adequate ways of accounting for much of what we observe.

Goffman's *Asylums*,[36] for example, with its portrayal of total institutions as engines of oppression, places engaged in mangling and reconstructing the selves of those souls unfortunate enough to be subjected to their baneful influence, paid scant attention to the pre-patient phase of the madman's moral career. Brief comments about inmates being 'betrayed' by their nearest and dearest into the clutches of the asylum and its associated tinkering trade coexisted unequally with lengthy dissections of the absence of autonomy, the shrinking of capacities, and the dehumanizing impact of ward life. In the face of Goffman's characteristic reticence about larger contextual issues, it was easy to assume that the primary source of the inmate's troubles was his institution, not his illness. Such, indeed, was the summary of Goffman's argument that his publisher put forth on the book's dust jacket, though it left the whole question of why society had ever embraced these museums of madness[37] a mystery.

Elsewhere, however, Goffman painted a very different picture, one which placed at its centre the character and extent of the havoc and disarray a mentally ill person could and did provoke among his (or, we would these days add, her) nearest and dearest, the wider social circle he was embedded in, and the social order more generally. So far from the mental patient being little more than the put-upon victim of an almost arbitrary social labelling process, Goffman suggested that 'the social significance of the confusion [the madman] creates may be as profound and basic as social existence can get'. 'Mental symptoms,' he insisted, 'are not, by and large, *incidentally* a social infraction. By and large they are specifically and pointedly offensive.... It follows that if the patient persists in his symptomatic behavior, then he must create organizational havoc and havoc in the minds of members.... It is this havoc that psychiatrists have dismally failed to examine and that sociologists ignore when they treat mental illness merely as a labeling process.'[38] Only by bringing pain and suffering, chaos and threat back into the picture could one begin to comprehend the societal reactions one sought to explain.

Hence the need to develop strategies for limiting and encapsulating the threats, both symbolic and practical, that the mentally ill pose to their immediate interactional partners and to the social order more generally – strategies that have clearly varied across time and space, but ways of coping that of necessity must allow for the more or less continuous employment of techniques of containment and damage limitation. The lunatic may be seen variously as the embodiment of extravagance and incoherence; incomprehensibility and ungovernable rage; melancholy or menace. The various manifestations of unreason – the rages of the raving, the dolour of the downcast, the grotesquely denuded mental life of the demented – each pose characteristic and to some extent distinct problems for society. But all these varieties of craziness serve to create almost unbearable disturbances in the texture of daily existence, disruptions that, the Szaszs[39] and the Scheffs[40] of this world notwithstanding, dictate, indeed *demand* some sort of organized and exclusionary response if organized social life is not to become chaotic or simply to collapse.

Through the end of the 1980s, Stan's work had displayed the great virtues of refusing to embrace the conventional happy talk about the evolution of the social control apparatus – not for him the Panglossian portrait of police, psychiatrists, prisons, madhouses as straightforward defenders of social order – while also increasingly resisting and rejecting those who sought to rationalise and relativise deviance out of existence. But a different kind of denial was about to monopolize his energies and attention: the involvement of the state – even a democratic state – in systematic torture and abuse; the ability of its politicians and bureaucrats to engage in doubletalk, redefine what they were up to, to avoid and evade the moral implications of their behaviour; and the deplorable ability of the rest of us to join in the process of avoidance and evasion, and in the process to ignore injustice, horror, unbearable pain.

Stan's unflinching revelations about Israeli torture of Palestinians have acquired a new resonance in the world of Gitmo, Abu Ghraib and extraordinary renditions. His early concerns with the sufferings of people living under systems of social control, evident particularly in his work with Laurie Taylor on the experience of long-term imprisonment,[41] during his time in Israel acquired a new moral urgency and force and an overtly political dimension. They also required a remarkable bravery: a willingness to suffer and to risk more than most of us are willing even to contemplate in the name of truth-telling. Wryly, Stan notes in the pages of his latest and most profound and disturbing book that 'doing something about your own country asks more of you, that you pay especially the price of standing up against the consensus: ostracism, isolation and stigmatization as a "traitor". You may even risk becoming a victim yourself.'[42] The autobiographical relevance of this remark should be clear to the rest of us, even though, quite characteristically, Stan modestly lets the matter slide. To refuse to embrace comfortable myths, to confront official denials and disinformation, to acknowledge violence and atrocities, and to refuse the role of the 'innocent' and wilfully ignorant bystander: these are just some of the lessons Stan Cohen has sought to teach those of us who study deviance and social control. To honour the man and to honour his contributions to the field is itself an honour and a privilege.

Notes

1 Stanley Cohen (ed.), *Images of Deviance*, Harmondsworth, Middlesex: Penguin, 1971.
2 Stanley Cohen, *Folk Devils and Moral Panics: The Creation of the Mods and Rockers*, London: McGibbon and Kee, 1972.
3 Andrew Scull, *Decarceration: Community Treatment and the Deviant: A Radical View*, Englewood Cliffs, NJ: Prentice-Hall, 1977.
4 Stanley Cohen and Andrew Scull (eds), *Social Control and the State: Historical and Comparative Essays*, Oxford: Martin Robertson, 1983.

5 David Garland and Peter Young (eds), *The Power to Punish: Contemporary Penality and Social Analysis*, London: Heinemann, 1983.

6 Michael Ignatieff, *A Just Measure of Pain: The Penitentiary in the Industrial Revolution, 1750–1850*, New York: Pantheon, 1978.

7 Frances Piven and Richard Cloward, *Regulating the Poor: The Functions of Public Welfare*, New York: Pantheon, 1971.

8 Michael Katz, *The Irony of Early School Reform: Educational Innovation in Mid-Nineteenth Century Massachusetts*, Cambridge, MA: Harvard University Press, 1968; David Tyack, *The One Best System: A History of American Urban Education*, Cambridge, MA: Harvard University Press, 1974.

9 Anthony Platt, *The Child Savers: The Invention of Delinquency*, Chicago: University of Chicago Press, 1969; Steven Schlossman, *Love and the American Delinquent: The Theory and Practice of 'Progressive' Juvenile Justice 1825–1920*, Chicago: University of Chicago Press, 1977. A more recent contribution is John Sutton's *Stubborn Children: Controlling Delinquency in the United States 1640–1981*, Berkeley, CA: University of California Press, 1988.

10 Michel Foucault, *Madness and Civilization: A History of Insanity in the Age of Reason*, London: Tavistock, 1971; trans. and abr. from *Histoire de la folie a l'âge classique*, Paris: Plon, 1961.

11 David Rothman, *The Discovery of the Asylum: Social Order and Disorder in the New Republic*, Boston: Little, Brown, 1971.

12 Erving Goffman, *Asylums: Essays on the Social Situation of Mental Patients and Other Inmates*, New York: Doubleday, 1961.

13 For a more extensive discussion of these differences, and a critique of Rothman's analytic stance, see Chapter 2 of my *Social Order/Mental Disorder: Anglo-American Psychiatry in Historical Perspective*, Berkeley, CA: University of California Press, 1989.

14 For anyone inclined to doubt the intellectual genealogy, Rothman subsequently acknowledged it in a Canadian interview. See Dorothy Chunn and Russell Smandych, 'An interview with David Rothman', *Canadian Criminology Forum*, 4, 1982, pp. 152–62.

15 David Garland, 'The rationalization of punishment', in Heikki Pihlajamäki (ed.) *Theatres of Power: Social Control and Criminality in Historical Perspective*, Helsinki: Matthias Calonius Society, 1991, p. 111.

16 Andrew Scull, *Decarceration: Community Treatment and the Deviant: A Radical View*, Englewood Cliffs, NJ: Prentice-Hall, 1977.

17 Gary Wills, 'The Human Sewer', *New York Review of Books*, 22, 3 April 1975, pp. 3–8.

18 F.C. Redlich, preface to W. Caudill, *The Psychiatric Hospital as a Small Society*, Cambridge, MA: Harvard University Press, 1958; A.H. Stanton and M.S. Schwartz, *The Mental Hospital: A Study of Institutional Participation in Psychiatric Illness and Treatment*, New York: Basic Books, 1954.

19 J.K. Wing and G.W. Brown, *Institutionalism and Schizophrenia*, Cambridge: Cambridge University Press, 1970; Russell Barton, *Institutional Neurosis* (2nd edn), Bristol: Wright, 1965.

20 Ivan Belknap, *Human Problems of a State Mental Hospital*, New York: McGraw-Hill, 1956, p. 212.

21 Erving Goffman, 'The Insanity of Place', p. 336; (see note 38).
22 Benedict Alper, 'Foreword' to Y. Bakal (ed.), *Closing Correctional Institutions*, Lexington, MA: D.C. Heath, 1973, p. viii.
23 Jerome Miller, 'The politics of change: correctional reform', in Y. Bakal (ed.), *Closing Correctional Institutions*, Lexington, MA: D.C. Heath, 1973, pp. 3–8.
24 Stanley Cohen, 'The punitive city: notes on the dispersal of social control', *Contemporary Crises*, 3, 1979, pp. 339–63; *idem*, 'Social control talk: telling stories about correctional change', in D. Garland and P. Young (eds), *The Power to Punish*, London: Heinemann, 1983.
25 Janet Chan and Richard C. Ericson, *Decarceration and the Economy of Penal Reform*, Toronto: University of Toronto Centre of Criminology, 1981, p. 55. See also Thomas Blomberg, 'Diversion and accelerated social control', *Journal of Criminal Law and Criminology*, 68, 1977, pp. 274–82.
26 Stanley Cohen, *Visions of Social Control: Crime, Punishment and Classification*, Cambridge: Polity Press, 1985.
27 Sir Roy Griffiths, *Community Care: Agenda for Action: A Report to the Secretary of State*, London: HMSO, 1988.
28 David Garland, 'The rationalization of punishment', p. 111.
29 *Ibid.*, p. 97.
30 See especially Durkheim's 'Two laws of penal evolution', reprinted as Chapter 4 in S. Lukes and S. Scull (eds), *Durkheim and the Law*, Oxford: Martin Robertson, 1983.
31 James B. Jacobs, 'The politics of prison construction', in his *New Perspectives on Prisons and Imprisonment*, Ithaca, NY: Cornell University Press, 1983.
32 S. Cohen, 'The punitive city', p. 350.
33 David Rothman, *Conscience and Convenience: The Asylum and Its Alternatives in Progressive America*, Boston: Little, Brown, 1980.
34 For earlier scholarly commentary on the California scene, see Franklin Zimring and Gordon Hawkins, 'The growth of imprisonment in California', *British Journal of Criminology*, 34, 1994, pp. 83–95.
35 See, for example, Andrew Scull, *Madhouse: A Tragic Tale of Megalomania and Modern Medicine*, New Haven, CT: Yale University Press, 2005.
36 Erving Goffman, *Asylums: Essays on the Social Situation of Mental Patients and Other Inmates*, Garden City, NY: Doubleday, 1961.
37 Andrew Scull, *Museums of Madness: The Social Organization of Insanity in Nineteenth Century England*, London: Allen Lane, 1979.
38 Erving Goffman, 'The insanity of place', Appendix to his *Relations in Public: Microstudies of the Public Order*, New York: Basic Books, 1971, pp. 356–7.
39 Thomas Szasz, *The Myth of Mental Illness* (rev. edn), New York: Harper and Row, 1974; *idem*, *The Manufacture of Madness*, New York: Harper and Row, 1970.
40 Thomas Scheff, *Being Mentally Ill*, Chicago: Aldine, 1966.
41 Stanley Cohen and Laurie Taylor, *Psychological Survival: The Experience of Long-Term Imprisonment*, New York: Pantheon, 1973.
42 Stanley Cohen, *States of Denial: Knowing About Atrocities and Suffering*, Cambridge: Polity, 2001, p. 19.

Part 5
The Theory and Practice of Denial

Chapter 19

Denial and responsibility

Nicola Lacey

Denial may be neither a matter of telling the truth nor intentionally telling a lie. The statement is not wholly deliberate, and the status of 'knowledge' about the truth is not wholly clear. There seem to be states of mind, or even whole cultures, in which we know and don't know at the same time.

Stanley Cohen, *States of Denial* (2001: 4–5).

[W]hatever is obscure about self-deception infects our understanding of what it is to be a person, what it is to know oneself, and what it is to act responsibly.

Herbert Fingarette, *Self-Deception* (1969: 1).

The dominant theories of responsibility in contemporary criminal law scholarship argue or assume that individuals or, more rarely, groups are responsible for criminal acts or omissions which engage their capacities for rational deliberation. Whether based on choice, opportunity or character, these agency-based theories typically attach importance to attitudes or states of mind such as knowledge, intention and recklessness, with dispositions such as carelessness or indifference featuring as secondary bases for the attribution of responsibility. In this chapter, I will reflect on the implications of Stanley Cohen's arguments, in his fascinating and outstandingly imaginative monograph *States of Denial* (Cohen 2001), about the structure and importance of denial for the shape of our practices of attributing criminal responsibility. To what extent does, and should, criminal law hold us responsible for taking risks we are unaware of, or for engaging in conduct the harmful or wrongful nature of which we are not conscious, where that lack of consciousness or awareness is due to 'states of denial'?

Cohen's arguments, I shall suggest, constitute a useful starting point to begin to think about the scope – and limits – of human responsibility, and about the relationship between the variegated understandings of responsibility which circulate in our complicated social world. In what follows, I shall begin by tracing the variety of conceptions of responsibility circulating in not only legal and philosophical but also in broader social discourse, noting the lack of fit between certain pervasive social understandings of, or feelings about, responsibility and legal or moral conceptions. I shall then go on to trace the influence of ideas of responsibility in practices of criminal exculpation and inculpation. I shall argue that this survey suggests that a more explicit dialogue between criminological, philosophical and legal conceptions of responsibility on the one hand and psychological/psychoanalytic and social conceptions of responsibility on the other hand can sharpen our appreciation of the practical imperatives of – and limits on – practices of formal 'responsibilisation'. Such a dialogue may also illuminate the ways in which formal mechanisms of responsibility attribution in fact draw upon certain informal understandings which they have tended not to acknowledge.

Feelings of responsibility versus conceptions of responsibility and mechanisms of 'responsibilisation'

It is hardly difficult to grasp the fact that the technical notions of human responsibility at work in social institutions such as the criminal justice system are not coterminous with the multifarious notions of responsibility at work in everyday life. None of us would want to live in a world in which the criminal law – or indeed moral conventions – held us responsible for everything we occasionally – or even persistently – felt guilty about, or responsible for. It is easy enough to see why this is the case. In her remarkable memoir, *The Year of Magical Thinking* (2005), Joan Didion explores her own feelings in the year following her husband's sudden death as a result of a heart attack. Despite a history of heart disease and various medical prognoses which might have led her – and did lead her late husband – to predict such an event, in the months following her husband's death she struggles to internalise emotionally the rational explanation available to her. Predominant among her feelings are those of responsibility, founded in – as she herself can see, though this does nothing to displace the feelings – an irrational sense of guilt. In essence, she feels that she is responsible for her husband's death: that she could have prevented it. Indeed, at the most extreme moments in her grief, she finds herself behaving in ways which only make sense on the premise of a belief that she could still bring him back.

Almost a year after the death, she finally receives the autopsy report. Its clear analysis helps her to begin to distance the feelings of responsibility which have haunted her, though she continues to be distracted and distressed – again, notwithstanding good scientific reasons for her to be sure of their irrelevance to her husband's sudden death – by phenomena such as adverts for products like aspirin which reduce the risk of heart attacks. Of the impact of these adverts and other similar prompts, Didion reflects:

> As I recall this I realize how open we are to the persistent message that we can avoid death.
> And to its punitive correlative, the message that if death catches us we have only ourselves to blame (Didion 2005: 206).

The feelings reported by Didion – of responsibility for outcomes and events which lie well outside the boundaries of rationalist philosophical theories of agency and human responsibility – are very common. They provide an ironic counterpoint to one of the central perplexities of established systems of criminal justice: systems which, notwithstanding a certain confidence about the normative basis of their own attributions of responsibility, in practice struggle to induce the kinds of subjective feelings of guilt and responsibility which Didion reports (on the techniques deployed to 'neutralise' such feelings, see Matza and Sykes 1957; Cohen 2001: Chapter 3). We expect our systems of criminal justice to respect the contours of some rationalist, philosophical principles: confining criminal responsibility to acts and outcomes which, variously, the defendant had chosen to do or bring about or had a fair opportunity to do/not do or bring about/not bring about; acts which genuinely expressed a vicious character or settled hostility to the relevant norm/s of criminal law; or, at the very least, acts with which the agent is intimately related in a causal sense (on these conceptions, see Hart 1968; Honoré 1988; Tadros 2004; Lacey 2007). *Feeling responsible* is not, in short, a sufficient condition for being *held responsible* in civic legal (or, indeed, moral) discourse. Indeed, the emotional aspects of responsibility are generally held at a considerable distance, the assumption being that a justifiable finding of criminal responsibility must be founded in good *reasons*.

Those actions and outcomes for which we are properly held criminally responsible, it is further assumed, must be grounded in capacities, decisions and motivations which can be recovered to the present mind. Increasingly, since the development of medical and psychological sciences in the nineteenth century, it is the state of that subjective mind which is assumed to be the primary object of testimony and proof of responsibility in a criminal trial. Even for those theorists drawn to the more evaluative, character-based conceptions of criminal responsibility, basic cognitive and volitional capacities – capacities of understanding and self-control – underlie the potentially transparent and essentially unitary conception of human subjectivity which informs the criminal law.

Yet, paradoxically, we worry about the failure of our robust practices of criminal responsibilisation to induce *feelings of responsibility* that often plague the genuinely (i.e., rationally) non-responsible. We puzzle over, deplore, regret, or feel despair about the incapacity of our public institutions of naming and shaming to induce in the formally responsible the sorts of subjective feelings to which those not, by legal standards, truly 'to blame' are all too often haunted. In the significant movements in many parts of the globe to rediscover and institutionalise mechanisms of 'restorative justice', whether through family group conferences, truth commissions or practices of mediation, we see an attempt to align, through institutional means, appropriate 'feelings of responsibility' with more or less formal mechanisms of response to wrongdoing founded on rational conceptions of responsibility (Braithwaite 1989). In attempting this alignment, restorative justice seeks to bring the rational and affective aspects of criminalisation into a more intimate relation with one another.

Responsibility beyond subjective consciousness?

In *States of Denial*, Stanley Cohen directs our attention to a further sphere relevant to, and yet distinct from, both the *feelings of responsibility* analysed by Didion and the *rational grounding of responsibility* defined by criminal law. In doing so, he illuminates a terrain converse to that exposed by Didion's testimony: a terrain in relation to which there might be a rational basis for responsibility, yet in relation to which the corresponding subjective feelings – even the possibility of acknowledgement – are structurally blocked or excluded. For over a century, we have been familiar with the idea that human psychology is not entirely captured by an analysis of the workings of the conscious mind: that individuals are not entirely present to themselves, because some of the most influential workings of the mind occur at a sub- or an unconscious level. Yet, with a few honourable exceptions, criminologists, and particularly criminal law theorists, have shown relatively little interest in the relevance of this unconscious dimension of human psychology, along with its accompanying mechanisms such as denial and repression, to criminal responsibility.

The reasons for this 'denial' of the unconscious in criminal legal discourse are not far to seek. The most firmly established aspects of criminal responsibility have, ever since the gradual emergence of legal doctrines defining and refining the relevant legal conceptions, focused primarily on cognitive states: states such as intention, knowledge, belief, foresight, and awareness. These essentially factual, subjective mental states are readily capable of representation: they can be made available to the forensic capacities of the finder of fact: that is, in predominant legal ideology if not in practice, the jury. Admittedly, this common-sensical, subjectivist picture is seriously compromised by the widespread dependence on 'objective' tests referring to what a ' reasonable man' (or, latterly, 'person') would have intended, believed, known, and foreseen. But this too has been rationalised without undue practical difficulty – if not with complete theoretical coherence – in terms of a further common-sensical picture of jury perception: the defendant's peers can be relied on, in a non-technical way, to understand what would and could have been expected of the reasonable citizen under the relevant circumstances. We shall return to the relevance of these reasonableness standards to the question of denial below.

Exculpation based on non-conscious factors

The volitional aspect of criminal responsibility has always been more controversial, and accordingly more fragile, than the cognitive aspect. Certainly, criminal responsibility is seen as founded in basic capacities not only of understanding but also of self-control: and this has generated a range of exculpatory arguments which do reach beyond the conscious aspects of human psychology. The notion of volitional dynamics beyond the control of human beings underpins the widespread existence of a range of mental incapacity defences and exemptions. But the defences based purely or primarily on volitional defects have always aroused suspicion: notably in the extended late Victorian debate about whether the McNaghten Rules on insanity should be extended to include cases of 'moral insanity' and of 'irresistible impulse' (Smith 1981). This debate was not resolved in England and Wales until the advent of the restricted and partial defence of diminished responsibility, introduced in section 2 of the Homicide Act 1957, with volitional defects acting up until that time – and, in non-homicide cases to which diminished responsibility is inapplicable, beyond it – only as mitigating factors at the sentencing stage.

This reluctance to confront and legally accommodate volitional defects is, I want to argue, of great significance in understanding the broader issue of criminal law's response to the question of (legal) responsibility for what we do unconsciously, and for which we have developed the sophisticated mechanisms of denial which Cohen charts in his book. Ostensibly, the resistance to the irresistible impulse defence has always been a very practical one: how will the law distinguish between a 'fabricated' claim of irresistible impulse, made up to rationalise, explain or excuse an action, and a genuine case of action determined by impulses beyond the defendant's control? The law is, understandably, chary of arguments which threaten to escape its relatively crude forensic reach. The broad plausibility of the idea that human beings are occasionally overwhelmed by impulses that no reasonable person can be expected to resist has led, over time, to the shaping of both mental incapacity defences and other defences and principles of mitigation such as provocation and duress. But a residual suspicion remains, and this connects to a general problem for criminal law: how to manage that which is difficult or impossible to render up as evidence in a courtroom within a trial process like the one familiar to late modern criminal justice systems.

In cases of diminished responsibility this anxiety has been overcome – to some extent – by the professionalisation of medical testimony as to established syndromes of mental illness, disorder or brain damage. In cases involving provocation or duress, there are external events – a piece of provoking behaviour, a threat – which are also susceptible to exhibition and examination in the courtroom. But if the exculpatory argument were to be founded on unconscious motivations – the power of the repressed to influence or even determine human conduct – the law's forensic credentials would be hard to establish. Criminal law is, after all, part of a system oriented to social control; and information which cannot be publicly validated and legitimated is likely to be defined as irrelevant. Little wonder, then, that defences based on evidence about inferences from the unconscious, or even later recoveries of formerly repressed experiences or motivations – post-traumatic stress disorder, and recovered memory syndrome, to name but two – have been slow to find exculpatory acknowledgement in systems of criminal justice. We might see this as connecting with the general irrelevance of motive to criminal liability – though, as many scholars have noted, this is an 'irrelevance' which has been massively exaggerated (Norrie 2001; Binder 2002: 15–27).

Inculpation via responsibility beyond consciousness

The potentially exculpatory effect of subconscious motivations therefore poses significant practical difficulties for criminal law. Less often noticed, however, has been the potentially inculpatory effect of an acknowledgement of responsibility for motivations and other psychological dynamics beyond consciousness. This far-reaching issue is raised by Cohen's acute analysis of denial in political discourse. How far may – indeed should – human beings be held positively responsible for conduct for which no basis in the engagement of conscious cognitive powers can be established? In terms of the Enlightenment discourses of human responsibility which dominate criminal law theory, it stands to reason, as it were, that human beings cannot be held responsible for actions and outcomes which lie beyond the scope of their conscious choices or control. The very unconsciousness of the unconscious, on this view, guarantees its irrelevance to the construction of individual responsibility. Unless the law can identify a moment at which the guilty knowledge was consciously repressed or denied, it escapes the analytic reach of the predominant theories of agency and responsibility. Doctrinal mechanisms of responsibilisation which dispense with these paradigm cognitive conditions – strict liability offences and certain versions of corporate responsibility, for example – tend to be marginalised as exceptions based primarily on the social control or deterrence imperatives of the criminal justice system.

I want to argue, however, that these and a number of other practical legal examples, troubling to predominant doctrines of criminal responsibility, should on the contrary not be dismissed as outside rational theories of agency and responsibility; and, moreover, that our broader discourses about denial and repression may be of significant help in understanding the issues, as a necessary preliminary to refining the relevant doctrinal mechanisms. I will argue, furthermore, that an analysis of these recurring doctrinal problems in terms of an implicit reference to the relevance of the unconscious in human agency may help us to rationalise the distinctive shape of certain legal practices of responsibility attribution. I shall try to establish this in relation to three examples: the debate about 'objective' responsibility standards in general, and about responsibility for conduct attendant on attitudes of 'practical indifference' in particular: the case of strict liability; and the case of corporate liability for serious crimes.

'Objective' responsibility based on fair opportunity or the evaluation of character: negligence and practical indifference

From a purely subjective, cognitivist point of view, it is problematic to suggest that a defendant should be held responsible not only for actions she has consciously chosen and circumstances of which she is actually aware but also for actions which a reasonable person would have avoided and for circumstances of which a reasonable person would have been aware. Actual systems of criminal law, however, standardly do apply such 'objective' tests of fault or responsibility both in offence definitions and in the construction of defences. To take some examples from the criminal law of England and Wales, defendants have long been held responsible for the offence of manslaughter on the basis of 'gross negligence' (Lacey, Wells and Quick 2003: Chapter 6.IV.c) – a serious departure from the standards of care or awareness of a reasonable person. Similarly, defences such as provocation, duress and even self-defence have long depended on the establishment of reasonable grounds: the provoked defendant is held to the standard of how a reasonable person would have reacted (Lacey *et al.* 2003: Chapter 6.IV.d.ii): the threatened person is assumed to be a person of reasonable firmness (Lacey *et al.* 2003: Chapter 4.II.e); the person defending herself is not excused for an unreasonably excessive response to the attack (Lacey *et al.* 2003: Chapter 6.IV.e). These 'objective', reasonableness tests are usually rationalised on a 'fair opportunity' version of a capacity-based understanding of responsibility: even if defendants were not fully aware of all the relevant circumstances, and even if they did not consciously choose to act as they did or to take the relevant risk, they are properly held responsible if the jury can be sure that, notwithstanding their limited cognitive awareness, they had a fair opportunity to conform their conduct to the relevant legal standard. As a practical system oriented to social control, the criminal law is entitled to hold us to this 'reasonable' standard, and, even on a character-based conception of responsibility, a negligent as well as a deliberately vicious disposition, when expressed in action, may form a proper object of the law's attention.

Interestingly, the structure of this argument for 'objective' standards of liability bears a close resemblance to one of the earliest psychoanalytically informed analyses of the relevance of the idea of the unconscious and associated notions such as denial for the philosophical question of responsibility. In a series of papers and books, Herbert Fingarette advanced an account which aspired to be both common-sensical and empirical (Fingarette 1950, 1967, 1969). In essence, his argument was that technical psychoanalytic references to a person's being 'in denial' or consigning unwanted knowledge or feelings to 'the unconscious' could be accurately rendered in terms of the proposition that under normal conditions such feelings would be present to the person's mind. As Fingarette (discussing Siegler 1962) puts it in his treatise on self-deception, 'to ascribe self-deception to someone is to attribute to him an erroneous belief which it is unreasonable to have, and to ascribe responsibility to him for this' (Fingarette 1969: 21). This exactly captures the legal mechanism of objective liability. (This is not to say that Fingarette equated legal with moral responsibility; on the contrary, he was careful to point out that legal responsibility is typically concerned with actions as well as states of mind, and is generally more circumscribed than moral responsibility: Fingarette 1967: 86. 92.) Though philosophers continue to puzzle over the paradox that in the case of self-deception, we are inclined to see ignorance as inculpatory, whereas in usual moral discourse 'ignorance and blindness exculpate, whereas knowledge, insight and foresight inculpate' (Fingarette 1969: 136), the social practices of responsibility attribution in both law and conventional morality appear to live quite happily with the apparent contradiction. This, I would argue, should lead us to question the emphasis laid in some influential theories of criminal responsibility on the centrality of conscious mental states.

Certainly, in some areas, the application of reasonableness standards has remained controversial. A particularly vivid example, stretching across many jurisdictions, is that of rape. From the time of the *Morgan* decision in 1976 (*Appeal Cases* 182; see Lacey *et al.* 2003: Chapter 5.II.b.iii and iv), English criminal law held that a defendant's honest mistake as to the victim's consent to sex entailed a lack of criminal intent even if there were no reasonable grounds for that mistaken belief: the man who honestly believed the person he was having sex with was consenting did not intend to rape, nor was he reckless as to the risk of rape. This position was recently reversed by the Sexual Offences Act 2003. But between the 1976 decision and the 2003 legislation, there arose a doctrinal debate of key significance to my analysis in this paper. This debate was concerned with how to classify defendants who, in effect, testified that they had given no thought to the question of consent: had gone ahead, as one judge somewhat unfortunately put it, 'willy-nilly': who 'couldn't have cared less' – or, perhaps, simply acted on the assumption of consent.

On a strictly subjectivist, cognitivist view, this should have been insufficient: the person who had given no thought to lack of consent cannot be shown to have had the subjective awareness of lack of consent which was essential to *mens rea* under the *Morgan* test. But, significantly, the courts were reluctant to accept this apparently logical conclusion.

Instead, they gradually developed a doctrine known as 'wilful blindness' or 'practical indifference' (*R* v. *Satnam* (1984) 78 *Criminal Appeal Reports* 149), accepting that these attitudes – it seems awkward to call them 'states of mind', because in some senses they are precisely the reverse – were sufficient to establish the *mens rea* of rape. This, I suggest, discloses a clear view on the part of the courts that human beings can indeed be held responsible for things which are not present to their conscious minds: that things which we 'repress' or 'deny' can ground responsibility even if there is no precise moment at which we can identify a conscious decision to repress or deny the relevant information. The repression or denial – like many of the examples canvassed in Cohen's book – may be attendant on long processes of acculturation or upbringing, or on more specific circumstances like the taking of alcohol or other intoxicants. Indeed, the criminal law's arrangements for holding voluntarily intoxicated defendants responsible (Lacey *et al.* 2003: Chapter 3.III.b) would provide another fertile example of the general legal practice to which I am drawing attention here: that of doctrinally constructing criminal responsibility for, as it were, states of mind beyond consciousness. (For an excellent philosophical discussion of responsibility for matters lying within our 'tacit knowledge', see Duff 1990, as well as Fingarette 1969: 120–1 on knowledge available to be 'spelled out'.) To rationalise this practice in terms of holding people responsible for things which they had a 'fair opportunity' to know, avoid, and be aware of might itself be taken as an implicit recognition of the idea of denial. Alternatively, some theorists would rather see such mechanisms in terms of an idea that when criminal law holds defendants responsible it is making an evaluation of the character displayed in their conduct. This idea of responsibility for a disposition exhibited or expressed in action itself invites an accommodation of criteria beyond consciousness as relevant to the court's evaluation. Nor, as Duff has pointed out, is this accommodation necessarily a case of 'objective' as opposed to 'subjective' liability: the standard may still be oriented to *this* defendant's 'indifference', the 'reasonableness' of that indifference merely operating as an evidentiary mechanism (Duff 1990: Chapter 7, in particular, pp. 149–57).

Strict liability and responsibility for outcomes

The criminal law of England and Wales, like that of many other countries, combines a strong attachment to the principle that defendants should be held responsible only for actions and outcomes for which they were genuinely responsible with the apparently contradictory practice of establishing a wide range of 'regulatory' offences of which defendants can be convicted without proof of a responsibility element such as intention, negligence, knowledge or belief. Such offences typically cluster in areas such as corporate conduct, taxation, the regulation of industries or road traffic, minor public order infractions and licensing. When criminal law commentators and theorists can curb their embarrassment about this apparent affront to the 'general principles of criminal law', their usual instinct is to rationalise these offences as exceptional, and as founded on an instrumental, utilitarian rationale. The social gains of strict liability offences in terms of deterrence, promoting important goods such as public health and safety, are such as to justify a sacrifice in terms of fairness and justice; the usual normative constraints are suspended in pursuit of collective goods. Except in cases where the offences are subject to 'due diligence defences', capacity-based theories of responsibility cannot provide any rationalisation here. For character-based theories of criminal responsibility, the impasse is hardly less complete: to infer that a single act of, for example, pollution, a single licensing infraction, or a single lapse of safety standards in a factory constitutes an expression of hostility to the relevant norm – the 'character' of a bad employer, or licensee, or industrialist – seems far-fetched. In practice, of course, we know that strict liability prosecutions are largely brought against repeat offenders. This might be seen as justifying such an inference, but – like an inference that this defendant really had had a fair opportunity to comply with the law – it would be at the level of hunch or induction rather than of proof beyond reasonable doubt.

A third way of conceptualising responsibility, however, suggests once again an interesting link between mechanisms of formal criminalisation and a recognition of the relevance of the unconscious to human agency. Some theorists have argued that what is at work in the strict liability area is a distinct principle of responsibility: that of 'outcome responsibility' (Honoré 1988). What we do – the effects which we have on and in the world – inevitably, whether or not we could have helped them or had the capacity to do otherwise, become part of our identity. A thought experiment helps to illuminate the argument. Imagine that X is driving, at a reasonable speed, along a road into which a small child runs out from behind a car. However fast X's reactions had been, there would have been no chance of avoiding the child, who is critically injured when X hits her. When interviewed by the police, X expresses no emotion or remorse: X simply says, 'It was an accident, and hence nothing to do with me'. Here some may feel we are bordering on the area of 'irrational' feelings of responsibility charted by Didion. But what would a world in which we so clinically distanced ourselves from the effects of our actions really look like? Both very different from our own, and distinctly unattractive. We may not hold people *as responsible* for what they do accidentally or unintentionally, but we do recognise that this is something for which they are, at some level answerable – and particularly so in the context of a risk-creating activity such as driving. This is a quite different case from that of practical indifference. But it is another example of the scope of responsibility beyond the reach of cognitive, conscious mental states; and we might regard X's testimony as a classic example of just the kind of denial which proves so troubling in the political examples canvassed by Cohen.

Corporate responsibility

One of the most persistent doctrinal debates of recent years in English criminal law has centred on the question of how far corporations may be held responsible for serious crimes. There are, of course, offences – notably many regulatory offences – designed specifically with corporations in mind. But offences against the person have historically been applied exclusively to human individuals, and the concepts of conduct and responsibility which have developed to structure their application have accordingly been based on assumptions about human psychology and action. With the increasing social importance – and impact – of corporations, there has gradually developed a demand to render corporations responsible for outcomes which, if accomplished by an individual, would amount to serious assaults or homicide. In the USA, the notorious Ford Pinto case illustrates the point (Lacey *et al.* 2003: Chapter 6.II.c): why should a corporation which had made a deliberate decision not to recall cars it knew were dangerous, on the basis of an economic calculation, not be held responsible for the deaths of those injured when the predicted dangers eventuated?

A more tricky example, however, and one closer to my subject of responsibility beyond consciousness, lies in the English case which reopened the debate about corporate manslaughter in the 1980s. It arose out of the tragic sinking of a ferry in Zeebrugge harbour, with the loss of several hundred lives (*P & O European Ferries Ltd.* (1991) 93 *Criminal Appeal Reports*. 72; *R* v. *Coroner for East Kent ex p Spooner* (1989) 88 *Criminal Appeal Reports* 10). What made this case difficult for criminal law was the fact that the rapid sinking of the ship was revealed in the subsequent inquiry to have its origins in a cluster of acts and omissions, not all of which could be traced to individual human beings. Certainly, the proximate cause of the sinking was the fact that the ship had sailed with its bow doors open – something which could be attributed to the negligent omissions of certain crew members. But, as the inquiry revealed, a number of other factors were in play: the crews were under pressure to meet a tight timetable set by the company, which more or less necessitated risk taking; proper safety practices and training systems were not in place; the corporation, in the memorable words of the inquiry, was 'infected by sloppiness' at every level. There was, in short, a diffusion of responsibility among actors and institutions, with a toxic mix of poor management and economic pressure conducing to a situation in which all relevant actors 'denied' the existence of a serious danger which was obvious *ex post*. But, as the subsequent court decisions revealed, it was difficult to incorporate this diffused responsibility within existing criminal law conceptions of responsibility: no one grossly negligent act or omission could be identified, and the courts refused to construct a composite state of corporate criminal negligence out of the aggregated negligence of crew members and high-ranking officials (Lacey 2000).

The dismissal of the case against P & O Ferries was widely criticised, and resulted in an extended (continuing) political process of consultation on a special law of corporate homicide. The question has to be debated, of course, as to whether criminalisation of corporations for this kind of management failure is the most effective way to promote safety standards and to prevent such tragedies. But confining our attention to the question of whether a conception of legal responsibility could have been constructed notwithstanding the lack of any one conscious agent on whom to 'pin the blame', it is apparent that the courts took an unduly unimaginative approach. As social commentary surrounding the case made clear, there now operates a popular conception of corporate responsibility, and – as the various reform proposals canvassed by the Law Commission and government (and indeed implemented in several other jurisdictions) show – this can readily be rendered intelligible in the terms of legal doctrine. These facts, once again, demonstrate that our practices of responsibilisation do not depend solely – or even primarily – on the identification of conscious states of awareness. A corporation which engages, particularly for profit, in a potentially dangerous activity, is justly held responsible for harmful outcomes, particularly where they are attendant on the corporation's failure to institute procedures to maximise the chances of good practice being observed. To say that the risks or dangers had not been present to the mind of any particular corporate executive – or to claim that they had been 'repressed', or that the corporation was in a 'state of denial' about them because its corporate focus was so firmly on the business environment – is unconvincing or even unconscionable. The corporate example makes more vivid what is already true in the individual case, and this perhaps explains why so many of the most compelling examples of unconvincing arguments about 'denial' have arisen in the context of actions by collectivities such as states.

In conclusion

Joan Didion's painful memoir reminds us that there are indeed rational limits to human or collective responsibility, and that to lose the ability to draw proper boundaries can amount to pathology. But her memoir also reminds us of the significantly affective dimension of our social understandings of responsibility – a dimension often lost from sight in criminal law discourse, though explicitly on the agenda of restorative justice. Stanley Cohen's analysis of states of denial, and of their implications for the attribution of responsibility, has much to teach theorists of criminal law. The criminal law already confronts, in a range of doctrinal and practical circumstances, the need to construct mechanisms for the attribution of responsibility beyond cases where individual subjective human consciousness at the time of the relevant conduct is available as evidence. In cases where it is present, this consciousness is an important component in constructing responsibility. But it is neither a necessary nor – as the case of McNaghten insanity shows (Lacey *et al.* 2003: Chapter 1.II.d) – a sufficient condition for criminal responsibility. The most influential theories of criminal responsibility, based on the criteria of capacity or character, have often struggled to understand and accommodate responsibility beyond consciousness. But, as I have argued, that accommodation is not beyond them. The judges have been ahead of the theorists on this matter, but it remains important for the theorists to direct their attention to these issues. For without a more nuanced normative debate, the application of ideas of responsibility beyond consciousness could easily become institutionally pathological: a means of increasing criminal law's power without adequate justification. My purpose in this chapter has therefore *not* been to argue for an expansion of responsibility for non-conscious attitudes. Rather, it has been to face up to the existence of mechanisms of responsibilisation beyond consciousness, as a necessary precursor to beginning a proper debate about what their limits should be.

Acknowledgements

My warm thanks go to Arlie Loughnan for research assistance and for her helpful comments on a draft of this paper.

References

Binder, G. (2002) 'The rhetoric of motive and intent', *Buffalo Criminal Law Review*, 6: 1–96.

Braithwaite, J. (1989) *Crime, Shame and Reintegration*. Cambridge: Cambridge University Press.

Cohen, S. (2001) *States of Denial: Knowing about Atrocities and Suffering*. Cambridge: Polity Press.

Didion, J. (2005) *The Year of Magical Thinking*. New York: Alfred A. Knopf.

Eigen, J.P. (1999) 'Lesion of the will: medical resolve and criminal responsibility in Victorian insanity trials', *Law and Society Review*, 33: 425.

Fingarette, H. (1950) '"Unconscious behaviour" and allied concepts. A new approach to their empirical interpretation', *The Journal of Philosophy*, 47: 509–20.

Fingarette, H. (1967) *On Responsibility*. New York and London: Basic Books.

Fingarette, H. (1969) *Self-Deception*. London: Routledge and Kegan Paul.

Hart, H.L.A. (1968) *Punishment and Responsibility*. Oxford: Clarendon Press.

Honoré, T. (1988) 'Responsibility and luck: the moral basis of strict liability', *Law Quarterly Review*, 104: 530 [reprinted in *Responsibility and Fault*, Oxford: Hart Publishing, 1999, p. 14.]

Lacey, N. (2000) 'Philosophical foundations of the common law: social not metaphysical', in J. Horder (ed.) *Oxford Essays in Jurisprudence* (Fourth Series). Oxford: Clarendon Press, p. 17.

Lacey, N. (2007) 'Character, capacity, outcome: towards a framework for assessing the shifting pattern of criminal responsibility in modern English law', in M.D. Dubber and L. Farmer (eds) *Modern Histories of Crime and Punishment*, pp. 14–28. Palo Alto, CA: Stanford University Press.

Lacey, N., Wells, C. and Quick, O. (2003) *Reconstructing Criminal Law* (3rd edn). Cambridge: Cambridge University Press.

Matza, D. and Sykes, G. (1957) 'Techniques of neutralization', *American Sociological Review*, 22: 664–70.

Norrie, A. (2001) *Crime, Reason and History* (2nd edn). Cambridge: Cambridge University Press.

Siegler, F.A. (1962) 'Demos on lying to oneself', *Journal of Philosophy*, 59: 469–75.

Smith, R. (1981) *Trial by Medicine*. Edinburgh: Edinburgh University Press.

Tadros, V. (2004) *Criminal Responsibility*. Oxford: Clarendon Press.

Chapter 20

The Israeli human rights movement – lessons from South Africa

Daphna Golan-Agnon[1]

One of the principal questions that Stanley Cohen posed during the years he lived and worked in Israel was this: Why do Israeli liberals not try to do more to change the political situation? In 1988, Stan delivered a lecture entitled 'The Psychology and Politics of Denial: The Case of Israeli liberals', to a group of Israeli and Palestinian psychologists and social workers, active in the cause of peace. He spoke about:

> the educated, enlightened, western-oriented sectors of the middle class; those supposedly receptive to messages of peace and co-existence; those who are first to condemn racism and human rights violations in South Africa or Chile; those who are 'like us' in every respect but one: their reluctance to actively engage with the political situation. They might be wringing their hands, saying how terrible things are – but not much else.[2]

Stan analysed this question while simultaneously trying to change the reality he was studying.[3] He proposed various kinds of activism for opposing the occupation, participated in demonstrations, helped establish the Public Committee Against Torture, built bridges of cooperation with Palestinian activists and publicly protested the fact that his Israeli academic colleagues at the Hebrew University, especially those in the Law Faculty, did not do enough to change the unjust reality in which they live.

He pushed the academic discussion in Israel to pose questions that were universal and obvious in other parts of the world, but seemed threatening enough to marginalise him in the Israeli liberal university establishment. In 1990, Stan delivered a lecture in the memory of

Michael Wade[4] on 'The Human Rights Movement in Israel and South Africa: Some Paradoxical Comparisons'. Perhaps this comparative perspective on Israel and South Africa that Stan proposed was most threatening. It angers and threatens Israelis in general, and liberal Israelis in particular, because it challenges the basic belief that the Israeli-Palestinian conflict was imposed upon Israel and that it is so unique that it cannot be compared with any other conflict in the world.[5]

Here I return to the questions Stan posed at the time and ask them again in the current context, in which liberal Israelis are still doing little to bring about reconciliation and justice. I ask these questions in order to examine which of Stan's perceptions are still relevant to Israeli reality at the start of the twenty-first century.

I begin with Stan's comparison of South African and Israeli organisational activism, using three principal distinctions that he suggests and considering the relevance of each to the current situation. Only then do I return to the issue of why Israeli liberals do virtually nothing to try to change the injustice that surrounds them. My premise is that understanding the limitations of activism among those who *are* involved will provide insights into why the voting public remains so uninvolved.

Human rights organisations in Israel and South Africa – what has changed since 1990?

Stan presented three essential differences between the activism of the human rights organisations in South Africa and Israel: the use of the tools and discourse of civil rights in Israel as opposed to the human rights discourse in South Africa; the attempt to be apolitical in Israel versus the politics of human rights in South Africa, and the emphasis on individual rights in Israel versus the focus on collective rights in South Africa. Before using these three differences to examine the human rights movement in Israel today,[6] I first situate Stan's unpublished presentation in the political context in which it was given, at the Faculty Club of the Hebrew University on Mt Scopus at the height of the first intifada.

The year 1990 was a milestone in South African history. This was the year that De Klerk announced the freeing of Nelson Mandela, the legalisation of the African National Congress (ANC), the freeing of political prisoners, and the beginning of negotiations between the government and the ANC. In Israel, the intifada was raging, Palestinians were rising up against their oppression in the Occupied Territories, and the Israeli army, following directives from the Israeli government, was trying to quash the uprising. Yitzhak Rabin, who would in time become the champion of peace, instructed the soldiers to break the Palestinians' bones. Thousands of Palestinians were arrested, many without trial. Though the Palestinians' uprising mainly took the form of stone throwing, more and more regulations and laws were enacted to prevent the Palestinians from organising, protesting, and demanding their independence. Dozens of Israeli human rights organisations were founded to protect Palestinian rights. Important organisations – such as B'Tselem, the Israeli Information Center for Human Rights in the Occupied Territories (1989), the Public Committee Against Torture (1990) (of which Stan was a founder), and Physicians for Human Rights (1988) – were just starting out, and joining other organisations to protect Palestinian rights.[7]

At the time Stan gave his lecture, these organisations were small, young, and angry, and Stan was the one of the few who thought they should be thought about, let alone researched, by academia. Not only were we in these organisations situated outside the Israeli consensus, but also outside the Israeli campuses. At the time, Stan and I were researching torture of Palestinians in Israeli prisons, but our activism was not part of our academic work. In fact, our activism was opposed by academia, which held that academic freedom excluded the bringing of politics on campus. Stan, with courage, charm, and academic brilliance, brought us onto the campus, into the prestigious seminar room in the faculty club and placed our activities at the centre of his lecture, along with the South African human rights movement that was celebrating its victory. Stan optimistically encouraged the Israeli human rights movements to learn from its South African counterpart, asking 'how [have] the different movements... resolved and expressed their shared commitment to the same values of legality and human rights?'

Civil rights and human rights

Stan noted:

> In the South African case, it was hardly possible to invoke the traditional discourse of civil liberties or civil rights. This discourse depends entirely on an existing structure of democratic citizenship. When such citizenship is denied to the bulk of the population, the question of justice must be framed within the stronger discourse of human rights, rather than the legalistic notion of civil liberties. In Israel, it was possible, certainly before 1967 (although perhaps the idea was compromised more than is generally acknowledged by the notion of a 'Jewish state'), to invoke the narrower concept of civil liberties.

This tension between the language of civil rights and human rights is still relevant for the study of Israeli human rights organisations, even though so much has changed in the use of the human rights discourse by both the state and by NGOs. In 1991, Israel signed six major international treaties, including the treaty against torture.[8] Thus, despite having added a caveat to the signature and failing to make the treaty part of Israeli legislation, Israel indicated to the international community that it was part of the family of nations that upholds human rights.

The legislation of the Basic Law on human rights in 1992 heralded the beginning of a constitutional revolution, bringing about a transformation of the legal status of human rights in Israel. The new law granted the High Court the authority to review Knesset legislation that violates rights protected by the Basic Law. Israeli human rights organisations have thus been able to use the new Basic Law, together with the international language of human rights, which has grown stronger, especially with the support of the International Court at the Hague.[9]

The number of human rights organisations in Israel, particularly the number of organisations dealing with Palestinians' rights, has increased dramatically. In 1990, we were a small community of activists. Today, each organisation employs dozens of people and many new organisations have emerged.[10] The successes of these organisations have been especially impressive.[11]

Nevertheless, with few exceptions, the human rights movement in Israel still uses civil rights tools or works within the Israeli legal system to repair it or to challenge it to improve itself, but does not question the system's legitimacy. The operational space occupied by the human rights movements in Israel is much wider than it was in South Africa. They are active in a society that has more freedom of expression, largely for Jews, but also to a large extent for Arab citizens. Many of the human rights activists believe that it is possible to change things from within, and oppose the intervention and pressure of the international community on Israel. There is great resistance not only to the threat of British academics to enforce an academic boycott on Israel because of violations of human rights of Palestinians, but also to the attempts to bring to trial in Europe or the USA Israeli officers who committed war crimes, are much criticized in Israel.[12]

The focus of human rights activity on the legal system is part of the 'legalisation' of Israeli society. There are more lawyers per capita in Israel than in any other country in the world.[13] Israel has no constitution and the High Court has become the main organ for deciding human rights issues. Thus, despite the fact that the court has accepted state and military positions on almost every issue pertaining to the Occupied Territories, by approving expropriation of territories and house demolitions, deportation and prolonged arrests without trial of Palestinians, the court still frequently seems the only possible avenue for some justice, and the number of appeals regarding Palestinians' rights in the territories has continued to grow steadily.[14]

The High Court never clearly acknowledged that the Occupied Territories are in fact occupied and, hence, that the Fourth Geneva Convention, which protects citizens living in occupied territories, applies. The High Court continues to disregard the opinion of the International Court at The Hague, which ruled that Jewish settlements in the Occupied Territories are illegal and the construction of a separating wall in the territories is against international law.

In rare cases, however, the court allows the human rights organisations and lawyers representing Palestinians a few victories, which indicate that it is still possible to effect change from within. For example, about a week after the International Court's ruling on the illegality of the wall and settlements in the territories was made public, the High Court ruled that the site of the wall should be changed in the Beit Sourik area.[15] Even so, this verdict, like a similar one delivered in the Alfei Menashe High Court case,[16] was very different from the International Court's ruling in that it did not state that the wall is illegal or that Jewish settlements in the territories are a violation of international law. The verdict indicates, however, that the High Court is not totally oblivious to the human rights organisations and to their civil rights language, particularly when legal authorities in the world support them publicly.[17]

As Stan himself showed, in some cases these languages of civil and human rights are the same. For example, the struggle against torture is the same absolute struggle for which many tools of civil and human rights were used, and the most striking victory of the human rights organisations was the court's ruling against torture on 6 September 1999.

In 1991, we published the first B'Tselem report on torture of Palestinian detainees.[18] This report and the public response to it encouraged Stan to research denial. As he writes in the introduction to his book *States of Denial*:

> Our evidence of the routine use of violent and illegal methods of interrogation was to be confirmed by numerous other sources. But we were immediately thrown into politics of denial. The official and mainstream response was venomous: *outright denial* (it doesn't happen); *discrediting* (the organization was biased, manipulated or gullible); renaming (yes, something does happen,

but it is not torture); and *justification* (anyway 'it' was morally justified). Liberals were uneasy and concerned. Yet there was no outrage. Soon a tone of acceptance began to be heard. Abuses were intrinsic to the situation; there was nothing to be done till a political solution was found; something like torture might even be necessary sometimes; anyway, we don't want to keep being told about this all the time.[19]

We then published a follow-up report that showed how the critique had led to significant changes but asserted that, as long as Israel continued to permit 'moderate physical pressure,' it would in fact be facilitating legal torture.[20]

Since 1991, Israeli lawyers have submitted hundreds of appeals, asking the High Court to permit them to meet with their Palestinian clients and to order the General Security Service (GSS) or the army to stop torturing them. There were two main objectives in petitioning the High Court. The first was to provide legal representation to help individual detainees. The second was to pressure the Israeli High Court of Justice into outlawing the use of torture and other cruel and inhuman treatment which were legally approved and termed 'moderate physical pressure'. 'Flooding the court' with appeals aimed to remind the justices that torture was a routine practice in Israel and to suggest that by permitting the GSS to torture prisoners, the court was in fact legitimising these actions.[21] After rejecting hundreds of appeals, the court decided to review seven appeals simultaneously and discuss the question of whether the GSS's interrogation techniques were legal. It took five years for the High Court justices to reach their decision; five years in which torture continued, while the justices took their time deliberating.

Finally, in September 1999, the president of the High Court, Justice Aharon Barak, read the verdict, signed by all nine High Court justices, which stated that the interrogation methods used by the GSS were illegal. The sought-after court victory had been achieved after years of struggle engaged in by dozens of individuals and organisations in Israel and Palestine. It was achieved after international judges and human rights organisations had criticised Israeli policy and made court appearances to indicate to the High Court justices that their verdict would have a significant effect on the standing of Israel in the international community and the judges' own standing in the legal world. The verdict itself was highly apologetic:

Deciding these applications weighed heavy on this Court. True, from the legal perspective, the road before us is smooth. We are, however, part of Israeli society. Its problems are known to us and we live its history. We are not isolated in an ivory tower. We live the life of this country. We are aware of the harsh reality of terrorism in which we are, at times, immersed. Our apprehension that this decision will hamper the ability to properly deal with terrorists and terrorism, disturbs us. We are, however, justices. Our brethren require us to act according to the law. This is equally the standard that we set for ourselves. When we sit to justice, we are being judged. Therefore, we must act according to our purest conscience when we decide the law.[22]

The High Court ruling did not put a decisive end to torture, but it did stop some of the horrific practices that were routinely employed, indicating clearly to interrogators that the use of torture is not legal.[23] This was a significant verdict, for which Stan had worked by simultaneously criticising the limitations of the liberal discourse and utilising it in the struggle against torture.

Human rights and politics

The second difference that Stan found between Israeli and South African organisations was that. 'While it would be literally inconceivable for human rights organisations in South Africa not to be against apartheid, it is possible to find human rights organisations in Israel which are not openly against the Occupation.' In order to comprehend this principal difference, Stan suggested the wider context of different perceptions of law and human rights in Israel and South Africa. 'In South Africa', he said, 'the struggle for legality and basic civil rights was inseparable from the overall political struggle.' In Israel, however, 'the *apparent* intactness of the rule of the law has allowed the liberal, consensual image to be sustained with some conviction.' He was referring not only to 'the normative ideal' (what is desirable and valued) but to 'what people think is actually happening'.

'In the Occupied Territories after 1967,' he said, 'the picture is entirely different.' Here, the model of liberal legalism cannot be applied by any stretch of the imagination. 'Law' operates through a baroque framework of military orders which are explicitly designed to serve the interests of the occupier and to regulate, govern and control the lives of the occupied. Only in the most rhetorical or analogical sense does this system fit the criteria of justice demanded by domestic Israeli law or international law.

Trying to understand how Israeli liberals, particularly in the legal community, can possibly resolve this major anomaly, Stan referred to a technique, which he called 'geographical magic'. He explained, 'In Israel itself, they claim, everything is okay, but "over there", across the Green Line, there is a military government, there is no rule of law, and there are no civil or human rights. Everyone understands this – and nothing can be done about it until there is a political solution.'

Stan criticised the Israeli liberal legal community not only for ignoring the fact that the Israeli legal system is itself deeply implicated in maintaining the occupation, but for lending the occupation its veneer of legality. 'The illusion that there is a boundary that marks the Occupation as a separate social territory,' he wrote, 'prevents full comprehension of how the norms of legality applied "over there" spreads into, penetrates and contaminates every element of the legal system in Israel itself – lawyers, courts, military police, ordinary police, the prisons, judges, academics.'[24] More than 16 years later and after further bloodshed, fear and hate and pain, there is still widespread conviction among liberal Israelis that if we separate here from there, everything will be all right.[25] Today, however, the imaginary lines are reinforced with real walls and checkpoints.

The Israeli human rights organisations work within this broader context, careful not to be seen as political, because the political solution in Israel does not correspond well with the language of human rights. In South Africa, work on behalf of human rights was part of the political struggle for a democratic South Africa. In Israel, the political solution is perceived as a demarcation of boundaries – a political act that does not fall within the human rights frame of reference. The human rights organisations have therefore never addressed the question of where the border between the states would be and what the peace agreement would look like. Instead, they focus on how they can, in the present setting, improve the human rights situation in the territories and how they can ensure that protection of human rights will be taken into consideration if peace agreements are signed.[26]

In recent years, the new Basic Laws have empowered the courts to review Knesset laws, resulting in a growing number of appeals to the High Court concerning human rights. The emphasis on legalisation has exacerbated the tendency among human rights organisations toward professionalization. If the founding generation was made up of radical Israelis, who saw the liberal language of human rights as a way of working against the occupation, a means of connecting with the global human rights movements and a source of new tools for activism, now the organisations have gradually become more and more professional and increasingly wary of taking a political stand. Because the public being targeted by the human rights organisations are policymakers and liberal Israelis, and because the prevailing view is 'if they only knew, they would do more', and because threats to the consensus in Israel are perceived as political, most of the Israeli human rights movements avoid broaching the issues which are defined by Israeli academics as political.

For example, B'Tselem, the Israeli Information Center for Human Rights in the Occupied Territories, the largest, most important and most reliable source of information on human rights violations in the territories, has issued many publications on particular infringements of human rights – freedom of movement of Palestinians, administrative detentions, torture, house demolition, and the wall – but not a single comprehensive publication on the human rights situation of Palestinians in the territories or recommendation on how to put an end to the occupation.[27]

As a further example, when staff members of B'Tselem proposed a study on the Palestinian right of return, the Board of Directors, consisting of Israeli academics, held a fierce debate and vetoed the proposed research by a large margin. Their principal justification was that Palestinian refugees' right of return is a political issue and not a human rights issue. The study was never conducted.

The right of return is an issue that is deeply threatening to Israeli society, not only to liberals, but also to many Israelis who are active against the occupation. The fear of even beginning to discuss the Palestinian right of return is so great that the very mention of the topic engenders panic in many Israelis. They react by claiming that there is nothing to talk about because they do not want four million Palestinians to come back and make them a Jewish minority in the state of Israel. The Palestinian refugees are the main taboo, their existence denied, their dreams neglected. They are pushed out of the human rights discourse in Israel, as are other issues, which challenge the feasibility of Israel's maintaining its status as both a Jewish and democratic state.

This brings us to the third difference that Stan referred to in his comparison between Israel and South Africa.

Individual versus collective rights

In the two cases we are comparing, we see that precisely the problem of the relation between the individual and the collective conceptions has rendered these human rights movements so different. In both cases, the heart of the conflict lies in the demands for group rights: control over natural resources, land, culture, nationality. In the South African case, however, the dominance of the demand for the collective rights of the majority black population is too obvious to even require comment.

However, in Israel, Stan said

> the collective concept poses too many anomalies. To fully concede the Palestinian case (historically or today) would be to call into question too many normative assumptions about the nature of Israeli democracy or (until recently, at least) the very existence of the state. This was never so in South Africa, where it has not ever been possible to sustain even the pretense of democracy. The paradox here is precisely because Israeli 'democracy' has seemed so intact (to Israeli Jews, at least), liberals hesitate to be drawn into a collectivist, political tradition – a tradition that is, which concedes that human rights have no separate existence from the idea of peoples' rights, collective rights.

This distinction still holds today, despite significant changes that have taken place over the years. I will present three important court rulings which attest to the tension between collective rights and individual rights and the process of change through which the discourse of collective rights has begun to form in Israel.

In 1995, the Association for Civil Rights (ACRI) petitioned the High Court on behalf of the Qa'adans, a Palestinian couple, Israeli citizens, who wished to build a house in Katzir. They were denied permission because they were Arabs and Katzir was built for Jews only.[28] The court accepted the application in a decision, which was perceived by the Israeli public as a groundbreaking case, since it allowed an Arab family to be included and integrated in the town of Katzir despite its having been explicitly intended to serve as a settlement for Jews.

This application was on behalf of an individual, not for the collective rights of Palestinian citizens as a national group residing in its homeland. The applicants in the *Qa'adan* case did not raise historic demands or question the legitimacy of the activity of the Jewish agency who founded the settlement. They accepted the ideological values of the state of Israel as a Jewish state.

The President of the High Court, Aharon Barak, cited the petitioners: 'The proxy for the petitioners does not question the important role of the Jewish Agency in the history of the State of Israel, nor does he criticize the policy that has been in place for many years regarding the establishment of Jewish settlements throughout the land.'[29] ACRI's petition did not seek recognition of the historical wrong that was done to Palestinians in Israel as a people as a result of a consistent policy of land confiscation, nor did they seek acknowledgement of their collective memory.[30]

In 1996, a group of Palestinian-Israeli lawyers (some of whom worked for ACRI) formed Adalah: The Legal Center for the Arab Minority in Israel. They employ strategies much more reminiscent of those used in South Africa. They see the legal struggle as part of the political struggle for full human rights in Israel and emphasise the collective rights of Palestinian Arabs and their historical connection with the land. Adalah has petitioned the High Court many times on behalf of collective rights in the areas of education, burial, land ownership and services.[31] One of the most important of these cases pertained to the use of the Arabic language as the language of the Palestinian Israeli minority.[32]

In the *Re'em Engineers* case,[33] the applicant wanted to place an advertisement in Arabic on the noticeboard of the municipality of Natzrat Illit, a Jewish town built on lands of Arabic Nazareth and the nearby Palestinian villages. The city rejected his request. The President of the High Court, Justice Barak, articulated the situation as a confrontation between two values: freedom of speech and expression, on the one hand, and the public interest in the Hebrew language on the other hand. Justice Barak, by way of a balancing act, concluded that the advertisement could be published, since its publication would not harm the dominance of the Hebrew language. Justice Dov Levin joined Justice Barak, saying that 'freedom of expression in a foreign language is at the center of our discussion, and not necessarily the freedom to use the Arabic language'. In this manner, the court avoided a discussion of the important issue of the status of Arabic as an official language of Israel.

In both the *Qa'adan* and *Re'em* cases, the High Court accepted that the policy preventing an individual from realising his or her personal freedom is discriminatory, yet, in both cases, collective rights were replaced by individual rights. Only the Jews are presented as a people, while the Arabs in Israel are presented as an ethnic minority.

Adalah and other human rights organisations operate in an environment in which Palestinian demands for collective rights are perceived as a threat to Israel as a so-called Jewish and democratic state. However, as a result of the deep denial that characterises Israeli society, there is no discussion of what exactly it is that those demands threaten. Instead, the court, facing obvious discrimination, accepted some demands on individual basis. These decisions of the High Court represent larger denial among Israeli liberals. For example, Professor Ruth Gavison, the president of the Association for Human Rights at the time it petitioned the High Court on behalf of the Qa'adans, included a footnote in dealing with land in general and the *Qa'adan* verdict in particular:

The establishment of the Jewish state, in the most minimal sense as one that has a large Jewish majority, damages the non-Jewish inhabitants of the State in an important way. In turns them into a minority in a state established on territory where they were once the majority. It is important to acknowledge this damage, and that it is ongoing and persistent. The Jewish state is also characterized by control over immigration and a systematic effort to increase the Jewish majority in the country. Moreover, the Jewish state 'celebrates' its Judaism in symbolic and formative ways. This exacerbates the alienation of its Arab citizens, upon whose misfortune the state was founded. But all these notions, as important as they may be for understanding the deep difficulties with which relations between Arab and Jewish citizens of the state of Israel are fraught, do not constitute discrimination.[34]

The denial expressed in this footnote – which so powerfully summarises the main difficulty of Israeli liberals, but claims that it does not constitute discrimination – is essentially similar to that in the High Court verdict from May 2006 regarding the law of citizenship – the third High Court case I describe.

On 14 May 2006, the Israeli High Court of Justice decided to uphold the Citizenship and Entry into Israel Law, which bars family reunification for Israelis married to Palestinians from the Occupied Territories. It targets Palestinian citizens of Israel, who make up a fifth of Israel's population, and Palestinian Jerusalemites, who often marry Palestinians from the West Bank and Gaza Strip. Five of the 11 High Court judges who ruled on this law, including the court's President, Justice Barak, voted against upholding it, recognising that it infringes human rights and violates the right of Israeli Arabs to equality. The verdict is 263 pages long, opening with a detailed description of terror victims in Israel and the security threat faced by Israeli citizens and 'inhabitants of the region' (this is what the court prefers to call Israeli settlers in the occupied Palestinian territories) and why the state of Israel, which is in danger, passed a law that tries to reduce the possibility of Palestinians immigrating to Israel in order to commit acts of terror. The verdict begins thus:[35]

In September 2000 the second Intifada broke out. Terror landed a fierce blow on Israel. Most of the attacks targeted civilians: men, women, the old and the young. Whole families lost loved ones. The attacks were meant to take lives. They were meant to sow fear and panic. They were meant to ruin the lives of Israeli citizens. The attacks take place inside Israel and in the region, at random venues. They target passengers on public transport, people in shopping centers and markets, cafes and inside homes and towns. The main targets of the attacks are the urban centers in Israel, but Israeli localities in the region and roads are also targeted. The terrorist organisations employ a variety of means including suicide bombings, car bombs, planting of explosive devices, Molotov cocktails and grenades, shootings, shells and rockets. A number of attacks on strategic targets have failed. From the beginning of these acts of terror to January 2006, over 1,500 attacks have been carried out in Israel. Over a thousand Israelis have lost their lives inside Israel. Some 6,500 Israelis have been injured. Many of these have been severely crippled. On the Palestinians' side too, the conflict has led to many dead and injured. Bereavement and pain wash over us.

Barak went on to clarify:

The objective at the foundation of these directives is security related. It is intended to prevent realization of the dangerous potential of a spouse from the region, who has permission to live in Israel with an Israeli spouse, helping hostile operatives, something that has occurred in the past. There is no demographic objective or intention to limit the growth of the Arab population in Israel underlying this law.

If the law is not rooted in a demographic objective, why did the President of the court see fit to say so? Perhaps because Justice Procaccia wrote about it explicitly in her minority position. She wrote:

While it is true that the state, in presenting the law, indicated that security considerations were the only considerations, the Knesset discussions show that the demographic issue hovered over the legislative process throughout and was a central issue in both the house and the committee for internal affairs. There were members of Knesset from different parties who felt that the demographic dimension was the main justification for the legislative arrangement that was adopted. Some of them, such as Minister Gidon Ezra (Likud, government-Knesset liaison at that time) and Speaker Ruby Rivlin (Likud), warned that family reunification[36] was a mechanism intended to constitute de facto realization of the right of return.

The state, as part of its position, was willing to declare that although the security consideration was the only one behind the legislation, had the demographic consideration been at the foundation of the policy that led to this legislation, it would still be legitimate, in keeping with the values of the state of Israel as a Jewish and democratic country.[37]

In other words, the state of Israel passed legislation that prevented Palestinians from living in Israel because it wanted to preserve the Jewish majority and feared that Palestinian immigration would mark the beginning of a 'return'. The High Court gave legal backing to this law and, with the exception of one justice, claimed that it was not about what the legislators explicitly said it was about – not a racist law intended to add another restriction to the many imposed on Arabs in Israel, but one born of security concerns. That ruling created another legal rubber stamp for the 40-year-old distinction between four categories of people, each with different levels of rights: inhabitants of the Occupied Territories who have no rights at all (the court calls them 'inhabitants of the region' so as not to indicate that they deserve protection as citizens of Occupied Territory); residents of East Jerusalem who are permitted to enter Israel but have no civil rights; Palestinian Israeli citizens whose standing as citizens with unequal rights was reaffirmed by this and previous rulings; and Jewish Israelis with full rights and privileges.

The High Court of Justice was divided on the question of whether this was legal discrimination. The day after the ruling was issued, the President of the High Court wrote a detailed letter to a friend at Yale University in which he described the ruling, after having headed a minority of five against six:

> As you can see, technically, my view lost, but in substance there is a very solid majority to my view that the Israeli member of a family has a constitutional right to family unification in Israel with a foreign spouse, and that the statute is discriminatory.[38]

Representatives of Adalah and other Palestinian organisations in Israel, such as Mossawa or the Arab Association for Human Rights, have to deal not only with the denial of Israeli liberals, who camouflage racist legislation as action against terror, but also with the support this denial receives from liberal legal practitioners in the Western world, most of whom see the High Court justices as representatives of a liberal enlightened institution.

The main difference between Israel and South Africa is that in the former, control of resources, anti-liberal legislation and discriminatory policy are made possible by legislation facilitated by the Jewish majority, and not by a minority group as was the case in the latter. Because the decisions are taken by a numerical majority that controls the political system, Jewish society can claim that the political system is democratic. This democratic self-image of the state of Israel,[39] is reinforced by the unconditional support of the USA, which has been reinforced recently by the struggle with the Muslim world, and the European states' fear of criticising Israel as a result of guilt following the horrors of the Holocaust.

The establishment of the Truth and Reconciliation commissions in South Africa attests to the realisation that questions of memory, truth and past pain have to be addressed in order to create a better future. In Israel, the human rights movement deals with the present, but not with the past and not with the future, because we have no collective vision. This is because in Israel, the past and future are repressed issues that are not only beyond the consensus, but not even talked about. Denial of the past and future is nourished by Israeli liberals' need to perceive the state of Israel as democratic. As long as the Jews are a majority, any discriminatory legislation and practice in the present is perceived as separate and not part of a historical continuum – legal because effected by the majority. The refusal to speak about the dispossession and expulsion of Palestinians in 1948, and the refusal to speak about the right of return, stem from the liberals' fear of some day finding themselves in the minority position. As long as there is a Jewish majority in the state of Israel, Israeli liberals can continue to believe they are living in a Jewish democratic state. They can continue to believe that the 'solution' to the Palestinian situation in the territories is a political solution towards which the political leadership has striven for years, 'reaching out a hand in peace,' but not finding a worthy Palestinian partner. 'There is no one to talk to.' In 2006, when the Palestinians elected a Hamas government which took the same 'there's no one to talk to' position, the Israeli liberals could maintain their sense of being right. They could continue to believe in the disconnection between the temporary occupation of the territories (which would be over if only there were a suitable Palestinian partner) and discrimination (which does not actually exist in Israel because the state is democratic and the majority rules via democratic process). The liberal High Court affirms this position.

Why do Israeli liberals not do more?

Israeli liberals and human rights organisations operate within the political system and within a social context in which only 29 per cent opposed the demand that a Jewish majority be required for decisions critical to the country's future, and 62 per cent support the demand that the government encourage Arab emigration from the country.[40]

Different groups in Israeli society hold different opinions on what needs to be done in order to reduce the number of Arabs in Israel: a large portion of the Israeli public believes in the religious obligation to 'liberate' as much territory as possible from non-Jewish control. In the 2006 elections, some 10 per cent supported a party that suggests transferring Arab Israeli citizens over the border. There are those who perceive themselves as liberals, and who agree that Arab citizens of Israel deserve equal rights, within a Jewish democratic country, but that all the Jews in the world must be allowed citizenship in Israel. Over a million people immigrated from the ex-Soviet Union to Israel in the last 15 years, and they make up almost a fifth of Israeli citizens. A similar number of Palestinians are citizens of Israel. But while the newcomers were given equal-rights citizenship, and many benefits to help them adapt in the new country, the doors were not open thus to the Arabs.

Israeli liberals want to believe that they are part of Europe, not the Arab world in which we are geographically situated. The new law that bars spouses of Palestinians from living here, the various laws that bar Palestinians from entering Israel, the confiscation of the identity cards of Palestinians in Jerusalem, and all the internal discrimination against Palestinians in Israel are all ways of denying the very reality that should be visible even to a child. There cannot be a democratic Jewish state, just as there cannot be an Muslim democratic state. What kind of a democracy would this be? There is an internal contradiction in this definition and, thus, in the possibility of such a democracy existing in reality.[41]

In his book *States of Denial*, in the section entitled 'Israel: a special case,' Stan writes:

> The Jewish public's assent to official propaganda, myth and self-righteousness results from a willing identification – not fear of arbitrary imprisonment, commissars or secret police. Many topics are known and not-known at the same time.[42]

Conclusion

If there is anything I can add to Stan's conclusions about why Israeli liberals do not do more, it is that they can do no more and still perceive themselves as liberals living in a democratic state. Unlike South African liberals, who were ostracised throughout the world, Israeli liberals, even those who do nothing politically, can pride themselves on a High Court that is considered enlightened and democratic, and an organised legal system based on the Jewish majority that makes use of all democratic devices. Unlike in South Africa, a country that was banned from international sports, Israeli teams play in European leagues. Unlike the cultural boycott of South Africa by artists, thousands of artists are eager to perform in Israel. Israel competes in the Eurovision song contest each year as if it were part of Europe.

My first simple conclusion is that Israeli liberals do not do more because they can avoid doing more and still be part of the Western world. They do not do more because they do not want to be a part of the Arab world in which they live, and the USA and Europe support them as a Western force within the Arab world, as 'the only democracy in the Middle East'. Israeli liberals do not do more because their dissonance is less pronounced than was that of South African liberals. They do not live in a country where a small minority oppresses a large majority, but in a country where the majority oppresses a minority.

They do not do more because legal language has taken over the public discourse in Israel. There is no talk of the future or the past – only argument over the present in legal terms. Are the territories occupied or 'held'? Do the human rights conventions or humanitarian law apply in the territories or, because of complicated legal reasons, do they not? This legal language allows cloaking terrible deeds in ostensible justice. The High Court, which is perceived as uncompromisingly rooted in moral values, can rule that Arabs have no right to marry and live with their elected spouses in Israel, and the day after the verdict is issued the President of the High Court can write that the decision was taken against his opinion but his failure to convince his colleagues not to discriminate between Jewish and Arab rights in Israel was only a technical failure.

They do not do more because, they say, they 'do not believe there is a solution to this conflict', possibly meaning that they do not believe there is a solution that will preserve their privileges as Jews.

South Africa taught us that in order to move toward a better future we have to return to old wounds. Israeli liberals do not do more, because they do not want to go back and look at the past and acknowledge the wrongs they have perpetrated and continue to perpetrate against the Palestinians, who were evicted from their homes and are prevented from returning. They feel that these Palestinians, were they to return, would threaten the Jewish majority and thus also the democratic self-perception of Israel. They do not do more because most Palestinians, as well as many other Arabs, do not acknowledge the historical connection of Jews to this piece of land (albeit this connection is partly imagined as Anderson suggests in 'imagined communities') and see them only as foreign conquerors.

In Israel, as in South Africa, it is not the liberals who will be the vanguard of change. Israeli liberals will join in if, and once, we do manage to consolidate a shared vision of how we see ourselves in the future, how Jews and Arabs will live here together, enjoying justice and reconciliation on the same piece of land, how we will atone for the pain of the past, how we will ask forgiveness. How will we, as Jews, live in the midst of an Arab region which has never accepted us, a region which we have done very little to be accepted by. I do not know when we will begin to talk about these issues. In the meantime, Israeli liberals enjoy the privileges which are shared mostly by Jews in Israel and at the same time regard themselves as liberals.

It has been painful for me to write this chapter. I have written with a sense of failure at having been active in the human rights movement for so many years while the situation deteriorates. Watching the recent terrible and ugly war, already called the Second Lebanon War, that should have never been fought, a war that has devastated millions of people, not only made me angry and sad and scared. It also made me wonder how Israeli liberals could support this war and still call themselves and be seen in the world as liberals.

Notes

1 Many thanks to Hagar Mushonov, Irith Ballas and Alaa Mahajna for their help in the research for this chapter, and to Janine Woolfson for translation.

2 S. Cohen, 'The psychology and politics of denial: the case of Israeli liberals', Lecture given at IMUT Conference: Psychological Barriers to Peace, Jerusalem, 24 May 1988.

3 S. Cohen and D. Golan, *The Interrogation of Palestinians During the Intifada: Ill-Treatment, 'Moderate Physical Pressure' or Torture?* Jerusalem: B'Tselem, 1991.

4 Professor Michael Wade, who died in 1990, was an expert on South African literature and a friend of Stan from their student days at the University of Witwatersrand.

5 After four years reporting from Jerusalem and more than a decade reporting from Johannesburg, the *Guardian*'s award-winning Middle East Correspondent, Chris McGreal, published an assessment of the comparison between Israel and South Africa. McGreal's fascinating articles were not translated or published in Israeli newspapers, but *Haaretz*, the liberal Israeli newspaper, did publish a scathing response to McGreal by Benjamin

Pogrund, who claimed that the comparison between Israeli and apartheid South Africa was unjustified. See, C. McGreal, 'Worlds apart', *Guardian*, 6 February 2006; C. McGreal, 'Brothers in arms – Israel's secret pact with Pretoria', *Guardian*, 7 February, 2006; and B. Pogrund, 'Why depict Israel as a chamber of horrors like no other in the world?', *Guardian*, 8 February 2006. Also published in *Haaretz*.

6 Until the end of the 1980s, the Association for Civil Rights, established in 1972, was the only civil rights organisation in Israel. For the first 15 years of its existence, the association did not petition the High Court with regard to Palestinian rights in the Occupied Territories. See N. Gordon, 'Human rights and social space: the strength of the Israeli civil rights movement', *Israeli Sociology* (2005) 1, pp. 23–44 and Na'ama Yishuvi, *Human Rights, That's All: The Human Rights Association Interim Report*, Jerusalem: The Association for Human Rights, 2002.

7 S. Cohen, 'The human rights movement in Israel and South Africa: some paradoxical comparisons,' *Occasional Papers*. Harry S. Truman Research Institute for the Advancement of Peace, no. 1, 1991, p. 2.

8 Basic Law: Human Dignity and Freedom, and Basic Law: Freedom of Occupation.

9 See C.A. (Civil Appeal) 6821/93 *Mizrahi Bank* v. *Migdal Co-operative Village* 49(4) P.D. 221. See H.C. 1715/97 *The Association of Investment Managers* in *Israel* v. *Minister of Finance*, 51(5) P.D. 367.

10 The last ten years have seen the establishment of new organisations dealing with two main issues: the rights of the Palestinian Israeli minority and social rights. With the widening economic gaps in the 1990s, due to the decline of the welfare state and the influx of approximately a million Russians and thousands of Ethiopians with simultaneous intensive growth of its high-tech industries, Israel became one of the countries with the most pronounced economic differences. There are dozens of human rights organisations that inform citizens of their rights, assist in the legislation of public housing, and petition the courts on issues of principle in the field of human and social rights and private cases. These organisations are not active at the grass-roots level but stress legal strategy. Most of them also lobby in the Knesset and have education and media departments.

11 Forty-eight employees work for the Association for Civil Rights in Israel. Some 60,000–80,000 people visit their website each month. B'Tselem – The Israeli Information Center for Human Rights in the Occupied Territories – (established 1989) has 27 office employees and eight field workers. About 2,000 people use their website daily. The Public Committee Against Torture employs 28 staff and four volunteers. Physicians for Human Rights (established 1988) has 19 employees and hundreds of volunteers, most of whom are medical doctors.

12 See, for example, the responses to the arrest warrant that awaited Major-General (ret.) Doron Almog in Great Britain for his alleged crime of the destruction of 59 civilian homes in Rafah refugee camp and dropping a one-ton bomb on Gaza City that killed 15 Palestinian civilians. Sima Kadmon, 'Where is the border?', *Yediot Ahronot*, 16 September 2005;

A. Fachter, 'Universal Hypocrisy', *NFC*, 18 September 2005 (both in Hebrew).

13 According to the Ministry of Trade and Industry's website, 511 new lawyers qualified in 1990, and 2271 in 2004. Israel has become the country with the most lawyers per capita in the world. http://www.moit.gov.il/NR/rdonlyres/D404E25B-257D-4845-BE8A-DAAF67C46487/0/X6532.doc.

14 In his book *The Occupation of Justice*, David Kretzmer studies the main rulings pertaining to the Palestinians in the territories which enabled the Israeli government to conduct deportations and house demolitions, and establish Jewish settlements on lands declared state property. He concludes: 'In its decisions relating to the Occupied Territories, the Court has rationalized virtually all controversial actions of the Israeli authorities, especially those most problematic under principles of international humanitarian law.' See D. Kretzmer, *The Occupation of Justice; the Supreme Court of Israel and the Occupied Territories*, Albany, NY: State University of New York Press, 2002.

15 HCJ 2056/04 *Beit Sourik Village Council* v. *The Government of Israel* http://elyon1.court.gov.il/files_eng/04/560/020/a28/04020560.a28.pdf.

16 HCJ 7957/04 *Maraaba* v. *The Government of Israel*.

17 To obtain the ruling ordering that the wall be moved and free five Palestinian villages from the threat of being surrounded and cut off from all their sources of income, Attorney Mohammed Dahala of Adalah 'recruited' a group of retired Israeli military figures who live in the Israeli town of Mevasseret Zion near the wall. They presented their professional military opinions that the proposed location of the wall was not in Israel's security interests. They had surveyors build a model of the proposed wall and display it before the court (Mohammed Dahala: lecture delivered to my students, 2005).

18 S. Cohen and D. Golan, op. cit.

19 S. Cohen, *States of Denial: Knowing about Atrocities and Suffering*, London: Polity, 2001, p. xi.

20 S. Cohen and D. Golan, *The Interrogation of Palestinians During the Intifada: Ill-Treatment, 'Moderate Physical Pressure' or Torture? – Follow-up Report*, Jerusalem: B'Tselem, 1992.

21 See my 'Victory at the High Court', in *Next Year in Jerusalem: Everyday Life in a Divided Land*, New York: The New Press, 2005.

22 HCJ 5100/94 *Public Committee Against Torture* v. *Israel* http://elyon1.court.gov.il/files_eng/94/000/051/a09/94051000.a09.pdf.

23 There are no statistical data on the use of torture in Israel today. The most recent report (not yet published) of the Public Committee against Torture in Israel (PCATI) covers 2004–5. In 2004–5, PCATI handled some 1360 cases. About 1100 of these involved detainees or prisoners who approached PCATI with complaints of torture and other ill treatment during arrest, interrogation and detention. The other 260 cases mostly involved the killing of civilians during military activities in the Occupied Territories.

24 S. Cohen, 'The human rights movement in Israel and South Africa: some paradoxical comparisons,' Occasional Papers, no. 1, Harry S. Truman Research Institute for the Advancement of Peace, 1991 p. 5.

25 This is reminiscent of a notion that prevailed among South African liberals. There, too, for years, white liberals described their country as consisting of two circles, the democratic one that whites lived in and the one where blacks had no rights.

26 It is worth noting that although the human rights organisations made an important contribution to exposing the horrors of the occupation and holding up a mirror to Israeli society so that it would have to address the evil it was perpetuating, they were not invited by either the Israelis or Palestinians to the many peace talks, all of which failed.

27 I have full respect and admiration for B'Tselem as well as other human rights organisations struggling against injustice. I was the founding research director, and I remember Stan telling me that we have a moral duty to witness. See my 'Compassion and the Language of Human Rights', in *Next Year in Jerusalem.*

28 *H.C. 6698/95, Qa'adan v. Israel Lands Administration, et. al*, P.D. 54(1) 258.

29 *H.C. 6698/95, Qa'adan*, paragraph 37.

30 Ten years later, the Qa'adans petitioned the High Court again as they still could not live on their land.

31 M. Dalal, 2000, 'The guest, the house, and the judge: a reading in the unread in the Qa'adan decision', *Adalah's Review*, 2, *Land*, pp. 40–7.

32 Another example is the petition to cancel the governmental decision which excluded the vast majority of Arab towns and villages in Israel from the list of National Priority Areas, thus denying their access to substantial economic and social benefits. On 27 February 2006, an expanded seven-justice panel of the Supreme Court of Israel unanimously accepted Adalah's petition, originally submitted in 1998, and overruled a governmental decision establishing 'National Priority Areas', finding that it discriminates against Arab citizens of Israel on the basis of race and national origin. See www. adalah.org.

33 H.C. 105/92 *Re'em Engineers and Contractors* v. *Upper Nazareth Municipality*, 47(5) P.D. 189.

34 R. Gavison, 'Jewish and Democratic', *Adalah's Review*, 2000, 2, *Land*, pp. 28–33, footnote 11.

35 H.C. 7052.03 *Adalah et al.* v. *Minister of Interior, et al.* delivered on 14 May 2006.

36 The justice refers to the minutes of meeting 276 of the 16th Knesset, Wednesday 27.7.2005, p. 15 and the Internal Affairs Committee on 29.7.2003.

37 Paragraph 169 to the state's summation from 16/12/2003, as quoted in paragraph 14 to Justice Procaccia's ruling in H.C 7052/03.

38 Yuval Yoaz, 'Barak: citizenship law will be voided if extended', *Haaretz*, 18 May 2006.

39 N. Ruhana and A. Sabar-Huri, 'Aggression, the space of tolerance and the privileged situation', in Hanna Herzog and Kinneret Lahad (eds) *Knowledge and Silence: On Mechanisms of Denial and Repression in Israeli Society* [in Hebrew], Van-Leer Institute Jerusalem/Hakibbutz Hameuchad Publishing House, 2006, pp. 68–71.

40 A. Arian, N. Atmor and Y. Hadar, *Auditing Israeli Democracy*, Israel Democracy Institute, 2006.
41 To examine this denial, of the past, of the present reality that Israel is situated in the midst of an Arab world and does nothing to be part of the region in which it is, we have focused here on the dominant, legal, discourse. But this denial is also maintained of course by other groups in Israeli society. For example, none of the Israeli textbooks discuss the Naqba, the expulsion of the Palestinians in 1948, or the refugee question. The Israeli education system continues to deny the history that is most relevant to Israeli students. Not only are Arab students prevented from studying their history, literature, and culture, but the Jewish students do not, at any point during their 13 years of schooling, learn about the origins of the Israeli-Palestinian conflict. On this issue as well as on other ways in which Palestinian students are discriminated against in Israel see my 'Separate but not equal: discrimination against Palestinian Arab students in Israel', in *American Behavioral Scientist*, 2006, 49 2006 1075-1084, and my book *Inequality in Education* [in Hebrew], Tel Aviv: Babel, 2004, as well as 'Separate but not equal' in my *Next Year in Jerusalem*.
42 Cohen, *States of Denial: Knowing About Atrocities and Suffering*, London: Polity, 2001, p. 157.

References

Adam, H. and Kogila, M. (2005) *Seeking Mandela – Peacemaking between Israelis and Palestinians*. Philadelphia: Temple University Press.
Amara, M.H. (2006) 'Real core or no core at all?', In D. Inbar (ed.), *Toward Educational Revolution?* Van Leer Educational Conference on Dovrat's Report. Tel Aviv: Hakibbutz Hameuchad, pp. 195–202.
Arian, A., Atmor, N. and Hadar, Y. (2006) 'Auditing Israeli democracy – 2006: changes in Israel's political party system: dealignment or realignment?', in *The President's Conference – Israeli Democracy Examined*. www.idi.org.il/english/article.asp?id=01052006145754.
Barak, E. (2003) 'I did not give away a thing', *Journal of Palestine Studies*, 33: 84–7.
Boraine, A. (2000) *A Country Unmasked: Inside South Africa's Truth and Reconciliation Commission*, Cape Town: Oxford University Press.
Boraine, A., Levy, J. and Scheffer, R. (eds) (1994) *Dealing with the Past: Truth and Reconciliation in South Africa*. Cape Town: IDASA.
Cohen, S. (1988) 'The psychology and politics of denial: the case of Israeli liberals', Lecture given at IMUT Conference: Psychological Barriers to Peace, Jerusalem.
Cohen, S. (1991) *The Human Rights Movement in Israel and South Africa: Some Paradoxical Comparisons*. Occasional Papers, no. 1, Harry S. Truman Research Institute for the Advancement of Peace.
Cohen, S. (2001) *States of Denial: Knowing about Atrocities and Suffering*. London: Polity.

Cohen, S. 'Cultural criticism and human rights – comments on Adi Ofir' (unpublished).

Cohen, S. and Golan, D. (1991) *The Interrogation of Palestinians During the Intifada: Ill-Treatment, 'Moderate Physical Pressure' or Torture?* Jerusalem: B'Tselem.

Cohen, S. and Golan, D. (1992) *The Interrogation of Palestinians During the Intifada: Ill-Treatment, 'Moderate Physical Pressure' or Torture? – Follow-up Report.* Jerusalem: B'Tselem.

Dalal, M. (2000) 'The guest, the house, and the judge: a reading in the unread in the Qa'dan decision', *Adalah's Review*, 2 (Land): 40–7.

Gavison, R. (2000) 'Jewish and democratic', *Adalah's Review*, 2 (Land): 28–33.

Golan-Agnon, D. (2004) *Inequality in Education*, Tel Aviv: Babel [in Hebrew].

Golan-Agnon, D. (2005) *Next Year in Jerusalem-Everyday Life in a Divided Land.* New York: New Press.

Golan-Agnon, D. (2006) 'Separate but not equal: discrimination against Palestinian Arab students in Israel', *American Behavioral Scientist*, 49: 8, 1075–1084.

Gordon, N. (2005) 'Human rights and social space: the power of the Association for Civil Rights in Israel', *Israeli Sociology*, 7: 23–44 [in Hebrew].

Gross A.M. (2004) 'The constitution, reconciliation, and transitional justice: lessons from South Africa and Israel', *Stanford Journal of International Law*, 40, 47–104.

Katz, Y. (2006) 'Core curriculum in Israel: common denominator for all educational sectors', in Inbar D. (ed.) *Toward Educational Revolution?* Van Leer Educational Conference on Dovrat's Report. Tel Aviv: Hakibbutz Hameuchad, pp. 186–94.

Kretzmer, D. (2002) *The Occupation of Justice; The Supreme Court of Israel and the Occupied Territories.* Albany, NY: State University of New York Press.

Kretzmer, D. (2005) 'The advisory opinion: the light treatment of international humanitarian law', *American Journal of International Law*, 99: 88–102.

Lawyers in Israel – Characteristics and Employment in the Last Decade (2005) Ministry of Industry, Trade and Labor. www.moit.gov.il/NR/rdonlyres/D404E25B-257D-4845-BE8A-DAAF67C46487/0/X6532.doc.

McGreal, C. 'Worlds apart', *Guardian*, 6 February 2006.

McGreal, 'Brothers in arms – Israel's secret pact with Pretoria', *Guardian*, 7 February 2006.

Pogrund, B. 'Why depict Israel as a chamber of horrors like no other in the world?' *Guardian*, 8 February 2006.

Rouhana, N.R. (2001) 'Reconciliation in protracted national conflict; identity and power in the Israeli-Palestinian case', in A.H. Eagly, V.L. Hamilton and R.M. Baron (eds) *The Social Psychology of Group Identity and Social Conflict: Theory and Practice.*

Ruhana, N. and Sabar-Huri, A. (2006) 'Aggression, the space of tolerance and the privileged situation', in Hanna Herzog and Kinneret Lahad (eds) *Knowledge and Silence: On Mechanisms of Denial and Repression in Israeli Society.* Van-Leer Institute Jerusalem/Hakibbutz Hameuchad [in Hebrew].

Roy, S. (2002) 'Why peace failed: an Oslo autopsy', *Current History*, 101: 651, 8–16.

Sagi, A. (2001) 'Law and society: rights discourse and identity discourse in Israel', *Bar-Ilan Law Studies – Journal of the Faculty of Law*, 16: 2 (in Hebrew).

Yashuvi, N. (2002) *Human Rights, That's the Whole Story: The Association for Civil Rights – Mid-summary.* Jerusalem: Association for Civil Rights.

Laws

Basic Law: Human Dignity and Freedom, and Basic Law: Freedom of Occupation.

Court rulings

H.C 7052/03 Adalah et al. v. *Minister of Interior et al.* delivered 14 May 2006.

H.C. 1715/97 The Association of Investment Managers in Israel v. *Minister of Finance*, 51(5) P.D. 367.

HCJ 2056/04 Beit Sourik Village Council v. *The Government of Israel et. al.* delivered 30 June 2004.

C.A. 6821/93 Mizrahi Bank v. *Migdal Co-operative Village* P.D. 49(4) 221.

HCJ 5100/94 Public Committee Against Torture in Israel v. *Israel*, P.D. 53(4) 817.

H.C. 6698/95, Qa'adan v. Israel Lands Administration, et al., P.D. 54(1) 258.

H.C. 105/92 Re'em Engineers and Contractors v. *Upper Nazareth Municipality*, P.D. 47(5) 189.

Chapter 21

Mediterranean poverty and conflict: applying a human rights strategy

Peter Townsend

Countries bordering the Mediterranean are rarely investigated as territories or populations constituting a distinct region with structural interconnections. In this particular region, the problem can be put into stark relief by the scale of impoverishment, for example, in Morocco, Albania, Egypt, Palestine and Lebanon. Progress in reaching the Millennium Development Goals has been slow, and, according to a number of authorities, the prospects of achieving substantial success by 2015 are virtually non-existent (Robinson 2003; Brown and Wolfensohn 2004; Vandemoortele 2005).

Compilations of evidence from recent years by the World Bank, the UN itself, the UN Development Programme (UNDP) and others (Townsend and Gordon 2002) substantiate this cautionary tale. There is concern because there is no scientific or political consensus about the exact definition, and therefore measurement, of the concept of poverty in the world. This means that exact comparisons between different countries bordering the Mediterranean regarding the severity of their condition cannot be drawn; and therefore that strategic and policy priorities for international agencies and national governments cannot be demonstrable as well as discernible.

The separation of the definition, study and measurement of poverty in the First and the Third Worlds, the preoccupation with individual, community and local factors in the 'transmission of poverty between the generations', and the failure to relate national poverty either to the international context or to overall social or political stratification are evident. Regional initiatives can of course prepare the way for wider international agreement. Moreover, realistic hopes of diminishing world poverty, and in particular poverty due to civil conflict and war, rest on a more active application of the instruments of human rights – as illustrated by assessment of conditions in the countries bordering the Mediterranean.

In this chapter I will do three things: 1) I will argue for the construction and adoption of a threshold poverty line for all countries; 2) I will argue for the development of major social security systems in poor countries, built on the examples established over many decades in the OECD countries or newly devised, with a predominant element being social insurance; and 3) I will call attention to those Articles of human rights that are particularly relevant to the discussion of Mediterranean anti-poverty strategy. The last is illustrated in Figure 21.1.

Establishing an international baseline

The nearest that we get contemporaneously to an agreed international usage is the World Bank's dollar-a-day per person and the European Union's 50 or 60 per cent of median household income. Both are objects of easy criticism. They have not been subjected to verifiable objective evidence independent of level of income.

The US dollar-a-day definition of poverty was an acceptable improvisation at the end of the 1980s as a convenient and understandable temporary standard on which to base investigation and policy. But two mistakes were made. One mistake was to take 1985 as the base year, and not to foresee that changes in the markets, and especially the division between what is free or subsidised and what has to be paid for, and changes in fulfilling individual roles at work, in family and society, with consequences for nutritional and dietary requirements, as well as other consumables and services, necessarily affect the threshold of income required to meet minimum human needs. The mistake was compounded when the bank underestimated the value of the poverty line in 1993 and later years following inflation (Kakwani and Son 2006).

The US dollar-a-day standard has also become tenuous to uphold with the adoption of a US 2-dollars-a-day as a standard for some countries, and then US 4-dollars-a-day as a standard for the transitional economies of the former Soviet Union and Eastern Europe (World Bank 2000). Differing standards have not been explained and justified in relation to levels of material and social deprivation.

The second mistake of the World Bank was in 1990 to state that the correct measure of poverty had two necessary elements but, after introducing the simplest practicable measure of $1 a day to cover the first element, to fail to explore how the second element could be

Authority	Social Security	Adequate Living Standard
Convention on the Rights of the Child (1989)	Article 26(I) – States parties shall recognize for every child the right to benefit from social security, including social insurance, and shall take the necessary measures to achieve the full realization of this right in accordance with their national law.	Article 27 (I) – States parties recognize the right of every child to a standard of living adequate for the child's physical, mental, spiritual, moral and social development. Article 27 (3) – …and shall in case of need provide material assistance and support programmes, particularly with regard to nutrition, clothing and housing.
International Covenant on Economic, Social and Cultural Rights (1966- came into force 1976)	Article 9 – The States Parties to the present Covenant recognize the right of everyone to social security, including social insurance.	Article 11 (1) – The States Parties to the present Covenant recognize the right of everyone to an adequate standard of living for himself and his family, including adequate food, clothing and housing, and to the continuous improvement of living conditions.
Universal Declaration of Human Rights (1948)	Article 22 – Everyone, as a member of society, has the right to social security and is entitled to realization, through national effort and international co-operation and in accordance with the organization and resources of each state, of the economic, social and cultural rights indispensable for their dignity and the free development of their personality.	Article 25(1) – Everyone has the right to a standard of living adequate for the health and well-being of their family, including food, clothing, housing and medical care and necessary social services, and the right to security in the event of unemployment, sickness, disability, widowhood, old age or other lack of livelihood in circumstances beyond their control.

Figure 21.1   The rights to social security and an adequate standard of living

properly added. Thus, in the 1990 *World Development Report*, the World Bank defined poverty as 'the inability to attain a minimal standard of living' consisting of 'two elements: the expenditure necessary to buy a minimum standard of nutrition and other basic necessities and a further amount that varies from country to country, reflecting the cost of participating in the everyday life of society' (World Bank 1990: 26).

Variations in the scale of poverty

The countries that border the Mediterranean straddle three conventionally defined regions of the world and include developing and industrialised countries that are seldom examined together. Despite having much in common, the countries vary greatly in the extent and severity of poverty that they have experienced historically and experience today. There are three principal groups (see Petmesidou and Papatheodorou 2006). Among the countries of southern Europe, the four member states of the European Union (EU), Italy, Spain, Portugal and Greece, have little poverty, by the standard of $2 per person per day, but among non-member states of southern Europe, such as Bulgaria, Macedonia, Romania and Albania, there is a significant or substantial extent. In the third group of Middle Eastern and North African countries, poverty, by the same standard, averages 23 per cent, and in some countries, such as Egypt, Yemen and Mauritania, is far more extensive. Tables 21.1 and 21.2 provide a summary (drawn from Petmesidou and Papatheodorou 2006). During the 1980s, there was a substantial percentage reduction in

Table 21.1 Poverty in Middle Eastern and North African countries

Year	Per cent below $2 per day at 1993 PPP	Number in population below $2 per day (million)
1981	28.9	51.9
1984	25.2	49.8
1987	24.2	52.5
1990	21.4	50.9
1993	20.2	51.8
1996	22.3	60.9
1999	24.3	70.4
2001	23.2	69.8

Source: World Bank 2004.

Table 21.2 Poverty and other social indicators in Middle Eastern and North African countries

Country	Expected years of life at birth (2002)	% under-nourished (1999–2001)	% children under 5 underweight (1995–2000)	% lacking access to sanitation facilities (2002)	% under $2 a day*	% under national poverty line*
Mauritania	52.3	10	32	67	68.7	46.3
Sudan	55.5	21	17	38	*	–
Yemen	59.8	33	46	62	45.2	41.8
Morocco	68.5	7	9	32	14.3	19.0
Egypt	68.6	4	11	2	43.9	16.7
Algeria	69.5	6	6	8	15.1	22.6
Iran	70.1	5	11	17	7.3	–
Turkey	70.4	–	8	10	10.3	–
Jordan	70.9	6	5	1	7.4	11.7
Syria	72.1	4	7	10	–	–
Saudi Arabia	72.1	3	14	0	–	–
Occupied Palestinian Territories	72.3	–	4	0	–	–
Libya	72.6	–	5	3	–	–
Tunisia	72.7	–	4	16	10.0	7.6
Lebanon	73.5	3	3	1	–	–

Source: cols. 2–5, see Petmesidou and Papatheodorou (2006).
*The examples given are for the latest available year (in the range 1995–2002).

poverty, but overall in the two decades there was an increase of some 18 million in the total numbers in poverty.

Some of the latest results for the second group of countries – the Balkan countries – are disturbing. Poverty is substantial and in some countries has deepened in the aftermath of the collapse of the Soviet Union. In most countries (except Macedonia, Croatia and Montenegro), poverty as measured in terms of $2 per person per day applies to between a fifth and over a quarter of the population. By nationally measured standards, the scale of poverty is the same, or smaller, though higher in Macedonia. Poverty is particularly prevalent because traditional measures to reduce poverty in those countries have been abandoned rather than used as a building block or object lesson in constructing society in a different world.

Compared with other European transition economies, the Balkan transition countries experienced larger increases in poverty and inequality (see, for example, Neri *et al.* 2004) and rapid deterioration of some features of economic and social well-being. While life expectancy is relatively high, the populations of most countries betray a marked extent of undernourishment and high levels of unemployment.

Where poverty is most severe: the case of Egypt

The third group of Middle Eastern and North African countries (MENA) must be given the most urgent attention. In comparing development across countries surrounding the Mediterranean and looking, in particular, at the extent and severity of poverty, this is the group of countries that provokes particular concern, as well as very mixed results in relation to poverty. This is not the place for systematic analysis, but only for three illustrations that suggest how concluding observations about international and national social development policies in the Mediterranean region might be newly shaped.

One country with a very high rate of poverty, by any standard, is Egypt. The history of poverty research in Egypt is extensive. In a 1996 report, Korayem showed that three definitions – the basic needs approach, the relative income definition and the government's indirect definition – that is, a threshold of income below which individuals were treated as eligible for social assistance – had been applied in a range of studies published from 1977 to 1994. A subjective definition of poverty had also been applied, though on a very small scale.

While there appear to have been marked trends in particular periods – for example, different authors trace a decline in poverty from 1974–5 to 1981–2, there is clear agreement that rural poverty has been, and remains, very high. For 1974–5, estimates range from 51 per cent to 61 per cent, and for 1990-91 from 21 per cent to 54 per cent (Korayem 1996: 193). Extreme poverty (near to starvation) in rural households in 1990-91 was estimated to be between 5 and 9 per cent by two sources but to be 22 per cent by a third (*ibid*.: 194).

Interpretations of the effects on poverty in Egypt of structural adjustment programmes, like those in many parts of Africa (see, in particular, Kanji, and Donkor, in Townsend and Gordon 2002), are diverse. Generally, the advocates of such programmes are positive about their long-term effects, even though these are impossible to measure, and they are defensively positive about the short-term effects, on the grounds that ameliorative social measures are enough to negate any ill-effects. But there remains little explanation why such programmes were launched at all without putting into place social protection measures, especially social security systems.

The main components of the structural adjustment and stabilisation policies in Egypt were currency devaluation, liberalisation of international trade, raising the price of utilities, reducing subsidies, and applying tight monetary and fiscal policies. After these programmes were introduced, the large-scale protests that ensued eventually resulted in agreement that the poor would be bound to suffer and that the social costs had to be minimised. But the elements of the World Bank/IMF poverty-alleviation strategy were inadequate, and perceived in Egypt to be inadequate. An alternative adjustment package was proposed – to increase the access of the poor to productive employment and assets, to invest in human capital, to promote the productive potential of the poor (such as investment in education, training, and health), and to begin establishing welfare measures through transfer payments and subsidies (Korayem 1996: 203).

Where poverty is most severe: the case of Palestine

In certain respects, the Palestinian Territory offers different, or additional, causes for a high rate of poverty. The consequences of protracted conflict, combined with the difficulties of setting up sustainable local and national forms of employment and minimal labour rights, account for a large share of experienced poverty. To the existing problems of economic development and growth have been added processes of material and social impoverishment. There have been imaginative improvisations to allay poverty. Substantial unemployment and irregular opportunities for paid employment have led to the strengthening of informal sector improvisations. In a reliable household survey, about 16 per cent of rural workers were found to be in the informal sector. Contrary to expectation, there were proportionally more men than women (Daghra and Al Saleh 2004).

A National Poverty Eradication Commission was established in 1997 and reported in 1998. A 'deep' poverty line reflecting absolute basic necessities, together with a 'relative' poverty line covering a broader range of necessities, including health care, education and housekeeping supplies, was formulated. The number of all households in Palestinian areas living under the relative poverty line declined slowly from 24 per cent in 1996, and 23 per cent in 1997 to 20 per cent in 1998, but then 'jumped to nearly three times that of its pre-September 2000 figure, that is, 60 per cent' (see Hilal, in Petmesidou and Papatheodorou 2006). 'Deep' poverty accounted for more than half those in relative poverty. Before the Intifada of September 2000, the decline in poverty had continued – because of 'the decline in unemployment rates resulting from an easing of closures by Israel on Palestinian areas, the increase in the employment opportunities in the Palestinian labour market and an increase in the average daily wage'. Severe restrictions on Palestinian labour, together with curfews and restriction of the movement of goods and people, preceded the second intifada of 2002. There were a number of research enquiries in different areas that showed conditions rapidly becoming worse. A World Bank report of February 2003 found that some 60 per cent of the population in the West Bank and the Gaza Strip were living under a poverty line of $2 per day. The number of poor tripled from 637,000 in 2000 to 2 million at the end of 2002 (*ibid.*; and see also research into new forms of social exclusion; for example, Abdalrahman 2004). The Palestinian economy had been dependent on the Israeli economy but then became completely dominated – through political, economic, and administrative restrictions, including military orders. Social cohesion was hard to foster under a policy of divide and rule, and skilful improvisations to engineer prosperity were obstructed.

What is distinctive about the Palestine case is the relatively successful tracking from year to year of economic and social conditions during civil conflict, and the combination of good internal and external research testimony about the entire situation and the causes of the deterioration of living conditions. The account by Hilal (in Petmesidou and Paptheodorou 2006) is therefore a model of what can be built upon elsewhere.

Mediterranean policies to restrict poverty: the case of Israel

Egypt and the Palestine Territory provide two different examples of severe poverty in a poor country, combined with impoverishment because of conflict. Israel is a very different third example of regional development. Between 1948 and 1952, the population of Israel tripled and welfare legislation began to be put in place. In 1953 the National Insurance Law was enacted. The aim was to eliminate poverty and ensure general well-being by means of wage and salary equity, progressive taxation, subsidies on basic consumption items and social insurance (Doron and Kramer 1991; Bar-Yosef 1996). A social transfer system on the lines of the schemes developed in many European countries came into being – as illustrated in Table 21.3. In these years, collective values were strong, and for long periods a Labour government was in power. This was a time when the kibbutz movement became strong (Talmon 1972). The list of transfer payments developed by government in those early years contains universal or group-benefit items – child allowance, maternity, old age and survivors, and unemployment benefits – and selective items – means-linked guaranteed income maintenance and housing subsidies. The transfers reduced poverty by nearly half. Nonetheless, in 1992, 17 per cent of individuals were found to be under the defined poverty line of 50 per cent of median income.

Although the Israeli poverty line reflects European practice and has come under repeated critical assessment, including examination of alternative options (see, for example, Silber and Sorin in Petmesidou and Papatheodorou 2006), the numbers estimated to be in poverty are high by European standards and appear to have grown (see also Alfandari 2004).

Table 21.3 Decline in overall inequality brought about by pensions and other social transfers, measured by the Gini index, and per cent of population in poverty, before and after transfers (2001)

Country	% decrease in inequality	Per cent in poverty – before transfers	Per cent in poverty – after transfers
Italy	–46.3	50.2	19.1
Greece	–36.6	47.5	21.8
Spain	–35.6	43.5	17.2
Portugal	–28.4	42.5	20.8

Note: Poverty defined in accordance with the EU convention of 60 per cent of median equivalised household income.
Source: Petmesidou and Papatheodorou, Tables 2.3 and 2.4.

The reasons given for continuing poverty are instability because of conflict, discontinuous forms of employment, dependence on arms and other imports, and growing inequality. The cost of the strategy followed during the 1990s and 2000s is now being impressed upon Israeli and world public opinion. Thus, a 2005 report by the Adva Centre in Tel Aviv, commissioned by Oxfam, concludes: 'The second intifada has hurt Israel deeply, resulting in a cessation of economic growth, in a lowering of the standard of living, in the debilitating of its social services, in the dilution of its safety net, and in an increase in the extent and depth of poverty' (McGreal 2005a, 2005b).

Lessons for the resolution of Mediterranean poverty

The illustrations I have given for some countries in the region convey three needs: (1) stronger regional organisation, together with collaborative economic and social development; (2) larger, and better systematized, redistribution of resources internationally and nationally, and (3) extension of anti-poverty policies to countries drastically impoverished by conflict. All three strands of argument gain from being placed within the framework of analysis of human rights.

Regional and political association and human rights

The representation of the four south European EU member countries, according to a variety of economic and social indicators, places them among the high-income, high human development group of countries in the world, and this differentiates them from most, if not all, of the countries in the rest of the region. This favourable position must, in part, be attributed to the convergence policies of the EU.

The recent and the proposed future stages of the enlargement of the EU have implications for the resolution of poverty throughout the Mediterranean region. Because of their history as national states and as member states, the countries of the EU are unlikely to dismantle the redistributive social transfer schemes that have greatly reduced poverty and enhanced social stability, and incidentally facilitated economic growth.

Criticism of the existing policy model and the need for a different model are illustrated separately for Algeria, Morocco, the Palestinian Territories, Lebanon and Turkey in Petmesidou and Papatheodorou (2006). For Europe, the Community Charter and the Maastricht Treaty avowed commitment to social policy within the EU, as did the later White Paper on *European Social Policy: A Way Forward for the Union.*

The core shared values included 'democracy and individual rights, free collective bargaining, the market economy, equal opportunity for all and social welfare and solidarity' (European Commission 1999). Minimum standards were needed for the cohesion of the union, along with high levels of employment and the European Social Model.

The alternative model would be one introducing substantial redistributive social services and social security, complemented by public employment-creation schemes and, through regional association and international development programmes, much higher levels of overseas aid.

Greater efforts to develop a job replacement and creation strategy in both public and private sectors; an expansion strategy for small businesses; a basic income strategy to bring together a minimum wage and a minimum level of benefit in coordinated form; and an NGO strategy to promote volunteer public service and environmental conservation, and improvement activities for particular groups of the population have all been argued (Townsend 1998: 23).

Overseas aid has been a policy priority in the union. Four of the EU countries are the only countries to have satisfied the agreement after the war to devote 0.7 per cent of GDP to overseas aid. There are proposals to increase the EU target to a flat 1 per cent of GDP (Atkinson 2002).

The right to social security: a Mediterranean policy?

What, therefore, might be the terms upon which an economic and social development strategy designed to defeat poverty might emerge from an organised regional association of countries encircling the Mediterranean? For each of the three groups of countries identified, there is a common theme of access, or access denied, to social security and to basic social services, in explaining a large part of the severity of poverty experienced. The four South European member states of the EU – Italy, Spain, Greece and Portugal – successfully reduced their inequality in the distribution of gross income through elaborate systems of social transfer. Table 21.3 gives a summary of measured reduction of income inequality, together with the poverty rate before and after social transfers.

The second group of countries – the Balkan countries – have social transfer systems which are both residual and embryonic – being the combined result of impoverishment and conflict after 1989 and slow progress toward the establishment or re-establishment of sufficient social transfers to reduce greatly the current poverty of large sections of the population, particularly those incapable of paid employment, but also those in part-time, temporary and low-paid employment.

In contrast to the first two groups, the third group of countries (MENA) appear to have meagre and patchy social transfer schemes.

The right to social security: current developments

The International Labour Organisation (ILO) has for many years played a leading role in reviewing developments in social security (for example, ILO 1984 and 2001). The organisation reported in 2001 that policies and initiatives which can bring social security to those who are not covered by existing systems were 'of the highest priority' (ILO 2001: 2). This meant necessary movement away from the informal economy and active promotion of employment programmes in countries with high rates of unemployment. There was little coordination of international and national anti-poverty policies. The problem of low coverage had 'taken a dramatic turn for the worse, as an increasing proportion of the urban labour force is working in the informal economy, inter alia as a result of structural adjustment' (ILO 2001: 57–8).

> The long-term challenge in social protection financing is global as well as national. If global economic players are allowed to undermine seriously the power of the nation state to levy taxes and social security contributions, then social security, which achieved such progress in the twentieth century, will face great uncertainties in the twenty-first. Governments must work together to preserve their sovereignty in these crucial areas (ILO 2001: 93).

Table 21.4 summarises total expenditure on social security by individual countries, expressed as a percentage of GDP, listing the Mediterranean countries, together with selected examples of other countries that are included for purposes of comparison. The table illustrates the sharp difference between the richest industrialised countries and both middle-income and low-income countries. Despite retrenchment by some countries in recent years, spending on public social security and services in the high-income countries has continued, on average, to grow. At similar levels of GDP, there remain wide differences in the commitment to social security of countries, with established outcomes for the numbers in poverty – whether assessed nationally or internationally.

There are examples of poor countries that are engaged in the rapid development of systems of social security. The two main types of social security in China are social assistance and social insurance. Schemes currently 'are either confined to urban or rural residents; as yet, there are none that cover the whole population. This will change

Table 21.4   Total public social security expenditure (including pensions and health care) as % GDP – selected countries – Mediterranean marked in bold lettering (1996)

Countries	Total	Pensions	Health care
High			
Sweden	34.7	13.8	6.1
Denmark	33.0	9.6	5.2
Finland	32.3	13.2	5.4
France	30.1	13.3	8.0
Germany	29.7	12.4	8.3
Norway	28.5	8.9	7.0
Netherlands	26.7	11.4	6.8
Austria	26.2	14.9	5.8
Israel	24.1	5.9	2.7
Italy	23.7	15.0	5.4
UK	22.8	10.2	5.7
Greece	22.7	11.7	4.5
Croatia	22.3	8.2	7.2
Spain	22.0	10.9	5.8
Middling			
Portugal	19.0	9.9	5.0
Canada	17.7	5.4	6.6
United States	16.5	7.2	7.6
Australia	15.7	4.6	5.7
Japan	14.1	6.8	5.6
Bulgaria	13.2	7.1	3.3
Romania	12.4	6.8	2.9
Brazil	12.2	2.4	2.1
Chile	11.3	5.9	2.3
Albania	10.9	5.7	2.4
Low			
Jordan	8.9	0.5	2.9
Tunisia	7.7	2.3	2.2
Algeria	7.6	3.3	3.4
Turkey	7.1	3.8	2.3
Egypt	5.4	2.3	0.9
Sri Lanka	4.7	2.4	1.5
Ethiopia	3.7	0.9	1.0
China	3.6	1.5	2.1
Morocco	3.4	0.5	1.0
India	2.6	–	0.9
Kenya	2.6	0.3	1.7
Ghana	2.2	1.1	1.0
Ecuador	2.2	1.2	0.3
Indonesia	1.7	0.0	0.6
Mauritania	0.8	0.2	–
Myanmar	0.7	–	0.5

Source: Adapted from ILO (2001: Statistical Annex).

as the Minimum Living Standard Insurance (MLSI), which, at present, is largely confined to the urban population, is extended to cover the whole rural population' (Hussain 2002). Extension of the MLSI to all rural areas was announced by the Chinese government in 2006.

The right to social security: the lessons of history

Universal protection against the risks of sickness, injury or disablement, unemployment and old age became a high priority for many governments in the war of 1939–45 and the early post-war years. This waned from the late 1970s into the 1980s and 1990s but is now being contemplated seriously again. Universalism – partly because of continuing developments in human rights – is back in fashion. Keynes was effectively Britain's chief negotiator at the UN at the time of its establishment and he was also a strong advocate of comprehensive social security (Townsend 2004). The USA had enacted a Social Security Act in 1935, and its scheme attracted wide interest when it began operation shortly before the country entered the war in 1941. The right to social security was included in the Declaration of Human Rights and later in the International Covenant and the Convention on the Rights of the Child.

The establishment of the interlocking social institutions of social security and social services was regarded in the industrialised countries as an achievement of the first magnitude. Inevitably, there were repercussions in the developing countries and especially those that remained colonised or were obtaining independence. What has to be explained is why, in later stages of development, poorer countries were denied the transitional schemes fathered by their predecessors on the road from poverty and pre-industrialisation.

Mahbub ul Haq, former special adviser to the UNDP, put the matter graphically:

> Rich nations channel an average of 15 per cent of their own GNP to their own 100 million people below a poverty line of around $5000 a year. The same nations earmark only 0.3 per cent of their GNP for poor nations which contain 1.3 billion people below an income level of $300 a year. What a telling contrast between national and international safety nets! (ul Haq 1995: 374).

Partly because of such demonstrable inequality, the International Labour Office has taken up the agreed decision, among other agreements for action, reached by 117 governments after the World Summit for Social Development in Copenhagen in 1995, to extend universal social security (see Figure 21.2).

307

Authority	Social Security	Adequate Living Standard
Copenhagen World Summit for Social Development (1995)*	**Action Programme: 38 –** Social protection systems should be based on legislation and … strengthened and expanded …to protect from poverty people who cannot work …Actions to this end should include: a) …programmes providing universal basic protection, and social security insurance programmes… b) developing … a strategy for a gradual expansion of social protection programmes that provide social security for all… c) ensuring that social safety nets associated with economic restructuring are considered as complementary strategies to overall poverty reduction and an increase in productive employment [and are] short term by nature… d) exploring a variety of means for raising revenues to strengthen social protection programmes…	**Action Programme: 8.** Equitable and non-discriminatory distribution of the benefits of growth among social groups and countries and expanded access to productive resources for people living in poverty. 35. Governments should cooperate to meet the basic human needs of all, by a) ensuring universal access to basic social services, with particular efforts to facilitate access by people living in poverty and vulnerable groups; b) creating public awareness that the satisfaction of basic human needs is an essential element of poverty reduction: these needs are closely interrelated and comprise nutrition, health, water and sanitation, education, employment, housing and participation in cultural and social life…

Figure 21.2

Note: *The 1995 Copenhagen Declaration and Programme of Action, following the World Summit for Social Development, was partly set within a human rights framework (see UN 1995: 50–5.)

Human rights at times of conflict and national impoverishment

Up to the present time, anti-poverty policies have concentrated largely on conditions in settled societies. Civil conflict and open warfare have marked countries that, for short or long periods, have resisted attempts to measure or monitor impoverishment, and the changes taking place in the living standards of different sections of population. As a consequence, many countries have been set aside in the tracking of worldwide poverty.

Yet, in retrospect, historians have shown that large-scale and immediately reactive policies, rather than grudging and often belated gradualist small-scale policies, have been needed in crisis situations affecting millions of people. In an individual's life, there are, of course, the risks of severe impoverishment – as a result of bereavement, disability, sickness, retirement and unemployment. But sudden, and catastrophically severe, impoverishment also applies to populations as a whole – as a result of economic collapse, earthquakes or tsunami, war and civil conflict. The framework of human rights becomes practically, as well as theoretically, relevant. The large-scale preventative/casualty-alleviating model, rather than the softer retrospective model, in dealing with sudden, crippling, poverty seems to deserve new scrutiny for its international potentialities as a better model on which to base future action.

Conclusion – creative use of the human rights framework

The increasing readiness by countries to recognise and ratify human rights is a source of inspiration for the creation of cooperative alliances of states in overcoming poverty. There are three principal reasons for such a conclusion, as dramatically illustrated in examining the Mediterranean. One is that the framework of human rights offers a basis for more systematic, and coordinated, and therefore more effective, anti-poverty policies, especially in countries not torn by conflict. The southern EU member states in the Mediterranean region have gone a long way in recent decades to establish social transfer systems to reduce poverty, and yet can still gain, in new global conditions, by judicious use of comprehensive entitlement to multiple material and social need. Thus, the right to social security (Article 22 of the Universal Declaration as well as Article 9 of the International Covenant and Article 26 of the Convention on the Rights of the Child) is universal and, therefore, poses serious questions for international programmes of aid that are strictly and often confusingly conditional or selectively discriminatory, as well as narrowly targeted.

Historically, the rich countries established universal systems of social security to meet the needs of large numbers in their populations who had become sick, disabled, bereaved, elderly or otherwise were in families with dependent needs. Schemes for social assistance or voluntary insurance were often replaced by group benefit or comprehensive social insurance schemes covering the needs of particular groups in the population. Sometimes, comprehensive coverage of certain groups – for example, children or the elderly of a particular age – was paid for through direct taxation. These systems were introduced to meet the needs of dependency and poverty. Economic and social prosperity was built partly on that basis. The systems are now elaborate and account for a substantial percentage of GDP.

These relatively prosperous countries, therefore, are ill-qualified to deter poor countries from attempting to go down the same path. There are precedents at the present time of countries in other regions that are now beginning to take social security more seriously – for example, in Brazil, South Africa and China – and of developing and middle-income countries steadily expanding social security as a system aiming for social stability as well as a minimum social platform on which to base economic production. In the Mediterranean region, the Maghreb countries, Algeria, and Turkey offer less emphatic illustrations of such a positive strategy. On the basis of historical and contemporary precedent, an urgent programme for the reduction of poverty might be developed for the poorest countries in the Mediterranean region – such as Egypt, as illustrated above, and for the region as a whole.

There is a second reason for deploying the human rights framework in eliminating poverty. There are acute problems of civil conflict in the region, involving countries that are often excluded from the international debate about the elimination of world poverty. The Palestinian Territories and Lebanon are discussed above. The problems of impoverishment as a result of conflict have been brought to the forefront in considering future international and national policies to resolve poverty. This transforms the nature of the anti-poverty strategies, and policies that must attract priority attention.

Third, the human rights instruments epitomise universal, or comprehensive, measures, and all Organisation for Economic Cooperation and Development (OECD) countries, in substantially diminishing national poverty, have developed and maintained elaborate systems of comprehensive social insurance and other group-directed non-means-tested schemes within social security. In examining the social security model, it is important to distinguish the past success of non-means-tested schemes within those systems. In nearly all OECD countries, it is the non-means-tested schemes that account for the bulk of redistribution, that continue to be popular, and that allow least obstructed entry to paid employment and enhanced hours of paid employment. It is this feature of social security that can accommodate and strengthen sustainable economic growth.

There is, therefore, redoubled need for a preventative anti-poverty strategy in the Mediterranean and elsewhere. This would take the form of accelerated protection of human rights, including the rights to social security, an adequate standard of living, minimum nutrition, safe water, sanitation, health, and education – through new cross-national measures. But it would also take the form of broader measures to prevent war as well as poverty, because, today, war and extensive civil conflict often generate collapse into severe poverty among the mass of the population. By means of such a dual strategy, the prospects of social stability, both internally and externally, can be greatly strengthened.

Altogether, then, there exists a strongly established, and widely accepted, human rights framework for developing successful anti-poverty agreements among the Mediterranean countries. The following conclusions can be drawn:

1 Regional initiatives are required to develop a strategic approach to anti-poverty policies in countries around the Mediterranean, drawing on the social transfer precedents in Europe.

2 Human rights instruments offer the best analytical and strategic framework for action to understand and reduce poverty.

3 Impoverishment of countries as a result of conflict can be remedied not only by a combination of resolute, quick reaction, and stronger UN forces but also by basic social security and social services for all.

4 International social policies have become essential – international laws, taxation and contributions via UN agencies, the G8 and the transnational corporations – to match domestic policies.

Acknowledgements

This chapter draws extensively on a concluding commentary of mine in M. Petmesidou and C. Papatheodorou (2006), *Poverty and Social Deprivation in the Mediterranean Area: Trends, Policies and Welfare Prospects in the New Millennium*, Centre for Research on Poverty (CROP), London, Zed Books. I wish to acknowledge the help I obtained from the editors of that book and Else Oyen, the director of CROP in Bergen, and also colleagues at the University of Bristol and the LSE, particularly David Gordon and Shailen Nandy, in the former, and Conor Gearty, Christine Chinkin and Athar Hussain, in the latter.

References

Abdalrahman, M. (2004) 'Expansion and Annexation Wall and social exclusion in the West Bank in Palestine', paper presented at the IAOSS-IASS Joint Conference on Poverty, Social Exclusion and Development: A Statistical Perspective, Amman (November).

Alfandari, Y. (2004) 'A new absolute measure of poverty in Israel', paper presented at the IAOSS-IASS Joint Conference on Poverty, Social Exclusion and Development: A Statistical Perspective, Amman (November).

Atkinson, A.B. (2002) '1% of £10,000 billion', in P. Townsend and D. Gordon (eds) *World Poverty: New Policies to Defeat an Old Enemy*. Bristol: Policy Press.

Bar-Yosef, R.W. (1996) 'Israel: resistance of poverty to change', in E. Oyen, S.M. Miller and S.A. Samad (eds) *Poverty: A Global Review. Handbook on International Poverty Research*. Oslo and Boston: Scandinavian University Press/UNESCO.

Braithwaite, J., Grootaert, C. and Milanovic, B. (2000) *Poverty and Social Assistance in Transition Countries*. New York: St. Martin Press.

Brown, G. and Wolfensohn, J. (2004) 'A New Deal for the world's poor', *Guardian*, 16 February.

Commonwealth Human Rights Initiative (2001) *Human Rights and Poverty Eradication*. New Delhi: CHRI.

Daghra, S. and Al Saleh, J. (2004) 'Informal sector as a determinant of poverty; the Palestinian Case', paper presented at the IAOSS-IASS Joint Conference on Poverty, Social Exclusion and Development: A Statistical Perspective, Amman (November).

Donkor K. (2002) 'Structural adjustment and mass poverty in Ghana', in P. Townsend and D. Gordon (eds) *World Poverty: New Policies to Defeat an Old Enemy*. Bristol: Policy Press.

Doron, A. and Kramer, R.W. (1991) *The Welfare State in Israel: The Evolution of Social Security Policy and Practice*. Boulder, CO: Westview Press.

European Commission (1994) *A White Paper – European Social Policy: A Way Forward for the Union*. Brussels: European Commission.

European Commission (1999) *A Concerted Strategy for Modernising Social Protection*. Brussels: European Commission.

Goodin, R.E., Headey, B., Muffels, R. and Dirven, H.-J. (1999) *The Real Worlds of Welfare Capitalism*. Cambridge: Cambridge University Press.

Haq, M. ul (1995) 'Putting people first', in U. Kirdar and L. Silk (1995) *People: From Impoverishment to Empowerment* (sponsored by UNDP). New York: New York University Press.

Hussain A. (2002) 'Urban poverty in China: incidence and policy responses,' in P. Townsend and D. Gordon (eds) *World Poverty: New Policies to Defeat an Old Enemy*. Bristol: Policy Press.

International Labour Organisation (2001) *Social Security: A New Consensus*. Geneva: ILO.

Kakwani, N. and Son, H.H. (2006) *New Global Poverty Counts*. Working Paper Number 20. Brasilia: UNDP International Poverty Centre.

Korayem, K. (1996) 'Egypt: comparing poverty measures', in E. Oyen, S.M. Miller and S.A. Samad S.A (eds) *Poverty: A Global Review. Handbook on International Poverty Research*. Oslo and Boston: Scandinavian University Press/UNESCO.

McGreal, C. (2005a) 'Israelis use barrier and 55-year-old law…', *Guardian*, 31 January.

McGreal, C. (2005b) 'Hidden costs of Israel's occupation policies', *Guardian*, 25 February.

Neri, L., Ballini, F. and Betti, G. (2004) 'Poverty and inequality mapping in Albania using census data', paper presented at the IAOSS-IASS Joint Conference on Poverty, Social Exclusion and Development: A Statistical Perspective, Amman (November).

Robinson, M. (2003) Speech at the Launch of Child Poverty in the Developing World, London School of Economics. Bristol: Policy Press.

Talmon, Y. (1972) *Family and Community in the Kibbutz*. Cambridge, MA: Harvard University Press.

Townsend, P. (1998) 'The future world of work', Proceedings of the European Social Policy Forum 98 (24–26 June). Brussels: European Commission.

Townsend, P. (2004) 'The restoration of "universalism" – the rise and fall of Keynesian influence on social development policies', in T. Thakandiwire (ed.) *Social Policy and Development*, Geneva: UNRISD.

Townsend, P. and Gordon, D. (2002) *World Poverty: New Policies to Defeat an Old Enemy* (especially chapters 14 and 17). Bristol: Policy Press.

United Nations (1995) *The Copenhagen Declaration and Programme of Action: World Summit for Social Development*. New York: United Nations.

World Bank (1990) *World Development Report 1990: Poverty*. Washington, DC: World Bank.

World Bank (2000) *Balancing Protection and Opportunity: A Strategy for Social Protection in the Transition Economies*. Washington, DC: World Bank.

World Bank (2004) *World Bank Indicators*. Washington, DC: World Bank.

Chapter 22

States of acknowledgement: the politics of memory, apology, and therapy[1]

Claire Moon

My memory, sir, is like a garbage heap.

Jorge Luis Borges

Thrown from a half-tamed horse, a 19-year-old Argentinian boy is left paralysed.[2] After his accident Funes is confined to bed, his eyes fixed on a fig tree in the back yard or contemplating the intricacy of a nearby spider's web. The 'chronometrical' Funes marks out his days by recalling his past in microscopic detail and with linear precision. He summons up the leaves, tendrils and fruit that made up a familiar grapevine, the forms of the southern clouds at dawn, and the dying flames of a fire that once had warmed him. Funes reminisces in 'real' time, taking a whole day to reconstruct the events of a whole day. Before his accident, Funes had been 'what all humans are: blind, deaf, addle-brained, absent-minded'. All his life he had 'lived as if in a dream, looking without seeing, listening without hearing, and forgetting everything'.[3]

'Looking without seeing', 'listening without hearing', 'forgetting everything': Borges presages unwittingly in these themes the problems to which a late-twentieth-century era of memorial politics promised to respond, and to which Stan Cohen's *States of Denial* attends. This politics of memory has been animated by many states in transition either from conflict or to democracy in diverse social and political contexts such as Chile, South Africa and East Timor in response to state denials of atrocity. It has attempted to come to terms with the legacy of state atrocity by challenging official denials that, for example, disappearances, torture and mass killings were an object of state policy, by establishing public records of past state crimes and endorsing new official memories of political violence. These processes have provided a counterpoint to past denials. They have endeavoured to 'look *and* see', to 'listen *and* hear', and to '*remember* everything'.

The political challenges of post-atrocity memorialisation have been concentrated around the following issues: *what* to remember and what to forget, *how* to remember and *when* to stop remembering in order to turn to the future and to prevent the social and political stagnation that might be an effect of dwelling upon the past too much, a condition upon which Funes's paralysis appears to be a parable. This, in Nietzsche's words, is the art of determining 'the boundary at which the past has to be forgotten if it is not to become the gravedigger of the present'.[4] The health of individuals and nations, he argues, is contingent on their ability to 'forget at the right time as to remember at the right time'.[5] These are compelling issues of perennial personal, social and political relevance, which in turn invoke a range of familiar clichés: 'coming to terms with' or 'closing the door on' the past, or 'turning the page' and 'closing a chapter' of history. The proverbial nature of these sayings makes them no less enigmatic, but in spite of their perplexing implications they have become the common leitmotifs shaping the recent political imagination of nation-states seeking to atone for the crimes of the past.

This chapter takes up Cohen's unique contribution to these questions. It concentrates upon the politics of acknowledgement, and the ways in which memory, apology and a therapeutic paradigm of understanding the consequences of atrocity are employed in its service. It argues, in particular, that more thought needs to be given to the implications of the therapeutic model because it has become one of the dominant frameworks through which the effects of atrocity have been thought out and 'healing' administered. Cohen has provided some important starting points for this agenda, and yet much needs to be done for the implications of therapy at the political level to be properly explored and understood.

Memorial politics: dealing with past injustice

For Cohen, acknowledgement is 'the active and infrequent opposite of denial', and one of the central empirical problems of *States of Denial* is 'to discover the conditions under which information is acknowledged and acted upon' at the political level. This, Cohen argues, is essential because denial – shutting out any awareness of the suffering of others – is not an aberration but 'the normal state of affairs'.[6] In order to understand how acknowledgement might be brought about, Cohen is first concerned with mapping out the multiple strategies of denial, both at the level of the individual and at that of the state.

Cohen's first explication of state denial appeared in an influential article in 1995, an article that played a pivotal role in initiating early debates on issues around how states might deal with a violent past, a practice and field of enquiry that came to be known as 'transitional justice'.[7] This article made a specific intervention into debates around lustration (purging individuals from public office) that was central to early discussions about transitional justice in Eastern Europe. In this article, Cohen delineates various strategies by which states repress or dispose of evidence of state crimes. His arguments constituted a crucial 'missing link' in thinking about dealing with the past, because he constructed a careful typology of state denial while connecting this typology to normative claims that were then being put forward by states in transition about the necessity of revealing the truth about past atrocity.

Since that article, Cohen has, characteristically, marked out a distinctive terrain within broader transitional justice debates. *States of Denial* appeared in 2001 to great critical acclaim, a culmination of many years' work and thinking about what he describes as 'the sociology of denial'.[8] The book integrates, in a unique assessment, social psychological, psychiatric, criminological and political insights about denial and its consequences at levels of state, society and individual. The book iterates in detail the grammar of denial, composed of multiple practices and states that collude to obviate, conceal and avoid the truths of human suffering. For Cohen, denial has three manifestations. 'Literal denial' is to state that 'this is not happening'. A literal state denial would be to deny the existence of a reported abuse such as disappearances. 'Interpretive denial' would be to suggest that what is happening is 'really something else'. Interpretive denial might acknowledge the facts of the matter ('yes, torture took place'), but it will use euphemisms ('moderate physical pressure') to conceal or to moderate the facts. 'Justificatory denial' will interpret the facts ('detention without trial') in relation to something else deemed to be of greater importance ('for the sake of national security'). As such, the atrocity might be admitted but will be subordinated to a grander scheme in which, for example, the curtailment of individual liberties is presented as necessary to the security of the collective.

Cohen's taxonomy presents an impressive account of state denials, but his is also a hopeful project in which he also presents a litany of modes of acknowledgement that might be used to 'deal with the past'. Overcoming the painful legacies of violent state repression at the collective level entails diverse and multiple strategies that are, at least initially, supposed to be traumatic before they are finally 'liberating'. Disinterring repressed truths about past violence frequently entails opening graves to assert that yes, against the official record, a massacre did happen, and yes, here are the bodies of those who had 'simply disappeared'. These strategies are crucial first steps in the process of acknowledging what had been denied all along, setting the record straight and 'freeing' individuals and nations from the terrors of the past.

From the 1980s to the present, the question of acknowledging and accounting for state crimes became especially relevant in the context of three sets of historical and geopolitical changes. First, it was intrinsic to a number of transitions from military regimes in Africa and Latin America; second, to the disintegration of the Soviet Union and the concomitant collapse of communist regimes in Eastern Europe; and third to the demise of apartheid in South Africa. The influence of the end of the Cold War and the bipolar order that it involved is implicated, to a greater or lesser degree, in all three contexts. The specific transitional contexts within which the question of dealing with the past has arisen have been twofold: first, from various forms of military regimes and dictatorships to more democratic orders; and second from civil conflict to peace. It is a mark of the increasing significance of international human rights regimes that the question of dealing with the past, of establishing the truth about, and accounting for past horror, has today become so crucial a feature of the governance of these particular transitional moments. Well-known examples include Chile in 1990, El Salvador in 1991 and, most notably, South Africa, which began a long process of investigating its apartheid past in 1995.

Transitional justice emerged out of political contexts circumscribed profoundly by compromises between either old and new regimes or parties to conflict, and it has seen its formalization in the institution of the truth commission, which, typically, has investigated past atrocity by soliciting testimonies from victims, and offering amnesties to perpetrators.[9] Truth commissions present a prime institutional site, in Cohen's words, 'for the symbolic recognition of what is already known but was officially denied'.[10] The truth commission emerged as a new instrument concerned expressly with revealing 'the truth' about past atrocity, a truth that had long been denied, concealed, repressed, covered up. Truth-telling and amnesty are often cast by its protagonists as having restorative objectives, directed toward reconciling old enemies, ethnic or racial groups, and reinstating the nation-state as the central moral community. As such, recent practices of remembering and dealing with the past have manifested not 'justice as we know it' but 'justice compromised'. That is to say, it has now become a truism that something must be sacrificed in the process of seeking justice during political transition if democracy is to be forthcoming. This sacrifice is retributive justice, which is frequently subordinated to the broader objective of establishing and consolidating upon political order and nation building. The memory of past atrocity and the type of justice that accompanies it are thus hitched to the evolution of a democratic polity, eventually becoming a footnote to a future democratic order.

Transitional memory has, at particular points in its history, gone under the injunction *nunca mas* ('never again'), indicating that, while retrospective, memory work is oriented ethically toward the future prevention of the conditions under which gross violations might come to be perpetrated yet again. Thus, memory is charged with a preventive mandate in which the past is seen as a repository of recoverable lessons by which the future might be guided.[11] The purported value of collective retrospection lies in the assumption that humanity might learn from its mistakes and make positive attempts to prevent the repetition of conditions giving rise to the perpetration of atrocities in the first place. On this account, the past is endowed with a moral gravity which demands a response in the present.[12]

South Africa's Truth and Reconciliation Commission (TRC) is the indisputable *locus classicus* to which all subsequent truth politics have referred. It was remarkable for bringing into the political domain the more usually private rituals of apology, remorse and atonement in recognition of past atrocity perpetrated by the state and its opponents. The TRC claimed to provide a 'road map to those who wish to travel into our past' in order that South Africa may 'reach out to a new future' of national unity and reconciliation.[13] But it recognised that remembering the past could undermine rather than further national unity and reconciliation. The TRC faced the problem of how to determine the point at which to stop remembering and look to the future, of when to draw the line between past and future, between retrospection and hope. The truisms 'turning the page' and 'closing the door on the past' help to convey the idea that too much remembering can hinder hope and action, which are essentially future-oriented. Borges' story presents a metaphor of this problem, of managing the process of remembering, of the 'recovery of the past', without becoming defined by that past at the expense of the present.

The TRC heralded an international transitional justice industry characterised by a proliferation of truth commissions, transitional justice institutes, and research centres. This industry was, in its early days, marked by exuberant plaudits for the truth commission, then a new institution, an exuberance that has since, and necessarily, been tempered by more critical evaluations of its aims, assumptions and achievements.[14]

Inevitably, and simultaneously with this new phenomenon of political praxis, the study from the mid-1990s of the TRC in particular and truth commissions more generally generated transitional justice as a new, although now thriving, academic subfield of the disciplines of politics, law, anthropology and sociology, which connected most forcefully to the field of human rights. This is a field into which Cohen has made characteristically striking and productive interventions. His 1995 contribution is remarkable for its persistent freshness and insight.[15] Long after many of these early debates have ceased to be relevant to the contemporary state of transitional justice, Cohen's appraisal of its practices and principles, developed in *States of Denial*, endures.

Technologies of acknowledgement: the political apology

One strategy of acknowledgement is the simple statement of apology. Cohen is unfashionably, although refreshingly, suspicious of this:

> To deny past horrors is immoral, but to make collective apologies for the past to whole groups (or their representatives on earth decades or even centuries later) is preposterous. In July 1999, the Florida-based Lutheran Orient Mission Society went on a Reconciliation Walk through the Middle East, tracing the path of the Crusaders from Cologne to Jerusalem. The 400 apology hikers ended up praying in Jerusalem to mark the 900 years since the Crusaders slaughtered Jews, Muslims and Eastern Rite Christians. Instead of being solemnly greeted and *thanked* by religious and political leaders, they should have been treated with total derision and told to pack their crosses and go back home.[16]

Cohen's dismissal notwithstanding, the apology has inserted itself with some force into the scene of transitional justice in particular, and into recent political life more generally.[17] This 'politics of regret'[18] has been widely pervasive, and has lodged itself within a broad range of reflective junctures and reparatory gestures in the life of the nation. It has been deployed by states seeking to atone for repressive policies or atrocities of the past, addressing a range of issues, including slavery, war crimes and the legacies of colonial rule. Japan and the USA have been among the most prolific issuers of apologies for past wrongs, some might say for important reasons, although these often have been issued in restricted ways that either deflect complete responsibility or obviate material consequences such as actual financial reparations. Japan has made official although limited apologies for wartime atrocities in

Nanking, and to the (inappropriately named) Korean 'comfort women', and in October 1998 the Japanese Prime Minister Keizo Obuchi issued a written apology to President Kim Dae Jung for abuses perpetrated during Japan's 35-year occupation of South Korea. The USA under Bill Clinton offered apologies on a whole range of issues, national and international in dimension. In 1993 Clinton endorsed an 'Apology Resolution' for the role of the USA in the overthrow of the kingdom of Hawaii in 1893. In 1997 Clinton openly considered a public apology for slavery in what has become a fiercely contested debate, although, notably, his intervention appeared to some as an attempt to deflect calls for financial reparations for slavery – far more costly and committed than a verbal apology.[19] In the same year, Clinton apologised to the black male victims of the notorious 40-year Tuskegee experiment in Alabama into the long-term effects of syphilis, between 1932 and 1972. Medical researchers enrolled 400 black, male, syphilis sufferers with the false promise of free health care. Despite the treatability of the disease, the men received no medication to prevent its deleterious effects. Elsewhere, France's Jacques Chirac apologised in 1995 for the French role in the persecution of Jews under German occupation; Britain's Tony Blair, in 1997, apologised for the English role in the Irish potato famine; and, in 2000, Australia's John Howard apologised for the decimation of the Aboriginal population. Australia even has a state sanctioned 'Sorry Day' to consecrate state remorse for federal policies that forcibly separated Aboriginal children from their families.

In light of these and other episodes, it has been suggested that the end of the last century is memorable precisely for what the Nigerian writer Wole Soyinka has called a *fin de siècle* 'fever of atonement'.[20] A wave of public contrition has accompanied national attempts to acknowledge and emerge from the legacies of past injustice, to which these numerous examples attest, and this has contributed to the appearance of a new national master narrative of remorse, atonement and healing of the individual and social body. The public theatricality of the apology lends dramatic force to this particular narrative. Roy Brooks has investigated this apologetic proclivity in some detail, arguing that political apologies are much more complex than the mere 'canonization of sentimentality'. For Brooks, public displays of accountability and remorse have a profound impact upon society, improving the 'national spirit and health' and consequentially raising its 'moral threshold'.[21] Brooks argues that apologies make a crucial contribution to establishing and acknowledging accountability for past wrongs, and, most importantly, apologies create the possibility of a future free from repeated abuses. However, the apology is a highly contentious and problematic mode of redress for a number of reasons, not least because its proliferation in recent political life has been widely lauded. First, accounts like Brooks' lend credence to a teleological account of the 'moral maturation' of a Western political sensibility, evidenced by the proliferation of apology as a political instrument.[22] Second, it is anything but clear that there is a causal relationship between apology and acknowledgement and reduced frequency of future abuses, as Mendeloff has argued.[23]

For Cohen, the absurdity of the political apology lies in two things; its collective nature and in the idea that it may be offered by proxy down through the generations and centuries. Cohen disparages the very possibility that an apology can be offered to a *group* of people, and yet this has very much become the mode of recent political apologies. In order to understand what this type of apology attempts, it is crucial to distinguish between micro-apologies and macro-apologies where the former typically involves one-to-one encounters, and the latter concerns interactions between large groups of people or nations. The form, function and meanings of the interpersonal apology are, inevitably, transformed by its transposition onto political life, in which the apology requires an institutional framework. Common to both interpersonal and political life is the attempt, through apology, to make amends, to restore a relationship and to establish a 'morally appropriate relationship' between parties.[24] The conditions of apology at the interpersonal level must also be met at the collective level. The apology should contain an expression of remorse, be sincere, and contain a promise on behalf of the apologiser to refrain from similar actions in the future. As such, the apology is Janus-faced, simultaneously looking backward to past wrongs, and forward to the future in its promise to prevent any repetition of the wrong.

However, the political apology and its public performance – it is not *just* about making amends with the offended group but about displaying a 'moral integrity' to other onlookers or interested parties – should make us suspicious of its sincerity. There is an extant, end-oriented functionality to the political apology, and the risk of offering the apology entails a specific gain to be achieved that in itself detracts from the sincerity of the 'true' apology that is offered without hope of any return, as Derrida has argued in his discussion of forgiveness.[25] In addition, the political contexts within which apologies are offered condition the very appearance of the apology in the first place. A new and stable regime is more likely to offer an apology for the abuses of the previous regime, as was the case in Aylwin's Chile. This apology serves the added purpose of providing a moral boost for the new regime which both distinguishes and distances itself from the previous regime through the act of apology. The apology thus functions as a strategy of national and international order whereby the new regime attempts to consolidate upon legitimacy nationally, simultaneously signalling to other states its readiness to belong to the liberal international order. Further reasons for Cohen's suspicion of this type of apology include its use to assuage a guilty conscience, an example of which could be Clinton's apology for late intervention in the Rwandan genocide; by perpetrators to escape punishment; or as a substitute for punishment in contexts where amnesty is a feature of transitional justice.[26]

More troubling, or at least more complex, perhaps, is the proxy apology offered on behalf of antecedents to descendants of those who suffered, who themselves may still suffer the effects of the 'original' deed as, for example, the proponents of reparations for slavery in the USA today argue.[27] To what extent can descendants make sincere declarations of responsibility for past harms? And to what extent do they have the authority to do so? One of the most thoughtful responses to this question to date has been presented by Nicholas Tavuchis. He negates the proxy apology because 'an authentic apology cannot be delegated, consigned, exacted, or assumed by the principals, without totally altering its meaning and vitiating its moral force'.[28] The proxy apology demands a particular theatricality, role-playing and a suspension of disbelief. The person offering the apology must play the role of the perpetrator, and those accepting the apology must act as those offended against. When an apology is granted, the apologiser is, by definition, giving up the 'moral high ground' by making an admission of culpability. S/he relinquishes power to the recipient of the apology, thereby, as Lazare notes, 'transferring the humiliation from the victims to the offenders'.[29] Tavuchis concurs with this by suggesting that the apology is a 'vulnerable expression', even a 'form of self-punishment' that elevates the offended against.[30]

Cohen's refusal to engage fully with the apology is, I suspect, symptomatic of his concern with the way in which the apology poses, problematically, as a moral rather than a political response to the past. Indeed, Cohen consigns his consideration of the apology to the heading 'post-modern acknowledgement' in which he argues that, while 'harmless enough', the apology is mainly a function of a time in which 'all history has become revisionist'.[31] Although Cohen does not elaborate further upon the apology, as his brief dismissal is at odds with the meticulous anatomy of denial and of the multiple strategies that might be brought to bear on its repudiation that he presents in the rest of his book. I would suggest, however, that the apology falls squarely within, and indeed is a prime exemplar of, the contemporary strategies and meanings of acknowledgement to which Cohen dedicates significant discussion.

Technologies of healing: the therapeutic model

For Cohen denial is a normal state of affairs. Yet, this interpretation is contrary to popular understanding. In popular psychology, denial is an abnormal condition that must be confronted and undermined. The instant recognisability of this platitude reflects the profound and widespread influence of the therapeutic model. This paradigm is grounded in a grammar of trauma and suffering that claims that repressed memory causes untold difficulties, that 'revealing' or truth-telling leads to healing, and that 'closure' on the past must be reached in order for the present to be lived and the future to be faced. Cohen notes the imperatives of this model thus: 'in populist psychology, denial is an aberrant state, something to be exposed, confronted and undermined. People must face up to their "troubling recognitions".'[32] He goes on: 'persistent denial is taken to indicate personal pathology (dissociation, disintegration, splitting) and political atrophy (living the lie, cultural amnesia)'.[33]

Transitional states have borrowed from this lexicon of individual pathology with the effect of creating the notion that the nation is a 'unitary self' to which pathologies of the self – dissociation, disintegration, splitting – are made to seem relevant to the political domain. In a set of pithy questions, Michael Ignatieff questions the ways in which states have appropriated therapeutic concepts.[34] He asks 'do nations, like individuals, have psyches? Can a nation's past make a people ill as we know repressed memories sometimes make individuals ill? Conversely, can a nation… be reconciled to the past, as individuals can, by replacing myth with fact and lies with truth?' Ignatieff's questions point to the problems inherent in the transposition of the therapeutic frame onto a political context. It entails a problematic conflation of individual suffering and psychological trauma with that of national suffering and trauma. And yet, as Cohen argues, 'psychological concepts cannot simply be transposed to the political level' because 'they are not grounded in roles and relationships' and neither are they 'universal brain mechanisms, but highly contextualised linguistic devices and cultural practices that vary across time and social space.'[35]

However, this fusion of the individual and national psyche has become the singular article of faith by which states in transition conduct investigations into the past, and therapeutic assumptions about healing the individual, social and political body have become the touchstones by which the effects of atrocity are understood and responses to it devised. Many of those who spoke before South Africa's TRC articulated suffering by recourse to popular psychotherapeutic metaphors such as 'healing' and 'closure'. Desmond Tutu, Chair of

South Africa's TRC and one the most charismatic and enthusiastic proponents of therapeutic justice, urged that 'the wounds of the past must not be allowed to fester'; that they must 'be opened', they must be 'cleansed' and 'balm must be poured on them so they can heal'.[36] The platitudes that underpin Tutu's assumptions are neatly summarised by this statement by Terry Dowdall:

> The Truth and Reconciliation Commission... can contribute to rehabilitation by breaking the culture of silence. *We all know* that concealing, suppressing or repressing painful memories commonly brings in its wake psychological symptoms: stress, anxiety, and depression. *We also know* that speaking about upsetting things in a supportive and affirming setting makes people feel better [emphasis added].[37]

Such commentaries enforced and compelled these assumptions by reflecting popular truisms about denial and mental health: that recalling buried memories or truths about past trauma can help to alleviate anxiety and emotional suffering, and prevent the unsettling and disruptive 'return' of the past.

This application of therapeutic assumptions to the political domain requires investigation because therapy as a moral frame of reference has distinctive features that produce particular political effects. Indeed, Cohen has recently noted that such an investigation is part of the 'unfinished agenda' of topics connected to acknowledgement. He suggests that the 'specific influence of the therapeutic model, with its lexicon of trauma, hidden suffering, repression, "closure" and belief that "revealing is healing" requires closer attention.[38]

The work of James Nolan on the 'therapeutic state' is helpful in furthering this agenda because he provides a useful map of the political deployment of therapy.[39] Nolan has argued that the therapeutic ethos, unlike traditional moral orders, is essentially self-referential and looks to the self rather than to natural law or divine reason to provide the moral boundaries of society and the means of its negotiation.[40] In processes of acknowledgement, such as truth-telling, perpetrators are required to hold up their 'inner selves' for public scrutiny and judgement, and to express remorse as an outward sign of inner change. Public belief in such confessions is grounded in an understanding that humans are generally inclined toward the good and are capable of reform.

Second, central to this ethos is an 'emotivist ethic' that emphasises open displays of emotion.[41] Displays of emotion, expressing in particular suffering or remorse, are intimately tied to truth. On this account, truth is accessible through emotional demonstrations rather than through the rational judgement and deliberation common to formal legal processes. Truth is also connected to the process of healing where catharsis and 'relief' are weighed in proportion to the open communication of feelings.

Third, the therapeutic perspective pathologises human action. Particular modes of behaviour are represented as if they were diseases needing proper diagnosis and medical treatment. A pathological approach concentrates on causal factors, symptoms and development of a condition, and upon the necessary professional interventions required to ameliorate disease.

These approaches to the treatment of the effects of wartime atrocities have a particular historical lineage that can be traced from the treatment of shell shock during the First World War to the invention of post-traumatic stress disorder (PTSD) in the wake of the Vietnam War, the key moment in the development of psychiatric responses to war trauma.[42] The incorporation of PTSD into the lexicon of psychiatric diagnostic categories in 1980 brought with it a shift in interpretation of soldiers' agency in war, since the diagnosis took into account the conditions under which war was fought rather than the 'intrinsic' psychological dispositions of individuals.[43] War trauma, or PTSD, came to be understood in terms of the structural and functional 'changes' produced by the experience of a 'psychologically traumatic event that is generally outside the range of usual human experience'.[44] Pathological perspectives on war trauma have particular implications for conceptions of human accountability for the perpetration of atrocity. As Derek Summerfield has argued, the invention of PTSD 'was a powerful and essentially political transformation: Vietnam veterans were to be seen not as perpetrators or offenders but as people traumatised by roles thrust on them by the US military' that 'legitimised their "victimhood" and gave them "moral exculpation"'.[45]

There are two important consequences of the therapeutic perspective. First, it is arguable that it contributes to a culture of impunity, for if everyone is a victim, no one is responsible. Achille Mbembe has argued that acknowledgement without punishment has created particular problems in post-TRC South Africa, where a culture of 'corruption, impunity and non-accountability is fast becoming the norm'. He states that 'public and private lives are conducted as if forgiveness was an inalienable right. Nobody is being responsible for his or her conduct, everybody is presumed innocent until proven guilty.'[46] Therapy has displaced the moral order represented by retributive responses to atrocity, operating *in place* of retribution and compelling 'self-reform' without punishment. This displacement, it seems to me, is but one effect of the amnesty process in South Africa for which therapy discourse attempted to compensate.

Second, therapeutic perspectives feed into and legitimise self-understanding as victimization. In South Africa, victims became the constitutive subject of the new political order. The political implications of this are astutely observed by Michael Humphrey, who notes that the TRC staged the 'spectacle of victim pain and suffering in order to publicly project the power of the state'.[47] In other words, the TRC inverted the logic of apartheid power thus: where the power of the former regime was founded on the state's capacity for terror, the power and legitimacy of the new order is grounded in the public performance of the state's power to restore and heal.

Concluding remarks

Funes thinks his immobility a 'minimum price to pay' for his now infallible memory, but he dies of congestion of the lungs not long after his accident. Certainly, it is arguable that, as Cohen has noted, personal and political life can be conjoined in one loose sense: excessive dwelling on the past may indeed impede action and prevent us from 'getting things done'.[48] Indeed, John Torpey has warned against the way in which the past has become the new horizon of political life.[49] He argues that reflective politics is inherently conservative because it is radically decoupled from a progressive political agenda that has its eyes on the future.

However, the time will come when this preoccupation with the past is replaced by a new understanding of the place and significance of atrocity within political life. Indeed, the so-called 'war on terror' and concomitant national 'security' agendas in the USA and the UK have already provided a new and public justificatory discourse for the resurgence of torture, suggesting a slippage back into an era of 'denial'. This development gives the lie, somewhat, to some of the assumptions embedded within the politics of acknowledgement – that knowledge ('truth') and acknowledgement ('official admission') – prevent the repetition of future abuses. However, Cohen is, typically, already ahead of the game. *States of Denial*'s incisive analysis of the strategies of denial offers powerful resources for the demolition of this discourse. It is my suspicion that Cohen will, once again, carve out the moral and political agenda through which the new justifications of state crimes can be challenged and repudiated.

Notes

1 My thanks go to Martin McIvor for his, as ever, lucid and insightful comments on an early draft.

2 I recount here the short story by Jorge Luis Borges, 'Funes the memorias', *Labyrinths*, London: Penguin, 1970, 87–95.

3 Borges, 'Funes the memorias', 91.

4 Friedrich Nietzsche, 'On the uses and disadvantages of history for life', *Untimely Meditations*, Cambridge: Cambridge University Press, 1993, 62.

5 Nietzsche, 'On the uses and disadvantages of history for life', 63.

6 Stanley Cohen, *States of Denial: Knowing About Atrocities and Suffering*, Cambridge: Polity Press, 2001, 249.

7 Stanley Cohen, 'State crimes of previous regimes: knowledge, accountability, and the policing of the past', *Law and Social Inquiry* (1995), 20:1, 7–50.

8 *States of Denial* won the Division of International Criminology, American Society of Criminology award for outstanding publication in 2001, the British Academy Book Prize in 2002, and it was a runner-up for the *Los Angeles Times* Book of the Year award in 2002.

9 The identification of a 'truth commission phenomenon' was precipitated by a now widely cited article in the mid-1990s: Priscilla B. Hayner, '15 truth commissions – 1974 to 1994: a comparative study', *Human Rights Quarterly* (1994), 16, 597–655. I would like to add a strong caveat to the general claim that amnesties have become a typical feature of transitional justice. There are multiple ways in which amnesty has been used, such that it is impossible to state that it is a singular and unified feature of such processes. In any investigation, each case of amnesty must be evaluated within the specific context in which the amnesty was instituted, and heed taken of the particular form it took – individual, blanket, in exchange for truth, and so on.

10 Cohen, *States of Denial*, 13.

11 The alleged relationship between remembering and prevention is one that, while widely assumed and promoted, has not been established empirically, as David Mendeloff argues in his article, 'Truth-seeking, truth-telling and post-conflict peace-building: curb the enthusiasm', *International Studies Review* (2004), 6, 355–380. However, it is difficult to suggest how a strict and causal relationship between the two might be established empirically. It is perhaps enough to suggest at this point that this is an under-explored assumption that founds much of the work of truth commissions.

12 The idea of 'coming to terms with the past' is not new, however. For a broader historical account, see Jon Elster, *Closing the Books: Transitional Justice in Historical Perspective*, New York: Cambridge University Press, 2004.

13 *Truth and Reconciliation Commission of South Africa Report*, Cape Town: TRC, 1998, 1 (1), 5–6.

14 Influential pieces of enthusiastic literature include Priscilla Hayner, *Unspeakable Truths: Confronting State Terror and Atrocity*, New York: Routledge, 2000, and Neil J. Kritz (ed.), *Transitional Justice: How Emerging*

Democracies Reckon with Former Regimes, vol 1–3, Washington, DC: United States Institute of Peace Press, 1995. Examples of more critical interventions include Mendeloff, 'Truth-seeking, truth-telling and post-conflict peace-building' and Richard A. Wilson's excellent book, *The Politics of Truth and Reconciliation in South Africa: Legitimizing the Post-Apartheid State*, Cambridge: Cambridge University Press, 2001.

15 Stanley Cohen, 'State crimes of previous regimes: knowledge, accountability, and the policing of the past', *Law and Social Inquiry* (1995), 20:1, 7–50.

16 Cohen, *States of Denial*, 248.

17 Examples of apologies in transitional justice include South African F.W. De Klerk's 1993 apology for apartheid, that of former Guatemalan president Álvaro Arzú in 1998 for atrocities perpetrated against indigenous Guatemalan citizens during the country's 36-year civil war, and that of former Chilean president Patricio Aylwin to the victims of the Pinochet regime in 1991 on publication of the Truth and Reconciliation Commission's final report.

18 Jeffrey K. Olick and Brenda Coughlin, 'The politics of regret: analytical frames', in John Torpey (ed.), *Politics and the Past: On Repairing Historical Injustices*, Lanham, MD: Rowman and Littlefield, 2003, 37–62.

19 For an overview of these debates, see John Torpey, 'Paying for the past: the movement for reparations for African-Americans', *Journal of Human Rights* (2004), 3:2.

20 Wole Soyinka, *The Burden of Memory, the Muse of Forgiveness*, New York: Oxford University Press, 1999, 90.

21 Roy Brooks (ed.), *When Sorry Isn't Enough: The Controversy over Apologies and Reparations for Human Injustice*, New York: New York University Press, 1999.

22 See Olick and Coughlin, 'The politics of regret' for an excellent refutation of this teleological account.

23 Mendeloff, 'Truth-seeking, truth-telling and post-conflict peace-building'.

24 Jean Harvey, 'The emerging practice of institutional apologies', *International Journal of Applied Philosophy* (1995), 9:2, 62.

25 Jacques Derrida, *On Cosmopolitanism and Forgiveness*, London: Routledge, 2001, part II.

26 For a discussion of some of these issues, see Trudy Govier and Wilhelm Verwoerd, 'The promise and pitfalls of apology', *Journal of Social Philosophy* (2002), 33:1, 67–82.

27 For an excellent discussion of this, see John Torpey, *Making Whole What Has Been Smashed: On Reparations Politics*, Cambridge, MA: Harvard University Press, 2006, Chapter 4.

28 Nicholas Tavuchis, *Mea Culpa: A Sociology of Apology and Reconciliation*, Stanford, CA: Stanford University Press, 1991, 49.

29 Aaron Lazare, *On Apology*, Oxford: Oxford University Press, 2004, 52.

30 Tavuchis, *Mea Culpa*, 8.

31 Cohen, *States of Denial*, 246–7.

32 Cohen, *States of Denial*, 249.

33 Cohen, *States of Denial*, 278.

34 Michael Ignatieff, 'Articles of faith', *Index on Censorship* (1996), 5, 110–122.

35 Cohen, *States of Denial*, 50.

36 Desmond Tutu, *Truth and Reconciliation Commission of South Africa Report*, Cape Town: TRC, 1998, 1 (1) 27.

37 Terry Dowdall, 'Psychological aspects of the Truth and Reconciliation Commission', in H. Russell Botman and Robin M. Petersen (eds), *To Remember and To Heal: Theological and Psychological Reflections on Truth and Reconciliation*, Cape Town: Human and Rousseau, 1996, 34.

38 Stan Cohen, book review of Torpey, *Making Whole What Has Been Smashed*, *Contemporary Sociology*, forthcoming. While Cohen makes this remark with regard to Torpey's book, it is a comment that may be applied more generally to the state of research on transitional justice.

39 James L. Nolan, *The Therapeutic State: Justifying Government at Century's End*, New York: New York University Press, 1998.

40 Nolan, *The Therapeutic State*, 3.

41 Nolan, *The Therapeutic State*, 5–7.

42 For a discussion of the historical development of psychiatric responses to war trauma, see Ben Shepherd, *A War of Nerves*, London: Jonathan Cape, 2000.

43 See American Psychiatric Association, *Diagnostic and Statistical Manual of Mental Disorders*, third edition (Washington, DC: APA, 1980), commonly referred to as 'DSM-III'.

44 DSM-III, 236.

45 Derek Summerfield, 'The invention of post-traumatic stress disorder and the social usefulness of a psychiatric category', *British Medical Journal* (2001), 322.

46 Achille Mbembe, 'South Africa's second coming: the Nongqawuse syndrome', *openDemocracy*, 15 June 2006 (www.openDemocracy.net).

47 Michael Humphrey, 'From victim to victimhood: truth commissions and trials as rituals of political transition and individual healing', *Australian Journal of Anthropology* (2003), 14:2, 171.

48 Stan Cohen, book review of Torpey, *Making Whole What Has Been Smashed*, *Contemporary Sociology*, forthcoming.

49 Torpey, *Making Whole What Has Been Smashed*, 19.

Chapter 23

Denial in Cambodia

Margo Picken

1

In the early 1990s, Cambodia was described as a war-torn society in need of reconstruction, then as post-conflict and in transition, and most latterly as a managed democracy.

Stan Cohen's *States of Denial* has often come to mind in a country where denial, and complicity with denial, seem to be present at so many levels. How is this possible and is it normal?

2

Norman Lewis in *A Dragon Apparent* describes Cambodia in 1950, then a protectorate of France, in somewhat idyllic terms even with insurgents fighting for independence in the remoter parts of the country. Cambodia became independent in 1953. Some now look back on the next years, by no means perfect, as halcyon. For what followed was the secret US bombing of Cambodia; the coup against the king in 1970 and the rise of Marshall Lon Nol; the Nixon Doctrine; Kissinger; Cambodia engulfed in the Vietnam War; furious bombing for peace; absolute control by Pol Pot and the Khmer Rouge from 17 April 1975 until defeat by Vietnam in early January 1979. Then retreat to camps on the Thai border, where the Khmer Rouge was rearmed for what were to be ten more years of cold war. The fall of the Berlin Wall in 1989. The adoption in Paris of Peace Agreements for a Comprehensive Political Settlement for Cambodia in 1991. The arrival of the United Nations Transitional Authority for Cambodia in I992 to oversee an end to armed conflict, neutralise Cambodia's political environment, and organise free and fair elections. Cambodia was equipped with a new constitution in September 1993, a new parliament, King Sihanouk back on the throne, a market economy, and hopes for a peaceful future.

Except that the political environment was not neutralised, the Constitution was not respected, and the past was not discussed, disclosed, closed, acknowledged or forgotten.

3

Many of Cambodia's educated people died or fled during the 1970s. Cambodia's history has been largely interpreted and written by outsiders – the French for the earlier period; Australians and Americans in more recent times. Modern history is not taught in the schools or universities. Discussion of history is not encouraged; official versions of history are mistrusted.

Official and personal records were lost and destroyed, leaving private memories, a slow piecing together of lives, a striving to understand what happened and why, and scope for invention and reinvention.

Recent history and the present are passionately contested by Cambodians and outsiders alike, full of hearsay, replete with ignorance and denial. Everyone is entitled to a view and opinion, and in the absence of records and authoritative voices, who is to say who is right and wrong?

History tends to be truncated and simplified, as if there were no underlying continuity, itself a form of denial, into the French colonial time, Prince Sihanouk's People's Socialist Community, the Lon Nol time, the Pol Pot time, the Vietnamese communist time, the UNTAC time, and the bewildering now.

For many, the landmarks are simple and few. When was this pagoda built? Before Pol Pot. Before the war. Which war?

The older generation speaks French, but English is now the main second language, seen as essential for Cambodia's integration into the global economy, the region and the world. Perhaps the more forward-looking learn Chinese. Cambodians sent on scholarships abroad in the 1980s came back with languages, now largely forgotten, from the Soviet Union, Eastern Europe, Cuba. Thousands of Cambodians were repatriated from camps on the Thai border in the early 1990s, some having spent a decade and more confined to small spaces. Cambodians, new citizens of Canada, Australia, the USA, France, often children when they fled or never having lived in Cambodia at all, came later, fluent in new languages, but not always in Khmer.

Cambodia's leadership has enjoyed extraordinary continuity, its prime minister now having served for more than 20 years, the longest serving head of government in the region. The reference point for this leadership is Pol Pot, a period from which Cambodia is held to be still emerging. Progress is measured by then and now; and failure is impossible in such a setting. Proud of having kept the peace, the leaders see and present themselves as the only force for stability. The monarchy has also survived, now a shadow of its former self.

4

Angkor with its splendid temples testifies to a glorious past, giving Cambodians their roots, and personal and national pride. Zhou Daguan, a Chinese envoy, who visited in the thirteenth century described daily life in Angkor. The empire disintegrated soon thereafter. France claims to have rediscovered the temples in the mid-nineteenth-century. They became a jewel in her Oriental crown. India came as temple restorer in the 1980s, France reclaiming her place in the early 1990s when UNESCO declared Angkor a World Heritage site. France and Japan now lead a never-ending project of temple restoration and conservation, while fending off get-rich-quick predators and *son et lumière*. Siem Reap has become a gold-rush town.

. Cambodia is best known for its temples and its killing fields. These are what most interest the tourists who come in ever increasing numbers. The children of Angkor sell pirated photocopied guides to both. The children are multi-lingual; their knowledge of world capitals is considerable. For the children, Angkor and Pol Pot are history. Whatever their understanding of that history is another matter.

5

This is one story, perhaps typical.

I am from a poor village. I was born in 1961. I can remember when I was eight. My father was then a rice farmer. We were very poor. Our house was made of wood, and the roof and walls of palm leaf. We all slept in one room, with our two cows. When he was not in the rice field, my father made wooden shutters and bamboo cages for fighting cocks. My primary school was about a kilometre from home, and my older sister and I walked there every day. I usually got up at 4 or 5 a.m. to help my parents. In the rainy season, I helped to plant rice. I also looked after the cows. My mother rarely bought food from the market, because we did not have enough money. My father and I fished in the pond near our house. We ate fish paste and eggs when there were not enough fish.

I was nine when the first war of my life started in 1970. In March, my father joined a demonstration against Lon Nol, who had made a *coup d'état* against King Norodom Sihanouk. There were two demonstrations that month. The first one was bloody. I do not remember the date, but at 9 a.m. an aeroplane flew over the demonstration and fired on demonstrators for several hours. There were many army trucks and soldiers who shot down people, and chased demonstrators who ran away, and killed them. One man who survived told us that wounded people who begged for their lives were killed instantly. Many people were injured and killed. In the days after these events, some people were arrested and killed in my village.

My village could be reached by both Lon Nol's soldiers and the force of the National United Front, which, at that time, was called the Force of the West because this force was always hiding in the mountains to the west of where we lived. Later it was called the Khmer Rouge. The Force of the West always came to my village at night to meet the villagers and to persuade them to join their force. When they came, all the dogs in the village started barking. This could be heard by government soldiers, who would then start shelling. After this happened several times, the Force of the West said that if any family had dogs that barked when they were there, the owners would be held responsible. So the villagers killed their dogs. We had a dog named Chak. No one in the family could bear to kill Chak, so we gave him to our neighbour. When he came, Chak sat on the bed and when our neighbour opened the sack, Chak jumped into the sack by himself, as if he understood the situation. All my family was very sad.

In 1971 and 1972, the presence of the Force of the West and Vietnamese soldiers, which were then called the Viet Cong, increased in my village. There was frequent fighting between the Lon Nol soldiers and the Force of the West. Our commune fell under the control of the Force of the West in 1973. That year I joined the commune youth organisation. We built dams, farmed and grew potatoes to support the soldiers at the front. In early 1974, I joined another youth group and built dams. Revolutionary music was played through a big loudspeaker, and at night there was theatre. We worked day and night. The dam still exists today and has been renovated.

A few months later, I and other young people in my village joined the Khmer Rouge army. We thought that there was no safe place for us, that it was better to fight to end the war faster. I first joined the commune, then the district army. I was the youngest in my group. I remember that when I stood my rifle on end, it was taller than me.

In early 1975, my group was integrated into the regional forces of South-West Region. Some friends of my age were not chosen. They selected older men, because forces were needed for fighting against

Phnom Penh. But, the commander of my group said I could join. Not long after, we were sent to Kandal province. Every 15 minutes, artillery shelling was launched from Phnom Penh. One day there was fierce fighting against government forces that had tanks and helicopters. Many of my colleagues were killed. Their bodies were indescribable; some were torn apart and covered with dark smoke. They were carried for burial up to 50 kilometres away. I think I was lucky again, because I was in the fighting but not at the front. Sometimes I was a messenger, sometimes a fisherman, sometimes I cooked for the soldiers.

After the war ended on 17 April 1975, my group was sent to Takeo province near the Vietnamese border. We travelled from Phnom Penh by ox cart and bicycle. We stopped at my village. My family did not own anything anymore. What we had had before, had become the property of the state and everything was decided by the village chief. My mother sent my younger sister to ask his permission to pick a coconut for me to eat from what used to be our coconut tree.

In early 1976, the soldiers had enough rice, and there was plenty of fish, but in late 1976, there was no rice and we ate gruel, and sometimes red corn. We built canals and dams day and night. Everyone had to dig and carry two cubic metres of earth a day. During that time, the authority was called Angkar. Angkar considered that those who had stayed with it since the war started and had never been on the government side were good people, and selected them to live along the border. My family was among them. I did not dare to ask permission to visit my family, but I could stop and see them because they lived on the road I travelled on. My mother was very ill. She got worse and worse, so I decided to tell my commander about her. He was a good man, and gave me some medicine for her. I managed to help a few times, but the commune medic was unhappy with me, because at that time people like my mother were unable to get good medicine. The medicines used in hospitals were made from the roots of trees by steaming or cutting and grinding them. Later my mother was sent to the provincial hospital. My father and sisters wanted to help look after her, but the hospital staff said no, that they would take care of her. I and my family have not had any information about my mother since.

In September 1978, I was sent to China to study oil refining. I went with about 150 persons. When we heard the news that Vietnam had invaded Camboidia we all felt anxious and lost hope. We stopped studying refining. My group learnt how to repair army trucks, and the other group learnt about landmines. We returned to Cambodia by ship. Some were assigned to fight inside Cambodia. I stayed on the border. At first, there were few people but more and more arrived from

Cambodia. Some could not walk because they had not eaten for a long time; others could walk but they were thin and pale.

In late 1984, all resistance groups at the border came under attack, and most were moved closer to the border. Civilians were moved inside Thailand into refugee camps. I moved to a camp in Tratar province. I got married at the camp. I studied English by myself and worked as assistant to the camp administrator. I returned to Cambodia in the middle of 1992, through the repatriation programme of UNHCR under the Paris Peace Agreements. I worked in an UNTAC warehouse in Phnom Penh. Now I take care of my five children. I work hard, and I wonder what will happen next.

6

The killing fields, Pol Pot and the trials.

This is what journalists come to Cambodia to write about; this is what captures the world's imagination; this is why they are sent. The trials will cost some $56 million, almost entirely funded by foreign governments, primarily Japan. They are budgeted to run for three years and to try six to ten senior leaders of the Khmer Rouge and those most responsible for the crimes committed during the period of Democratic Kampuchea which lasted for three years, eight months and 20 days.

No before and no after.

And yet, Cambodians need and want to understand that terrible period when from one-quarter to one-third of the population are estimated to have died. They live with their broken lives, confused about what happened and why. Everyone lost someone, and everyone now over 30 was directly affected. The stories they tell are the stories of victims, and are often eagerly told. Yet many must have done what they knew was wrong, witnessed or stood by in order to survive. These are the stories that are harder to tell, that you do not always want to hear, that need to be listened to. Revenge can be sour, as George Orwell said.

Denial compounding denial for Cambodia was also victim of a larger world. China, Vietnam, Thailand, the USA, France, the USSR, and others have their own stories to tell, all played their part.

Sometimes it seems that the outside world is more preoccupied with the trials than Cambodians themselves. For time has gone by and most have found ways of coping. They struggle to manage difficult lives in a harsh modern world. They are looking for justice now and for a better future for themselves and their children.

Will the trials bring Cambodians the understanding and answers they are looking for? Will they explain what happened and why?

Will they open a discussion about before and after? Will they help to establish a common memory that all can acknowledge and agree on? Or will they send Cambodians back into a past, to be punished again in the name of justice? Will they condemn a few while exonerating the many for crimes committed yesterday and today? Will they put an end to impunity? Or will they be another form of denial in disguise? Will the court be an instrument of denial or will it help to bring about its downfall?

Will the trials open up a road to better lives?

7

Cambodia has a large expatriate population. Half the national budget is provided by foreign governments and bilateral and multilateral agencies, its development 'partners' helping Cambodia to recover, with staff staying for three, four, or at most five years.

Transients helping transients.

Known as the donors, they are valued not so much for the ideas, but for the money they bring. Money is what matters. Consultants with a thousand recipes for recovery, generating papers and plans and reports and assessments, and PowerPoint displays.

A world apart. A parallel universe, as one author has described it.

The donors are also the captive of a government whose good faith many doubt. While assisting, donors also legitimise and rescue it from its responsibilities. They can also be blamed when things go wrong, and they are under pressure from home to report stories of success. Is having international helpers present a means and method of denial?

In such a setting, human rights organisations often bring bad news which is not welcome. They are pressed to be balanced and constructive, not to speak out, to attribute the wrongs not to a problem of accountability, but to one of capacity, the result of the Khmer Rouge. Are they also at risk of becoming accomplices to denial?

Democracy through technical assistance, advisory services, government ownership, donor coordination, capacity building, deconcentration and decentralisation in a constant tug of war. The OECD guidelines call for coordination, simplification and harmonization, but finding common ground can sometimes be difficult.

Is it getting better? Is it getting worse? Is the cup half-full? Is the cup half-empty? What do the statistics say? Are the statistics reliable? Is poverty being reduced? By how much and for whom? And what about corruption, corruption, corruption? What do we do about that? Is it inherent? Is it endemic? Should we have a law? What kind of law? Should assets be declared? By whom to whom?

Counter-terrorism compromising safety, the language of development masking and cluttering reality. Treaties replaced by goals. Human rights too radical an agenda. Justice to be advanced by stealth.

When to speak out? When to be silent? What is the reality that cannot be talked about?

The realists, the pragmatists, the cynics, the sceptics, the optimists, the balanced ones, the impatient ones, the long view and next generation ones, the idealists, the ideologues, the arrogant ones, the muddled ones, the meddling ones, the well-meaning ones. Diplomats pursuing diverse interests.

Some donors say the people must be consulted; the people must participate; their voices must be heard; they must be empowered. Participation and consultation, seminars and workshops in grand hotels, training for building capacity, the drafting of laws. Donors say that there must be the rule of law, that unless the law rules investors will not come. The private sector upon which Cambodia's future is held to rest. The garment factories trucking young women to work in better conditions than in neighbouring countries, the lucky ones with a monthly minimal pay of $45.

8

Turning a blind eye; looking on the bright side.

Cambodia has seen high levels of GDP in the last decade. Almost all its wealth is concentrated in Phnom Penh where 15 per cent of the population lives.

Phnom Penh, a city on the make, its back turned on rural Cambodia, and the poor.

Win Win.

Huge villas, drug dealers, traffickers, brothel owners, child sex, casinos, murky companies, unknown shareholders, humvees, AK-47s, Chivas whisky, Lexus cars, diamond rings.

And oil in the offing.

The poor, the 'beneficiaries' wait.

They wait to become less poor.

Step by step.

Uncertain and afraid.

'We can see everything, we have pineapple eyes', the Khmer Rouge said, and the expression has stayed.

How many generations will it take?

Why do we need to wait? What about now?

The ship sails on. You will go. We will stay.

What is to be done?

9

Is a Cambodia possible, not of the very rich, of vast plantations, economic export zones, factories producing on the cheap, but of smallholders, community-managed forests and fisheries, family businesses, and people living decent lives in peace? Is it possible to rekindle hopes, to pay doctors, nurses, teachers, civil servants a living wage, to stop the stripping and stealing of Cambodia's land and forests in the name of development? Is this possible and more for this small country of 13 million people that yearns for and deserves better?

Could such a vision find inspiration in the Hindu creation myth, a centrepiece of the temple of Angkor Wat, in which the gods of heaven and demons of the underworld together churn the sea of milk to produce the elixir of life?

Could it capture world imagination in the same way as the Khmer Rouge trials do? If not, why not? Perhaps that should be the starting point, the first question.

Note: The views expressed are those of the author alone.

Chapter 24

'Does any of this matter?' Transitional justice and the Israeli–Palestinian conflict*

Ron Dudai

In a book honouring Stanley Cohen, it may be appropriate to start with a *New Yorker* cartoon. One dog is talking to another; the caption reads:

> There they were, sitting around the dinner table, knocking off a bottle of Côtes-du-Rhône and blathering about the Middle East – you've never heard such shallow, simplistic reasoning in your life – and one of them turns to me and says, 'And what do you think, Barney? What do you think we should do?' and all I could come up with was 'Woof.' I felt like such an ass.

Indeed, the volume of commentary being produced about the Israeli-Palestinian conflict is overwhelming, and by now hardly any of it is deep or original. One does often feel like an ass. Yet, one avenue has remained under-explored: the potential contribution of the field of transitional justice, or truth and reconciliation, to the prognosis and diagnosis of this gloomy conflict. Stanley Cohen was one of the very few scholars who pursued this line of enquiry. In a short paper written immediately after the 1993 Oslo Agreement, Cohen engaged in a rare attempt to apply the themes of transitional justice, much in vogue in Chile and South Africa at the time, to the Israeli-Palestinian case. He started with presenting the basic ideas of this field: the keywords of justice, truth and reconciliation; the demand to 'confront the past'; the assumption that a political transition has to be complemented, or followed, by mechanisms that acknowledge past abuses, in order to move forward to a more peaceful and stable future. He then moved on to the particularities of the Middle East, and posed a simple question: 'Does any of this matter?'[1]

This was not a rhetorical question. Achieving the first, interim, agreement between Israelis and Palestinians was precarious enough, and to add to this challenge the burden of 'dealing with the past' may have seemed imprudent. Moreover, transitional justice was usually applied in different contexts, of moving from oppression to democracy in a single society, rather than in the framework of separation into two states that the Israeli-Palestinian process entailed.

At the time, Cohen suggested two potential answers. One position was that 'no just resolution is possible without an honest confrontation of the past. Without a full acknowledgment of injustices, the ghost of history will return.' Yet, the other position was that 'it does not matter what goes on in people's heads, hearts or souls. A structure of political and legal compulsion has to be implemented which gives people no choice but to conform.'[2] This chapter revisits the question more than a decade afterwards and with the benefit of hindsight it argues: Yes, it does matter.

Transitional justice and the Israeli–Palestinian peace process: it did matter

Transitional justice can be broadly defined as: 'a field of activity and inquiry focused on how societies address legacies of past human rights abuses'.[3] Societies emerging from periods of repression or violent conflict around the world have turned to diverse models of truth commissions, prosecutions in domestic and international courts, 'lustration' or disqualification from public office of offenders, opening government files for public scrutiny, compensations and reparations, public apologies and acts of commemoration and memorization.[4] None of these has featured throughout the Israeli-Palestinian peace process, and proposals for such mechanisms have not been engaged with even in the margins of the political process.

Since the beginning of the peace process in 1993, the political leaderships – Israeli and Palestinian, as well as American and other foreign actors – seem to have adopted Cohen's second suggested position. They have reasoned that the best chances of achieving wide support for compromise is through selling their constituencies a 'realistic' agreement, one that will not necessitate anyone's acknowledgement of past wrongdoing. The focus was on 'security' discourse and instrumental arguments, while moral and international law aspects were ignored. Indeed, there was hardly any mention of human rights throughout the process.[5] In sum, 'the leaderships of both the Labour Party and the PLO, bent on pragmatism, may not have considered human rights language, trying to dispense with rhetorical burden'.[6]

This position was taken early on: 'During the early negotiations of the Oslo Accords, the negotiators decided not to debate historical issues, realizing that neither could convert the other to its view of the past'.[7] It has remained intact in the later final-status negotiations as well. An emblematic position was articulated during the 2000 Camp David Summit by Elyakim Rubinstein, then Israel's attorney-general and one of its chief negotiators: 'the peace process should not be the arena in which historical truth is pronounced'.[8] Sandy Berger, who was a senior member of the American team in these negotiations, expressed a typical view: 'The key is to get the parties talking about what they will do, not what others have done to them – endless diatribes from Israelis about the grievous sins of the Palestinians and the Palestinians about the grievous sins of the Israelis [...]. The key here is to get them to focus on the future and not the past.'[9] Yael Tamir, an Israeli philosopher and peace activist, was similarly hostile to the idea: 'If the peace process is to move forward, it cannot proceed on the basis of an investigation of the past', she argued.[10]

Yet retrospective conclusions were different. A recent study by the US Institute for Peace, on the failure of the Israeli-Palestinian negotiations, for example, found that 'a clear conclusion' is that 'history cannot be ignored in negotiations of communal conflict'.[11] Why is that the case? Bell argued that in many conflicts there is also a 'meta-conflict', or 'a conflict on what the conflict is about'.[12] This is undoubtedly true for the Israeli-Palestinian conflict, which is immersed in collective memories. As Makovsky observed, 'Outsiders often assume that the main source of conflict between the Israelis and the Palestinians is how to deal with the West Bank and Gaza. In fact, the conflict runs far deeper. Palestinians and Israelis have radically different historical narratives [...] they go to each side's self-conception as a historical victim, and they have engendered much mutual hatred.'[13] It can be argued that it is not so much the questions of how to handle the water resources or Jerusalem which prevent the two sides from reaching peace; there are agreed tentative principles regarding how to solve all of these issues. Yet, these questions are not confronted directly and honestly by either side, because the 'meta-questions' – is it an anti-colonial struggle or exterminatory war; who is the aggressor and who acts in self-defence; and so on – prevent both sides from dealing sincerely with the substantial issues on the table.

The decision not to engage with the past and acknowledge human rights violations by both sides has sustained the meta-conflict, and thus made resolving the conflict much harder. For example, in their post-mortem of the Camp David summit, Agha and Malley note how the lack of recognition of the past by Israel led to bitterness and impasse over the negotiated issues such as land and settlements: when Israelis were 'offering' land and being 'generous', the Palestinians felt that the 'land was not given, but given back';[14] this was perhaps more important to the failure than disagreements over percentage of land transfer. As Quandt sums, 'historically rooted sensitivities on both sides had a clear effect on negotiations'.[15]

Three communal conflicts that captured the international attention in the 1980s have advanced to interim peace agreements in the 1990s that won their architects a Nobel Prize for peace: South Africa, Israel/ Palestine and Northern Ireland. That only the South African prize seems today not premature is but one indication that a formal agreement between leaderships is not enough and that 'unless a negotiated settlement is underwritten by other efforts to bring two antagonists together, it may not last'.[16] In 1993, soon after the signing of the first Oslo Agreement, Yitzhak Rabin, then Israel's prime minister, said that 'in order to bring an end to the state of war in the reality of the Israel-Arab conflict, there must be a change in the psychological components, the perceptions and interests, not only of governments and diplomats, but also of the people involved in the conflict'.[17] Unfortunately, neither he nor his Palestinian counterparts did enough to respond to this task. One of the lessons from the successful South African process, where the leaderships not only negotiated among themselves but also made sure their constituencies confronted the legacy of past mutual demonization, is that 'it would be wrong to suggest that subjective factors simply "arise" fortuitously. It is the task of political actors to *create* the circumstances for them to occur.'[18]

The sidelining of 'dealing with the past' ignored the fact that issues of collective memory are crucial in the two parties' consciousness and without responding to them the chances of moving forward are rather low. Zerubavel argued that 'the Israeli-Palestinian conflict grew out of this clash between their respective memories and their refusal to acknowledge the problems inherent to their divergent reconstructions of the past'.[19] Cohen noted that while often 'historical appeals' come only from leaders and intellectuals, in some cases, such as the Israeli-Palestinian, 'individual participants on each side have an acute political conscience and a detailed historical sense', and as he describes: 'The discourse is melodramatic: legendary heroes and persecuted victims, conquest and defeat, blood and revenge [...] this is like a Verdi opera – killers on both sides pause between firing to recite nostalgic and epic texts'.[20] It is important to understand the special nature of the Israeli society in that respect: 'The Israeli culture of denial does not derive from state communism or military dictatorship [...] denial of the injustices and injuries inflicted on the Palestinians is built into the social fabric. The Jewish public assent to official propaganda, myths and self righteousness results from willing identification.'[21]

Yet many of the negative features of Israeli culture are mirrored also by the Palestinian side; Jamal accurately observes that 'the most salient feature in the Israeli discourse is Palestinian guilt and Israeli innocence'[22] – but the reverse is also true. On both sides, notions of exclusive collective victimhood are prevalent and have adversely affected attempts of conflict-resolution. Gladstone once observed that the root of the Anglo-Irish conflict is that 'The English remember nothing, while the Irish forget nothing'. Translating this diagnosis to the Middle East, we could say that both sides remember nothing of their own crimes, and forget nothing about the crimes committed against them. The decision not to confront the past means that the collective notions of exclusive victimhood, among both Israelis and Palestinians, inform their behaviour during the long process of negotiations. Thus, each violent attack by extremists from either side easily derails the process, 'confirming' for each side that the other only wishes to destroy them.

Responding to these denials and myths is no less important than any attempt to reach yet another sophisticated technical formula for security arrangements or control of Jerusalem. While the latter are indeed at the core of the peace process, it has to be complemented by addressing past abuses. As Fateh Azzam, a Palestinian human rights activist, has put it, we need 'to confront the denial of reality that exists on both sides of the political fence [...] unless we acknowledge what happened in the past, it will continue to come up'.[24] Uzi Benziman, one of Israel's leading commentators, wrote recently that 'One hundred years of mutual blood-letting weighs on both sides' consciousness [...] it would be difficult to quiet this emotional maelstrom with diplomatic agreements alone [...] what is needed is therapeutic intervention, which could be supplied by launching a process of reconciliation'.[25]

What kind of truth?

This recognition is the first step, but we need to transform the abstract notion of 'therapeutic intervention' into concrete truth-seeking mechanisms. And in order to understand what exactly is the 'truth' that needs to acknowledged, we need to look at the exact type of denials that were used. Cohen has identified several types of official denials of atrocities:

- Literal denial (e.g., X was not tortured; he was never even detained)

- Interpretative denial (e.g., it was not torture, just tough interrogation)
- Implicatory denial (the suspect was a ticking bomb: torture was justified).[26]

Denials of the first type were common in South Africa, for example. The government denied that some anti-apartheid activists were detained or killed, but claimed, for example, that they had escaped and gone undercover. The regime employed secret death squads, activists were killed and their bodies were thrown into secret graves.[27] Similar literal denials were common in some Latin-American countries, embodied by the practice of 'disappearances'. This has led, in most countries, to transitional justice mechanisms that sought factual knowledge: finding out the fate of the disappeared, designating guilt to specific security services.

Yet, by contrast, Israel's human rights violations are performed, broadly speaking, in an open and acknowledged way. Blunt literal denial is rare in Israel, and so is denial of responsibility. When the South African government wanted to assassinate an opponent, it did so either without claiming responsibility or detained the person and killed him while pretending that 'he had an accident' in custody. Israel's government, on the other hand, has an open policy on assassinations: the prime minister announces that Sheikh Yassin is to be killed, an F16 is being sent, and at a press conference, the government takes responsibility. That is also true for the Palestinian atrocities: they do not deny the existence of suicide bombings, nor do they put the blame for them on foreign or unknown actors. Most human rights violations (the collective punishment of house demolitions, for example) are lawful under Israeli law, unlike the gross human rights violations that the TRC investigated, most of which were officially illegal under South African domestic law during apartheid.

A full and updated list of the names of Jewish and Arab casualties of the conflict already appears, for example, on the website of the human rights group B'Tselem.[28] This is in stark contrast with many other pre-transition contexts[29] and will make the task of truth-seeking mechanisms different than elsewhere. The challenge is to find ways in which truth mechanisms could tackle not so much the factual forensic details of the violations but the broad societal justifications that were given to them. If the South African TRC helped to 'narrow the range of permissible lies' regarding the apartheid years,[30] in Israel/Palestine, truth and reconciliation mechanisms would have to confront what Cohen called the 'official propaganda, myths and self righteousness, [and] pious kitsch'.[31] Here, they should perhaps try to 'narrow the range of permissible political and historical clichés'.

What kind of commission(s)?

Ideally, the best way to confront the past in the Middle East would be to follow the South African TRC model: an institution established by the political leadership, covering the whole range of abuses in one all-encompassing high-profile mechanism. However, the feasibility of such a project in the Israeli-Palestinian context is low. The separation into two states would mean that the 'discontinuity of the regime', which enabled successive governments to deal with the past elsewhere, would not be a feature here: 'When the Palestinian state is in place, there will be two sovereign governments, each representing more continuity than change and both with a history of involvement in individual, group and state terror.'[32] Nonetheless, this should not mean that any attempt to deal with the past would be unfeasible. A more suitable model could be an incremental process, involving less ambitious mechanisms, and with a larger role for civil-society initiatives.

One option is to address just one specific topic. The issue of Palestinian refugees is an example of an issue in which diplomatic agreements are unlikely to be achieved without recognition of the past. Examining and acknowledging the creation of the refugee problem could be done in the framework of a truth commission. It should be emphasized that addressing the historical injustice through a truth and reconciliation mechanism is meant to complement, rather than supplant, political-legal mechanisms such as return, relocation and restitution. The idea here is that part of a package deal regarding the refugees is likely to include an Israeli recognition, acknowledgement or apology regarding its historical responsibility, a step that may smooth the negotiations regarding the right of return and its implementation,[33] and to include 'reparations' within the agreement. Reparations could and should include not just monetary compensation, but acts such as public apologies and commemoration.[34] Such a 'narrow' commission could perhaps lead the way to other single-topic inquiries, such as regarding torture (by both Israel and the Palestinian Authority), or killing of civilians by both sides.

Another option is to establish official truth and reconciliation commissions by each side, to address issues relevant to the conflict from an internal perspective. In Israel, such an issue could be the Palestinian population inside Israel: the 20 per cent of Israeli citizens who are Palestinians. While they always have been granted some basic civil liberties by the Israeli government, most notably voting rights, and have not been subject to the full range of human rights violations experienced by Palestinians in the Occupied Territories, there is an important legacy of discrimination and oppression of them. This legacy is often neglected, mainly due to the emphasis of the conflict in the Occupied Territories. The eruption of the uprising in the Occupied Territories in early October 2000 was accompanied by week-long, unprecedented violent demonstrations of Israeli-Palestinians inside Israel, which were met by the excessive force of the Israeli police, leaving 13 Palestinians dead. From one perspective, the issue of the Arab minority in Israel is a transitional justice issue by itself, and some have suggested establishing 'forums in the spirits of truth and reconciliation commissions'[36] to address the legacy of discrimination against Arabs within the state of Israel. But it is, of course, also related to the 'major' conflict: Israeli Palestinians have the potential to serve as a 'bridge to peace', but if their grievances are not addressed, this issue will remain potentially explosive in the relations between Israel and a Palestinian state. This might be the first avenue to start the whole Israeli-Palestinian truth and reconciliation project, especially as it would be easier – politically and legally – for the Israeli government and public to address human rights violations of the country's own citizens rather than of the Palestinians in the occupied territories.

A Palestinian internal truth and reconciliation initiative could deal, for example, with collaboration. This phenomenon creates a complex legacy: some Palestinians who were cooperating with the Israeli establishment have contributed directly or indirectly to human rights abuses against their fellow Palestinians. Israel's methods of 'recruitment' have often included illegal forms of blackmail. In addition, hundreds of real and alleged collaborators have been killed by Palestinians in 'street justice' and a few by official executions.[37] In similar transitions, addressing the phenomenon of collaboration in an adequate manner proved challenging.[38] Yet, given the scope and negative effects of collaboration in the Palestinian context, the issue must be confronted.[39] The collaboration-related violence is of course related to the Israeli-Palestinian conflict as such, but it would allow Palestinians to examine the past from a local perspective, which, as with Israeli society, might be easier. A potential precedent is the internal truth commission established by the ANC regarding its abuses of alleged collaborators.[40] This commission preceded the all-encompassing Truth and Reconciliation Commission (TRC), and to a degree paved the way for its establishment.

Finally, while, in general, truth commissions are official bodies with vested authority from the State, there is scope for truth and reconciliation initiatives by civil society. If this work would be done by the already established human rights NGOs, its effects might be limited, but we should perhaps reject a rigid dichotomy of oppositional NGOs on the one hand and official governmental sponsorship on the other hand. While this was true in dictatorial Brazil, for example, both

Israeli and Palestinian societies are richer, and there is a space between these two poles, which include public figures who are not 'tainted' as NGO activists but who are also not part of the executive. An illustration for such a model is the recent TRC in Greensboro, North Carolina, which addressed the legacy of racial violence and especially the killing of human rights activists by the Ku Klux Klan in 1979.[42] While not officially commissioned or authorized by the Executive, the commission's design involved figures such as a mayor, a district court judge and a member of the House of Representatives: this distinguished it from a purely NGO-based initiative. In Israel/Palestine, we should seek involvement of low-level politicians, mayors, intellectuals, former soldiers or religious figures, which could have an impact, even if the body is not sponsored by the Israeli and Palestinian prime ministers.

The key would be to move from simple documentation of abuses to more complex ways to counter denial. Let me give three examples of such projects. First, an Israeli group called 'Zochrot' ('remembering' in Hebrew), which focus on commemoration of the Palestinian villages that were destroyed by Israel in 1948.[43] They have recently succeeded in pressuring the Israeli government (including through Supreme Court petition) to install commemorative plaques on sites of destroyed Palestinian villages inside Israel.[44] Such actions could have significant effects: 'Collective memory can be assuaged by reports on "peace and reconciliation" that document human rights violations of the past. Non-tangible gestures that do not necessarily carry any price tag can also become a catharsis for healing the wounds.'[45] Another group, called 'Combatants for Peace', includes former Israeli soldiers and former Palestinian militants who have renounced violence.[46] Much of their activity is based on telling their personal stories of involvement in atrocities. Finally, a project called 'Shared Histories' has brought together Palestinians and Israeli historians to discuss their narratives of the conflict.[47] The point of such projects is not for each side to convince the other of the accuracy of its narrative, but rather to acknowledge both narratives as legitimate. The principle could be based on a distinction made by Charles Maier, who suggested distinguishing two forms of acknowledgement: in the first, one party is appreciating the pain the other has experienced; in the second, there is an identification of one version of the facts as authoritative. Maier argued that there are more chances for the first form to succeed in the Middle East: an Israeli could appreciate the pain suffered by a Palestinian refugee, without necessarily accepting the Palestinian version of the history that led to this suffering.[48]

Such isolated civil society initiatives will not transform the Middle East overnight, but with time they can accumulate into a larger and more influential movement. Like the suggested internal commissions or a narrow-based joint commission, they can set a precedent, and at least establish the principle of the importance of dealing with the past. As a result of the particularities of the Israeli-Palestinian case, the model presented above is based on a wider, more inclusive, understanding of what could and should be included under the heading of transitional justice. Analytically, it moves away from viewing a 'moment' of transition; rather, it looks for a longer period of time, without one clear demarcation.[49] Correspondingly, in terms of prescription, it does not seek to locate transitional justice mechanisms in one such moment, to have a single, all-encompassing mechanism in a short and defined stage. Rather, it views transitional justice mechanisms as a series of 'small' incremental, steps.

Proposing truth and reconciliation mechanisms for the conflict in the Middle East necessitates striking a balance between what is considered desirable and what is considered 'realistic'. While there is a clear need to avoid utopian thinking, we should also avoid what du Toit called, during the early discussions on a possible truth commission for South Africa, 'loaded realism': a way of thinking in which the issue is posed in a question-begging way, and the problems are 'built into the question so one is going to arrive at the conclusion that the project is not feasible'.[50] In answering, 'does any of it matter' to the Middle East, it would perhaps also be useful to think of transitional justice not as a yes/no question, but rather as a spectrum: the question should not be 'Can we have transitional justice or not?', but rather 'How much transitional justice can we have?'

Does any of *this* matter?

Let us conclude where we started: a *New Yorker* cartoon. This one shows two academics chatting happily in a conference; the caption reads: 'Want to have a drink after the genocide panel?'. For academics who deal with human rights, this one, as they say, is 'a bit too close to home'. It captures this familiar sense of uneasiness, the feeling that the academic studies of violence and conflict operate in a sphere of their own, advancing our careers and giving us some good times, but not affecting reality in any way. Cohen himself once wrote, in uncharacteristically dark mood, about 'the tragedy of knowing that all these academic labours – the institutes, fees, models, royalties, conferences, journals – will not come to much in even foreseeing let alone preventing the next horror'.[51] Yet here, for once, he might have been wrong. The mechanisms of transitional justice were to a large degree based on the work of engaged academics. Prof. Carlos Nino influenced the policies in Argentine; in Chile Prof. Jose Zalaquett articulated the importance of truth about the past and presided over the truth commission; Prof. Kader Asmal was extremely instrumental in creating the South African TRC. Indeed, the foundations of the TRC mandate were laid in, of all places, an academic conference (on 'Dealing with the Past', which took place in Cape Town in February 1994). Throughout the world, the transitional justice field, both as an academic discipline and as a practical activity, was developed through an 'international learning process' of activists, politicians and, yes, scholars.[52]

The work of Stanley Cohen in exposing the mechanisms of denial, especially in the Israeli context, would inform any potential discussions on truth commissions in this country. Lawyers may dominate the human rights field, but the role of the social scientists is crucial. If any transitional justice mechanism were to be established in the Middle East, it would not be because of this or that international law clause, but because of recognition of the destructive role of denial and the need to acknowledge past wrongs in order to secure a better future, for both Palestinians and Israelis. This sentiment, the basis of transitional justice, was expressed in numerous works, but perhaps never better articulated than in the poignant words of another former university lecturer, Albie Sachs:

> There are no perpetual enemies, perpetual victims, perpetual oppressors. The crucial thing is not so much to condemn the past as to break the sense of inevitability that cloaks the continuing inequality of the present. It did not just come to pass, it was brought about. We find the truth of the past in the present, not the other way around; we negate and liberate the past by the confident way we bear ourselves in the present. The future will not just come to pass, we will bring it, too, about.[53]

If and when this message reaches both Palestinians and Israelis, we would be one big step closer to a lasting peace.

Notes

*I would like to thank the International Center for Transitional Justice and the Institute for Justice and Reconciliation for co-sponsoring a research fellowship in South Africa, which has widely contributed to the development of the ideas presented here. I'm also grateful to Heribert Adam, Alex Boraine, Hillel Cohen, Andre du Toit and Noam Hoffstater for valuable comments on an early version of this piece.

1 Stanley Cohen, 'Justice in transition? prospects for a Palestinian-Israeli truth commission', Middle East Report, (May–August 2005).
2 *Ibid.* p. 5.
3 Louis Bickford, 'Transitional Justice', in Dinah L. Shelton (ed.), *Encyclopedia of Genocide and Crimes Against Humanity*, New York: Macmillan, 2004.
4 See Neil Kritz, *Transitional Justice: How Emerging Democracies Deal with Former Regimes*, Washington DC: US Institute of Peace, 1995; Stanley Cohen, 'State crimes of previous regimes: knowledge, accountability and the policing of the past', *Law and Social Inquiry*, (1995), 20(1), pp. 7–50; Ruti Teitel, Transitional Justice, Oxford: Oxford University Press, 2000.
5 Mustafa Mari, 'The negotiation process: the lack of human rights component', *Palestine-Israel Journal*, (2003) 10(3), pp. 5–16.
6 Edward Kaufman and Ibrahim Bisharat, 'Introducing human rights into conflict resolution: the relevance for the Israeli-Palestinian peace process', *Journal of Human Rights* (2002) 1(1), pp. 71–91, at 79.
7 William Quandt, 'Israeli-Palestinian peace talks: from Oslo to Camp David II', in Tamara Cofman Wittes (ed.), *How Israelis and Palestinians Negotiate: A Cross-Cultural Analysis of the Oslo Peace Process*, Washington, DC: United States Institute of Peace, 2005, p. 15.
8 Quoted in Charles Enderlin, *Shattered Dreams: The Failure of the Peace Process in the Middle East 1995–2002*, New York: Other Press, 2002, p. 198.
9 See www.usip.org/events/2005/0607_beberger.pdf.
10 See the Harvard Roundtable on Truth Commissions at <www.law.harvard.edu/programs/hrp/Publications/truth3.html>.
11 Tamara Cofman Wittes, 'Conclusions' in *idem* (ed.), *How Israelis and Palestinians Negotiate: A Cross-Cultural Analysis of the Oslo Peace Process*, Washington, DC: United States Institute of Peace, 2005, p. 144.
12 Christine Bell, *Peace Agreements and Human Rights*, Oxford: Oxford University Press, 2000, p. 15.
13 David Makovsky, 'Middle East peace through partition', *Foreign Affairs* (2001) 80(2), pp. 28–45, at 30.
14 Hussein Agha and Robert Malley, 'Camp David: the tragedy of errors', *New York Review of Books*, (2001), 48(13), 9.
15 Quandt, *supra*, note 7, p. 16.
16 Heribert Adam and Kogila Moodley, *Seeking Mandela: Peacemaking between Israelis and Palestinians*, Philadelphia: Temple University Press, 2005, p. 155.
17 Cited in Amal Jamal, 'The Palestinians in the Israeli Peace discourse: a conditional partnership', *Journal of Palestine Studies*, (2000), 30(1), pp. 36–51, at 37.
18 Nicholas Haysom, *Negotiating the Political Settlement in South Africa: Are There Lessons for Other Countries?*, Cape Town: University of Cape Town Press, 2002, p. 15 [emphasis in original].
19 Yael Zerubavel, *Recovered Roots: Collective Memory and the Making of Israeli National Tradition*, Chicago: University of Chicago Press, 1995, p. 215.
20 Stanley Cohen, *States of Denial: Knowing about Atrocities and Suffering*, Cambridge: Polity Press, 2001, pp. 96–7.

21 *Ibid*, p. 157.
22 Jamal, *supra,* note 16, p. 40.
23 Quandt, *supra,* note 6, pp. 14–16.
24 See Roundtable on Truth Commissions, *supra*, note 10.
25 Uzi Benziman, 'Needed: reconciliation', *Haaretz*, 12 October 2005.
26 Cohen, *supra*, note 20, pp. 104–12.
27 See Piers Pigou, 'The apartheid state and violence: what has the Truth and Reconciliation Commission found?', *Politikon* (2001), 28(2), pp. 207–33.
28 See www.btselem.org/English/Statistics/Casualties.asp.
29 In Peru, for example, the Truth and Reconciliation Commission's finding that 69,000 people were killed during the civil war has shocked local and international observers who thought the numbers were much lower. Reuters, 'Peru doubles estimate of political war deaths', 28 August 2003.
30 Michael Ignatieff, 'Articles of Faith', *Index on Censorship* (1996) 25(5), pp. 100–22, at 113.
31 Cohen, *supra*, note 20, p. 157.
32 Kaufman and Bisharat, *supra*, note 6, p. 84.
33 See also Yoav Peled and Nadim N. Rouhana, 'Transitional justice and the right of return of the Palestinian refugees', *Theoretical Inquiries in Law* (2004), 5(2).
34 Elazar Barkan, *The Guilt of Nations: Restitution and Negotiating Historical Injustices*, New York: Norton, 2000.
35 For background and an overview of the Israeli Arabs' situation, see International Crisis Group, *Identity Crisis: Israel and Its Arab Citizens*, March 2004.
36 Dan Rabinowitz and Khawla Abu-Baker, *The Stand-Tall Generation*, Jerusalem: Keter, 2002, p. 92 [in Hebrew].
37 On Palestinian collaboration see also Salah Jawwad, 'Collaboration', *Palestine Report* (2002), 9(3); Eyad El-Sarraj, 'Spare thy neighbour', *The Jerusalem Report*, 26 October 1998.
38 The issue of informers was dealt with extensively – and controversially – in post-communist East Germany and Czechoslovakia; see Tina Rosenberg, *The Haunted Land: Facing Europe's Ghosts after Communism*, New York: Vintage, 1995.
39 Ron Dudai and Hillel Cohen, 'Triangle of betrayal: collaborators and transitional justice in the Israeli-Palestinian conflict', *Journal of Human Rights*, (2007) 6(1) pp. 37–58.
40 Priscilla Hayner, *Unspeakable Truths: Facing the Challenge of Truth Commissions*, New York: Routledge, 2002, pp. 60–61.
41 *Ibid*. p. 14.
42 For background, see the commission's website, www.greensborotrc.org.
43 See the organization's website: www.nakbainhebrew.org.
44 Yuval Yoaz, 'The Palestinian past of Canada Park is forgotten in JNF signs', *Haaretz*, 12 June 2005.
45 Kaufman and Bisharat, *supra* note 6, p. 84.
46 See the website: www.combatantsforpeace.org.

47 See Walid Salem and Benjamin Pogrund (eds), *Shared Histories: A Palestinian-Israeli Dialogue*, California: Left Coast Press, 2006.
48 See Roundtable on Truth Commissions, *supra* note 10.
49 An analysis that may also be true for the Northern Ireland experience; see Fionnuala Ni Aoláin and Colm Campbell, 'The paradox of transition in conflicted democracies', *Human Rights Quarterly* (2005) 27(1), pp. 172–213.
50 Quoted in Alex Boraine *et al.* (eds) *Dealing with the Past: Truth and Reconciliation in South Africa*, Cape Town: IDASA, 1994, p. 132.
51 Stanley Cohen, 'The meaning of genocide', *New Humanist*, November 2005.
52 Andre du Toit, 'The South African Truth and Reconciliation Commission: local history, global accounting', *Politiques Africaines*, (2003) 92.
53 Albie Sachs, 'Guilt and atonement: unmasking history for the future', paper presented at the New Nation Writers' Conference, University of the Witwatersrand, December 1991.

Part 6
Ways Ahead

Chapter 25

'I sang in my cell because I wouldn't sing' and other tales

Albie Sachs

I was 39 years old and teaching law at Southampton University when I discovered I was a terrorist, and the title of the first of the four tales about terrorism that I am going to relate in the course of this chapter in this book honouring my great friend Stan Cohen is as follows:

I sang in my cell because I wouldn't sing

How did I discover that I was a terrorist? I had been invited by the Contemporary History Department at Yale University in Connecticut to attend a conference on contemporary South African history and I applied for a visa. I discovered that I couldn't get a visa because I was a terrorist. Why was I a terrorist? Because I belonged to the African National Congress (ANC) which had been classified as a terrorist organization, and any member of a terrorist organization is, and was, a terrorist. Happily, the lobby group for the ANC in the USA dealing with the Department of Immigration, which had classified me as a terrorist, turned out to be a little more persuasive than the lobby group against the ANC. And so I discovered that after all I wasn't a terrorist, and yet the description resonated, and irritated. I wouldn't say it hurt. It irritated because we knew who we were and who we weren't, but it rankled.

It reminded me of a largely vain mission which I'd undertaken to Amnesty International (AI) some years earlier in Stockholm to try and persuade Amnesty to adopt Nelson Mandela as a prisoner of conscience. Today – oh, how they wish, how they wish, how they wish they had adopted him! But AI didn't. It said: 'He's obviously an admirable person, but he was involved in planning violence against the state in South Africa, he doesn't meet our criteria, we can't adopt him.' In vain I replied: 'If his conscience had simply left him immobilized, sitting in his house and doing nothing against apartheid, and he was picked up, then you could adopt him. But if his conscience led him to give up his career, break up his family, go underground, and take all the risks that he took – changing his name, his appearance, dedicating his whole life to bringing about change; if his conscience could tell him to do all that *and* to risk his life physically by confronting the state that was denying him and his people their rights, then he doesn't qualify?' Sometimes good does come out of bad. We did persuade Amnesty that if they couldn't adopt Nelson Mandela as a prisoner of conscience, at least they could deal with two other issues. First there was the question of capital punishment. Nobody, whoever they are, even if they plan violence, should be executed by the state. I believe that was the moment when Amnesty embarked upon what turned out to be one of its greatest contributions to contemporary human history and civilization – putting international focus on the question of capital punishment. Secondly, we said: 'Even if Mandela is somebody who was involved in violence who can't be adopted by yourselves, he and others being imprisoned like himself in South Africa should not be subjected to torture.' So Amnesty was persuaded to take up the issue of torture, which became the second major platform of Amnesty's work, in addition to helping particular political prisoners who met their definitions.

Unlike Nelson Mandela, I did qualify as one of the prisoners of conscience. The key law in South Africa was called the Ninety Day Law. The South African security forces had told the government they simply couldn't deal with terrorism in South Africa if they didn't have power to lock up the people whom they knew were planning to overthrow the state. 'We need to be able to lock them up for 90 days, and then we'll nip all their plans in the bud.' It became known as the Ninety Day Law, and I was detained under the Ninety Day Law. It was simply enough that they had suspicion that I had information which could help them in dealing with anti-state activity. No charge, no trial, no access to lawyers – solitary confinement. I think everybody has known loneliness. Solitary confinement is something different. It is the loneliness of being on your own, of being isolated, but it's also the loneliness of being in a world without human beings, without association, without the sounds of ordinary life. It's existentially absurd, and punishing to a degree that only those who've been through it can understand, whether hijacked, or kidnapped in Iraq, or locked up in solitary confinement by the Nazis or in the gulags – it's that same kind of experience. I was kept in solitary confinement simply on the grounds that I was suspected of being a terrorist, or somebody who had information about terrorism, or who was connected to terrorists. I had to find stratagems to keep myself in touch with myself, to feel I was still a human being, not just a creature kept in a cube. I would go through the alphabet, singing songs beginning with A, *Always*, B *Because*, C *Charmaine*, D... and I had problems I remember with X, so I used *Deep in the Heart of Texas*, that was the closest I could get. *Always*, that song, it's strange isn't it, using that Noel Coward song to fight loneliness in a South African prison cell: 'I'll be living here, always/ Year after year, always / In this little cell that I know so well / I'll be living swell, always, always. / I'll be staying in, always / Keeping up my chin, always / Not for but an hour / not for but a week / not for 90 days, but always.' I would waltz around on my own, keeping myself company, with my voice giving me some kind of courage and hope.

And of course 90 days was only the start. The next time I was detained, it was under the 180 Day Law. And for people who were detained after that it was the Terrorism Act, permitting indefinite detention. Everything that was to become especially vicious in our law enforcement – the tortures, the disappearances, the violations – started with the Ninety Day Law. Suddenly, there was that space in which those in command were not subject to the almost taken-for granted restraints on power in a legal society. South Africa was always unjust and unfair; grossly unfair, with rights being reserved explicitly for white people, such as ownership of land – 87 per cent of the land was legally owned by the whites, only whites voted for the parliament, or could be president, white judges, whites in command of everything, controlling everything. But it was done according to the law. Here was the law now creating a vacuum, a space, a totally extra-legal area, with only the conscience or system of command of the authorities to prevent abuse of people locked up. Suddenly, we started having deaths in detention. Suddenly we started having people disappearing. Suddenly we would have people brought to court after two years in prison because after 90 days they would be released for three minutes, as happened to me, and then brought back for another 90 days. It's endless, you don't know how long it's going to be. The whole criminal justice system was turned inside out. In effect, instead of the judiciary being the agency that was in control – making the basic decisions as to whether people were branded as criminals, sent to prison or not – it was the police who were making those decisions. They lined up the witnesses, the judiciary became a kind of a backstop. A few very wonderful judges were alert and provided some space for people to protest about conditions and expose torture. But by and large, the basic decisions on innocence or guilt were now not being made by the judges, but by the security police.

And draconian as they were, these measures didn't stop us. We now honour far too many martyrs in our country. But the Ninety Day Law didn't change anything, except give a false sense of power to the authorities. If anything, it created a greater sense of anger and resistance, and a feeling of intolerability about our society. Now not only was it unjust, it was also manifestly cruel. Books were written about imprisonment by persons branded terrorists. Breyten Breytenbach was locked up for seven years; a poet and activist (not a particularly good political operative, but a wonderful writer) entitled his memoirs, *True Confessions of an Albino Terrorist*. So the word 'terrorist' became a word of proud irony for those labelled with it. Terrorism, or, rather, anti-terrorism, was given a bad name, inverting the very objective intended to be achieved by the use of extraordinary measures. The thing about extraordinary measures is they are never extraordinary enough. Once you start breaking that membrane called the rule of law (I'm not speaking about bending – you can bend up to a certain point; you can make adjustments; you can take account of realities, of emergency situations), once you start rupturing that membrane of principles and rules developed by humanity over centuries, based on bitter, painful experiences, then the simple tear is never enough. When 90 days wasn't enough, they needed 180 days – 'But that's not enough, we need indefinite detention because they always exploit the fact they know they can come out after a certain period.' And it's not stopping the fight, the resistance, the bombs going off, the international protests, the general strikes. It's not achieving its intended objects, and so you have to extend and extend and extend the emergency measures. That's the problem with the exceptional. The exceptional becomes the normal, and then it becomes too little and then you have to make it more exceptional and more exceptional and more exceptional. And the dagger aimed at the enemy in the end is plunged into your own innards, perforating the very character of your own society and rupturing precisely what these laws were said to be supposed to be defending.

The core of our whole constitutional set-up in South Africa is a total inversion of the way that power was applied in the past. Once more, it is the good that comes out of the bad. I think our constitution is the only one in the world that actually includes the words 'No detention without trial'. We put those words in not simply as part and parcel of the ordinary adjuncts of the rights of freedom, of *habeas corpus*. There is an express injunction, 'no detention without trial', because detention without trial was the weapon, the instrument that was used to pervert the whole of our criminal justice system. Everything else flowed from that. I might mention that I was one of the authors at the early constitution-making stage and if anybody says, 'Well, that was Albie putting his own footprint in the constitutional cement,' I won't deny it. Yet after I was on the court and the final constitutional text was adopted by parliament, and I was no longer involved in the drafting, that phrase survived, 'No detention without trial'. It was in the interim constitution, and it is in the final constitution.

I did go to Yale. I recall at the conference the total support I got from everybody when I went through the Universal Declaration of Human Rights and was able to show that South Africa violated every single article in the Declaration of Human Rights, except for the one on copyright. People were with me, completely on board, but when I said, 'One day in South Africa we're going to have a non-racial democratic country. That's what we're fighting for, that's what we believe in', I just saw their eyes glaze over. It was total incredulity. Total disbelief that we could ever have a non-racial, democratic South Africa. I repeat that because there are other places in the world where people feel it's impossible, that the situations are intractable. As we proved, anything that humans make, humans can unmake.

The second story about terrorism explains why we succeeded when even our closest supporters predicted a racial bloodbath.

King Sabata, who made us laugh five minutes late

I first met King Sabata in my exile in Mozambique. He was one of the traditional leaders who didn't play along with apartheid. Eventually he went into exile. He told me he didn't realize he was a king, he thought he was just a paramount chief, until he went into exile and the ANC called him King Sabata. I enjoyed the title, I looked after his family, took his children to the beach, and lent him my bathing costume. I'd never lent my bathing costume to a king before, and I called him 'comrade king'. A little while afterward we had a very important conference in a small town called Kabwe in Zambia. This was 1985. The Eminent Persons Group of the Commonwealth had tried to broker some kind of arrangement with the South African government to get Mandela released and get negotiations started, and the only result in the end had been that the securicrats took over, the negotiations collapsed completely, and there were bombing raids to kill us in Zambia. So we were quite on our alert at that time, and the conference was surrounded by Zambian troops in case there was another commando raid to wipe out the couple of hundred delegates of the ANC.

There were two big themes on the agenda. The first was how to destroy racist power in South Africa; we used to use the phrase people used to speak about, the 'seizure of power'. They loved the word 'seizure'; it was just like an onomatopoeic, imaginative expectation of storming the Union buildings at Pretoria and hoisting the ANC flag, and seizing power. But together with that were also negotiations and getting authority for negotiations. I knew that the king was down to speak and I was very curious to know what his take would be on the seizure of power. One of the themes was self-imposed limitations on the instruments being used by the ANC. There was a certain impatience from some quarters as to the kinds of targets to be hit, and similar levels of irritation with the proposition that you don't go for civilian targets.

I thought back to the first big debates we'd had in exile on this question. It was the time of the Black September when planes were being hijacked. One of the figures, Leila Khaleed, became quite famous internationally, and some of the members of the ANC were saying, 'What's wrong with our leadership? Look what the Palestinians are doing! They're capturing these planes, they're getting headlines, they're putting their struggle on the map! And our leadership carry their little briefcases and they pass resolutions. Are we scared?' There were very intense debates, and the word came down from the leadership: 'We don't believe in hijacking. One very obvious reason is the leaders of the ANC might be on the plane, who knows? and you're hijacking and putting at risk your own leaders.' But that wasn't the main reason. The main reason was 'that's just not the way we fight, that's not the enemy, those are not the targets, and if you do that, you are playing into the hands of those who want to project us simply as wild people who have no respect for human dignity, for the rights of others, who are so driven by rage and anger that they will destroy anybody and everybody simply to make their point. And it undermines the very justice of our cause, it detracts from the human dignity at the centre of what we're fighting for.' So the leadership in command of all the operations persuaded the membership not even to think along those lines. That was in the late 1960s and early 1970s.

But by the time of our meeting in Zambia, it was the mid-1980s, a very difficult period in South Africa. Many people were being tortured to death in the prisons, shot down in the streets, with commando raids in various frontline states, and some of the members were asking what was the matter with us? Why weren't we fighting back? It was in that context that King Sabata went to the platform. He spoke in Xhosa and that's why, when we laughed, we laughed five minutes late. About 90 per cent of the audience could understand, while about 10 per cent of us, because of our cultural limitations, couldn't, and we had to wait for the translation. And he's talking away, and talking away, and the people are laughing, and laughing; not uproariously but strongly and firmly. Then five minutes later, we get our chance to laugh. The king had been telling a story about two men who are fighting. They are very, very angry, their families are quarrelling. They are fighting with sticks and battering one another, and their wives are with them and urging them on, and eventually the wife of one says, 'Husband, what's the matter with you? You are stronger than your opponent and yet he's beating you over the head, over the back, everywhere! If you are stronger, why is he crushing you? Because you are holding your stick in one hand and covering your nakedness with a blanket in your other hand. Drop the damn blanket! Use both your hands and smash him to bits!' That was when everybody burst out laughing. Laughter was the polite African way of saying we hear you, and admire your gifts as a storyteller, even if we do not accept your conclusions. After the king, we heard other people saying, 'They are killing our children. School kids are being mowed down. We bury them every week. Until their children are being killed, until their parents feel the pain of burying their children, they will never understand our pain, and they will never give way.' That was a strong, emotional argument that had a certain measure of support, and the king, who hadn't been politically all that active, couldn't understand why the ANC was imposing very strict restraints on its fighting capacity. These were generally but not always followed. The whole philosophy was to go for military targets, to go for physical targets, but not to go for civilian targets. The matter was debated and debated and debated, and overwhelmingly the conference decided, 'We don't go for civilian targets. We don't change our policy.'

The reasons were partly tactical; going for civilians gives you a bad name internationally. You lose friends. But there were lots of things that gave us a bad name internationally, that embarrassed our friends. Many people didn't like the sporting, economic and cultural boycotts. Certainly, many people – great supporters of ours – didn't like the armed struggle at all. Yet there was no other way. There had to be some kind of physical confrontation to raise the popular fighting spirit, even though in the end it wasn't the physical armed struggle that proved decisive. There were also powerful strategic reasons for not going for civilians. It was important to disaggregate the opposition, to try and win over as many people as possible to at least be neutral, if they couldn't be on our side. If your targets are indiscriminate, then you are pushing everybody into one camp and they feel 'Well, they gave us no option, we can't speak to these people, we can't have anything to do with them because our children are at risk'.

361

But I don't think even that, strong though it was, was the primary factor. The primary factor was not only what indiscriminate killing did to the opposition, to the other side, but what it did to us. If I become a killer of children, what am I fighting for? Who am I? If I dedicate my life to simply being an instrument of death, indiscriminate death, who am I? What am I doing to our struggle? We simply become instruments. We rob ourselves, and our struggle, of its heart, of its dignity, of its central core. I can't separate techniques of struggle from objectives of struggle, from the personality of struggle, from the kind of people that we are. We weren't pacifists, we were using violence, but it was violence that was targeted. It was proportionate. It was directed. It was always part and parcel of a political struggle. And it's important today to emphasize that fact, not to say what jolly good fellows we were, although it's nice to get a pat on the back occasionally. It turned out to be fundamental. Because we rejected terrorism, we got a country, we got a constitution, we got our dignity. It worked! Idealism works! Principle works! There's a reason why these things have emerged as beacons for humanity. It is not simply dreaming of one beautiful day, of imagining a future millennarian society. Humanity has found that cooperating, working together, believing in democracy, in fairness, in justice, in human dignity, actually helps to solve problems. Idealism is intensely practical.

So here we were, the terrorists, who were anti-terrorism. As Stan Cohen will well remember, we lived then in a world of 'isms'. Not just capitalism and socialism, imperialism, fascism, and Nazism. We had our own internal 'isms' in our struggle. My father was expelled from the Communist Party for 'right-wing deviationism', which was as bad as 'left-wing deviationism'. Then I remember you had 'adventurism', which was where the political groups went too far ahead, as opposed to 'tail-ism' where you didn't take enough initiative. But 'terrorism' was a dirty word in our ranks, because terrorism was seen as the alternative to serious political struggle, and it was one of those concepts that was negating what we were really aiming at, which was a transformation of society, of human relationships. Targeting individuals, races, groups, personalities was regarded as actually undermining what we intended to achieve.

I can't leave the 'isms' without mentioning my favourite one, from the Chinese Revolution. It was 'mountaintop-ism'. That was a very serious offence where instead of joining in the general revolutionary struggle, you simply consolidated your base on top of a mountain. I've often thought of university rectors being accused of mountaintop-ism; as long as we are all right, as long as my turf is OK, we don't have to worry. I am sure that Stan was never a mountaintop-ist.

And my third story is about the great 'ism' of our times, racism, and a man whose profession it was through state terrorism to defend it.

Henry, whose hand shook

I am now a judge of the Constitutional Court. My telephone rings and a voice says, 'Reception here. There's a man called Henry to see you. He says he has an appointment', and I say, 'Send him through.'

I went to the security gate and opened it with some excitement because Henry had telephoned me to say that he had organized the placing of the bomb in my car in Maputo. Now he was going to the Truth Commission to ask for amnesty, and was I willing to see him? I opened the door and here's this man, a bit younger than myself, also a bit thin, looking at me – I'm looking at him. 'So this is the man who tried to kill me', and I could see in his eyes, 'So this is the man I tried to kill'. We had never met; we hadn't fought over anything; we hadn't been angry with each other; yet he'd tried to exterminate me because I belonged to the enemy. And now I'm looking at the person whom I used to call the enemy.

He told me he went to the Potchefstroom University for Christian Higher Education. He had been a very good student, had been recruited into the army and had risen rapidly in the ranks. He was put in charge of special operations and had organized the explosives that were put in my car. I tried to understand why he would have tried to kill me, somebody whom he didn't know. Had he seen himself as a Christian defending his faith, his civilization, his values? Had he regarded me as part of an organized group of ideologues threatening to bring chaos, oppression and violence to his country? Happily, as we conversed, he didn't say 'I'm sorry, I apologise'. How can you say to someone, 'Sorry I blew off your arm?' Eventually, after talking for some time, I stood up. I said, 'Henry, I have to get on with my work. Normally, when I say goodbye to someone, I shake their hand. I can't shake your hand. But go to the Truth Commission. Tell them what you know. Do something for South Africa. Maybe we'll meet one day, who knows?'

The Truth Commission did something very, very special for our country. It's highly controversial. Some people feel it wasn't radical enough – it allowed killers and murderers and torturers to walk freely on the streets. Others felt it was unfair; it targeted certain groups. There wasn't due process of law. I think it's in the nature of truth not to be clean and compact and neat. It's inconvenient, it's painful and contradictory. As life is. But one thing the commission did that cannot be contested – it showed us to each other, not as faceless caricatures,

363

but as human beings. We watched on television, we heard on the radio, we saw faces and voices. It wasn't just facts, data, information, detail we received; it was converting knowledge into acknowledgement.

We heard the tears, we saw the faces of people we knew. It was the accents of people we knew. It was the stories we found so credible because they were told uninterruptedly. It brought human beings into contact with other human beings; it brought the pain out. Even those who had done terrible things were coming forward and acknowledging their criminality, not because they had been tortured into doing so, but to free themselves from the legal threat, and maybe from the psychological burden of what they had done; they were telling the country what they had done in their own voices. It personalized, even humanized, terrible episodes in our lives. It wasn't some strange persons called 'the security police' who did this; it was 'Sergeant So and So' and 'Officer This or That'. The victim wasn't some anonymous poor black person living in a township, it was someone with a name. The process enabled us in our torn country to start living together as people and to begin to share our memories and our associations.

When the Truth Commission had been functioning for a little while, I went to a party. I was enjoying being there, listening to the music, when suddenly I heard a voice say, 'Albie!' I turned around. 'Albie!' 'My God, it's Henry.' He was beaming. He came up to me and said, 'I got in touch with the Truth Commission and I spoke to Bobby and Sue and Farouk [other people who had been in exile in Mozambique with me who also could have been the targets of a bomb] and I told them everything, and you said, "one day'…"' And I said, 'Henry, I've only got to look at your face to know that what you are telling me is the truth.' And I put out my hand and I shook his hand. He went away absolutely elated and I almost fainted. I heard afterward that in fact he went home after the party and cried for two weeks. And in a curious way, that moved me quite a lot. I feel relieved that he isn't that blind exterminator – blind in the sense of not even knowing me – out there. He's become another person like myself; engaged in activities at a particular moment, and now we've both just become South Africans getting on with our lives in a relatively peaceful country. Which brings me to my fourth and last tale.

A rendition of a man called Mohamed

I'm now sitting in my green robes, one of 11 judges on the bench of the Constitutional Court, hearing an urgent appeal from the Cape High Court.

The case was brought by a Capetonian who was a confectioner in an area in which mainly Muslim people lived. He'd gone to the Cape High Court because an amiable young Tanzanian refugee he called Ishmael, who'd been working as a pastry chef with him, had gone to have his immigration permit renewed, and had been whisked off; just disappeared. The baker didn't know what had happened, but he felt in the new South Africa, these things just don't happen. So he had gone to the High Court for our equivalent of a writ of *habeas corpus*. In the High Court, it came to light that in fact Ishmael's real name was Mohamed, and he wasn't just a nice pastry cook – he was a mass murderer, who had apparently organized the moving of explosives to the American Embassy in Dar es Salaam. It blew up, killing many people, mostly Tanzanians and some Americans. It was a brutal, bitter, terrible action. He'd come to South Africa under a false name, had been given status as a political refugee – he had some kind of cover story – and began working quietly there. And he'd been deported. The Cape High Court said, 'Well, he was in our country under a false name. He lied to the immigration authorities, and he's been deported. He's out of the country, and there's no scope for *habeas corpus* now, and there never really was anything a court could or should have done.'

The case came to us. We felt there was something very wrong. In the first place, whatever he'd done, whoever he was, the owner of the pastry shop wanted Ishmael/Mohamed to have a lawyer. He had *employed* a lawyer, and the lawyer was simply turned away. Now that is a violation of a most basic right in a constitutional state. But there was something else that we regarded as critical. He'd been whisked off in an American military plane to stand trial in New York on a charge of murder. We had no problem about the fact that he was being charged with murder, and that American courts had jurisdiction; in fact, there was every reason why it was important that he be put on trial. But South Africa has proper legal processes, and whether you call it deportation or extradition, however a person is being sent out of the country, it has to be remembered that our court had held that capital punishment was inconsistent with the values of our constitution. Just as you don't hand someone over to a country where they might be tortured, you don't hand somebody over to a country where they face a risk of being executed. Our government should have got an assurance from the American government before handing him over that whatever the finding of the jury, he would not face capital punishment. This is what the German government had done with one of his co-conspirators who'd been picked up in Germany before being deported or extradited to the USA to face trial. In the case of Germany, it was due process of law with respect for fundamental

365

rights. In the case of South Africa, it was what the documents referred to as rendition.

In any event, our court gave a judgment that was very strong in terms of its legal philosophy, even if not so strong in terms of its practical impact. It said that the South African authorities had acted in a way inconsistent with our constitution, (a) by not giving Mohamed a lawyer and (b) by not insisting, before he was handed over to be flown to the USA, that the American government give an assurance that he would not be executed.

What could we do in those circumstances? In fact, it was very difficult to see what our government could do; by then, Mohamed had been found guilty and the only issue was whether he would get the death sentence or not; this would be placed before the jury. So we sent our judgement to the trial judge in New York in the hope that if he felt any of the material was relevant to the question of sentence, he would place it before the jury. American courts are in general not very enthusiastic about international jurisprudence, and are even less enthusiastic about a finding in relation to a matter that they themselves are hearing. Yet, somehow or another, the matter did come through to the jury. It split, I think, 7:5 for capital punishment, and so Mohamed was not sent to death row. And we felt some relief that our action had had some practical effect. This was before 9/11, a couple of months before, I should mention.

Now, why do I bring this case up? Well, one could say it's OK for judges sitting in Johannesburg, far away from the problems of terrorism, to write a beautiful, pure judgement, of little practical import. The fact is, bombs were going off in Cape Town at the time. We *were* faced with what we would have defined as terrorism. A police investigator and then a magistrate were assassinated by what was said to be a Muslim fundamentalist group. It was a real threat to us. And yet we didn't allow the fact that we were living in a very difficult time in Cape Town, with a lot of anxiety and fear around, to influence the decision that we took.

There were many voices, some in leadership positions, saying we needed detention without trial; there was no other way that we could deal with these new forms of violence. When leaders say there is a time when you have got to keep your nerve, they usually mean more troops, more power. Yet, there are times when you've got to keep your nerve in standing for legality, the rule of law, and basic democratic principles. And we kept our nerve. In fact, the killers, the bombers were caught through good police intelligence, through their ranks being penetrated, through well-prepared prosecutions. The primary breakthroughs came because, politically, their group had become totally isolated. They had no real community base. And the more isolated they became, the easier it was to get people to inform about their activities, and the more difficult it was for them to get collaborators and safe houses. And now for five years or so, we haven't had any activities of that kind in Cape Town, and our constitution remains intact.

I think anybody sitting on a high court in any land must feel the pressures in public life of grossly troubling, offensive, threatening and disturbing events. It would be odd if one didn't respond to these realities as a judge, as a human being, as a person. Yet, we live in a period when I have felt myself exceptionally proud not only to be a judge in a freedom-loving court in South Africa (we are an activist court, with an activist constitution, so we don't have some of the dilemmas judges in other parts of the world might have), but also to belong to a worldwide community of judges who think that the basic freedoms matter and have to be upheld. I feel a surge when I see that colleagues of mine in the US Supreme Court take a principled and carefully motivated stand on Guantànamo Bay; when I see that colleagues in the House of Lords Appellate Committee in the UK take equally principled and reasoned positions on torture and on basic issues involving fundamental notions of what it means to live in a free society. I feel that if we are not there for *that*, to say something profound about what our country stands for, what it is all about when it is being tested, then we are not truly fulfilling our vocation as judges. And to the extent that I've seen colleagues of mine in other countries that don't have the same facilitative constitutional texts that we have, taking positions that are honourable, that keep alive in a meaningful way – not a demagogic way, a meaningful way – these deep, deep values, then I get a sense of hope; not just pride in our profession, but hope that what Lincoln called the 'better angels of ourselves' can emerge most forcefully, precisely at the moments when we are most troubled.

Chapter 26

Restorative justice – answers to deficits in modernity?

Nils Christie

Restorative justice has been quite a remarkable growth area in several modern states throughout the last decade. Measured by the number of articles, books, small and large conferences, and concrete initiatives, not much can compete within other fields of penal policies.

Why this surge in interest just now? That will be my theme here.

The reappearance of roots

First, highly industrialized societies have been increasingly interested in and aware of their roots, as with Maoris in New Zealand, North American Indians, or Inuits in the far North. The culture of the original inhabitants gets more attention – maybe there was after all something of value here? One of their values increasingly deemed useful, even for modernity, is their way of solving conflicts with an emphasis on creating peace rather than internal war. A particular stimulation for the interest in restorative justice has been what happened in the famous truth and reconciliation commissions of South Africa after apartheid, and in a great number of other states where severe repression has taken place. And we have seen another interesting example in New Zealand, where elements of Maori law are built into the child welfare system.

The overextension of the penal system

As a result of profound changes in our social system, more and more of those acts seen as unwanted are considered crimes. The whole system of formal control and punishment thereby takes a more dominant position.

More people are apprehended by the police; more appear before the judges as accused, witnesses, or victims; and more receive punishment – pain intended as pain. In my country, Norway, complaints to the police of behaviour seen as crimes have increased more than ten times throughout the last 50 years. The prison population has doubled and has now reached the, for us, unheard-of figure in modern times of 70 per 100,000 of the population. In the USA, more than 700 per 100,000 are in prisons.[1]

This puts more and more pressure on the criminal justice system for control. The penal courts have become machineries for mass production, as reflected in attempts to standardise the procedure by the use of sentencing tables, and in the steady increase in the prison population. The abundance of research reports on the lack of utility in what the courts are doing and, in view of the moral dilemmas in delivering pain without purpose, the difficulties built into criminal courts become increasingly clear.

Many societies are troubled by the idea of intentionally inflicting pain on other human beings, especially those perceiving themselves as welfare states, or as Christian ones, where some ideas of kindness and forgiving lurk in the background. The increase in the use of formal punishment makes the contradictions increasingly felt. It might soften the conflict to turn to some of the major theories on the reasons for punishment. Here we meet arguments on the *usefulness* of punishment. First of all, we are told that delivery of pain is good for deterrence. If we did not punish person A for his bad acts, persons B, C, and D would soon follow.

If arguments about deterrence are not enough to carry the moral burden of inflicting severe pain on fellow human beings, arguments of treatment come up. The culprit needs punishment to learn his lesson. At least, it might be seen as useful to get rid of the person for a period – even if most of us know that she or he will be even more problematic after that lesson.

A large body of research indicates that the penal system does *not* reach these goals. But such findings have no great impact. This is not surprising. Without good, measurable reasons based on utility, we would be forced to accept that we had other reasons for punishment, – or that we did it without reasons at all.

Here another type of argument for punishment appears. Evil acts might need evil counter acts. A value has been hurt, and punishment might be seen as a way of restoring the dignity of that value. In addition, it is said that the population – the whole or in parts – is angry and cries for vengeance. If punishment were not applied, the population might be unhappy and disintegrate. Criminal courts might here, in a 'Durkheimian' perspective, function as organisations to give anger an outlet and thereby restore the dignity of the value.

But again trouble arises, this time due to a clash in values. Generally, we hail such values as kindness, care and forgiveness. And some states insist they are welfare states – and actually provide welfare for large parts of their populations. Most ideologies in such states claim that a major goal is to reduce pain, not to use it for the purpose of vengeance. In addition, there is the question of whether values can be restored by penal actions – is the value of life protected by killing the killer?

Then, to a third factor behind the growth of restorative justices:

The lack of room for grief and anger in modern societies

One of the worst curses you might inflict upon another person in medieval times was to say: I hope you will die suddenly far from home! Philippe Ariès (1981) describes this in his beautiful book on death and dying.[2]

Why was this curse so terrible? Because it meant that you were removed from participation in your own death. Even if you were among the most humble of persons, you had one moment in life where you were at the centre of everybody's attention. In the ideal case, the priest arrived, neighbours likewise, relatives, friends – they were all there, talking about you, refreshing past history, creating a picture of the person that was to leave. When you had heard enough, you left this earth, while some of those around you remained in the room to prevent the devil from snatching your soul before its arrival in heaven. But first and foremost, it was a conscious death with many to bear witness. Then came the funeral. It would be beyond comprehension if all those with even a minimum of relation to the deceased were not there. Outsiders also paid respect to funeral rituals. I am old enough to remember my father standing attentively at the roadside with hat in hand if a funeral procession in cars passed us. Black clothing, a veil for the widow, and months of mourning were obligatory. A reminiscence of it can still be seen in royal families.

What a contrast to our time.

The great majority of deaths in modern Western societies occur in hospitals or nursing homes. Death takes place concealed from the person's ordinary network and also often concealed from the dying person – who has been given false hope of survival and therefore is unaware of what is to happen, and/or has been drugged to stupor. The announcement that death has occurred will sometimes appear after the funeral has taken place.

What does it mean?

It can be read as a reflection of our type of society. We are less involved in one another's lives and therefore also in one another's deaths, and we are to a limited extent part of networks with a binding importance to us. The modern funeral reflects, and also intensifies, all this. One more lost opportunity for sharing emotional experiences and also a lost opportunity for reunions above the wear and tear of daily life.

Nonetheless, normally, it is not *all* gone. Funerals are one of the few arenas left where it is still legitimate to express feelings. Tears are here not signs of weakness, but of belonging to humanity. Crocodile tears might appear, but that derogatory term tells how despised they are.

It seems safe to say that funerals by and large are arenas for expressive behaviour. It is a place for *expression of grief with no other purpose than expression of grief*. A rational mind might see this as a waste of opportunity. Why not have some posters in or out of church or crematorium, saying: 'If he had not smoked, we would not be here now.' Or, 'Smoking kills', 'Don't drive after drinking', 'Eat more fruit!' It can't be done, and we know it.

As a preliminary conclusion: Death and death rituals are still important also at the personal level. But we have less of the real death, more of the plastic one. The death we take most part in is death in the media, types of death that at the same time are very close and very remote. At home we can daily observe death; while we eat, wash the dishes, play with the children. A glance at the TV reveals the usual slaughter in Iraq, Afghanistan or Palestine. For relaxation, we might watch a crime story. We are enmeshed in plastic deaths, habituated to the irrelevance of dying.

Death and funerals have waned, while crime and punishments have waxed. This has several social consequences.

Less that unites and more that divides

Funerals might unite us in sorrow – possible antagonists keep away, or keep their thoughts for themselves. However, criminal courts are arenas that emphasize conflicts. Criminal courts are deep in a process of fact finding; what happened, how and when? The accused person has a major enemy in the court, the prosecutor, but also a friend, the defending counsel. So also with many among the witnesses, they have potential enemies in the room, the representative for the other party or among listeners in from the street. This is not a situation for openness, but for guarded statements and for limits on information given; keep quiet, or it might harm your own position. Typically, only witnesses are by law obliged to tell the truth; from the accused, no honesty is expected.

Good values versus bad ones

Funerals are also situations emphasizing positive contributions, not negative ones. British newspapers are famous for their honest obituaries of public figures, an art slightly shocking to those of us outside the UK. But in ordinary social life related to the funeral, it is the good deeds that are remembered; how kind she or he had been, what a kind father, good worker, what a stimulating companion. Activities around the dying person, and later at the funeral can be seen as emphasizing the positive values in life. It is a sort of resurrection of positive values, exemplified from the life of the deceased.

Funerals might be the beginning of the end of mourning. It can't be changed; she is dead. There is a sort of closure, as the coffin disappears. Tears and despair, but in the good cases also some solemn relief. A picture can be painted in the mind of the survivors, a picture of ideals that the deceased comes to exemplify.

In criminal courts, it is the negative values that reign. Someone has probably done something wrong. If so, she or he will have to suffer. Bad deeds are at the centre of attention. Positive values are there only as underlying premises when the bad acts are condemned. Also here a picture is painted, but this time a picture of disgusting acts and people. It becomes a celebration of badness, not goodness. And it becomes a situation where major actors often leave in dissatisfaction, finding the punishments much too mild. A picture of a monster will often remain in the victim's mind, the harmed values are not restored, and wish for vengeance might become the dominant theme for a long time.

The whole person, versus the parts

Not all is told about the dying or deceased, only parts of the story, parts seen as right to present in this situation. But the selected elements are not challenged, there and then. To do so would not serve any interest and would be seen as highly unkind. We get a concentration on the positive parts. When it comes to the other parts, we hide them behind RIP – rest in peace.

The contrast to the criminal court could not be greater. Criminal courts are solemn arenas for concentrating attention on blame and pain. Is the person guilty and, if so, what would be the right amount of suffering? To protect against abuse, ancient rules of procedure have been developed, symbolized by Lady Justice: blindfolded with sword in hand, but also holding the scales of justice aloft. Equal cases are to receive an equal amount of pain. But cases – acts and their perpetrators – are never equal. Therefore, they have to be *made* equal. Eliminating complicating information makes sure that this happens. Legal training is to a large extent training in what is *not* relevant and therefore not acceptable to bring up in court. Courtrooms are therefore not places for revealing the *whole* story – only those bits and parts that the judiciary deem relevant. What the parties might feel to be of central importance might be seen as irrelevant and therefore cut off in court. Again and again, we meet the same complaints both from victims and from persons sentenced: 'The attendance in court was the worst part of it all. I never got a chance to present the whole story.'

A fertile ground for restorative justice

Restorative justice can in this whole perspective be seen as an answer to a deficit situation in modernity. This type of justice comes in many forms. Central to them all is their fact-finding activity – but then *facts as the parties see these facts*. Fact finding is the dominant question in several Latin-American countries that now are free from military dictatorship: what happened? Where are they, those that disappeared? My grandchildren, are they still alive, now as adults, here or in another country? Or my wife, I know she was killed, but where are her remains hidden? Or, on the more trivial level in Europe: you robbed me – why me? Maybe I am still in danger? And what sort of person are you, who could do this? You have created anxiety, or in more extreme cases, you have destroyed so much of my life; how could you do such a thing?

Peacemakers

Most forms of restorative justice have also another element in common: they strive, in one way or another, to create peace. Peace by finding some sort of truth.[3] Or peace created through some sort of understanding of why the other party acted as he or she did, or through the acceptance of some sort of excuse or compensation.

Criminal law also makes a claim of creating peace between parties, but this is often an unfounded claim. Growing up in an occupied and Nazified country, I later experienced how little peace was created though the severe punishments that followed after the war. Observing everyday penal processes, I see the same: long rows of mostly poor and deprived people on their way into prison; the same persons, only more deprived and damaged, on their way out again. If punishment were to have any meaning in the creation of peace, there should be an orchestra outside all exits from prisons. Out they should come, all those who had purged their sins, and great ceremonies should have been arranged in their honour to celebrate their homecoming.

No sword in hand

The most important among the differences between criminal courts and arrangements for mediation is that the mediators have no sword in hand. They are there to find out what happened, and hopefully come closer to some sort of solution that might be acceptable to the parties, but they are not there to decide on guilt or innocence, or to inflict pain if guilt is found.

Without the sword, most is changed. Particularly, the need for control of the controllers is diminished. When punishment is not central, the emphasis on equal treatment of equal cases is reduced. Mediators are not to the same extent as criminal court judges forced to limit the information to what is seen as 'legally relevant'. *Relevance is more what the parties find relevant.* This opens up the space for expressive behaviour. Crying, or expressing anger or joy, becomes possible, sometimes encouraged. 'The Kleenex-commission' was a half-way derogatory term now and then used for the South African Restorative Justice Commission (Tutu 1999). These are not arenas for cool reasoning leading to conclusions on the degree of guilt and decisions on the amount of intended pain the offender is to suffer. It is not a system that makes it rational for the parties to keep back emotions.

On form

An essential feature of restorative justice is openness as to what sort of phenomenon stands at the centre of attention. Much is done *not* to activate the terminology from criminal law. One of the ideals is *not* to use terms such as 'victim' and 'offender', but instead to talk about 'parties' in a conflict. In tune with this, it is seen as useful to emphasize 'information as the parties see it' – attempting to bring to the forefront the meaning the acts have for the participants in the process. This is essential. So often, it is not the concrete acts that are disputed, but the *meaning* of these acts, how they were intended, how they turned out. At the core of a mediative process lies the intention to bring variations in these meanings into the open, thereby also creating an opening for changes in the meaning given to the acts by one or both parties.

On the advantage of ordinary language

For civil – and civilizing – purposes, it is important to try not to be captured by the terminology of the specialists. Maybe most citizens within highly industrialized countries are better educated than before. But we are at the same time poorer when it comes to language. Highly specialized groups monopolize so many of the terms. Particularly dangerous in this connection are psychiatrists and lawyers. They tell us what things are with concepts from law books or diagnostic tables. To escape the dominance of the specialists, it might be helpful to use a more narrative form. For mediation or restorative justice, it is both important and possible to let parties tell the whole story, instead of letting specialists translate bits and pieces of the occurrences into their professional terminology. Storytelling, often in the form of short novels, or poetry, might provide more adequate linguistic tools for creating common understanding between common people – of the type we all actually are.

Liberated from the terminology of law and psychiatry, participants will be more able to take part in decisions about their own story.

But if a crime has occurred?

To get my point across, I will be blunt and brutal and say: crime does not exist. Acts are not, they become – their meanings are created through a complex interplay between cultural heritage, power relations within the social system, and various, often conflicting, interests among the directly involved parties. Who has the motivation as well as the power to get the acts branded as crime? Acts considered crimes are thus a product of cultural, social and mental processes. Crime is thus a product of cultural, social and mental processes. For all acts, including those seen as unwanted, there are dozens of possible ways to understand them: bad, mad, evil, misplaced honour, youth, bravado, political heroism – or crime. The 'same' acts can thus be met within several parallel systems such as judicial, psychiatric, pedagogic or theological. And as stated above, as a result of profound changes in our social system, more and more unwanted acts are considered crime. The whole penal system assumes a more dominant position.

This is exactly what is counteracted by restorative justice. This is what makes it so important *not* to be captured by the criminal law terminology of crime, victim/offender or amount of punishment. Words are dangerous tools, they capture our minds, shape our thoughts. In the old days, a considerable amount of killing took place in the valleys of Norway. If three reliable men saw the killings as accidents – it might have been play or competition among slightly drunk young males – the king was not informed.[4] The case could be resolved with compensation and peace might be re-established in the valley (Sandmo 1999).

Major gains

Institutions for restorative justice let the sorrow come out and be expressed publicly. There are no narrow limits on relevance in a mediative process. What is relevant to the parties is relevant to the process. It is a ceremony which creates an opportunity to express deep grief. It is a situation that gives opportunities to expose how awful the losses have been. Anger and blame can also be expressed, since this is not directly connected with decisions on the degree of guilt and on what in this situation would be the correct amount of pain. It is a forum for expression of sorrow and blame, but without decisions on the delivery of pain attached.

Organizations for mediation or restorative justice create possibilities to convert anger to sorrow, while the criminal court process to a larger extent confirms anger and bitterness and often strengthens these feelings. It is a situation built for opposition and fight, and the punishment will often be seen as 'wrong' by both parties. Anger might lead to further destruction and increased conflicts. Sorrow might, with some support, lead to relief and possibilities for peace.

Funeral ceremonies and criminal court proceedings are places of obvious significance in most modern societies. Most of us cannot imagine death without some sort of ceremonial ending. When the body of the supposed dead person is not found, mourning takes longer. My supposition is that ceremonies for restorative justice little by little will be seen as a completely natural part of any well-functioning society. This is what is developing, just in these days.

Dangers ahead

Fine. And not so fine. Nothing might destroy like success. Many are attracted by the activity level, enthusiasm and expansion within this field. It has in some countries evolved into a growth industry. This threatens some of the basic ideas behind restorative justice, particularly the idea that ordinary people should get access to their own conflicts – and also that it is important that the surrounding society should be involved. This very idea is more important now than ever. We live in situations where important parts of civil society are weakened. This is particularly so within 'highly developed societies'. It is a result of the expanding educational system within these societies. An increasingly large part of the population is receiving high school or university diplomas, often of an unspecified type. This means that they are highly educated for tasks not yet specified. But they need a career to make a living, and are eagerly on the outlook for opportunities. Conflicts are fine. Entrepreneurs create training courses and establish firms – and little by little, we have a new profession of mediators. One more specialty. Good for those earning a living by it, but at the same time one more challenge removed from civil society. One more of those tasks people of all sorts could unite around. Instead of strengthening civil society, this trend might remove challenging tasks. We will know that mediators know best, and we abdicate. Soon there are no tasks left in the neighbourhood, and we can safely retreat to privacy and leave everything else to experts. They certainly know what is best.[5]

Notes

1 I describe the mechanisms behind this development in *A Suitable Amount of Crime* (Christie 2004).
2 A beautiful description of Nordic rituals can be found in Troels Lund (1929– 1931).
3 See Vanspauwen *et al.* (to be published).
4 Happily, he had his throne far away in Denmark at that time.
5 I discussed some of the dangers in that success in a paper on the thirtieth anniversary of criminology at Sheffield in September 2006.

References

Ariès, P. (1982) *The Hour of our Death*. New York: Vintage Books.
Christie, N. (2004) *A Suitable Amount of Crime*. London and New York: Routledge.

Sandmo, E. (1999) *Voldssamfunnets undergang. Om disiplineringen av Norge på 1600-tallet*. Oslo: Universitetsforlaget.

Troels, L. (1929–31) *Dagligt Liv i Norden i det Sekstende Aarhundrede*. Ved Knud Fabricius. Bind IV, Fjortende Bog; *Livsavslutning. Gyldendalske Boghandel 1929–31*.

Tutu, D. (1999) *No Future Without Forgiveness*. (In Norwegian: Ingen fremtid uten tilgivelse. Pax 2000.)

Vanspauwen, K., Parmentier, S. and Weitekamp, E. (2005) *Restorative Justice for Victims of Mass Violence. Reconsidering the Building Blocks of Post-Conflict Justice*. Manuscript.

Chapter 27

The flow of boundaries: gays, queers and intimate citizenship

Ken Plummer

> We are confronting a universe marked by tremendous fluidity; it won't and can't stand still. It is a universe where fragmentation, splintering, and disappearance are the mirror images of appearance, emergence and coalescence.
>
> Anselm Strauss (1993: 19)

I wish to start with some strong assertions. The first is (the currently very unfashionable view) that identities and citizenship both imply some sense of a core, a boundary, a unity. Thus, to have an identity is also to suggest a non-identity (who one is not); and to be a citizen is also to suggest a non-citizen (someone who does not belong to a specified citizen group). This unity is also to be found between identity and citizenship; each is implicated in the other: it is hard to be a citizen without an identity (though we could have identities that are not linked to citizenship). As Isin and Wood (1999: 20) say, 'The affinity between citizenship and identity is that they are both group markers. Citizenship marks out the members of a polity from another as well as members of a polity from non-members. Identity marks out groups from each other as well as allowing for the constitution of groups as targets.' My second assertion (almost) contradicts this. It is that as modernity accelerates into a new kind of social order (postmodern, late modern, liquid, informational, network, etc.), identities are more readily seen as unstable, shifting, and fragmented while citizenship likewise is becoming flexible (Ong 1999), differentiated (Kymlicka 1995), and pluralistic (Ellison 1997). Therefore, the centre no longer seems to hold. And my third assertion is that when we come to specific identities such as 'the gay and lesbian identity', we find these issues clearly and sharply exemplified: some believe only the former – gay identity is indeed fixed – and some stress the latter – to the point that gay identity is itself a fiction or a strategy of control. It is with these tensions that this chapter is concerned.

There are several reasons that these debates are so popular today. One is that late-modern societies highlight in major ways the fragmentation, splits, flows, mobilities, and differences rather than the (supposed) harmonies and unities of social life. In many ways, though, this is not necessarily a new view: it is the world of Heraclitus's 'flux', and the world of the pragmatic symbolic interactionist. As the late Anselm Strauss (1993) put it: we live in a world of 'continual permutations of action'.

Another reason is that it serves to highlight some classic problems of social theory: does rapid social change bring chaos? How much transgression can a society take? Are there limits? How can we handle taboo, dirt and pollution? Do all societies have them? How much difference can we live with? Must societies and people have moral boundaries? Are classification systems needed? Can we find links between social classifications and personal classifications? We can find it being discussed in some of the classics of social theory. For Cooley (1998), it is a distinction between the ingroup and the outgroup. For Weber, some of these ideas hover around the notion of 'ideal type'. Even for Marx, there is a diffuse sense of class ('in itself') and a more tightly bound, self-aware 'class for itself'. The problems of boundaries (and transgression) are perennials of social analysis (Jenks 2003).

A third reason for the popularity of the debate concerns the rise of multiculturalism and the politics of all kinds of 'difference groups', and in the case here, sexual minorities – the clashes over essentialism and phenomenalism, and the links to social movements politics, rights and 'the politics of identity'. I will return to these concerns later.

Boundary problems

The opening question, then, is can we live without borders, boundaries, frameworks, classifications, order? Some radical – anarchist? – tendencies do indeed want to see this; but most philosophers and sociologists would see this as neither sociologically possible, nor humanly desirable. Writing in his magisterial *The Sources of the Self*, Charles Taylor can say:

I want to defend the strong thesis that doing without frameworks is utterly impossible for us; otherwise put, that the horizons within which we live our lives and which make sense of them have to include these strong qualitative discriminations. … The claim is that living within such strongly qualified horizons is constitutive of human agency, that stepping outside these limits would be tantamount to stepping outside what we would recognize as integral, that is undamaged, human personhood (Taylor 1989: 27).

Earlier, the sociologist Durkheim saw the normal and the pathological as twin processes, bound up with the conditions of social life. For him, the simple classification of the normal and the pathological served to mark out moral boundaries, and unite people against common enemies. It establishes that there is a 'we' and the 'Other', and it is hard to find instances of societies which do not do this.

Therefore, many have argued the need for classification grids of order on both the personal and the societal levels, of the need for common frameworks (Durkheim 1964a, 1996b, 1971; Mauss 1970; Bourdieu 1993), so that the liberal sociological critic Alan Wolfe is compelled to say: 'It is impossible to imagine a society without boundaries' (Wolfe 1992: 323).

Inclusive democracy and exclusive group centeredness are necessary for a rich but just social life. Without particular groups with sharply defined boundaries, life in modern society would be unbearable. … Yet if the boundaries between particular groups are too rigid, we would have no general obligations…. We would live together with people exactly like ourselves, unexposed to the challenge of strangers, the lure of cosmopolitanism, and the expansion of moral possibility that comes with responsiveness to the generalized other (Wolfe 1992: 311).

By its very terminology, some would argue that the idea of identity also implies some sense of sameness, commonality, continuity: if not actually present, the search is nevertheless at least on for an identity – a project of knowing who one is or what one's nation is. The category behind the identity is presumed and is often stridently clear. 'I am what I am.' From nation states to individual psyches, it speaks metaphorically to a constant concern of the day: sameness, unity, commonality – as opposed to conflicts, differences, fragmentation. It derives from the Latin *idem*, the same (Late Latin = *identitas*) and enters the English language around 1570 (defined as 'the quality or condition of being the same; absolute or essential sameness; oneness').

A further linked concept – that of citizenship – also traditionally highlights the boundaries and margins of societies or groups. To be a citizen – whether as status or participant – is to imply being inside a particular frame, to belong; and simultaneously to imply someone who is not a citizen, and hence outside that frame. In the past, the term 'citizenship' has usually been a term of unity and hence, by implication, a term of exclusion. And identity and citizenship are closely linked. To speak of citizenship must really imply a person, a voice, a recognized type, an identity, a locus, a position from which the citizenship claims can be made. In the past, this may have a been a universalized person (usually a white, privileged male).

In short, classification systems are needed in order to make sense of the world and boundaries are needed to mark out 'group belonging' (the we) from others. Many agree, then, that a clear case can be made that classifications and boundaries are needed for identities, citizenship and, indeed, societies. But there are some who argue that it may well have been modernity itself which brought this current preoccupation with issues of *classification* and its partner *ambivalence*. In this problem of classification lies the search for order. Every act of classification is an act of inclusion and exclusion, and as Bauman says 'ambivalence is a side product of the labour of classification; and it calls for yet more classifying effort ... the struggle against ambivalence is, therefore, both self destructive and self propelling' (1991: 3).

Likewise, 'order is what is not chaos; chaos is what is not orderly. Order and chaos are *modern* twins' (p. 4) This is our modernist plight. I find this slightly paradoxical, but it does raise many issues. In our zeal to classify and categorize, we fail. The world is too complex to manage this effectively. And so in the process of classifying, we find the need to search out more and more forms of classification. I sense this may be true of all societies, though maybe it is more intense in modernist ones, for, as Mary Douglas says in *Purity and Danger*:

> Dirt is the by-product of a systematic ordering and classification of matter, in so far as ordering involves rejecting inappropriate elements.... Dirt ... appears a residual category, rejected from the normal scheme of classification (Douglas 1966/1970: 48).

And the existence of 'dirt' leads to the zeal to classify more and more, and expunge and annihilate the dirt that this may leave.

Boundaries and hostilities: constructing the 'Other' and the enemy

Borders and boundaries can be perfectly tame, harmless and useful. A garden fence can be a helpful marker. But they can also be harbingers of hatred. Many have commented upon this – I often recall the famous statement by Thomas Szasz that the 'the first law of the jungle is kill or be killed', while 'the first law of human society was stigmatize or be stigmatized'. It is precisely because the inside/outside debate so often leads to enemies – with all the mocking injury and terrorist exterminations they can bring – that is especially potent. In many ways, as Beck (1997: 81) says, 'enemy stereotypes empower'. The invention of the Other galvanizes animosity. In a telling phrase, Bauman remarks:

> Woman is the other of man, animal is the other of human, stranger is the other of native, abnormality the other of norm, deviation the other of law abiding, illness the other of health, insanity the other of reason, lay public the other of expert, foreigner the other of state subject, enemy the other of friend (Bauman 1991: 8).

While William Connolly turns it into a major 'problem of evil':

> Doubts about self identity are posed and resolved by the constitution of an other against which the identity may define itself. To explore this territory is to struggle against the evil by attempts to secure the surety of self identity. Responding to the second problem of evil involves challenging those political tactics of self reassurance: problematising conceptions of identity, ethics, responsibility, politics, order, democracy, sovereignty, community and discourse through which solutions to the first problem are sustained; and exposing rituals of sacrifice concealed by established presentation of these themes (Connolly 1991: x).

There are many theories which attempt to understand this process: from scapegoating, moral indignation, class conflict, status politics and the like. The point simply here is that the drawing of boundaries is usually not a matter to be taken too lightly, and it can be a matter of great seriousness. A lot is at stake with our boundaries: people are known to die literally for them.

The flows of boundaries

But there is a seeming contradiction in much of this: while boundaries and classifications are needed, they are persistently moving, changing and even sometimes dissolving. In fact, I do not see this as a contradiction at all. For while we are always in need of boundaries, these boundaries themselves are open to flows, movements, mobilities.

They are constantly being reworked, redrawn, reshaped. Although there are clear needs for boundaries – in societies, identities, citizenship, etc. – for human functioning, the nature of these boundaries is constantly changing. They become more and more subject to flows, fluidities, transformations, amorphousness, networks, contingencies, movement, escapes. John Urry's recent influential book *Sociology Beyond Societies* (1999) talks of *mobilities* and suggests that in such a world, borders and boundaries cannot remain fixed. They can be present, but they become a shifting presence, as the edges are always being renegotiated.

Oddly, if we look back over the history of the term 'identity', it can soon be seen that the whole concept is stuffed full of change and precariousness. It is far from being a stable and well-bounded entity. The fluctuant, processual nature of identity and self is easily seen in the full lineage of interactionist thought – from Cooley's swirling looking-glass imagery (1998) through James to Mead on identities 'in crisis' for at least the last 75 years: the 'other-directed' self, the impulsive self, the mutable self, the protean self, the homeless mind, and on to Goffman's 'presented self'. The idea that the self is invented, produced socially, open to constant change and in crisis is very far indeed from being a new idea (though many recent writers seriously overlook this matter!). In all these views, then, identity is not really very well bounded at all: it is permanently unsettled, destabilized, under provisional construction, very much a project and never a thing (see also Baumeister 1986).

And just as identity is open to this debate, so too is citizenship. Will Kymlicka in his influential book *Multicultural Citizenship* (1995) makes a powerful claim for minority rights within citizenship frameworks. He is concerned with the growing clash of majorities and minorities within a given state over such things as language rights, education curriculums, immigration policies, and national symbols like public holidays. Although he is primarily talking about the clash of ethnic groups with 'dominant cultures' across the world as he develops his theory of 'multicultural' citizenship, I think his thesis also has relevance to other sorts of minorities, including gays and lesbians. His theory is a major defence and development of liberalism in which he tries to find some universal common grounds along with a recognition of differences. As he says, 'Citizenship should be a forum where people transcend their differences, and think about the common good' (Kymlicka 1995: 175). But if this is so, how can we deal with what falls outside? And indeed, must something fall outside? Taking his argument to the situation of women, who have traditionally been excluded from citizenship, Ruth Lister seeks what she calls a 'differentiated universalism': 'a universalism that stands in a creative tension to diversity and difference and that challenges the divisions and exclusionary inequalities which stem from this diversity' (Lister 1997: 66). However, as she wisely remarks, the difficulties in this project 'are not to be underestimated' (Lister 1997: 90).

So the issue is really not just the *existence* of boundaries but the *nature* of these boundaries. Contemporary identity and citizenship debates live on the borders of this very problem – recognizing the necessity of boundaries and classifications while at the same time wishing to stretch them to include multiple differences and change. Maybe the task ahead is to develop further ideas of 'differentiated universalisms' whereby boundaries remain present but shift and sway, are less permanently settled, less rigid and divisive, and become more porous, more archipelago-like, more open to change. Boundaries are always being reworked and are not permanently settled. They become the recurrent sites for debates about what is good and what is not: they display 'moral effervescence'. And all this would lead to recognition of the continuous need for both a simultaneous drive toward a common good and what has been called 'a pluralization ethos'.

The stability of classification with which I started has now gone. We arrive, then, at the classic problems of universals and differences: of who is inside or outside, is included or excluded, both within and across social worlds. Often such processes of boundary making have had strong patriarchal, racializing and homophobic elements – drawing boundaries that tacitly (and sometimes not so tacitly) exclude others on gendered, race and sexual grounds. Rightly, the last decades of the twentieth century have seen a lot of analysis that has attempted to remove these boundaries and that celebrated a politics of difference. *So the issue is really not just the existence of boundaries (which may be necessary) but the nature of these boundaries.*

Sexual boundaries and classifications

Among the many boundary systems of a society are ones based on sexuality. All societies are likely to create symbolic orders which render some sexual experiences acceptable, others less so and some strictly taboo. Much talk of transgression of boundaries is indeed connected to 'the sexual' – Foucault's writing (notably *The History of Sexuality* (1976/9)) is deeply concerned with the emergence of sexual classificatory systems in the nineteenth century, and the ways in which they served to regulate people's lives. Embedded in such classification systems lie the workings of power. Likewise, Murray Davis, in *Smut*, talks of a structure which divides 'normal sex' from 'perverted sex' (Davis 1982), while Gayle Rubin (1984) has depicted the classifications of a sex hierarchy alongside the invention of a charmed circle, whereby some sexualities are acceptable and others are not. Sadomasochism (S/M) and child sexualities are often seen as the patterns of sexualities that defy any sense of social order: they are deeply transgressive and not capable of being constrained (Semiotext 1981/1995). For many societies, same-sex relations act as boundary challenger. To end this chapter I will look at this in a little more detail.

Queers, post-gays and the rest: the challenges to identity and citizenship

Ever since its arrival in academia during the 1970s, lesbian and gay studies has been haunted by the issue of categorization (and indeed the identity problem) (cf. Plummer 1981, 1992). To speak of lesbian and gay identities, then, is to create the potential for lesbians and gays to be recognized, have rights and become citizens. And such identities bring pasts, presents and futures: a sense of past histories, a defining 'Other' different from you, and hints for future conduct based in part on this 'otherness'. In the past, these 'identities of citizenship' were usually those of a universalized person and were made to seem rather solid, permanent, fixed, essential. (It was indeed usually a white, privileged, male.) But 'gay identity' brings a series of traps – it extends a polarity or dualism of 'them' and 'us'. It brings a category problem – who does and who does not 'fit'. It reifies same-sex experience into *an essence* – it cannot begin to capture the full complexities of what we might provisionally sense as 'same-sex experience', which may be youthful or old, black or white, disabled or non-disabled – to engage in just a few of the most simplistic variations. So our notions of identities from which to speak have to become more varied, pluralized and open than this, while acknowledging some kinds of continuities and boundaries. Fixed, clear voices seem now to have become weakened, identities ebb and flow, and voices now speak from a multiplicity of shifting and unsettled positions. The voices are always in dialogic process, and people speaking from various identities and positions may well find these have to shift in the very processes of argumentation. But they cannot speak at all if they do not recognize the categories at all – however humblingly inadequate they may be. We need what might be called a *thin essentialism*.

But this also raises the issue as to whether citizenship can ever allow for a radical or transgressive or queer identity (Bell and Binnie 2000; Phelan 2001). Ideas of citizenship falter around transgression and assimilation: how, in short, can you stay 'queer and radical' and yet be a 'good citizen'. Citizenship may well work directly against the 'bad gays' and foster social exclusion processes. In one sense, the modern history of the lesbian and gay movement has been a history of conflict between assimilationists and radicals. The former want to argue that homosexuality is normal, that gays and lesbians should get equal rights, and that gays and lesbians should be 'good citizens'. They want to be inside the boundaries set by a patriarchal and heteronormative society. They want to find their *'place at the table'* (Bahr 1993), and want to be *'virtually normal'* (Sullivan 1995). They have entered the mainstream of normalisation. Assimilationists want gays and lesbians to enter the 'charmed circle', and nothing should be done to weaken this – public sex, drugs, drag, or even radical marches are taboo.

By contrast, 'radicals' argue that homosexualities and other transgressive sexualities are invariably 'outside'. To get rights and become a citizen is to become normalized and to reinforce the dominant values. Radicals usually celebrate sexual desire in all its hedonistic forms as providing a 'seductive (and dangerous) vision of alternative possibilities'. They claim, indeed, that (male) homosexuals are 'obsessed' with sex, that homosexuality is a 'flight' from the responsibilities of mature sexuality and celebrates the world of S/M, leather sex, the fetish scene and the whole world of what we might call 'polysexualities'. Sex, sex and more sex in all its forms is the name of the game. Homosexuality is not meant to fit in; transgressive radicals are meant to pose challenges, create dangers, be a menace, bring about radical changes, and lie outside the borders and the boundaries. They are the sexual outlaws. For lesbians, too, the issue of being a lesbian is seen as much more threatening than mere assimilation. The issue of butchness is on the agenda; the lesbian is a threat and a menace; radical dykes, drag kings and other forms of 'female masculinity' (Halberstam 1998) work as a threat.

Queering identity

The more radical tendency has since the late 1980s (in North America, largely as a humanities/multicultural-based response to a more limited 'lesbian and gay studies') been through 'queer'. Queer is most definitely meant to take us beyond the boundaries and borders of heteronormativity. The roots of queer theory (if not the term) are usually seen to lie in the work of Eve Kosofsky Sedgwick. She argues that the central classifying device of the nineteenth and twentieth centuries – the overarching borders of society – are composed of the hetero/homo binary divide:

... many of the major nodes of thought and knowledge in twentieth century Western culture as a whole are structured – indeed fractured – by a chronic, now endemic crisis of homo/heterosexual definition, indicatively male, dating from the end of the nineteenth century ... an understanding of any aspect of modern Western culture must be, not merely incomplete, but damaged in its central substance to the degree that it does not incorporate a critical analysis of modern Homo/heterosexual definition (Sedgwick 1990: 1).

The heart to queer theory, then, must be seen as a *radical stance around sexuality and gender that denies any fixed categories and seeks to subvert any tendencies toward normality within its study.* 'Queer' may be seen as partially deconstructing our own discourses and creating a greater openness in the way we think through our categories. It is, to quote Michael Warner, a stark attack on 'normal business in the academy' (Warner 1993: 25). Queer theory explicitly challenges any kind of closure or settlement, and so any attempts at definition or codification must be non-starters. Queer theory is really post-structuralism (and postmodernism) applied to sexualities and genders in a stance in which sexual categories are seen to be open, fluid and non-fixed: both the boundaries of heterosexual/homosexual and sex/gender are challenged. Indeed, categories such as gay, lesbian and heterosexual become 'deconstructed'. There is a decentring of identity. Along with this, both the so-called deviance paradigm and the minority/majority frameworks are abandoned and the interest lies in a logic of insiders/outsiders and transgression.

Liberation and rights give way to transgression and carnival as a goal of political action – what has been called a 'politics of provocation' – and all normalizing, assimilationist and accommodationist strategies are shunned. Its most common objects of study are textual – films, videos, novels, poetry, visual images – and its academic work becomes ironic and paradoxical. Its most frequent interests include a variety of sexual fetishes, drag kings and drag queens, gender and sexual playfulness, cybersexualities, polyarmoury, sadomasochism and all the social worlds of the so-called radical sexual fringe that can be seen to break beyond boundaries. But there are problems here – the main concern is that queer theory itself brings a category/boundary problem: what Josh Gamson has described as a queer dilemma. He claims that while it is important to have queer/deconstructive ideas that break down categories, there is also, for Gamson and others, a clear need for a gay public collective identity (around which activism can galvanize). As he says: 'fixed identity categories are both the basis for oppression and political power' (Gamson 1996/8: 408). There are very many from within the lesbian, gay, bisexual and transgender movement (LGBT, as it is currently clumsily called) who also reject the tendency to deconstruct the very idea of gay and lesbian identity, hence abolishing a field of study and politics when it has only just got going. So all is not well in the house of queer.

A rival strategy: toward (postmodern?) intimate citizenship in a fuzzy world

Perhaps the major rival – albeit an often co-opted rival – to the constructing of queer theory has been the development of claims for 'sexual citizenship' (I prefer the term 'intimate citizenship' which can have a much wider and more amorphous meaning). In the writings of theorists such as Shane Phelan (2001), David Evans (whose book of that title appeared as early as 1993), Jeffrey Weeks (1998) and Diane Richardson (1998), it has become a key idea. In one sense, of course, it is far from new and it sounds deeply conventional, stuck within the borders and boundaries of the patriarchal and homophobic past. And it is indeed true that much of the work of the early lesbian, gay, and women's movements was built on 'constructed' assumptions of sexual rights. It was just not always made very clear that 'rights' were a key foundation, although nowadays this is being made very explicit (Plummer 2006). Yet, whatever its distant presence may have been in citizenship debates, it was largely hidden. Both political and social theory tend to deny the sexual – 'the intimate' is routinely minimized, written out, 'trashed'. But in a sense, all citizenship is 'sexual citizenship, as citizenship is inseparable from identity, and sexuality is central to identity' (Bell and Binnie 2000: 67). And yet the borders are policed around heterosexual families, homophobia, patriarchy and sex negativism. There is a core. And lesbians and gays do not easily sit within.

The trouble with such sexual citizenship is that it also highlights the clear need for boundaries. It marks out a mode, once again, of who is in society (the citizen) and who is outside (the non-citizen). To create, for example, gay citizens, lesbian citizens, transgendered citizens, S/M citizens, etc. is, significantly to shift the core through which boundaries are drawn – to stretch and pull it in new ways. Until recently, that core was clearly patriarchal (women were not citizens), heterosexist (gays were not citizens), sex negative (most non-heterosexual forms of sexuality were taboo and certainly not citizens') and familist (the model being the heterosexual nuclear family). All that is perhaps being stretched somewhat and the boundaries are in motion. Once again, we see flows, fluidities, transformations, networks, movements, scapes and mobilities. This is not to suggest that the boundaries are collapsing, but only that they are shifting. And with that comes some sense that there is a shifting notion of the Other or the enemy. In the UK, the category that does the most work as 'enemy' at present – as the boundaries otherwise enlarge – is that of the 'paedophile'.

The idea of 'intimate citizenship' broadens the boundaries even more. It is an idea that is part of a wide sociology of intimacy that highlights *the doings of gender, eroticism, relationships, reproduction, feelings and identities*. It is concerned with all those matters linked to our most intimate desires, pleasures and ways of being in the world. Some of this must feed back into the traditional citizenship [of civil, political and social rights], but equally much of it is concerned with new spheres, new debates and new stories…. People have to make decisions around the *control (or not) over* one's body, feelings, relationships; *access (or not) to* representations, relationships, public spaces etc; and *socially grounded choices (or not) about* identities, gender experiences, erotic experiences (Plummer: 1995: 151). It does not imply one model, one pattern, one way … it is a loose term which comes to designate a field of stories, an array of tellings, out of which new lives, new communities and new politics may emerge (1995: 152). It is a 'sensitizing concept … open and suggestive' (Plummer: 2003: 13). It suggests a bridge between the personal and the political. It 'recognizes emerging intimacy groups and identities, along with their rights, responsibilities and the need for recognition in emerging zones of conflict, and suggests new kinds of citizen in the making' (Plummer: 2003: 66). It designates 'public discourse on the personal life'. To capture an array of elements that need considering, the ideas were couched as 'the square of intimate citizenship' (2002) and subsequently as the 'intimate citizenship project' (2003). The basic elements of this project suggest the need to look at changes, moral conflicts, citizenships and rights, the making of new public spheres, the grounded moral stories of everyday life and the global context.

Continual permutations of boundary making and boundary closing

I have tried in this chapter to suggest (a) that boundaries are bound up with social life and persistently lead to stuff that is 'inside' and stuff that is 'outside'; (b) that boundaries, however, are never fixed, they are always on the move; (c) that they are best seen as flows, as continual permutations of groupings and classifications being reworked through and by groups; and (d) that, politically, social movements are a prime mover of such boundaries. Sexual boundaries are a classic instance of all this, and in the final sections of the chapter I suggest the continuing movements between gay and lesbian, queer, and intimate citizens as they engage in continuous struggles to mark out new boundaries and close others.

References

Bahr, B. (1993) *A Place at the Table*. New York: Simon & Schuster.

Bataille, G. (ed.) (1985) *Visions of Excess: Selected Writings*. Manchester: Manchester University Press.

Bauman, Z. (1993) *Post-Modern Ethics*. Cambridge: Polity.

Bauman, Z. (1991) *Modernity and Ambivalence*. Cambridge: Polity.

Baumeister, R. (1986) *Identity: Cultural Change and the Struggle for Self*. Oxford: Oxford University Press.

Beck, U. (1997) *The Reinvention of Politics*. Cambridge: Polity.

Bell, D. and Binnie, J. (2000) *The Sexual Citizen: Queer Politics and Beyond*. Cambridge: Polity Press.

Bourdieu, P. (1993) *The Field of Cultural Production*. Oxford: Polity.

Bowker, G. and Starr, L.S. (2000) *Sorting Things Out*. Cambridge, MA: MIT Press.

Butler, J. (1999) *Gender Trouble*. London: Routledge.

Calhoun, C. (ed.) (1994) *Social Theory and the Politics of Identity*. Oxford: Blackwell.

Califia, P. (1994) *Public Sex: The Culture of Radical Sex*. San Francisco: Cleis.

Connolly, W. (1991) *Identity/Difference: Democratic Negotiations of Political Paradox*. Ithaca, NY: Cornell University Press.

Connolly, W. (1995) *The Ethos of Pluralization*. Minneapolis, MN: University of Minnesota Press.

Cooley, C.H. (1998) *On Self and Social Organization*. Edited by H.-J. Schubert. Chicago: University of Chicago Press.

Davis, M. (1982) *Smut: Erotic Reality/Obscene Ideology*. Chicago: University of Chicago Press.

D'Emilio, J. (1984) 'Capitalism and gay identity', in A. Snitow *et al.* (eds) *Powers of Desire*. London: Virago.

Doty, A. (2001) *Flaming Classics: Queering the Film Canon*. London: Routledge.

Douglas, M. (1966) *Purity and Danger*. London: Routledge [1970: Penguin]

DuBay, W.H. (1987) *Gay Identity: The Self Under Ban*. London: McFarland.

Durkheim, É. (1964a) *The Division of Labour*. New York: Free Press.

Durkheim, É. (1964b) *The Rules of Sociological Method*. New York: Free Press.

Durkheim, É. (1971) *The Elementary Forms of the Religious Life*. London: Allen and Unwin.

Ellison, N. (1997) 'Towards a new social politics: citizenship and reflexivity in late modernity', *Sociology*, 31: 697–717.

Evans, D. (1993) *Sexual Citizenship*. London: Routledge.

Foucault, M. (1979) *The History of Sexuality*. Harmondsworth: Penguin.

Fraser, N. (1997) *Justice Interruptus: Critical Reflections on the Postsocialist Condition*. London: Routledge.

Fuss, D. (1990) *Essentially Speaking*. London: Routledge.

Gamson, J. (1998) 'Must gay identities self destruct'?, in S. Seidman (ed.) *Queer Theory/Sociology*. London: Routledge.

Geertz, C. (1983) *Local Knowledge*. New York: Basic Books.

Gergen, K. (1999) *An Invitation to Social Construction*. London: Sage.

Gergen, K. (1991) *The Saturated Self*. New York: Basic Books.

Goffman, E. (1956) *The Presentation of Self in Everyday Life*. Edinburgh: Edinburgh University Press.

Halberstam, J. (1998) *Female Masculinity*. Durham, NC: Duke University Press.

Isin, E.F. and Wood, P.K. (1999) *Citizenship and Identity*. London: Sage.

James, W. (1982) *Psychology: The Briefer Course*. New York: Henry Holt.

Jenks, C. (2003) *Transgression*. London: Routledge.

Kirk, M.K. and Madsen, H. (1989) *After the Ball*. New York: Doubleday.

Kymlicka, W. (1995) *Multicultural Citizenship*. Oxford: Oxford University Press.

Lister, R. (1997) *Citizenship: Feminist Perspectives*. London: Palgrave-Macmillan.

Marshall, T.H. (1950) *Citizenship and Social Class and Other Essays*. Cambridge: Cambridge University Press.

Mauss, M. (1970) *The Gift*. London: Routledge.

Mead, G.H. (1933) *Mind, Self and Society*. Chicago: University of Chicago Press.

Mohr, R. (1994) *A More Perfect Union: Why Straight America Must Stand Up for Gay Rights*. Boston: Beacon Press.

Ong, A. (1999) *Flexible Citizenship: The Cultural Logics of Transnationality*. London: Duke University Press.

Phelan S. (1989) *Identity Politics*. Philadelphia: Temple University Press.

Phelan S. (2001) *Sexual Strangers*. Philadelphia: Temple University Press.

Plummer, K. (ed.) (1981) *The Making of the Modern Homosexual*. London: Routledge.

Plummer, K. (1975) *Sexual Stigma: An Interactionist Account*. London: Routledge.

Plummer, K. (1983) 'Going gay', in J. Hart and D. Richardson (eds) *The Theory and Practice of Homosexuality*. London: Routledge.

Plummer, K. (1992) *Modern Homosexualities*. London: Routledge.

Plummer, K. (1995) *Telling Sexual Stories*. London: Routledge.

Plummer, K. (2001) *Documents of Life-2*. London: Sage.

Plummer, K. (2002) 'The square of initimate citizenship', *Citizenship Studies*, 5: 237–53.

Plummer, K. (2003) *Intimate Citizenship*. Seattle, WA: University of Washington Press.

Plummer, K. (2006) 'Inventing human rights', in L. Morris (ed.) *Rights: Sociological Perspectives*. London: Routledge.

Ponse, B. (1978) *Identities in the Lesbian World*. Westport, CT: Greenwood.

Richardson, D. (1998) 'Sexuality and citizenship', *Sociology*, 32: 83–100.

Rubin, G. (1984) 'Thinking sex', in C. Vance (ed.) *Pleasure and Danger*. New York: Routledge.

Sedgwick, K.E. (1990) *Epistemology of the Closet*. Berkeley: University of California.

Seidman, S. (ed.) (1998) *Queer Theory/Sociology*. London: Routledge.

Semiotext (e) (1981/1995) *Polysexuality*. New York: Columbia University Press.

Strauss, A. (1993) *Continual Permutations of Action*. New York: Aldine.

Sullivan, A. (1996) *Virtually Normal*. London: Picador.

Taylor, C. (1989) *Sources of the Self*. Cambridge, MA: Harvard University Press.

Troiden, R. (1988) *Lesbian and Gay Identity*. New York: General Hall.

Urry, J. (1999) *Sociology Beyond Societies: Mobilities for the Twenty-First Century*. London: Routledge.

Warner, M. (1999) *The Trouble with Normal: Sex, Politics and the Ethics of Queer Life*. Cambridge, MA: Harvard University Press.

Warner, M. (1993) *Fear of a Queer Planet*. Minneapolis, MN: University of Minnesota Press.

Warren, C.A.B. (1994) *Identity and Community in the Gay World*. New York: Wiley.

Weeks, J. (1998) 'The sexual citizen', *Theory, Culture and Society*, 15: 35–52.

Weeks, J. *et al.* (2001) *Same Sex Intimacies: Families of Choice and Other Experiments*. London: Routledge.

Wolfe, A. (1992) 'Democracy versus sociology: boundaries and their consequences', in M. Lamont and M. Fournier (eds) *Cultivating Differences*. Chicago: University of Chicago Press, pp. 309–26.

Young, I.M. (1990) *Justice and the Politics of Difference*. Princeton, NJ: Princeton University Press.

Chapter 28

The fates of solidarity: use and abuse

Fred Halliday

Human rights are the last grand narrative.
  Stan Cohen, over lunch in LSE Senior Common Room, 2000

Introduction: a crisis of universalism

In the course of the twentieth century, something strange and distorting appears to have happened to the concept of 'solidarity'. If we can take 'solidarity' as a rough rendering of the third of the great ideals of the French Revolution, of 'Fraternity', along with 'Liberty' and 'Equality', then the word, as both ideal and concept, admits of multiple interpretations, and in at least four dimensions: first, fraternity, or solidarity, within countries, between similar social groups, communities and, in the language of modern socialism above all, classes; secondly, international solidarity, in the conventional sense of supporting legitimate struggles, of workers, or ethnic groups, in other countries; thirdly, support for those within countries who are in some way *different* but who have a claim based on common humanity, or at least derived from common exploitation by a shared system of oppression, such as women, ethnic groups, or immigrants, this often subsumed in appeals to cultural pluralism or multiculturalism; finally, support for those who are *not* from the same social or class group, who are outside or foreign to the community in question, but to whom support, what Kant termed *Hospitalita*, is due, or toward whom, in modern terminology, 'duties toward strangers' are owed.

A survey even as brief as this should serve to illustrate that from its original, and apparently unproblematic, origins in the late eighteenth century the concept of solidarity has travelled a long way. Yet at its core, and in keeping with its origins in the Enlightenment and the French Revolution, solidarity rests on one important principle, namely, that of the shared moral and political value, the moral equality, of all human beings, and of the rights that attach to them. *The concept of solidarity presupposes that of rights.* In the vocabulary of the French Revolution, the term *citoyen/ne*, 'citizen', stood for the equality of all as against the differential system of estates, with the monarchy and the aristocracy at the top, that had hitherto prevailed. In the revolutionary proclamation of the Rights of Man, the basis upon which the French state justified its support for rebellion across Europe, the two principles, rights and solidarity, were so conjoined.

Solidarity is therefore at its core a value enjoining support for other people whose rights, collective or individual, are being denied. The reason to support others within our own society or in others is that they, too, have rights, by dint of the humanity we share. Hence the centrality, even if not always admitted or articulated, of a concept of rights within solidarity. Stan Cohen's observation, quoted at the beginning of this chapter, encapsulates the historical origins and contemporary destiny both of solidarity, conceived as support for other human beings, and of human rights themselves. The French Revolution has, as we know too well, bred many grand narratives; yet that of rights remains, arguably, the most important. It is the foundational narrative for others, be they nationalism, socialism, feminism or revolution, and it has proven to be the most enduring, given the failure of quite a few other narratives on the way, these two and a bit centuries past.

It is against this background that it becomes possible to assess the current difficulties into which discussions of human rights and, in related vein, of solidarity have fallen. The briefest look at the contemporary world will show how solidarity as a concept has travelled a very long way from the aspirations of 1789: it has served, amidst the political tensions of the twentieth century, as much to confuse and besmirch, as to realise in any ideal sense, the political programme of those who supported it, not least the socialist and liberal movements. Among the many ironies of this process has been the way in which solidarity has been declared with states, movements and individuals who, in their practice, deny the very concepts of rights by which the solidarity is supposedly justified in the first place. This has above all been the case in regard to interethnic conflicts, where the partisans of one side present their own as innocent, and the others as perpetrators of the most terrible crimes. At the same time, the ideal and practice of solidarity has been turned against those, in the communist movement, who most espoused it. Communist states, from 1917 to 1991, sought to mobilise and use solidarity movements, but to ends that suited their, state, purposes. Indeed, in 1928, Stalin defined 'internationalism', a principle closely associated with solidarity, as unswerving loyalty to the USSR. Thus, communist solidarity entailed not only support for the guerrillas of Vietnam, but also for the entry of Soviet forces into Hungary in 1956 and into Czechoslovakia in 1968, as, earlier, it had entailed support for the annexation of Georgia in 1921 and the Moscow trials of 1936–8. It was one of the many ironies of the late twentieth century that the greatest internal challenge to a European communist state should have come from a movement of the industrial working class that adopted as its slogan the ideal that communism had so proclaimed and corrupted, *Solidarnosc.*

The 1990s saw a major resurgence in liberal internationalism, with the end of the two-bloc confrontations of the Cold War, and the adoption by the UN of a commitment to 'humanitarian intervention'. The sense, widely held, was that in regard to the protection of Kuwait against the Iraqi occupation in 1990–1, the UN had acted decisively and along the lines of the Charter, as it had not done on so many previous occasions (most flagrantly, and very much in the minds of those who took the Security Council decisions of 1990, when Iraq, in a clear breach of the Charter, invaded Iran in September 1980). Perhaps now, a more consistent, and active international enforcement of human rights might be possible. No wonder that in this context, too, liberal individuals and organisations sought to intervene in the public realm, and to support, or seek to recruit to their causes, the major states on the international arena. NGOs and others lobbied for a range of progressive causes, from women's rights and the environment, to development aid and debt relief. As the wars in the Balkans began in 1992, there were many who, with varying degrees of misgiving, called for direct military intervention on the part of the USA, NATO or the UN, something that, in time, from Bosnia in 1995 to Kosovo in 1999, they got.

This upsurge in liberal internationalist sentiment was accompanied by apparently major advances in the development of the system of what was now termed 'global governance', the international institutions associated with the liberal project: consolidation and expansion of the European Union, the Kyoto Protocol on the environment, and the International Criminal Court. Side by side with 'global governance' 'global civil society' appeared on the scene, linking activist groups in many countries, and, with a clamour of many demands and agenda, lobbying major states, institutions and companies, for more transparency and more responsible policies. Episodically, if with decreasing enthusiasm, on the fiftieth anniversary of 1995 and the sixtieth of 2005, there was talk of reforming the UN itself. Even if the institutions of the UN itself were largely frozen, there was considerable policy development in the organisation itself, as reflected in the high-level reports on peacekeeping, the 'Brahimi Report', and *The Responsibility to Protect*.[1]

However, instead of a new liberal order, where the UN, backed by a benign 'coalition of the willing', enforced global standards, we saw a rapid deterioration of the international situation, first with the failed or belated interventions of the mid-1990s (Somalia, Bosnia, Haiti, Rwanda), and then with the apparent failure of the preferred liberal alternative to military intervention, namely, sanctions (Iraq, Iran, Afghanistan, Serbia). All of this culminated in the disastrous military intervention in Iraq in March 2003, a supposedly easy operation that turned into a nightmare for the Iraqi people themselves and a brutal lesson in the limits of power for the USA. Thus, within a few years of the onset of the hopefully more engaged post-Cold War world, and in a more rapid rerun of disillusion following from the earlier risky associations of liberal optimism with global trends seen in the days of colonialism and in those of communism, matters soon came to look very different. Not only did much of the liberal agenda come to little, but the attempt to relate such an agenda, with all its hopes and qualifications, to the policies of major powers came back to discredit the very principles and sentiments that had underlain the association in the first place: it was one year and four months from the publication in December 2001 of the UN report *The Responsibility to Protect* to the US invasion of Iraq in March 2003.

Many reasons for this outcome can be adduced, from an inherent lack of realism in much of what was originally envisaged during the 1990s, to the long-term shift in political centre of gravity within the USA to the right that became evident in the 2000 election campaign, to the very serious and negative consequences of the 9/11 and subsequent *jihadi* attacks on the USA and, to a growing extent, on Western European opinion and policy as well. Two events above all impelled developments in the direction they took, the Al Qaida attack on the USA in September 2001 and the subsequent US occupation of Iraq in March 2003. Between them, these developments served seriously to undermine the commitment of the 1990s to universalism and to human rights in the international arena within the public opinion of both Western and Middle Eastern states. If 9/11 dealt a serious blow to liberal optimism about the world, and to US commitment to global values and institutions, the invasion of Iraq, and all that followed, served more than any other event to discredit the cause of humanitarian intervention and of any Western commitment to human rights and respect for the rules of war: if it was only a year and a half from the publication of the Evans/Sahnoun report distilling the wisdom of the 1990s, *The Responsibility to Protect*, and the *droit d'ingérence* espoused by Kouchner and others, to the battle lines of Falluja and Anbar province, it was an era of understanding that separated them. That the March 2003 invasion was associated in the antecedent months, and in many later incidents, with outright lying, denial and hypocrisy on the part of the USA and its allies, most notably on the question of Iraq's possession of weapons of mass destruction, and was in no significant manner accompanied by attempts to promote human rights elsewhere in the Middle East, only served the more to discredit this venture, and any post-1991 global optimism.

The moral and political implications of this twist should not be understated. What the Soviet invasions of Hungary in 1956 and of Czechoslovakia in 1968 were to the cause of international communism, the US invasion of Iraq in 2003 was to the ideals and legality of humanitarian intervention. Thus, on the left, in the developed and Third worlds, there is now, even more than was the case during the debates on former Yugoslavia in the 1990s, widespread disparagement of rights, either on the grounds that they reflect the values and pretexts of the imperialist and hegemonic countries or because, as if this is an argument in itself, they are a product of the oppressive, rationalist, Enlightenment, this latter held as the source of most, or even all, of our current ills. The practical implications of this are manifold, from support for nationalist and culturally specific derogation from universal principles and conventions, to blind endorsement of guerrilla and armed groups even when they violate the conventions of war, to wholesale opposition to humanitarian intervention on the grounds that this only masks imperial interests.

Much of the critique of human rights and universal standards emanates from writers in the metropolitan countries, or by nationalist and secular left politicians and intellectuals in the Third World. But others too have joined the fray, as in the rhetoric deployed by Osama bin Laden against Western values, and framed in a moral context that explicitly rejects universalism, appealing to the followers of one religion, and only the Sunni part of them, and celebrating, as in the declarations made about Hurricane Katrina, the misfortunes of others, on the grounds that these were the punishment of God. Thus, the contribution made by militant Islamism to the weakening of universalism lies not only in the way in which it has emboldened and hardened the Right, or in its grotesque celebratory contempt for the rules and norms of war, and of any claim to humane treatment of prisoners, but also in the very moral particularism it espouses in such declamatory terms.[2]

This crisis of solidarity, and the related crises of universalism and of human rights, pervade not only those who are the self-conscious or self-proclaimed inheritors of the radical and liberal traditions of the Enlightenment, but also much of the Right as well. Of course, conservatism was from the start broadly opposed to human rights and of a politics deriving from a shared humanity, but the contribution of the Right to denigrating rights, and to undermining the international institutions and conventions on which the rights regime is based, has certainly become stronger in recent years. On the Right, and sometimes building, as Margaret Thatcher did in the 1980s, on earlier denials of rights, we have also seen a widespread embrace of nationalism, not to mention of foreign policy based on national interests, as the basis for internal action, a growing resiling from international conventions, most spectacularly from the Geneva Convention on treatment of prisoners of war by the USA, coupled with growing opposition to the institutions tasked with implementing an international legal and, by implication, humanitarian order, by the the UN, or the European Union, or, in the case of the International Criminal Court established in 1998, by rejection on the part of three out of five of the permanent members of the UN Security Council.

All of this has been made easier by the failure of political elites and others in the West to take seriously the lesson of the end of the Cold War, namely, that it was not, as the Reagan Right in the USA argued, the pressure of Western military power and expenditures that played the decisive role in breaking the authority and power of Soviet communism, but rather the commitments the USSR entered to in regard to human rights, in particular the Helsinki Accords of 1975, and the broader demonstration effect of Western society, not least of the European Union, in combining broad respect for democratic and human rights values with sustained economic growth. In the collapse of communism in 1989–91 there were those, particularly some opposition intellectual leaders in Eastern Europe, who did give credit where it was due, with international insistence on human rights, but many in the West did not hear the message.[3]

The Middle East

If the discussion so far has focused on the general interaction of liberal and radical universalism with historical forces and states, there is also a need to see how, in regard to particular regions of the world, the concept and practice of solidarity has run into difficulties. Here again we can see how an initially open and internationalist support for other peoples or states, derived from a concept of their shared entitlement to rights, can easily become something else, partial, instrumental, and in denial as to the violation of rights by the very peoples and states to whom solidarity is being offered. Such an examination is possible in regard to many parts of the world where social and ethnic conflict has taken place in recent decades, from Indo-China and southern Africa to Cyprus, the Balkans, and Ireland. Yet, arguably, no region of the world so illustrates the claims and counterclaims of international moral discourse, and the contradictions this can lead to, than the Middle East, this being understood as the broad west Asian region within which the Arab-Israeli question is significant. This can be observed by examining many episodes in the recent history of the Middle East, where issues of solidarity and political engagement arose, but in conditions of confusion and disarray. Thus, the Iranian revolution of 1978–9 prompted very different responses outside, as well as inside, that country, with much of the international Left supporting the clerical regime that emerged from that revolution, even as it imprisoned, tortured and executed members of left-wing parties. When, at the same time as the Islamic revolution took power in Iran, a communist regime was established in neighbouring Afghanistan, it received almost no international support, above all when it called on Soviet troops to protect it.

Yet, it was out of that war in Afghanistan, in the 1980s, that there was to emerge the transnational *jihadi* movement that crystallised around Al Qaida and which led to 9/11 and all that followed. Other events in that region were also to show up the inadequacies of international discussion: the Iranian condemnation of Salman Rushdie in 1989, and the Iraqi invasion of Kuwait in 1990. In regard to Rushdie, what was, in essence, a matter of free speech was met by many with condemnation of the author and a set of mawkish appeals to relativism, 'respect' for the authority of clerics and much else beside. In regard to Kuwait, most of the Left opposed the UN decision to expel the Iraqi invaders, even though it was as clear a case of state aggression and violation of the Charter as could be imagined. It is as if the Middle East has been the graveyard not only of imperial ambitions, British, French, Russian and now American, but also of clear-headed moral and legal discussion of the challenges it poses.

Confusion has reigned above all, of course, in regard to the Palestine question, the most prominent, if far from the only, of the interethnic and interstate conflicts that the region contains. Here there has been a history of one-sidedness and partisan engagement, albeit with quite dramatic shifts of partisanship on the way. In its origins, the state of Israel was widely supported by the Left. The USSR recognised Israel before the USA and supplied, directly and indirectly, the arms that helped the Israelis win that war and establish their state. In the 1950s and early 1960s, the overall liberal and socialist consensus was in favour of Israel, and paid scant attention to the rights of the Palestinians. This was a time before the emergence of the Palestinian guerrilla movement: the PLO had been set up in Cairo a few months earlier, in January 1964, initially under the control of the Arab states, and of Egypt in particular, but its first armed action was to come a few weeks later, in January 1965, in an attack on a water-pumping station near Galilee. For nearly everyone in the West, of left or right, the Palestinian issue was not one of a people's right to land or self-determination, but one of 'the refugees'. The focus was on the obstacles to resettlement (by Israel and the Arab states respectively), as if the Palestinians were in some way, this only 20 years after World War II, but a late addition to the millions of displaced persons and others whom the European conflict had shunted across frontiers.

For much of the world, 'solidarity', understood as respect for the rights and political aspirations of the group it supported, attached to Israel. Israel enjoyed enormous authority, not so much as a close ally of the West, which at that time it was not (the alliance with the USA was consolidated only in the late 1960s), but as the site of an experiment in socialist economics and living, epitomised by the kibbutz system. If there was, on the Left, sympathy for 'Arab' causes, it focused more on the experiment in 'Arab socialism' under Nasser in Egypt and on the experiences of workers' control and peasant cooperatives that had arisen out of the Algerian revolutionary war of 1954–62, and perhaps also, for a few, backing for the remote but reputedly resolute Imamate of Oman (which had, by 1959, ceased to exist). All of this was to change, of course, after the war of 1967, with the emergence of the Palestinian resistance movement in the West Bank and in Jordan, and the gradual loss of sympathy for Israel across much of the world. This latter process did not take place overnight: Cuba, for example, maintained relations with, and admiration for, Israel until after the war of 1973.

With 1967 came the redrawing of the battle lines, on the ground in the Middle East, with the conquest by Israel of all of mandate Palestine, and the rise, on the left internationally, of a movement of solidarity with the Palestinian people. The June 1967 war was 40 years ago, but amidst all the controversies that have followed, the issues, much of the language of identification and rejection, and the historical points of dispute, have done little but bring us much of the same. In the mass of material spoken and written since the explosion of the Lebanese-Israeli conflict in the summer of 2006, there was little, in argument, explanation, or sentiment that is new.

Universalist objections

To gauge how little discussion of the Arab-Israeli cause has advanced over recent decades, it is worth recalling some earlier assertions of a universalist position on this conflict, one, by Isaac Deutscher, from an independent Marxist perspective, and the other by Hannah Arendt from that of a courageous liberalism.[4] Deutscher struck a note that is almost wholly absent in more recent debates, where claims of identity prevail over universal principle, and where identification with one side or the other predominates in a war where both are guilty of atrocities of war and massive and callous political blunders. Deutscher's argument rested on three clear and courageous premises: that both leaderships, Arab and Israeli, were guilty of demagogy and misleading their own people, above all by promising a victory that was unattainable and by stoking hatred of other peoples and religions; that the antecedent histories of both peoples, genocide in Europe for the Jews, and denial of national rights for the Palestinians, could not be deployed to legitimate the maximal current claims of either side; and, resolutely adhered to throughout his argument, that the Israelis and Palestinians were peoples with legitimate claims that should be recognised on a sensible, and lasting, territorial and political basis. Above all, in the tones of anti-clerical and universalist disdain, something all too lacking in these days of grovelling before 'identity', 'tradition' and 'faith communities', he was clear in his rejection of the invocation of the sacred, the God-given, in political debate; of Talmudic obscurantism and bloodthirsty Arab calls for vengeance alike. He would have had little time for the Orthodox rabbis of the West Bank or the discourses of Sheikh Fadlallah.

The other author who, in work not directly related to the Arab-Israeli question but with immense relevance to it, and to the arguments taking place in the broader world about it, laid down an internationalist position was Hannah Arendt. A German philosopher who had lived in the USA during the war, she published a work on the trial in Jerusalem in 1961 of the Nazi war criminal and organiser of the gas chambers, Adolf Eichmann. This work, *Eichmann in Jerusalem,* was best known for the controversial phrase in the subtitle of the book, born of listening to the account given by the accused, 'the banality of evil'. This denoted not the banality of Eichmann, the organiser of mass murder, but the banal, routine and everday, manner in which he told of his crimes.

The claims of community

What was much more controversial was Arendt's critique of the legal and moral case made by the Israeli prosecutors against Eichmann. For, whereas the Nuremberg trials of the Nazi war criminals had been conducted under what at least purported to be some form of 'international' law, the precursor of later codes of universal jurisdiction, crimes against humanity and the International Criminal Court, Eichmann was prosecuted for the taking of *Jewish* lives and in the court of a Jewish state. What had, in 1946, been a case, weak in some points of principle, but confident in its universalist aspirations, of the International Military Tribunal, had in the early 1960s been converted into something derived from the ethnicity of the victims. And this ethnicisation of the victims was, at the same time, deemed to convey a particular right, if not responsibility, on the state that lay claim to representing those victims, namely Israel.

Herein lies the core of much contemporary confusion, and passion, about the Arab-Israeli question and, indeed, of the numerous other interethnic conflicts across the world where local rhetoric and partisan international solidarity prevail, as if one side were angels and the other devils – Cyprus, Bosnia, Nagorno-Karabagh, Northern Ireland. In regard to the Middle East, Muslims and Arabs across the world identify with the Palestinians or, in recent times, Hizbullah on ethnic, religious and communitarian lines; many Jews do the same, in support of Israel. Even many of those Jews who oppose the policies of the state of Israel speak as Jews ('not in my name'). Yet there is, arguably, a regression here, of ominous import, insofar as membership of a particular community, or claims of affinity, ethnicity or religious association with others, are deemed to convey either particular rights, or particular moral clarity, on those making such claims. In purely logical, and rational, terms, this is in fact nonsense. To take the example of the war of 2006: the crimes of the Israelis in wantonly destroying Lebanon, and denying Palestinians their national rights, and the crimes of Hizbullah and Hamas, placing the lives and security of their peoples recklessly at risk, hurling thousands of missiles at civilian targets in Israel and fomenting religious and ethnic hatred, do not require particularist denunciation; that is, that the one killed Arabs or Muslims, and the other spilt Jewish blood. They are crimes on the basis of universal principles, of law, decency, humanity, and should be identified as such. Particularism undermines the very basis of the denunciation.

Current political orthodoxy in Europe and the USA inclines to giving a legitimate, even privileged, place to 'communities' with a particular concern on international issues, from Armenians and Kashmiris, to Irish, Muslims and Jews. However, the opposite argument can and should be made: ethnic and religious communities abroad are, in this regard, the last people to turn to, for either rational explanation or moral compass in regard to such events.[5]

Human rights and the norms of war

Developments in regard to human rights in general and debate on the Arab-Israeli dispute in particular can lead us back to the need to reaffirm some of the core principles that inform the concept of solidarity and of human rights.[6] Equally, a condemnation of the actions of these militarised states and guerrilla groups needs to be based not only on a rejection of their demagogy and chauvinism, but also on something central to the body of rights and legal instruments we have, and that was long neglected, above all by the Left, and is still trampled on in much discussion of the war in Iraq, namely, *respect for the laws and norms of war*, as in the Geneva Protocols of 1949, the Additional Protocols of 1977 and other related documents. Today we see across the world movements of solidarity with the 'Iraqi resistance', Hamas or Hizbullah that, while invoking universal principles of war against Israelis, fail completely to apply the same principles to the behaviour of the guerrillas and other groups, many of them guilty of terrible acts of barbarism, murder, intimidation of civilians, and fostering of intercommunal hatred. While voices of the Western Left, high on their anti-imperialist rectitude, revel in the slaughter of civilian UN officials in Iraq, others condone the killing of children in Israel, and the wanton sacrificing of the security, stability, indeed sanity of the whole population of Lebanon in the name of a self-proclaimed 'national resistance'. And all of this from groups, in Palestine and Lebanon, who for years sought to destroy the one chance for co-existence and peace between Israelis and Palestinians that did arise, in the Oslo Accords of 1993, and then, egged on by their fellow-travelling intellectual acolytes in the West, proceeded to trample on Oslo's grave.[7]

Solidarity today, if it is true to the universalist premises of the original concept, is not embodied in partisan and morally one-eyed campaigns of support for one group of combatants or another, let alone in the denunciation of crimes by one side and apologia or silence with regard to the other. It rests with those who go beyond this partisanship, whose moral authority, and factual accuracy, transcend those of the 'solidarity' groups. This would include the work of journalists and diplomats who honestly seek to document and draw attention to human rights violations in war, and those, particularly in the human rights organisations, such as Amnesty International and Human Rights Watch, who resolutely, calmly and with as much accuracy as war and propaganda allow, document and condemn the crimes, and political follies, of both sides. Advocacy of respect for the rules of war, and protection of combatants and civilians alike in war, has long been the priority of the International Committee of the Red Cross. It is their courage, and their sustained independence and clarity of vision, that should guide commentary on current conflicts. Human rights may be the last grand narrative, but it is one with more than sufficient intellectual and moral authority to carry us many years into the future.

Acknowledgement

This chapter forms part of a broader research project on contemporary cosmopolitanism, its opportunities and problems, which was carried out with the support of the Leverhulme Trust. The latter's generous support in this regard is gratefully acknowledged.

Notes

1 Commission on Global Government, *Our Global Neighbourhood*, London: 1995; Report of the International Commission on Intervention and State Sovereignty, Gareth Evans and Mohamed Sahnoun, co-chairs, *The Responsibility to Protect*, Ottawa: International Development Research Centre, December 2001.
2 Bruce Lawrence (ed.), *Messages to the World. The Statements of Osama bin Laden*, London: Verso, 2005.
3 On the long-term social and political processes that led to the end of communism, see Nicholas Bisley, *The End of the Cold War and the Causes of the Soviet Collapse*, Basingstoke: Palgrave/Macmillan, 2004.
4 Isaac Deutscher, 'On the Arab-Israeli war', *New Left Review*, 44, 1967, reprinted in Isaac Deutscher, *The Non-Jewish Jew*, Oxford: Oxford University Press, 1984; Hannah Arendt, *Eichmann in Jerusalem: A Report on the Banality of Evil*, London: Penguin Books, 1977 (originally Viking Press, 1963).
5 In early 2005, when interviewed by a panel set up by the governors of the BBC to consider accusations of bias in regard to coverage of the Arab-Israeli dispute, I was given a list of the British-based groups the panel had consulted – Muslim and Arab on one side, Jewish and Zionist on the other; my recommendation to the panel was to take note of the political weight they had, but in terms of assessing the objectivity of coverage to ignore completely what any of them said and to question whether they should have any special standing in the matter.

6 Any hope, which lingered among some Marxists and socialists even into the 1970s, that a solution to this, or any other, interethnic conflict could be found on the bases of proletarian solidarity must be dispelled as ineffectual at best, and dangerous at most: proletarian solidarity did not save the Jews of Europe in the 1940s and has not reconciled Arabs and Jews thereafter. For one excellent account of the attempt by communists and socialists in Egypt and Israel to sustain such a position against the rise to power of the nationalist state, see Joel Beinin, *Was the Red Flag Flying Here? Marxist Politics and the Arab-Israeli Conflict in Egypt and Israel, 1948–1965*. Within the Arab world, while some of the militant and chauvinist rhetoric about Israel came from the self-proclaimed 'Marxist-Leninist' Left, e.g., the Popular Front for the Liberation of Palestine, it was also left-wing leaders within Palestine who continued to adopt a principled, internationalist, position on the conflict (e.g. the communist leader Emile Touma, and the novelist Emile Habiby).

7 Beinin argues that while the Left could not claim responsibility for the two-state compromise reached at Oslo, it could claim 'moral credit' for having long, and in difficult conditions, defended this principle.

Chapter 29

Criminology as a vocation

Robert Reiner

At the end of *Visions of Social Control*, Stan Cohen quotes a parable by Saul Alinsky, the radical American community organiser. It poses a tragic dilemma (Cohen 1985: 236). A fisherman sees a body floating downstream, and jumps in to rescue it. The same thing happens a few minutes, later, and then again, and again. When a tenth body floats down, the fisherman ignores it and starts running upstream. 'Where are you going?' shouts an observer, 'why aren't you rescuing that poor man?' The fisherman replies that he's going to find out how to stop these people getting pushed into the water in the first place.

This chapter will explore the tension pinpointed by this parable. How do we reconcile the responsibility to alleviate pressing concrete problems with the more uncertain search for their fundamental sources in the hope of reducing or eliminating them altogether?

Stan Cohen has grappled with the issue many times in his explorations of the ethical and political dilemmas of criminology (Cohen 1975, 1979, 1988, 1998), always attempting to keep in balance the conflicting pulls of commitment, analysis and action, with a sensitivity to how their priority shifts in changing circumstances. Criminologists, he has argued, have 'a triple loyalty: first, an overriding obligation to honest intellectual enquiry itself (however sceptical, provisional, irrelevant and unrealistic); second, a political commitment to social justice; and third (and potentially conflicting with both), the pressing and immediate demands for short-term humanitarian help. We have to appease these three voracious gods' (Cohen 1998: 122). As these remarks imply, this tension cannot be resolved in a universal and timeless fashion. How the voracious gods are to be appeased depends on our – always tenuous and contested – assessments of the current balance of voraciousness.

407

In the essay from which the above quotation comes, Stan Cohen also celebrated the 'deconstructionist impulse' that has gripped critical criminology since the mid-1960s (*ibid*.: 101). Many aspects of this are unequivocal advances, above all the questioning of taken-for-granted notions of criminal law and the operation of criminal justice. But there are aspects of 'deconstruction' that this chapter will question. In the last 30 years, the significance – even the reality – of macrosocial structural processes shaping crime and control has been 'deconstructed' by the culturalist and post-structuralist 'turns' in theory, and, from a very different direction, by the rise of 'realism', especially on the political Right, spearheaded by James Q. Wilson's no-holds-barred attack on 'root-cause' perspectives (Wilson 1975).

There has been a similar pincer movement, between post-1960s radical criminology and conservative 'realists', about the ethics of crime and justice. Stan Cohen long ago pinpointed the 'shrill moral innocence' of the project of 'appreciation' of deviance as diversity (Cohen 1979). The erstwhile new criminologists, become Left realists in the 1980s, took this argument about the harmful reality of crime further. On the other side, Right (and New Labour) realism simply slipped back into taken-for-granted acceptance of the standpoint not so much of the law as of 'the decent, the people who show respect and expect it back', as Tony Blair recently put it (Blair 2006).

These conflicting ways of changing the subject submerged the social democratic analysis and critique of crime and criminal justice that at least tacitly informed criminology before the late 1960s (Reiner 2006a). The still vital kernel of this was that crime often involves real harm, but is constructed in ways that reflect inequalities of power, and that while offenders have some degree of moral responsibility for their conduct, they are also pressured by circumstances not of their choosing (or even understanding). In a nutshell, social injustice shapes both crime and its control.

Criminology as a vocation: realism versus ultimate ends

The classic analysis of the ethics of social science was Max Weber's famous 'vocation' lectures, to which the title of this chapter alludes (Weber [1917/1919] 2004). The first, 'Science as a Vocation', was delivered on 7 November 1917, shortly after the Bolshevik October Revolution. The second, 'Politics as a Vocation', was presented on 28 January 1919, in a context of seething revolutionary conflict (the Spartacus League leaders, Rosa Luxemburg and Karl Liebknecht, had been assassinated less than two weeks earlier).

Weber's basic premise was 'the incompatibility of ultimate possible attitudes and hence the inability ever to resolve the conflicts between them' (Weber 1917: 27). In a disenchanted world, conflicting cultures, values, 'gods' rage. But to act – as politician, judge, police officer, anyone who has contracted with 'the diabolic means of power' – it is necessary to decide between them, knowing that not only are the facts not yet in, but they never will be, and in any case they could not resolve the ethical dilemmas.

Weber contrasted two moralities that politicians may be guided by: the ethics of responsibility, and the ethics of conviction, or 'ultimate ends'. These are usually treated as polar opposites, and indeed Weber himself introduced them as 'fundamentally different, irredeemably incompatible maxims' (Weber 1919: 83). However, although 'a profound abyss' exists between them, this 'does not mean that an ethics of conviction is identical with irresponsibility or an ethic of responsibility with a lack of conviction' (*ibid.*).

Weber's polemical thrust was directed against the utopianisms that swirled around him, oblivious of the icy limits of possibility in the dark circumstances after the Great War. But Weber also admired Luther's affirmation, 'Here I stand, I can do no other'. 'In this sense', comments Weber, 'an ethics of conviction and an ethics of responsibility are not absolute antitheses but are mutually complementary, and only when taken together do they constitute the authentic human being who is capable of having a "vocation for politics"' (*ibid.*: 92). Responsibility without at least a tacit utopian ideal goes nowhere. 'Politics means a slow, powerful drilling through hard boards, with a mixture of passion and a sense of proportion… what is possible could never have been achieved unless people had tried again and again to achieve the impossible in this world' (*ibid.*: 93).

'Science as a vocation' also has a crucial practical role. Weber insisted that science can never establish particular values, and he castigated the abuse of the lecture platform to propagandise for particular standpoints (Weber 1917: 25–31). But 'science' has a vital part to play in clarifying the conditions of realisation of ideologies, and their consequences.

I will suggest that in contemporary criminology Weber's primary fear of the ethics of ultimate ends should be reversed. For 30 years, criminology has lived with excessive 'responsibility', or, in its own terminology, 'realism', in part because of a self-imposed penance for earlier irresponsible idealism. It has been dominated by pragmatic 'what works' concerns, which lose sight of the wider conditions of existence of their own success or failure. But without an explicit conception of 'ultimate ends' pragmatic realism is irresponsible and chimerical. The next section will seek to show that contemporary crime and criminal justice cannot be understood without a macroanalysis drawn from political economy. It suggests that humane and effective crime control is threatened by neo-liberalism but facilitated by social democracy.

Crime, criminal justice and political economy

Political economy as a criminological perspective

Political economy has a venerable pedigree in criminology (Reiner 2007a), from (*avant la lettre*) the 'science of police', via (among others) Bonger, Merton, and 1970s 'new criminology', to a few contemporary survivors. Political economy is not economic determinism; it emphasises the embeddedness of the economic in other dimensions of existence (Polanyi [1944] 2001). There is a mutual shaping of structure and action, voluntarism and determinism – in Marx's celebrated aphorism, people make their own history, but not under circumstances of their own choosing (Marx 1852). The economic looms large in these circumstances but cannot be isolated from other dimensions, and the meaning of economic factors varies with cultural context.

Post-war Britain as a case study

Understanding crime trends requires a plausible narrative showing how the elements of crime were affected by economic, political, social and cultural changes (Reiner 2007b). This draws upon what we know about the criminogenic significance of different factors, based on econometric, survey and observational research. Three broad periods can be distinguished over the last half-century, in terms of crime trends.

Late 1950s–1970s – recorded crime rise

From the mid-1950s, recorded crime rose on an unprecedented scale. How far was this a rise in offending and victimisation, and how much was due to changes in reporting or recording practices? It is impossible to be sure, of course, because of all the familiar problems in interpreting official crime statistics (Maguire 2002). What is beyond doubt is that by the early 1970s the increasing recorded crime rate was becoming a major political issue. It facilitated the politicisation of law and order by Margaret Thatcher, playing a key role in the 1979 Conservative victory (Downes and Morgan 2002).

However, a major proportion of the increase probably was a recording phenomenon. During the 1970s, the General Household Survey included a question on burglary victimisation. This showed that most of the rise in recorded burglary was due to increased reporting by victims. Between

1972 and 1983, recorded burglary doubled, but victimisation only grew by 20 per cent. The spread of domestic household contents insurance, reflecting the advent of a new mass consumer culture, induced more reporting. It is plausible that similar processes applied to other volume property crimes. Thus, at least a substantial part of the crime wave that launched the politics of law and order (and the profound shifts in political economy and culture attributable to Thatcherism) was probably a recording phenomenon.

The culture and social structure of the new mass consumerism generated higher offending levels, not just greater reporting by victims. Most obviously, this resulted from the spread of tempting targets for crime: cars, radios and other equipment in cars, television sets, videos, computers, mobile phones, etc. These all increased the opportunities for relatively easy, lucrative thefts.

The increasingly materialistic culture of mass affluence emphasised monetary success rather than the means of achieving it, breeding anomie (Merton [1938] 1957; Messner and Rosenfeld 2006). The stimulation of consumption by advertising explicitly undermined norms of deferred gratification – 'live now, pay later', 'take the waiting out of wanting'. The pervasive stress on the desirability of must-have consumer products for all increased the sense of relative deprivation among those sectors lacking legitimate opportunities. This was predicted by social democratic criminologists at the dawn of the era of mass affluence (Longford Study Group 1964: 5; Downes 1966, 1998: 103–9), although Jock Young's idea of an 'aetiological crisis' aptly characterises the puzzlement of many policymakers and commentators who simplistically associated crime with absolute poverty (Young 1986; Bottoms and Stevenson 1992).

There was also some erosion of social controls, informal and formal. The rise of youth culture and broader aspects of desubordination threatened internalised restraints against offending. As recorded crime began to rise, pressures on the police increased and detection rates fell, weakening the deterrence and incapacitation effects of criminal justice.

In sum, after the late 1950s, a variety of interlinked consequences of mass consumerism fed rising crime rates. The reporting of crime was stimulated, as were opportunities and motivations for offending. Both informal and formal social controls weakened.

1980–92: crime explosion

The huge increases in recorded crime during the 1980s were largely in line with the estimates of increasing victimisation from the regular British Crime Surveys (BCS) launched in 1981. Only a small proportion of the rise was due to reporting/recording changes. From 1981 to 1993, recorded crime rose 111 per cent to a record height, and BCS crime by 77 per cent.

The crucial cause of the 1980s crime explosion was the brutal displacement of the consensus, Keynesian, welfare state policies of the post-war decades by neo-liberal monetarist policies. This produced the massive social dislocations of de-industrialisation and resurgent mass unemployment – indeed, long-term never-employment for increasing numbers of young men, especially among ethnic minorities and inner-city areas. Inequality sharpened into a yawning chasm between the top and bottom of the economic hierarchy, and poverty began to rise after a long historical process of increasing social incorporation and inclusion. Industrial and political conflict was sparked on a scale not experienced for half a century or more, with much more violent disorders.

Informal social controls of all kinds were eroded as whole communities lost the material basis of settled life. Neo-liberalism undermined stable – or any – family life and 'morality' far more than the 'permissiveness' that the Right railed against. Moral laissez-faire followed the economic. A culture of egoism, the 'me society', was stimulated under the guise of the ethic of individual responsibility. 'Greed is good' was the infamous watchword of a new Gilded Age. The unbridled turbo-capitalism of the Thatcher years had devastating consequences for order that far outweighed the strong state measures introduced to control it in a Canute-like effort to stem the social tsunami.

The Thatcher government shrilly denied any link between unemployment and crime, and the evidence in the 1980s was equivocal (Box 1987). But the data analysed up to the mid-1980s were drawn from the post-war full-employment decades, when unemployment was mainly transitional and voluntary. There is a plethora of evidence from recent econometric studies of links between crime, the business cycle, and inequality (for overviews, see Hagan and Peterson 1995; Fielding *et al*. 2000; Marris 2000; Garside 2004a; Hale 2005; Reiner 2006b, in press a).

A striking confirmation of the role of political economy in the explanation of the crime rise is a recent study of homicide trends by Danny Dorling (2004). Between 1967 and 2002, the number of homicides in Britain went up from around 350 per annum to around 800. Despite this huge increase, however, most of the population are less at risk of murder than they were a quarter of a century ago. 'The increase in murder was concentrated almost exclusively in the poorer parts of Britain and most strongly in its poorest tenth of wards' (*ibid*.: 186). The rise in murder is concentrated among men who left school at 16 in 1981, just as the de-industrialisation engendered by Thatcherite monetarist policies began to bite, and subsequent cohorts of the poorest young men, never-employed or marginally employed, who constituted a new surplus population. As Dorling concludes, 'Those who perpetrated the social violence that was done to the lives of young men starting some 20 years ago are the prime suspects for most of the murders in Britain' (*ibid*.: 191).

1992 onward: falling crime, rising fear

In the 1990s, the recorded crime and victimisation statistics began to point in different directions. Between 1992 and 1997, the recorded crime rate fell, but the BCS continued to rise until 1995. The surveys showed this was because reporting by victims and recording by the police declined. Since 1995, victimisation has fallen sharply according to the BCS, but the police recorded rate has increased in most years, mainly due to changes in official counting rules and procedures in 1998 and 2002.

The divergence in the statistical series roughly coincided with the election of New Labour in 1997. Michael Howard's years as Conservative Home Secretary (1993–7) saw a decline in recorded crime but a rise in the BCS. Tony Blair has governed in a period of sharp decline in the BCS (to its lowest level since its 1981 inception), but (ambiguously) rising police recorded statistics. So whether Tory Michael Howard or New Labour Tony Blair is the greatest crime buster since Batman depends on whether we go by the BCS or the police statistics. Is it a coincidence that Tory think tanks and newspapers have begun to rubbish the BCS? (Dennis and Erdos 2005; Green *et. al.* 2005).

During the 1990s, recorded crime figures and victimisation survey rates fell in most Western countries (Tonry and Farrington 2005). This has caused a reverse 'aetiological crisis' like that associated with the 1950s crime rise (Young 2004: 24–5). No 'grand narrative' seems satisfactory. Neo-liberalism, the Left's prime suspect, retains its global economic hegemony. But conversely, there has not been any reversal of 'permissiveness', the Right's main *bête noire*.

Few criminologists or policymakers doubt that there has been a decrease. But while victim surveys are not subject to the same problems as the police recorded figures, they have limitations of their own (Garside 2004b; Young 2004: 17–22). It could be that trends in the nature of crime make the BCS increasingly under-record victimisation, producing a spurious decline. For example, several studies have suggested that one consequence of better domestic and car security is that potential thieves switch to robbery (Fitzgerald *et al.* 2003; Hallsworth 2005), in particular of young people. As the BCS samples only people over 16, if there is a trend toward disproportionate victimisation of younger people, it could produce an increasing underestimate of crime. The homeless are

413

a severely victimised group (Newburn and Rock 2004), and are not sampled by the BCS. An increase in crimes against homeless people would not be registered by the survey. It would be implausible to conclude that the apparent trend toward falling crime is spurious. But it may be that, at any rate, a partial solution to the mystery of the falling crime rate is that it did not fall as much as the survey statistics suggest.

Policing changes undoubtedly played some part in the British crime drop of the 1990s. Since the early 1980s urban riots, there has been a stream of attempts to reform policing. A variety of innovative crime control strategies to remedy the weakness of traditional random patrol and detection have developed, and management and performance measurement became more 'businesslike'. This received a boost with New Labour's 1998 Crime and Disorder Act and Crime Reduction Programme. At first, the main focus was on 'smart', community-oriented tactics. The watchwords were intelligence-led, evidence-based, partnership. There has also been an increasing stream of legislation expanding police powers, without the safeguards associated with PACE (many of the latter have recently been abandoned), especially following the 'war on terror'.

There has also been a considerable toughening of punishment. Imprisonment has followed a marked upward trend. The contribution of this to falling crime rates is debatable. There may be some temporary incapacitation, but there is little evidence of deterrence (and what there is suggests that probability, not severity, of punishment was important (cf. Farrington and Jolliffe 2005)) or rehabilitation.

Within the array of explanations, economic factors are certainly significant, if peculiarly unheralded by governments wishing to appear 'tough on crime' (Downes 2004). Unemployment has certainly been at much lower levels than during the crime explosion of the 1980s, although this has been achieved largely by the expansion of secondary labour market jobs. Unemployment levels do track recent crime trends quite well (Deadman and Macdonald 2002; Farrington and Jolliffe 2005).

New Labour has succeeded in reducing child poverty substantially. The introduction of the minimum wage had a significant crime reduction effect in some areas (Hansen and Machin 2002). But, overall, there has not been any significant change in the extreme level of economic inequality and insecurity that New Labour inherited, despite welcome improvements in crucial aspects of poverty (Hills and Stewart 2005). The crime drop in Britain remains something of a mystery, defying any simple account. But economic factors are an important part of the explanation, as they were of the spectacular crime rise before that.

Comparative penal systems and crime

Political economy locates the role of economic factors within a holistic framework of interdependent cultural and social processes. These form different complexes of meaning and morality that are related to systematic variations in patterns of crime and violence, and the style of criminal justice they develop.

A recent comparative study of 12 industrial, liberal democratic countries (Cavadino and Dignan 2006) has demonstrated that different types of political economy correspond to clear variations in penal policy and culture, as measured for example by data on official imprisonment rates (shown in Figure 29.1). Neo-liberal political economies are far more punitive than social democracies, with European corporatism in between. Other recent research confirms the inverse relationship between welfare and punitiveness, in comparative studies of variation within and between different societies (Beckett and Western 2001; Downes and Hansen 2006).

There is no equally systematic comparative evidence on the relationship between crime and political economy. The International Crime Victims Survey (ICVS: van Kesteren *et al.* 2000) attracted particular media attention in the UK, because it shows England and Wales leading the 17 countries surveyed in overall incidence of reported victimisation, as well as being in the top three for every specific offence category (*ibid.*: Chapter 2). The USA, often assumed to be the world's crime capital, comes eleventh. The ordering of the countries by the ICVS bears no relationship to types of political economy nor to rankings of punitiveness. It is thus equally mysterious to political economists or deterrence theorists. When crimes are weighted by their seriousness, as judged by the public in the surveys, the pattern approximates more closely to political economy (van Kesteren *et al. ibid.*: 48). The top three countries are neo-liberal England and Wales, Australia, and the USA. The bottom three are social democratic Denmark and Finland, and 'oriental corporatist' Japan. But the archetypal social democracy, Sweden, remains in fourth place. As Jock Young suggests, these 'maverick results' run so counter to expectation that it is plausible that higher-ranked societies paradoxically may be ones where the relative absence of serious violence makes respondents more sensitive to low-level incivility, and thus more likely to report incidents (Young 2003: 36–7).

There are fewer problems in international comparison of homicide statistics, because there is less diversity in legal definitions and recording practices. The international pattern of homicide rates does correspond systematically to variations in political economy, along with penal policy, as shown by Figure 29.1.

	Imprisonment rate	Homicide rate
Neo-liberal countries		
USA	701	5.56
South Africa	402	55.86
New Zealand	155	2.5
England and Wales	141	1.6
Australia	115	1.87
Conservative corporatist		
Italy	100	1.5
Germany	98	1.15
Netherlands	100	1.51
France	93	1.71
Social democracies		
Sweden	73	1.1
Finland	70	2.86
Denmark	58	1.02
Norway	58	0.95
Oriental corporatist		
Japan	53	1.05

Sources: Cavadino and Dignan (2005), Barclay and Tavares (2003).

Figure 29.1 Political economy, imprisonment and homicide

The overall conclusion is clear: rates of lethal violence, as well as punitive penal policies, are highest in neo-liberal political economies, and lowest in social democracies.

Murder on the Orient Express *meets* Prime Suspect: *the New York murder mystery*

The big puzzle for the thesis I have been advancing is the 1990s crime drop in the USA, and especially New York City. Accounts of the overall US crime drop give political economy some weight (e.g. Bernstein and Houston 2000; Grogger 2000; Karmen 2000; Western 2001; Rosenfeld 2004), but stress criminal justice and other factors (Levitt 2004). In popular culture, the cops have got the credit: 'Crime is down in New York City: blame the police', as former Chief Bratton boasted, although academic analyses question this (see Bowling 1999 and the essays collected in Newburn 2005: Chapters 28–31). Most American analyses (e.g. Blumstein and Wallman 2000; Karmen 2000; Rosenfeld 2004) are the criminological equivalent of Agatha Christie's *Murder on the Orient Express*, where everyone dunnit, rather than *Prime Suspect*, where, as in Dorling's analysis of the UK, one offender is unmasked at the end (in that case Mrs Thatcher).

Altogether, the 1990s US trends are mysterious in the light of the extensive evidence of clear relationships between inequality and homicide patterns, demonstrated by over 40 different studies (Wilkinson 2005: 47–51). In the light of this, it is very hard to understand why US homicide rates have declined while incomes and wealth have become more unequal – although the US murder rate remains comparatively high (and is beginning to rise again in Washington, DC, and some other cities, fuelled, according to William Chambliss, by sharply growing visible inequality (cf. Goldenberg 2006: 25). One possible element in the overall decline of US crime may be paradoxically that inequality in much of the USA has reached such a degree that the poor are largely segregated from the more prosperous by spatial barriers. Increasing swathes of the life of the relatively advantaged are lived in 'mass private property' (Shearing and Stenning 1983; Davis 1992) – a pattern appearing around the world but to nothing like the same degree as in North America.

Conclusion: policing or political economy? – the irresponsibility of realism

The US 1990s experience has been a major ingredient in the resurgence of 'can do' optimism among police and criminal justice policymakers and agents around the world. But relying on prisons or policing to stem crime and disorder marks a sad decline from classical liberalism, which regarded state force as an evil, albeit occasionally a necessary one. At best, policing was seen as a short-term palliative, as Raymond Chandler summed it up in *The Long Goodbye*: 'Crime isn't a disease, it's a symptom. Cops are like a doctor that gives you aspirin for a brain tumour.'

In view of the evidence of the relationship between inequality and violence (Currie 1997; Hall and Winlow 2003, 2004), it seems hazardous to conclude that the lid can be held down indefinitely on injustice. The analysis of British and comparative patterns clearly suggests that there are 'root causes' shaping crime and penal trends, related to variations in political economy. They indicate that social democratic political economies suffer less homicide, violence and serious crime, and fewer punitive penal policies. This is plausibly due to cultural differences in the moral quality of individualism. Social democracies

417

reflect and encourage reciprocal individualism, in which there is some mutual concern for the welfare of all, as distinct from the competitive individualism of neo-liberalism, which fosters a Darwinian struggle in which only the strongest flourish.

To neglect structural causes of crime and seek suppression alone is the fallacy that Paul Rogers, in the context of the 'war on terror', has called 'liddism'. Has the New York Police Department really found the criminological Holy Grail, a new policing paradigm that can hold the lid down on growing inequality and exclusion? The dependence of social harmony on justice is not just a post-Enlightenment, modernist grand narrative, outmoded in a postmodernised, globalised era, but an ancient perception. Psalm 127 tells us that 'if the Lord does not guard the city, the watchman keeps watch in vain', and the precondition was the pursuit of justice. Roman statecraft postulated, '*si vis pacem, para iustitiam*'.

In recent years, a few theorists have reminded us of the inescapable and creative role of utopian sensibilities about ultimate ends (Young 1992; Loader 1998; Zedner 2003) as necessary elements even of pragmatic intervention. I would claim that the ethics of responsibility now requires emphasising what we know about the relationship between neo-liberal political economy, serious violent crime and harsh criminal justice. Social democracies offer an actually existing more benign and peaceful alternative, which also prevailed in the UK and the USA not very long ago. Exclusive concentration on immediate policy debates about criminal justice reform is not ethically responsible. The dangers now are the opposite of those that haunted Weber's vocation lectures. To return to the dilemma faced by Stan Cohen's fisherman, it is time to go upstream and point out where the bodies are coming from.

Acknowledgement

An earlier version of this chapter was given at a Hoffinger Colloquium, New York University, 27 March 2006. The author is grateful for the useful discussion.

References

Barclay, G. and Tavares, C. (2003) *International Comparisons of Criminal Justice Statistics 2001*. London: Home Office.

Beckett, K. and Western, B. (2001) 'Governing social marginality: welfare, incarceration and the transformation of state policy', *Punishment and Society*, 3: 43–59.

Bernstein, J. and Houston, E. (2000) *Crime and Work.* Washington, DC: Economic Policy Institute.

Blair, T. (2006) 'Britain's liberties: the great debate', *The Observer* 23 April.

Blumstein, A. and Wallman, J. (eds) (2000) *The Crime Drop in America.* Cambridge: Cambridge University Press.

Bonger, W. ([1916] 1969) *Criminality and Economic Conditions.* Bloomington, IN: Indiana University Press.

Bottoms, A. and Stevenson, S. (1992) 'What went wrong? Criminal justice policy in England and Wales, 1945–70', in D. Downes (ed). *Unravelling Criminal Justice.* London: Macmillan.

Cavadino, M. and Dignan, J. (2006) *Penal Systems: A Comparative Approach.* London: Sage.

Cohen, S. (1975) 'It's alright for you to talk: political and sociological manifestos for social work action', in R. Bailey and M. Brake (eds) *Radical Social Work.* London: Arnold.

Cohen, S. (1979) 'Guilt, justice, and tolerance: some old concepts for a new criminology', in D. Downes and P. Rock (eds) *Deviant Interpretations.* London: Martin Robertson.

Cohen, S. (1985) *Visions of Social Control.* Cambridge: Polity.

Cohen, S. (1988) *Against Criminology.* New Brunswick, NJ: Transaction.

Cohen, S. (1998) 'Intellectual scepticism and political commitment: the case of radical criminology', in P. Walton and J. Young (eds) *The New Criminology Revisited.* London: Macmillan.

Currie, E. (1997) 'Market, crime and community: toward a mid-range theory of post-industrial violence', *Theoretical Criminology*, 1: 147–72.

Davis, M. (1992) *City of Quartz.* London: Vintage.

Deadman, D. and Macdonald, Z. (2002) 'Why has crime fallen? An economic perspective', *Economic Affairs*, 22: 5–14.

Dennis, N. and Erdos, G. (2005) *Cultures and Crimes.* London: Civitas.

Dorling, D. (2004) 'Prime suspect: murder in Britain', in P. Hillyard, C. Pantazis, S. Tombs and D. Gordon (eds) *Beyond Criminology.* London: Pluto.

Downes, D. (1966) *The Delinquent Solution.* London: Routledge.

Downes, D. (1998) 'Back to the future: the predictive value of social theories of delinquency', in S. Holdaway and P. Rock (eds). *Thinking About Criminology.* London: UCL Press.

Downes, D. (2004) 'New Labour and the lost causes of crime', *Criminal Justice Matters*, 55: 4–5.

Downes, D. and Hansen, K. (2006) 'Welfare and punishment in comparative perspective', in S. Armstrong and L. McAra (eds) *Perspectives on Punishment.* Oxford: Oxford University Press.

Downes, D. and Morgan, R. (2002), 'The skeletons in the cupboard: the politics of law and order at the turn of the millennium', in M. Maguire, R. Morgan and R. Reiner (eds) *The Oxford Handbook of Criminology* (3rd edn). Oxford: Oxford University Press.

Farrington, D. and Jolliffe, D. (2005) 'Crime and punishment in England and Wales, 1981–1999', in M. Tonry and D. Farrington (eds) *Crime and Punishment in Western Countries, 1980–1999.* Chicago: Chicago University Press.

Fielding, N., Clarke, A. and Witt, R. (eds) (2000) *The Economic Dimensions of Crime.* London: Macmillan.

Fitzgerald, M., Stockdale, J. and Hale, C. (2003) *Young People and Street Crime.* London: Youth Justice Board.

Garside, R. (2004a) 'Is it the economy?', *Criminal Justice Matters*, 55: 32–3.

Garside, R. (2004b) *Crime, Persistent Offenders and the Justice Gap.* London: Crime and Society Foundation.

Goldenberg, S. (2006) 'Fear and loathing on DC's streets as summer crimewave reaches the elite', *Guardian*, 20 July: 25.

Green, D., Grove, E. and Martin, N. (2005) *Crime and Civil Society.* London: Civitas.

Grogger, J. (2000) 'An economic model of recent trends in violence', in A. Bloomstein and J. Wallman (eds) *The Crime Drop in America.* Cambridge: Cambridge University Press.

Hagan, J. and Peterson, R. (eds) (1995) *Crime and Inequality.* Stanford, CA: Stanford University Press.

Hale, C. (2005) 'Economic marginalization and social exclusion', in C. Hale, K. Hayward, A. Wahidin and E. Wincup (eds) *Criminology.* Oxford: Oxford University Press.

Hall, S. and Winlow, S. (2003) 'Rehabilitating Leviathan: reflections on the state, economic regulation and violence reduction', *Theoretical Criminology*, 7: 139–62.

Hall, S. and Winlow, S. (2004) 'Barbarians at the gates: crime and violence in the breakdown of the pseudo-pacification process', in J. Ferrell, K. Hayward, W. Morrison and M. Presdee (eds) *Cultural Criminology Unleashed.* London: Glasshouse.

Hallsworth, S. (2005) *Street Crime.* Cullompton: Willan.

Hansen, K. and Machin, S. (2002) 'Spatial crime patterns and the introduction of the UK minimum wage', *Oxford Bulletin of Economics and Statistics*, 64: 677–97.

Hills, J. and Stewart, K. (eds) (2005) *A More Equal Society?* Bristol: Policy Press.

Karmen, A. (2000) *New York Murder Mystery.* New York: New York University Press.

Levitt, S. (2004) 'Understanding why crime fell in the 1990s: four factors that explain the decline and six that do not', *Journal of Economic Perspectives*, 18: 163–90.

Loader, I. (1998) 'Criminology and the public sphere: arguments for utopian realism', in P. Walton and J. Young (eds) *The New Criminology Revisited.* London: Macmillan.

Longford Study Group (1964) *Crime: A Challenge to Us All.* London: Labour Party.

Maguire, M. (2002) 'Crime statistics: the data explosion and its implications', in M. Maguire, R. Morgan and R. Reiner (eds) *The Oxford Handbook of Criminology* (3rd edn). Oxford: Oxford University Press.

Marris, R. (2000) *Survey of the Research Literature on the Economic and Criminological Factors Influencing Crime Trends.* London: Volterra Consulting.

Marx, K. ([1852] 2002) *The 18th Brumaire of Louis Napoleon*. London: Pluto.

Merton, R. 1938 'Social structure and anomie', *American Sociological Review*, 3: 672–82. Revised in R. Merton (1957) *Social Theory and Social Structure*. London: Free Press.

Messner, S. and Rosenfeld, R. (2006) *Crime and the American Dream* (4th edn). Belmont, CA: Wadsworth.

Newburn, T. (ed.) (2005) *Policing – Key Readings*. Cullompton: Willan.

Newburn, T. and Rock, P. (2004) *Living in Fear: Violence and Victimisation in the Lives of Single Homeless People*. London: Crisis.

Polanyi, K. ([1944] 2001) *The Great Transformation*. Boston: Beacon.

Reiner, R. (2006a) 'Beyond risk: a lament for social democratic criminology', in T. Newburn and P. Rock (eds) *The Politics of Crime Control*. Oxford: Oxford University Press.

Reiner, R. (2006b) 'Neoliberalism, crime and criminal justice', *Renewal*, 14.

Reiner, R. (2007a) 'Political economy, crime and criminal justice', in M. Maguire, R. Morgan and R. Reiner (eds) *The Oxford Handbook of Criminology* (4th edn). Oxford: Oxford University Press.

Reiner, R. (2007b) 'Law and order: a 20:20 vision', in *Current Legal Problems 2006*. Oxford: Oxford University Press.

Rosenfeld, R. (2004) 'The case of the unsolved crime decline', *Scientific American*, 290: 82–90.

Shearing, C. and Stenning, P. (1983) 'Private security: implications for social control', *Social Problems*, 30: 493–506.

Tonry, M. and Farrington, D. (2005) (eds) *Crime and Punishment in Western Countries, 1980–1999*. Chicago: Chicago University Press.

Van Kesteren, J., Mayhew, P. and Nieuwbeerta, P. (2000) *Criminal Victimisation in Seventeen Industrialised Countries: Key Findings From the 2000 International Victims Survey*. The Hague: Ministry of Justice.

Weber, M. ([1917/19] 2004) *The Vocation Lectures*. Indianapolis, IN: Hackett.

Western, B. (2001) 'Incarceration, unemployment, and inequality', *Focus*, 21: 32–6.

Wilkinson, R. (2005) *The Impact of Inequality*. New York: New Press.

Wilson, J.Q. (1975) *Thinking About Crime*. New York: Vintage.

Young, J. (1986) 'The failure of criminology: the need for a radical realism', in R. Matthews and J. Young (eds) *Confronting Crime*. London: Sage.

Young, J. (2003) 'Winning the fight against crime? New Labour, populism and lost opportunities', in R. Matthews and J. Young (eds) *The New Politics of Crime and Punishment*. Cullompton: Willan.

Young, J. (2004) 'Voodoo criminology and the numbers game', in J. Ferrell, K. Hayward, W. Morrison and M. Presdee (eds) *Cultural Criminology Unleashed*. London: Glasshouse.

Young, P. (1992) 'The importance of utopias in criminological thinking', *British Journal of Criminology*, 32: 423–37.

Zedner, L. (2003) 'Useful knowledge? Criminology in post-war Britain', in L. Zedner and A. Ashworth (eds) *The Criminological Foundations of Penal Policy*. Oxford: Oxford University Press.

Chapter 30

Conflict, suffering and the promise of human rights

Ruth Jamieson and Kieran McEvoy[1]

> The voyager studied the harrow with a frown. The information about the judicial process had failed to satisfy him. All the same, he had to remind himself that this was a penal colony, that special measures were necessary here, and that military procedures had to be adhered to throughout.
>
> Kafka, *The Penal Colony* (2000: 133)

> What is the space between us and the collective suffering of others?
>
> Cohen (2001: 295)

Introduction

A significant element of Stan Cohen's political and intellectual energy in the past decade has been focused on the relationships between sociology, politics and human rights (1993, 1995, 1996a, 1996b, 2001, 2005). As criminologists who live and work in a former conflict zone wherein precisely that intersection has informed much of our own work, we have been hugely influenced by Cohen's writings and example of political and scholarly commitment. Throughout his career, he has demonstrated a remarkable capacity to visualise and theorise with precision about what is actually occurring in a range of different types of conflict. Whether he is unpicking the violent societal reaction to mods and rockers, or internecine disputes within the disciplines of criminology and sociology through to the human and social destruction of political violence, Cohen's particular knack has been to *see* clearly through the smoke of conflict and to *speak* authoritatively above the din. A key feature of conflict is confusion. Cohen's unique gift is intellectual, political and moral clarity in the midst of that confusion.

In a recent interview (2002: 3–4), Cohen described *States of Denial* as the most personal and most political book he has ever written. Working on it involved him in making an autobiographical journey retracing his formative experiences of growing up in apartheid South Africa and living in Israel in order to make 'sociological sense' of the problems that had always troubled him. The starting point of his journey was the issue of people's complacency and failure to respond to the very visible social injustices and suffering of others around them (Cohen 2002: 3–4). He was especially keen to theorise how states neutralised and denied the abuses they committed. He wanted also to understand the relationship between our knowing about the social suffering of others and the compulsion (or not) to action (1990, 1993, 1995, 1996a, 1995b). While working on the book he also wrote extensively for both academic and human rights NGOs about these issues.

During his time as Director of the Institute of Criminology at the Hebrew University of Jerusalem (1980–94), Cohen found himself in the eye of the storm (the 1982 invasion of Lebanon, the Palestinian uprising in 1987 and subsequent measures taken by the Israeli state to repress it). It was a protracted and violent political conflict in which there were mass violations of Palestinians' rights in the form of displacements, house demolitions and sealings, tear gassing, mass arrests, military administration, administrative detention and mistreatment of suspects under interrogation (see Golan 1989; Cohen 1990; and *Journal of Palestine Studies*, Special Report, 1991). As Cohen himself observed around the time of the first intifada, his political and intellectual engagement with these issues prompted him to move from doing criminology' to 'doing human rights'. He co-founded the Committee Against Torture in Israel and was also an active member of B'Tselem, the Center for Human Rights in the Occupied Territories, for which he wrote a report with Daphna Golan-Agnon on the abuse of Palestinian detainees during the intifada, detailing their ill treatment and torture during interrogation (Cohen and Golan-Agnon 1991). He describes the response of mainstream Jewish Israeli society to the report as one of 'passive indifference' – they knew about the abuses of Palestinians but carried on acting as if they did not. For Cohen, this was the single most important impetus to writing *States of Denial* (2002: 9).

In rereading this and much of his other work in preparation for this chapter, we found these themes of knowing about and better understanding human suffering, as well as the compulsion to action, emerging as key features for us. We seek to tease out the implications of some of these discussions in the particular context of political conflict and the ways in which common humanity is often negated in such settings in justification of the infliction of suffering. We begin by examining the broader relationship between justice, institutionalism and the notion of suffering. We then explore the ways in which the recognition or non-recognition of suffering maps onto possible moral responses. Finally, we explore the intersection between the 'energy' which typically accompanies violent political conflict and the potential of human rights discourses to serve as the key vehicle for praxis in response to the suffering that is often intrinsic to such conflicts.

Justice, institutionalism and the centrality of suffering

Cohen's preoccupation with the suffering of others in *States of Denial* and much other work centres upon the nature of our relationship to such pain, as academics, individuals, and members of social movements or particular polities. Of course, as criminologists, such concerns are not new to our discipline. Alvin Gouldner, a sociologist who was to be a major inspiration for emergence of a 'new' critical criminology in the UK and the USA in the late 1960s and early 1970s,[2] was explicit about the centrality of suffering in the thinking of sociologists who 'make a commitment'. As Gouldner (1968: 105) argued: The essential thing about the underdog is that he suffers, and that his suffering is naked and visible. It is this that makes and should make a compelling demand upon us.'[3] Gouldner argues that all suffering that is 'unavoidable, tragic and truly part of the human condition deserves sympathy and consideration', but that suffering that is a product of social injustice is especially deserving of our attention because it is less likely to be known and more likely to contain much that is avoidable (Gouldner 1968: 106). Social injustice is in effect suffering that is 'man-made', politically produced and replicated by the state or other powerful institutional forces. For Gouldner, the scholarly responsibility is to communicate 'not only the character of such suffering, its peculiar sources and special intensity but the underdog's attempts fight against it' (Gouldner 1968: 105).

Significantly influenced by Cohen himself, the ideological and political empathy of criminologists to the suffering of others has contributed significantly to a range of developments within the field. While some are more explicit than others, suffering and our responses to it are a theme around which many criminological discourses coalesce. Critical criminologists, drawing from the example of Gouldner, would almost certainly underline their awareness of the suffering of prisoners, marginalised youth, those labelled as criminal or deviant, and so forth as key intellectual and political undercurrents to their work (e.g. Taylor *et al.* 1973, 1975; Scraton *et al.* 1991; Carlen 1996). The self-professed 'new realists' emerged in part because of a sense that critical criminology had done too little to acknowledge and explore the suffering through crime of others such as women, people of colour, the poor and the elderly (Lea and Young 1984; Lea 2002). Victimology is premised upon the explicit assertion that the suffering of victims as a result of crime is a central rationale for the criminological enterprise (Mawby and Walkgate 1994; Karmen 1995). Peacemaking criminology rejects the war metaphor in tackling crime and seeks to explore the suffering of 'the real human beings' caught up in the criminal justice process based on a myriad influences including Buddhism, Marxism and humanist sociology (Pepinksi and Quinney 1991; Thomas *et al.* 2003). Restorative justice similarly privileges the human suffering of victims and communities affected by crime in seeking to repair relationships damaged by crime and anti-social behaviour (Johnstone 2001; Sullivan and Tift 2006). For many of these and other variants of criminology, a basic premise of analysis is that often the institutions of the criminal justice system, which are in theory designed to respond to suffering (or at least inflict punishment upon those who have inflicted pain upon others), are in fact deeply implicated in the production and reproduction of human misery (Matza 1969).

The state's response to suffering caused by crime works on a number of underlying rationales and practices. The state interposes itself between and above the perpetrator and victim through its justice-delivering institutions. These institutions are designed in theory to depersonalise the relationship between victim and perpetrator, remove the likelihood of arbitrariness, and calibrate the delivery of appropriate punishment (Sanders and Young 2006). The state adjudicates on the blameworthiness of perpetrator and victim and metes out suffering (or satisfaction) through the infliction of punishment on the officially culpable (Lacey 1988). In so doing, the state reconstitutes the suffering of the victim as its own through forensically reworking the suffering as a ritualised truth contest (Douglas 1992). Suffering becomes reshaped, commodified and packaged for its public and didactic salience.

Of course, despite its claims to rationality, that particular version of a state 'doing justice' experienced by those who suffer will inevitably reflect the specific institutional configurations, niches, logics, constraints, rigidities, thought styles, values and feelings of its personnel and the political context in which the institutions operate (Douglas 1986; Dunn 1990). If 'all human institutions are as they are and act as they act in part because some of their participants think and feel as they do', then they are all susceptible to being shackled not only to the false (illusory) necessity of their particular personnel and practices (Unger cited in Dunn 1990: 170)[4] but also to their capriciousness. This contingent aspect of social arrangements for protecting people from injury and injustice also makes them precarious in the sense that social institutions in dealing with contingency, uncertainty and risk are often inadequately run, inequitable in their operation, and an arena of fierce competition among powerful groups (Turner 1993: 501–2).

All of these dynamics are discernible in 'normal' criminal justice proceedings tasked with dealing with 'ordinary' crimes. However, we would argue, like Cohen (1996b), that they are particularly visible when states are responding to politically motivated violence or unrest that directly challenges the state's legitimacy or monopoly on the use of coercion. In such instances the suffering engendered by the agencies of the criminal justice system is more than an unfortunate by-product of the institutionalism of justice – never a particularly persuasive argument in our view – but rather part of a deliberate and calculated counter-insurgency strategy. Thus, for example, the resort to the torture and disappearances of political opposition in Chile, Argentina or Egypt; rendition (in Afghanistan, Pakistan and elsewhere); administrative detention without trial of suspected terrorists in Northern Ireland, Israel, Afghanistan, Cuba and elsewhere – these and similar measures can all be legitimately analysed as the strategic infliction of suffering for political purposes (e.g. Levinson 2004; Wilson 2005a; Paglen and Thompson 2006). The processes through which the inhuman and degrading treatment or torture of people detained by the state becomes routinised, bureaucratised and professionalized through institutional training, sequestration, victim 'othering', and so forth have been well documented by Crelinsten and Schmid (1994, especially the chapter by Kelman), Huggins *et al.* (2002) and others. Indeed, these abuses are usually the end point of the state's appropriation of judicial process as a modality of political and/or security repression.

To recap, we would argue that the centrality of suffering underscores important developments, either implicit or explicit, both within our own discipline of criminology and more broadly. Criminologists and sociologists in particular who take an interest in suffering normally regard it as axiomatic that the institutions of the state are themselves a source of considerable suffering; indeed, much critical work in these fields has been expository in nature – essentially detailing and theorising about the causes and consequences of such pain. From our perspective, the context wherein that institutionally driven suffering is most prevalent is the response of the state to political violence. Given that many of the darker arts of state-sponsored suffering tend to be practised in ways that makes them *deniable* (Cohen 2001; Jamieson and McEvoy 2005), nowhere is the vulnerability of the individual more *visible* than in political trials or special emergency procedures whereby the state adjudicates on its internal or external enemies (Kirchheimer 1961; Balbus 1977; Hain 1985). The contours of the dialectic between repression and resistance are most evident in the Soviet show trial, the Diplock court, the military commission at Guantánamo or similarly 'charged sites' (Jansen 1982; McEvoy 2000; Steyn 2004). It is in such locations that state power is most likely to be curtailed by the strictures of legal formalism and the protections of international human rights standards. It is also often through the evidence which emerges in such settings that we are afforded the opportunity to recognise the wider institutional capacity for the infliction and alleviation of suffering.

Suffering, recognition and the emergence of moral obligation

In the final scene of *The Trial*, Kafka describes Joseph K.'s feelings about the manner of his impending death and the banality of his two executioners as feelings of shame: 'With failing eyes K. could still see the two of them, cheek leaning against cheek, immediately before his face, watching the final act. "Like a dog!" he said. It was as if the shame of it must outlive him.' In trying to understand his own feelings with regard to his time at Auschwitz, the ultimate in a system of bureaucratised and rationalised suffering, Primo Levi has written appreciatively about how strongly Kafka's writing resonates for him. Reflecting on his own translation of *The Trial* and the emotions felt by K. he wrote:

> In this shame I sense another component that I know: Joseph K., at the end of his anguished journey, experiences shame because there exists this occult, corrupt tribunal that pervades everything surrounding him … It is in the end a human, not a divine, tribunal: it is composed of men, and made by men and, Joseph K. with the knife already planted in his heart is ashamed of being a man[5] (Levi 1991: 108–9).

Levi's point about shame (and by extension about its cognate emotions of humiliation and indignation) is that, despite institutional pretensions to objectivity, neutrality, rationality and so forth, shame is an inherently relational emotion. It arises in the relation of the victim to the perpetrator, or indeed the witness/bystander to the suffering other(s). In the moment of his death, Joseph K. is face to face with his two warders and is ashamed for them for their failure to recognise his humanity and for himself that he should be treated in this way (like a dog).[6] K. is ashamed for his warders, but they do not appear to feel shame for themselves (Scheff 2003), or if they do, they do not *recognise* it.[7] Kafka's portrayal of K. as being unable to escape his moral relation to his executioners, who are 'cheek leaning against cheek, immediately before his face', resonates with Emmanuel Levinas' argument about the nature of moral obligation, that the immediate presence of the 'Other' ('the face') places an absolute moral obligation on the 'Self' (Blum 1983: 151). Thus, morality is not the product of a reasoned calculation of obligation predicated on some anticipated reciprocity. Nor, indeed, is adherence to a set of legal rules or regulations. As both Levinas (1989: 82–4) and Bauman (1989) have argued, the self's obligation to the Other exists *prior* to the prevailing legal forms or moral codes of any particular time or place. It is relational, it is existential, it is based upon a shared humanity.

The practical challenge for us is how to translate that *recognition* of a common humanity from the philosophical or intuitive level into practical action, particularly in times of political or military conflict. As Durkheim observes, collective sentiments like patriotism in war tend to 'cast all feeling of sympathy for the individual into the background' and to 'silence feelings of pity and sympathy' (1997: 115). If, as C. Wright Mills (1940) has argued, action including moral action is socially situated and context specific, then how does one overcome the powerful institutional forces which inevitably silence feelings of empathy with the 'Other' in such a conflict? K.'s fastidiously dutiful warders and their leering counterparts at Abu Ghraib (or Camp Rhino, Birkenau, Hola, Foča, Omarska) committed their acts against prisoners (Levinas' immediately present 'Other'), acting as agents of the state and in the presence of a 'generalised [situational] Other'; that is, the prevailing social and institutional norms about what is or is not acceptable in that particular context (Mills 1940: 444). If we understand 'moral action' in such contexts as the acceptance of *responsibility to action* that is designed to ameliorate suffering in such a situation (e.g. a refusal to participate in such abuses, 'whistle-blowing', attempting to protect those who are suffering, etc.), then it might be useful to begin by unpacking the rationales deployed whenever such responsibility is refused.

We suggest there are at least three forms of refusal: retreat or turning in, making an exception and outright abdication of responsibility.

The first form of refusal involves a complete lack of engagement with the fact of social suffering and a retreat from recognising what is going on in the social world. Hannah Arendt (1955: 19) recalls observing this sort of *'turning in'* or 'inner emigration' among people during the Third Reich:

In that darkest of times, inside and outside Germany the temptation was particularly strong, in the face of a seemingly unendurable reality, to shift from the world and its public space to an interior life, or else simply to ignore that world in favour of an imaginary world 'as it ought to be' or as it once upon a time had been.

This form of inner emigration deals with the problem of obligation by denial certainly, but a denial that involves a significant disengagement from all others, not just those who suffer.

The second mode of refusal involves making an *exception* to one's normal relation of moral obligation to the Other on the grounds of necessity. Here there is still a recognition of a moral obligation to the Other (on the basis of shared humanity), but the exceptional suffering is deemed to be a *necessity* due to some exceptional exigency such as war (e.g. Ignatieff 1998). Soldiers who are 'obeying orders'; bureaucratised systems, training and the inculcation of military cultures which are specifically designed to negate empathy; and soldiers or militia members who fear for their own lives or those of their families – these are variants of military 'necessity' which underpin abuses in times of conflict (see especially Osiel 2001). In many such instances, refusal to acknowledge humanity on the basis of exception overlaps to an extent with racist or colonial excusatory frameworks where abuse is inflicted upon subordinated others as a necessity that is seen to emanate out of their 'difference' (Fanon 1963). This was the justification asserted, for example, for the 'unfortunate necessity' of the violent repressing of colonial Algerians by the French (Le Cour Grandmaison 2001). In such settings, humanity is often *suspended* until the dirty business is completed and a predetermined natural order is reasserted (e.g. the prisoner has talked or the uprising is suppressed) and the abuser can revisit his (*sic*) humanity on his own terms.

The third mode of refusal does not invoke necessity or difference, but involves a more or less complete *abdication* of the obligation to a dehumanised or thing-like other (Lifton 1986; Kelman and Hamilton 1989; Bauman 1989, 1995). The suffering of the Other is not recognised as human suffering and therefore no obligation is seen to arise from it. The Self–Other existential referent is negated. Often this is manifest as complete dehumanisation, wherein the Other is cast out of the human literally into another species (e.g. rat, snake, cockroach) by a process of 'pseudospeciation' (Lifton 1986: 502), the end point of which may be annihilation (Jamieson 1999). Those who are on the receiving end of abuses inspired by this form of abdication are usually painfully aware of their own compelling need to reassert their humanity in the eyes of their abusers. For example, Nils Christie (1974) noted that prisoners who asserted their humanity to Norwegian concentration camp guards (e.g. by showing them family photographs) increased their chances of escaping inhumane treatment and surviving. Similarly Varese and Yaish (2000) found that Jews in Nazi Germany who made a direct appeal for help on the basis of their common humanity with potential rescuers were far more likely to escape persecution.

In understanding these various means by which moral action is 'refused', it is important to stress again that the space between us and the moral suffering of others is defined not only by the obligations inherent in the self–Other ethical relation, but also by a historically contingent set of understandings about 'what's right' or acceptable (Shay 1994; Mills 1940). Both moral actions toward specific others (others in the existential sense) and the more generic 'socially moral' actions to which C. Wright Mills refers, are powerfully cathected (negatively and positively, consciously and unconsciously). Keeping the recognition of suffering of others at bay through processes of denial (Cohen 2001) and relinquishing agency (Milgram 1974: 143 *et seq.*) are both processes involving considerable emotional intensity and energy (Scheff 2003: 735; Katz 1999). All of these modes of refusing obligation – turning in, exception, abdication – require a discursive reframing of the relation of suffering and obligation through the deployment of situated vocabularies of motive (Mills 1940: 452). Often it requires euphemistic language rules to transform murder into granting a mercy death (Arendt 1994: 108), torture into moderate physical pressure or in-depth interrogation (Cohen 1991, 2001, 2006), and a range of other techniques of neutralisation (Sykes and Matza 1957) to render refusal or infliction socially acceptable.

In the current context of the war on terror, the blatancy of the torture at Abu Ghraib and elsewhere and the embracing of necessitarian justifications for it have led Cohen (2005) to conclude that we are now in an era of 'post-moral' torture. It is increasingly difficult to avoid despairing realist commentaries on the prospects for upholding human rights or humanitarian norms in the current international context (Glennon 2005). Much of the legal and criminological commentary on the Abu Ghraib and related abuses has been concerned with issues of legal norms and the sovereign power of states to deploy law to define threats, necessity and exception; to use proxies to disguise agency; and to create extra-juridical spaces for 'threatening others' (Greenberg and Dratel 2005; Jamieson and McEvoy, 2005; Kramer and Michalowski 2005). It is, of course, of paramount importance that such processes are understood. However, as Cohen (2002: 12) points out, the focus on human rights as being founded in legal norms and state praxis has a downside in so far as debates about legality, expressed in 'UN speak', can discourage 'the expression of ordinary moral and emotional sensitivity of the kind envisaged by Levinas'. In the next section we explore how we might adopt a human rights perspective on our obligations to others that suffer that is grounded in the existential rather than the contingent social.

Energy, suffering and human rights as praxis

It is undoubtedly true that conflict brings with it a certain energy to social and political discourses. When David Matza was asked whether he thought social and political context influenced the way people 'did' sociology, his response was 'In polarised times I think there are bursts of consciousness' (Weis and Matza 1971: 45). In theory at least such increased consciousness of suffering can compel the impulse to understand, interpret, critique and name. For example, the Holocaust certainly gave rise to and continues to inspire an abundance of intellectual energy and impulse to bear witness to the suffering and atrocity of the Holocaust in fiction (Levi 1979; Speigelman 1986, 1992), personal accounts (Frankl 2004; Bettleheim 1986), and scholarship on issues such as obedience, conformity, the banality of perpetrators or the passivity of bystanders (Arendt 1994; Milgram 1974; Lifton 1986). There was a similar upsurge in work on torture and genocide during the Vietnam and Cambodia era (Kelman 1973; Lifton 1973), during the 'dirty wars' in Latin America (Crelinsten 1995), the war in the former Yugoslavia (Mestrovic, 1996; Ignatieff 1998), the genocide in Rwanda (Barnett 2003; Van den Herik 2005), and the current war in Iraq and the war on terror (Crahan *et al.* 2004; Wilson 2005a).

Greater consciousness of moral suffering can clearly generate 'energy' that can also serve as a powerful driver for change at specific historical conjunctures (Habermas 1989; Wilkinson 2005). Human rights discourses and institutions are often viewed as key vehicles designed to give practical expression to that energy. For example, Glendon (2003) has written about the experience of a number of Latin American countries that, having experienced a period of 'democratic euphoria' after emerging from economic depression and previous variants of authoritarian rule, became actively engaged in the drafting of the Universal Declaration of Human Rights. The political will which led to the drafting of the European Convention on Human Rights is inevitably linked with the suffering endured by many of the countries occupied by the Nazis during the Second World War (Dembour *et al.* 2006; Greer *et al.* 2006). In South Africa, Sachs (2005) has argued that resistance to suffering during apartheid translated into a particular energy to

431

transform South African society, much of which was underpinned by the notion of human rights protections as the benchmark for a new society. More recently, the rapid developments within international criminal justice with the creation of the ad hoc tribunals concerning the conflicts in Rwanda and the former Yugoslavia as well as the permanent International Criminal Court have been viewed explicitly as giving institutional expression to the commitment of the United Nations to end impunity for abuses and promote human rights (e.g. Kittichaisaree 2001; Cassese 2003). Across a wide range of contemporary peacemaking efforts, the centrality of human rights concerns has become a symbolic expression of the suffering of the past and of practical commitments to ensure that such suffering does not recur in the future (Bell 2005).

Despite the centrality of human rights, we would share Cohen's concern that the dominance of legalism within human rights discourses places a limitation upon their capacity to express ordinary human and moral sensitivity to the suffering of others – particularly among non-lawyers. Critiques of the privileging of legalism in human rights have come from a broad range of sources (see e.g. Meckled-García and B. Çali 2005; Gearty 2006, especially Chapter 3). Philosophically, some commentators doubt the intellectual rigour with which human rights are claimed (e.g. Douzinhas 2000), while others point to the Western and imperialist bent to some human rights talk (Baxi 2002), the predominance of first-generation civil and political rights over social and economic rights (Woodiwiss 1998; Jones and Stokke 2005) and the tendency to a variant of legal formalism in staking human rights claims that denies the political nature of the argumentation or the fact that rights claims may well conflict (Ignatieff 2001; Kennedy 2002). The legalisation of human rights promotes a 'top-down' conception of justice that 'thins out' the complexities of life on the ground in conflicted societies and positivises the norms which underpin them into international conventions and tribunals, national constitutions, and the domestic courts (McEvoy 2007). The absence of thinking about the wider political, social or cultural contexts that have led to violence in the first place correspondingly curtails the power of human rights institutions to prevent future violence (Wilson 2005b). The translation of moral outrage at abuses into a complex legalistic language that is often understood by few outside the legal community can in turn reify lawyers' 'ownership' of such outrage (Christie 1977). The institutionalisation of such outrage, in the form of major international bodies such as ad hoc tribunals, the International Criminal Court, or even national level tribunals or hybrid institutions (usually housed in the national capital and often hundreds of miles from where abuses took place), accentuates the distinction between what Gready (2005) has described as 'distant justice' and justice that is actually 'embedded' in those communities that have been directly affected by violence and conflict.

Based upon our own experiences working in a conflict zone, we would propose a number of overlapping strategies designed both to guard against these dangers inherent in legalism and to maximise the potential for human rights discourses as channels for moral action in response to abuses.

First, we would advocate a range of strategies designed to *engender legal humility*.[8] During the Cold War era, when international law was so self-evidently malleable by the military and economic will of the two competing superpowers, the scholarship on this variant of law was at times arguably characterised by a variant of defensive legal positivism that was out of sync with the mainstreaming of critical, feminist and socio-legal analysis in legal scholarship more generally (Koh 1997; Charlesworth and Chinkin 2000; Koskenniemi 2002). However, with the emergence of human rights as the new 'lingua franca' of the post-Cold War era (Ignatieff 2001), and the instructional clout given to international law through the International Criminal Court and the various ad hoc tribunals, there is arguably a great space currently for lawyers to acknowledge both that they do not 'own' human rights and that human rights cannot and does not have all the answers. Human rights may work better as a vehicle for moral action in conflict zones when it is accompanied by other complementary approaches such as restorative justice or related indigenous forms of peacemaking (Sarkin 2001; McEvoy 2003, Wardak 2004).

Second, in tandem with this process of lawyers ceding their monopoly on the meaning and implementation of human rights, we would argue for processes designed to *embed human rights in bottom-up conflict transformation.* There is already a rich literature in development studies and anthropology that charts the role and potential for mainstreaming human rights discourses in grass-roots community and civil society organisations (see e.g. Wilson 1997; Hausermann 1998; Cowan *et al.* 2001; Sen 2001; Donnelly 2002, especially Chapter 11). As Braithwaite has argued, dejargonised language, proper training, and appropriately constructed accountability structures and bottom-up involvement in the development of standards of practice by those involved in peacemaking or restorative work after conflict are among the most effective ways of moving human rights standards beyond 'armchair pontifications from above' (Braithwaite 2002: 576). In societies such as Northern Ireland, where the 'contact hypothesis' (that increased social contact between Catholics and Protestants would decrease sectarianism and reduce civil strife) is now largely discredited (Connolly 2000), respect for the human rights of historical enemies is increasingly viewed as a more appropriate template for better 'community relations with teeth' (McEvoy *et al.* 2006). Similarly, in a number of societies that have experienced serious intercommunal conflict, education about the human rights of the 'Other' has become a central plank in the citizenship education of future generations (Freedman *et al.* 2004; McEvoy and Lundy 2007). Embedding human rights values and working practices in local communities, civil society organisations, schools and other 'non-legal' settings is central to the potential of realising human rights potential for praxis.

Third and directly related to such a process is the need to *'see' justice beyond the state.* As was discussed above, one of the key social and political processes associated with industrialisation has been the monopolisation of justice by the state or state-like social institutions. Legalism leads to 'stateism', and the weakness of that perspective is well developed in a range of disciplines. Human rights scholars in particular are prone to 'seeing like a state' (McEvoy 2007). For anthropologists, as James C. Scott (2001) has noted, one of the weaknesses of 'seeing like a state' in any exercise of power is that often it entails failing to take sufficient account of local customs and practical knowledge, and this, in turn, may lead to incompetence and maladministration. Similarly, a standard criminological critique of the state is that despite its long-term dominance in the delivery of justice services, the state's incapacity to effectively deliver such services has necessitated the development of a range of complex partnership arrangements (Crawford 1999; Loader and Walker 2007). We would argue that the reality of contemporary shared sovereignty over justice 'above' the state (e.g. in suprastate transnational policing structures), 'alongside' the state (e.g. in the private sector), or 'below' the state (in the community or voluntary sector) requires a broader, deeper and less 'state-centric' human rights perspective if the potential for moral action is to be realised.

Conclusion

Iain Wilkinson (2001, 2005) has argued for a sociology of suffering that can find a vocabulary to communicate the lived experience of human suffering, what it does to people, its emotional and moral meaning, and the implications for action. Rereading Stan Cohen's formidable body of work for this chapter, we have been reminded that he does all of this consistently, rigorously and with moral authority. Elsewhere, we have drawn approvingly from Cohen's oft-quoted scholarly obligation that we should serve the three voracious gods of honest intellectual enquiry, political commitment to social justice, and 'the pressing and immediate demands for short-term humanitarian help' (Cohen 1998). In tracing the relationship between conflict and our understanding of suffering, the emergence of moral obligation and the potential for human rights as praxis (all within the context of the contemporary war on terror), we are reminded that intellectual scepticism cannot become an excuse for political nonengagement (Cohen 1998: 126). Stan Cohen has shown us the way.

Notes

1 We are extremely grateful to the editors of this collection for their patience and support, particularly David Downes, who was, as ever, despite our tardiness, the perfect gentleman.
2 See Gouldner's 1973 foreword to *The New Criminology*.
3 Gouldner (1968) makes this argument about sociology and suffering in the context of his critical reappraisal of 'the sociologist as partisan' stance exemplified by Howard S. Becker's work, particularly his 1967 *Social Problems* essay, 'Whose side are we on?'
4 Unger's project was to reconceptualise social possibility and to imagine other possible social arrangements for doing justice that were not fettered by what he refers to as 'false necessity' (see Unger 1987).
5 Levi (1991: 108) goes on to say: 'I, a survivor of Auschwitz, would never have written it, or never in that way: out of inability, or insufficient imagination, certainly, but also out of a feeling of shame before death that Kafka did not know, or if he did, rejected; or perhaps out of lack of courage.'
6 In a similar vein, Moazzam Begg (2006: 112) has reported that one of the most humiliating experiences at Camp Rhino (Kandahar) was 'witnessing the abuse of others, and knowing how utterly dishonoured they felt. […] I felt that everything I held sacred was being violated, and they must have felt the same.'
7 Similarly, the faces of the guards in the infamous Abu Ghraib photographs betray no sense of shame at violating the inherent dignity in those they are abusing. But, as Joanna Bourke argues, 'We [the viewer] cannot escape complicity: the Abu Ghraib snapshots were deliberately intimate and confrontational: there was no place for us to look but straight into the perpetrators' eyes' (Bourke 2005: 390).
8 For a discussion on the relationship between lawyers and arrogance, see McEvoy and Rebouche (2007).

References

Arendt, H. (1955) 'On humanity in dark times: thoughts about Lessing', in H. Arendt, *Men in Dark Times*, pp. 3–31. New York, Harcourt Brace.

Arendt, H. (1994) (rev. edn) *Eichmann in Jerusalem: A Report on the Banality of Evil*. London/New York: Penguin Books.

Balbus, I. (1977) *The Dialectic of Legal Repression*. New Brunswick, NJ: Transnational Publishing.

Barnett, M. (2003) *Eyewitness to a Genocide: The United Nations and Rwanda*. Ithaca, NY: Cornell University Press.

Bauman, Z. (1989) *Modernity and the Holocaust*. Cambridge: Polity.

Bauman, Z. (1995) *Life in Fragments: Essays in Post-Modern Morality*. Oxford: Blackwell.

Baxi, U. (2002) *The Future of Human Rights*. Oxford: Oxford University Press.

Becker, H.S. (1967) 'Whose side are we on?', *Social Problems*, 14: 239–47.

Begg, M. and Brittain, V. (2006) *Enemy Combatant: A British Muslim's Journey to Guantanamo and Back*. London: Free Press.

Bell, C. (2005 reprinted) *Peace Agreements and Human Rights*. Oxford: Oxford University Press.

Bettelheim, B. (1986) *Surviving the Holocaust*. London: Flamingo.

Blum, R.P. (1983) 'Emmanuel Levinas' theory of commitment', *Philosophy and Phenomenological Research*, 44 (2): 145–68.

Bourke, J. (2005) 'Sexy snaps', *Index on Censorship*, 34: 39–45.

Braithwaite, J. (2002) 'Setting standards for restorative justice', *British Journal of Criminology*, 22: 563–77.

Carlen, P. (1996) *Jigsaw: A Political Criminology of Youth Homelessness*. Buckingham: Open University Press.

Cassese, A. (2003) *International Criminal Law*. Oxford: Oxford University Press.

Charlesworth, H. and Chinkin, C. (2000) *Boundaries of International Law: A Feminist Perspective*. Manchester: Manchester University Press.

Christie, N. interviewed by Annika Snare (1974) 'Dialogue with Christie', *Issues in Criminology*, 10: 35–47.

Christie, N. (1977) 'Conflicts as property', *British Journal of Criminology*, 17: 1–15.

Cohen, S. (1990) 'The intifada in Israel: portents and precarious balance', *Middle East Report*, No. 164/165, Intifada Year Three, pp. 16–20 and 78.

Cohen, S. and Golan, D. (1991) *The Interrogation of Palestinians During the Intifada: Ill-Treatment, 'Moderate Physical Pressure' or Torture?* Jerusalem: B'Tselem – The Israeli Information Center for Human Rights in the Occupied Territories.

Cohen, S. (1993) 'Human rights and crimes of the state: the culture of denial', *Australia and New Zealand Journal of Criminology*, 26: 97–115.

Cohen, S. (1995) 'State crimes of previous regimes: knowledge, accountability, and the policing of the past', *Law and Social Inquiry*, 20: 7–50.

Cohen, S. (1996a) 'Government responses to human rights reports: claims, denials, and counterclaims', *Human Rights Quarterly*, 18: 517–43.

Cohen, S. (1996b) 'Crime and politics: spot the difference', *British Journal of Sociology*, 47: 1–21.

Cohen, S. (2001) *States of Denial: Knowing About Atrocities and Suffering*. Cambridge: Polity.

Cohen, S. (2002) 'Preparing my next mistake', interview with Stan Cohen, *Social Science Teacher* Nov.

Cohen, S. (2005) 'Post moral torture: from Guantanamo to Abu Ghraib', *Index on Censorship*, 34: 24–38.

Cohen, S. (2006) 'Neither honesty nor hypocrisy: The legal reconstruction of torture', in T. Newburn and P. Rock (eds) *The Politics of Crime Control Essays in Honour of David Downes*. Oxford: Oxford University Press.

Connolly, P. (2000) 'What now for the contact hypothesis? towards a new research agenda', *Race, Ethnicity and Education*, 3: 169–93.

Cowan, J., Wilson, R. and Dembour, M. (eds) (2001) *Culture and Rights: Anthropological Perspectives*. Cambridge: Cambridge University Press.

Crahan, M., Goering, J. and Weiss, T. (eds) (2004) *The Wars on Terrorism and Iraq: Human Rights, Unilateralism and US Foreign Policy*. London: Routledge.

Crawford, A. (1999) *The Local Governance of Crime: Appeals to Community and Partnerships*. Oxford: Oxford University Press.

Crelinsten, R. and Schmid, A.P. (1995) *The Politics of Pain: Torturers and Their Masters*. Boulder, CO: Westview Press.

Crelinsten, R. (1995) 'In their own words: the world of the torturer,' in R. Crelinsten and A.P. Schmid (eds) *The Politics of Pain*, pp. 35–64. Boulder, CO: Westview Press.

Dembour, M., Twining, W. and McCruddent, C. (2006) *Who Believes in Human Rights?: Reflections on the European Convention*. Cambridge: Cambridge University Press.

Donnelly, J. (2002) *Universal Human Rights: Theory and Practice* (2nd edn). Ithaca, NY: Cornell University Press.

Douglas, M. (1986) *How Institutions Think*. New York: Oxford University Press.

Douglas, M. (1992) *Risk and Blame: Essays in Cultural Theory*. London: Routledge.

Douzinhas, C. (2000) *The End of Human Rights*. Oxford: Hart.

Dunn, J. (1990) *Interpreting Political Responsibility: Essays 1981–1989*. Cambridge: Polity Press.

Durkheim, E. (1997) (with a new preface by Bryan S. Turner) *Professional Ethics and Civic Morals*. London: Routledge.

Fanon, F. (1963) *The Wretched of the Earth*. New York: Grove Books.

Frankel, V. ([1946] 1984) *Man's Search for Meaning*. New York: Washington Square Press.

Freedman, S., Deo, K., Samuelson, B., Innocent, M., Immacule, M., Evode, M., Mutabaruka, J., Weistein, H., and Longman, T. (2004) 'Confront the past in Rwandan schools', in E. Stover and H. Weinstein (eds) *My Neighbour: My Enemy*. Cambridge: Cambridge University Press.

Gearty, C. (2006) *Can Human Rights Survive?* Cambridge: Cambridge University Press.

Glendon, M.A. (2003) 'The forgotten crucible: the Latin American influence on the Universal Declaration of Human Rights idea', *Harvard Human Rights Journal*, 16: 27–39.

Glennon, M.J. (2005) 'How international rules die', *Georgetown Law Journal*, 93; 939–92.

Golan, D. (1989) 'The military judicial system in the West Bank', Jerusalem: B'Tselem.

Gouldner, A. (1968) 'The sociologist as partisan: sociology and the welfare state', *The American Sociologist*, 3: 103–6, reprinted in P. Rock (1994), *History of Criminology*, pp. 553–66.

Gready, P. (2005) 'Reconceptualising transitional justice: embedded and distanced justice', *Conflict Security and Development*, 5: 2–21.

Greenberg, K. and Dratel, J. (2005) *The Torture Papers: The Road to Abu Ghraib*. Cambridge: Cambridge University Press.

Greer, S., Gormley, L. and Shaw, J. (2006) *European Convention on Human Rights: Achievements, Problems and Prospects*. Cambridge: Cambridge University Press.

Habermas, J. (1989) 'The new obscurity: the crisis of the welfare state and the exhaustion of utopian energies', in *The New Conservatism: Cultural Criticism and the Historian's Debate*. Cambridge: Polity Press.

Hain, P. (1985) *Political Trials in Britain*. London: Allen Lane.

Hausermann, J. (1998) A human rights approach to development: a discussion paper commissioned by the Department for International Development of the UK government. In *Preparation of the Government White Paper on International Development*. London: Rights and Humanity.

Huggins, M., Haritos-Fatouros, M. and Zimbardo, P.G. (2002) *Violence Workers: Police Torturers and Murderers Reconstruct Brazilian Atrocities*. Berkeley, CA: University of California Press.

Ignatieff, M. (1998) *The Warrior's Honour: Ethnic War and the Modern Conscience*. London: Chatto & Windus.

Ignatieff, M. (2001) *Human Rights as Politics and Idolatry*. Princeton: Princeton University Press.

Jamieson, R. (1999) 'Genocide and the social production of immorality', *Theoretical Criminology*, 3 (2): 131–146.

Jamieson, R. and McEvoy, K. (2005) 'State crime by proxy and the juridical other', *British Journal of Criminology*, 45: 504–27.

Jansen, M. (1982) *A Show Trial Under Lenin: The Trial of the Socialist Revolutionaries, Moscow*. The Hague: Nijhoff.

Johnstone, G. (2001) *Restorative Justice: Ideas, Values, Debates*. Cullompton: Willan Publishing.

Jones, P. and Stokke, K. (eds) (2005) *Democratising Development: The Politics of Socio-Economic Rights in South Africa*. Leiden: Brill.

Journal of Palestinian Studies (1991) 'Intifada human rights violations data', Special Report, 20 (3): 112–16.

Kafka, F. (2005) *The Trial*. London: Vintage Books.

Kafka, F. (2000) 'The penal colony', in *The Metamorphosis and Other Stories*. London: Penguin Books, pp. 127–53.

Karmen, A. (1995) *Crime Victims: An Introduction to Victimology*. Belmont, CA: Wadsworth Publishing.

Katz, J. (1999) *How Emotions Work*. Chicago: University of Chicago Press.

Kelman, H. (1973) 'Violence without moral restraint', *Journal of Social Issues*, 29: 25–61.

Kelman, H. and Hamilton, V. (1989) *Crimes of Obedience*. New Haven, CT: Yale University Press.

Kennedy, D. (2002) 'The international human rights movement: part of the problem?' *Harvard Human Rights Law Review*, 15: 101–27.

Kirchheimer, O. (1961) *Political Justice: The Use of Legal Procedure for Political Ends*. Princeton, NJ: Princeton University Press.

Kittichaisaree, K. (2001) *International Criminal Law*. Oxford: Oxford University Press.

Koh, H. (1997) 'Why do nations obey international law?' *Yale Law Journal*, 106: 2599–2660.

Koskenniemi, M. (2002) *The Gentle Civilizer of Nations: The Rise and Fall of International Law 1870–1960*. Cambridge: Cambridge University Press.

Kramer, R. and Michalowski, R. (2005) 'War, aggression and state crime: a criminological analysis of the invasion and occupation of Iraq', *British Journal of Criminology*, 45: 446-69.

Lacey, N. (1988) *State Punishment*. London: Routledge.

Lea, J. and J. Young (1984) *What Is to Be Done About Law and Order?* London: Penguin.

Lea, J. (2002) *Crime and Modernity: Continuities in Left Realist Criminology*. London: Sage.

Le Cour Grandmaison (June 2001) 'Liberty, equality, colony', *Le Monde diplomatique* online at http://mondediplo.com/2001/06/11torture2.

Levi, P. (1991) 'Translating Kafka', in *The Mirror Maker: Stories and Essays by Primo Levi*. London: Minerva, pp. 106–9.

Levi, P. (1979) *If This Is a Man*. London: Penguin Books.

Levinas, E. and Hand, S. (eds) (1989) *The Levinas Reader*. Oxford: Blackwell.

Levinson, S. (2004) *Torture: A Collection*. Oxford: Oxford University Press.

Lifton, R.J. (1973) *Home from the War*. New York: Simon & Schuster.

Lifton, R.J. (1986) *The Nazi Doctors*. New York: Basic Books.

Loader, I. and Walker, N. (2007) *Civilizing Security*. Cambridge: Cambridge University Press.

Matza, D. (1969) *Becoming Deviant*. Englewood Cliffs, NJ: Prentice-Hall.

Mawby, R. and Walkgate, S. (1994) *Critical Victimology*. London: Sage.

McEvoy, K. (2000) 'Law, struggle and political transformation in Northern Ireland', *Journal of Law and Society*, 27: 542–71.

McEvoy, K. (2003) 'Beyond the metaphor: political violence, human rights and "new" peacemaking criminology', *Theoretical Criminology*, 7: 319–46.

McEvoy, K. (2008) 'Beyond legalism: towards a thick theory of transitional justice', *International Journal of Transitional Justice*, 5 (in press).

McEvoy, K. and Rebouche, R. (2007) 'Mobilising the professions; lawyers, politics and the collective legal conscience', in J. Morrison, K. McEvoy and G. Anthony (eds) *Judges, Human Rights and Transition*. Oxford: Oxford University Press, pp. 275–314.

McEvoy, L. and Lundy, L. (2007) 'In the small places: education and human rights culture in conflict-affected societies.', in J. Morrison, K. McEvoy and G. Anthony (eds) *Judges, Human Rights and Transition*. Oxford: Oxford University Press, pp. 495–514.

McEvoy, L., McEvoy, K. and McConnachie, K. (2006) 'Reconciliation as a dirty word: conflict, community relations and education in Northern Ireland', *Journal of International Affairs*, 60: 81–106.

Meckled-García, S. and Çali, B. (eds) (2005) *The Legalisation of Human Rights: Multi-Disciplinary Perspectives on Human Rights and Human Rights Law.* London: Routledge.

Mestrovic, S. (ed) (1996) *Genocide After Emotion: The Postemotional Balkan War.* Abingdon: Routledge.

Milgram, S. (1974) *Obedience to Authority.* New York: Harper & Row.

Mills, C.W. (1940) 'Situated actions and vocabularies of motive', *ASR* 5, 6, reprinted in I.L. Horowitz (ed.) (1967) *Power Politics and People: The Collected Essays of C. Wright Mills.* London: Oxford University Press.

Paglen, T. and Thompson, A. (2006) *Torture Taxi: On the Trail of the CIA's Rendition Flights.* New York: Melville House.

Pepinsky, H. and Quinney, R. (eds) (1991) *Criminology as Peacemaking.* Bloomington, IN: Indiana University Press.

Osiel, M. (2001) *Obeying Orders: Atrocity, Military Discipline and the Laws of War.* New Brunswick, NJ: Transaction Publishers.

Sachs, A. (2005) Speech at the opening of the Institute for Transitional Justice, University of Ulster, June 2005.

Sanders, A. and Young, R. (2006) *Criminal Justice* (3rd edn). London: Butterworths.

Sarkin, J. (2001) 'The tension between justice and reconciliation in Rwanda: politics, human rights, due process and the role of the Gacaca courts in dealing with the genocide', *Journal of African Law*, 45: 143–72.

Scheff, T.J. (2003) 'Shame in self and society', *Symbolic Interaction*, 26 (2): 239–62.

Scott, J.C. (2001) *Seeing like a State.* Princeton, NJ: Princeton University Press.

Scraton, P., Sim., J. and Skidmore, P. (1991) *Prisons Under Protest.* Buckingham: Open University.

Sen, A. (2001) *Development as Freedom.* Oxford: Oxford University Press.

Shay, J. (1994) *Achilles in Vietnam: Combat Trauma and the Undoing of Character.* New York: Scribner.

Speigelman, A. (1986) *Maus: A Survivor's Tale: My Father Bleeds History.* New York: Random House.

Speigelman, A. (1992) *Maus: A Survivor's Tale: And Here My Troubles Began.* New York: Random House.

Steyn, J. (2004) 'Guantanamo Bay: the legal black hole', *International and Comparative Law Quarterly*, 53: 1–16.

Sullivan, D. and Tift, L. (2006) (eds) *A Handbook of Restorative Justice.* London: Routledge.

Sykes, G. and Matza, D. (1957) 'Techniques of neutralization: a theory of delinquency', *American Sociological Review*, 22: 664–70.

Taylor, I., Walton, P. and Young, J. (1973) *The New Criminology, For a Social Theory of Deviance.* London: Routledge & Kegan Paul.

Taylor, I., Walton, P. and Young, J. (1975) *Critical Criminology.* London: Routledge and Kegan Paul.

Thomas, J., Capps, J., Carr, J., Evans, T., Lewin-Gladney, W., Jacobson, D., Maier, C., Moran, S. and Thompson, S. (2003) 'Critiquing the critics of peacemaking criminology: some rather ambivalent reflections on the theory of 'being nice'', in K. McEvoy and T. Newburn (eds) *Criminology, Conflict Resolution and Restorative Justice*. London: Palgrave.

Turner, B.S. (1993) 'Outline of a theory of human rights', *Sociology*, 276: 489–513.

Unger, R.M. (1987) *False Necessity: Anti-Necessitarian Social Theory in the Service of Radical Democracy*. Cambridge: Cambridge University Press.

Van den Herik, L. (2005) *The Contribution of the Rwanda Tribunal to the Development of International Law*. Leiden: Brill Academic Publishing.

Varese, F. and Yaish, M. (2000) 'The importance of being asked: the rescue of Jews in Nazi Germany', *Rationality and Society*, 12: 307–34.

Wardak, A. (2004) 'Building a post-war justice system in Afghanistan', *Crime, Law and Social Change*, 41: 319–41.

Weis, J.G. and Matza, D. (1971) 'Dialogue with David Matza', *Issues in Criminology*, 6: 33–53.

Wilkinson, I. (2001) 'Thinking with suffering', *Cultural Values*, 5: 421–44.

Wilkinson, I. (2005) *Suffering: A Sociological Introduction*. Oxford: Polity.

Wilson, R. (1997) *Human Rights, Culture and Context: Anthropological Perspectives*. London: Pluto Press.

Wilson, R. (ed.) (2005a) *Human Rights in the 'War on Terror'*. Cambridge: Cambridge University Press.

Wilson, R. (2005b). 'Is the legalisation of human rights really the problem: genocide in the Guatemalan Historical Clarification Commission', in S. Meckled-García and B. Çali (eds) *The Legalisation of Human Rights: Multi-Disciplinary Perspectives on Human Rights and Human Rights Law*. London: Routledge.

Woodiwiss, A. (1998) *Globalisation, Human Rights and Labour Law in Pacific Asia*. Cambridge: Cambridge University Press.

Name Index

Subject Index